Diagnosing and Treating Children and Adolescents

A Guide for Mental Health Professionals

BRANDÉ FLAMEZ
CARL J. SHEPERIS
Lamar University

Library of Congress Cataloging-in-Publication Data:

Diagnosing and treating children and adolescents : a guide for mental health professionals / [edited by] Brandé Flamez,
    Carl J. Sheperis.
    pages cm
    Includes bibliographical references and index.
    ISBN 978-1-118-91792-3 (pbk.), 978-1-118-91794-7 (ePDF), 978-1-118-91793-0 (epub)
1. Child mental health–Handbooks, manuals, etc. 2. Child psychiatry–Handbooks, manuals, etc. 3. Adolescent
psychiatry–Handbooks, manuals, etc. I. Flamez, Brandé, editor. II. Sheperis, Carl, editor.
    RJ499.3.D53 2015
    618.92'89–dc23
                                        2015018217

Cover Image: © echo3005/Shutterstock
Cover Design: Wiley

Printed in the United States of America

10 9 8 7 6 5 4 3 2 1

To my children, Evelyn and Braeden.
Thank you for all the love and laughter you bring to my life.
You have been a gift from the beginning.
I love you more than all the sand on the beach and the stars in the sky.— Brandé

For my children, Ellis, Jake, Joe Lee, Emily, and Laura Beth—your
smiles, kisses, laughter, and hugs are some of the best things in life.— Carl

Contents

Preface

We decided to write *Diagnosing and Treating Children and Adolescents: A Guide for Mental Health Professionals* because of the often-difficult task of framing mental health symptomology with this population. We aim to help future and current counselors, behavioral health care clinicians, and other helping professionals become better at navigating decision trees in light of developmental considerations, assessment information, presenting symptoms, comorbidity, levels of severity, prevalence data, research, and other relevant factors. We also strive to provide a clear, evidence-based pathway from appropriate diagnosis to treatment planning. Child and adolescent mental health services are distinctly different from adult services, and those clinicians working with children and adolescents require a specialized knowledge base to be effective. Numerous changes occurred to the diagnostic process, assessment procedures, and diagnostic nomenclature with the publication of the *DSM-5*. As such, both current and future practitioners have a learning curve to navigate. Our hope is to provide the essential information that will help you, the reader, to rise to the top of the curve by developing a better conceptualization of mental health symptomology in children and adolescents and by developing the knowledge base to make best practice decisions for working with this vulnerable population.

We believe that diagnosis and treatment planning have a symbiotic relationship. Having skills in both areas is necessary to address client problems effectively. Throughout our textbook, we stress the need to identify the correct diagnosis accurately and to use that diagnosis to inform a plan for evidence-based intervention. To diagnose accurately, clinicians require in-depth knowledge of the *DSM-5*, related assessments, and the professional literature. Although no resource can substitute for the diagnostic manual, a focused exploration of the disorders as they relate to children and adolescents can provide a valuable means for organizing a vast amount of complex information. Throughout this textbook, we provide you an overview of the various disorders as they specifically relate to children and adolescents so that you can become more competent in the diagnostic and treatment-planning processes.

This textbook has two primary goals. The first goal is to ground readers in the comprehensive diagnostic process that has evolved with the publication of the *DSM-5*. Our second goal is to provide a framework for applying the *DSM-5* to child and adolescent mental health. To meet these goals, the textbook is divided into two parts that provide contemporary perspectives on child and adolescent mental health, procedures for diagnosis, fundamentals of treatment planning, diversity issues in diagnosis, and exploration of each diagnostic category related to children and adolescents. These parts include Stages of the Comprehensive Diagnostic Process and Diagnostic Categories of Psychiatric Disorders. An introduction to Part I immediately follows, and an introduction to Part II is before the start of Chapter 5 ("Autism Spectrum Disorder").

Acknowledgments

Completing a project of this scope would not have been accomplished without the dedication, hard work, and wonderful contributions of the contributing authors. To each of you, we extend our sincere appreciation for helping create a text that introduces the *DSM-5* and discusses the integral role it assumes in assisting mental health professionals in diagnosing and treating children and adolescents.

We would like to thank those at John Wiley & Sons who helped turn our vision into reality, especially our editor, Rachel Livey. Your support, patience, and encouragement are invaluable, and this book would not have been possible without your involvement. Finally, we would like to give a warm thank-you to Patricia Rossi, our acquisitions editor, for her helpful and enthusiastic responses.

—Brandé and Carl

Specific Acknowledgements

Words cannot express my gratitude for my family—especially Matthew and my parents, Rosemary and John. I thank you for your love and support during the many hours spent on this project. Your words of encouragement are like light switches. They light up a room of possibilities for me.

I appreciate the support from my department chair, Dr. Carl J. Sheperis. I would like to thank and acknowledge my friend and colleague Dr. Jason H. King for his generous recommendations and his insights throughout the process. I am grateful to Dr. Melinda Haley for her assistance with the manual. And to all the families and clients I have been privileged to serve, thank you for being an ongoing source of inspiration. Each one of you has my sincere appreciation and gratitude.

—Brandé Flamez

This project would not have been possible without the support of my wife (Donna Sheperis) and my family. Their patience and love is the essential ingredient in my success. I want to acknowledge the privilege I have had to work with thousands of children and adolescents throughout my career. Their lived experiences have helped make me the mental health counselor I am today.

—Carl Sheperis

About the Editors

Brandé Flamez, PhD, NCC, LPC, is a licensed professional counselor and clinical professor in the Counseling and Special Populations department at Lamar University. Dr. Flamez is also the CEO and founder of the nonprofit Serving and Learning Together (SALT) world Inc., which provides volunteer services to developing countries. Her clinical background includes working with children, adolescents, and families in community-based and private counseling settings both nationally and internationally. In addition, Dr. Flamez helped design an outpatient program for court-referred adolescents and specializes in diagnosis and assessment. Dr. Flamez is active in the counseling profession. She has served on the American Counseling Association (ACA) Governing Council for the International Association of Marriage and Family Counselors, ACA Finance Committee, ACA Investment Committee, and chaired the ACA Publications Committee. She is also the Past President for the Association for Humanistic Counselors (AHC) and President-elect for the International Association of Marriage and Family Counselors.

Dr. Flamez is on the editorial board for The Family Journal. She has presented numerous times at the nationally and internationally level and coauthored several book chapters and articles. Dr. Flamez is the co-author of the assessment textbook *Counseling Assessment and Evaluation: Fundamentals of Applied Practice* and *Diagnosing Children and Adolescents: Guide for Mental Health Practitioners.* She is the recipient of numerous national awards including the 2015 Counselor Educator Advocacy Award, 2014 ACA Kitty Cole Human Rights Award, 2012 ACA Gilbert and Kathleen Wrenn Award for a Caring and Humanitarian Person, and the 2012 IAMFC Distinguished Mentor Award.

Carl J. Sheperis, PhD, NCC, ACS, LMHC, LPC, serves as chair of the Department of Counseling and Special Populations at Lamar University. He is a past president of the Association for Assessment and Research in Counseling, associate editor for quantitative research for the *Journal of Counseling & Development*, and a director for the National Board for Certified Counselors. He has worked with the American Counseling Association as the chair of the Research and Knowledge Committee and has served as the editor of the *Journal of Counseling Research and Practice.*

In addition to this textbook Dr. Sheperis is an author of *Assessment Procedures for Counselors and Helping Professionals*; *Research in Counseling: Quantitative, Qualitative, and Mixed Methods*; *Clinical Mental Health Counseling: Fundamentals of Applied Practice*; *The Student Handbook for Online Counselor Education*; and *The Peace Train.* He is also published in various textbooks, academic journals, and reference volumes. A frequent speaker and presenter at professional conferences and workshops as well, Dr. Sheperis has appeared at such recent events as the American Counseling Association World Conference, the Association for Counselor Education and Supervision Conference, the National Assessment Conference, and the National Head Start Conference.

List of Contributors

Sue C. Bratton, PhD, LPC-S, RPT-S, is a professor at the University of North Texas (UNT) and director of the UNT Center for Play Therapy with over 20 years of experience as a university professor, researcher, and clinician. She is a nationally and internationally known speaker and author with over 65 publications in the area of child counseling, play therapy, and Child Parent Relationship Therapy (CPRT). Her most recent books are *Child Parent Relationship Therapy (CPRT): A 10-Session Filial Therapy Model*, *Child Parent Relationship Therapy (CPRT) Treatment Manual*, *Child-Centered Play Therapy Research: The Evidence Base for Practitioners*, and *Integrative Play Therapy*.

Tracy K. Calley, PhD, is an adjunct professor of counseling at Texas State University and Texas A&M University–San Antonio. She has a passion for working with adolescents, particularly at-risk youth and children in need. Her research interests with respect to adolescents include sand tray therapy, animal-assisted therapy, and adventure therapy.

Tara Chandrasekhar, MD, is a clinical assistant professor of psychiatry at the University of North Carolina (UNC) at Chapel Hill. She is a double-board-certified psychiatrist, in general psychiatry and child and adolescent psychiatry. She participates in clinical research with the UNC Adolescent, School-age and Preschool Psychiatric Intervention Research and Evaluation (ASPIRE) Program, teaches medical students and resident physicians, and cares for children and adults in outpatient clinics in rural North Carolina. She currently treats a number of children and adults with schizophrenia and related disorders, providing medication management and supportive therapy, and coordinating care with other providers.

SeriaShia Chatters-Smith, PhD, LMHC, is an assistant professor and coordinator of the Clinical Mental Health Counseling in Schools and Communities Program in the Department of Educational Psychology, Counseling, and Special Education at the Pennsylvania State University. She has taught courses in diagnosis and treatment of mental disorders, child and adolescent counseling, and multicultural counseling. She also has coauthored articles on bullying, cyberbullying, and depression in special populations.

Laura H. Choate, EdD, LPC-S, NCC, is an associate professor of counselor education at Louisiana State University with 15 years' experience as a therapist. She is the author of three books: *Girls and Women's Wellness: Contemporary Counseling Issues and Interventions* (2008), *Eating Disorders and Obesity: A Counselor's Guide to Prevention and Treatment* (2013), and *Adolescent Girls in Distress: A Guide to Mental Health Treatment and Prevention* (2013). She has 40 publications in journals and books, most of which have been related to girls' and women's mental health.

Richard J. Cicchetti, PhD, is a core faculty member in the Mental Health Counseling Program at Walden University. He also works in private practice with clients who have discomfort from process addictions, veterans with discomfort from readjustment syndrome, clients with disabilities, and clients with substance abuse and relationship issues.

Ryan M. Cook, MA, LPC, is a doctoral candidate in the Counselor Education and Supervision Program at Virginia Tech. He previously worked at a crisis stabilization facility and at an outpatient community mental health clinic.

Joshua John Diehl, PhD, is the chief strategy officer for Autism Services at LOGAN Community Resources, Inc. In addition, he holds positions as an adjunct assistant professor of psychology at the University of Notre Dame and as associate editor of the *Journal of Autism and Developmental Disorders*. His research focuses on the diagnosis and treatment of individuals with autism spectrum disorder.

Joshua D. Francis, PhD, LPCC-S, LICDC-CS, owns and operates a private counseling and consultation practice and is an adjunct counselor educator at Xavier University. Josh's clinical specialties and areas of research include child and adolescent mental health, marriage and family therapy, high-conflict divorce, trauma, counselor ethics, counselor wellness, and process/behavioral addictions.

Gary G. Gintner, PhD, LPC, is an associate professor and program leader of the Counseling Program at Louisiana State University. He has published numerous articles on topics such as the *DSM-5*, differential diagnosis, mood disorders, substance abuse, and best practices for the treatment of psychiatric and substance use disorders. From 2010 to 2013 he served as chair of the *DSM-5* Task Force for American Mental Health Counselors Association (AMHCA), charged with reviewing drafts of the *DSM-5* and providing feedback to the American Psychiatric Association. He is currently a member of the Global Clinical Practice Network for the World Health Organization and is participating in field trials for *ICD-11*.

Laura R. Haddock, PhD, LPC-S, NCC, is the program coordinator for the Counselor Education and Supervision Program at Walden University. She has been a counselor educator since 2001, supported by more than two decades of work as a mental health counselor. Her research interests include counselor wellness and secondary trauma, spirituality, sexuality, cultural diversity, and supervision.

Brooks Bastian Hanks, PhD, LCPC, is a core faculty member in the Mental Health Counseling Program at Walden University. Her research interests include child sexual abuse, forensic interviewing, vicarious trauma, and mental health accessibility. She has experience working with children who have been sexually abused and their families, and she works as a forensic interviewer and custody evaluator. She also has experience working with clients who have dual diagnoses, with obsessive-compulsive disorder being one of those diagnoses.

Gregory T. Hatchett, PhD, LPCC, is an associate professor and director of the Clinical Mental Health Counseling Program at Northern Kentucky University. He teaches courses in diagnosis, treatment planning, assessment, and research design. His research interests include the diagnosis of mood disorders, premature termination, and the assessment of the preferences that college students have for counseling.

Lindsey M. Hazzard, MSW, LCSW, is a research instructor in psychiatry on the ASPIRE research team at the University of North Carolina at Chapel Hill School of Medicine. Her work contributes to the advancement of pediatric clinical research in autism, bipolar, and early-onset psychotic disorders. She has participated in over 30 pediatric clinical research studies and is trained on several standardized assessments.

Nicole R. Hill, PhD, LPC, is the chair of the Department of Counseling and Human Services at Syracuse University. Her research interests include working with children and adolescents, multicultural counseling competencies, professional development of faculty and graduate students, and mentoring. Her clinical experience is focused on counseling children and adolescents.

K. Michelle Hunnicutt Hollenbaugh, PhD, LPC-S, is an assistant professor in the Department of Counseling and Educational Psychology at Texas A&M University–Corpus Christi. She has worked in a variety of clinical settings with varying populations, including inpatient, outpatient, intensive outpatient, college counseling center, and crisis stabilization. She specializes in practice and research related to Dialectical Behavior Therapy and currently is working to analyze the mechanisms that contribute to its effectiveness.

Claudia E. Howell, MEd, NCC, is a doctoral candidate in the Counselor Education and Supervision doctoral program at Virginia Tech. Her clinical experience includes residential work with adolescent males, as well as adults with HIV/AIDS.

Gregory S. Hupp, PhD, LP, works in private practice. He specializes in clinical neuropsychology and behavioral medicine and has particular expertise in the diagnostic assessment of developmental disorders, traumatic brain injury (TBI), and degenerative disorders. He has worked with children with autism spectrum disorder, soldiers with combined post-traumatic stress disorder (PTSD)/TBI, and visually impaired children and adults.

Jason H. King, PhD, DCMHS, ACS, CAS, is the student development coordinator for the master's and doctoral School of Counseling Programs at Walden University. He also owns an outpatient mental health and substance abuse clinic that collected data for the American Psychiatric Association's Routine Clinical Practice field trials that informed the *DSM-5* revision process. He served as an AMHCA and American Counseling Association (ACA) *DSM-5* Proposed Revision Task Force member and has given over 180 national and international seminars on the *DSM-5*. He completed a podcast and webinar on the *DSM-5* with the ACA and wrote 18 monthly articles on the *DSM-5* in ACA's *Counseling Today.*

Jason D. Kushner, PhD, LPC, CSC, is a professor of counselor education at the University of Arkansas at Little Rock. Concurrent with his experience as a counselor educator, he is a contributing therapist in an outpatient counseling clinic. His past experience includes positions as a high-school English teacher, professional school counselor, and college counselor.

Chloe Lancaster, PhD, CSC, is an assistant professor and school counseling coordinator at the University of Memphis. She previously worked as an elementary-school counselor and as a middle-school special education teacher and department chair, and ran counseling groups for court-referred youth at a local community counseling center. She also is engaged in research with community stakeholders to promote more effective services for foster care and adoptive children with histories of trauma and neglect.

Gerard Lawson, PhD, LPC, NCC, ACS, is an associate professor in the Counselor Education Program at Virginia Tech. He has presented at national and international conferences on a range of topics, including counselor wellness, crisis response and resilience, and clinical supervision. He was instrumental in helping coordinate the counseling response to the tragic shootings at Virginia Tech in 2007, and he is the principal author of Virginia Tech's first disaster mental health plan. He chaired the ACA Crisis Response Planning Task Force and has authored several articles and book chapters on crisis response. He has served as a consultant for school systems across the region, providing guidance and support for crisis response planning.

A. Stephen Lenz, PhD, LPC, is an assistant professor and Clinical Mental Health Counseling Program coordinator at Texas A&M University–Corpus Christi. He also works with adolescents and young adults in an intensive outpatient program for individuals with eating disorders. His research interests include community-based program evaluation, counseling outcome research, single-case research, instrument development, and holistic approaches to counseling, counselor education, and supervision.

Jacob J. Levy, PhD, LP-HSP, is an associate professor and director of the Ph.D. program in counseling psychology at the University of Tennessee, Knoxville. His research involves the intersection of personal characteristics with environmental demands, especially as it relates to career development, multicultural counseling, and counseling gifted and talented populations. He also is a licensed psychologist and maintains a part-time private practice.

Timothy M. Lionetti, PhD, LP, is a core faculty member and the coordinator of the school, counseling, and clinical psychology specializations at Walden University. His clinical and research interests include improving student reading, health promotion, effects of age on academic success, behavioral disorders, and the linking of the mental health and school systems. He works with children, schools, and families within the school and mental health systems and private practice using both direct and consultative services.

Christina G. McDonnell, MA, is a doctoral student in clinical psychology at the University of Notre Dame and a research assistant in the Development and Psychopathology Laboratory. Her research has focused on understanding the processes that confer risk and resilience across development within the context of child trauma, and she is interested in the translation of this research into empirically based interventions for at-risk families. She is currently working on a randomized controlled trial of an intervention for maltreating families and their children that a National Institutes of Health (NIH) grant is funding. She also has worked in a wide range of clinical and community settings, providing psychological assessment and services to at-risk children and families.

Ruth Ouzts Moore, PhD, LPC, NCC, is a core faculty member in the Mental Health Counseling Program at Walden University. She has worked in community mental health agencies, private practice, and inpatient/residential facilities. She has also provided consultation, training, and crisis intervention in schools. She also is a frequent presenter at the state, national, and international levels on topics including play therapy, abuse/trauma, high-conflict divorce/parental alienation, creative counseling techniques, and expert witness and courtroom testimony.

Nicole R. Motley, M.S., is a recent graduate of the Clinical Mental Health Counseling Program at Northern Kentucky University. She completed an internship at the Northern Kentucky University Training and Development Center, where she provided counseling services in both outpatient and residential settings. Her interests include creativity in counseling, integrated care, chronic illness, trauma treatment, and the study of process addictions.

Michelle Perepiczka, PhD, LMHC, CSC, RPT, NCC, is a core faculty member in the Mental Health Counseling Program at Walden University. Her clinical experiences include providing counseling and play therapy services in agency, hospital, and school settings to children and adolescents presenting with developmental, emotional, academic, and abuse-related concerns. Her research interests include wellness, humanistic philosophies, and the impact of alternative teaching models in higher education.

Torey Portrie-Bethke, PhD, NCC, is a core faculty member in the Mental Health Counseling Program at Walden University. She specializes in providing counseling services for children, adolescents, and families, using experiential counseling methods, such as adventure-based counseling, play therapy, and sandplay. Her scholarly interests include counseling supervision, adventure-based counseling, online counselor education, childhood sexual abuse, vicarious trauma, and experiential teaching methods.

Dee C. Ray, PhD, LPC-S, NCC, RPT-S, is a distinguished teaching professor in the Counseling Program and director of the Child and Family Resource Clinic at the University of North Texas. She specializes in the practice, supervision, and research of child-centered play therapy. In her position as clinic director, she supervises counseling services for over 150 clients per week, with a specific expertise in children and adolescents. She has studied the effects of child-centered play therapy on children with disruptive behavior disorders, ADHD, anxiety and those with significant functional impairment.

Varunee Faii Sangganjanavanich, PhD, LPCC-S, is an associate professor in and coordinator of the Counselor Education and Supervision doctoral program in the School of Counseling at the University of Akron. She has authored and coauthored numerous publications, including peer-reviewed journal articles, book chapters, and encyclopedia entries. Her research interests are in the areas of transgender issues in counseling, gender nonconforming youth, gender transition, and career development of transgender individuals.

Linmarie Sikich, MD, is an associate professor at the Duke University Department of Psychiatry and Behavioral Sciences. She is the associate director of the Duke Center for Autism and Brain Development and part of the Translational Neuroscience Team at the

Duke Clinical Research Institute. She is a board-certified child and adolescent psychiatrist. Her research focuses on developing and rigorously evaluating treatments for psychiatric and neurodevelopmental disorders affecting children and adolescents and their families. She has played a leading role in several long-term studies of children and adolescents with psychosis and has participated in clinical trials for children and adolescents with autism, fragile X, and pediatric bipolar disorder that the federal government, Autism Speaks, and individual pharmaceutical companies funded.

Anneliese A. Singh, PhD, LPC, is an associate professor in the Department of Counseling and Human Development Services at the University of Georgia. Her clinical, research, and advocacy interests include resilience of transgender youth and people of color, survivors of trauma, social justice and empowerment training, resilience of South Asian survivors of child sexual abuse, and empowerment interventions with survivors of trauma. Dr. Singh is the past president of the Southern Association of Counselor Education and Supervision and the past president of the Association of Lesbian, Gay, Bisexual, and Transgender Issues in Counseling (ALGBTIC).

Joy-Del Snook, PhD, LPC, is an assistant professor in the Department of Counseling and Special Populations at Lamar University. She is a supervisor in the community clinic on the university campus as well as the practicum coordinator within the department. Her research interests and experience include wellness for children, adolescents, and adults with mobility impairments; animal-assisted therapy for children and adolescents; advocacy; PTSD; addictions; supervision; and bridging research and practice.

Shawn L. Spurgeon, PhD, LPC, is an associate professor and coordinator of the Clinical Mental Health Counseling Program at the University of Tennessee, Knoxville. He served on the American Counseling Association's 2014 Ethics Revision Task Force and currently serves on the editorial board of the *Journal of Counseling Research and Practice* and the *Journal of the Professional Counselor*. He is the president for the Association for Assessment and Research in Counseling (AARC) and as president-elect for the Southern Association of Counselor Educators and Supervisors (SACES). He has published articles on African American male development and professional-counselor identity. He has previously worked as a mental health counselor in a family services agency, a private practice, and a community mental health center. His work has included couples, families, and adolescents with emotional and behavioral problems.

Hayley L. Stulmaker, PhD, LPC, NCC, RPT, is an assistant professor in the Department of Counselor Education at Sam Houston State University. She has experience working with children, adolescents, and families in community-based, elementary-school, and private counseling settings. She has worked with diverse clients with many presenting concerns, recently specializing in children who are anxious. Her research interests include play therapy effectiveness, understanding mediators and moderators of counseling processes, and finding treatments for children with anxiety and trauma experiences.

Gary M. Szirony, PhD, CRC, NCC, is a core faculty member in the College of Social and Behavior Sciences at Walden University. He serves on the editorial board of the international IOS journal, *Work: A Journal of Prevention, Assessment & Rehabilitation*, has published several peer-reviewed articles and book chapters, and presented at local, state, and national conferences. His research interests include neuropsychology, wellness, counseling and psychotherapy, distance learning, and, most notably, the development of the synergistic integration model.

Lee A. Teufel-Prida, PhD, LMHC, LPCC, NCC, is currently a core faculty member in the Marriage, Couple, and Family Counseling Program at Walden University. Her research interests include counseling and advocating for children and families affected by abuse, trauma, significant life stress, or military service. She has presented at several community, state, national, and international conferences and workshops, including those of the ACA and Association of Counselor Education and Supervision (ACES).

Kathleen Jones-Trebatoski, PhD, LPC-S, NCC, is in private practice, where she also supervises interns and provides community consultation. Her area of expertise is a focus on wellness and stress management. She also introduced Animal Assisted Therapy, a free community youth counseling program that involved the use of certified animals in counseling.

Kristin Valentino, PhD, is the William J. Shaw Center for Children and Families associate professor of psychology at the University of Notre Dame and is director of the Development & Psychopathology Laboratory. Her research evaluates how the integration of biological, psychological, and environmental factors can inform our understanding of the development of memory and self among maltreated children. In addition, Dr. Valentino focuses on the translation of developmental research into interventions for maltreated children and their families. Her current research, supported by the National Institute of Child Health and Human Development, is evaluating the effectiveness of a brief intervention for maltreated preschool-aged children and their mothers.

Holly H. Wagner, PhD, LPC, NCC, is an assistant professor in the Department of Counseling and Family Therapy at the University of Missouri–St. Louis. Her research interests include school counseling; counselor development; feminist pedagogy; cultural competence; lesbian, gay, bisexual, transgender, queer, questioning, intersex, and ally (LGBTQQIA) competence and advocacy; and social justice issues in counselor education. She also previously worked as a school counselor.

Julia L. Whisenhunt, PhD, LPC, NCC, is an assistant professor of counselor education and college student affairs in the Department of Clinical and Professional Studies at the University of West Georgia. She has presented and published in the areas of self-injury, suicide, sandtray therapy, play therapy, trauma, and posttraumatic growth, but her primary research concentrations are self-injury and suicide. She also has clinical experience working with child, adolescent, and adult clients who experience a variety of therapeutic issues.

Lisa A. Wines, PhD, LPC-Intern, CSC, is an assistant professor in the Counseling and Special Populations Program at Lamar University. She has worked within hospital, school, and university settings with children, adolescents, and graduate students. Her research interests are concentrated in the areas of qualitative methodology, school counseling, and multicultural endeavors.

Carlos P. Zalaquett, PhD, LMHC, is a professor and coordinator of the Brain Focused Laboratory for the study of biofeedback and neurofeedback treatments in the Department of Educational Psychology, Counseling, and Special Education at The Pennsylvania State University. He is a nationally and internationally recognized expert on mental health, diversity, and education; and is the author or coauthor of six books and more than 60 scholarly publications. He is the Vice-President for the US and Canada of the Society of Interamerican Psychology and serves as a visiting faculty in several academic programs abroad. He is the Associate Editor of the Journal of Multicultural Counseling and Development. He has conducted workshops and lectures in eight countries on the topics of clinical mental health counseling, psychotherapy, crisis intervention, bullying, and stress management.

Part I

Stages of the Comprehensive Diagnostic Process

Part I of this textbook focuses on the underlying principles and foundations of diagnosis and treatment planning. We designed this section to provide counselors and other helping professionals a foundation in the diagnostic process. Chapter 1 sets the stage for the remainder of the textbook by presenting a model for using the *Diagnostic and Statistical Manual of Mental Disorders, Fifth Edition* (*DSM-5*), in the diagnostic process with children and adolescents. Chapter 2 focuses on the assessment process for *DSM-5* disorders, stressing the use of various assessment sources, including instruments the American Psychiatric Association provided. Chapter 3 presents the process for using an accurate diagnostic process to guide the development of evidence-based treatment plans. Chapter 4 grounds the clinician in the diversity issues that can affect the diagnostic and treatment process. It is critical that clinicians consider gender, culture, diversity, age, and other demographic information in the determination of an accurate diagnosis. Although each of the chapters in Part I is important for understanding the diagnostic process, Chapter 4 is essential in the conceptualization of each disorder. After reading the chapters in Part I, clinicians should have a clear process for understanding each of the disorders presented in Part II.

Chapter 1

Conceptualizing DSM-5 Disorders in Children and Adolescents

BRANDÉ FLAMEZ, JASON H. KING, AND JOSHUA D. FRANCIS

Introduction

The creation of the *Diagnostic and Statistical Manual of Mental Disorders, Fifth Edition* (*DSM-5*; American Psychiatric Association [APA], 2013a), was a controversial and multi-faceted process. Early drafts of the manual created considerable debate within the mental health field, as some argued that it was not as grounded in science as it should be, while others argued that it seemed to lack clinical utility. The initial changes appeared as if they would be substantial reworkings of the *Diagnostic and Statistical Manual of Mental Disorders, Fourth Edition, Text Revision* (*DSM-IV-TR*), diagnoses and criteria, although they ended up not being quite as intense as originally thought.

Nonetheless, the *DSM-5* contains significant revisions, especially concerning the breadth and depth of the diagnostic criteria, inclusion of dimensional conceptualization, consolidation of many disorders, and acknowledgment of cultural factors. Although the *DSM-IV-TR* multiaxial system was eliminated, the new diagnostic categories provide more room for specifiers that will enable the clinician to provide a richer and more thorough description of the client's symptomatology. This should aid in both case conceptualization and treatment planning. These revisions also place a greater emphasis on changes across the lifespan and developmental issues. Although this emphasis certainly affects adult disorders, it has particular significance for disorders of childhood. Thus, it is important for the clinician to understand how these changes will affect clinical work with clients, particularly when working with children and adolescents.

This chapter will provide a framework for conceptualizing the array of mental health symptomology that child and adolescent patients may present. The chapter includes an overview of the differences in definitions of a mental disorder across editions of the *DSM*, including the current distress/impairment criterion for arriving at a diagnostic decision. In addition, the information in this chapter illuminates how the developmental process and age-related factors play a role in diagnosis. We dedicate specific attention to the critical role of neurodevelopment in the conceptualization of a *DSM* diagnosis among children and adolescents and review differences in categories for *DSM* diagnoses.

Defining a Mental Disorder

A mental disorder is generally a construct that requires a clustering of identifiable cognitive, affective, behavioral, or physical symptoms resulting in marked functional impairment. Because psychiatric symptoms often manifest on a spectrum of severity, frequency, and duration, and may be present within both normal and abnormal human development, the definition of a mental disorder is complex. To understand this complexity, this section reviews the historical influences that define a mental disorder and how the definition has evolved since the publication of the *DSM-I* (1952).

HISTORY OF DEFINITION

Publication of the *DSM-I* in 1952 heralded the first classification of diagnostic categories and provided a nosological system consistent with the concepts of modern psychiatry and neurology. This diagnostic scheme generically used the term *disorder* to designate a group of related psychiatric syndromes, with each group further divided into more specific psychiatric conditions termed *reactions*. The use of the term *reaction* in the manual reflected the influence of Adolf Meyer's (president of the APA from 1927 to 1928) *psychobiological* view that mental disorders were reactions of the individual's personality struggle for adjustment to psychological, social, and biological stressors, rather than biologically specifiable natural disease entities. As such, mental disorders in this manual were divided into the following groups (APA, 1952, p. 9):

1. "Those in which there is disturbance of mental function resulting from, or precipitated by, a primary impairment of the function of the brain, generally due to diffuse impairment of brain tissue."
2. "Those which are the result of a more general difficulty in adaptation of the individual, and in which any associated brain function disturbance is secondary to the psychiatric disorder."

The *DSM-I*'s Diseases of the Psychobiologic Unit included disorders caused by, or associated with, impairment of brain tissue function (neurocognitive disorders), mental deficiency (intellectual developmental disorder), disorders of psychogenic origin (bipolar-related, schizophrenia spectrum, and other psychotic disorders), psychophysiologic disorders (somatic symptom disorders), psychoneurotic disorders (anxiety, dissociative, conversion, phobic, obsessive-compulsive, and depressive disorders), personality disorders (paraphilic, addictive, elimination, speech, learning, and personality disorders), and transient situational personality disorders (adjustment disorders). This nomenclature "enabled to offer a completely new classification in conformity with newer scientific and clinical knowledge, simpler in structure, easier to use and virtually identical with other national and international nomenclatures" (APA, 1952, p. 1), such as the *Standard Classified Nomenclature of Disease* the New York Academy of Medicine published in 1933.

In the development of the *DSM-II*, the product of an international collaborative effort that started in 1957, a decision was made to base the classification on the mental disorders section of the Eighth Revision of the World Health Organization's *International Classification of Diseases* (*ICD-8*) to reflect "the growth of the concept that the people of all nations live in one world" (APA, 1968, p. vii). Since this time, all *DSM* editions have paralleled, with varying degrees of harmonization, the ongoing *ICD* revisions. Like the *DSM-I*, the second edition of the manual did not provide a formal definition of mental disorder. The *DSM-II* significantly expanded the *DSM-I*'s diagnostic nomenclature to include eight sexual deviations (i.e., homosexuality, fetishism, pedophilia, transvestitism, exhibitionism, voyeurism, sadism, and masochism), nine drug dependence classifications (i.e., opium, synthetic analgesics, barbiturates, other hypnotics and sedatives, cocaine, cannabis sativa, other psychostimulants, and hallucinogens), tic and other psychomotor disorders, encopresis, feeding disturbance, and cephalalgia.

Important nosological categories added in the *DSM-II* included Behavior Disorders of Childhood and Adolescence (i.e., hyperkinetic reaction, withdrawing reaction, overanxious reaction, runaway reaction, unsocialized aggressive reaction, group delinquent reaction, and other reaction) and Conditions Without Manifest Psychiatric Disorder and Non-Specific Conditions (i.e., social maladjustments without manifest psychiatric disorder, marital maladjustment, social maladjustment, occupational maladjustment, dyssocial behavior, and other social maladjustment). Despite the marriage of the *DSM-II* with the *ICD-8* and its resulting name changes to some of the mental disorders (e.g., *chronic brain syndrome* becomes *organic brain syndrome*; *mental deficiency* becomes *mental retardation*; *schizophrenic reaction* becomes *schizophrenia*; *neurosis* replaces *reaction* for anxiety, dissociative, conversion, phobic, obsessive-compulsive, and depressive disorders; and *disorder of sleep* replaces *somnambulism*), "the change of label has not changed the nature of the disorder" (APA, 1968, p. ix)—thus the overall conceptualization of mental disorders in the *DSM-II* paralleled the conceptualization of mental disorders in the *DSM-I*.

The *DSM-III*, published in 1980, provided a descriptive approach that was atheoretical with regard to pathophysiological processes of mental disorders, and it reflected the importance of having common language between research investigators and clinical practitioners. Unlike the First and Second Editions, the *DSM-III* emphasized that accurate diagnostic assessment was essential to treatment planning and therefore included "such new features as diagnostic criteria, a multiaxial approach to evaluation, much-expanded descriptions of the disorders and many additional categories" (APA, 1980, p. 1). The *DSM-III* also differed from the *DSM-I* and the *DSM-II* in that clinical field trials, sponsored by the National Institute of Mental Health, were conducted to identify classification problems, test solutions to these problems, and evaluate diagnostic reliability among clinicians in diverse settings and of varying theoretical orientations. The *DSM-III* further noted that boundaries between disorders were discontinuous and lacked precision.

Most important, the *DSM-III* provided the first discussion in the manual on the subjective concept *mental disorder* by highlighting two important aspects (APA, 1980, p. 6):

1. "Each of the mental disorders is conceptualized as a clinically significant behavioral or psychological syndrome or pattern that occurs in an individual and that is typically associated with either a painful symptom (distress) or impairment in one or more important areas of functioning (disability)."

2. "There is an inference that there is a behavioral, psychological, or biological dysfunction, and that the disturbance is not only in the relationship between the individual and society."

Seven years later, the *DSM-III-R* (APA, 1987) retained this definition of *mental disorder*—sparking controversial dialogue among mental health professionals regarding the overall clinical utility of a definition focused on an individual's distress, disability, or dysfunction resulting from a psychiatric syndrome (Wakefield, 1992; Spitzer, 1999).

DSM-IV DEFINITION

Published in 1994, the *DSM-IV* resulted from comprehensive and systematic reviews of the published literature, reanalysis of already collected data sets, and extensive issue-focused field trials. This manual also acknowledged the term *mental disorder* arbitrarily implied that a distinction exists between *physical* disorders (medical conditions) and *mental* disorders (psychological conditions)—although such is not the case. The manual further recognized that "the concept of mental disorder … lacks a consistent operational definition that covers all situations" and "the term persists in the title of *DSM-IV* because we have not found an appropriate substitute" (APA, 1994, p. xxi). As such, the *DSM-IV* retained the definition of *mental disorder* published in the *DSM-III* and the *DSM-III-R*; however this definition contained reordering of some words and addition of other words to the first half of the definition. In the *DSM-IV*, the phrase "that is typically associated with either a painful symptom (distress)" is changed to read "that is associated with present distress (e.g., a painful symptom)," and the phrase "or impairment in one or more important areas of functioning (disability)" is changed to read "or disability (i.e., impairment in one or more important areas of functioning)." Finally, the phrase "or with a significantly increased risk of suffering death, pain, disability, or an important loss of freedom" is added and is the concluding language of the first half of the definition. Similar to the *DSM-III* and the *DSM-III-R*, culturally sanctioned response patterns (e.g., the death of a loved one) were excluded from the *DSM-IV* definition of *mental disorder*, and deviant behavior had to be directly manifest to a symptom of a dysfunction in the individual.

The *DSM-IV-TR* (APA, 2000) retained the definition of *mental disorder* published in the *DSM-IV*. Grossman (2004) provided an analysis of this definition by challenging the implication that mental disorders are located within the individual and that mental disorders cannot be merely the result of environmental factors, as proposed in the *DSM-I*'s *psychobiological reactions*, and the associated ascriptions of responsibility upon the individual for preventing the mental disorder.

DSM-5 DEFINITION

The Fifth Edition of the *DSM*, published in 2013, acknowledged that capturing all aspects of all syndromes within the definition of *mental disorder* is challenging. Developed for clinical, public health, and research purposes, the *DSM-5*'s required elements that define *mental disorder* retain language from the *DSM-III*, the *DSM-III-R*, the *DSM-IV*, and the *DSM-IV-TR* that "significant dysfunction, distress, or disability in social, occupational, or other important activities are usually associated with mental disorders" (APA, 2013a, p. 20). Like its predecessors, the *DSM-5* excludes culturally expected responses to a common stressor from the definition and requires that social deviancy result directly from a dysfunction in the individual; and it requires clinical utility to "determine prognosis, treatment plans, and potential treatment outcomes" (APA, 2013a, p. 20). New to the *DSM-5* definition are the words *disturbance*, *cognition*, *emotion regulation*, and *developmental processes underlying mental functioning*.

The conceptualization of mental disorder in the latest manual further incorporates empirical evidence from "antecedent validators (similar genetic markers, family traits, temperament, and environmental exposure), concurrent validators (similar neural substrates, biomarkers, emotional and cognitive processing, and symptom similarity), and predictive validators (similar clinical course and treatment response)" (APA, 2013a, p. 20). The most important conceptual change to the definition of mental disorder in the *DSM-5* is the significantly expanded use of *course* specifiers that communicate symptom progress (e.g., in partial remission, in full remission), *descriptive* specifiers that communicate symptom distinctiveness (e.g., with good to fair insight, in a controlled environment), and *severity* specifiers that communicate symptom intensity (e.g., mild, moderate, severe). Finally, the *DSM-5* conceptualization of *mental disorder* more richly encompasses gender differences, cultural issues, and developmental and life span considerations to facilitate a dimensional approach to clinical case formulation.

The *DSM-5* definition of *mental disorder* has already spurred discussion in the professional literature. First and Wakefield (2013) critiqued the requirement of establishing the presence of *dysfunction* in the individual and offered helpful requirements to ensure that the disorder meets the requirements of the definition of mental disorder. Some of these requirements include the following:

- A minimum duration and persistence
- That the frequency or intensity of a symptom exceed that seen in normal people
- Disproportionality of symptoms, given the context
- Pervasiveness of symptom expression across contexts, adding specific exclusions for contextual scenarios in which symptoms are best understood as normal reactions.

In 2013, Kecmanovic provided an overview of the extraordinary difficulty encountered when defining *mental disorder*. Kecmanovic championed the *DSM-5*'s continuation of the *DSM-III*'s addition of "clinical significance" to the definition of mental disorder to reduce diagnosing normative individuals as mentally disordered. However, an important critique this author provided is that the *DSM-5* definition does not operationalize how serious a dysfunction should be, or how much cognitions, emotions, or behavior should be dysfunctional, to qualify as clinically significant. Similarly, Bingham and Banner (2014) noted that relying on scientific theory or values to define *mental disorder* fails to safeguard the diagnostic status of individuals in oppressive societies and risks excessive inclusion of mental or behavioral states, such as same-sex attraction, that happen to be negatively valued in the individual's social context. This criticism is targeted toward the *DSM-5*'s retained language from *DSM-III* that the definition of *mental disorder* restricts "socially deviant behavior (e.g., political, religious, or sexual) and conflicts that are primarily between the individual and society" and "results directly from a dysfunction in the individual" (APA, 2013a, p. 20).

The Clinical Significance Criterion in Diagnosis

In the *DSM-IV-TR*, the definition of mental disorder included the requirement that there be significant distress or impairment for a diagnosis to be made. The concept of impairment was quite straightforward: It typically related to social, emotional, or occupational dysfunction and could be fairly easily quantified. For example, someone diagnosed with alcohol abuse or dependence frequently would report strained relationships with friends and family or having difficulties completing work responsibilities. These symptoms would be sufficient to satisfy the impairment requirement.

On the other hand, the concept of distress is quite murky. There is not an agreed upon universal definition within the mental health community, and it can be very difficult to quantify. For instance, children may deny feeling any distress, although they may exhibit acting-out behaviors. A trained clinician might view the behaviors as symptoms of distress, but that leaves it up to individual interpretation, which is problematic from a scientific perspective.

Another problem with using distress (or even impairment) as a diagnostic criterion is that the *ICD* criteria do not include it. When the authors of the *DSM-5* began developing the new manual, their original intent was to remove the clinical significance criterion from the diagnostic categories to align better with the *ICD-10*. However, a majority of the work groups for the various diagnoses found that it was simply not possible to remove the criterion. Thus, although the clinical significance criterion is not a requirement for a mental disorder in the *DSM-5*, it is a requirement for many diagnostic categories.

One prominent example of this is in the diagnosis of gender dysphoria in children (formerly gender identity disorder). The clinical significance criterion is listed as Criterion B after eight other symptoms are included under Criterion A. To make the diagnosis, the client has to display six of the eight symptoms from Criterion A, as well as exhibit significant distress or impairment. In fact, the presence of distress is particularly important in making this diagnosis because the name of the disorder was changed to reflect the unpleasant feelings that occur when there is a disconnect between one's assigned gender and expressed gender rather than focusing on identity issues.

Although some notable disorders do not require the clinical significance criterion (e.g., substance use, tic disorders, pyromania, etc.), most of the other disorders still require that the client experience distress or impairment. Despite the authors' attempts to better align the *DSM* diagnostic criteria with the *ICD*, it simply was not feasible in this version of the manual. Still, the decision not to require that the clinical significance criterion be met in the definition of mental disorder was a major shift in the *DSM-5*.

The Developmental Process

The *DSM-5* reflects important conceptual and practical differences between the *DSM-IV-TR* related to developmental impacts on presenting symptomology for children and adolescents. The former manual lumped the variations in the presentation of a disorder that are attributable to an individual's developmental stage in a subheading of the disorder descriptive text titled "Specific Culture, Age, and Gender Features." In contrast, the *DSM-5* carves out the developmental focus into a subheading of the disorder descriptive text titled "Development and Course." The "Diagnostic Features" section of the new manual further contains the following developmental focus additions:

- *Bipolar and related disorders* (i.e., "these symptoms are recurrent, inappropriate to the context, and beyond what is expected for the developmental level of the child"; "developmentally inappropriate sexual preoccupations"; "children of the same chronological age may be at different developmental stages"; "the child's symptoms must exceed what is expected in a given environment and culture for the child's developmental stage"; APA, 2013a, pp. 127–129).

- *Depressive disorders* (i.e., "temper outbursts are inconsistent with developmental level" and "developmentally appropriate mood elevation … should not be considered as a symptom of mania or hypomania"; APA, 2013a, pp. 156).
- *Anxiety disorders* (i.e., "differ from developmentally normative fear or anxiety by being excessive or persisting beyond developmentally appropriate periods"; "anxiety exceeds what may be expected given the person's developmental level"; "it is important to assess the degree of impairment and the duration of the fear, anxiety, or avoidance, and whether it is typical for the child's particular developmental stage"; APA, 2013a, pp. 189, 191, & 200).
- *Obsessive-compulsive and related disorders* (i.e., "differ from developmentally normative preoccupations and rituals by being excessive or persisting beyond developmentally appropriate periods"; "individuals may experience developmental difficulties"; "easily distinguished from developmentally adaptive saving and collecting behaviors"; APA, 2013a, pp. 235, 240, & 249).
- *Trauma- and stressor-related disorders* (i.e., "developmentally inappropriate attachment behaviors"; "often co-occurs with developmental delays"; "developmental regression, such as loss of language in young children, may occur"; "reluctance to pursue developmental opportunities in adolescents"; APA, 2013a, pp. 266, 276–277).
- *Feeding and eating disorders* (i.e., "children and adolescents who have not completed growth may not maintain weight or height increases along their developmental trajectory"; "nor does it include developmentally normal behaviors"; "developmental impairments that reduce an infant's responsiveness to feeding"; "associated developmental and functional limitations"; APA, 2013a, pp. 334–336).
- *Sleep-wake disorders* (i.e., "comorbidity during these developmental phases of the lifespan"; "associated with the normal developmental process"; APA, 2013a, p. 365).
- *Neurocognitive disorders* (i.e., "that are acquired rather than developmental" and "may be reflected in delays in reaching developmental milestones"; APA, 2013a, pp. 591, 626).

The *DSM-5* text furthermore includes developmental-related factors, such as symptom presentation and prevalence differences in certain age groups, specific to mental disorders. To assist with accurate clinical case formulation, the authors added these developmental-related factors to the diagnostic criteria, where applicable, as a note. Specific additions include the following:

- "Developmentally appropriate mood elevation, such as occurs in the context of a highly positive event or its anticipation, should not be considered as a symptom of mania or hypomania" (APA, 2013a, p. 156) for disruptive mood dysregulation disorder.
- "In children, the anxiety must occur in peer settings and not just during interactions with adults" (APA, 2013a, p. 202) for social anxiety disorder (social phobia).
- "Young children may not be able to articulate the aims of these behaviors or mental acts" (APA, 2013a, p. 237) for obsessive-compulsive disorder.
- "In children older than 6 years, repetitive play may occur in which themes or aspects of the traumatic event(s) are expressed"; "In children, there may be frightening dreams without recognizable content"; and "In children, trauma-specific reenactment may

occur in play" (APA, 2013a, pp. 271, 280–281) for both posttraumatic stress disorder and acute stress disorder.

- "For children younger than 5 years, the behavior should occur on most days for a period of at least 6 months … For individuals 5 years or older, the behavior should occur at least once per week for at least 6 months" (APA, 2013a, p. 462) for oppositional defiant disorder.

The most prominent developmental focus additions to the *DSM-5* are reflected in pediatric-specific diagnostic criteria for posttraumatic stress disorder (PTSD) and gender dysphoria. Compared with children and adolescents older than 6 years, clinicians use distinct criteria to diagnose PTSD in this preschool subtype, such as language, to detect trauma events the child's parent or primary caregiving figure experienced and three symptom clusters requiring four minimum of 18 possible symptoms to satisfy the diagnostic threshold (compared with four symptom clusters requiring six minimum of 20 possible symptoms to satisfy the diagnostic threshold). Diagnostic criteria language also focuses on constriction of play, socially withdrawn behavior, and "clinically significant distress or impairment in relationships with parents, siblings, peers, or other caregivers or with school behavior" (APA, 2013a, p. 274).

Examples of developmental issues related to a PTSD diagnosis in children and adolescents, compared with adults, include the following (APA, 2013a, p. 277):

A wide range of emotional/mood or behavioral changes

Focus on imagined interventions in play or storytelling

Preoccupation with trauma and stressor reminders

Experiencing co-occurring traumas

Difficulty identifying onset of symptomatology in chronic circumstances

Restricted exploratory behavior and reduced participation in new activities

Judging themselves as cowardly

When diagnosing gender dysphoria, clinicians now use criteria specific to children (typically ages 2 to 10) that are distinct from criteria for adolescents (typically ages 11–17). For children with gender dysphoria, six of eight symptoms minimum are required for the diagnosis compared with two of six symptoms minimum required for adolescents—with criteria sets focused on cross-gender preferences manifest in dressing or clothing, roles in play, activities, toys, games, and playmates for children. Because young children are less likely to express extreme and persistent anatomic dysphoria and because child cognitive development is concrete in nature, gender dysphoria diagnostic criteria reflect this concreteness and are framed in a more behavioral manner for children than those for adolescents. The most important example of developmental issues relating to a gender dysphoria diagnosis include factors related to distress and impairment:

A very young child may show signs of distress (e.g., intense crying) only when parents tell the child that he or she is "really" not a member of the other gender but only "desires" to be. Distress may not be manifest in social environments supportive of the child's desire to live in the role of the other gender and may emerge only if the desire is interfered with. In adolescents and adults, distress may manifest because of strong incongruence between experienced gender and somatic sex. Such distress may, however, be mitigated by supportive environments and knowledge that biomedical treatments exist to reduce incongruence. (APA, 2013a, p. 455)

Age-Related Factors

The human life is expansive, covering vast and broad changes in the physical, biochemical, and emotional realms. When viewed on a continuum, the aging process is essentially a developmental process, with aging contributing greatly to many factors associated with mental and psychological health. The authors of the new diagnostic manual were determined to improve clinical utility through organizing the document on developmental and life span considerations (APA, 2013a) and shift from a strong emphasis on behavioral symptoms to more prominence placed on developmental processes (Insel, 2014). In the development of the *DSM-5*, the human life span continuum played a significant role in the organizational structure and classification of clinical disorders (Zupanick, 2013). Additionally, a distinct change in the publication of the *DSM-5* is the inclusion of age-related factors within the diagnostic criteria section of each disorder.

MENTAL HEALTH SYMPTOMOLOGY ACROSS THE LIFE SPAN

Within the newly accentuated age-related organization of the *DSM-5*, mental health symptomology is seen as occurring developmentally over the entire life span. The human life span covers a broad and vast expanse, both within the single life of an individual and across the incredible diversity of over 7 billion collective human beings walking the earth. Although the *DSM-5* does not overtly make the claim, its intention is to identify and delineate the symptomology of all current mental health issues across the vast human domain. With the new emphasis on developmental processes, the *DSM-5* is trying to view mental health symptomology as factors interacting as a fluid process of growth, change, and adaptation. Factors considered include the age at which disorders first occur, how diagnoses and symptoms may change over the life span, and how disorders may evolve into new disorders over the life span (APA, 2013d).

AGE-RELATED FACTORS AND DIAGNOSES SPECIFIC TO CHILDREN AND ADOLESCENTS

Age-related factors also contribute greatly to mental health diagnoses specific to children and adolescents. The authors of the *DSM-5* made discernible efforts to provide more precise descriptions of disorders that accurately reflect the most recent scientific data on matters such as onset, etiology, prognosis, and treatment of child and adolescent conditions (APA, 2013b). Age-related factors contribute to all aspects of the diagnostic spectrum, from birth to death. The distribution of mental illness varies with many factors, including age, socioeconomic status, gender, and locale, with the prevalence of mental illness higher in children (Lakhan & Ekúndayò, 2015). Although mental health issues are diagnosed more frequently in children and adolescents, growing evidence has emerged that has shown declines in the prevalence of mental illness over the adult years and with age (Charles & Carstensen, 2009; Hudson, 2012). Age-related factors, whether onset, frequency, or other diagnostic variables, affect the assessment and diagnosis of mental illness in children and adolescents. Many of the age-related phenomena are in the new neurodevelopmental disorders chapter of the *DSM-5*, addressing disorders commonly formed in the early years of human life.

PREVALENCE WITH CHILDREN AND ADOLESCENTS

The prevalence of mental illness among children and adolescents varies depending on a number of conditions. The World Health Organization ([WHO], 2005) found prevalence rates of psychiatric disorders ranged from 12 percent to 29 percent worldwide, with a 21 percent rate in the United States. Similarly, the National Institute of Mental Health (n.d.) found that just over 20 percent of U.S. children either currently, or at some point in their life, suffer from a debilitating mental disorder. Regrettably, the vast majority of children and adolescents suffering from mental health issues go untreated.

DSM-5 and Life Span Approach to Diagnosis

The authors of the *DSM-5* purposefully organized the document in a linear fashion, consistent with the chronological timeline of the human life span. Evidence of this design is in the *DSM-5*'s chapter structure, text outline, and criteria revisions, consistently identifying age and development as part of the clinical diagnosis and classification process (Varley, 2013). The manual begins with disorders thought to reflect clinical processes that develop early in life, proceeds to disorders that present in adolescence and young adulthood, and ends with disorders more common in adulthood and later life (APA, 2013). Accordingly, the neurodevelopmental disorders (disorders most likely to occur early in the life span) are the first in the sequence of disorders covered in the manual (p. 31), whereas neurocognitive disorders (disorders most likely to occur later in the life span) are covered much later (p. 591). Other examples of disorders that are covered later in the manual, hence generally occurring later in the life span, are personality disorders (generally a condition of adulthood) and paraphilic disorders (generally a condition of postpubescence).

Within the sphere of child and adolescent mental health disorders, this chronological continuum also occurs. Immediately following the neurodevelopmental disorders are the schizophrenia spectrum and other psychotic disorders, which contemporary research is demonstrating occur earlier in the life span (Eranti, MacCabe, Bundy, & Murray, 2013; Liu, Norman, Manchanda, & De Luca, 2013). Following these disorders are bipolar and related disorders and depressive disorders, continuing progressively through the life span and average onset of the disorders.

DSM-5 Changes in Age-Related Issues

Numerous and significant changes are found in the *DSM-5* related to both developmental and age-related issues. Most prominently, the *DSM IV-TR* chapter classification Disorders Usually First Diagnosed in Infancy, Childhood, or Adolescence is now completely reconceptualized in the manual. Within this previous chapter classification, 10 disorders were disseminated into other chapter classifications of the *DSM-5*, with the remaining disorders found in the new Neurodevelopmental Disorders chapter classification.

Table 1.1 provides a comprehensive table listing the changes from the *DSM-IV-TR*'s Disorders Usually First Diagnosed in Infancy, Childhood, or Adolescence to their new location in the *DSM-5*.

TABLE 1.1   The Transition or Relocation of the *DSM-IV-TR's* Disorders Usually First Diagnosed in Infancy, Childhood, or Adolescence to Their New Position in the *DSM-5*

DSM-IV-TR *Disorders Usually First Diagnosed in* *Infancy, Childhood, or Adolescence*	*DSM-5* *Location in* DSM-5: *New chapters and titles noted*

Mental Retardation
  Mild, Moderate, Severe, Profound, Severity
    Unspecified
	Neurodevelopmental Disorders
	  Intellectual Disability
	    Mild, Moderate, Severe, Profound
	    Global Developmental Delay (new)
	    Unspecified Intellectual Disability

Learning Disorders
  Reading Disorder
  Mathematics Disorder
  Disorder of Written Expression
  Learning Disorder NOS [Not Otherwise
    Specified]
	Neurodevelopmental Disorders
	  Specific Learning Disorder
	    With Impairment in Reading
	    With Impairment in Written Expression
	    With Impairment in Mathematics
	    (Mild, Moderate, Severe)

Motor Skill Disorder
  Developmental Coordination Disorder
	Neurodevelopmental Disorders
	  Developmental Coordination Disorder

Communication Disorders
  Expressive Language Disorder
  Mixed Receptive-Expressive Language
    Disorder
  Phonological Disorder
  Stuttering
  Communication Disorder NOS
	Neurodevelopmental Disorders
	  Language Disorder
	  Speech Sound Disorder
	  Childhood-Onset Fluency Disorder
	    (Stuttering)
	  Social (Pragmatic) Communication Disorder
	  Unspecified Communication Disorder

Pervasive Developmental Disorders
  Autistic Disorder
  Rett's Disorder
  Childhood Disintegration Disorder
  Asperger's Disorder
  Pervasive Developmental Disorder NOS (PDD
    NOS)
	Neurodevelopmental Disorders
	  Autism Spectrum Disorder
	  (Rett's Disorder, Childhood
	    Disintegration Disorder, Asperger's
	    Disorder, Pervasive Developmental
	    Disorder—Eliminated)

Attention Deficit and Disruptive Behavior Disorders
 Attention-Deficit/Hyperactivity Disorder
  Combined Type
  Predominantly Inattentive Type
 	
    Predominantly Hyperactive-Impulsive Type
    Attention-Deficit/Hyperactivity Disorder
      NOS
  Conduct Disorder
  Oppositional Defiant Disorder
  Disruptive Behavioral Disorder NOS
	Neurodevelopmental Disorders
	 Attention-Deficit/Hyperactivity Disorder
	  Combined Presentation
	  Predominantly inattentive presentation
	  Predominantly hyperactive/impulsive
	    presentation
	  Other Specified
	    Attention-Deficit/Hyperactivity Disorder
	  Unspecified Attention-Deficit/Hyperactivity
	    Disorder

Feeding and Eating Disorders of Infancy or Early Childhood
  Pica
  Rumination Disorder
  Feeding Disorder of Infancy or Early Childhood
	Feeding and Eating Disorders (new chapter)
	  Pica
	  Rumination Disorder
	  Feeding Disorder of Infancy or Early
	    Childhood renamed to Avoidant/
	    Restrictive Food Intake Disorder

(*continued*)

TABLE 1.1   (*continued*)

DSM-IV-TR *Disorders Usually First Diagnosed in* *Infancy, Childhood, or Adolescence*	*DSM-5* *Location in* DSM-5: *New chapters and titles noted*

Tic Disorders
    Tourette's Disorder
    Chronic Motor of Vocal Tic Disorder
    Transient Tic Disorder
    Tic Disorder NOS
	Neurodevelopmental Disorders
	    Motor Disorders
	      Tic Disorders
	        Tourette's Disorder
	        Persistent (Chronic) Motor or Vocal
	          Tic Disorder
	        Provisional Tic Disorder
	        Other Specified Tic Disorder
	        Unspecified Tic Disorder

Elimination Disorders
    Encopresis
    Enuresis
	Elimination Disorders (**new chapter**)
	    Enuresis
	    Encopresis

Other Disorders of Infancy, Childhood, or
Adolescence
    Separation Anxiety Disorder
    Selective Mutism
    Reactive Attachment Disorder of Infancy or
      Early Childhood
    Stereotypic Movement Disorder
    Disorder of Infancy, Childhood, or Adolescence
      NOS
	Anxiety Disorders
	    Separation Anxiety Disorder
	    Selective Mutism
	Trauma and Stressor-Related Disorders
	    Reactive Attachment Disorder
	Neurodevelopment Disorders
	    Motor Disorders
	      Stereotypic Movement Disorder

The *DSM-5*'s diagnostic criteria of PTSD demonstrate one of the most significant inclusions of age-related phenomena in the new manual. In addition to the expansive changes in criteria from the *DSM-IV-TR* to the *DSM-5*, PTSD now emphasizes a developmental perspective with diagnostic thresholds lower for children and adolescents than for adults (APA, 2013). Additionally, distinct criteria have been added for children with PTSD and ages 6 and younger. For example, for children ages 6 or younger, the *DSM-5* provides distinct alterations in arousal and reactivity associated with the traumatic events, different from older children and adults. These symptoms include irritable behaviors and angry outbursts, hypervigilance, exaggerated startle response, problems with concentration, and sleep disturbance. Overt and higher-processing behaviors, often seen in older children and adults, are not as concrete or formalized within the developmental stages of children under age 6, therefore creating the need to modify these criteria for the younger age group.

Neurodevelopment and Neurodevelopmental Disorders

The introduction of the neurodevelopmental disorders chapter in the *DSM-5* brings significant attention and consideration to the area of neurodevelopment. Neurodevelopment and neuroprocesses have emerged as important areas of both clinical and research elements in the social sciences (Kindsvatter & Geroski, 2014). Once predominantly the work of the fields of neurology and neuropsychology, mental health professionals are now finding themselves assessing, diagnosing, and treating an array of neurodevelopmental issues identified in the *DSM-5*. Neurodevelopmental disorders' onsets are usually found in childhood but often persist into adulthood, resulting in impairment or delay in various central nervous system functioning. The disorders rarely experience remission or relapses and commonly follow a stable course over time (WHO, 2014).

The assessment, diagnosis, and treatment of neurodevelopmental disorders is very challenging, because early developmental trajectories are inherently unpredictable, influenced by complex genetic, biological, environmental, and psychosocial factors (Insel, 2014). Recent advances in pediatric neuroscience have revealed increasingly complex systems that continue to evolve and change (Fine & Sung, 2014). A diverse and comprehensive understanding of the concepts and processes associated with neurodevelopment is needed for a deep understanding of child and adolescent issues in the new diagnostic manual.

DEFINITION OF NEURODEVELOPMENT

Various scientific and technical terminologies are applicable when defining neurodevelopment. Simply stated, neurodevelopment is generally understood as the series of processes and progressions that generate and form the nervous system throughout the human life span. Much of the dynamic development occurs in youth, especially the first several years of life (Perry, 2008). A more detailed definition identifies neurodevelopment as a complex, multifaceted, dynamic process that involves gene–environment interactions resulting in both short- and long-term changes in gene expression, cellular interactions, circuit formation, neural structures, and behaviors over time (National Institute of Mental Health [NIMH], 2014). Emerging research continues to demonstrate that neurodevelopment includes a complex interaction between genetic inheritance and environmental factors, mediated by epigenetic processes, that forms and shapes the brain from conception to adulthood (Fine & Sung, 2014).

Neurodevelopmental disorders are identified as such because of the onset of the condition occurring in the developmental period of the individual's life span.

THE NEURODEVELOPMENTAL PROCESS

Healthy and unobstructed neurodevelopment has long been regarded as essential for proper life functioning. Although research continues to emphasize the importance of the complex series of developmental progressions that shape early life directions, our understanding of these processes remains insufficient (NIMH, 2014). Normal neurological development usually follows a consistent sequence in every person and adheres to these stages throughout the developmental process, beginning with conception and continuing throughout the human life span. Although the *DSM-5* views the neurodevelopmental disorders as occurring during childhood, the manual contains no references to the ages when the neurodevelopmental period ends and adulthood begins (Wills, 2014). According to the Environmental Protection Agency ([EPA], 2013) neurodevelopmental disorders affect up to 15 percent of children in the United States ages 3 to 17 years. Of all of these conditions, attention-deficit/hyperactivity disorder and learning disabilities are the most common.

Table 1.2 provides a table of neurodevelopment stages within the mental health of children and adolescents and identifies important cognitive, social, and emotional phenomena, as well as potential signs of impairment during these stages.

TABLE 1.2   Neurodevelopmental Stages and Mental Health (Based in Part on the Institute for Human Services for the Ohio Child Welfare Training Program, 2007)

Age	Cognitive Development	Social Development	Emotional Development	Signs of Delays/ Disturbances
0 to 6 months	Sensory-motor exploration of environment; significant brain cell development; curiosity, coos	Seeks comfort from parent; responsive to social stimuli; facial expression of emotion	Learns trust in self and caretakers; attachment; craves nurturance; complete dependence	Delays in gross and fine motor skills; poor muscle tone; colicky
6 to 12 months	Babbles, begins to imitate sounds; discriminates between parents; basic problem solving	Socially interactive; some stranger anxiety; separation anxiety; solitary play	Frequent giggles and laughing; occasional feelings of upset or distress	Problems with attachment; overly clingy; unable to be comforted or soothed
12 to 24 months	Recognition; responding to verbal cues; single word use; receptive language; imitating complex behaviors	Peer imitation and learning; some parallel and symbolic processing; play with peers and caregivers	Stubborn, defiant; displays of anger	Language and speech delays, absence of speech; unable to discriminate significant people
2 to 4 years	Begins to understand sequences; multiple-step tasks and processes	Invested play with others; strong attachments to parental figures or caregivers; more trust in others	Pride, embarrassment; recognizes distress and pain in others; emotional attachments to objects; need for security	Passive, withdrawn, apathetic; depressed, anxious, fearful
5 to 8 years	Use of language as primary communication tool; recognizes others' perspectives	Understands concept of right and wrong; situation-specific friendships; relies upon rules or norms for appropriate behavior	Increased self-esteem; strategies for dealing with emotions more diverse; sensitive to others' opinions	Feelings of worthlessness; immature play; unable to recipro-cate emotions; oppositional defiant behaviors
9 to 12 years	Recognizes difference between behavior and intent; can understand and consider others' points of view	Rules can be bended or negotiated; begins to understand social roles; takes on more responsibility; begins loyalty to friends	General understanding and curiosity of sex and gender differences; sexual activity can begin; experiences more complicated emotions	Anger outbursts; low frustration tolerance; poor impulse control; anxiety; poor peer relations; strong mistrust; emo-tional disturban-ces; conduct disturbances

(continued)

TABLE 1.2   (*continued*)

Age	Cognitive Development	Social Development	Emotional Development	Signs of Delays/ Disturbances
12 to 14 years	Thinks hypothetically; considers consequences; considers possibilities; begins to think more logically	Grows distant from parents; strong identity with peer group; need to be independent from adults; indifference about romantic relationships; sense of pride	Self-conscious about physical appearance, development and body image; sensitive to parental criticism; risky behaviors begin; rejection of adult standards; strong reliance on peer group for emotional support	Emotional disturbances (mood swings, anger, depression, and anxiety); identity confusion; antisocial behavior
15 to 18 years	Thinks more abstractly and hypothetically; deeper insight and perspective; systematic problem solving; cognitions affected by emotions	Emphasis on loyalty and trust in friendships; increased morality; begins sexual activity	Strong identity formation; begins to see self as whole; concept of self-image	Engaging in self-destructive and sabotaging behaviors; unable to maintain peer relations; difficulty managing emotions; antisocial behaviors

THE ROLE OF NEURODEVELOPMENT WITHIN MENTAL HEALTH

Healthy neurodevelopment is essential for the mental health of all individuals. Because the human brain is the organ that governs most behavioral, social, cognitive, and emotional functioning, abnormal neurodevelopment can result in altered functioning of the brain systems or various states of psychopathology (Perry, 2008). Accordingly, the specific nature of the mental health dysfunction is a result of which areas, networks, and stages are altered. A key element in understanding the nature of a neurodevelopmental disorder is identifying the etiology or cause of the malady (Thome, Drossos, & Hunter, 2013). Most neurodevelopmental disorders have multiple etiological contributors, including genetic, biological, psychosocial, and environmental (EPA, 2013). The following list identifies some of the multiple causes of neurodevelopmental disorders:

- Genetic Causes
  - Fragile X syndrome
  - Down's syndrome
  - Rett syndrome
- Biological Causes
  - Traumatic brain injury
  - Disease
  - Nutritional factors

- Psychosocial Causes
  - Emotional trauma
  - Neglect
  - Abuse/Maltreatment
- Environmental
  - Exposure to toxins
    — Alcohol, tobacco, drugs (in utero)
    — Mercury
    — Lead
  - Chaotic family (divorce, foster care, substance abuse, lack of nurturance)
  - Poverty

Neurodevelopmental, Behavioral, and Intellectual Symptomology

It is also important to differentiate neurodevelopmental disorders from intellectual disability and neurocognitive disorders, both distinct disorders identified in the *DSM-5*. The difference can often be found in separating the behavioral elements of the neurodevelopmental disorders from the intellectual symptomology found in the same category of disorders. Although intellectual disability and specific learning disorders are in the neurodevelopmental disorders chapter, they occupy a distinct process from the other disorders in the chapter because of deficits in cognitive capacity beginning in the developmental period (APA, 2013b). Another change in the *DSM-5*, and a distinction inherent in the intellectual disabilities, is the departure from relying exclusively on IQ scores as the determinant of disability. Although IQ testing can still assist in scaling the level of intellectual disability (*DSM-IV-TR*'s cutoff for mental retardation was 70), new criteria resulting from the assessment of adaptive functioning levels are also needed to determine severity (Moran, 2013).

Additionally, neurocognitive disorders are similar to but distinct from the neurodevelopmental disorders. Neurocognitive disorders are conceptualized as deficits in cognitive function that are *acquired* rather than *developmental* (APA, 2013a). The assessment and diagnostic process related to neurocognitive disorders often involves the determination of the cause, or etiology, of the disorder. Clinicians must also consider age-related factors in differentiating these two classifications. For example, an individual may demonstrate symptoms of communication impairment at an advanced age because of the onset of Alzheimer's disease. The communication issue occurs through the acquiring of the disease. In contrast, a child can develop a similar issue with communication because of the progression of autism spectrum disorder. The latter communication issue occurs through the development of the disorder.

Neurodevelopmental Disorders and the *DSM-5*

The *DSM-5* defines *neurodevelopmental disorders* as "a group of conditions with onset in the developmental period" (APA, 2013a, p. 31). The manual describes the variety of disorders as occurring early in the developmental years (often before grade school), and resulting in an array of impairments in personal, social, academic, or occupational functioning (APA, 2013a). The neurodevelopmental disorders cover a vast and expansive range, from extremely low-functioning, catatonic behavior, such as severe autistic spectrum disorder, to incredibly high functioning, such as a minor tic disorder. Such a broad expanse creates incredible diversity in the family of disorders, requiring an ongoing awareness and competency to assess, diagnose, and treat the conditions adequately.

A particular diagnostic challenge facing clinicians when interacting with the neurodevelopmental disorders is the extremely high frequency of comorbidity and dual diagnosis (a phenomenon discussed further in Chapter 2). The combinations of behavioral, psychological, and functional symptom presentations, in addition to the cultural and environmental factors, all exist on a continuum across development. This multitude of factors creates a complex clinical profile for many children with neurodevelopmental disorders, leading to high levels of diagnostic comorbidity (Thome et al., 2013). It is common for a child to receive multiple diagnoses within the area of neurodevelopmental disorders. For example, Tommy is a 6-year-old boy struggling academically, behaviorally, and socially in the first grade. Behavioral observations show he is having a hard time sitting still and difficulty concentrating and is failing most classes. He is also very socially isolated and struggles with connecting with peers and engaging in play. Upon advanced psychological testing, Tommy is diagnosed with attention-deficit/hyperactivity disorder, specific learning disorder with impairment in reading, and mild autistic spectrum disorder.

See Table 1.3 for a list of the neurodevelopmental disorders as identified in the *DSM-5*.

TABLE 1.3   *DSM-5* **Classification of Neurodevelopmental Disorders**

Category/Disorder	*Subtype/Disorder*

Intellectual Disabilities	• Intellectual Disability (Intellectual Developmental Disorder)
	  ◦ Mild
	  ◦ Moderate
	  ◦ Severe
	  ◦ Profound
	• Global Developmental Delay
	• Unspecified Intellectual Disability (Intellectual Developmental Disorder)

Communication Disorders	• Language Disorder • Speech Sound Disorder • Childhood-Onset Fluency Disorder (Stuttering) • Social (Pragmatic) Fluency Disorder • Unspecified Communication Disorder

Autistic Spectrum Disorder	• Autistic Spectrum Disorder
	  ◦ Specify:
	  ◦ Association with other condition (medical, genetic, environmental, another neurodevelopmental, mental, behavioral disorder)
	  ◦ Current severity
	    — With or without accompanying impairment (intellectual, language); with catatonia.

(continued)

TABLE 1.3   *(continued)*

Category/Disorder	Subtype/Disorder
Attention-Deficit/Hyperactivity Disorder	• Combined Presentation • Predominantly inattentive presentation • Predominantly hyperactive/impulsive presentation • Other Specified Attention-Deficit/Hyperactivity Disorder • Unspecified Attention-Deficit/Hyperactivity Disorder

Specific Learning Disorder	• Specific Learning Disorder
	  ○ Impairment in reading
	  ○ Impairment in written expression
	  ○ Impairment in mathematics

Motor Disorders	• Development Coordination Disorder
	• Stereotypic Movement Disorder
	• Tic Disorders
	  ○ Tourette's Disorder
	  ○ Persistent (Chronic) Motor or Vocal Tic Disorder
	  ○ Provisional Tic Disorder
	  ○ Other Specified Tic Disorder
	  ○ Unspecified Tic Disorder

Other Neurodevelopmental Disorders	• Other Specified Neurodevelopment Disorder • Unspecified Neurodevelopmental Disorder

Changes in Diagnostic Categories from the *DSM-IV-TR* to the *DSM-5*

As discussed in this chapter, the *DSM-5* represents a fundamental shift in mental disorder classification and conceptualization. Some of these clinical modifications include greater inclusion of culture issues and gender issues within diagnostic criteria and descriptors. Expanded discussion of these factors in the latest diagnostic manual enhances clinical case formulation and individualized treatment planning—essential elements to conceptualization. When clinicians engage in assessment and diagnosis of mental disorders in children and adolescents, they are likely to appreciate an additional change reflected in the *DSM-5* that aligns with current scientific evidence: the infusion of neurobiological validators (i.e., antecedent, concurrent, and prospective). Inclusion of these biopsychiatric markers facilitated the *DSM-5*'s new organizational structure (the way in which disorders are grouped) with the goal of improving clinical utility and disorder classification relationships based upon shared symptoms, shared genetic and environmental risk factors, and shared neural substrates. "By reordering and regrouping the existing disorders, the revised structure is meant to stimulate new clinical perspectives and to encourage researchers to identify the psychological and physiological cross-cutting factors that are not bound by strict categorical designations" (APA, 2013a, p. 10). Clinicians will notice how harmonization with the *ICD-10*, a dimensional approach to diagnosis, and developmental and life span considerations generate an empirically supported clinical framework to effectively understand internalizing (depression, anxiety, and somatic symptoms) and externalizing factors (impulsivity, disruptive conduct, and substance use symptoms) in child and adolescent mental disorders. They will also notice that mental disorders are sequenced developmentally (typical age of onset) in the *DSM-5* classification chapters (e.g., depressive disorders, anxiety disorders, trauma- and stressor-related disorders, feeding and eating disorders, and disruptive, impulse-control, and conduct disorders).

OVERVIEW OF THE CHANGES THAT OCCURRED SPECIFIC TO CHILDREN AND ADOLESCENTS

The *DSM-5* neurodevelopmental disorders chapter represents the most substantial changes in the entire manual. Most of the mental disorders from the previously titled *DSM-IV-TR* chapter "Disorders Usually First Diagnosed in Infancy, Childhood, or Adolescence" are renamed, relocated, reconceptualized, or removed. Specifically, pica, rumination disorder, and feeding and eating disorder of infancy or early childhood located in the *DSM-IV-TR* subcategory Feeding and Eating Disorders of Infancy or Early Childhood are relocated to the new *DSM-5* feeding and eating disorders chapter; and eating disorder of infancy or early childhood is renamed and reconceptualized as avoidant/restrictive food intake disorder and relocated to this chapter. Encopresis and enuresis, located in the *DSM-IV-TR* subcategory Elimination Disorders are relocated to the new *DSM-5* elimination disorders chapter. Oppositional defiant disorder and conduct disorder, located in the *DSM-IV-TR* subcategory Attention-Deficit and Disruptive Behavior Disorders, are relocated to the new *DSM-5* disruptive, impulse-control, and conduct disorders chapter. Separation anxiety disorder and selective mutism, located in *DSM-IV-TR* subcategory Other Disorders of Infancy, Childhood, or Adolescence, are relocated to the *DSM-5* Anxiety Disorders chapter. Also located in this *DSM-IV-TR* subcategory, reactive attachment disorder of infancy or early childhood is reconceptualized and renamed as reactive attachment disorder and disinhibited social engagement disorder—with both disorders being relocated to the new *DSM-5* trauma- and stressor-related disorders chapter.

The *DSM-IV-TR* subcategory and diagnosis Mental Retardation is renamed and reconceptualized in the *DSM-5* to intellectual disability (intellectual developmental disorder) and is located in the new subcategory Intellectual Disabilities. The disorder rename parallels the *ICD*'s use of *intellectual developmental disorder* and is the preferred term of the American Association on Intellectual and Developmental Disabilities.

> Moreover, a federal statute in the United States (Public Law 111–256, Rosa's Law) replaces the term mental retardation with intellectual disability, and research journals use the term intellectual disability. Thus, intellectual disability is the term in common use by medical, educational, and other professions and by the lay public and advocacy groups. (APA, 2013a, p. 33)

For children who are unable to complete systematic assessments of intellectual functioning because they are too young (e.g., under age 5), clinicians can use the new *DSM-5* diagnosis global developmental delay to indicate deficient developmental milestones in several areas of intellectual functioning. This mental disorder does not contain diagnostic criteria and is to be used until the child presents as a reliable candidate for standardized testing (i.e., over age 5).

The *DSM-IV-TR* Communication Disorders subcategory is retained in the *DSM-5*; however, the *DSM-IV-TR* expressive language disorder and mixed receptive-expressive language disorder are reconceptualized into the *DSM-5* language disorder, and the *DSM-IV-TR* phonological disorder is renamed and reconceptualized in the *DSM-5* to speech sound disorder. The *DSM-IV-TR* stuttering diagnosis is reconceptualized and renamed to childhood-onset fluency disorder (stuttering). Social (pragmatic) communication disorder, also referred to as pragmatic language impairment in the scientific literature, is new to the *DSM-5*. This disorder classifies persistent difficulties in the social uses of verbal and nonverbal communication in children typically over age 5. This syndrome is distinct from language disorder and speech disorder because syntax, articulation, pronunciation, and fluency, are intact; and this syndrome cannot be diagnosed in the presence of restricted repetitive behaviors, interests, and activities—key psychiatric markers of autism spectrum disorder.

The *DSM-IV-TR* subcategory Pervasive Developmental Disorders is renamed Autism Spectrum Disorder and contains the newly reconceptualized *DSM-5* autism spectrum disorder. This classification "encompasses disorders previously referred to as early infantile autism, childhood autism, Kanner's autism, high-functioning autism, atypical autism, pervasive developmental disorder not otherwise specified, childhood disintegrative disorder, and Asperger's disorder" (APA, 2013, p. 53). The *DSM-IV-TR*'s Rett's disorder and childhood disintegrative disorder are removed as classifications in the *DSM-5* and become descriptive specifiers, when applicable, to autism spectrum disorder.

Grouped in the *DSM-IV-TR* subcategory Attention-Deficit and Disruptive Behavior Disorders, attention-deficit/hyperactivity disorder is located in the new *DSM-5* subcategory Attention-Deficit/Hyperactivity Disorder.

The *DSM-5* removes the *DSM-IV-TR* reading disorder, mathematics disorder, disorder of written expression, and learning disorder not otherwise specified located in the *DSM-IV-TR* subcategory Learning Disorders and makes these conditions descriptive specifiers to the newly reconceptualized *DSM-5* specific learning disorder located in the new subcategory Specific Learning Disorder.

The *DSM-IV-TR* subcategory Motor Skills Disorder is renamed Motor Disorders in the *DSM-5* and contains the renamed and reconceptualized developmental coordination disorder. Stereotypic movement disorder, located in the *DSM-IV-TR* subcategory Other Disorders of Infancy, Childhood, or Adolescence, is reconceptualized and relocated to this new *DSM-5* subcategory. Located in the *DSM-IV-TR* subcategory Tic Disorders, Tourette's disorder is relocated to the *DSM-5* subcategory Motor Disorders; chronic motor or vocal tic disorder is renamed to persistent (chronic) motor or vocal tic disorder and relocated to this new *DSM-5* subcategory; and transient tic disorder is reconceptualized and renamed to provisional tic disorder and is relocated to this new *DSM-5* subcategory.

One of the most important additions to the neurodevelopmental disorders in *DSM-5* is that clinicians may include the descriptive specifier *associated with a known medical or genetic condition or environmental factor* to any of the classifications in this chapter.

> This specifier gives clinicians an opportunity to document factors that may have played a role in the etiology of the disorder, as well as those that might affect the clinical course. Examples include genetic disorders, such as fragile X syndrome, tuberous sclerosis, and Rett syndrome; medical conditions such as epilepsy; and environmental factors, including very low birth weight and fetal alcohol exposure. (APA, 2013a, pp. 32–33)

See Table 1.4 for a listing of new *DSM-5* disorder titles for children and adolescents.

TABLE 1.4   New *DSM* Disorder Titles for Children and Adolescents

- Intellectual Disability (Intellectual Developmental Disorder)
- Global Developmental Delay
- Language Disorder
- Speech Sound Disorder
- Childhood-Onset Fluency Disorder (Stuttering)
- Social (Pragmatic) Communication Disorder
- Autism Spectrum Disorder
- Specific Learning Disorder
- Disruptive Mood Dysregulation Disorder
- Persistent Depressive Disorder (Dysthymia)
- Premenstrual Dysphoric Disorder
- Social Anxiety Disorder (Social Phobia)
- Agoraphobia
- Trichotillomania (Hair-Pulling Disorder)
- Excoriation (Skin-Picking) Disorder
- Reactive Attachment Disorder
- Disinhibited Social Engagement Disorder
- Depersonalization/Derealization Disorder
- Somatic Symptom Disorder
- Illness Anxiety Disorder
- Conversion Disorder (Functional Neurological Symptom Disorder)
- Avoidant/Restrictive Food Intake Disorder
- Binge-Eating Disorder
- Insomnia Disorder
- Hypersomnolence Disorder
- Non–Rapid Eye Movement Sleep Arousal Disorders
- Nightmare Disorder
- Rapid Eye Movement Sleep Behavior Disorder
- Restless Legs Syndrome
- Gender Dysphoria
- Substance Use Disorders

EXAMPLE OF NEW CRITERIA INCLUDING SEVERITY INDEX

Characterized by deficits in general mental abilities, intellectual disability (intellectual developmental disorder) receives new criteria and severity indices in the *DSM-5*. Modifications from *DSM-IV-TR* (APA, 2000, p. 49) to *DSM-5* (APA, 2013a, p. 33) for this disorder include the following:

> **Criterion A**—changed the focus from "significantly subaverage intellectual functioning, defined by an IQ of approximately 70 or below," to a focus on "deficits in intellectual functions, such as reasoning, problem solving, planning, abstract thinking, judgment, academic learning, and learning from experience, confirmed by both clinical assessment and individualized, standardized intelligence testing."

Criterion B—changed from "Concurrent deficits or impairments in present adaptive functioning" to "Deficits in adaptive functioning that result in failure to meet developmental and sociocultural standards for personal independence and social responsibility." Language added to this criterion includes "Without ongoing support, the adaptive deficits limit functioning." Finally, Criterion B threshold was lowered from "at least two of the following areas" to "in one or more activities of daily life … across multiple environments … "

Criterion C—changed from "the onset is before age 18 years" to "onset of intellectual and adaptive deficits during the developmental period."

In *DSM-IV-TR*, severity index of mental retardation was determined by the child's IQ score as follows:

Mild—IQ level 50 to 55 to approximately 70

Moderate—IQ level 35 to 40 to 50 to 55

Severe—IQ level 20 to 25 to 35 to 40

Profound—IQ level below 20 or 25

Moreover, it was possible to diagnose mental retardation in children with IQ scores between 71 and 75 if they displayed significant deficits in adaptive behavior characteristic of borderline intellectual functioning. However, it is important for clinicians to understand that an IQ score may involve a measurement error of approximately five points and that "IQ measures are less valid in the lower end of the IQ range" (APA, 2013a, p. 33), and "problems in adaptation are more likely to improve with remedial efforts than is the cognitive IQ, which tends to remain a more stable attribute" (APA, 2000, p. 42). Consequently, the *DSM-5* removes the *DSM-IV-TR* requirement that IQ score solely determines the disorder severity index. Clinicians now determine severity index (i.e., mild, moderate, severe, profound) by "using both clinical evaluation and individualized, culturally appropriate, psychometrically sound measures" (APA, 2013a, p. 37) to assess the child's ability to cope with common life demands and meet the standards of personal independence relative to age and culture in *conceptual* (knowledge and judgment), *social* (empathy and communication), and *practical* (learning and self-management) adaptive functioning domains. For accurate severity index determination, clinicians are encouraged to use "Table 1: Severity levels for intellectual disability (intellectual developmental disorder)" located in the *DSM-5* on pages 34 to 36.

SAMPLE *DSM-5* DIAGNOSIS

Removal of the multiaxial system in *DSM-5* helps clinicians detect and communicate porous psychiatric symptoms in a more clinically informative framework. For example, using the *DSM-IV-TR*, clinicians reporting a childhood Asperger clinical profile used this format:

Asperger's Disorder (this style of classification format significantly limits clinical case formulation and hinders individualized treatment planning).

In contrast, clinicians using the *DSM-5* descriptive specifiers and "Table 2: Severity levels for autism spectrum disorder" (APA, 2013a, p. 52) now report a childhood Asperger clinical profile using this format:

Autism Spectrum Disorder—requiring substantial support for social communication and social interaction (level 2 moderate); requiring support for restricted repetitive behaviors, interests and activities (level 1 mild); without accompanying intellectual impairment; without accompanying language impairment; without catatonia.

Notice the diagnostic precision the *DSM-5* offers in comparison with the vague *DSM-IV-TR* classification. Conceptualizing autism as a spectrum disorder allows for dimensional specificity and facilitates developmental and life span–sensitive treatment interventions. For example, the moderate severity index *requiring substantial support* for social communication conveys the child's "marked deficits in verbal and nonverbal social communication skills; social impairments apparent even with supports in place; limited initiation of social interactions; and reduced or abnormal responses to social overtures from others" (APA, 2013a, p. 52). These deficits become primary targeted behavior management areas. The mild severity index *requiring support* for restricted repetitive behaviors (RRBs) indicates that the child's "inflexibility of behavior causes significant interference in one or more contexts. Difficulty switching between activities. Problems of organization and planning hamper independence" (APA, 2013a, p. 52). These deficits become secondary targeted behavior management areas. Clinicians are encouraged to read the *DSM-5*'s use of the manual chapter (pp. 19–24) to properly understand the new approach to clinical case formulation, elements of a diagnosis, and assessment and monitoring tools displayed in this sample diagnosis.

Summary

This chapter began with a discussion of the evolution of the *DSM* up to the current Fifth Edition, with a particular focus on identifying, and defining, the term *mental disorder*. From there, it moved to looking at diagnostic issues specific to childhood and adolescence and the changes that occurred in the new manual. The new diagnostic criteria and categories were thoroughly discussed, and case examples were provided to help illustrate the changes. Finally, the chapter concluded with a sample diagnosis that highlighted the differences between the diagnostic criteria in the *DSM-IV-TR* and the *DSM-5*.

References

American Psychiatric Association. (1952). *Diagnostic and statistical manual of mental disorders*. Washington, DC: Author.

American Psychiatric Association. (1968). *Diagnostic and statistical manual of mental disorders* (2nd ed.). Washington, DC: Author.

American Psychiatric Association. (1980). *Diagnostic and statistical manual of mental disorders* (3rd ed.). Washington, DC: Author.

American Psychiatric Association. (1987). *Diagnostic and statistical manual of mental disorders* (3rd ed., rev.). Washington, DC: Author.

American Psychiatric Association. (1994). *Diagnostic and statistical manual of mental disorders* (4th ed.). Washington, DC: Author.

American Psychiatric Association. (2000). *Diagnostic and statistical manual of mental disorders* (4th ed., text rev.). Washington, DC: Author.

American Psychiatric Association. (2013a). *Diagnostic and statistical manual of mental disorders* (5th ed.). Arlington, VA: American Psychiatric Publishing.

American Psychiatric Association (2013b). *DSM-5 and diagnoses for children*. Retrieved from http://www.psychiatry.org/file%20library/practice/dsm/DSM-5/DSM-5-diagnoses-for-children.pdf

American Psychiatric Association (2013c). *Highlights of changes from DSM-IV-TR to DSM 5*. Retrieved from http://www.dsm5.org/Documents/changes%20from%20DSM-IV-TR%20to%20DSM-5.pdf

American Psychiatric Association (2013d). *Lifespan developmental approaches*. Retrieved from http://www.dsm5.org/MeetUs/Pages/LifeSpanDevelopmentalApproaches.aspx

Bingham, R., & Banner, N. (2014). The definition of mental disorder: Evolving but dysfunctional? *Journal of Medical Ethics*, *40*(8), 537–542. Retrieved from http://search.proquest.com/docview/1606006293?accountid=166133

Charles, S. T., & Carstensen, L. L. (2010). Social and emotional aging. *Annual Review of Psychology*, *61*(1), 383–409.

Environmental Protection Agency. (2013). *Neurodevelopmental disorders*. Retrieved from http://www.epa.gov/ace/pdfs/Health-Neurodevelopmental.pdf

Eranti, S. V., MacCabe, J. H., Bundy, H., & Murray, R. M. (2013). Gender difference in age at onset of schizophrenia: A meta-analysis. *Psychological Medicine*, *43*(1), 155–167. doi:10.1017/S003329171200089X

Fine, J. G., & Sung, C. (2014). Neuroscience of child and adolescent health development. *Journal of Counseling Psychology*, *61*(4), 521–527. doi:10.1037/cou0000033

First, M. B., & Wakefield, J. C. (2013). Diagnostic criteria as dysfunction indicators: Bridging the chasm between the definition of mental disorder and diagnostic criteria for specific disorders. *The Canadian Journal of Psychiatry*, *58*(12), 663–669. Retrieved from http://search.proquest.com/docview/1492674819?accountid=166133

Grossman, C. I. (2004). Labels and language: Implications for prevention of the DSM definition of mental disorder. *The Journal of Primary Prevention*, *24*(4), 513–522. 10.1023/B:JOPP.0000024804.56658.ea

Hudson, C. G. (2012). Declines in mental illness over the adult years: An enduring finding or methodological artifact? *Aging & Mental Health*, *16*(6), 735–752. doi:10.1080/13607863.2012.657157

Insel, T. R. (2014). Mental disorders in childhood: Shifting the focus from behavioral symptoms to neurodevelopmental trajectories. *JAMA: Journal of the American Medical Association*, *311*(17), 1727–1728. doi:10.1001/jama.2014.1193

The Institute for Human Services for the Ohio Child Welfare Training Program. (2007). *Developmental milestones chart*. Retrieved from http://www.rsd.k12.pa.us/Downloads/Development_Chart_for_Booklet.pdf

Kecmanovic, D. (2013). The *DSM-5* definition of mental disorder. *Australian and New Zealand Journal of Psychiatry*, *47*(4), 393–394. Retrieved from http://search.proquest.com/docview/1413433590?accountid=166133

Kindsvatter, A., & Geroski, A. (2014). The impact of early life stress on the neurodevelopment of the stress response system. *Journal of Counseling & Development*, *92*(4), 472–480.

Lakhan, R., & Ekúndayò, O. T. (2015). National sample survey organization survey report: An estimation of prevalence of mental illness and its association with age in India. *Journal of Neurosciences in Rural Practice*, *6*(1), 51–54. doi:10.4103/0976-3147.143194

Liu, J. J., Norman, R. M., Manchanda, R., & De Luca, V. (2013). Admixture analysis of age at onset in schizophrenia: Evidence of three subgroups in a first-episode sample. *General Hospital Psychiatry*, *35*(6), 664–667. doi:10.1016/j.genhosppsych.2013.07.002

Moran, M. (2014, October 22). *DSM-5* provides new take on neurodevelopmental disorders. *Psychiatric News*. Retrieved from http://psychnews.psychiatryonline.org/doi/full/10.1176%2Fappi.pn.2013.1b11

National Institute of Mental Health. (n.d.). *Any disorder among children*. Retrieved from http://www.nimh.nih.gov/health/statistics/prevalence/any-disorder-among-children.shtml

National Institute of Mental Health. (2014). *Transformative neurodevelopmental research in mental illness: Report of the National Advisory Mental Health Council's Workgroup*. Retrieved from http://www.nimh.nih.gov/about/advisory-boards-and-groups/namhc/neurodevelopment_workgroup_report_33553.pdf

Perry, B. D. (2008). Child maltreatment: A developmental perspective on the role of trauma and neglect in psychopathology. In T. Beauchaine & S. P. Hinshaw (Eds.), *Child and Adolescent Psychopathology* (pp. 93–129). Hoboken, NJ: John Wiley & Sons.

Spitzer, R. L. (1999). Harmful dysfunction and the DSM definition of mental disorder. *Journal of Abnormal Psychology*, *108*(3), 430–432. 10.1037/0021-843X.108.3.430

Thome, J., Drossos, T., & Hunter, S. J. (2013). Neurodevelopmental disorders and associated emotional/behavioral sequelae. In L. A. Reddy, A. S. Weissman, & J. B. Hale (Eds.), *Neuropsychological assessment and intervention for youth: An evidence-based approach to emotional and behavioral disorders* (pp. 271–298). Washington, DC: American Psychological Association.

Varley, C. K. (2013). *Overview of DSM-5 changes*. Retrieved from http://www.omh.ny.gov/omhweb/resources/providers/DSM-5-overview.pdf

Wakefield, J. C. (1992). Disorder as harmful dysfunction: A conceptual critique of DSM-III-R's definition of mental disorder. *Psychological Review*, *99*(2), 232–247. 10.1037/0033-295X.99.2.232

Wills, C. D. (2014). DSM-5 and Neurodevelopmental and Other Disorders of Childhood and Adolescence. *Journal of the American Academy of Psychiatry Law*, *42*(3), 165–172.

World Health Organization. (2005). *Child and adolescent mental health policies and plans*. Retrieved from http://www.who.int/mental_health/policy/Childado_mh_module.pdf

World Health Organization. (2014, October). *Mental disorders*. Retrieved from http://www.who.int/mediacentre/factsheets/fs396/en/

Zupanick, C. E. (2013). *The new DSM-5: Changes to childhood disorders*. Retrieved from http://www.amhc.org/1418-DSM-5/article/51958-the-new-DSM-5-changes-to-childhood-disorders

Chapter 2

Effective Strategies for Assessing DSM-5 Disorders

Joshua D. Francis and Laura R. Haddock

Introduction

Counseling professionals working with children and adolescents are charged with providing comprehensive, culturally sensitive care to their clients. The *Diagnostic and Statistical Manual of Mental Disorders*, Fifth Edition (*DSM-5*), emphasizes the need to use clinical assessment to help establish a rich and precise interpretation of presenting problems. Effective strategies to assist clinicians in accurately assessing client needs are a key to establishing treatment plans and choosing interventions. This chapter will include a guide for counseling professionals working with children and adolescents and strategies for assessing *DSM-5* disorders. Beginning with a review of diagnostic challenges and special considerations when working with children and adolescents, this chapter provides a thorough explanation of the movement away from categorical diagnosis and toward dimensional, nonmultiaxial approaches. Assessment strategies, such as tests and inventories, checklists and rating scales, interviews, and observations are all included. Direction for establishing diagnostic validity and differential diagnosis will guide counselors through application of diagnostic criteria and through what to do when faced with diagnostic ambiguity. Finally, a clinical case formulation demonstrates the integration of social, psychological, and biological factors when assessing children for treatment.

Diagnostic Challenges and Special Consideration When Working with Children and Adolescents

CRITERIA FOR CLINICAL SIGNIFICANCE

Counselors are ever striving for intervention outcomes that show real and practical differences in the daily lives of clients. Whether symptoms change a lot, change a little, or do not change but the client is better able to cope with them, the current emphasis on evidence-based practice has resulted in significant advances in the evaluation of intervention effects, prevention, and education. The crucial precursor for establishing treatment goals is the identification of symptoms that are clinically significant. The *DSM-5* includes a clinical significance criterion for a great many of the diagnostic criteria sets, which requires that symptoms cause "clinically significant distress or impairment in social, occupational, or other important areas of functioning" (APA, 2013c, p. 1). The clinical significance criterion offers counselors the opportunity to diagnose accurately when the symptom criteria do not necessarily indicate pathology. The definition of mental disorder in the introduction to *DSM-5* requires that there be clinically significant distress or disability beyond an expectable or culturally sanctioned response. To highlight the importance of considering this issue, the criteria sets for most disorders include a clinical significance criterion, which helps establish the threshold for the diagnosis of a disorder in those situations in which the symptomatic presentation by itself is not inherently pathological. In children and adolescents particularly, mild forms of symptoms may be encountered in individuals for whom a diagnosis of mental disorder would be inappropriate and could represent developmentally appropriate behavior. Assessing whether a client meets this criterion, especially in terms of role function, is an inherently difficult clinical judgment and an integral part of the assessment process. This appeal to clinical judgment serves to remind counselors to evaluate not only the presence of symptoms within the criteria set but also the context of severity, developmental appropriateness, and cultural framework.

SPECTRUM APPROACH TO DIAGNOSIS

Although all disorders in *DSM-5* remain in specific categories, measures indicating degree of severity have been integrated for a number of combined diagnoses. This approach offers counselors the opportunity to employ assessment models that focus on the acuteness of symptoms when gathering information, fostering accurate diagnostic assignment and treatment plan development. For example, new in the *DSM-5* is the explicit recognition of the spectrum nature of autism and the removal of categorical subgroups into a single umbrella term *autism spectrum disorder* (ASD). The *DSM-5* characterizes ASD in two behavioral domains and provides a severity scale to capture the spectrum nature of the disorder (Lai, Lombardo, Chakrabarti, & Baron-Cohen, 2013). In addition, the *DSM-5* proposes a more inclusive age-of-onset criterion, recognizing that although symptoms present in early childhood, they may not emerge as fully evident until social demands exceed the capacity of the child or adolescent to cope with them (Lord & Jones, 2012). This umbrella approach to ASD, accompanied by individualized assessment of therapeutic need, has the potential to be quite useful in clinical settings, especially to individualize the required levels of support for all individuals on the spectrum who are in need of interventions from educational or health care systems. ASD will be covered in greater detail in Chapter 5.

Previous versions of the *DSM* had a more constricted categorical approach, which narrowed the assessment of potentially important clinical information. The spectrum approach to diagnosis promotes more individualized, contextual assessment with greater depth of detail about symptoms, recognizing the dynamic nature of development and how individuals interact with their environment. This integrated approach provides counselors an opportunity to tailor a diagnosis to a specific child or adolescent, with potentially significant implications for diagnosis, treatment planning, prognosis, and treatment outcomes. Details regarding how to use the criterion for clinical significance and the application of the new spectrum approach to diagnostics when planning treatment are covered in depth in Chapter 3.

STAGES OF DEVELOPMENT

The *DSM-5* updates revised diagnostic criteria to capture the experiences and symptoms of children and adolescents more precisely (American Psychiatric Association [APA], 2013b). The updated version of the *DSM-5* also takes a life span approach, which captures how childhood conditions manifest at different stages of life and the implications of the developmental stages of life with regard to symptom development and assignment of diagnosis.

FAMILY STRUCTURE AND ENVIRONMENTAL CONTEXT

According to the APA (2013c), consumer and family advocacy groups contributed valuable feedback during the revision process. Because many of the *DSM-5* diagnostic criteria require feedback for behaviors that are observed by parents or individuals within the child's or adolescent's environment who observe them regularly, the feedback solicited during the revisions helped frame that perspective. It is both proper and crucial for primary caregivers to contribute to the assessment process. Further discussion regarding appropriate sources of information during assessment is offered a little later in this chapter.

CULTURAL IDENTITY

Culture affects every nuance of client care in counseling, including how clients choose to share their experiences of illness and suffering (Kirmayer, 2006), the interpretation of the experience (Kleinman, 1977), and the approaches counselors use to understand and recognize symptoms in terms of mental health diagnoses (Kleinman, 1977). Culture also shapes clients' perceptions of treatment, including what types of interventions are satisfactory and for how long (Lewis-Fernández et al., 2013). Even when counselors are culturally competent, culture affects treatment through other influences on identity, such as those due to gender, age, class, race, occupation, sexual orientation, and religion (Lu, Lim, & Mezzich, 1995). Cultural factors can also influence the expression and interpretation of signs and symptoms for counselors. For instance, African Americans have historically been disproportionately diagnosed with schizophrenia, as opposed to depression, when compared with whites (Johnson, 2013). Trierweiler et al. (2010) found that a counselor's racial identity can serve as a critical decision-making variable in diagnostic decision making. Social, cultural, and economic considerations must be acknowledged when attempting to identify and classify behavior diagnosed as maladaptive. Culture is threaded through the clinical encounter for each client and counselor; thus it is an essential component of any comprehensive assessment.

The *DSM-5* simplifies the consideration of cultural factors, a revision that promotes cultural competence for counselors. The *Diagnostic and Statistical Manual of Mental Disorders, Fourth Edition, Text Revision* (*DSM-IV-TR*) used a multiaxial system and global assessment of functioning (GAF) scale, which did not promote cross-cultural diagnosis. The inclusion of a dimensional model within *DSM-5* simplifies the incorporation of cultural identity into the diagnostic process. The dimensional assessments included with categorical diagnosis are designed to assist counselors with diagnosis and treatment planning (Jones, 2012). Unlike the former categorical system, dimensional assessments measure disorders on a continuum and represent degrees of a behavior (Sue, Sue,

Sue, & Sue, 2014). This approach allows counselors to consider individual differences and the influences of race and culture on diagnosis and treatment (Johnson, 2013). Because mental disorders are not static, "the cross-cultural precision of diagnosis using the *DSM-5* is contingent upon assessing the presence of a disorder on a continuum or dimension" (Johnson, 2013, p. 18). The dimensional approach within the *DSM-5* allows counselors more freedom to assess the severity of a condition and design an intervention that responds with an individualized approach to the client's identified level of acuteness. When a specifier or subtype has an associated code, it is listed below the diagnostic criteria. If the specifier or subtype is not associated with its own code, the name of the diagnosis with subtype or all relevant specifiers should be recorded in the medical record along with the code for the disorder. In relation to culture, these assessment options offer an evidenced-based approach to monitor therapeutic progress. Measuring a child's presenting symptoms, which reflect culturally based disorders, may improve with *DSM-5*'s dimensional approach: "Dimensional models provide more reliable scores (e.g., across raters and across time), help to explain symptom heterogeneity and the lack of clear boundaries between categorical diagnoses" (Trull, Tragesser, Solhan, & Schwartz-Mette, 2007, p. 52).

In addition to the dimensional assessments, the *DSM-5* contains descriptions associated with cultural identity. Psychosocial factors are integrated by using V codes from the World Health Organization's ([WHO], 1979) *International Classification of Diseases, Ninth Revision, Clinical Modification* (*ICD-9-CM*) and Z codes from the *International Classification of Diseases, 10th Revision* (*ICD-10*; WHO, 1992). In addition, three new terms are introduced in the *DSM-5*: *cultural idiom of distress, cultural syndrome,* and *cultural explanation or perceived cause* (Pomeroy & Anderson, 2013). They define cultural syndromes as "clusters of symptoms and attributions that tend to co-occur among individuals in specific cultural groups, communities, or contexts ... that are recognized locally as coherent patterns of experience" (p. 758); cultural idioms of distress represents "ways of expressing distress that may not involve specific symptoms or syndromes, but that provide collective, shared ways of experiencing and talking about personal or social concerns" (p. 758); and cultural explanations of distress or perceived causes identifies "labels, attributions, or features of an explanatory model that indicate culturally recognized meaning or etiology for symptoms, illness, or distress" (p. 758). Critical to understanding individuals and their distress is the capacity to conceptualize a child's story within the sociocultural context in which he or she lives.

For example, anxiety could represent a cultural concept in relation to diagnosis. In Western culture, generalized anxiety disorder is represented by a cluster of symptoms within the *DSM-5*. However, anxiety could also be considered an *idiom of distress*, in the sense that Westerners commonly talk of feeling anxious in everyday life. The *DSM-5* Glossary of Concepts of Distress lists nine of "the best-studied concepts of distress around the world": *ataque de nervios* ("attack of nerves"), *dhat* syndrome ("semen loss"), *khyâl cap* ("wind attack"), *kufingisisa* ("thinking too much"), *maladi moun* (literally "human-caused illness"), *nervios* ("nerves"), *shenjing shuairuo* (reglossed as "weakness of the nervous system"), *susto* ("fright"), and *taijin kyofusho* ("interpersonal fear disorder"; p. 833).

Cultural influence on mental health assessment is also integrated into the *DSM-5* with the inclusion of the Cultural Formulation Interview (CFI; APA, 2014; Pomeroy & Anderson, 2013). The CFI was established to advance cross-cultural diagnostic assessment and was produced from the Outline for Cultural Formulation (OCF) of the *DSM-IV-TR* (Aggarwal, Nicasio, DeSilva, Boiler, & Lewis-Fernández, 2013). In keeping with multicultural competence models, the CFI provides a vehicle for counselors to explore and understand children's experiences and worldviews, as well as cultural descriptions of distress. When counselors approach each child as an individual and seek to understand his or her experiences, accurate diagnosis and ethical practice are more likely (Swartz-Kulstad & Martin, 1999). There are also 12 supplementary modules to the CFI, which provide additional questions to flesh out domains assessed briefly in the 16-item CFI (e.g., cultural identity) as well as questions for use during the cultural assessment of particular groups, such as children and adolescents, older adults, immigrants and refugees, and caregivers. Chapter 4 addresses client diversity throughout the diagnostic process in more detail. See Sidebar 2.1 for a concise overview of the *DSM-5* revisions related to culture.

SIDEBAR 2.1

Cultural identity has far-reaching implications for counselors. Threaded through background information, case conceptualization, and all the way through the diagnostic process, an individual's cultural identity has a presence. The *DSM-5* has made a number of revisions that highlight the importance of cultural identity. Here are a few changes, at a glance:

- Examples have been added to criterion items to facilitate application across the life span.
- Acknowledgment of international differences in descriptions of deficits.
- Some diagnostic thresholds have been lowered for children and adolescents.
- Notes have been added to some criteria to provide guidance on the frequency typically needed for a behavior to be considered symptomatic of the disorder.
- Minimum age limits have been established for diagnoses that may be difficult to distinguish from developmentally acceptable behavior.

NORMATIVE AGE-APPROPRIATE BEHAVIOR AND TEMPERAMENTAL ANTECEDENTS

One new chapter in the *DSM-5* includes disruptive, impulse-control, and conduct disorders (APA, 2013b). All the behavioral disorders included in this chapter are characterized by problems in the self-control of emotions and behaviors that violate the rights of others or that bring the individual into significant conflict with societal norms or authority figures. Of critical importance in this new chapter is that the frequency, persistence, pervasiveness across situations, and impairment associated with the behaviors indicative of the diagnosis be considered relative to what is normative for a person's age, gender, and culture when determining whether he or she is symptomatic of a disorder. The authors added criteria to guide counselors with regard to the frequency needed for a behavior to be considered symptomatic of a disorder. Additionally, a completely new diagnosis of disruptive mood dysregulation disorder was added, which offers counselors a more accurate classification for children and adolescents presenting with chronic, severe, persistent irritability and frequent temper outbursts (instead of a bipolar-related classification; APA, 2013b).

Building on a developmental foundation, when using the *DSM-5* counselors will be challenged to identify behavioral symptomology that is pervasive and persistent across settings and observable by others. Thus, because of the routine difficulty in distinguishing developmentally appropriate temper tantrums, the *DSM-5* includes age limits and developmental equivalents in the diagnostic criteria.

Classification Models

Complicated sets of information require consistent organization and structure to present the material in a clear fashion. The *DSM-5* uses an established classification system to identify and organize the vast range of material it covers. Significant disagreements exist on the classification of psychopathology and the specific criteria for different disorders (APA, 2013b). Two approaches to the classification of mental and emotional disorders, categorical and dimensional models, have been used. The authors made an effort in the development of the *DSM-5* to introduce an integration of a dimensional approach to diagnosis and classification within the current categorical model (APA, 2013d). This effort was rooted in the intention to move the classification of mental disorders into a broader dimensional sphere, rather than the traditional categorical approach to diagnosis.

CATEGORICAL APPROACH

The publication of the *DSM-5* brought about numerous changes in both the clinical content and the organizational structure of the manual. Previous editions of the diagnostic manual relied heavily upon the categorical approach to the classification of psychopathology. Categorical approaches to the classification of diagnoses label an individual as either having or not having a disorder based on established diagnostic criteria (APA, 2013b; Kraemer, Noda, & O'Hara, 2004). Jones (2012) asserted that the categorical approach to diagnosis has only two values: either the presence of, or absence of, a disorder. For example, upon integrating all assessment information on an adolescent with myriad oppositional defiant behaviors, a clinical assessor consults with the *DSM* criteria to conclude whether the individual possesses the minimal number of symptoms to qualify for the specific disorder. To diagnose the adolescent with oppositional-defiant disorder, there must be evidence (for at least six months) of at least four of the eight symptoms listed in the diagnostic criteria.

Numerous strengths and weaknesses of the categorical approach to diagnosis are identified. Strengths of the categorical approach to diagnosis include ease of professional communication, reliable and consistent descriptions of disorders, understandable outcome measures, accurate clinical decision making, and better distinction between the presence or absence of mental illness (Bjelland et al., 2009; Kamphuis & Noordhof, 2009). Limitations of the categorical approach to diagnosis include the presence of diagnostic comorbidity, an underappreciation of the importance of variations in categorical symptoms, failure to recognize the complexity and uniqueness of contributing factors of the disorder, and failure in addressing the etiology of disorders (Stein, 2012). In recognizing that previous editions of the diagnostic manual considered each disorder as categorically separate from other conditions and diagnoses, previous editions of the *DSM* did not acknowledge the sharing of symptoms and criteria readily found in studies on comorbidity (APA, 2013). Lastly, the clinical assessor must be reminded that although the *DSM-5*'s categories cover vast diagnostic ground, "mental disorders do not always fit completely within the boundaries of a single disorder" (APA, 2013, p. xii).

DIMENSIONAL APPROACH

A common criticism of past editions of the *DSM* and their categorical reliance was in its overly narrow view of each separate disorder. This narrow view was not conducive to the mutual sharing of symptoms and risk factors across many disorders (APA, 2013d). This constricted view of mental disorders led many clinical assessors to use *not otherwise specified* (NOS) diagnoses as a means of communicating their diagnostic uncertainty. Studies of comorbidity among disorders found high rates of shared symptomology (Cummings, Coporino, & Kendal, 2014) and will be discussed in more detail later in this chapter. These factors have contributed to changes in the *DSM-5* categorization of the NOS designation. In an effort to enhance diagnostic specificity, the *DSM-5* has taken on a more dimensional approach to the classification of psychopathology, offering the clinician more freedom to assess the severity of the condition and not to imply a distinct threshold between normality and abnormality (APA, 2013d). Take, for example, the case study found in Sidebar 2.2.

SIDEBAR 2.2

Darius is a 9-year-old boy struggling with inattention, difficulty focusing, and impulsivity in his third-grade classroom. He is also assessed as gifted in reading, creativity, and math. Darius's teacher recommended his mother take him to his pediatrician for an attention-deficit/hyperactivity disorder (ADHD) assessment. Upon doing so, Darius was prescribed a psychostimulant. Unfortunately, psychostimulant medications can have numerous side effects. Darius's mother wants further testing to determine the degree of his symptoms and to make a more informed decision. After a thorough, multidimensional assessment, the clinical assessor dimensionally scales Darius's ADHD as mild to moderate and recommends a more challenging educational environment and other behavioral interventions. These changes allowed greater intellectual stimulation and alleviated most of his problematic symptoms.

The dimensional approach to the classification of mental disorders provides a diagnosis or classification to exist on a scale or spectrum, with higher scores indicating greater degrees of the disorder (Kraemer et al., 2004). Dimensional assessments are rating scales that measure a variety of features of a disorder, including frequency, duration, and severity, providing additional information to assist the clinician with diagnosis, treatment planning, and treatment monitoring (Jones, 2012). Strengths of the dimensional approach to the classification of mental disorders include allowing the clinician the ability to assess disorder severity, identify subclinical elements of the disorder, and measure changes in symptoms over time (Lebeau et al., 2012). Additionally, disadvantages of the dimensional approach include its inconsistency with the prevailing and current system used in the

DSM, the lack of consistency among literally hundreds of different scales of measures, and the potential higher costs of dimensional assessments (Hudziak, Achenbach, Althoff, & Pine, 2010).

A common phenomenon in the use of dimensional approaches for the classification of psychopathology is for the dimensional approach to be translated back eventually to the categorical approach, regardless of the intention of the clinical assessor (Stein, 2012). For example, a clinical assessor can use a full battery of assessment instruments to measure the severity of anxiety in a child, providing robust data and detailed measures of this disorder. However, in the current *DSM-5* categorical system, the assessed levels must still apply exclusively to the specific diagnostic criteria provided to meet the requirements of the disorder. As long as the categorical model of the classification of disorders dominates the *DSM*, diagnosis will essentially remain a binary process (Lebeau et al., 2012).

Identifying Sources of Information

All information acquired in the course of a mental health assessment must come from a source through which the information is originated. Sources of information can be broad and vast, because the ultimate purpose of assessment in mental health is simply to accumulate as much diverse information as possible. The more accurate information the assessor receives, providing detailed context to the client's circumstances, the more comprehensive the clinical assessment. The assessor should consider all information received in the course of a clinical assessment valuable and valid (information is simply information); however, not all information is necessarily accurate. It is the challenge of the competent assessor to seek out sources of viable information from a multitude of sources and formats, integrate all information received, and ultimately draw from this information accurate and comprehensive clinical conclusions.

Diverse and abundant sources of information give the clinician a host of advantages in formulating an accurate assessment and diagnosis. Multiple sources of information are used to lessen the risk of malingering or other forms of secondary gain. Malingering is the intentional feigning of symptoms for personal gain (APA, 2013b). To reduce the potential for malingering, clinical assessors may use diverse sources of information to cross-check the accuracy of all sources. Assessors gather information relevant to diagnostic assessment from numerous sources, with the most common sources covered in more detail.

DIRECT REPORT

Receiving information and data directly from the client is the most common form of information collected in the assessment process. Direct report in the context of the clinical interview offers an abundance of valuable information coming firsthand from the client. Acquiring assessment information through direct report also allows for the honoring of the client as the authority on his or her own life (Watson & Flamez, 2014), further adding to the therapeutic allegiance between client and assessor.

Prior to beginning the face-to-face assessment process, assessors can gather various information through an age-appropriate life history questionnaire the client fills out. When assessing children and adolescents, parents or caregivers can fill out life history questionnaires if the client is too young to communicate the information in written form. Common components of a life questionnaire include a conceptualization of the problem, background information, activities of daily living, hobbies and interests, description of family relations or dynamics, and other information specific to the assessment or treatment environment.

Gathering assessment information through direct report is highly dependent on the type and nature of questions asked. A key element in using questions is to differentiate open-ended questions from closed-ended questions. Closed-ended questions are simply questions that one can answer with one word—usually a yes or no. Alternatively, open-ended questions cannot be answered with just one word and require a longer and more detailed response. For example, when attempting to solicit information from adolescents about their relationship with their parents, an example of a closed-ended question is "Do you have a good relationship with your parents?" This question invites clients to respond easily with a yes or no and avoid any detail or depth in their response. An example of an open-ended question examining the same topic is "Tell me about your relationship with your parents?" This question challenges clients to provide a deeper level of elaboration to the information begin solicited. It also provides additional information for the assessor to integrate into other lines of questioning, based on the specifics of the more detailed responses offered from the open-ended questions.

PARENTS, CAREGIVERS, AND FAMILY

In addition to gathering information directly from the client, information from adults who have significant interaction with the client is also very valuable. Quickly assessing the child's or adolescent's home environment can identify parents, parental caregivers, or family members who possess valuable assessment and diagnostic information about the client. Biological parents frequently have the greatest breadth of historical information about the client; however, other caregivers or family members with substantial interaction with the client can also prove valuable sources of information. These can include grandparents, foster parents, legal guardians, aunts and uncles, siblings, pastors and clergy, and community elders. Overall, the primary caregivers are often a key source of information regarding day-to-day living with the identified client.

When gathering information from parents, caregivers, or family, it is important to begin with broad, open-ended questions and then proceed to further questioning that solicits greater detail. Table 2.1 provides examples of both specific and broad questioning to a parent or parent figure to elicit more information.

TABLE 2.1   Questions for Parents and Parental Caregivers

Broad/Molar Questions	*Specific/Molecular Questions*
"Tell me about (child's name)?"	"How is your child's appetite, energy, and sleep?"
"So tell me what is going on with (child's name)?	"What are the specific triggers to your child's anger outbursts?"
"Tell me what brings you here today?"	"What is your child afraid of?"
"What concerns you about your child?"	"When did the child's symptoms first appear?"
"Please describe for me what is bothering your child?"	"How is the child's school performance?"

TEACHERS OR EDUCATORS AND IMPORTANT COMMUNITY MEMBERS

Teachers or Educators—Children and adolescents typically spend a significant amount of time in structured educational settings, offering abundant time for observation by professionals. Gathering information from school administrators (principals, superintendents, deans of students), teachers, aides, school counselors and psychologists, and other school staff can have tremendous diagnostic value. Teachers and educators can provide information about a child's or adolescent's behaviors, moods, concentration or focus, peer relations, anxiety or fears, and other diagnostically relevant symptomology. With appropriate releases of information, assessing clinicians can request school records, or even more efficiently, simply call the various school personnel associated with the area of concern. School personnel are often very willing and interested in offering collaborative information about a child's or adolescent's emotional or behavioral health.

Peers—When assessing a child or adolescent occurs in an environment that provides interaction and contact between the assessor and the client's peers, the assessor should take advantage of the information offered through this contact. Schools, inpatient treatment facilities, and residential treatment centers can be examples of this assessment opportunity. Children and adolescents often share information with peers that they do not share with adults. Casually interacting with peers and asking questions about the child in concern, without jeopardizing the reputation or identity of the child, is important. The assessment information derived from this interaction does not have to come specifically through conversation with peers but rather can result from hanging out in common areas of peer interaction and making direct observations.

Medical or pediatric professionals—Valuable information can be gathered through various medical professionals who have previously treated or assessed the child. Current treating physicians or medical professionals often possess vital information about the child necessary for an accurate clinical assessment. This information can include current or past diagnoses and medical conditions, current or past medications, or medical procedures. Medical interventions can have significant impact on the mental health of a client, as can physical health conditions. It is critical for an assessing clinician to maintain a general fund of knowledge and awareness of medical conditions, medications and their side effects, and the connection between physical illness and mental health.

Other sources of information—Further reinforcing the idea that any information gathered in the course of a comprehensive assessment can be valuable, information from unique and diverse sources can be significant. Children and adolescents often express feelings in nonverbal or covert ways. Uncovering these hidden feelings can be challenging for the clinical assessor, requiring creative thinking and sometimes innovative requests. Valuable sources of alternative information can include client journals, poetry, song lyrics, drawings or any type of personal artwork (paintings, sketches, pottery, or figures). With the recent increase in use of social media, smartphones, and tablets, it can be very useful to ask a client to show any pictures, videos, or social media material he or she would like to share. Some children and adolescents may be reluctant to share this material, but others will gladly cooperate, enhancing the emotive expression and building rapport with the assessor. Items can also be gathered from parents and caretakers.

In addition, other sources of information can be assembled from a unique line of questioning during the clinical assessment. Various forms of the *miracle question* can be asked to ascertain problems areas in the client's life and changes that he or she would like to see occur. For example, ask, "If you could wake up tomorrow and your life is just the way you would like it to be, describe what it would look like?" A variation of this question is the *Aladdin* question: "If you had a magic genie and could ask for any three wishes, what would they be?" Lastly, the *time machine* question asks: "If you had a time machine and could go back in time, knowing what you know now, and change anything, what would you change?" The intent of these questions is to get the child or adolescent expressing emotion and potentially to identify problematic symptoms, sources of trauma or adversity, or levels of insight and judgment.

Finally, it can also provide great insight to ask children and adolescents about selective interests and pastimes. Favorite movies, television shows, musicians or genres of music, and video game preferences can all be helpful in gathering more information about the individual, aiding in the clinical assessment. Interpreting and understanding client answers to these questions require a broad knowledge base on the part of the assessor, emphasizing the importance of clinical assessors being in touch with current events and trends. See Sidebar 2.3 for a case illustration of the value of investigating interests and keeping abreast of current events.

SIDEBAR 2.3

Danielle is a 15-year-old high school freshman suffering from depression, isolation, bullying, and family chaos. Her mother had taken her to a therapist for an assessment, but Danielle refused to talk. Her mother tried again and brought her to your office, because you have the reputation of being able to get through to difficult and resistant teenagers. Part of your success is found in taking a unique and creative approach to assessment. Instead of focusing exclusively on Danielle's dysfunction in the assessment session, you simply focused on rapport building and creating a safe and empathic environment. One question you asked was whether she enjoyed music and whether she had any favorite musicians. Danielle quietly answered, and you immediately looked up the group on your tablet and together watched a video of the group, commenting on how cool the music was, compelling Danielle to relax slightly and offer further information.

Assessment Strategies

INTERVIEWS

Diagnostic interviews are the primary method used to form a clinical diagnosis (Lewis et al., 2014). Methods of interviewing in a clinical assessment can be broad and vast and are often customized to the individual clinical assessor. Although many approaches to the interview exist, the purpose is to investigate competently the specific diagnostic features categorized in the *DSM-5* (APA, 2013b). Interviewing children and adolescents requires a particular skill set encompassing both clinical skill and interpersonal finesse (Sommers-Flanagan & Sommers-Flanagan, 2009).

Establishment of Trust and Rapport

Imperative to the accuracy of any mental health evaluation is the establishment of trust and rapport between the client and the mental health professional. A lack of trust and rapport can result in limited or inaccurate information, resulting in an incomplete assessment. It is important for clinical assessors to place priority on the therapeutic attending behaviors accrued in the course of their clinical training and experience. Basic attending behaviors, such as active listening skills, paraphrasing and restatement, positive regard, and empathy all assist in garnering a therapeutic alliance and establishing trust and rapport in the assessment process. Rogers (1942) identified congruence, unconditional positive regard, and accurate empathy as three core conditions in establishing a therapeutic relationship with a client.

Especially important when assessing children and adolescents is an awareness of one's office environment, personal attire, and disposition. Essentially, an assessor should make every attempt to view things from the eyes of the client he or she is assessing and accommodate to make that client comfortable and at ease. Casual dress and a comfortable, relaxed environment are recommended when assessing children and adolescents. Paying special attention to the physical environment assists in helping a young client feel at ease and lessens the gap that may exist in the assessing relationship.

Communication between two people involves the sending and receiving of messages. Although simple in concept, human communication can be a complex phenomenon, occurring even when two people are not talking (Sommers-Flanagan & Sommers-Flanagan, 2009). The assessing clinician must pay attention to the nonverbal elements of communication, including the use of silence, to both gather information and build trust and rapport. Becoming comfortable with silence can be challenging for novice clinicians but can be an essential part of mental health assessment.

Clinical Interview

The clinical interview is exactly what the name implies: a formal interview process that takes place in a clinical setting. Sommers-Flanagan and Sommers-Flanagan (2012) suggested that the clinical interview be both a scientific and a relational process, possessing therapeutic value inherent in the assessment process itself. There are three commonly accepted types of clinical interviews: structured, semistructured, and unstructured (Jones, 2010). The structured clinical interview consists of standard questions, which one must read to the client exactly as written. Common structured interviews used with children and adolescents include the:

- Child Assessment Schedule (CAS)
- Diagnostic Interview Schedule for Children (DISC-IV)
- Diagnostic Interview for Children and Adolescents (DICA-IV)
- Child and Adolescent Psychiatric Assessment (CAPA)

Semistructured interviews are less standardized than structured interviews and offer some flexibility for the clinical assessor to direct the interview as he or she feels is appropriate based on the issues the client presents. A popular and frequently used example of the semistructured interview is the Structured Clinical Interview for DSM Disorders (SCID). Currently in development to integrate the *DSM-5*, the SCID offers multiple diagnostic modules for a clinician to use depending on the disorders he or she is assessing.

In addition, the SCID has a version specifically developed for use with child and adolescent disorders called the KID-SCID. The KID-SCID uses many of the same questions the adult version popularized, but uses language more conducive to children and adolescent populations (Matzner, Silva, Silvan, Chowdhury, & Nastasi, 1997). Both the child and the parent(s) or caregiver(s) answer each question based on diagnostic symptomology to achieve a score. A KIS-SCID diagnosis can be found if a client meets the required number of symptoms (Steensel, Bogels, & Bruin, 2012). Lastly, unstructured clinical interviews are the most frequently used type of clinical interview and allow the clinical assessor complete autonomy in the questions asked because of a lack of standardization of questioning or recording of responses (Watson & Flamez, 2014).

Depending on the age and developmental level of the child or adolescent being assessed, components of the child clinical interview are similar to those of an adult clinical interview. Common components of clinical interviews (based in part on American Psychiatric Association's Psychiatric Evaluation of Adults, 2006) include:

- Identifying information
- Presenting problem(s)
- Relevant history:
  - History of present emotional symptoms
  - History of past emotional symptoms
  - Medical history
  - Substance abuse or addictions history
  - Developmental history
  - Psychosocial and sociocultural history
  - Employment and military history
  - Legal history
  - Family history
- Functional assessment or strengths assessment
- Mental status examination
- Assessment summary
- Diagnosis
- Recommendations

OBSERVATIONS

Mental Status Examination

A primary observational component of all clinical assessment is the mental status examination (MSE). The MSE is a method of assessing and organizing clinical observations relating to a client's current mental state or condition (Sommers-Flanagan & Sommers-Flanagan, 2013). A skilled and experienced clinical assessor can transform conversational elements of the clinical interview into a rich and robust set of diagnostic data in the form of an MSE (Polanski & Hinkle, 2000). The MSE should be an essential part of all clinical assessments of *DSM-5* disorders. A frequently used and comprehensive example of an MSE is the Folstein Mini-Mental Status Examination (MMSE; Folstein, Folstein, & McHugh, 1975). The Folstein MMSE is a scoreable instrument designed to scale mental states and can be helpful in working with all clinical populations, including

TABLE 2.2   Mental Status Examination Components and Descriptors

Mental Status Examination Component	Elements/Descriptors
Appearance	Weight, grooming, age congruence, dress, prominent features
Behaviors	Movements, walk or gait, activity, repetition
Speech	Rate, intelligibility, volume, quality, quantity
Attitude toward examiner	Openness, expression, hostility level, guardedness
Affect and Mood	Expression, mood or affect congruence, appropriateness, happy or sad, tearful
Thought Content	Suicidal or homicidal ideation, obsessions, compulsions, delusions, phobias
Thought Process	Pace or speed of thoughts, logical, goal directed, disorganized
Attention and Concentration	Distractibility, tracking, focus
Orientation	×4: person, place, time, situation
Memory	Recall, short term or immediate, long term
Judgment and Insight	Good, fair, poor, guarded

children and adolescents. Clinicians frequently use the MMSE to measure changes in cognitive states and response to treatment (Pradier et al., 2014). See Table 2.2 for the most common components of an MSE and the elements measured.

CULTURAL FORMULATION INTERVIEW

The *DSM-5* (APA, 2013b) introduced the CFI as a means of assisting the assessing clinician in determining the impact of culture on key components of a client's clinical presentation. The CFI is a brief, semistructured interview consisting of 16 questions designed to strengthen the cultural validity of diagnostic assessment. The instrument is based on the revised Outline for Cultural Formulation and is based on five categories: cultural identity of the individual, cultural conceptualizations of distress, psychosocial stressors and cultural features of vulnerability and resilience, cultural features of the relationship between the individual and the clinician, and overall cultural assessment. The assessing clinician should strongly consider cultural elements in all clinical assessment of children and adolescents.

TESTS AND INVENTORIES

An abundance of tests and inventories exist in an effort to measure client phenomenon during the assessment process objectively. Although standardized instruments are common in mental health research, the use of tests and inventories is often lacking in clinical assessment and practice (Ford et al., 2013). In using established tests and inventories, it is imperative for the assessing clinician to be familiar with each instrument being utilized (American Academy of Child and Adolescent Psychiatry, 2011). It is important to note both the strengths and the limitations of tests and inventories in the assessment process. Strengths of the use of tests and inventories in the assessment process are numerous:

- Objectivity
- Lack of bias
- Reliability and validity

- Common language among distinct mental health professions
- Leads to appropriate and uniform treatment

Limitations of the use of tests and inventories in the assessment process also exist:

- High cost
- Time-consuming
- Limited holistic profile
- Detached
- Limited therapeutic value

CHECKLISTS AND RATING SCALES

In addition to tests and inventories used during the clinical assessment of children and adolescents, numerous checklists and rating scales are valuable to the clinical assessor. Checklists and rating scales are generally shorter and easier to use than tests and inventories and usually comprise only important dimensions being observed and rated (Drummond & Jones, 2010). Rating scales often use the services of an *informant*, or source of information. Informants are typically teachers, parents, and others who interact with the client being assessed. The informant can also be the clinical assessor or clients themselves.

Checklists use similar sources of information as rating scales and assist in forming diagnostic conclusions from the derived data. Checklists help clarify the types and extents of mental health symptoms that might be diagnostically relevant with a child or adolescent. It is important to note that checklists are best used as screening devices and should not be used with singularity in the formation of a mental health diagnosis. The most frequently used checklist in the assessment of children and adolescents is the Child Behavior Checklist/6–18 (Achenbach & Rescorla, 2001), a comprehensive instrument designed for evaluating behavioral and emotional problems in children aged 6 to 18.

SYMPTOM AND SEVERITY MEASURES

The *DSM-5* enhanced its online and digital presence with the creation of its cross-cutting symptoms measures (APA, 2013b). The assessment measures were designed for use both at the initial assessment meeting and in any follow-up meetings to measure symptoms' improvement or change. A thorough description of the cross-cutting symptoms measures will be presented in Chapter 3 of this text.

PROJECTIVE PERSONALITY TESTING

Children and adolescents often struggle in their ability to express verbally the complicated set of human emotions felt during these years. A viable option available to clinical assessors is the use of projective testing to develop more profound insight into the emotional processes of this age group. Projective tests comprise a plethora of techniques thought to allow the child or adolescent to give free-form responses to sets of ambiguous stimuli (McGrath & Carroll, 2012). When assessed competently, the child's responses to the ambiguous stimuli create themes and concepts, which one can interpret in conjunction with other assessment data. Projective testing can be very informative; however, clinical diagnosis conclusions based exclusively on projective personality testing is rarely warranted.

Projective Drawings

Rooted in elements of psychoanalytic theory, projective drawings use interpretations from the children's drawings as a means of elaborating and validating themes found elsewhere in the assessment process (Thornton, 2014). Projective drawings are commonly perceived as one of the oldest forms of child and adolescent mental health assessment (Whitcomb & Merrell, 2012). Child drawings are believed to contain nonverbal hints about the child's deeper feelings and emotional issues (Watson & Flamez, 2014). Two of the most commonly used projective drawings are the House-Tree-Person Technique (HTP; Buck, 1948)

SIDEBAR 2.4

FIGURE 2.1 An Example of an HTP Drawing of a 10-Year-Old Boy

The clinical assessor should note the mobile nature of the house, the potted tree, the child himself standing on top of the house, and the fire drawn on the left of the picture. The hand-drawn picture illustrates several of this particular client's potential issues, including multiple family moves (the mobile house and potted tree), the desire and need for power and control on part of the child (standing on top of the house), and a turbulent and traumatic past (fire and smoke).

and the Kinetic Family Drawing (K-F-D; Burns & Kaufman, 1970). Although different applications of these techniques are prolific, the essence of the drawings is simply to ask the child or adolescent to draw specific objects or people, with different elements of the drawings representing certain emotional dynamics. Interpretations derived from projective drawings have limitations, however, as most projective tests have failed to provide research support in the establishment of adequate reliability and validity. See Figure 2.1 and Sidebar 2.4 for an example of a House-Tree-Person drawing and brief interpretation.

An additional set of pragmatic projective assessment techniques are sentence completion tasks. Sentence completion tasks ask clients to finish a specific sentence when provided a brief prompt. Administration and responses may be either written or oral and, when interpreted in their entirety, can elicit broad themes and insights into the client's emotional profile. The Rotter Incomplete Sentence Blank (RISB; Rotter, Lah, & Rafferty, 1992) is one of the best-known and commonly used techniques with children and adolescents (McCloskey, 2014). Again, the clinical assessor is tasked with the challenge of identifying commonalities in the responses the client gives and integrating this information with all other assessment data.

Establishing Diagnostic Validity

The concept of validity is present throughout the sciences. Validity simply refers to the degree to which evidence and theory supports the interpretation of scores and assessments (American Educational Research Association [AERA], American Psychological Association, & National Council on Measurement in Education, 2014). In other words, validity asks whether the claims and decisions made on the basis of assessment are sound, meaningful, and useful for the intended purpose of the results. Validity is often a matter of degree, meaning that it does not exist on an all-or-none basis (Watson & Flamez, 2014; Miller, Linn, & Gronlund, 2012). Diagnostic validity mimics this concept, because the establishment of a clinical diagnosis is usually not a clearly delineated process. The *DSM-5* uses a variety of approaches to assist the clinical assessor in determining the quality of a given diagnosis. The quality of a diagnosis is defined by its validity and reliability (Kraemer et al., 2004); therefore these measures should be factors in all assessment processes being used.

CLINICAL UTILITY

A primary goal in the clinical assessment of a child or adolescent is ultimately to reach an accurate and precise mental health diagnosis. Of equal importance is for the diagnosis to have clinical utility. The clinical utility of a diagnosis helps the assessing clinician in determining the prognosis, treatment plan, and treatment outcome for the client (APA, 2013d). One can view the clinical utility of an assessment instrument or application as the pragmatic elements of the tool. High clinical utility is often related to both high reliability and high validity (Morey, Skodol, & Oldham, 2014) but is more commonly seen as a practical by-product of the diagnosis or application in the eyes of the clinical assessor.

CRITERIA FOR CLINICAL SIGNIFICANCE

A prominent factor in the validity of a mental health diagnosis is whether a set of symptoms meet the criteria for clinical significance according to the *DSM* guidelines. Because of the ambiguity often found in a child's or adolescent's clinical profile, an uncertainty can exist in the degree to which symptoms are normal or pathological. The *DSM* provides a statement as a guide to assist the assessing clinician in determining the clinical significance of symptoms. Diagnostic criteria provided for each primary disorder covered in the *DSM-5* include a generic criterion offered to establish disorder thresholds: "the disturbance causes clinically significant distress or impairment in social, occupational, or other important area of functioning" (APA, 2013b, p. 21). Assessing and applying this statement, on a case-by-case basis, with each individual being assessed, is the task of the clinical assessor.

For example, when diagnosing a child with social anxiety disorder, the degree of impairment the symptoms cause is often a primary factor in determining the clinical significance of the diagnosis. A child could meet many of the diagnostic criteria for the disorder, including marked, persistent, and avoidant fear or anxiety about one or more social situations; however, if it is assessed that the fears do not constitute significant distress or impairment in functioning, a diagnosis is not justified.

ELEMENTS OF A DIAGNOSIS

Consistent and established elements must be present to warrant a formal diagnosis. A primary task of thorough clinical assessment is the challenge of identifying these elements and conceptualizing their meaning within a diagnostic framework. The lack of significant symptomology and features of mental disorders ultimately lead to ambiguity and diagnostic uncertainty. In an effort to guide the clinical assessor in the conceptualization of emotional disorders, the *DSM* provides a comprehensive system of investigative symptoms (criteria) to use as the foundational elements of formal diagnosis.

Diagnostic Criteria and Descriptors

The *DSM-5* offers an abundance of diagnostic criteria as guidelines for the formulation of clinical diagnoses (APA, 2013b). Diagnostic criteria are simply written descriptions of clinical symptoms, provided along with a list of other related symptoms corresponding to each specific disorder. For a set of symptoms to meet the degree necessary to warrant a diagnosis, a minimal number of criteria must be endorsed. For example, in diagnosing an adolescent with generalized anxiety disorder, the *DSM-5* provides six (items A thru F) criteria that he or she has to meet to elicit a full diagnosis. Additionally, under item C, six specific symptoms are also included. To diagnose a child with this disorder, at least one of the symptoms has to have been present for more days than not over the past six months. The current diagnostic system weighs each specific criterion equally, with each criterion counting the same toward meeting the diagnostic threshold. A limitation can be found in this system, however, because researchers argue that certain criteria are more useful than others in determining the associated mental disorder (Cooper & Balsis, 2009).

Further information about specific individual disorders, as well as each diagnostic chapter, is provided in text descriptions to help support a clinical diagnosis. In addition to diagnostic criteria, the *DSM* provides information about disorder severity, diagnostic features, prevalence, development and course, and risk and prognostic factors.

This information is useful in further determining the precise diagnosis based on the assessment information. For example, in the newly identified disruptive mood dysregulation disorder (DMDD), information contained in the diagnostic features section further extrapolates on the clinical presentation, severity, and prominent research on the disorder. Information on the prevalence of the DMDD finds that 2 percent to 5 percent of children and adolescents suffer from the disorder, and risk and prognostic factors include temperamental, genetic, and physiological aspects of the disorder.

Subtypes and Specifiers

In an effort to provide greater detail to each clinical disorder, a variety of additional information can be communicated in the formulation of a specific diagnosis. Subtypes and specifiers are usually coded on the fourth, fifth, or sixth digit of the numeric code and are offered for increased specificity and diagnostic description (American Counseling Association, 2013). Subtypes describe mutually exclusive subgroupings within a specific diagnosis. Specifiers, in contrast, are not intended to be mutually exclusive and can therefore include more than one specifying feature. Severity specifiers are also provided to assist clinicians in assessing the intensity, frequency, duration, symptom count, or other severity indicator of the disorder (APA, 2013b). Not every clinical disorder includes subtypes and specifiers in the *DSM-5*.

Assessment Instrument Validity and Reliability

For any standardized assessment instrument to contribute accurately to a comprehensive clinical assessment, both reliability and validity measures of the instrument have to be established. Applied to various assessment instruments (inventories, surveys, quotients, tests, scales, etc.), validity refers to whether the claims and decisions based on assessment results are sound, meaningful, and useful, whereas reliability speaks to the degree to which an instrument's scores are consistent, dependable, and reproducible (Watson & Flamez, 2014). Assessment instruments must be both reliable and valid for the results of the study to have credible results. Additionally, reliablity and validity must be examined, determined, and reported for each assessment instrument to be viable for use in a clinical assessment (Sullivan, 2012).

Reliability is often viewed as a component of the assessment of validity. Reliability constructs need to be established within different items of a test, with different forms of a test, and with repeated administrations of a test. Common methods of estimating the reliability of an assessment instrument include test-retest, alternate form, internal consistency reliability, split-half reliability, coefficient alpha (Cronbach's Alpha), and interrater reliability (Watson & Flamez, 2014).

Validity of an assessment instrument also requires significant evidence to verify that the instrument measures what it is supposed to measure (Watson & Flamez, 2014). Common sources of validity evidence include test content, response processes, internal structure, relations to other variables, and consequences of testing (AERA et al., 2014). The process of test validation can be ongoing and demanding but is vital to ensure accountability in the assessment and diagnosis of mental disorders, especially among children and adolescents.

Conducting a Differential Diagnosis

Many of the disorders affecting children and adolescents, similar to disorders in adults, include an abundance of diagnostic ambiguities that add to the complexity of the assessment process. One of the most challenging elements of a competent clinical assessment and diagnosis of children and adolescents is found in the world of differential diagnoses. Differential diagnosis is the act of distinguishing one disorder from another disorder that has similar presenting characteristics (APA, 2013b). In other terms, differential diagnosing challenges the assessor to ask the question: *What else could be contributing to the client's symptoms?* A general fund of diagnostic awareness is needed to connect the diagnostic dots and relationships of various disorders that relate to the presenting problem.

According to the *DSM-5 Handbook of Differential Diagnosis* (First, 2013), a significant problem in the area of mental health assessment is the premature diagnostic conclusion assessing clinicians arrive at. Many assessing clinicians determine a diagnosis within the first few minutes on a clinical assessment. The clinician unfortunately spends the rest of the assessment simply justifying this diagnosis through the already determined, biased lens. In an effort to combat this tendency, it is strongly encouraged to consider all other diagnostic candidates and ultimately to choose the disorder that best describes the presenting symptoms.

In an effort to assist the assessing clinician in being more aware of potential differential diagnoses, the *DSM-5* provides alternative diagnoses with each of the clinical disorders described (APA, 2013b). For example, differential diagnoses to be considered when evaluating a diagnosis of oppositional defiant disorder include conduct disorder, attention-deficit/hyperactivity disorder, depressive and bipolar disorders, disruptive mood dysregulation disorder, intermittent explosive disorder, intellectual disability, language disorder, and social anxiety disorder. All of these disorders share common symptomology that could potentially apply to both disorders. It is the responsibility of the clinical assessor to thoroughly delineate the primary diagnosis from secondary diagnoses or differential diagnoses. In Chapters 5 through 18 you will learn more about these specific disorders in children and adolescents and differential diagnoses.

It is important in the early stages of diagnostic assessment and conceptualization to start with a broad and molar view of the symptomology and begin ruling out potential diagnostic contributors. To assist in this endeavor, the *DSM-5 Handbook of Differential Diagnosis* (First, 2013) provides a six-step process of differentiating *DSM-5* diagnoses: (1) ruling out malingering and factitious disorder, (2) ruling out a substance etiology, (3) ruling out an etiological medical condition, (4) determining the specific primary disorder(s), (5) differentiating adjustment disorder from the residual Other Specified and Unspecified conditions, and (6) establishing the boundary with no mental disorder.

COMORBIDITY

Comorbidity refers to the existence of more than one disorder occurring at the same time (First, 2013). Comorbidity is also commonly referred to as dual disorders or co-occurring disorders. Although differential diagnosis generally refers to the idea that an assessing clinician is selecting a single diagnosis from a larger pool of similar diagnosis, comorbidity occurs when diagnoses are not mutually exclusive. In cases such as these, multiple diagnoses are needed to describe and cover the presenting symptomology adequately. Criticisms against past editions of the *DSM* have cited rampant comorbidity disorders as a prominent limitation of this document (Kamphius & Noordhof, 2009). Certain psychiatric disorders in children and adolescents have higher rates of comorbidity with other disorders. For example, children diagnosed with autistic spectrum disorder have high rates of comorbidity with others disorders, such as depression, anxiety, attention-deficit/hyperactivity disorder, and behavioral disorders (van Steensel, Brögels, & de Bruin, 2013).

Another common example of comorbidity in children and adolescents of particular challenge to clinical assessors is the diagnoses of anxiety and depression. Increasing research recognizes the shared symptomology of these disorders, with some research finding a comorbidity rate of up to 75 percent (Cummings, Caporino, & Kendal, 2014). The latest findings are begging the question of whether depression and anxiety are actually different versions of the same disorder. Many researchers suggest that comorbidity is a byproduct of an imperfect diagnostic system to be further examined in future diagnostic manuals (Cummings et al., 2014). The phenomenon of comorbidity exemplifies the importance of a competent and thorough clinical assessment. The successful differentiation between two or more disorders is often in the minute nuances of the subtle symptoms of the disorder. The skilled clinician uses diverse assessment resources to delineate these symptoms and develop the most appropriate diagnostic profile.

Clinical Case Formulation

Assessment strategies in children and adolescents always involve a type of clinical case formulation or clinical case conceptualization. Clinical case formulation is a broad term used to describe the integration of multiple judgments about the problems, history, and causal variables that influence and affect the focus and strategy of the assessment and diagnosis process (Godoy & Haynes, 2011). A case formulation is often theory dependent, with distinctive components coming from various theories, such as cognitive-behavioral, psychodynamic, humanistic, and eclectic perspectives.

Three distinct steps have been identified in the case formulation process (Neukrug & Schwitzer, 2006). The first step is for the clinical assessor to *evaluate* the client through assessment, observation, and appropriate testing of symptoms. The second step is for the clinician to organize the assessment information into *patterns and themes* in the client's symptomology. Lastly, the clinical assessor chooses a *theoretical orientation*, or set of theoretical orientations that aids in the interpretation, explanation, or clinical judgments about client experiences.

SOCIAL, PSYCHOLOGICAL, AND BIOLOGICAL FACTORS

An integral part of any holistic assessment of children and adolescents is the attention the assessor pays to the social, psychological, and biological components of the client's life. The biopsychosocial (BPS) approach is one of the most common, comprehensive, and integrative frameworks used in a mental health assessment (Meyer & Melchert, 2011). This comprehensive assessment system offers a holistic model to organize and integrate complex assessment data. Additionally, numerous professional practice guidelines, standards of practice, and ethical codes within multiple mental health disciplines emphasize that biological and sociocultural considerations be incorporated into mental health assessment and case conceptualization.

The *DSM-5* (APA, 2013b) suggests that a case formulation for a client should include a detailed clinical history and summary of the biological, social, and psychological elements that have influenced the development of a particular disorder. The *DSM-5* promotes a balanced approach to case formulation, which recognizes "the combination of predisposing, precipitating, perpetuating, and protective factors has resulted in a pathological condition" (APA, 2013b, p. 19). Furthermore, a thorough case formulation can aid the clinical assessor in the accurate formulation of a comprehensive treatment plan.

Comprehensive Case Study

Consider the following comprehensive case study as an application of the elements of this chapter:

> Brittany is a 14-year-old Caucasian female. At the time of the assessment and admission to treatment, her presenting problem was mild to moderate behavioral acting out, oppositional behaviors, anger outbursts, anxiety, and self-injury (superficial cutting on arm). She also has a past diagnosis of attention-deficit/hyperactivity disorder and is currently prescribed a psychostimulant by her pediatrician. The applications and instruments used to assess Brittany were a semistructured clinical interview, mental status examination, Child Behavior Checklist/6–18, House-Tree-Person Drawing, Kinetic Family Drawing, and the Rotter Incomplete Sentence Blank.

CLINICAL INTERVIEW

Significant historical information was collected from a multitude of sources. Primary information was provided by Brittany and her adopted parents of four years. Collateral information was also gathered through her past clinical counselor, pediatrician, school counselor, children's services worker, and biological grandparent. Additionally, upon the clinical assessor's requests, copies of grade cards, hand-drawn pictures and artwork, and a scrapbook created by Brittany's adopted parents were also reviewed. Specific questions were asked of her cultural background and early life experiences, although some of the information was limited because of her adopted status.

Brittany was born in southern Ohio and is of Appalachian decent. Her biological parents were never married and split up when Brittany was very young. From the ages of 1 until adoption at age 10, Brittany resided at 18 different residences, including a combination of second-degree relatives (grandparents, aunts and uncles) and therapeutic foster homes. There is no evidence of physical or sexual abuse, but there is a significant history of verbal and emotional abuse in the form of yelling and screaming and of degrading and harsh parenting techniques. There is some question among the children's services workers whether malnutrition and neglect were present during the ages 0 to 4. Her parents adopted her four years ago. Since this time, she has lived a middle-class lifestyle and is the only child of her adoptive parents.

MENTAL STATUS EXAMINATION

Brittany presented as a 14-year-old Caucasian female with bright red hair, fair skin, and freckles. She wore eyeglasses and was casually, but neatly, dressed in attire that was more consistent with younger children. Brittany appeared two to three years younger than her stated age because of her short height (approximately 4'2''–4'6'' and 70–80 lbs.). She had very small features, including small feet and hands. Her speech was appropriate, with a healthy volume, tone, and slightly elevated rate. She was talkative and open to the examiner and did not show any signs of mistrust or suspiciousness. There were no unusual movements or behaviors, although she had mild difficulty sitting still and fidgeting. Her thought processes were also slightly rapid, and she was verbose. Several times throughout the interview she had to be redirected to stay on topic. Her insight and memory were good, as she demonstrated a deep awareness of her past and was a very good historian. She was oriented × 4 to person, place, time, and current situation. Her judgment was also good, as she answered all related questions comprehensively.

CHILD BEHAVIOR CHECKLIST/6–18

Significant symptoms were presented on the checklist in the areas of inattention, poor concentration, and impulsivity. Additionally, symptoms were found to be elevated in symptoms of anger outburst, emotionality, anxiety, and excessive feelings of guilt and regret.

HOUSE-TREE-PERSON DRAWING

Interpretation of the drawing found multiple themes related to Brittany's profile. Interpretation of the person (how she views herself) could indicate a poor self-concept and lack of ego strength. The house (how she views her family) could indicate a past history of instability, family change, and chaos. The tree (how she views her life in its entirety) indicated a lack of foundational support and further instability.

KINETIC FAMILY DRAWING

Brittany's family drawing represented her current adoptive family and did not include any other relatives. Her picture demonstrated a sense of closeness to her parents with a strong allegiance and possible dependency on her adoptive mother.

ROTTER INCOMPLETE SENTENCE BLANK

An analysis of Brittany's completed sentences found strong themes of inadequacy, fears of abandonment, and low self-esteem and self-confidence. She indicated numerous anxieties and worries about the future, especially with her family and well-being.

CASE SUMMARY AND DIAGNOSIS

Integrating all assessment information finds numerous areas of clinical concern. Biologically, Brittany has a strong family history of depression, anxiety, and schizophrenia.

Environmentally, she has been through multiple caregivers and probable early life neglect. Socially, Brittany is occasionally the victim of bullying and stands out physically from her peers because of her delayed development, small features, poor school performance, and behavioral acting out. Based on the assessment, Brittany meets the *DSM-5* diagnostic criteria for attention-deficit/hyperactivity disorder, combined presentation (314.01), oppositional defiant disorder (313.81), and unspecified anxiety disorder (300.00). Other diagnoses that should be considered upon further assessment are posttraumatic stress disorder, reactive attachment disorder, and major depressive disorder. Treatment recommendations include outpatient psychotherapy, medication management, and group therapy to increase her social skills.

Summary

Providing individualized, culturally competent treatment to children and adolescents can be challenging for even the most seasoned counseling professional. Proper assessment of each individual is a critical element to that end. The *DSM-5* includes a number of important updates that pose critical implications for counselors when assessing presenting problems and determining client needs. The paradigm shift with expanded criteria for clinical significance and the inclusion of a spectrum approach to some diagnostic categories have profound implications for assessment and treatment planning. This chapter opened with challenges and special considerations for counselors working with children and adolescents followed by a comprehensive explanation of the movement away from categorical diagnosis and toward dimensional, nonmultiaxial approaches. Guidance for best practice regarding assessment strategies and establishing diagnostic validity and differential diagnosis were included. A clinical case formulation demonstrating the integration of social, psychological, and biological factors when assessing children for treatment was included. As best practice, a counselor's assessment process will provide individualized, contextual assessment with great depth of detail recognizing the dynamic nature of development and how children and adolescents interact with their environment.

References

Achenbach, T. M., & Rescorla, L. A. (2001). *Manual for the ASEBA school-age forms & profiles*. Burlington, VT: University of Vermont, Research Center for Children, Youth, and Families.

Aggarwal, N. K., Nicasio, A. V., DeSilva, R., Boiler, M., & Lewis-Fernández, R. (2013). Barriers to implementing the DSM-5 Cultural Formulation Interview: A qualitative study. *Culture, Medicine, and Psychiatry, 37*(3), 505–533. doi:10.1007/s11013–013–9325-z

American Academy of Child and Adolescent Psychiatry. (1997). Practice parameters for the psychiatric assessment of children and adolescents. Retrieved from http://download.journals.elsevierhealth.com/pdfs/journals/0890–8567/PIIS0890856709625910.pdf

American Academy of Child and Adolescent Psychiatry. (2011). Practice parameter for child and adolescent forensic evaluations. Retrieved from http://download.journals.elsevierhealth.com/pdfs/journals/0890–8567/PIIS0890856711008835.pdf

American Educational Research Association, American Psychological Association, & National Council on Measurement in Education (2014). *Standards for educational and psychological testing*. Washington, DC: American Educational Research Association.

American Psychiatric Association. (2006). *Psychiatric evaluation of adults* (2nd ed.). doi: 10.1176/appi.books.9780890423363.137162

American Psychiatric Association. (2013a). *Cultural Formulation Interview (CFI)—Informant version*. Retrieved from http://www.psychiatry.org/file%20library/practice/dsm/dsm-5/culturalformulationinterviewinformant.pdf

American Psychiatric Association. (2013b). *Diagnostic and statistical manual of mental disorders* (5th ed.). Arlington, VA: American Psychiatric Publishing.

American Psychiatric Association. (2013c). *DSM-5 and diagnoses for children*. Retrieved from http://www.psychiatry.org/file%20library/practice/dsm/dsm-5/dsm-5-diagnoses-for-children.pdf

American Psychiatric Association. (2013d). *DSM-5's integrated approach to diagnosis and classifications*. Retrieved from http://www.psychiatry.org/file%20library/practice/dsm/dsm-5/dsm-5-integrated-approach.pdf

American Psychiatric Association. (2014). *Online assessment measures*. Retrieved from http://www.psychiatry.org/practice/dsm/dsm5/online-assessment-measures

Bjelland, I., Lie, S. A., Dahl, A. A., Mykletun, A., Stordal, E., & Kraemer, H. C. (2009). A dimensional versus a categorical approach to diagnosis: Anxiety and depression in the HUNT 2 study. *International Journal of Methods in Psychiatric Research, 18*(2): 128–137.

Bozarth, J. D. (1991). Person-centered assessment. *Journal of Counseling & Development, 69*(5), 458–461.

Buck, J. N. (1948). The H-T-P test. *Journal of Clinical Psychology, 4*(2), 151–159.

Burns, R. C., & Kaufman, S. H. (1970). *Kinetic family drawings (K-F-D)*. New York, NY: Brunner-Mazel.

Cooper, L. D., & Balsis, S. (2009). When less is more: How fewer diagnostic criteria can indicate greater severity. *Psychological Assessment, 21*(3), 285–293. doi:10.1037/a0016698

Cummings, C. M., Caporino, N. E., & Kendal, P. C. (2014). Comorbidity of anxiety and depression in children and adolescents: 20 years after. *Psychological Bulletin, 140*(3), 816–845. doi:10.1037/a0034733

Drummond, R. J., & Jones, K. D. (2010). *Appraisal procedures for counselors and helping professionals*. (7th ed.). Upper Saddle River, NJ: Pearson Education.

Erford, B. T. (2013). *Assessment for counselors* (2nd ed.). Belmont, CA: Brooks/Cole.

First, M. B. (2013). *DSM-5 handbook of differential diagnosis*. Arlington, VA: American Psychiatric Publishing.

Folstein, M., Folstein, S. E., & McHugh, P. R. (1975). "Mini-mental state": A practical method for grading the cognitive state of patients for the clinician. *Journal of Psychiatric Research, 12*(3), 189–198.

Ford, T., Last, A., Henley, W., Norman, S., Guglani, S., Kelesidi, K., … Goodman, R. (2013). Can standardized diagnostic assessment be a useful adjunct to clinical assessment in child mental health services? A randomized controlled trial of disclosure of the Development and Well-Being Assessment to practitioners. *Social Psychiatry and Psychiatric Epidemiology, 48*(4), 583–593. doi:10.1007/s00127-012-0564-z

Godoy, A., & Haynes, S. N. (2011). Clinical case formulation: Introduction to the special section.

European Journal of Psychological Assessment, 27(1), 1–3. doi:10.1027/1015-5759/a000055

Hudziak, J., Achenbach, T., Althoff, R., & Pine, D. (2007). A dimensional approach to developmental psychopathology. *International Journal of Methods in Psychiatric Research, 16*(1), 16–23.

Johnson, R. (2013). Forensic and Culturally Responsive Approach for the DSM-5: Just the FACTS. *Journal of Theory Construction & Testing, 17*(1), 18–22.

Jones, K. D. (2010). The unstructured clinical interview. *Journal of Counseling & Development, 88*(2), 220–226.

Jones, K. D. (2012). Dimensional and cross-cutting assessment in the DSM-5. *Journal of Counseling & Development, 90*(4), 481–487. doi:10.1002/j.1556-6676.2012.00059.x

Kamphuis, J. H., & Noordhof, A. (2009). On categorical diagnoses in DSM-V: Cutting dimensions at useful points? *Psychological Assessment, 21*(3), 294–301.

Kirmayer, L. J. (2006). Beyond the 'new cross-cultural psychiatry': Cultural biology, discursive psychology and the ironies of globalization. *Transcultural Psychiatry, 43*(1), 126–144.

Kleinman, A. (1977). Depression, somatization and the "new cross-cultural psychiatry." *Social Science & Medicine, 11*(1), 3–10.

Kraemer, H., Noda, A., & O'Hara, R. (2004). Categorical versus dimensional approaches to diagnosis: Methodological challenges. *Journal of Psychiatric Research, 38*(1), 17–25.

Lai, M., Lombardo, M. V., Chakrabarti, B., & Baron-Cohen, S. (2013). Subgrouping the Autism "Spectrum": Reflections on DSM-5. *PLoS Biology, 11*(4). 1–8. doi:10.1371/journal.pbio.1001544

Lebeau, R. T., Glenn, D. E., Hanover, L. N., Beesdo-Baum, K., Wittchen, H., & Craske, M. G. (2012). A dimensional approach to measuring anxiety for DSM-5. *International Journal of Methods in Psychiatric Research, 21*(4), 258–272. doi:10.1002/mpr.1369

Lewis, A., Bertino, M. D., Bailey, C. M., Skewes, J., Lubman, D. I., & Toumbourou, J. W. (2014). Depression and suicidal behavior in adolescents: A multi-informant and multi-methods approach to diagnostic classification. *Frontiers in Psychology, 51*–24. doi:10.3389/fpsyg.2014.00766

Lewis-Fernández, R., Balán, I. C., Patel, S. R., Sánchez-Lacay, A. J., Alfonso, C., Gorritz, M., … Moyers, T. B. (2013). Impact of motivational pharmacotherapy on treatment retention among depressed Latinos. *Psychiatry, 76*(3), 210–222.

Lord, C., & Jones, R. M. (2012). Annual research review: Re-thinking the classification of autism spectrum disorders. *Journal of Child Psychiatry, 53*(5), 490–509.

Lu, F. G., Lim, R. F., & Mezzich, J. E. (1995). Issues in the assessment and diagnosis of culturally diverse individuals. In J. M. Oldham & M. B. Riba (Eds.), *Review of psychiatry* (Vol. 14; pp. 477–510). Arlington, VA: American Psychiatric Press.

Matzner, F., Silva, R., Silvan, M., Chowdhury, M., & Nastasi, L. (1997). *Preliminary test-retest reliability of the KID-SCID.* Paper presented at the scientific proceedings of the American Psychiatric Association Meeting, Washington, DC.

McCloskey, L. C. (2014). Construct and incremental validity of the Rotter Incomplete Sentences Blank in adult psychiatric outpatients. *Psychological Reports, 114*(2), 363–375. doi:10.2466/03.09.PRO.114k22w7

McGrath, R. E., & Carroll, E. J. (2012). The current status of "projective" "tests." In H. Cooper, P. M. Camic, D. L. Long, A. T. Panter, D. Rindskopf, & K. J. Sher (Eds.), *APA handbook of research methods in psychology, Vol. 1: Foundations, planning, measures, and psychometrics* (pp. 329–348). Washington, DC: American Psychological Association.

McWilliams, N. (1999). *Psychoanalytic case formulation.* New York, NY: Guilford Press.

Meyer, L., & Melchert, T. P. (2011). Examining the content of mental health intake assessments from a biopsychosocial perspective. *Journal of Psychotherapy Integration, 21*(1), 70–89. doi:10.1037/a0022907

Miller, M. D., Linn, R. L., & Gronlund, N. E. (2012). *Measurement and assessment in teaching.* (11th ed.). Boston, MA: Pearson.

Morey, L. C., Skodol, A. E., & Oldham, J. M. (2014). Clinician judgments of clinical utility: A comparison of DSM-IV-TR personality disorders and the alternative model for DSM-5 personality disorders. *Journal of Abnormal Psychology, 123*(2), 398–405. doi:10.1037/a0036481

Neukrug, E., & Schwitzer, A. M. (2006). *Skills and tools for today's counselors and psychotherapists: From natural helping to professional counseling.* Belmont, CA: Brooks/Cole.

Polanski, P. J., & Hinkle, J. (2000). The mental status examination: Its use by professional counselors. *Journal of Counseling & Development, 78*(3), 357.

Pomeroy, E. C., & Anderson, K. (2013). The DSM-5 has arrived. *Social Work, 58*(3), 197–200. doi:10.1093/sw/swt028

Pradier, C., Sakarovitch, C., Le Duff, F., Layese, R., Metelkina, A., Anthony, S., … Robert, P. (2014). The Mini Mental State Examination at the time of Alzheimer's Disease and related disorders diagnosis, according to age, education, gender and place of residence: A cross-sectional study among the French National Alzheimer Database. *PLoS ONE, 9*(8), 1–8. doi:10.1371/journal.pone.0103630

Rogers, C. R. (1942). *Counseling and psychotherapy: Newer concepts in practice.* Boston: Houghton, Mifflin.

Rotter, J. B., Lah, M. I., & Rafferty, J. E. (1992). *Rotter Incomplete Sentences Blank manual* (2nd ed.). San Antonio, TX: Psychological Corporation.

Sommers-Flanagan, J., & Sommers-Flanagan, R. (1995). Intake interviewing with suicidal patients: A systematic approach. *Professional Psychology: Research and Practice, 26*(1), 41–47. doi:10.1037/0735–7028.26.1.41

Sommers-Flanagan, J., & Sommers-Flanagan, R. (2009). *Clinical Interviewing* (4th ed.). Hoboken, NJ: John Wiley & Sons.

Stein, D. (2012). Dimensional or categorical: Different classifications and measures of anxiety and depression. *Medicographia, 34*, 270–275.

Sue, D., Sue, D. W., Sue, D., & Sue, S. (2014). Essentials of understanding abnormal behavior (2nd ed.). Belmont, CA: Cengage Learning.

Sullivan, G. M. (2011). A primer on the validity of assessment instruments. *Journal of Graduate Medical Education, 3*(2), 199–120.

Swartz-Kulstad, J. L., & Martin, W. E. (1999). Impact of culture and context on psychosocial adaptation: The cultural and contextual guide process. *Journal of Counseling & Development, 77*(3), 281–293. doi:10.1002/j.1556-6676.1999.tb02451.x

Thornton, V. (2014). Using the emotional impact of domestic violence on young children. *Educational and Child Psychology, 31*(1), 90–100.

Trierweiler, S. J., Neighbors, H. W., Thompson, E. E., Munday, C., Jackson, J. S., & Binion, V. J. (2010). Differences in patterns of symptom attribution in diagnosing schizophrenia between African American and Non-African American clinicians. *American Journal Orthopsychiatry, 76*(2), 154–160, doi:10.1037/0002-9432.76.2.154

Trull, T. J., Tragesser. S. L., Solhan, M., & Schwartz-Mette, R. (2007). Dimensional models of personality disorder: Diagnostic and Statistical Manual of Mental Disorders Fifth Edition and beyond. *Current Opinion in Psychiatry, 20*(1), 52–56.

van Steensel, F. J. A., Bögels, S. M., & de Bruin, E. I. (2013). Psychiatric comorbidity in children with Autism Spectrum Disorders: A comparison with children with ADHD. *Journal of Child and Family Studies, 22*(3), 368–376.

Vrshek-Schallhorn, S., Wolitzky-Taylor, K., Doane, L. D., Epstein, A., Sumner, J. A., Mineka, S., … Adam, E. K. (2014). Validating new summary indices for the childhood trauma interview: Associations with first onsets of major depressive disorder and anxiety disorders. *Psychological Assessment, 26*(3), 730–740. doi:10.1037/a0036842

Watson, J. C., & Flamez, B. (2014). *Counseling assessment and evaluation: Fundamentals of applied practice.* Thousand Oaks, CA: SAGE.

Whitcomb, S. A. & Merrell, K. W. (2012). *Behavioral, social, and emotional assessment of children and adolescents* (4th ed.). New York, NY: Routledge.

World Health Organization. (1992). *International statistical classification of diseases and related health problems* (10th revision). Geneva, Switzerland: Author.

Chapter 3

Developing and Evaluating Client Treatment Plans

LAURA R. HADDOCK, MICHELLE PEREPICZKA, AND RUTH OUZTS MOORE

Introduction

When clients enter the therapeutic process, a plan is necessary to identify the issues that will be addressed, as well as the approach that will be used to address them. Ideally, a treatment plan sets specific goals allowing the client, or in the case of a child, allowing the client and the parents to understand the particular focus of treatment, the expected outcome, and the methods necessary to monitor ongoing progress. The treatment plan will be reviewed and updated throughout the duration of counseling.

This chapter will provide a guide for developing a comprehensive treatment plan that will allow clinicians to determine where to begin with the direction of treatment, where they want to go, and how they will get there. This chapter builds on Chapter 2 and includes an overview of the components of a treatment plan, including initial case conceptualization, the development of goals and objectives, and *DSM-5* cross-cutting and disorder-specific assessment measures that clinicians may use to inform the process of goal development. In addition, the information in this chapter illuminates diagnostic challenges that counselors may face when using the *DSM-5* to develop treatment plans, as well as practical strategies for how to assess treatment plan effectiveness and issues related to third-party reimbursement for practitioners. Differences between school settings and clinical settings will be highlighted.

Assessment Measures for Children (6–17) in the *DSM-5*

The *Diagnostic and Statistical Manual, Fifth Edition* (*DSM-5*), is a tool for mental health clinicians that guides in assessment and diagnosis. Although it contains a wealth of information related to the characteristics of various disorders, it does not include specific guidelines for the treatment of any disorder. The *DSM-5* provides a framework that assists clinicians in developing a comprehensive approach to treatment through the integration of cultural and social context along with clinical diagnostic information. Determining an accurate diagnosis is the first step in appropriately treating any mental disorder. Therefore, the *DSM-5* includes a variety of patient assessment measures that one can administer during the initial patient interview and throughout the course of treatment to monitor progress, and clinicians should become well oriented with these assessments. The following section provides an overview of the new *DSM-5* assessment measures that one may use as part of the treatment planning process.

Dimensional Aspects of Diagnosis versus Dichotomous Methods

DSM-5 diagnoses emphasize multidimensional aspects of disorders to more specifically capture the nuances of disorders, such as specific symptoms, number of symptoms present, onset and duration, and level of intensity or severity (American Psychiatric Association [APA], 2013b). These factors allow practitioners to more accurately identify a diagnosis along a continuum, for example, instead of a categorical method of criteria, such as met or not met. This dimensional approach allows practitioners to address and account for degrees of symptom occurrence within and between disorders. Historically, the *Diagnostic and Statistical Manual, Fourth Edition, Text Revision* (*DSM-IV-TR*), used a dichotomous method of diagnosing, which sometimes left clinicians forced to opt in or out of clinical characteristics of a disorder and did not allow for a middle ground resulting from a unique patient's age, gender, and cultural factors. Do note monothetic and polythetic criteria are both used in the diagnostic process in the *DSM-5* (APA, 2013b). Monothetic criteria require all listed symptoms for that particular diagnosis to be present for that particular diagnosis to be accurately selected. Examples of monothetic diagnoses are selective mutism, social anxiety disorder, and specific phobia. Polythetric criteria allow a certain number of a longer list of particular symptoms to be present for the diagnosis to be selected. Examples of polythetric diagnoses are separation anxiety disorder and panic disorder. Some diagnoses combine the use of monothetic and polythetric aspects, such as generalized anxiety disorder, where the list of six criteria must be met, but one criterion has a subset of symptoms where at least one item must be present in children. Clinicians are also able to notate symptoms, severity, or additional factors related to the diagnosis.

Subjective Client Reports versus Subjective Combined with Cross-Cutting Symptom Measures Tool

Previous diagnostic practices relied on subjective client reports of symptoms during initial screenings, comprehensive biopsychosocial assessments, and repeat measures assessments over the course of treatment to assess progress. The drawback to relying solely on subjective client reports is that clinicians can miss critical information from clients (Association for Assessment in Research and Counseling [AARC], n.d.).

A multipoint assessment has been considered best practice (AARC, n.d.). The challenge with current standardized instruments is that these have not been specifically recommended by the *DSM* as the scales to use across the helping professions related to making mental health diagnoses. For instance, an instrument Agency A uses to assess for depression may not be the same instrument Agency B uses. The reasons for such differences may relate to cost to administer or score an instrument, multidimensional cultural characteristics of the population served, time needed to complete the assessment, language availability, and more. Essentially, the mental health diagnostic community has lacked a common standard; however, there was general agreement among helping professionals regarding the need for both subjective client reports and standardized instruments for the clinician to interpret and compare to the *DSM-5* criteria. Thus, the cross-cutting symptom measures are now available to assist in the diagnostic decision-making process (APA, 2013b).

CROSS-CUTTING SYMPTOM MEASURES TOOL

The cross-cutting symptoms measures were developed to assess comprehensive aspects (or domains) of mental health from initial screening to thorough diagnosis (APA, 2013b). There are two levels of the cross-cutting symptoms measures tool: Level 1 and Level 2. Level 1 could be conceptualized as a tool to draw attention to main areas related to diagnosis that the clinician can use to inform decisions about areas needing additional assessment (APA, 2013c). Level 2 could be considered the more in-depth assessment of the areas flagged as a concern in Level 1 (APA, 2013d). Both Level 1 and Level 2 measures consist of 12 key psychiatric domains for which the minor's (ages 6 to 17) parent or guardian would rank severity, or symptom intensity. A self-assessment is available for children ages 11 to 17 to complete if the adolescent desires and parent or guardian provides written consent. When both the parents or guardians and the child complete the assessments, the clinician would interpret the scores and add this information to the comprehensive intake information collected to use for diagnostic decision making.

Clinicians should make note that there are limitations to the cross-cutting measures. Just like other forms of child data collection or assessment, they are used only to collect data points to inform decision making about diagnosis (Watson & Flamez, 2014). These are not tools that tell the clinician what diagnosis to select. For best practices, clinicians should use the cross-cutting measures to supplement other forms of data, such as medical records, developmental history, academic records, family history, history of symptoms, and other biopsychosocial questionnaires. The counselor would deduct the diagnosis from comprehensive data collected from the child, caregivers, third parties in the child's life (such as teachers), and direct interviews or observations completed by the clinician.

Level 1

The Level 1 measure for children and adolescents consists of 12 domains (APA, 2013c). The domains are considered the major areas of mental health that should be screened for most commonly reported psychiatric concerns. The 12 domains include the following: somatic symptoms, sleep problems, inattention, depression, anger, irritability, mania, anxiety, psychosis, repetitive thoughts and behaviors, substance use, and suicidal ideation or suicide attempts. Make note that the Level 1 domains for children differ from the adult domains.

The parent or guardian Level 1 assessment includes 25 questions, which equates to about two questions per domain, related to how frequently the parent or guardian perceives the child to be affected by symptoms pertaining to the matching domain within the past two weeks (APA, 2013c). The child form, which children between the ages of 11 to 17 can complete based on clinician discretion and parent or guardian approval, follows the same format; however, the questions are written to address the child's self-perception (APA, 2013d). Clinicians score the Level 1 measure separately for each domain (APA, 2013b). The scoring is done by identifying the highest score the informant (parent or guardian or the child) reported within the bundle of items related to that particular domain. For instance, if there are two items on the anxiety domain and the informant reported a severity rating of 2 for mild on one question and a severity rating of 3 for moderate on the second question, then the clinician will score that domain with this highest indicated response of a 3. The highest score will be used to make clinical judgments for the next step in the assessment process. This will be repeated for all domains. There is not a comprehensive or overall scoring considering all the domains.

Clinicians can interpret the Level 1 score for children in the following ways: (a) items with a rating of 2 (moderate) or higher indicate a need for additional assessment by the clinician consisting of self-reports or the appropriate Level 2 cross-cutting symptom measure, appropriate disorder-specific severity measure, or appropriate clinician-rated severity measure for the symptom domains of clinical concern, (b) inattention and psychosis scales with a rating of 1 (mild) or greater would indicate a need for additional follow-up consisting of the appropriate Level 2 cross-cutting symptom measure, appropriate disorder-specific severity measure, or appropriate clinician-rated severity measure (especially the Clinician-Rated Dimensions of Psychosis Symptom Severity measure on *DSM-5* pages 742 through 744 or http://www.psychiatry.org/practice/dsm/dsm5/online-assessment-measures), and (c) a rating of affirmative or unknown for the suicide ideation and attempts as well as the substance use questions would indicate need for further clinical attention by using the *DSM-5* Clinician-Rated Severity of Nonsuicidal Self-Injury and the LEVEL 2—Substance Use—Parent/Guardian of Child Age 6–17 (adapted from the NIDA-modified [National Institute on Drug Abuse] ASSIST [Alcohol, Smoking and Substance Involvement Screening Test]) or LEVEL 2—Substance Use—Child Age 11–17 (adapted from the NIDA-modified ASSIST; APA, 2013b; APA, 2013c).

Level 2

After the domains of concern are identified from the Level 1 measurement, clinicians can choose to use the Level 2 Cross-Cutting Symptom Measures to explore the symptomology further (APA, 2013b). There is a matching Level 2 measurement for all of the 12 domain areas except for suicidal ideation or attempts. Some of the domains (depression, anxiety, and psychosis) also have measurements to determine the severity of symptomology in that particular domain (APA, 2013b). See Table 3.1 for the Level 2 measurements as well as severity assessments (to be completed by the informant or the clinician) aligned with the 12 original Level 1 symptom domains.

PERSONALITY FUNCTIONING

Personality disorders are considered with children and adolescents because onset may appear in childhood and continue unchanged into adulthood (APA, 2013b). In the situation where a minor's symptomatic personality functioning affects multiple areas of his or her life, maladaptive function has been present for over one year (note less time is acceptable for antisocial personality disorder), and unhealthy functioning is unrelated to other disorders, then personality disorders may be applicable.

There are currently two measures available online (http://www.psychiatry.org/dsm5) to aid in assessment of personality disorders in children: the Personality Inventory for *DSM-5* (PID-5; Krueger, Derringer, Markon, Watson, & Skodol, 2013b) and the Personality Inventory for *DSM-5*—Brief Form (PID-5-BF; Krueger, Derringer, Markon, Watson, & Skodol, 2013a). The PID-5 consists of 220 questions addressing individualized personality traits (Krueger et al., 2013b). Children asked to answer the questions rate how well or not a given question seems to describe themselves. The answers range from 0 (never true) to 4 (very true). The individualized personality traits can also be bundled into personality domains. The personality traits assessed include anhedonia, anxiousness, attention seeking, callousness, deceitfulness, depressivity, distractibility, eccentricity,

TABLE 3.1   Level 2 and Severity Measurements

Domain	Parent or Guardian (children 6–17) Level 2 Measure	Child Self-Report (11–17) Level 2 Measure	Informant Report (11–17 only) Severity Assessment	Clinician Report (11–17 only) Severity Assessment
Somatic	Patient Health Questionnaire 15 Somatic Symptom Severity Scale (PHQ-15)	Patient Health Questionnaire 15 Somatic Symptom Severity Scale (PHQ-15)		Severity of Somatic Symptom Disorder
Sleep	Patient Reported Outcomes Measurement Information System (PROMIS)—Sleep Disturbance—Short Form	PROMIS—Sleep Disturbance—Short Form		
Inattention	Swanson, Nolan, and Pelham, version IV (SNAP-IV)			
Depression	PROMIS Emotional Distress— Depression— Parent Item Bank	PROMIS Emotional Distress— Depression— Pediatric Item Bank	PHQ-9 modified for Adolescents (PHQ-A)	
Anger	PROMIS Emotional Distress— Calibrated Anger Measure—Parent	PROMIS Emotional Distress— Calibrated Anger Measure—Pediatric		Severity of Oppositional Defiant Disorder, Severity of Conduct Disorder
Irritability	Affective Reactivity Index (ARI)	Affective Reactivity Index (ARI)		
Mania	Adapted from the Altman Self-Rating Mania Scale (ASRM)	Altman Self-Rating Mania Scale		
Anxiety	Adapted from PROMIS Emotional Distress— Anxiety—Parent Item Bank	PROMIS Emotional Distress— Anxiety—Pediatric Item Bank	Severity Measure for Separation Anxiety Disorder, Severity Measure for Specific Phobia, Severity Measure for Social Anxiety Disorder, Severity Measure for Panic Disorder, Severity Measure for Agoraphobia, Severity Measure for Generalized Anxiety Disorder, Severity of Posttraumatic Stress Symptoms, National Stressful Events Survey PTSD Short Scale (NSESS), Severity of Acute Stress Symptoms, National Stressful Events Survey Acute Stress Disorder Short Scale	

(continued)

TABLE 3.1 *(continued)*

Domain	Parent or Guardian (children 6–17) Level 2 Measure	Child Self-Report (11–17) Level 2 Measure	Informant Report (11–17 only) Severity Assessment	Clinician Report (11–17 only) Severity Assessment
Psychosis			Severity of Dissociative Symptoms, Brief Dissociative Experiences Scale (DES-B)	Dimensions of Psychosis Symptom Severity
Repetitive Thoughts and Behaviors		Adapted from the Children's Florida Obsessive Compulsive Inventory (C-FOCI) Severity Scale		
Substance Use	Adapted from the NIDA-Modified ASSIST	Adapted from the NIDA-Modified ASSIST		
Suicidal Ideation or Suicide Attempts				Severity of Nonsuicidal Self-Injury Severity of Autism Spectrum and Social Communication Disorders

Note: The Level 1, Level 2, and Severity Scales are available online at www.psychiatry.org/dsm5.

emotional lability, grandiosity, hostility, impulsivity, intimacy avoidance, irresponsibility, manipulativeness, perceptual dysregulation, perseveration, restricted affectivity, rigid perfectionism, risk taking, separation insecurity, submissiveness, suspiciousness, usual beliefs and experiences, and withdrawal. The assessment also includes a list of the personality domains and the individual personality traits that are bundled within the domains. Extended details on scoring and interpretation are available within the PID-5 manual guide.

The PID-5-BR consists of 25 questions addressing only the personality domains (negative affect, detachment, antagonism, disinhibition, and psychoticism; Krueger et al., 2013a). Children asked to answer the questions rate how well or not a given question seems to describe themselves. The answers range from 0 (never true) to 4 (very true). Extended details on scoring and interpretation are available within the PID-5-BF manual guide.

EARLY CHILDHOOD DEVELOPMENT AND HOME BACKGROUND

An assessment is also available for collecting information about early childhood milestones and the current home environment. The Early Development and Home Background (EDHB) Form—Parent/Guardian consists of 19 questions aligned to one of the three areas: early development, early communication, and home environment (Shaffer, 2013b). Informants may choose from responses such as No, Yes, Can't Remember, and Don't Know or responses that quantify frequency of events from Less than Once a Month to Most Days. This particular assessment is intended to increase holistic understanding of the child's experience and improve comprehensive care for the child. In addition, this assessment may aid the clinician in possibly detecting early development-based risk factors for

DSM-5 trauma- and stressor-related disorders, such as reactive attachment, disinhibited social engagement disorder, pediatric posttraumatic stress disorder, acute stress disorder, and adjustment disorder (APA, 2013b).

Following the parent or guardian completing the EDHB Form—Parent/Guardian assessment, the clinician will complete a separate assessment called the Early Development and Home Background (EDHB) Form—Clinician (Shaffer, 2013a). The clinician will review the 19 items the parents completed and will critically analyze whether there is any indication of early central nervous symptom problems; early disturbances within the home environment, such as abuse or neglect; and home environment concerns related to caregiver emotional ability and current depression level. Indication of concerns in any of these areas would inform clinical decisions for treatment planning; clinical follow-up time intervals; referrals to other pediatric specialists; reports to child protective agencies; referrals for services for the caregiver; referrals to community support networks, such as housing or government social services; and additional mental health assessment.

CULTURAL FORMULATION INTERVIEWS

As mentioned in Chapter 2, cultural formulation interview protocols are available to assist the clinician with collecting holistic data to better understand the child within individualized context. The Cultural Formulation Interview (CFI)—Informant Version would be used to guide the clinical interview through the cultural definition of the problem; cultural perceptions of the cause, context, or support; cultural factors affecting self-coping and past help seeking; and cultural factors affecting current help seeking (APA, 2013a).

The Supplementary Modules to the Core Cultural Formulation Interview (APA, 2013c) provide additional areas to explore with the caregiver or parent completing the CFI. These questions are designed to identify more about the child's development, relationships with family members, gender relations, and more. For adolescents, additional questions related to thoughts about transitioning to adulthood or being mature are included.

TIMELINES FOR INITIAL ASSESSMENT AND REASSESSMENT

The Level 1 cross-cutting, Level 2 cross-cutting, and disorder-specific severity measures are designed to be used for the initial assessment of a client as well as follow-up assessments to track the impact of treatment on functioning of a client (APA, 2013b). The time span between progress points can be customized to the needs of the client in terms of his or her symptom stability, intensity, or treatment compliance and progress.

The parent or guardian as well as the clinician completing the original assessment on the child should remain the same across the follow-up assessments to maintain consistency (APA, 2013b). If it is not possible to have the same parent or guardian complete the assessment, then another person who is close to the child is acceptable. The clinician would need to consider this when reviewing the information and possibly ask follow-up questions. If a new clinician takes up the case, best practice would include review of previous files and, if possible, communicating with the previous therapist (Balkin & Juhnke, 2014).

Children who receive repeated high scores on the same domains would trigger the need for additional assessment, critical treatment planning, and consistent follow-ups to track progress. Children with scores that fluctuate from high at times to low at others would highlight a need for the clinician to follow up. The clinician may want to start with reviewing the assessment process to identify what may potentially be interfering with data collection. The clinician may want to do additional assessment to try to identify what may inform the changes or supplement existing information with data such as changes in treatment, irregular treatment compliance, modification in family, or possibly change in treating clinicians (Watson & Flamez, 2014).

DIFFERENTIAL DIAGNOSIS DECISION MAKING

After a clinician completes a full assessment, the next step would be analyzing the information obtained to make a diagnosis. A *DSM-5 Handbook of Differential Diagnosis* is available to guide a clinician through the decision-making process when multiple diagnoses may need to be eliminated (First, 2013). The handbook outlines the decision-making process with six steps and decision-making trees, as well as with the use of tables. It is up to a trained clinician to process the information obtained during the assessment to make an appropriate diagnosis.

Process

Chapter 2 provided a comprehensive overview of the process of establishing a differential diagnosis. A number of tools may assist clinicians in determining a differential diagnosis.

Decision-Making Trees and Tables

Twenty-nine decision-making trees are currently available, including: (a) poor school performance, (b) behavioral problems in a child or adolescent, (c) speech disturbance, (d) distractibility, (e) delusions, (f) hallucinations, (g) catatonic symptoms, (h) elevated or expansive mood, (i) irritable mood, (j) depressed mood, (k) suicidal ideation or behavior, (l) psychomotor retardation, (m) anxiety, (n) panic attacks, (o) avoidance behavior, (p) trauma or psychosocial stressors involved in the etiology, (q) somatic complaints or illness/appearance anxiety, (r) appetite changes or unusual eating behavior, (s) insomnia, (t) hypersomnolence, (u) sexual dysfunction in a female or a male, (v) aggressive behavior, (w) impulsivity or impulse-control problems, (x) self-injury or self-mutilation, (y) excessive substance use, (z) memory loss, (aa) cognitive impairment, and (bb) etiological medical conditions.

Tables

Sixty-six differential diagnosis tables are available and address the following *DSM-5* disorders: (a) neurodevelopmental disorders, (b) schizophrenia spectrum and other psychotic disorders, (c) bipolar and related disorders, (d) depressive disorders, (e) anxiety disorders, (f) obsessive-compulsive and related disorders, (g) trauma- and stressor-related disorders, (h) dissociative disorders, (i) somatic symptom and related disorders, (j) feeding and eating disorders, (j) sleep-wake disorders, (k) sexual dysfunctions, (l) gender dysphoria, (m) disruptive, impulse-control, and conduct disorders, (n) substance-related and addictive disorders, (o) neurocognitive disorders, (p) personality disorders, and (q) paraphilic disorders. The tables begin with the clinician's working diagnosis and offer the clinician an exhaustive list of *DMS-5* disorders with similar symptomology to consider further or be eliminated from the decision-making process. This assists the clinician in comprehensively considering all diagnostic possibilities.

Case Conceptualization

Following the intake and assessment process, case conceptualization provides clinicians with a road map for treatment plan development and selection of interventions. Conceptualization includes the integration of the client's identified problems, etiology of the issues, and diagnosis to promote understanding of the client's needs (Leppma & Jones, 2015). The emphasis on the evolution of the client's presenting problem helps facilitate the development of an effective treatment plan (Meier, 2003). Professional counseling literature suggests that treatment protocols established through case conceptualization show improved treatment outcomes (Leppma & Jones, 2015). Particularly when clients present with multiple issues, clinicians can have difficulty teasing apart which elements are most important. Case conceptualization can help clinicians manage and simplify multidimensional information. In addition, as a counselor learns a client's history, he or she ethically obligated to carefully consider factors of diversity when determining diagnoses and establishing an intervention plan (American Counseling Association [ACA], 2014). The guidelines for the American Counseling Association (2014) and the American Mental Health Counselors Association (AMHCA, 2010) both indicate that counselors should understand the cultural implications for a client's presenting problem. Case conceptualization promotes comprehensive consideration of each client's particular circumstance.

Although many specific models of case conceptualization exist, a number of common themes emerge in the literature (Kendjelic & Fells, 2007; Kuyken, Padesky, & Dudley, 2009; Leppma & Jones, 2015; Messer & Wolitzky, 2008). The general goal, regardless of the specific model or theoretical orientation, is to formulate a comprehensive picture of the client, including factors that may have caused or contributed to the development of the distress. Elements of case conceptualization common across a number of models include:

- Identify the client's presenting problem.
- Determine how the identified problems are causing current distress for the client.
- Identify any events that precipitated the onset of the problems.
- Identify the client's current strengths.
- Formulate a clinical diagnosis based on *DSM-5* criteria.
- Articulate an overall impression of the client's problem.

Ultimately, the clinician synthesizes information to create a summary explanation about the client's circumstance. This big picture will identify relationships among existing issues, precipitating factors, causal factors, and the client's strengths that may be used to combat the distress. Ideally, the clinician will make the conceptualization brief and concise to promote clarity. Take a moment to consider the case study of Jason found in Sidebar 3.1. Use the information presented to develop an initial case conceptualization that may serve as a foundation for next steps.

SIDEBAR 3.1

Jason is a 16-year-old high-school junior referred to his school counselor after excessive absences from after-school meetings required for his work on the school yearbook committee. The teacher, being concerned, first called Jason's mother, who indicated that she has also noticed changes in Jason's behavior at home. He has become apathetic, is not bathing, and is refusing to participate in any family activities. It became noticeably worse after Jason's father repeatedly told Jason he would pick him up for Christmas and then didn't show up. On the actual day his father didn't show up, Jason attempted to show indifference and emphatically claimed that he didn't care because he didn't want to go anyway. However, his mother saw a Facebook post that said, "Still waiting on Dad. Guess, once again, I am not worth showing up for." In spite of his decreased extracurricular activity, Jason has maintained a 3.5 grade point average (GPA) and is well liked by his peers.

Diagnosing

Once background information is obtained and the client has been appropriately assessed, clinicians are charged with determining an appropriate diagnosis. This will ultimately play an important role in the case conceptualization as well as the treatment planning process. The case conceptualization may be incomplete without a diagnosis; however, the conceptualization process can assist in the development of a treatment plan and selection of interventions with or without a formal diagnosis. The following section explores key elements for consideration when diagnosing children and adolescents.

GIVING AN ACCURATE DIAGNOSIS

Assigning an accurate and culturally justified diagnosis is an important part of the treatment planning process; however, this process can be clinically challenging. Clients frequently do not meet all the criteria for a particular disorder, or they may have overlapping symptoms across multiple disorders that warrant clinical attention (APA, 2013b). Thus, the boundaries between various disorders can easily become blurred, which can lead to misdiagnosis. To address this concern, the *DSM-5* disorders were rearranged into a new organizational structure (APA, 2013b). Some of the disorders listed in the *DSM-5* now contain clearly identified clusters of symptoms; however, many disorders are included on a spectrum with other closely related disorders (APA, 2013b). For example, autism and schizophrenia/other psychotic disorders are conceptualized dimensionally; symptom severity is rated on a spectrum in the *DSM-5*, whereas they were not in the *DSM-IV-TR*. The organization of such disorders on a spectrum in the *DSM-5* stems from the realization that the *DSM-IV-TR* subgroups of these disorders were not distinctly separate; rather the symptoms ranged in severity on a continuum from mild to severe impairments (APA, 2013b). Classifying certain disorders on a spectrum increases the accuracy of the diagnosis, because attention is given to unique client developmental aspects and evolutionary gene–environment interactions (APA, 2013b). Leigh (2009) stated that psychiatric disorders were the result of an interaction between genes and early exposure to environmental stressors, which affects the adaptive functions of the brain. The author proposed the use of a continuum model when considering psychiatric diagnoses. By identifying and communicating diagnostic information on a continuum, the clinician is able to outline specific treatment goals based on the client's level of impairment (APA, 2013b; Leigh, 2009).

Deciding upon diagnostic accuracy can become further complicated by the fact that clinicians often feel pressured to give a diagnosis fairly quickly, particularly when seeking third-party reimbursement or when speed is required by agency policies and procedures. And, although a diagnosis should not be assigned solely for reimbursement purposes, giving a diagnosis is often a time-sensitive process. Mental health professionals risk psychological harm to clients when an inaccurate diagnosis is given, because the diagnosis serves as a guide in the treatment planning process. For example, a clinician would not want to diagnose a child with attention-deficit/hyperactivity disorder if the child actually had a diagnosis of generalized anxiety disorder. Although there may be similarities in the symptom presentations of both disorders, the treatment options for those disorders are clinically distinct. Thus, it is essential that counselors conduct a comprehensive assessment before constructing a diagnosis and treatment plan. The ACA Ethics Code (2014) E.5. a encourages counselors to carefully consider and select appropriate assessment measures to ensure that they give an appropriate diagnosis. Counselors also need to understand the reciprocal relationship that exists between diagnosis and treatment planning. They are interrelated and never static. Counselors continuously assess the client's level of functioning, progress, and treatment needs (ACA, 2014, E.5.a); the treatment plan is modified throughout the counseling process, particularly as the counselor obtains more information. It can be challenging to develop a comprehensive treatment plan without a fully established diagnosis, and there are potential risks involved in giving a diagnosis prematurely. Thus, it is easy to see how the diagnostic and treatment planning process can seem obscure. What should counselors do when they feel a sense of urgency in giving a diagnosis? How can counselors feel confident that they have given an accurate diagnosis and outlined the appropriate treatment recommendations? The use of symptom severity scales, specifiers, and provisional diagnoses can help circumvent many challenges encountered during the diagnostic process. Take a moment to examine Sidebar 3.2, which includes a practical example of how more than one diagnosis can present with similar symptoms, which can complicate case conceptualization.

SIDEBAR 3.2

It is critically important for counselors to be very clear on the nuances of each particular client, including symptom presentation, frequency, duration, and severity. As mentioned previously, a counselor who is not clearly acquainted with a client's needs could potentially misdiagnose the presenting problem. Take a moment to give thoughtful consideration to how the following diagnoses might present as similar:

Jack is a 12-year-old male brought into treatment by his parents. He is described as shy and "afraid of his own shadow." He has few friends and avoids group activities. Jack performs poorly in school, particularly in reading and math. He frequently daydreams and loses track of what is going on. His mother reports she has a history of anxiety and fears Jack is suffering from the same thing.

Looking at this initial information, it would be virtually impossible to accurately diagnose Jack. What would your next steps be in developing a treatment plan?

Subtypes, Specifiers, and Severity

As introduced in Chapter 2, many *DSM-5* disorders contain subtypes, specifiers, and severity measures, which are often coded on the fourth, fifth, or sixth digit (APA, 2013b). *Subtypes* are mutually exclusive subgroupings within a given disorder that one can use to provide greater clarity regarding the diagnosis. Subtypes contain the directive "Specify whether" (APA, 2013b, p. 21). On the contrary, *specifiers* are not mutually exclusive; therefore more than one can be given. Specifiers are indicated by the instruction, "Specify if" (APA, 2013b, p. 21). *Severity* refers to the level and intensity of symptomology and is indicated by "Specify current severity" (APA, 2013b, p. 162). For example, suppose an adolescent client has a diagnosis of major depressive disorder. The diagnostic code is based on whether it is a single or a recurrent episode. The client's current severity may be "moderate," but the client may have additional specifiers of "with anxious distress" and "with seasonal pattern" (APA, 2013b, p. 162). The use of subtypes, specifiers, and severity measures can help professionals communicate the diagnosis with greater clarity and guide them when constructing culturally informed and developmentally sensitive treatment plans.

Other Specified Disorders and Unspecified Disorders

In lieu of the *not otherwise specified* diagnosis used in the *DSM-IV-TR*, the *DSM-5* now contains the options of *other specified disorder* and *unspecified disorder*. These terms are used when a client has clinically significant symptoms or impairment but the symptoms do not fit in one structured diagnostic category. *Other specified disorder* is used when the client does not fully meet the diagnostic criteria, and then the reason is stated. *Unspecified disorder* is used when the diagnostic criteria are not met; however, the clinician is unable to provide specifics based on the clinical presentation of symptoms. For example, suppose a client of Latino descent presents in therapy with symptoms of anxiety and other trauma-related symptoms but does not meet the criteria for posttraumatic stress disorder; a diagnosis of other specified trauma- and stressor-related disorder, *ataque de nervios,* could be given. However, if there is insufficient information to specify, then unspecified trauma- and stressor-related disorder would apply. The use of other specified disorders and unspecified disorders gives clinicians a better understanding of the client's symptoms, which also eliminates the need to code 799.9, deferred diagnosis, as was previously used in the *DSM-IV-TR*.

Provisional Diagnoses

There may be times when professionals feel fairly certain that a client has a particular diagnosis; however they are unable to give a definitive diagnosis at the given moment (APA, 2013b.) For example, a client may meet many of the diagnostic criteria for a particular disorder, but there may not have been enough information gathered during the initial session to support that all the necessary criteria have been met. Moreover, some diagnoses require that symptoms are present for a certain period, and there may be uncertainties about the length of time that the symptoms have been present. In such cases a *provisional* diagnosis can be given (APA, 2013b). Once the needed information is obtained, then the definitive diagnosis can be assigned.

Rule-Outs

The term *rule out* is not an official diagnostic term in the *DSM-5*; however, it is often used informally by mental health professionals and reflected on the treatment plan

(Neukrug & Fawcett, 2015). The use of a rule-out suggests that the client is experiencing some of the symptoms associated with one or more disorders, but not enough symptoms are present to distinguish between these disorders or to make a diagnosis (Neukrug & Fawcett, 2015). If a professional indicates that one should rule out a particular disorder, the nature, frequency, and intensity of the symptoms should be explored further in future sessions (Neukrug & Fawcett, 2015). For example, a child whose parents recently divorced may present with anxiety, declining grades, and impaired concentration. The professional may want to rule out a diagnosis of attention-deficit disorder versus adjustment disorder with anxiety.

CULTURAL FACTORS

When outlining treatment goals, professionals must consider the relevant psychosocial and cultural factors that affect treatment. "Cultural, ethnic, and racial identities can be sources of strength and group support that enhance resilience, but they may also lead to psychological, interpersonal, and intergenerational conflict or difficulties in adaptation that require diagnostic assessment" (APA, 2013b, p. 749). The *DSM-5* contains the Outline for Cultural Formulation, which provides a framework for assessing cultural identity, conceptualization of distress, psychosocial stressors and cultural features of vulnerability and resilience, cultural features of the relationship between the individual and the clinician, and an overall cultural assessment (APA, 2013b, pp. 749–750). The Cultural Formation Interview is also included in the *DSM-5* and is based on those outlined key areas. It is a 16-item assessment that can be used in the initial session to assess background and specifics about the client's current situation and life stressors (APA, 2013b). The informant version of the Cultural Formation Interview can be used with children and adolescents when they are unable to provide the necessary information. Cultural competence is of utmost importance among treatment team members, because treatment is most likely to be successful when the plan is based on the family's preferences and culture (Bruns Sather, Pullman, & Stambaugh, 2011; Walker & Schutte, 2005).

ETHICAL CONSIDERATIONS

The ACA Ethics Code (2014) E.5.d. guides counselors in refraining from making or reporting a diagnosis if it could potentially cause harm to the client or others. Associated with each diagnostic label is a diagnostic code, which is typically used by institutions and agencies for data collection and billing purposes. However, if counselors cannot fully substantiate a diagnosis, it would be unethical to assign one. Additionally, assigning a diagnosis can be controversial. Many professionals assert that diagnostic labels add to the stigmatization of mental illness and depersonalization of the individual who is suffering. For example, consider a client who is referred to as *a schizophrenic* or *an alcoholic*. The use of such language implies that the client is defined by the diagnosis instead of the diagnosis serving as an indicator of the types of challenges the individual may encounter. It would be more appropriate and respectful to say that *the individual has a diagnosis of schizophrenia* or *the client has issues with substance use*. ACA Code (2014) E.5.b. encourages counselors to be aware of social and historical prejudices related to the diagnosis of psychopathology. Diagnoses are descriptive and helpful for professionals in using the same language to discuss clients. There is a need for a stable, agreed-upon language for mental health professionals to study human behavior and treatment reliably and accurately. However, when clients learn they have been labeled with a particular diagnosis, it can be discouraging and disempowering. Livingston and Boyd (2010) stated that individuals who internalize stigma associated with their diagnoses are more likely to experience severe psychiatric symptoms and are less likely to be compliant with treatment. Thus, the diagnosis should not become a pejorative label for the client; rather it is a term to help the client and other professionals understand the individual's treatment needs. When giving a diagnosis, outlining the treatment plan, and collaborating with other health professionals, counselors will want to use professional language. Counselors must also be cognizant of the fact that information contained in a mental health record can have long-lasting implications and should not be treated lightly.

Best practice for counselors would be to withhold from making a diagnosis in the absence of sufficient data. Kaplan (2006) asserted that it can be harmful to record a formal diagnosis if it "can be used against the client by a third party" (para. 8). Additionally, it is important to consider cultural or environmental circumstances before assigning a diagnosis (ACA, 2014, E.5.b.). Western philosophical perspectives do not capture all life experiences that other cultures view as part of normal life experiences. For example, some cultures view visions of family members following death as typical, and a diagnosis of hallucinations could be harmful to the client (Kaplan, 2006). Another important consideration would be occupational elements. Premature assignment of a diagnosis could result in pilots losing flight privileges or military personnel losing security clearance. As such, it would be important to highlight the issue of diagnosis and insurance reimbursement during your informed-consent process.

Components of a Comprehensive Treatment Plan

An effective treatment plan is made up of multiple parts. For instance, the clinician will need to identify clear goals, objectives, and timelines to assess progress. Focus of treatment plans can vary depending on whether a counselor is in a clinical mental health setting or a school setting. In this section, the typical components of treatment plans are outlined, including variations between mental health and school settings and the implications those differences have in relation to planning.

GOALS

When setting treatment goals, counselors should make them as specific as possible. Precise, individualized goals are the gold standard. Counselors must determine families' and children's perspectives and concerns before identifying and prioritizing treatment needs (Bruns et al., 2011; Walker & Schutte, 2004; Walker & Schutte, 2005). Treatment planning builds on the client and family's strengths and reflects the family's preferences regarding treatment and outcomes (Bruns et al., 2011; Walker & Schutte, 2004; Walker & Schutte, 2005). To build upon the existing strengths, the treatment plan goals will be geared toward building self-efficacy and social support (Bruns et al., 2011). Children and families who are in need of intensive treatment often feel overwhelmed by the treatment planning process (Walker & Schutte, 2005). They may not know what services are vital, and they may have difficulty coordinating those services and monitoring whether progress has been made. Furthermore, there may be times when parents may not have the insight or judgment to determine what is in the best interest of the children (Walker & Schutte, 2005).

Therefore, the treatment provider may need to educate the family about potential treatment options and provide guidance when establishing the treatment goals. When the focus on self-efficacy and social support is maintained, children and families are likely to feel more empowered in the treatment planning process.

During the initial evaluation and assessment, clients and families may discuss a variety of issues. The counselor must determine which issues present as most significant so that decisions may be made regarding how to focus the treatment process. Typically, a primary problem rises to the surface, though secondary problems frequently exist. Counselors must be prepared to identify which issues to target for treatment and which issues can wait. An effective treatment plan will deal with only a few select issues at any given time (Jongsma, Peterson, McInnis, & Bruce, 2014). Each child and family will present with unique issues, and problems that appear similar between clients will have individual nuances for each individual or system. Goals should be individualized to meet the specific needs of each client or family. Counselors working in a clinical mental health setting will likely use the *DSM-5*, the *International Classification of Diseases* (*ICD*), or both to identify clinical diagnosis based on the evaluation of the client's complete clinical presentation. Treatment goals are typically geared toward resolution of the identified problem or symptoms of the prescribed diagnosis and indicate a desired outcome for the treatment intervention. See Sidebar 3.3 for an experiential exercise to practice initial treatment goal development.

SIDEBAR 3.3

Edith is a 12-year-old female who is brought to counseling by her mother. Edith's parents are recently divorced. Edith has withdrawn from her friends and family. She spends hours alone in her room or riding her bicycle. Her mother reports hearing Edith cry at night several times per week, but she is nonresponsive when she asks whether she is okay. Her art teacher at school reports that Edith has limited all of her art to the use of red and black paint. She was sent to in-school suspension after being caught hiding in the bathroom during gym class. Edith reports she didn't want to go to gym because she didn't want to change clothes in front of other kids.

How many issues can you identify from this initial assessment?

Which of the issues would you identify as the primary focus of treatment?

Can you identify one treatment goal?

Can you identify one desired outcome?

In a school setting counselors follow a similar process in terms of treatment planning. A key difference is that the treatment plan stems from an Individualized Education Plan (IEP; U.S. Department of Education, 2005) that is centered solely on academic concerns as related to personal/social, career, and academic development (American School Counselor Association [ASCA], 2004). Diagnostic codes are routinely left out of treatment planning because treatment for mental health issues is routinely outside of the scope of a school counselor's role. Thus, the treatment plan in a school would focus on how student challenges affect academic performance, how student strengths can help him or her overcome the current struggles, and what interventions would be put in place to help the student overcome barriers in school (Geltner & Leibforth, 2008). One additional caveat in a school setting is that the intervention team is expanded beyond the counselor and parents (ASCA, 2004). The school system, including regular education teachers; special education teachers; school counselors, school social workers, or school psychologists; parents; and the student when appropriate may be involved in treatment planning. Representatives from each of these areas would be involved in the comprehensive treatment plan because each would play a role in addressing the student's academic-related need (U.S. Department of Education, 2005).

OBJECTIVES

For each therapeutic goal, counselors need specific steps for accomplishing the goal. The steps outline specific actions the client will take to accomplish each goal. For every step that is put into place, the counselor should communicate with the client or parent, making changes if needed. Each step should include consideration for the client's cultural identity, abilities, and limitations. Ideally, allowing the client to have small successes may act as a foundation for bigger ones.

In contrast with long-term goals, objectives may be short-term, measurable parts of a greater whole. The objectives are clearly assessed for progress so that health insurance providers and counselors alike may clearly identify when the client has made progress and when continued treatment attention is needed. This allows the client's progress to be easily tracked and promotes accountability for treatment providers.

In a school setting, an IEP will outline the goals and related objectives. The format consists of identifying the long-term goal, concretely describing related short-term objectives for each goal, and identifying who will provide what intervention to address the specific objective. Progress indicators of the student moving toward the goal will be included, which consist of behavioral signs of progressing, how often the targeted behavior would occur by when, and how the behavior would be measured (U.S. Department of Education, 2005). Sidebar 3.4 offers an opportunity to examine the differences and similarities of short- and long-term goals when establishing treatment goals for a child with disruptive behavior.

SIDEBAR 3.4

Compare and contrast a long-term goal with a short-term objective for a child referred for disrespectful and disruptive behavior:

Long-term goal

Terminate intimidating behavior and treat others with respect and kindness.

Short-term objective

Identify two situations, thoughts, or feelings that trigger angry feelings or problem behaviors.

How are the long-term and short-term goals similar?
How do the goals differ?

TIME FRAME

Counselors must establish a timeline for each treatment plan. With the client, a time frame is established to accomplish each goal. If appropriate, a timeline may be put into place for each individual step of a prescribed intervention. In general, most treatment plans include long-term goals, though it is also common for short-term objectives to be implemented. Managed-care organizations may ask for frequent updates to approve ongoing care (Haddock & Moore, 2015).

It is also important to determine how often progress will be assessed. This could mean examining progress during each session, weekly, or monthly, depending on the goal and what is appropriate for each case. Treatment providers will routinely have standing time frames for follow-up. For example, treatment plan reviews are automatically conducted 30 days after onset of the intervention to allow counselors to verify the accuracy of the plan or revise if needed. This allows counselors to maintain appropriate treatment plans as well promote professional accountability.

INDIVIDUALIZED PLANS

The treatment plan is essentially a blueprint for a counselor's work with a client. Treatment plans address the presenting problem as identified by the client (and family or teachers as appropriate) and the case conceptualization as established by the clinician. A treatment plan should be individualized for each particular client. Thus, every plan should ideally be based on each client's distress and history and be a fit for the client's needs. In other words, the treatment plan should be customized instead of generic. Although there are often similarities in plans when treating clients with similar complaints, each plan should give careful consideration to each client's experience. This would likely include abilities, lifestyle, socioeconomic status, educational history, cultural identity, religion, and family values (Jongsma & Bruce, 2010; Walker & Schutte, 2005). Treatment plans should also include emphasis on each client's individual strengths.

Challenges in the Treatment Planning Process

Federal and state laws, including Public Law 94-142 and the Individuals with Disabilities Act (IDEA), require that children with emotional, behavioral, and learning disorders be given a diagnosis to receive services and accommodations (Neukrug & Fawcett, 2015). A clinical diagnosis is also necessary when requesting reimbursement from managed-care organizations and insurance companies, because they will base the number of authorized therapy sessions on the diagnosis and treatment plan goals. The *DSM-5* is an important tool in determining a client's diagnosis and should be used in combination with clinical interviews, family assessments, and standardized assessment instruments when developing a treatment plan (Neukrug & Fawcett, 2015).

COLLABORATION AMONG HELPING PROFESSIONALS

Developing a treatment plan is a complex process. There are often multiple helping professionals involved in a case, and the treatment plan must reflect the goals of all the service providers involved. For example, mental health counselors, school counselors, psychologists, and behavioral specialists may have simultaneous involvement with children in agency or school settings. Any of these professionals may be the first to diagnose a child with a mental disorder (Neukrug & Fawcett, 2015). Once the diagnosis is determined, specific treatment goals and interventions must be clearly outlined. Therefore, collaboration among the professionals involved is essential to ensure that the child's service needs are identified, the interventions are clearly documented on the treatment plan, and the methods of ongoing assessment and outcome measures are established.

The terms *multidisciplinary collaboration* and *interdisciplinary collaboration* are often used interchangeably in the mental health field. However, McLoughlin and Geller (2010) insisted that the terms are distinctly different. The authors proposed that multidisciplinary teamwork involves separate treatment plans created by professionals from different disciplines, whereas interdisciplinary collaboration promotes a mutual sharing of information and ideas so that the treatment plan can be constructed as a team. Interdisciplinary collaboration ensures that there is cohesion among the service providers and that the multifaceted aspects of treatment are implemented effectively. Interdisciplinary teamwork is frequently known as *wraparound* team planning in the practice of children's mental health, particularly when working collaboratively with service providers for children and families and with complex emotional and behavioral difficulties (Bruns et al., 2011; Walker & Schutte, 2004; Walker & Schutte, 2005). Because of the intricacies of these cases, children and families are often in need of frequent and intensive services from multiple agencies (Walker & Schutte, 2005). Children are best served when an individualized plan of care is created in partnership with the children and families involved (Bruns et al., 2011). Therefore, the New Freedom Commission on Mental Health (2003) outlined specific recommendations to enhance the quality of mental health for children and families. Those recommendations serve as the basis for wraparound team planning, which is widely used among mental health service providers when developing and implementing treatment plans (Bruns et al., 2011; Walker & Schutte, 2005). In fact, wraparound planning has become one of the primary strategies for improving services and outcomes for children and families in need of comprehensive treatment (Bruns et al., 2011). But how do professionals work together to create, implement, and monitor progress on treatment goals? How is it possible to coordinate quality services and support across systems and among various helping professionals?

Bruns et al. (2011) discussed the need to create an infrastructure when collaborating with other helping professionals. Ideally, there should be an individual who serves as the team leader who coordinates treatment. The team coordinator will ensure that the child and family receive the appropriate interventions and are able to use existing support networks. The team leader will also monitor progress on designated outcome measures, regularly review the treatment plan goals, and make changes as needed throughout the treatment process.

Teamwork in Determining the Diagnosis

According to the *DSM-5,* "The diagnosis of a mental disorder should have clinical utility: it should help clinicians to determine prognosis, treatment plans, and potential treatment outcomes for their patients" (APA, 2013b, p. 20). When conducting wraparound team planning, the family is an integral component in determining the diagnosis and treatment goals (Bruns et al., 2011; Walker & Schutte, 2004; Walker & Schutte, 2005). The diagnostic nomenclature of the *DSM-5* is an effective way to communicate with the service providers involved (Jensen-Doss, Youngstrom, Youngstrom, Feeny, & Findling, 2014; Neukrug & Fawcett, 2015). The helping professionals will summarize the client's characteristic symptoms and share the comprehensive assessment data to make a diagnosis. The diagnosis can then be explained to the client or family to help them understand the need for services, the client's prognosis, and what to expect from treatment (Neukrug & Fawcett, 2015).

Psychosocial Factors

One significant change in the *DSM-5* is that it does not contain the multiaxial system that existed in the *DSM-IV-TR* (APA, 2013b). Psychosocial stressors were previously coded on Axis IV in the *DSM-IV-TR*; however, with the removal of the five-axial diagnostic system in the *DSM-5*, they are now systematically listed so that helping professionals can document additional issues that may be encountered in clinical practice (APA, 2013b). These conditions are found in the section Other Conditions That May Be a Focus of Clinical Attention and include problems or issues that may be the focus of clinical attention or affect the diagnosis or course of treatment (APA, 2013b). These conditions are coded using the *International Classification of Diseases, Tenth Revision, Clinical Modification (ICD-10-CM)*, and are particularly useful in explaining the need for a particular test or treatment (APA, 2013b). The *ICD-10-CM* conditions are typically coded as Z codes. Psychosocial stressors and related conditions can greatly affect parent–child and family relationships, as well as affect how children and families respond to treatment (Cunningham, 2007). Thus, gaining a thorough understanding of the family's psychosocial stressors is essential in assessment and treatment planning (Cunningham, 2007). The stressors listed in the Other Conditions That May Be a Focus of Clinical Attention (APA, 2013b) section and their corresponding codes can be used to guide the construction of treatment plan goals. For example, if a client were diagnosed with V15.81 (Z91.19), nonadherence to medical treatment, and V62.3 (Z55.9), academic or educational problem, the team may desire to formulate specific treatment goals to increase compliance with treatment, as well as to improve academic performance.

Cross-Cutting Considerations in Treatment Planning

Earlier in the chapter, we discussed cross-cutting assessment measures in the diagnostic process. Cross-cutting assessment is also relevant when determining treatment plan goals, in that a cross-cutting goal on a treatment plan could address a symptom or troubling behavior that is affecting the client in multiple ways or settings. For example, a child with disruptive mood dysregulation disorder might exhibit temper outbursts at home, at school, and with peers. A treatment goal could be established to address the problem behavior as it spans multiple settings. You will notice in the case of Larry in Sidebar 3.5, not only is he receiving services in school and agency settings, but he also has problem behaviors that he is exhibiting in multiple environments. Certainly, we can see that Larry's case is quite complex. The treatment team would collaborate to determine the appropriate goals and interventions.

SIDEBAR 3.5

Larry is an 8-year-old male who was diagnosed with attention-deficit/hyperactivity disorder, combined type. Larry is currently taking lisdexamfetamine dimesylate (Vyvanse) as prescribed by his psychiatrist, whom he sees monthly at a local mental health center. Larry's teacher recently expressed concern about his declining grades and angry outbursts in class. Larry reported to the school counselor that he does not like school, because he gets in trouble for hitting other children. Larry attributes his outbursts to his being provoked by his peers. Larry's mother informed the school counselor that Larry often yells, kicks the wall, and throws things when he gets angry at home. Larry's parents are in the process of divorcing, and he has little contact with his father. How could a cross-cutting goal be written to address the angry outbursts in both home and school settings? What other goals should be created?

There is general consensus among helping professionals that research-informed treatment is most effective (Beutler, 2011). Therefore, treatment teams use evidence-based principles and tailor them to meet the specific treatment needs of the client (Beutler, 2011). Regardless of whether the goals on the treatment plan are related to psychosocial stressors or pharmacological treatment, the interventions are empirically supported (Beutler, 2011). The cross-cutting goals on the treatment plan are written in such a manner that when there is a change in the severity of the symptoms, it will be evident over time. Thus, the professionals will be better able to assess the client's responsiveness to treatment.

Ongoing Assessment and Outcomes

Treatment planning is an ongoing process, and professionals closely monitor the child and family to assess progress on treatment goals. Treatment goals need to be updated, changed, or removed over time. Suppose a client has a provisional diagnosis of generalized anxiety disorder. Once the needed diagnostic information is obtained, the provisional diagnosis should be removed and replaced with a definitive diagnosis. Rule-outs and provisional diagnoses should be resolved as quickly as possible so that the treatment plan goals reflect the specific diagnosis and its severity (Neukrug & Fawcett, 2014).

Having an integrated team in place increases the likelihood that the treatment plan will accurately depict the client's current level of need, as well as that cross-system, solution-based problem solving occurs (Bruns et al., 2011). When establishing the treatment plan, attention will also be given to outcome measures (Bruns et al., 2011). That is, how will the team assess whether treatment is working? How will they determine whether the client has met a particular goal within a particular time frame? Ongoing assessment procedures and outcome measures ought to be clear, concise, and objective.

TRANSITIONING TREATMENT PLANS FROM THE *DSM-IV-TR* TO THE *DSM-5*

When conducting treatment planning, professionals will likely encounter clients who have existing diagnoses and treatment plans based on the *DSM-IV-TR* criteria. In such cases, professionals must adjust the diagnoses and treatment plans to reflect the diagnostic criteria in the *DSM-5*. Such considerations are particularly important when working with children with diagnoses that have been revised. For example, the *DSM-5* states, "Individuals with a well-established *DSM-IV-TR* diagnosis of autistic disorder, Asperger's disorder, or pervasive developmental disorder not otherwise specified should be given the diagnosis of autism spectrum disorder" (APA, 2013b, p. 51). The federal Interagency Autism Coordinating Committee recently issued a statement indicating that children with an autism spectrum disorder under the *DSM-IV-TR* criteria will retain their diagnosis and will not be required to be reevaluated according to the *DSM-5* criteria (U.S. Department of Health and Human Services, 2014). Professionals must be familiar with the pertinent changes in the *DSM-5* when developing treatment plans to ensure that the treatment plan is an accurate representation of the client's diagnosis and treatment goals.

Strategies to Maximize Treatment Plan Effectiveness

EVIDENCE-BASED PRACTICE

The *DSM-5* is also helpful in measuring the effectiveness of treatment, because dimensional assessments assist clinicians in assessing changes in severity levels as a response to treatment.

Providing evidence-based treatment requires treatment providers to use interventions that have been scientifically proved in research trials to be efficacious (Jongsma et al., 2014). This means that therapists are charged with not only knowing what interventions are appropriate for use with their clients but also staying abreast of current literature regarding the successful implementation of the interventions. The support of scientific proof is of critical importance to the mental health community because insurance companies routinely link payment for treatment to the incorporation of evidence-based practice (Haddock & Moore, 2015). Commonly, evidence-based treatments are short-term, problem-oriented treatments that focus on improving current problems or symptoms related to a client's presenting problem. Of course, treatment providers must choose interventions with consideration of options that are recognized as useful but might not yet have received empirical scrutiny. Those treatments defined as empirically sound have undergone a clinical trial or large clinical replication series that have features reflective of good experimental design (Leppma & Jones, 2015). Well-established evidence-based treatments frequently have more than one study demonstrating their efficacy. Because new literature is produced all the time, this means that clinicians must not only stay abreast of current research but also possess competence to read and understand the research.

STRUCTURING A TREATMENT PLAN

Developing a treatment plan is a process. It starts with an exploration of client needs, followed by assessment of symptoms and finally by development of a case conceptualization. A diagnosis must be established and individualized goals and objectives developed, complete with identified time frames for ongoing assessment and evaluation of progress.

From a practical perspective, when a clinician actually sits down to write the treatment plan, it should be specific and measurable. The clinician and the client should each know what he or she must do to make progress. Ideally the plan will focus on reducing distress and increasing desired behaviors. Feasibility of the plan is critical, as the client and the counselor should both clearly understand the goals and desired outcomes as well as both agree with the choice of goals and potential for goal achievement.

Another consideration is that treatment plans are written with measurable goals and objectives to track client progress. This not only demonstrates change in clients but also holds the treatment provider accountable for the plan and the interventions. The inclusions of ratings, numeric accomplishments, or changes in frequency are easy ways to document change. For example, reductions in scores on an assessment instrument or reduced number of incidents of problematic behavior through the course of a week are both clear ways to show a measurable change (or lack thereof). Just verify that the goals are specific and realistic. If you have concerns about a client accomplishing a particular goal, it is perfectly reasonable to have him or her accomplish one step of a larger goal. For example, if the ultimate goal is for the client to complete a general education development (GED) program, an initial goal might be simply to identify options for GED programs and secure the details of enrollment requirements rather than setting a goal for GED completion. As time progresses and the client works toward the goal, the plan can be updated to include next steps.

Treatment Plan Development

Review the following case example. Give thoughtful consideration to the background information and the proposed case conceptualization. Review the sample goal and objective, and add another of your own development.

BACKGROUND INFORMATION

Clair is a 9-year-old African American female. She is referred to counseling by her parents after Clair received in-school suspension for bullying another child who was chosen as captain of the kickball team and demonstrating excessive anger when she was confronted about her behavior by her teacher. Her parents are both educated, employed business professionals who describe themselves as highly driven and successful. They have always been proud of Clair's extroverted personality and minimized her problems with interpersonal relationships with peers and adults, saying it was "just a phase" in spite of Clair displaying an irritable mood most days. Clair has demonstrated repeated episodes of angry outbursts toward peers and adults with increased frequency for the past year. This behavior has occurred at home with kids in the neighborhood, at church when participating in her youth group, and at school. According to the school, Clair is routinely disrespectful to peers and several times a week participates in behaviors such as name-calling and laughing when other children cry or are hurt. Clair is very bright, with strong verbal skills, though she is highly competitive and anxious when she is not selected first for teams or teachers do not choose her to answer questions when her hand is raised.

CASE CONCEPTUALIZATION

Based on the information included in the background information, let's give consideration to the elements for case conceptualization:

1. Determine how the identified problems are causing current distress for the client.
   - Clair has received in-school suspension.
   - She has difficulty with interpersonal relationships.

2. Identify any events that precipitated the onset of the problems.
   ∘ Clair was triggered by not being chosen as team captain and being confronted by her teacher.
   ∘ Clair's parents have historically dismissed her disrespectful behavior and viewed it as part of her personality.
   ∘ Clair's parents are both highly driven, and Clair also demonstrates a high drive to succeed.
3. Identify the client's current strengths.
   ∘ Clair is bright and developmentally intact.
   ∘ She is motivated to achieve.
4. Formulate a clinical diagnosis based on *DSM-5* criteria.
   ∘ Assess for disruptive mood dysregulation disorder.
5. Articulate an overall impression of the client's problem.
   ∘ Clair is a 9-year-old African American female with recurrent temper outbursts out of proportion to the precipitating event. These outbursts occur at home, church, and school, multiple times per week and have been ongoing for at least one year.

TREATMENT GOALS

1. React appropriately to important social cues and follow expected rules at home, school, and church.
2. Decrease angry outbursts by using self-calming exercises during times of frustration.

OBJECTIVES

1. Clair will identify one feeling, thought, or situation that causes her to feel angry or upset.
2. Clair will decrease the frequency of her temper outbursts from three to four times per week to two or fewer times per week according to parent report, teacher report, and self-report.
3. Clair's parents will increase the frequency of praise and positive reinforcement for Clair's positive social behaviors and good impulse control to a minimum of one time per day when appropriate.

INTERVENTION

1. Explore with Clair possible stressors or frustrations that might cause negative behaviors to emerge.
2. Design a reward system for Clair to reinforce identified positive behaviors and reduce the frequency of disruptive behaviors.
3. Assign the parents readings to increase their knowledge and understanding about effective disciplinary techniques.

TIME FRAME

1. Objective 1: one month
2. Objective 2: six months
3. Objective 3: four months

Summary

Developing a plan to address a client's issues and identify the approach that will be used to address them is a nuanced and sometimes challenging task for a mental health provider. Effective treatment planning requires that clinicians tailor each plan to the individual needs of each individual. Family dynamics, cultural factors, diagnoses, and symptom patterns must all be simultaneously considered when developing a treatment strategy. This chapter includes practical guidance and strategies for elements to include in a plan, use of the *DSM-5*, and considerations of best practice. An exercise in treatment plan development is included. Ultimately, clinicians are charged to find a balance between drawing on clinical experience and supporting choices with evidence-based treatment. Through case conceptualization and the new *DSM-5* assessment protocols, clinicians have tools to develop individualized, measurable goals and objectives that will address client concerns and promote effective mental health care.

References

American Counseling Association. (2014). *Code of ethics*. Alexandria, VA: Author.

American Mental Health Counselors Association. (2010). *2010 AMHCA code of ethics*. Retrieved from http://c.ymcdn.com/sites/www.amhca.org/resource/resmgr/Docs/AMHCA_Code_of_Ethics_2010_up.pdf

American Psychiatric Association. (2013a). *Cultural Formulation Interview (CFI)—Informant version*. Arlington, VA: American Psychiatric Publishing.

American Psychiatric Association. (2013b). *Diagnostic and statistical manual of mental disorders* (5th ed.). Arlington, VA: American Psychiatric Publishing.

American Psychiatric Association. (2013c). *DSM-5 parent/guardian-rated level 1 cross-cutting symptom measure—Child age 6–17*. Arlington, VA: American Psychiatric Publishing.

American Psychiatric Association. (2013d). *DSM-5 self-rated level 1 cross-cutting symptom measure—Child age 11–17*. Arlington, VA: American Psychiatric Publishing.

American Psychiatric Association. (2013e). *Supplementary Modules to the Core Cultural Formulation Interview (CFI)*. Arlington, VA: American Psychiatric Publishing.

American School Counselor Association. (2004). ASCA National Standards for Students. Alexandria, VA: Author.

Association for Assessment in Research and Counseling. (n.d.). *Standards for assessment in mental health counseling*. Retrieved from http://aarc-counseling.org/assets/cms/uploads/files/AACE-AMHCA.pdf

Balkin, R. & Juhnke, G. (2014). *The Theory and Practice of Assessment in Counseling*. Upper Saddle River, NJ: Pearson Education

Bruns, E. J., Sather, A., Pullman, M. D., & Stambaugh, L. (2011). National trends in implementing wraparound: Results from the state wraparound survey. *Journal of Child and Family Studies, 20*(6), 726–735. doi:10.1007/s10826–011–9535–3

Beutler, L. E. (2011). Prescriptive matching and systematic treatment selection. In J. C. Norcross, G. R. VandenBos, & D. K. Freedheim (Eds.), *History of psychotherapy: Continuity and change* (2nd ed.; pp. 402–407). Washington, DC: American Psychological Association.

Cunningham, C. (2007). A family-centered approach to planning and measuring the outcome of interventions for children with attention deficit hyperactivity disorder. *The Journal of Pediatric Psychology, 32*(6), 676–694.

First, M. B. (2013). *DSM-5 handbook of differential diagnosis*. Arlington, VA: American Psychiatric Publishing.

Geltner, J. A., & Leibforth, T. N. (2008). Advocacy in the IEP process: Strengths-based school counseling in action. *Professional School Counseling, 12*(2), 162–165.

Haddock, L., & Moore, R. (2015). Working within the managed care system. In D. S. Sheperis & C. J. Sheperis (Eds.), *Clinical mental health counseling: Fundamentals of applied practice* (pp. 150–177). Upper Saddle River, NJ: Pearson Education.

Individuals with Disabilities Education Act. (2004). *Building the legacy: IDEA 2004*. Retrieved July 23, 2008 from http://idea. ed.gov/.

Jensen-Doss, A., Youngstrom, E. A., Youngstrom, J. K., Feeny, N. C., & Findling, R. L. (2014). Predictors and moderators of agreement between clinical and research diagnoses for children and adolescents. *Journal of Consulting and Clinical Psychology, 82*(6), 1151–1162. doi:10.1037/a0036657

Jongsma, A. E., & Bruce, T. J. (2010). *Evidence-based psychotherapy treatment planning: DVD facilitator's guide*. Hoboken, NJ: John Wiley & Sons.

Jongsma, A. E, Peterson, L. M., McInnis, W. P., & Bruce, T. J. (2014). *The child psychotherapy treatment planner* (5th ed.). In A. E. Jongsma (Series Ed.), Practice Planners. Hoboken, NJ: John Wiley & Sons.

Kaplan, D. (2006, August 7). Permission to refrain from making a diagnosis. *Counseling Today*. Retrieved from http://ct.counseling.org/2006/08/ct-online-ethics-update-6/

Kendjelic, E. M., & Fells, T. D. (2007). Generic psychotherapy case formulation training improves formulation quality. *Psychotherapy: Theory, Research, Practice, Training, 44*(1), 66–77.

Krueger, R. F., Derringer, J., Markon, K. E., Watson, D., & Skodol, A. E. (2013a). *The personality inventory for DSM-5—Brief form (PID-5-BF)—Child age 11–17*. Arlington, VA: American Psychiatric Publishing.

Krueger, R. F., Derringer, J., Markon, K. E., Watson, D., & Skodol, A. E. (2013b). *The personality inventory for DSM-5 (PID-5)—Child age 11–17.* Arlington, VA: American Psychiatric Publishing.

Kuyken, W., Padesky, C. A., & Dudley, R. (2009). *Collaborative case conceptualizations: Working effectively with clients in cognitive-behavioral therapy.* New York, NY: Guilford Press.

Leigh, H. (2009). A proposal for a new multiaxial model of psychiatric diagnosis: A continuum-based patient model derived from evolutionary developmental gene-environment interaction. *Psychopathology, 42*(1), 1–10. doi:10.1159/000173698

Leppma, M., & Jones, D. (2015). Case conceptualization and treatment planning. In D. S. Sheperis & C. J. Sheperis (Eds.), *Clinical Mental Health Counseling* (pp. 127–149). Upper Saddle River, NJ: Pearson Education.

Livingston, J. D., & Boyd, J. E. (2010). Correlates and consequences of internalized stigma for people living with mental illness: A systematic review and meta-analysis. *Social Science & Medicine, 71*(12), 2150–2161. doi:10.1016/j.socscimed.210.09.030

McLoughlin, K. A., & Geller, J. L. (2010). Interdisciplinary treatment planning in inpatient settings: From myth to model. *Psychiatric Quarterly, 81*(3), 263–277. doi:10.1007/s11126–010–9135–1

Meier, S. T. (2003). *Bridging case conceptualization, assessment, and intervention.* Thousand Oaks, CA: SAGE.

Messer, S. B., & Wolitzky, D. L. (2007). The psychoanalytic approach to case formulation. In T. D. Fells (Ed.), *Handbook of psychotherapy case formulation* (2nd ed.; pp. 67–104). New York, NY: Guilford Press.

Neukrug, E. S., & Fawcett, R. C. (2015). *Essentials of testing and assessment: A practical guide for social workers, counselors, and psychologists* (3rd ed.). Stamford, CT: Cengage Learning.

New Freedom Commission on Mental Health. (2003). *Achieving the promise: Transforming mental health care in America: Final report* (DHHS Pub. No. SMA-03-3832). Rockville, MD: Author.

Shaffer, D. (2013a). *The early development and home background (EDHB) form—Clinician.* Arlington, VA: American Psychiatric Publishing.

Shaffer, D. (2013b). *The early development and home background (EDHB) form—Parent/Guardian.* Arlington, VA: American Psychiatric Publishing.

U. S. Department of Health and Human Services. (2006, October 4). Individualized Education Program. Retrieved from http://idea.ed.gov/explore/view/p/,root,dynamic,TopicalBrief,10,

U. S. Department of Health and Human Services. (2014, April 2). *Interagency Autism Coordinating Committee statement regarding scientific, practice and policy implications of changes in the diagnostic criteria for autism spectrum disorder.* Retrieved from http://iacc.hhs.gov/publications/2014/statement_iacc_dsm5_changes_criteria_040214.shtml

Walker, J. S., & Schutte, K. M. (2004). Practice and process in wraparound teamwork. *Journal of Emotional and Behavioral Disorders, 12*(3), 182–192. doi:10.1177/10634266040120030501

Walker, J. S., & Schutte, K. (2005). Quality and individualization in wraparound team planning. *Journal of Child and Family Studies, 14*(2), 251–267. doi:10.1007/s10826–005–5052–6

Watson, J. C., & Flamez, B. (2014). Counseling assessment and evaluation: Fundamentals of applied practice. Thousand Oaks, CA: SAGE.

Chapter 4

Addressing Client Diversity throughout the Diagnostic Process

JACOB J. LEVY AND SHAWN L. SPURGEON

Introduction

Conducting a sound diagnostic assessment—one that is accurate, thorough, and impartial—is a multidimensional, multifaceted process. It involves the ability to conceptualize the overall process of progressive decision making as well as to infuse cultural information into the process. The purpose of this chapter is to help counselors address clients' cultural diversity throughout the diagnostic process. We will begin by operationalizing the concepts of culture and multiculturalism and provide a discussion of culture in diagnostic decision making. Next, we will address how cultural information has (and has not) been incorporated in the American Psychiatric Association's (APA) *Diagnostic and Statistical Manual of Mental Disorders* (*DSM*) over the years, with particular attention to expansions in multicultural assessment present in its latest edition (*DSM-5*; APA, 2013), most notably the Cultural Formulation Interview (CFI). We will then suggest how to incorporate the CFI within a multicultural assessment process in an effort to make more accurate, culturally informed diagnostic decisions. Finally, we will illustrate this process in a hypothetical case example.

Culture and Multiculturalism

In the *DSM-5*, *culture* is defined as "systems of knowledge, concepts, rules, and practices that are learned and transmitted across generation" (APA, 2013, p. 749). Also noted is the relationship between culture and socially constructed concepts, such as race, and culturally constructed group identities, such as ethnicity. The *DSM-5* also acknowledges the multidimensional nature of culture and that individuals are exposed to and identify with multiple cultural identities throughout their lives. This broad and inclusive conceptualization of culture yields advantages and disadvantages. Hays (1996) asserted that the primary advantage of such a broad and inclusive definition is that "it allows for the consideration of overlapping and integrated cultural influences in the lives of individual clients" (p. 334), thus, not limiting one's conceptualization of culture to narrow variables, such as race or ethnicity. Hays (1996) provided this example:

> Many Muslims identify themselves primarily by their religion, but because Muslim Americans include people of diverse ethnicities and nationalities (e.g., Pakistanis, Africans, Arabs, Indonesians, Cambodians, East Indians, and African Americans), they do not fit the definition of an ethnic group. Thus, when multicultural counseling defines culture solely in terms of ethnicity, Muslim Americans are left out. (p. 334)

Conversely, the inclusive definition of culture has a critical disadvantage. Locke (1990) noted that the broad definition of culture includes virtually any group of people, thus allowing the dominant culture to study and consider culture without attending to the difficult and painful topic of oppression. Thus, a narrow definition of culture, with a focus on those affected by these power differentials (initially racial and ethnic minorities), allowed for issues of inequities in the psychiatric diagnosis process to begin to be addressed (Hays, 1996).

The broad and narrow definitions of culture correspond to two separate approaches to multicultural counseling research and practice. The etic approach focuses on aspects of human experience that transcend, or at least apply to, many cultures (Fukuyama, 1990). Such an approach can result in widely ignoring the impact cultural factors have on one's psychological presentation (Swartz-Kulstad & Martin, 1999). The second, the emic approach, emphasizes the need to focus on the culturally specific factors and to develop an intimate awareness of the knowledge base of the culture of every individual (Hays, 1996). This approach can result in focusing too narrowly on certain cultural variables (e.g., race and ethnicity) to the point that other variables (e.g., religion or sexual orientation) are ignored (Swartz-Kulstad & Martin, 1999).

Hays (1996) suggested a solution to the definitional dilemma by synthesizing both the etic and emic approaches into what she referred to as the transcultural-specific perspective. This perspective is represented in the working model of multicultural counseling, called the ADRESSING model. This model identifies nine cultural factors (and the corresponding minority group) that counseling and psychological research have shown to be in need of special attention (Hays, 1996). These factors include **A**ge and generational influences; **D**isability status; **R**eligious affiliation; **E**thnicity (including race); **S**ocial status (e.g., socioeconomic status, formal education, urban or rural origins, family name, etc.); **S**exual orientation; **I**ndigenous cultural heritage; **N**ational origin; and **G**ender. Thus, using the first letter of each factor creates the slightly misspelled acronym. Consider exploring your own multicultural identity in Sidebar 4.1.

SIDEBAR 4.1:   SELF-REFLECTION

An important aspect of becoming a culturally competent counselor is to gain insight and awareness of your cultural influences and biases. We are all people of culture. Compose a two- to three-page summary of the cultural factors that have influenced you. With which cultures or subcultures do you identify? What values and beliefs influence your actions? What cultural experiences have you had (positive and negative) that have shaped your views and perceptions of the world?

Culture is not only multidimensional; it is also interactive. The influence of multiple cultural identities acting within a person can and does affect his or her understanding and perceptions. For example, various researchers have found the existence of negative attitudes toward homosexuality among African American communities (Clarke, 1983; Icard, 1985; Peterson, 1992). However, in their survey of African American heterosexuals' attitudes toward lesbian women and gay men, Herek and Capitanio (1995) found African American men have stronger negative attitudes than African American women toward gay men; and both male and female African American who were well educated, single, registered to vote, and not religious tended to have more positive attitudes toward gay men and lesbian women. Such findings illustrate the need to understand the influence of multiple cultures interacting within a given individual or client. Take for example a client who is an African American gay male seeking treatment for depressive symptoms. If this client were raised in a religious, socially conservative, and poorly educated family and social environment, the potential cultural influences on their symptoms may be quite different from an African American gay man raised in nonreligious, socially liberal, and well-educated family and social environment.

The process by which counselors and other helping professionals develop the understanding of the psychological presentation of clients is generally referred to as psychological assessment, or clinical decision making. When incorporating the interactions and influences of various cultural dimensions in the clinical decision-making process, it is commonly referred to as multicultural assessment (Ridley, Li, & Hill, 1998). The next section will provide a review of literature of the impact of culture variables on diagnostic decision making.

Culture and Diagnostic Decision Making

Historically, the idea that culture affects the appraisal of one's psychological presentation has been met with discrepant views regarding how and whether to alter the diagnostic process (Dana, 1993; Draguns, 1996; Fabrega, 1989; Sue & Sue, 2003). Researchers have feverishly supported the notion that diagnosis needs to be based on empirically grounded evidence (Cheng & Robinson, 2013; Fernando, 2012; Gureje & Stein, 2012). Seligman and Reichenberg (2014) argued that diagnosis serves as the cornerstone of effective treatment planning. They highlighted the relevance of the therapeutic relationship and how this relationship elicits important clinical information necessary for clinicians to make accurate and meaningful diagnoses. Sue (2010) advocated for cultural adaptation as a way of effectively conceptualizing a client's core issues. The *DSM-5* also supports a clearly defined, dimensional decision-making process that incorporates elements of the individual's self, including culture. However, researchers have repeatedly noted the disparity in the relationship among clinical assessment, psychiatric misdiagnosis, and culture (Berg, Mimiaga, & Safren, 2008; Cho & Kim, 2012; Dodd, 2011; Flaskerud, 2000).

Fulford, Christodolou, and Stein (2011) posited that the debate continues to rage in the mental health arena as to whether mental disorders truly capture social and ethnic values. This debate focuses on the notion that diagnostic assessments and evaluations are based in part on individual values and beliefs. As such, the political, social, and familial systems in which we reside have powerful influence on our conceptualization of mental health. Fulford et al. (2001) also argued for the relevance of universal standards through which individuals in the mental health diagnostic community formulate criteria for evaluation. It is clear that there does not seem to be one universal principle that guides the method by which clinicians evaluate diagnostic material.

It is beyond the scope of this chapter to highlight all the relevant cultural and ethnic groups counselors will work with in the clinical setting (e.g., African American and Afro-Caribbean groups, Cambodians, East Asian women, Euro-Canadian women, Latin Americans and other Latino groups, Native Americans, Non-Latino Caribbean Blacks, Non-Latino Whites, and Vietnamese). However, are some relevant cultural differences among general categories merit further review and evaluation. Clinicians will undoubtedly encounter a member of one of the groups mentioned below in their practice. It is imperative that clinicians understand the historical and inherent challenges of these groups as well as develop a clearer picture of the disparities so that their diagnostic decision making can be clearer and more focused.

RACE AND CLASS

Fernando (2012) stated that race, based largely on physical appearance, serves as the source of discrimination and bias toward others. As the country becomes more racially diverse, the experiences of racial minorities as they relate to mental health cannot be ignored (Cho & Kim, 2010). As such, the awareness of race and class as it relates to diagnostic decision making has been well documented in the literature. Race-based diagnostic measures have influenced both inpatient and outpatient service access for minority populations.

INPATIENT SERVICES

Minorities seeking services for inpatient hospitalization have dealt with ineffective, biased assessment measures (Eack & Newhill, 2012; Sohler & Bromet, 2003). These measures are concurrent with the disparity between minorities and Whites on a number of measures, including suicide rates and homicide rates in inpatient settings (Kupfer, Frank, Grochocinski, Houck, & Brown, 2003).

The challenges related to inpatient services for minorities are clearly delineated in the literature. For example, Sohler and Bromet (2003) noted that psychiatric hospitalizations in the 1940s and 1950s were often based on biased, racist ideas about mental health. As a result, the disparity between the numbers of Blacks hospitalized for schizophrenia as opposed to the number of Whites was alarming. Assessments were based on the notion that Blacks were more likely to have severe illnesses and less likely to suffer from mood problems. Also, Eack and Newhill (2012) advocated for improved mental health assessment approaches for African Americans to facilitate better access to services. In their study, they concluded that African Americans released from psychiatric hospitalization received poorer assessments, were less likely to be connected to available resources, and were more likely to carry the stigma associated with psychiatric hospitalization than their Caucasian counterparts.

OUTPATIENT SERVICES

These challenges are not limited to inpatient treatment for minorities; there are major disparities in treatment access and attainment for outpatient services as well (Husky, Kanter,

McGuire, & Olfson, 2012). The challenge lies in identifying salient aspects of minorities' individual and cultural development and then linking them with appropriate services (Schnittker, Pescosolido, & Croghan, 2005). This challenge is exacerbated by the fact that many assessment measures designed to evaluate critical data related to culture are not designed to incorporate cultural variables (Redmond, Galea, & Delva, 2009). The clinician is left to assess culture using his or her acquired clinical skill set, which may or may not incorporate cultural components.

Cho and Kim (2010) stated that mental health service providers often struggle when assessing minority groups for outpatient services because of the limited number of minorities who choose to access services. Given the fact that knowledge of satisfaction with services is an integral part of improved outpatient quality, most outpatient assessment agencies do not adequately meet the needs of racial minorities because they have limited information about what works for them. If clinicians want to increase minority participation in outpatient services, there needs to be a stronger commitment to understanding minority issues during the diagnostic assessment process (Qureshi & Collazos, 2011).

GENDER

Rowan-Szal, Joe, Bartholomew, Pankow, and Simpson (2012) attributed the increase in women's incarceration rates partially to poor assessment strategies treatment providers used. They attributed this problem to limited resources and assessment measures designed to delineate differences between men and women. As such, clinical characteristics unique to the female population are often overlooked and categorized in the same manner as those of male offenders (Wilhelm & Turner, 2002). Taxman, Perdoni, and Harrison (2007) advocated for the use of brief screening measures designed to highlight distinguishing characteristic differences between males and females; however, budget restraints have severely limited the implementation of such measures. Lahey et al. (2007) assessed the predictive validity of the *Diagnostic and Statistical Manual of Mental Disorders, Fourth Edition, Text Revision (DSM-IV-TR)* related to attention-deficit/hyperactivity disorder (ADHD) and found distinct gender differences among the characteristics and clinical variables. Their results highlighted the subtle differences between girls and boys when assessing for ADHD traits and supported the notion that clinicians sometimes miss these critical differences. A key point of their research is the notion that differences do exist between men and women and that clinicians need to increase their awareness of these important differences. For example, Seligman and Reichenberg (2014) noted the fact that explosive behaviors in men often mask depression and mood disorders. However, the underlying mood problems are not effectively diagnosed in men but are an essential part of an intake assessment for women. A notable revision and expansion of information in the *DSM-5* is the presentation of potential differences between men and women in the expression of mental illness, especially with regard to risk factors associated with both biological sex and individual representation—psychological, behavioral, and social consequences of one's perceived gender (APA, 2013, p. 15). Such discussions are uniquely addressed in the Gender-Related Diagnosis Issues section of relevant disorders and presented independently from the Culture-Related Diagnostic Issues section. These types of challenges are further exacerbated by sexuality and sexual orientation. See Sidebar 4.2.

SIDEBAR 4.2:   GENDER DIFFERENCES IN SYMPTOM MANIFESTATION

Review the gender-related diagnostic issues for social anxiety disorder (*DSM-5*, p. 206) and posttraumatic stress disorder (*DSM-5*, p. 278), and discuss in small groups possible cultural and environmental factors that may contribute to gender difference in expression of these disorders.

SEXUALITY AND SEXUAL ORIENTATION

Sexual minorities face unique stressors related to their development, including harassment, fear of rejection, and discrimination (Berg, Mimiaga, & Safren, 2008). As such, assessment measures oftentimes fail to capture the essence of their core issues. The clinician could miss critical information related to their development, resulting in an inaccurate assessment and diagnosis.

Rutherford, McIntyre, Dailey, and Ross (2012) noted major disparities for lesbian females seeking accurate and effective mental health services. The researchers noted that these sexual minorities are 2.5 times more likely to have attempted suicide and are 1.5 times more likely to struggle with depressive symptoms. Similarly, Berg et al. (2008) stated that the level of distress among sexual minority men seeking mental health services continues to be significant, even though there is an increased emphasis on developing methods for understanding this population.

Though there is increased interest and focus on diagnostic decision making with culturally diverse groups, many deficits need to be addressed. The challenge of developing inclusive, comprehensive measures for assessing mental distress continues to serve as the impetus for research and evaluation (Dodd, 2011). Gureje and Stein (2012) advocated for a comprehensive, inclusive assessment approach designed to incorporate salient variables related to culture. They believed that health is more than merely the absence of disease and that contextual variables merit consideration in the assessment process.

Cultural Concepts of Distress

Distress is conceptualized as an important component of mental illness and a key to understanding what happens to an individual when the presence of symptoms denotes a change in the individual's behavior, attitude, or physical appearance (Kendell, 1975). This concept is critical when assessing clients for mental health disorders because it helps the clinician understand the severity of a given situation (Seligman & Reichenberg, 2014). The ability to accurately assess an individual's situation, including a keen understanding of the severity of the situation, is crucial to clinicians for effective treatment planning and insurance reimbursement (Gureje & Stein, 2012). As such, treatment outcomes not rooted in an understanding of the relationship between culture and distress can be seen as deficient (Sue, 2010).

Clinicians need to understand that society and culture affect the way in which distress variables present themselves in the clinical setting (Qureshi & Collazos, 2011). For example, researchers readily agree that men's expressions of emotions are often rooted in their behaviors (Spurgeon, 2012). However, African American men understand that this behavioral expression can lead to severe consequences (e.g., incarceration) and are therefore less likely to display aggressive acts toward others. They internalize their emotions and avoid outward expression of them, leading to further mental health challenges, such as depression and suicide. The suicide rate among African American males has more than doubled since 1980 (Williams, 2008).

The above example highlights the important role cultural variables have in assessing distress in clients. As such, diagnostic criteria need to include relevant cultural variables that may affect the client's behavior (Lewis-Fernández et al., 2014). The interplay between cultural adaptations in treatment and diagnostic assessment is critical in understanding the client and the client's core concerns.

Culture and the *DSM*

Dana (2008) noted that psychiatric diagnosis, based on the *DSM*, did not include any consideration of invariance in psychological presentation based on cultural factors until the publication of the fourth edition of the *DSM* in 1994 (i.e., *DSM-IV*)—thus, the *DSM* operated from the etic perspective prior to this time. For the *DSM-IV*, and its text revision, the *DSM-IV-TR* (APA, 2000), intentional efforts were made to acknowledge the importance of cultural context when making psychiatric diagnoses. This was accomplished primarily by incorporating a discussion of ethnic and cultural considerations in the introduction to the manual and by creating an Outline for Cultural Formulation and Glossary of Culture-Bound Syndromes (Good, 1996). The Outline for Cultural Formulation was designed to "supplement the multiaxial diagnostic assessment and to address difficulties that may be encountered in applying the *DSM-IV* criteria in a multicultural environment" (APA, 2000, p. 897); whereas the Glossary of Culture-Bound Syndromes identified select "recurrent, locally-specific patters of aberrant behavior and troubling experiences that may or may not be linked to a particular DSM-IV diagnostic category" (APA, 2000, p. 898).

In its most recent edition, the *DSM-5* (APA, 2013) expands its cultural formulation outline into a well-articulated, semistructured interview—the Cultural Formulation Interview (discussed later in this chapter). In addition, the manual expands its coverage of cultural-related diagnostic issues throughout (cf. Intellectual Disability, p. 39; Autism Spectrum Disorder, p. 57; Attention-Deficit/Hyperactivity Disorder, p. 62; Specific Learning Disorder, pp. 72–73; Stereotypic Movement Disorder, p. 79; Tic Disorders, p. 83; Schizophrenia, p. 103; Schizoaffective Disorder, pp. 108–109; Major Depressive Disorder, p. 166; all of the Anxiety Disorders, pp. 193, 201, 205, 211, 216, 220, and 224; Obsessive-Compulsive Disorder, p. 240; Reactive Attachment Disorder, p. 267; Posttraumatic Stress Disorder, p. 278; Acute Stress Disorder, p. 285; Somatic Symptom Disorder, p. 313; Pica, p. 331, Avoidant/Restrictive Food Intake Disorder, p. 336; Anorexia Nervosa, p. 342; Bulimia Nervosa, p. 348, and Binge Eating Disorder, p. 352). For example, in its coverage of schizoaffective disorder, the *DSM-IV-TR* highlighted cultural issues relative to age (e.g., more common in younger adults), and gender (e.g., incidence rate higher in women than men), whereas in the *DSM-5* references to research citing "overdiagnosis of schizophrenia compared with schizoaffective disorder in African American and Hispanic populations" (APA, 2013, pp. 108–109) are presented. Other notable culture-related expansions and specifications can be found in the discussion of social anxiety disorder and panic disorder. In the discussion of panic disorder in the *DSM-IV-TR*, it was noted in some cultures, "Panic Attacks may involve intense fear of witchcraft or magic" (APA, 2001, p, 234), whereas in the *DSM-5*, much more detailed information is provided:

> The rate of fears about mental and somatic symptoms of anxiety appears to vary across culture ... a Vietnamese individual who has a panic attack after walking into a windy environment (*trúng gió;* "hit by wind") may attribute the panic attack to exposure to wind as a result of the cultural syndrome that links these two experiences. (APA, 2013, p. 211)

Similar discussions are offered with regard to adjustment disorders, oppositional defiant disorder, and sexual dysfunctions whereby interpretations of adjustment, sexual, and oppositional issues necessitate examination within the cultural context the behavior is manifested, although it is yet to be determined whether these revisions have yielded "a better instrument for understanding human distress and suffering and for guiding cultural responsive, effective, and equitable care" (Alarcón et al., 2009).

We suggest that the challenges related to a culturally appropriate diagnostic assessment center on three types of issues:

1. Issues explicitly related to client's cultural differences
2. Issues related to the interaction of the client's culture(s) and environmental demands
3. Issues related to the clinician's cultural bias in the decision-making process

The first type involves knowledge base competencies—that is, information related to psychiatric conditions, or expressions of psychiatric conditions, that exist within a particular cultural context. For example, in the *DSM-5*'s Glossary of Cultural Concepts of Distress, nine syndromes or conditions are presented that describe the cultural expressions of distress (similar to disorders described in the *DSM*'s anxiety and mood disorders) in non-Western or non-White cultural contexts. The second set of issues concern person–environment interactions, in particular, clients' experiences with marginalization, discrimination, and other forms of oppression. Relatedly, the third type involves counselors' biases, beliefs, or ignorance regarding the influences of cultural variables on one's psychological presentation.

It is beyond the score of this chapter to provide a comprehensive presentation of issues explicitly related to client's cultural differences. The *DSM-5* does a fairly good job summarizing the major research findings in cultural differences in symptom presentation and prevalence in the discussions of individual disorders. In addition, several texts are devoted to culture and other environmental factors in psychopathology and psychiatric disorders (cf. Freeman & Stansfeld, 2008; Mezzich, Kleinman, Fabrega, & Parron, 1996; Tseng & Streltzer, 1997). Thus, we will focus our attention on the issues and challenges related to the process counselors face when attempting to make sound diagnostic decisions with culturally diverse clients.

The Process of Multicultural Assessment

The inherent difficulty in infusing cultural information into the assessment process is the reality that no two individuals internalize culture in the same way. In paraphrasing an old Asian proverb, Sue and Sue (2003) stated: "All individuals, in many respects, are (a) like no other individuals, (b) like some individuals, and (c) like all other individuals" (p. 11). The truism leads to an inability to use cultural-specific (emic) or universal (etic) assessment approaches decisively, because reliance on either approach neglects the inherent uniqueness of the individual (Swartz-Kulstad & Martin, 1999).

In describing the two types of decision-making errors counselors can make when attempting to assess clients from culturally diverse backgrounds, Neighbors, Jackson, Campbell, and Williams (1989) noted:

1. They can assume that minority and nonminority clients are necessarily similar.

2. They can assume minority clients and nonminority clients are inherently different or attribute all of the psychological presentation to cultural variables.

The first error corresponds to the notion of culture blindness, for example, "I don't see you as being a minority, just another human" (Ridley, 2005, p. 67), whereas the latter refers to the notion of culture consciousness, for example, "The reason you have an alcohol addiction is because you are Native American" (Ridley, 2005, p. 68). The result is that counselors make assessment decisions that are inaccurate, incomplete, and partial. It has been posited that this incompetence arises from several factors: (a) the inability to conceptualize the overall assessment process, (b) the inability to infuse cultural data into the process adequately, and (c) the failure to coordinate and integrate the various competencies required in multicultural assessment (Levy & Plucker, 2003, 2008; Ridley et al., 1998; Ridley, Hill, Thompson, & Ormerod, 2001).

> We chose to use the terms *culture blindness* and *culture consciousness* as opposed to the terminology cited in Ridley (2005)—*color blindness* and *color consciousness*—in an effort to reflect a broader and more inclusive view of cultural diversity.

Ridley et al. (1998) developed the Multicultural Assessment Procedure (MAP) to assist counselors in making purposeful and scientifically based decisions. The MAP consists of three dynamic phases (identifying, interpreting, and incorporating cultural data) that a counselor must work through to arrive at sound assessment decisions, which is the final phase of the process. Below is a brief description of the MAP.

THE MULTICULTURAL ASSESSMENT PROCEDURE (MAP)

Phase One: Identify Cultural Data

The goal of this phase is to establish rapport and work toward understanding, from the client's point of view, the nature of his or her cultural contexts. Using clinical interviews, counselors obtain information related to the client's presenting concerns and cultural background. In the *DSM-5*, the Cultural Formulation Interview (CFI) is a tool designed to collect such data.

The *DSM* has, since its inception, struggled with the notion of culture and the relevance of cultural variables as they relate to assessment. With each iteration, researchers attempted to bridge the gap between effective assessment and these important variables. The *DSM-IV* developed an outline for cultural adaptation of clinical variables, including diagnostic categories and cultural narratives connected to each class of disorders (Seligman & Reichenberg, 2014). The Outline for Cultural Formulation (OCF) was designed to give clinicians a systematic method for assessing cultural variables (Aggarwal, Nicasio, DeSilva, Boiler, & Lewis-Fernández, 2013). The result of this addition was an enhanced appreciation and understanding of efforts to validate the *DSM-IV-TR* as a diagnostic assessment tool.

The *DSM-5* further expanded this notion with the development of the CFI, designed to help clinicians complete culturally appropriate diagnostic interviews. Because there were inherent challenges with the internal structure and administration of the OCF, the CFI serves as an operationalization of the data used in the OCF (Lewis-Fernández et al., 2014). The intended goal of the CFI is to provide a baseline assessment tool that would incorporate relevant cultural variables that may be readily missed with other assessment measures.

Cultural Formulation Interview

The CFI is composed of 16 questions designed to assess 12 areas of functioning. Each question is structured to elicit a specific response from the client, which then helps the clinician gain a better understanding of the client's core concerns and of how connected those concerns are to the client's cultural development (Lim, 2013). For example, question 2 asks: "Sometimes people have different ways of describing their problem to their family, friends, or others in their community. How would you describe your problem to them?"(APA, 2013, p. 752). This question is designed to help the clinician understand how others see the client's problem. As such, it provides the clinician with important socio-cultural information necessary for effective and competent assessment (Lewis-Fernández et al., 2014).

There are some challenges related to the CFI's implementation and usage (Aggarwal, 2012; Aggarwal et al., 2013; Lewis-Fernández et al., 2014). However, the CFI represents a cogent attempt to operationalize relevant cultural and ethnic variables often overlooked in clinical practice. One of the most important aspects of the CFI is that it helped increase the awareness of culture and provided a framework from which others could operate in developing their own approach to cultural assessment. The increased attention to cultural variables in clinical practice only serves to strengthen clinicians' assessments and to provide more specific information for the clients with whom they work. Examine what it is like to experience a CFI in Sidebar 4.3.

SIDEBAR 4.3:   CFI ROLE PLAY

Imagine that you are a client seeking counseling for a mock (i.e., imagined) issue but from your personal culture background. Partner with a classmate and work through the CFI (*DSM-5*, pp. 749–759) to examine how your issue might be interpreted depending on your cultural context.

Phase Two: Interpret Cultural Data

After the counselor has gathered sufficient information about the client's clinical and cultural background, the next phase is to interpret the data. Ridley et al. (1998) noted that this interpretive process involves (a) differentiating the client's cultural data (i.e., data expected of any client from the client's culture) and idiosyncratic data (i.e., data unique to the client and not necessarily expected of other members of the client's culture), (b) applying base rate information to cultural data, (c) differentiating dispositional from environmental stressors, and (d) differentiating clinically significant data from clinically insignificant data. The previous interpretation then leads the counselor to formulate working hypotheses. Levy and Plucker (2003) recommended the use of a divergent hypothesis strategy in multicultural assessment by intentionally generating alternative hypotheses for a client's behavior (i.e., examine the possible function of the behavior in addition to examining the possible dysfunction). See Sidebars 4.4 and 4.5 for exercises related to interpreting cultural data.

SIDEBAR 4.4:   STEREOTYPE THREAT 1

"Clinical identification rates [for ADHD] in the United States for African American and Latino populations tend to be lower than for Caucasian populations" (*DSM-5*, p. 62). What cultural or environmental factors do you think might contribute to this discrepancy? Discuss in small groups.

SIDEBAR 4.5:   STEREOTYPE THREAT 2

"Specific learning disorder is more common in males than females (ratios range from about 2:1 to 3:1)" (*DSM-5*, p. 73). Discuss in a small group what you think or have been told about gender differences in learning disabilities. Then, review the gender-related diagnostic issues for specific learning disabilities. Is this finding because of cultural bias? Was the information consistent with what was discussed in your group?

Phase Three: Incorporate Cultural Data

The next task is to test the hypotheses generated in Phase Two by: (a) ruling out any possible medical (physiological) explanations for the client's clinical presentation; (b) using psychological testing to confirm or refute the clinical hypotheses; and (c) comparing the interpreted data to diagnostic criteria listed in the *DSM-5* in a culturally appropriate manner. As noted earlier, the *DSM-5* includes a section in the discussion of many disorders that notes cultural deviations in presentation, as well as a glossary of culture-bound syndromes to consider when testing clinical hypotheses.

Phase Four: Arrive at a Sound Assessment Decision

According to Ridley et al. (1998), working through the first three phases of the MAP enables counselors to arrive at a sound assessment decision. Arriving at such a decision involves being able to answer two questions: "What is the nature of the client's psychopathology, if any?" and "How does nonpathological but clinically relevant information fit into the assessment conclusion?" It is important to note that arriving at an assessment decision does not necessarily constitute an end point. The MAP is recyclable by nature, and as more clinical and cultural information is identified throughout the course of treatment, the counselor may need to reinterpret and reincorporate that data.

Case Example: Alon

In this example, we hope to illustrate the process and complexities of cross-cultural diagnostic decision making in the hypothetical case of Alon, age 12, a boy referred to counseling because of his frequent school tardiness. We will begin by presenting a brief description of the presenting concern, followed by summary of responses to a CFI from both Alon and his mother. Next we will describe the process of generating clinical hypotheses to help explain Alon's behavior. We will then test these hypotheses by comparing the behaviors to *DSM-5* criteria in a culturally appropriate manner as we try to arrive at a diagnostic decision.

PRESENTING CONCERN

Alon, age 12, was referred for counseling following being repeatedly late (i.e., tardy) for school—arriving at least 45 minutes late every day. The school contacted Alon's mother following his tardiness during the first three days of school. Alon's mother was quite confused about why her son was late, because she had dropped him off at his bus stop prior to leaving for work each day. According to the school bus driver, Alon had never ridden the bus (either to or from school) and was not present at the bus stop when the bus arrived in the morning. When questioned about his bus-riding behavior, Alon stated that he did not want to ride the bus and instead walked the 3 miles to and from school. Because his mother did not arrive home until after 5 PM, Alon was able to make the walk home from school before she returned; thus, his lack of bus riding home had gone unnoticed. Alon was referred to a mental health professional to aid in diagnostic decision making and to make recommendations for possible counseling or other services. Alon presented with his mother, and both were separately interviewed.

BACKGROUND INFORMATION

Alon's mother was born in the United States and is of Israeli decent. A Jewish American woman, his mother met and later married Alon's father (an Israeli native) while in college in New York. They moved to Israel shortly after graduation, and Alon's father enlisted in the Israeli military. He was killed during a training exercise when Alon was 2 years old. Alon and his mother remained in Israel for 10 years, until his mother was able to secure a promotion at her job that allowed for a transfer back to the United States. Alon and his mother recently moved to a small suburban town in the northeastern United States during the early summer months, and they had lived there for approximately three months prior to Alon starting school. He expressed no concerns to his mother about starting school. Alon was fluent in English and a strong academic student.

SUMMARIES OF CFIs WITH ALON AND HIS MOTHER

Cultural Definitions of the Problem

When describing how he understood the problem that brought him to counseling, Alon stated that he didn't want to ride the bus but didn't understand why it was a big deal. He stated that "buses aren't safe," and he thought he was being pretty smart by walking to school instead. He stated that he had walked to school "before moving here," and it had never been a problem before. Although he didn't particularly like being late to school, he thought it better than the alternative of being "blown up on a bus."

Alon's mother provided a bit of context to Alon's statements. She noted that she and her son had recently moved to the United States from Israel. She noted that while living in Israel, it was not uncommon for buses to be targets for bombings. Neither she nor Alon had ever directly been affected by or ever witnessed such an incident, but she noted that one "must always be on guard when living in the Middle East." His mother noted that "personal safety" was a key motivator in her desire to return to the United States.

Cultural Perceptions of Cause, Context, and Support

Though he never witnessed or was involved in a bomb attack, Alon stated it was "common knowledge" that buses are unsafe. He stated he never rode on a bus in Israel. When his mother dropped him off at the bus stop for the first day of school, he remembered feeling very nervous, but because he knew how hard his mother had worked to bring them to the United States, he did not want to disappoint her by telling her of his fear. He said he knew how to get to the school because they had visited it several times while he was preparing to enroll. He didn't think it was too far, so he decided to walk. He said his teachers really didn't seem to care he was late until the third day.

Alon reported feeling "very embarrassed" about being seen by a psychologist. Although he felt "nervous a lot," he did not think it was a big deal and thought that "all kids feel that way." He stated he felt at his best when he was alone or with his mother. He noted he was an observant Jew and was finding it difficult living in a community with a "much smaller Jewish community" than he was accustomed to in Israel. He did not want to burden his mother and just wanted to "do the right things." He stated that he had very few friends, both currently and while growing up in Israel. He reported caring for his mother, greatly, and wanting her to be happy.

His mother reported having a very close relationship with Alon. She noted that after her husband had died, she devoted all her energies to caring for him and working toward a time when she could move them to the United States. She reported having her family nearby, and she liked being "back in the States." She thought Alon would like it, too, "once he got used to it," but now was not be so sure.

Cultural Factors Affecting Self-Coping and Past Help Seeking

Both Alon and his mother denied any previous counseling or psychiatric treatment. Alon's mother noted she had a difficult time following her husband's death and raising her young son in a foreign land. She did not seek professional help but "dived into work" and focused her energies on gaining the necessary resources to facilitate moving herself and her son to America. This was the first time either Alon or his mother had presented for psychological services.

Cultural Factors Affecting Current Help Seeking

Alon stated the only reason he presented to counseling was to appease his mother. He did not think he had a "problem." His mother, however, was quite concerned. She feared that the problem might be greater than she cared to admit and was concerned he never told her of his fear of buses or that he was walking to school. She noted that Alon had "always been quiet and very sensitive." She was very surprised by his tardiness, because he had never had any problems at school before. When she asked him about his tardiness, he told her "not to worry," that he was "fine" and just wanted to walk to school instead of riding the bus and would leave earlier in the future so that he "would not cause her any more trouble."

GENERATING CLINICAL HYPOTHESES

Several cultural variables are potentially relevant in conceptualizing the psychological presentation of Alon, including being raised in a perceived volatile and potentially dangerous environment and recently immigrating to a new country where he was now a religious minority. Based on the information gathered during the clinical and cultural formulation interviews, it is reasonable to hypothesize that Alon may meet criteria for one or several *DSM-5* diagnoses, including trauma- and stressor-related disorders, such as posttraumatic stress disorder (PTSD) or adjustment disorder with anxiety, and anxiety disorders, such as specific phobia (riding buses) or generalized anxiety disorder. The underlying premise of the former (PTSD and adjustment disorder) is that clinical distress has manifested following exposure to some traumatic or stressful event (APA, 2013), whereas anxiety disorders tend to be internally oriented (i.e., fear deemed excessive or persisting relative to developmental norms). Although it is certainly possible that other diagnostic possibilities or other clinical hypotheses could be made that describe Alon's behavior, we will focus on these for illustrative purposes. Alon's symptoms meet criteria for:

1. PTSD
2. Adjustment disorder with anxiety
3. Generalized anxiety disorder (GAD)
4. Specific phobia—bus riding.

It is also possible that his presentation (5) does not meet criteria for psychiatric diagnosis at all—this hypothesis should also be rigorously examined. For more detailed discussions of these disorders, see Chapter 12, which discusses trauma- and stressor-related disorders, and Chapter 10's coverage of anxiety disorders.

COMPARING CLINICAL HYPOTHESES WITH *DSM-5* CRITERIA

As noted earlier in this chapter, the MAP suggests two strategies for testing clinical hypotheses in addition to comparing with *DSM-5* criteria—ruling out other medical or physical conditions and the use of psychological testing. For the sake of illustration, all potential medical or physical explanations for Alon's behavior have been ruled out via a physical exam by his pediatrician. We will integrate psychological testing results in our discussion of comparing our hypotheses with *DSM-5* criteria.

In testing out our first hypothesis (PTSD), we first reviewed the Culture-Related Diagnostic Issues section of the description of PTSD in the *DSM-5*. It was noted that expression of symptoms and characteristics may vary greatly cross-culturally and that it is important to view these manifestations in the appropriate cultural context. Review of the diagnostic criteria revealed that Alon's presentation does not meet Criteria A because he did not experience exposure to "actual or threatened death, serious injury, or sexual violation" (APA, 2013, p. 280). Although he heard of, or was warned of, accounts of bus bombings, Alon had not been directly affected by one (e.g., witnessing, learning of the loss of loved ones, or repeated or extreme exposure to adverse details). Thus, when testing this hypothesis, it does not appear that Alon's presentation is consistent with PTSD.

As a possible differential diagnosis, we next examined the possibility of Alon's presentation being consistent with an adjustment disorder. The *DSM-5* notes that adjustment disorders should be considered in cultural context in terms of nature of and response to the stressor (APA, 2013). Several questions arise when comparing Alon's presentation with the criteria for adjustment disorders as well. To meet the criteria, Alon's presentation would need to include "marked distress" or "significant impairment" (APA, 2013, p. 286) in functioning in response to an identifiable stressor. Alon's symptoms have resulted in school tardies, and school officials and his mother expressed concerns. Whether this constitutes significant impairment is subject to debate. Before we debate it, we will examine the other hypotheses.

Our next two hypotheses (GAD and specific phobia) were related to concerns raised by Alon's mother that he was "very sensitive" and Alon's admission that he was "nervous a lot." As noted in the *DSM-5*, it is important to examine whether worries or anxiety is excessive in certain cultural contexts (for both GAD and specific phobia). Alon's mother noted that being vigilant and "on guard" was typical of those living in the Middle East. Criteria for GAD include excessive anxiety across several activities manifested by some combination of cognitive, behavioral, and somatic symptoms of anxiety. Review of the diagnostic criteria for specific phobic revealed some consistencies with Alon's behavior, most notably the active avoidance of riding a bus, and fear out of proportion with immediate threat. Again, questions remain regarding the relative severity of anxious symptoms.

To help address the questions related to significant impairment and relative severity of symptoms, we used psychological testing. Inventories such as the Minnesota Multiphasic Personality Inventory-Adolescent (MMPI-A; Butcher et al., 1992) and the Personality Assessment Inventory-Adolescent (Morey, 2007) provide normative comparisons of personality and psychopathological symptoms (for a review of the inventories in the context of multicultural assessment, see Leong, Levy, Gee, & Johnson, 2007). Alon's responses to such an inventory revealed he is quite introverted and has experienced a moderate level of anxiety but not at a level that would be considered clinically significant. No other psychopathology was revealed in the testing.

ARRIVING AT A CULTURALLY INFORMED DIAGNOSTIC DECISION

After comparing Alon's symptoms with *DSM-5* criteria and using psychological testing, we arrived at the decision that Alon's current psychological presentation does *not* meet diagnostic criteria for any major psychiatric disorder. Because Alon only recently immigrated to the United States, and he is not manifesting significant distress or impairment, as evidenced by his psychological testing and prior history, it appears his refusal to ride a bus is best conceptualized as related to acculturation stress, not a psychiatric disorder. Alon would likely benefit from counseling or support groups to help ease his transition to the United States. If his avoidant or other anxious symptoms continue to manifest after such interventions, reassessment of his psychological condition would be warranted.

SIDEBAR 4.6: CASE EXAMPLE

The authors provided an example of working through the MAP and ultimately arrived at a clinical decision of no diagnosis. Do you agree with their rationale? Would your opinion change if Alon had different cultural information (e.g., was not a recent immigrant) or represented a different ethnic or cultural group? Discuss the various possibilities in small groups.

Summary

As noted throughout this chapter, the process of addressing client diversity throughout the diagnostic process is complex. Historically, clients from underrepresented or marginalized groups have been adversely affected by a diagnostic approach that relied on an etic perspective, where the context of manifested behaviors and other presentations was rarely considered. Counselors and other helping professionals have made, and continue to make, substantial progress in the last few decades to help address these and other disparities in health service delivery to culturally diverse client populations. We reviewed a conceptual approach to multicultural assessment and integrated it with the CFI found in the *DSM-5*. Culture is always relevant in the diagnostic process. Sometimes cultural variables can help explain the presentation of apparent aberrant behavior (as illustrated in the case example described in this chapter); however, it is equally important to test out all of our hypotheses and not to fall into the trap of cultural consciousness. Psychiatric disorders exist in every culture, though their nature, expression, and prevalence may differ.

References

Aggarwal, N. K. (2012). Hybridity and intersubjectivity in the clinical encounter: Impact on the cultural formulation. *Transcultural Psychiatry*, *49*(1), 121–139.

Aggarwal, N. K., Nicasio, A. V., DeSilva, R., Boiler, M., & Lewis-Fernández, R. (2013). Barriers to implementing the DSM-5 Cultural Formulation Interview: A qualitative study. *Culture, Medicine, and Psychiatry*, *37*(3), 503–533. doi:10.1007/s11013-013-9325-z

Alarcón, R. D., Becker, A. E., Lewis-Fernández, R., Like, R. C., Desai, P., Foulks, E., … Primm, A. (2009). Issues for DSM-V: The role of culture in psychiatric diagnosis. *Journal of Nervous and Mental Disease*, *197*(8), 559–560. doi:10.2097/NMD.0b013e3181b0cbff

American Psychiatric Association. (1994). *Diagnostic and statistical manual of mental disorders* (4th ed.). Washington, DC: Author.

American Psychiatric Association. (2000). *Diagnostic and statistical manual of mental disorders* (4th ed., text rev.). Washington, DC: Author.

American Psychiatric Association. (2013). *Diagnostic and statistical manual of mental disorders* (5th ed.). Arlington, VA: American Psychiatric Publishing.

Berg, M. B., Mimiaga, M. J., & Safren, S. A. (2008). Mental health concerns of gay and bisexual men seeking mental health services. *Journal of Homosexuality*, *54*(3), 293–306. doi:10.1080/00918360801982215

Butcher, J. N., Williams, C. L., Graham, J. R., Archer, R. P., Tellegen, A., Ben-Porath, Y.S., & Kaemmer, B. (1992). *Minnesota Multiphasic Personality Inventory-Adolescent professional manual*. Minneapolis, MN: University of Minnesota Press.

Cheng, T. C., & Robinson, M. A. (2013). Factors leading African Americans and Black Caribbeans to use social work services for treating mental health and substance use disorders. *Health & Social Work*, *38*, 99–109.

Cho, H., & W. J. Kim. (2010). Racial differences in satisfaction with mental health services among victims of intimate partner violence. *Community Mental Health Journal*, *48*(1), 84–90.

Clarke, C. (1983). The failure to transform: Homophobia in the Black community. In B. Smith (Ed.), *Home girls: A Black feminist anthology* (pp. 197–208). New York, NY: Kitchen Table/Women of Color Press.

Dana, R. H. (1993). *Multicultural assessment perspectives for professional psychology*. Boston, MA: Allyn & Bacon.

Dana, R. H. (2008). Clinical diagnosis in multicultural populations. In L. A. Suzuki & J. C. Ponterotto (Eds.), *Handbook of multicultural assessment: Clinical, psychological, and educational applications*. San Francisco, CA: Jossey-Bass.

Dodd, K. (2011). Race equality training and values-based practice. *Mental Health Practice*, *15*(2), 28–32.

Draguns, J. G. (1996). Multicultural and cross-cultural assessment: Dilemmas and decisions. In G. R. Sodowsky & J. C. Impara (Eds.), *Multicultural assessment in counseling and clinical psychology* (pp. 37–84). Lincoln, NE: Buros Institute of Mental Measurements.

Eack, S. M., & Newhill, C. E. (2012). Racial disparities in mental health outcomes after psychiatric hospital discharge among individuals with severe mental illness. *Social Work Research*, *36*(1), 41–52. doi:10.1093/swr/svs014

Fabrega, H. (1989). Cultural relativism and psychiatric illness. *The Journal of Nervous and Mental Disease*, *177*, 415–425.

Fernando, S. (2012). Race and culture issues in mental health and some thoughts on ethnic identity. *Counselling Psychology Quarterly*, *25*(2), 113–123.

Freeman, H., & Stansfeld, S. (2008). *The impact of the environment on psychiatric disorder*. New York, NY: Routledge.

Fukuyama, M. A. (1990). Taking a universal approach to multicultural counseling. *Counselor Education and Supervision*, *30*(1), 6–17.

Fulford, K. W. M., Christodolou, G. N., & Stein, D. J. (2011). Values and ethics: Perspectives on psychiatry for the person. *International Journal of Person Centered Medicine*, *1*(1), 161–162.

Good, B. J. (1996). Culture and DSM-IV: Diagnosis, knowledge, and power. *Culture, Medicine, and Psychiatry*, *20*(2), 127–132.

Gureje, O., & Stein, D. J. (2012). Classification of mental disorders: The importance of inclusive decision-making. *International Review of Psychiatry*, *24*(6), 606–612. DOI: 10.3109/09540261.2012.726214.

Hays, P. A. (1996). Addressing the complexities of culture and gender in counseling. *Journal of Counseling & Development*, *74*(4), 332–339.

Herek, G. M., & Capitanio, J. P. (1995). Black heterosexuals' attitudes toward lesbian and gay men in the United States. *Journal of Sex Research, 32*, 95–106.

Husky, M. M., Kanter, D. A., McGuire, L., & Olfson, M. (2012). Mental health screening of African American adolescents and facilitated access to care. *Community Mental Health Journal, 48*(1), 71–78.

Icard, L. D. (1985). Black gay men and conflicting social identities: Sexual orientation versus racial identity. *Journal of Social Work & Human Sexuality, 4*(1–2), 83–93.

Kendell, R. E. (1975). The concept of disease and its implications for psychiatry. *British Journal of Psychiatry, 127*(4), 305–315.

Kupfer, D. J., Frank, E., Grochocinski, V. J., Houck, P. R., and Brown, C. (2003). African-American participants in a bipolar disorder registry: Clinical and treatment characteristics. *Bipolar Disorders, 7*(1), 82–88.

Lahey, B. B., Hartung, C. M., Loney, J., Pelham, W. E., Chronis, A. M., & Lee, S. S. (2007). Are there sex differences in the predictive validity of DSM–IV ADHD among younger children? *Journal of Clinical Child and Adolescent Psychology, 36*(2), 113–126.

Leong, F. T. L., Levy, J. J., Gee, C., & Johnson, J. (2007). Clinical assessment of ethnic minority children and adolescents. In S. R. Smith & L. Handler (Eds.), *The clinical assessment of children and adolescents: A practitioner's handbook* (pp. 547–574). Mahwah, NJ: Lawrence Erlbaum.

Levy, J. J., & Plucker, J. A. (2003). Theory and Practice: Assessing the psychological presentation of gifted and talented clients: A multicultural perspective. *Counselling Psychology Quarterly, 16*(3), 229–247.

Levy, J. J., & Plucker, J. A. (2008). A multicultural competence model for counseling gifted and talented children. *Journal of School Counseling, 6*(4), 1–47.

Lewis-Fernández, R., Aggarwal, N. K., Bäärnhielm, S., Rohlof, H., Kirmayer, L. J., Weiss, M., … Lu, F. (2014). Culture and psychiatric evaluation: Operationalizing cultural formulation for DSM-5. *Psychiatry, 77*(2), 130–154.

Lim, R. (2013). What's new in *DSM-5* for cultural psychiatry? *Psychiatric News.* Retrieved from http://psychnews.psychiatryonline.org/newsarticle.aspx?articleid=1757008

Locke, D. C. (1990). A not so provincial view of multicultural counseling. *Counselor Education and Supervision, 30*(1), 18–25.

Mezzich, J. E., Kleinman, A., Fabrega, H., & Parron, D. L. (Eds.). (1996). *Culture and psychiatric diagnosis: A DSM-IV perspective.* Arlington, VA: American Psychiatric Publishing.

Morey, L. C. (2007). *Personality Assessment Inventory Adolescent professional manual.* Lutz, FL: Psychological Assessment Resources.

Neighbors, H. W., Jackson, J. S., Campbell, L., & Williams, D. (1989). The influence of racial factors on psychiatric diagnosis: A review and suggestions for research. *Community Mental Health Journal, 25*(4), 301–311.

Peterson, J. L. (1992). Black men and their same-sex desires and behaviors. In G. Herdt (Ed.), *Gay culture in America: Essays from the field* (pp. 147–164). Boston, MA: Beacon Press.

Qureshi, A., & Collazos, F. (2011). The intercultural and interracial therapeutic relationship: Challenges and recommendations. *International Review of Psychiatry, 23*(1), 10–19.

Redmond, M. L., Galea, S., & Delva, J. (2009). Examining racial/ethnic minority treatment experiences with specialty behavioral health service providers. *Community Mental Health Journal, 45*(2), 85–96.

Ridley, C. R. (2005). *Overcoming unintentional racism in counseling and therapy* (2nd ed.). Thousand Oaks, CA: SAGE.

Ridley, C. R., Hill, C. L., Thompson, C. E., & Ormerod, A. J. (2001). Clinical practice guidelines in assessment. In D. B. Pope-Davis & H. L. K. Coleman (Eds.), *The intersection of race, class, and gender in multicultural counseling.* Thousand Oaks, CA: SAGE.

Ridley, C. R., Li, L. C., & Hill, C. L. (1998). Multicultural assessment: Reexamination, reconceptualization, and practical application. *The Counseling Psychologist, 26*(6), 827–910.

Rowan-Szal, G. A., Joe, G. W., Bartholomew, J. P., Pankow, J., and Simpson, D. D. (2012). Brief trauma and mental health assessments for female offenders in addiction treatment. *Journal of Offender Rehabilitation, 51*(1–2), 57–77. doi:10.1080/10509674.2012.633019

Rutherford, K., McIntyre, J., Daley, A., & Ross, L. E. (2012). Development of expertise in mental health service provision for lesbian, gay, bisexual, and transgender communities. *Medical Education, 46*(9), 903–913. DOI: 10.1111/j.1365-2923.2012.04272.x.

Schnittker, J., Pescosolido, B. A., & Croghan, T. W. (2005). Are African Americans really less willing to use health care? *Social Problems*, *52*(2), 255–271.

Seligman, L., & Reichenberg, L. W. (2014). *Selecting effective treatments: A comprehensive, systematic guide to treating mental disorders* (4th ed., update). San Francisco, CA: Jossey-Bass.

Sohler, N. L., & Bromet, E. J. (2003). Does racial bias influence psychiatric diagnoses assigned at first hospitalization? *Social Psychiatry and Psychiatric Epidemiology*, *38*(8), 463–472. doi:10.1007/s00127-003-0653-0

Spurgeon, S. L. (2012). Counseling men. In C. C. Lee (Ed.), *Multicultural issues in counseling: New approaches to diversity* (4th ed., pp. 127–138). Alexandria, VA: American Counseling Association.

Sue, S. (2010). Cultural adaptations in treatment. *The Scientific Review of Mental Health Practice*, *7*(2), 31–33.

Sue, D. W., & Sue, D. (2003). *Counseling the culturally diverse: Theory and practice* (5th ed.). Hoboken, NJ: John Wiley & Sons.

Swartz-Kulstad, J. L., & Martin, W. E. (1999). Impact of culture and context on psychosocial adaptation: The cultural and contextual guide process. *Journal of Counseling and Development*, *77*(3), 281–294.

Taxman, F. S., Perdoni, M. L., & Harrison, L. D. (2007). Drug treatment services for adult offenders: The state of the state. *Journal of Substance Abuse Treatment*, *32*(3), 239–254.

Tseng, W., & Streltzer, J. (1997). *Culture and psychopathology: A guide to clinical assessment.* New York, NY: Brunner/Mazel.

Wilhelm, D. F., & Turner, N. R. (2002). Is the budget crisis changing the way we look at sentencing and incarceration? *Federal Sentencing Reporter*, *15*(1), 41–49.

Williams, J. E. (2008). Suicide watch. *Essence*, *38*, 134.

Part II

Diagnostic Categories of Psychiatric Disorders

Part II of the textbook builds on the Stages of the Comprehensive Diagnostic Process section by exploring the specific diagnoses that are relevant to children and adolescents. We structured the content of our text to mirror that of the *Diagnostic and Statistical Manual of Mental Disorders, Fifth Edition (DSM-5)*, to provide an easy-to-use crosswalk between the two. Each chapter in Part II is dedicated to a specific diagnosis or category of diagnoses (e.g., autism spectrum disorder, depressive disorders, and sleep-wake disorders). This edited volume encompasses multiple viewpoints of practicing counselors and behavioral health care professionals from a diverse spectrum of work settings across the United States. Each author has firsthand clinical experience practicing in the areas on which he or she wrote (both in terms of diagnoses discussed and treatment strategies recommended).

The chapters in Part II are designed to guide readers in the assessment of signs and symptoms indicative of each specific disorder, how they can identify or create empirically based treatment plans, and how they can assess client progress and treatment success specific to children and adolescents. We believe that formatting the chapters in this manner will help strengthen readers' ability to integrate these complicated clinical tasks. Because the intent is to be able to apply the diagnostic process to real-world practice, we supplement most chapters with real-world case examples. Each example is designed to improve readers' clinical decision-making process, including the selection of appropriate diagnostic data-gathering tools, differential diagnosis, and formulation of individualized treatment plans aimed at addressing the particular diagnosis determined. Our intent is to provide readers an evidence-based resource that they can apply in clinical practice with children and adolescents. Although the *DSM-5* was published in 2013, it was in development for many years. Because of the lengthy development process, much of the research in the *DSM-5* is already several years old. The information contained in each chapter of this textbook reflects more recent research and developing conceptualizations of each disorder.

Part II includes chapters focused on autism spectrum disorder; attention-deficit/hyperactivity disorder; schizophrenia spectrum and other psychotic disorders; bipolar and related disorders; depressive disorders; anxiety disorders; obsessive-compulsive and related disorders; trauma- and stressor-related disorders; feeding and eating disorders; sleep-wake disorders; gender dysphoria; disruptive, impulse-control, and conduct disorders; substance-related disorders; major and mild neurocognitive disorders because of traumatic brain injury; and other conditions that may be a focus of clinical attention when working with children and adolescents. Each chapter provides an introduction and overview of the disorder or category of disorders, a description of the disorder, a review of *DSM-5* criteria, an in-depth discussion of each disorder in the category, an exploration of the differential diagnosis process, a review of assessment strategies, evidence-based treatment strategies and interventions, evaluation strategies, useful websites, and a number of sidebars that include real-world examples.

Our textbook provides a guide for applying the *DSM-5* to children and adolescents. Although the information in this textbook is comprehensive, it should be used in conjunction with the *DSM-5* rather than as a sole resource. In addition, we encourage clinicians to obtain supervised training in the assessment and diagnostic process. We ask that clinicians dedicate themselves to becoming lifelong learners about child and adolescent mental health and to continuing to improve upon clinical skills. Children and adolescents are vulnerable clients and deserve the best qualified clinicians to serve them.

Chapter 5

Autism Spectrum Disorder

JOSHUA JOHN DIEHL, CHRISTINA G. MCDONNELL, AND KRISTIN VALENTINO

Introduction

Autism spectrum disorder (ASD) is a neurodevelopmental disorder that encompasses a range of difficulties in social communication and behavior that first appear in infancy or early childhood. Just as *awareness* of autism has risen considerably over the past two decades, so too has our *knowledge* about ASD. ASD is an evolving diagnosis that has gone through several conceptual changes in the past three decades. Despite the amount of attention ASD receives in the media these days, it is a relatively new diagnosis that has gone through a number of changes in the past few decades in the *Diagnostic and Statistical Manual of Mental Disorders* (*DSM*). Table 5.1 provides a timeline of the evolution of the ASD diagnosis with each revision of the *DSM*. The most recent edition of the *DSM* (*DSM-5*; American Psychiatric Association [APA], 2013) represents a substantial change in the conceptualization of the disorder that moves away from categorical diagnostic subtypes and toward a spectrum model. In this chapter we examine a number of aspects of ASD, including diagnosis, assessment, treatment, and clinical challenges in the context of the new diagnostic criteria.

Description of the Disorder

ASD is a neurodevelopmental disorder that is characterized by social communication and social interaction impairments along with restricted, repetitive patterns of behavior, interests, or activities (APA, 2013). In contrast with neurodevelopmental disorders with a known biological etiology (e.g., Down's syndrome and Williams-Beuren syndrome), ASD is diagnosed and characterized by observed behavior rather than an etiological pathway. In this way, it is more similar to *DSM-5* disorders such as attention-deficit/hyperactivity disorder and specific learning disorder, which are also diagnosed based on behavior. Perhaps because of ASD's high heritability (Constantino et al., 2013; Fombonne, 2005), much focus has been placed on discovering a simple (predominantly biological) etiology for ASD, which could then be cured or prevented (Hyman, 2010; Lord & Jones, 2012). Decades of research, however, have shown that the etiology of ASD is anything but simple and characterizing ASD as a strictly categorical diagnosis is misleading (Kamp-Becker et al., 2010). In *DSM-5* there is shift toward behavioral, dimensional conceptualizations and considering ASD symptoms along a continuum of severity

103

TABLE 5.1   ASD in the *DSM* through the Years

DSM Version	*Overarching Category*	*Subcategory*	*ASD and Related Conditions were Called:*
DSM-I (1952)	N/A	N/A	Not recognized; most children with ASD were likely diagnosed as having schizophrenic reaction—childhood type
DSM-II (1968)	N/A	N/A	Not recognized; most children with ASD were likely diagnosed as having schizophrenic reaction—childhood type
DSM-III (1980)	Disorders Usually First Evident in Infancy, Childhood, or Adolescence	Pervasive Developmental Disorders	Infantile Autism, Childhood Onset Pervasive Developmental Disorder, Atypical Pervasive Developmental Disorder
DSM-III-R (1987)	Disorders Usually First Evident in Infancy, Childhood, or Adolescence	Pervasive Developmental Disorders	Autistic Disorder, Pervasive Developmental Disorder—Not Otherwise Specified
DSM-IV (1994) and *DSM-IV-TR* (2000)	Disorders Usually First Diagnosed in Infancy, Childhood, or Adolescence	Pervasive Developmental Disorders	Autistic Disorder, Asperger's Disorder, Rett Syndrome, Childhood Disintegrative Disorder, Pervasive Developmental Disorder—Not Otherwise Specified
DSM-5 (2013)	Neurodevelopmental Disorders	N/A	Autism Spectrum Disorder

(i.e., across social-communicative functioning) rather than attempting to define distinct categorical subgroups, such as autistic disorder and Asperger's disorder.

According to estimates from the Centers for Disease Control and Prevention, about 1 in 50 children has been identified with an ASD, a rate that in recent years has been steadily increasing (Blumberg et al., 2013). It is very important to note, however, that the most recent prevalence numbers are based on *DSM-IV-TR* criteria (APA, 2000) and might not be representative of the prevalence of the *DSM-5* diagnostic criteria. For example, preliminary studies have suggested that 91 to 93 percent of people who met *DSM-IV-TR* criteria will meet *DSM-5* criteria, whereas the remaining 7 to 9 percent will be characterized as having social (pragmatic) communication disorder (Huerta, Bishop, Duncan, Hus, & Lord, 2012; Mazefsky, McPartland, Gastgeb, & Minshew, 2013). It should be noted that the *DSM-5* specifically states that "individuals with a well-established *DSM-IV-TR* diagnosis of autistic disorder, Asperger's disorder, or pervasive developmental disorder not otherwise specified should be given the diagnosis of autism spectrum disorder" (APA, 2013, p. 51), but research suggests that the new criteria will have an effect on the prevalence of newly diagnosed cases. As such, this research suggests that current prevalence numbers might not be representative of future estimates. ASD appears to be four to eight times more common in males than females (Blumberg et al., 2013; Kogan et al., 2009; Volkmar, Lord, Bailey, Schultz, & Klin, 2004). This number partially reflects genetic factors that affect heritability and etiological pathways related to the X chromosome (Belmonte & Bourgeron, 2006) but also might reflect gender biases in diagnosis (Giarelli et al., 2010, also see Diagnostic Challenges, this chapter).

Age of onset is very early in development, with almost half of all parents expressing concerns within the first year of life and 90 percent of parents identifying difficulties by age 2 (Lord & Richler, 2006; Volkmar, Klin, & Chawarska, 2008; Wimpory, Hobson, Williams, & Nash, 2000). Table 5.2 provides examples of representative developmental milestones in the first two years of life that are often used as important indicators of developmental delays. Given the high heritability of ASD, tracking infant siblings from birth allows researchers to examine a population considered at high risk for developing the disorder. These studies have revealed several different patterns of development in infants eventually diagnosed with ASD. In the first pattern, there are clear developmental delays or a developmental plateau in the emergence of typical developmental milestones. A second pattern involves a developmental regression, or loss of documented skills over time. Developmental regressions were thought to be relatively rare in the development of ASD, with most children displaying persistent developmental delays. However, findings from prospective research by Ozonoff et al. (2010) indicated that most infants who were later diagnosed with ASD demonstrated declining trajectories of social communication behavior and loss of skills. It is important to note that developmental patterns in ASD are not categorical and should not be restricted to delay versus regression as was once thought (Ozonoff et al., 2010) and that there are variations of development, delay, plateau, and regression among the population.

Prospective sibling research has also been used to identify a prodrome (i.e., a set of signs that precede the onset) of ASD. Such efforts have indicated the presence of several behavioral markers at 12 months of age (but not at 6 months) that differentiate infants who develop ASD from those who do not (Ozonoff et al., 2010; Zwaigenbaum et al., 2005). Risk markers have generally included atypical or poor eye contact, gaze to faces, orienting to name, shared or social smiles, imitation, vocalizations to others, and social interest. Data accrued from retrospective analysis of early home videos of children diagnosed with ASD similarly indicate various behavioral indices of attention, communication, social behavior,

TABLE 5.2 **Language and Communication Milestones in Infancy and Toddler Development**

Age	Key Skills
1 to 6 months	Cooing, laughing; alternates making sounds with another person
6 to 12 months	Babbling consonant-vowel combinations; sounds resemble speech; responds to name
12 to 18 months	Utterance of first words; symbolic gesturing; tries hard to make self understood
18 to 24 months	Uses two-word sentences; beginning of language and naming explosion; average child goes from 50 to 900 words over six-month period

and so on, but overall research has not cohered to identify any consistent developmental prodrome (Yirmiya & Charman, 2010).

DSM-5 CRITERIA

Although there were characterizations of autism in the early twentieth century (Asperger, 1944; Kanner, 1943), *infantile autism* did not appear as a diagnosis in the *DSM* until 1980 (*DSM-III*; APA, 1980), and the diagnostic criteria have gone through several substantial revisions in the past 30 years. The most recent revision reflects a departure from the categorical diagnoses contained in the *DSM-IV-TR* (APA, 2000), such as autistic disorder and Asperger's disorder, and the introduction of one overarching ASD diagnosis. Table 5.3 compares how the *DSM-IV-TR* and *DSM-5* categorize ASD and related diagnoses. The *DSM-5* states that ASD "encompasses disorders previously referred to as early infantile autism, childhood autism, Kanner's autism, high-functioning autism, atypical autism, pervasive developmental disorder not otherwise specified, childhood disintegrative disorder, and Asperger's disorder" (APA, 2013, p. 53). Although pervasive developmental disorders (PDDs) were not originally conceptualized as being part of an autism spectrum, over time research showed considerable overlap between the disorders (Kamp-Becker et al., 2010). In *DSM-5*, the section titled Disorders Usually First Diagnosed in Infancy, Childhood, or Adolescence is renamed Neurodevelopmental Disorders, and this category includes ASD, attention-deficit/hyperactivity disorder (ADHD), intellectual disability, and communication disorders, among a number of other diagnoses (APA, 2013). Table 5.3 provides an explanation of the rationale for this change. The neurodevelopmental disorders are characterized by limitations of learning, deficits with control of executive functions and motor movements, and global impairments of social skills or intelligence that most often become apparent in early childhood and can effect everyday functioning (e.g., interpersonal, academic, occupational). There is no longer a PDD subcategory, and most (but not all) individuals formerly in this category now meet criteria for an ASD, with the remaining 7 to 9 percent likely meeting criteria for social (pragmatic) communication disorder (Huerta et al., 2012; Mazefsky et al., 2013).

SIDEBAR 5.1:   WHERE DID CHILDHOOD GO?

In *DSM-5*, the section titled Disorders Usually First Diagnosed in Infancy, Childhood, or Adolescence was renamed Neurodevelopmental Disorders. This represents a broader philosophical change throughout the *DSM* away from the idea that there were childhood and adult disorders and toward the philosophy of development as a process that is dynamic throughout the lifespan.

The essential diagnostic features of ASD according to the *DSM-5* include impairments across two domains of functioning: (1) social communication and social interaction and (2) restricted, repetitive patterns of behavior, interests, or activities. Moreover, these symptoms must be present in early childhood. Importantly, symptoms and behaviors may change over time as social demands increase with age, or they may be obscured

TABLE 5.3 *DSM-IV-TR* and *DSM-5* Comparison

	DSM-IV-TR	*DSM-5*
Overarching group of conditions	Disorders Usually First Diagnosed in Infancy, Childhood, or Adolescence	Neurodevelopmental Disorders
Autism-related diagnostic categories	Autistic Disorder Asperger's Disorder Pervasive Developmental Disorder—Not Otherwise Specified (PDD-NOS) Childhood Disintegrative Disorder Rett's Disorder	Autism Spectrum Disorder
Severity levels	None. By definition, individuals with Autistic Disorder manifested at least two social communication impairments compared to individuals with Asperger's Disorder or PDD-NOS, but the degree and the severity of these symptoms varied greatly within each diagnosis	A separate severity level for each diagnostic criterion (social communication and social interaction; restricted, repetitive patterns of behavior, interests, or activities)
What if the individual does not meet full diagnostic criteria?	PDD-NOS represented a broad category that captured many individuals who manifested problematic symptoms but did not meet criteria for any of the other PDD diagnoses. This clinical profile was often described as part of the autism spectrum	Social (Pragmatic) Communication Disorder is a new diagnostic category for individuals with marked deficits in social communication but without restricted, repetitive patterns of behaviors, interests, or activities. This diagnosis is mutually exclusive with ASD Other Specified Neurodevelopmental Disorder replaces *DSM-IV-TR* Not Otherwise Specified and is used when an individual shows marked functional impairment but his or her symptom profile does not meet ASD criteria, and the clinician chooses to specify the reason. This classification can be used for non-ASD profiles Unspecified Neurodevelopmental Disorder is a new diagnostic category in which an individual shows marked functional difficulties typical of neurodevelopmental disorders but does not meet criteria for a Neurodevelopmental Disorder, or there is insufficient information available at the time of diagnosis. This classification can be used for non-ASD profiles

by compensatory strategies or services and supports. Therefore, detailed developmental information is needed, because diagnoses of ASD can be given based on case history even if behaviors are not currently present. These symptoms must also be associated with significant impairment across multiple indices of everyday functioning (i.e., social, educational, or occupational). Finally, these behaviors should be differentiated from intellectual disability or global developmental delay.

DEFICITS IN SOCIAL COMMUNICATION AND SOCIAL INTERACTION

A major change from the *DSM-IV-TR* to *DSM-5* is that social interaction and social communication impairments, formerly separate diagnostic criteria in autistic disorder requiring three of seven possible symptoms, are combined into one category representing both social communication and social interaction and requiring symptoms to be present in each of three related subcategories (social-emotional reciprocity, nonverbal communication, and developing, maintaining, and understanding relationships). The current literature supports this clustering of symptoms, given close relationships between language, communication, and social interaction (Gotham, Risi, Pickles, & Lord, 2007; Guthrie, Swineford, Wetherby, & Lord, 2013). According to the *DSM-5* (APA, 2013), deficits in social communication and social interaction must be manifested by impairments in (1) social-emotional reciprocity, (2) nonverbal communicative behaviors, and (3) developing, maintaining, and understanding social relationships. These deficits must be persistent and present in multiple environments (e.g., school and home). First, deficits in social-emotional reciprocity, the ability to interact with others and share thoughts and feelings in age-appropriate ways, must be present. In younger children, this may be manifested as reduced interest or initiation of interactions with peers, one-sided language, or infrequent behavior imitation. In adults, deficits in social-emotional reciprocity are primarily seen as difficulty interpreting and engaging with social cues (APA, 2013). Second, nonverbal communication deficits may include abnormal use of eye contact, gestures, or facial expressions. Young children with ASD commonly present with joint attention difficulties (Meindl & Cannella-Malone, 2011), and adults with ASD may show reduced use of gestures or facial expressions during interactions with others. Third, difficulty forming relationships may be observed by lack of joint play or by play that is constrained by rigid rules during early childhood. In adulthood, individuals with ASD tend to have difficulty understanding friendships and modifying behavior to fit certain situations or may evidence reduced interest in peers.

RESTRICTED, REPETITIVE PATTERNS OF BEHAVIOR, INTERESTS, OR ACTIVITIES

The presence of restricted, repetitive patterns of behavior, interests, or activities either currently or during childhood must be indicated by at least two of the following symptoms: (1) stereotyped motor movements, use of objects, or speech; (2) insistence on sameness or ritualized routines; (3) highly restricted, fixated interests; or (4) hyperreactivity or hyperactivity to sensory input (APA, 2013). Stereotyped behaviors include repetitive motor movements (e.g., hand flapping and rocking), use of objects (e.g., lining up objects or using them in atypical ways), and speech (e.g., echolalia; Leekam, Prior, & Uljarevic, 2011). Insistence on sameness may be evident as difficulty transitioning from activities, rigid rule adherence, or ritualized behaviors, including repetitive questioning or pacing (APA, 2013). Highly fixated interests may be manifested as obsessive, unusually intense, circumscribed preoccupations that may be pursued at the expense of more normative interactions or activities (Attwood, 2003).

One important difference between the *DSM-IV-TR* and the *DSM-5* is the addition of sensory sensitivity to the restricted and repetitive behaviors diagnostic criteria. Previously, sensitivity to sensory stimuli was considered an associated characteristic, whereas research indicates that sensory issues are common (Boyd et al., 2010). Hyperreactivity or hyporeactivity to sensory input may be observed as overresponsiveness or underresponsiveness to sensory stimulation, including fascination with lights, reactivity to loud noises, extreme responses to touch, and so on.

SPECIFIERS

Applicable specifiers should be recorded in diagnostic considerations of ASD. Primarily, severity is specified separately for both domains (social communication and repetitive behaviors or interests). According to the *DSM-5*, severity should be specified on a scale from mild, moderate, or severe—with the recognition that severity may vary by context and fluctuate over time. Clinicians should use Table 2: Severity Levels for Autism Spectrum Disorder (*DSM-5*, p. 52) and the Clinician-Rated Severity of Autism Spectrum and Social Communication Disorders (located at http://www.psychiatry.org/practice/dsm/dsm5/online-assessment-measures). Level one mild (requiring support) indicates that deficits in social communication and repetitive behaviors significantly interfere with everyday functioning and are associated with observable impairments. With supports, these deficits are significantly less apparent. Level two moderate (requiring substantial support) indicates that marked deficits in social communication and repetitive behaviors are apparent even with supports, frequently occur such that they are readily apparent to a casual observer, and are associated with significantly impaired functioning. Level three severe (requiring very substantial support) indicates profound deficits in social communication and inflexible behavior that are associated with severely impaired functioning in all domains, very limited social skills, minimal social responses, and significant distress adjusting to transitions. For example, an individual who presents with level three severity may have extremely impoverished language skills (e.g., only a few words) or initiate social interactions solely to fulfill immediate needs (APA, 2013).

In addition to the severity specification, five additional specifiers should be considered along with a diagnosis of ASD according to the *DSM-5*. These include:

1. With or without intellectual impairment

2. With or without language impairment

3. Associated with a known medical or genetic condition or environmental factor

4. Associated with another neurodevelopmental, mental, or behavior disorder

5. Catatonia

The intellectual impairment specifier involves estimates of verbal and nonverbal cognitive abilities, knowledge of which is necessary for interpreting other diagnostic features and informing intervention approaches. The language impairment specifier involves consideration of expressive and receptive language skills, and the individual's verbal functioning should be explicated (e.g., nonverbal, single words only, or fluent speech). The third specifier should be recorded if the individual presents with concomitant medical (e.g., epilepsy), genetic (e.g., fragile X syndrome), or environmental (e.g., premature birth, low birth weight, or fetal alcohol syndrome) conditions. If an individual also meets criteria for comorbid disorders (e.g., ADHD, anxiety, depression, disruptive behavior), his or her diagnosis should be specified as "associated with another neurodevelopmental, mental, or behavior disorder." Finally, catatonia, which is "marked psychomotor disturbance that may involve decreased motor activity, decreased engagement during interview or physical examination, or excessive and peculiar motor activity," (APA, 2013, p. 119) should be specified if present. These specifiers aid in the interpretation of an individual's presenting profile and inform treatment efforts based on patterns of strengths and weaknesses. Can you think of an example of how a description of ASD with specifiers might look? Sidebar 5.2 provides a description of ASD with specifiers.

SIDEBAR 5.2: HOW IS A *DSM-5* DIAGNOSIS OF ASD WITH SPECIFIERS COMMUNICATED?

299.00 Autism Spectrum Disorder; Requiring Substantial Support for deficits in Social Communication and Social Interaction (moderate severity); Requiring Support with Restricted Repetitive Behaviors, Interests, and Activities (mild severity); Without Accompanying Intellectual Impairment; Without Accompanying Language Impairment.

Differential Diagnosis

Given that ASD encompasses a complex set of deficits in social-emotional reciprocity; deficits in nonverbal communicative behaviors; deficiency in developing, maintaining, and understanding relationships; and restricted, repetitive patterns of behavior, interests, or activities that may vary along a continuum, distinguishing ASD from other neurodevelopmental disorders or psychopathological conditions is critical (Matson, Nebel-Schwalm, & Matson, 2007). According to the *DSM-5*, several differential diagnoses should be considered in the context of evaluation for ASD. These include selective mutism, language or communication disorders, intellectual disability, stereotypic movement disorder, ADHD, and schizophrenia. Other important differential diagnoses include other genetic conditions (e.g., fragile X syndrome and Rett syndrome). It is possible that an individual can meet criteria for both ASD and ADHD (because research indicates about 30 percent of ASD individuals have comorbid ADHD and ASD; Simonoff et al., 2008) or can have a medical condition (e.g. fragile X syndrome) and still meet criteria for ASD, but clinical judgment is important for determining whether a single diagnosis or multiple diagnoses are necessary.

Selective mutism is an anxiety disorder that refers to a consistent failure to speak in social situations, despite showing the ability to speak in other contexts (APA, 2013). Selective mutism is primarily associated with social anxiety (Chavira, Shipon-Blum, Hitchcock, Cohan, & Stein, 2007), although it can be difficult to distinguish from ASD

(Cline & Baldwin, 2004). Selective mutism is distinct from ASD in that individuals with selective mutism likely possess appropriate communication abilities in some settings and do not typically show deficits in social interaction or patterns of restricted or repetitive behaviors. Moreover, Leonard and Dow (1995) suggest that failure to speak associated with selective mutism is usually unique to school, whereas communication deficits are evident across multiple contexts in ASD.

Communication disorders, including social (pragmatic) communication disorder, are conceptualized as persistent deficits in language use involving either comprehension or production (APA, 2013). Language disorders are not commonly associated with nonverbal social communication difficulties or restrictive and repetitive behaviors. Criteria for social (pragmatic) communication disorder may be met when an individual presents with social communication difficulties but does not have a history of nor presents with the restricted, repetitive behaviors essential to an ASD diagnosis. There is some debate as to whether the two diagnoses are also distinguishable by their social communication profiles, although there is still considerable research needed to examine similarities and differences between the (relatively) new diagnostic categories (e.g., Gibson, Adams, Lockton, & Green, 2013; Reisinger, Cornish, & Fombonne, 2011).

Intellectual disability, or intellectual developmental disorder, is diagnosed following evidence of deficits in intellectual abilities and adaptive behaviors (APA, 2013), and intellectual disability and ASD are frequently comorbid (Matson & Shoemaker, 2009). According to the *DSM-5*, comorbid diagnoses should be given when social communication abilities are significantly low for one's age compared with an individual's nonverbal skills. Intellectual disability without ASD should be diagnosed if this disparity between social-communicative and broader cognitive abilities is not observable. Moreover, presence of restricted, repetitive behaviors is essential for a diagnosis of ASD but not for intellectual disability.

The *DSM-5* also suggests that stereotypic movement disorder, ADHD, and schizophrenia may be considered as differential diagnoses in relation to ASD. Ritualized motor patterns are an essential diagnostic feature of ASD; thus, stereotypic movement disorder should be considered as an additional diagnosis when repetitive motor behaviors are associated with self-injury and harm and require targeted intervention (APA, 2013). Further, although attention deficits and hyperactivity are also commonly associated with ASD, a comorbid diagnosis of ADHD is suggested if attention difficulties are significantly elevated for one's age (APA, 2013; Taurines et al., 2012). ADHD was a mutually exclusive diagnosis with autistic disorder in the *DSM-IV-TR* (Goldstein & Schwebach, 2004), even though it was common to make this dual diagnosis in clinical practice. The *DSM-5* now allows for both ASD and ADHD diagnoses to be given simultaneously. Finally, schizophrenia, a psychotic disorder manifested by delusions, hallucinations, disorganized speech or behavior, and negative symptoms, such as diminished expressiveness, is often characterized by a prodromal state of social difficulties and atypical interests and beliefs (APA, 2013). Therefore, the behavioral presentation associated with a prodromal state of schizophrenia may be confused with ASD, although autism is not characterized by hallucinations and delusions. Moreover, schizophrenia is not associated with delayed achievement of early developmental milestones or developmental regression, unlike ASD; and the psychotic features of schizophrenia typically emerge between the late teens and the mid-30s; onset prior to adolescence is rare (APA, 2013). Detailed consideration of the aforementioned differential diagnoses informs clinical information regarding current symptoms and clinical course, aids in diagnostic interpretation, and facilitates the development of individualized treatment plans for ASD.

Finally, consideration of disorders with known biological origins that might share phenotypic characteristics with ASD is important. This includes disorders such as Rett syndrome and fragile X syndrome. For many of these disorders, genetic testing is often a useful addition to behavioral testing if these disorders are suspected. Rett syndrome was previously included in the *DSM-IV-TR*, but given its known etiological pathway, it is closer to other neurodevelopmental disorders, such as fragile X syndrome, and was not included in the *DSM-5* as a categorical diagnoses. For ASD that is associated with a known medical or genetic condition or environmental factor, counselors would record ASD associated with *name of condition, disorder, or factor* (e.g., autism spectrum disorder associated with Rett syndrome; APA, 2013).

Assessment Strategies

To promote the best outcomes for children with ASD, early assessment, identification, and intervention are necessary. Over half of parents express concerns within the child's first year of life, and almost 90 percent of parents express concerns by the time the child is 2 years old (Matson & Sipes, 2010). Typical early concerns include delayed language development, regression or loss of skills, not responding to verbal commands, and developmental delays compared with siblings (Wetherby et al., 2004). Early diagnosis can be difficult, given that many of the social deficits in ASD are in skills that do not emerge until later in development (even for typically developing peers) and given that a number of children with ASD display a pattern of developmental regression (Ozonoff et al., 2010). Thus, assessment for ASD should be comprehensive and multidisciplinary and integrate information from multiple settings and informants (Sheperis, Doggett, & Henington, 2005). Moreover, it is important that clinicians use standardized instruments that have good psychometric properties to aid their clinical judgment. It is critical that assessment approaches be individualized to a child's unique clinical profile and broader ecological environment, especially given that ASD is conceptualized as a spectrum of behaviors varying along a continuum of severity.

Assessment for ASD primarily involves a detailed developmental history across multiple contexts along with clinical observations of social interaction and play situations. One of the most challenging procedures of assessing for ASD is that it is a social disorder; therefore, observations must include opportunities for age-appropriate social interaction. Moreover, a child's behavior can vary greatly across contexts, so it is crucial to determine whether the behavior is specific to the situation. A number of scales and assessment measures exist for the evaluation and diagnosis of ASD (Barton, Dumont-Mathieu, & Fein, 2012; Matson & Sipes, 2010). In fact, "standardized behavioral diagnostic instruments with good psychometric properties, including caregiver interviews, questionnaires and clinician observation measures, are available and can improve reliability of diagnosis over time and across clinicians" (APA, 2013, p. 55). With this in mind, we now describe some of the most commonly used assessment tools.

ADI-R AND ADOS

The Autism Diagnostic Interview-Revised (ADI-R; Rutter, Le Couteur, & Lord, 2003) and the Autism Diagnostic Observation Schedule, Second Edition (ADOS-2; Lord et al.,

2012), are well-established assessment methods for ASD. Even before the publication of the *DSM-5*, these measures treated autism-related symptoms on a spectrum. The introduction of the autism spectrum concept in the *DSM-5* made these measures even more useful as part of the diagnostic process. Although these tools are often described as the gold standard assessment tools for ASD, it is important to note that neither of these tools provides a definitive diagnosis; they both constitute ways to gather information on the child as part of a clinical evaluation (Lord et al., 2012; Rutter et al., 2003). Clinical judgment based on *DSM-5* criteria should always be part of the diagnostic process as well.

The ADI-R is a comprehensive, standardized interview administered to a parent or caregiver who can report on a child's developmental history and current functioning. The interview can be used for both children and adults and contains 93 items that assess three functional domains:

1. Language/communication
2. Reciprocal social interactions
3. Restricted, repetitive, and stereotyped behaviors and interests

Moreover, the items on the ADI-R cover a broad content of behaviors and symptoms associated with ASD, including eight content areas (demographics, overview of behavior, early development and milestones, language acquisition, current functioning, social development and play, interests and behaviors, and clinically relevant concerns, including aggression and self-injury).

The ADOS-2 is a semistructured, standardized clinical assessment of communication, social interaction and play, and restricted or repetitive behaviors (Lord et al., 2012). The ADOS involves the presentation of a set of standard activities designed to elicit behaviors associated with ASD. Structured activities and materials and less structured interactions provide standard contexts in which social, communicative, and other behaviors relevant to ASD are observed during a 45-minute to 1-hour period. In particular, the examiner presents the individual being assessed numerous opportunities to exhibit behaviors of interest in the diagnosis of ASD through standard *presses* for communication and social interaction. *Presses* consist of planned social interactions in which it has been determined in advance that a behavior of a particular type is likely to appear. The ADOS-2 consists of five modules that can be used for individuals of different ages and language abilities. The ADI-R and ADOS-2 have been used together to diagnose ASD and have been validated in numerous empirical studies (Ben Itzchak & Zachor, 2009; Hus, Pickles, Cook, Risi, & Lord, 2007; Lord & Risi, 1998).

PARENT REPORT INSTRUMENTS FOR ASSESSMENT OF ASD

A number of parent report measures have been developed and validated for use in the assessment of ASD. Some are designed for early identification, whereas others focus on a broader age range for identification. It is critical to integrate information from parent report with clinical observations and interviews, because evaluation of child functioning across multiple contexts is essential for the proper diagnosis of ASD. Many of these parent reports provide cutoff scores that should be interpreted as indicators of the need for more extensive ASD evaluation, rather than as definitive markers of having or not having a diagnosis. Moreover, it is important to follow up on the answers parents give to determine whether the answers the parents give are consistent with the intended meaning of the question.

The most widely used and accepted parent report scales include the Modified Checklist for Autism in Toddlers (M-CHAT; Robins, Fein, Barton, & Green, 2001); Baby and Infant Screen for Children with aUtIstic Traits (BISCUIT; Matson et al., 2009); Childhood Autism Rating Scale, Second Edition (CARS-2; Schopler & Van Bourgondien, 2010); Gilliam Autism Rating Scale, Third Edition (GARS-3; Gilliam, 2014); Early Screening of Autistic Traits Questionnaire (ESAT; Dietz, Swinkels, van Daalen, van Engeland, & Buitelaar, 2006); and Social Communication Questionnaire (SCQ; Rutter, Bailey, Berument, Lord, & Pickles, 2003). These instruments have been empirically validated for use in the assessment of ASD in combination with clinical observation methods (e.g., Allen, Silove, Williams, & Hutchins, 2007; Scambler, Hepburn, & Rogers, 2006; Snow & Lecavalier, 2008). Whereas the M-CHAT, BISCUIT, and ESAT are designed for early identification, the CARS-2, SCQ, and GARS-3 were developed to assess ASD across a broader age range.

Related Assessment Strategies for ASD

A number of broader assessment strategies and instruments have been suggested to clarify individual profiles of strengths and weaknesses across a broad range of functioning within the context of evaluation for ASD. For example, it is necessary to obtain measures of cognitive abilities, as well as expressive and receptive language functioning. In particular, this is necessary to determine whether an individual also presents with intellectual or language impairment. Furthermore, these measures can help distinguish ASD from differential diagnoses, including intellectual disability, language disorders, or social (pragmatic) communication disorder. Achievement testing (e.g, Woodcock-Johnson III Tests of Achievement) would also help clarify whether specific learning difficulties are also present.

In addition to cognitive and language assessment, it is also recommended to obtain measures of adaptive behavior and socioemotional symptoms. An important component of the *DSM-5* ASD criteria is that the ASD symptoms interfere significantly with some aspect of social, occupational, or other important areas of current functioning. Clinically relevant deficits in the areas of adaptive behavior, communication, daily living skills, and socialization are commonly measured using the Vineland Adaptive Behavior Scales, Second Edition (Sparrow, Balla, & Cicchetti, 2005). Moreover, it would also be informative to assess ADHD-related behaviors at school and home, because abnormalities of attention are often present among individuals with ASD. Further assessment of socioemotional systems (e.g., home environment, peer group, school, or social support networks) would provide information regarding comorbid symptoms that may interfere with an individual's functioning or treatment progress (e.g., anxious distress, self-harm, and aggression). Finally, medical evaluations may consider motor function abilities, hearing, or concomitant medical conditions that may further influence an individual's everyday functioning. Genetic testing is also recommended in many cases. For example, fragile X, DiGeorge, and Rett syndromes (among others) are commonly associated with ASD behaviors, and DNA analysis would provide diagnostic clarity. Therefore, comprehensive, multidisciplinary assessment that incorporates information from multiple sources and environments is needed to inform intervention efforts for individuals with ASD. The ASD

Video Glossary (https://www.autismspeaks.org/what-autism/video-glossary) is a helpful resource for parents and professionals who are learning to identify early signs of ASD.

Treatment Strategies and Interventions

It should not be surprising that, for a disorder defined by behaviors, treatments that target behaviors are often the most successful. Among the wide range of treatment options available for children and adolescents with ASD, treatment approaches using applied behavior analysis (ABA) strategies have received the most empirical support (Vismara & Rogers, 2010). Broadly, ABA techniques involve the application of basic learning principles to social interactions and problem solving. As such, primary elements of ABA are derived from behavioral principles of reinforcement and extinction (Granpeesheh, Tarbox, Dixon, Carr, & Herbert, 2009). Reinforcement refers to the strengthening of behavior associated with desirable consequences, whereas extinction refers to the reduction of behavior when reinforcement is removed. Reinforcement and extinction can be probed through four primary teaching methods: (1) prompting (presentation of cues or assistance to facilitate behavior), (2) fading (gradual removal of prompt so that behavior continues independently), (3) shaping (scaffolding successive approximations to promote desired behavior), and (4) chaining (chunking complex behaviors into a sequence of smaller, simpler behaviors that are successively taught; Granpeesheh et al., 2009). ABA intervention approaches integrate these behavioral elements across different modalities and can generally be classified into two broad categories: those that are designed as comprehensive to address all developmental domains, and those that are skills based and focused on a more specific set of goals.

Discrete trial training (Lovaas, 1981; Smith, 2001) involves breaking down skills into small components and teaching each component through blocks of adult-structured learning trials. Systematic contingent reinforcement, shaping, and explicit prompting are all used to elicit and maintain child production of target responses or skills to each trial. A variety of behaviors have been facilitated through discrete trial training, including speech in nonverbal children (Tsiouri, Simmons, & Paul, 2012), conversation (Krantz, Zalenski, Hall, Fenske, & McClannahan, 1981), and receptive and expressive language skills (Howlin, 1981; Lovaas, 1977). Lovaas (1987) also found that discrete trial training was associated with higher intellectual and emotional functioning among children with ASD. Though quite successful, this approach has also been criticized for its lack of generalizability in more naturalistic settings where there is not such tight stimulus control and adult structure (Vismara & Rogers, 2010).

More recent interventions that have focused on using naturalistic learning opportunities include incidental teaching (McGee, Daly, Izeman, Mann, & Risley, 1991) and pivotal response training (PRT; Koegel, Koegel, Harrower, & Carter, 1999). PRT places emphasis on pivotal areas likely to affect broad aspects of functioning, such as improving social motivation, a core deficit associated with impairments in ASD (Dawson, Webb, & McPartland, 2005). In particular, Vismara and Bogin (2009) emphasized that PRT should involve sequential steps that address "pivotal learning variables," including motivation, responding to multiple cues, self-management, and self-initiation. Moreover, a central feature of PRT is that instruction is integrated within child-centered activities that provide a naturalistic opportunity for the child to communicate and socialize within the context of play.

Interventions for children with ASD have also focused on the facilitation of communication, language, and social interaction skills. For example, Verbal Behavior Therapy uses ABA techniques to promote four primary communicative behaviors: requesting, commenting, responding, and repeating (Sheperis, Mohr, & Ammons, 2014). Both verbal and nonverbal forms of communication have been shown to be enhanced with Verbal Behavior Therapy (Carbone, Sweeney-Kerwin, Attanasio, & Kasper, 2010; Kelley, Shillingsburg, Castro, Addison, & LaRue, 2007). In addition to Verbal Behavior Therapy, several intervention approaches have integrated various strategies to promote language and social skills. For example, social pragmatic strategies use the child's individual interests as a framework for promoting social interaction and language production that is tailored to the home environment (Ingersoll, Dvortcsak, Whalen, & Sikora, 2005).

A range of naturalistic interventions have focused on promoting communication and social skills within the child's unique environment and involving parents and families. The most common example of this type of approach is the Developmental, Individual-Difference, Relationship-Based (DIR) model, or Floortime. This approach relies on parent engagement in joint activities with the child to promote social awareness, shared attention, and problem-solving skills (Greenspan & Wieder, 1997). A defining characteristic of this approach is that the parent follows the child's lead and operates at the child's level, whatever the child might be doing at the time. This approach is often integrated as part of a broader treatment approach that includes ABA-based therapeutic approaches.

DEVELOPMENTAL FRAMEWORK FOR ABA INTERVENTIONS

A number of interventions have integrated ABA techniques within a developmental framework to assess and intervene with children with ASD (Dawson et al., 2010; Rogers & Vismara, 2008). These programs, which include the Denver Model and the Early Start Denver Model (ESDM; Dawson et al., 2010), involve rigorous initial assessments of child functioning across multiple developmental domains, which are used to create individual profiles of functioning. These individual developmental profiles then inform the development of specific interventions tailored to each child's needs. In particular, ESDM involves the instruction of developmental, social, and communicative skills that can be implemented in various settings and delivered by parents. In a two-year randomized control trial of ESDM, children receiving the ESDM treatment showed significant gains in IQ, adaptive functioning, and language relative to children who received treatment as usual in the community (Dawson et al., 2010).

A second notable treatment approach is the Treatment and Education of Autistic and Related Communication Handicapped Children (TEACCH) program (Mesibov, Shea, & Schopler, 2004). Similar to the Denver Model, TEACCH also emphasizes the role of comprehensive assessment and individual profiles of strengths and weaknesses as central to informing intervention. Additionally, TEACCH includes a heavy focus on psychoeducation, parental collaboration and involvement in treatment, and using parents as cotherapists in the intervention (Schopler, Mesibov, & Baker, 1982). Overall, the TEACCH model is associated with improvements in parent skills as well as in child outcomes and meets criteria for an evidence-based, comprehensive treatment model for children with ASD (Odom, Boyd, Hall, & Hume, 2010).

Efforts to promote socioemotional functioning further among children with ASD have been manifested in a novel treatment approach known as Social Communication,

Emotional Regulation, and Transactional Support (SCERTS; Prizant, Wetherby, Rubin, Laurent, & Rydell, 2006). This model integrates ABA methods that have been previously shown to enhance social communication with techniques for promoting emotion regulation and transactional support (Prizant, Wetherby, Rubin, & Laurent, 2003). Emotion regulation techniques focus on facilitating the child's ability to self-regulate, seek support from others, and recover from dysregulation. Techniques designed to foster transactional support involve promotion of support across multiple domains of the child's environment (e.g., education and learning, interpersonal, and family). This intervention approach has been shown to promote communication and positive affect among children with ASD (Wetherby & Woods, 2006).

Moving forward, increasing research emphasis on intervention outcomes and mechanisms supporting or thwarting intervention effectiveness is needed. As Karst and van Hecke (2012) noted, it will be particularly essential for ASD interventions to include parent and family outcomes to fully understand effectiveness of treatment. Additionally, given recent evidence that some children with ASD are able to achieve optimal outcomes following intervention such that they no longer meet criteria for an ASD, it will be essential for research to better delineate the factors and mechanisms contributing to this positive developmental trajectory (Kelley, Naigles, & Fein, 2010). Further identification of specific mediators and moderators of improvement in ASD symptomatology in the context of intervention studies will provide guidance on where, when, and how to intervene to support children with ASD best.

Evaluation Strategies

There is a growing corpus of data showing that many individuals with ASD can achieve positive outcomes. One challenge in discussing prognosis is that there are differences in how ASD is viewed that can affect how prognosis, treatment goals, and treatment effectiveness are interpreted. For example, some individuals with ASD and some researchers have argued that ASD isn't as much a disorder as it is a different way of processing the world (Happé, 1999). Others have used a medical model to argue that autism is a disease or an epidemic that needs to be cured (see Gernsbacher, Dawson, & Hill Goldsmith, 2005 for a critique of this view). These examples are extremes, and there are many views of ASD that lie in between these examples. Regardless of one's own perception of the disorder, it is important to understand the factors that affect outcomes and the best way to evaluate the effectiveness of an approach.

We are just beginning to understand risk or protective factors that can lead to different outcomes in ASD. Part of the reason for the lack of information on outcomes stems from the fact that the diagnosis itself is relatively new (APA, 1980) and the criteria have been evolving over time. Only recently has there been a growth in long-term data on predictors of outcomes for individuals with ASD. Even these data have been inconsistent. For example, one review indicated that reports of individuals who no longer meet criteria for autism range from 3 to 25 percent (Helt et al., 2008), and these findings are complicated by the fact that some of these individuals might have been initially misdiagnosed (Sutera et al., 2007).

Data on prognosis falls into two types: (1) long-term outcomes and (2) optimal outcomes. The two types of information look at outcomes from two perspectives. One line of research examines common outcomes for a broad range of individuals with

ASD, regardless of their life trajectory. The major finding in this research has been that outcomes for individuals with ASD are variable, with some individuals showing great improvements, some showing stability of functioning, and others showing a deterioration of functioning over time (Levy & Perry, 2011). Factors that have been found to influence outcomes include severity of autism symptomatology, level of cognitive functioning, language development, comorbid psychopathology, and access to services (Levy & Perry, 2011). It has been demonstrated that outcomes do not differ based on onset of symptoms (regression versus early delays; Shumway et al., 2011). Importantly, recent research has shown that early and intensive behavioral treatments have had a very significant impact on outcomes for individuals with ASD, both in the short term and the long term (e.g., Eikeseth, Klintwall, Jarh, & Karlsson, 2012). It is important to note that a reduction in ASD symptomatology does not always directly translate into positive long-term outcomes in other areas of functioning. Howlin (2013) found that for many adults with ASD, social inclusion remained very limited even with improvements in autism symptomatology with age. Therefore, it is important for clinicians to consider the broader social difficulties related to ASD beyond the symptoms.

A second line of research that contributes to our understanding of prognosis is *optimal outcomes* research. This research examines individuals with ASD who no longer meet criteria for the disorder and examines factors that might have contributed to these optimal outcomes.

Although this recovery pattern has been acknowledged as a provocative finding (Elsabbagh & Johnson, 2010; Rogers, 2009), recent research has shown that optimal outcomes are a legitimate pathway and not related to a misdiagnosis (Ozonoff, 2013). This line of research is in its infancy, but early findings have shown that major predictors involve lower difficulties in the social domain—repetitive behaviors and language deficits were not related to optimal outcomes—and early and intensive behavioral treatment (Fein et al., 2013; Sutera et al., 2007).

Monitoring the effectiveness of a treatment approach is an ongoing challenge in the ASD field. Social behavior and play is complex and changes over time; therefore, it is difficult to develop measures that are sensitive to these changes. As such, a staggering number of outcome measures are used in treatment research, a fact that can be overwhelming to a practicing clinician (Bolte & Diehl, 2013). Clinicians who are monitoring the effectiveness of their approach need to consider several factors. First, it is important to look for improvement beyond the skill therapy is targeting. For example, are improvements in social communication also reducing repetitive behaviors? Second, even if clients are showing improvement in social skills, are these skills translating into real-world situations (i.e., social performance)? Finally, the most effective approaches will not only affect core characteristics of ASD, but they will also have an impact on adaptive behavior. It is important to consider progress in terms of the entire individual, not just the characteristics of the individual that relate to ASD.

Diagnostic Challenges

Broadly speaking, the biggest challenge facing clinicians working with individuals with ASD is the ability to stay current on assessment best practices because about 70 percent of individuals with ASD may have one comorbid mental disorder, and 40 percent may have two or more comorbid mental disorders (Simonoff et al., 2008). For example, the substantial changes in the diagnostic criteria, including the introduction of levels of severity, will be a challenge for clinicians in the near future as they shift from a categorical to a spectrum conceptualization. Moreover, it will take time and ongoing psychometric validation for assessment measures to change from *DSM-IV-TR* categorical criteria to *DSM-5* dimensional criteria. It will be important for clinicians to be aware of the status of the measures used. Additionally, not all state education agencies' and local school districts' special education criteria changed with the introduction of the *DSM-5*, so clinicians must be adept with the *DSM-5* and how to communicate and advocate collaboratively with various professionals. The addition of social (pragmatic) communication disorder will present diagnostic challenges. The major diagnostic difference in the *DSM-5* between ASD and social (pragmatic) communication disorder is the presence of restricted, repetitive behaviors in ASD at some point during the child's developmental history. These restricted or repetitive behaviors might not be present at the time of diagnosis, so clinicians will need to rely on parent report measures and developmental history to determine the appropriate diagnosis. There is still considerable research needed on the presence or absence of differential diagnostic profiles in other areas of functioning, so clinicians will need to stay up-to-date on the latest research comparing these two diagnoses.

Early identification and diagnosis continues to be a challenge for parents and clinicians. Despite the fact that, for many, symptoms become apparent in the first 18 months of life, the average age of first evaluation is still much later (Giarelli et al., 2010). Even after first evaluation, there is an average gap of 12 to 15 months before children receive their first diagnosis, and children on average do not receive their first diagnosis until two to three years after their first symptoms are identified (Giarelli et al., 2010). This is a significant issue, given that early diagnosis and subsequent access to empirically supported treatment are some of the most important predictors of outcomes. Moreover, clinicians must be aware that typical development followed by regression in the first two years of life is much more common than previously reported and should be considered one of the many possible pathways to an ASD diagnosis.

There are several issues related to females with ASD and low socioeconomic status (SES) families as well. Boys are more likely than girls to receive an ASD diagnosis even when presenting with similar symptoms, whereas girls are more likely than boys to be diagnosed with another condition, such as intellectual disability or general developmental delay (Giarelli et al., 2010). Moreover, it takes longer for girls to receive a diagnosis of ASD after a first evaluation than boys (Giarelli et al., 2010). There is considerable evidence that genetic factors in part contribute to the difference in prevalence between boys and girls (Volkmar et al., 2004), but it is important for researchers and clinicians to consider possible biases in applying the diagnosis.

Families from low-income, higher-risk communities may have less access to health care services (Hansson, 2003). In particular, disparities in insurance coverage and in the geospatial availability of mental health service providers constitute primary barriers for individuals seeking care in low-income communities (Guagliardo, 2004; Hansson, 2003). These service barriers are compounded by a host of other factors that influence the accessibility and use of health care services, including perceived stigma of mental illness, automobile accessibility, and public transportation availability (Ronzio, Guagliardo, & Persaud, 2006). Furthermore, previous estimates suggest low availability of specialized services in schools (Adelman & Taylor, 1993; Braden, DiMarino-Linnen, & Good, 2001; Flaherty, Weist, & Warner, 1996) and the prevalence of youth services have been shown to be more strongly related to supply variables (e.g., grants and funding) than to demonstrated need for services (Esparza, 2009). Thus, it is necessary to consider service accessibility for ASD, especially among high-risk communities where there may be significant barriers to health care access and use.

Clinicians must also consider that individuals with ASD are part of a family, and families of individuals with ASD face certain challenges that stem from the diagnosis. For example, the economic impact on a family of raising a child with ASD has been estimated to be three to five million dollars more than raising a typically developing child (Lord & Bishop, 2010). Generally, ASD diagnoses have been associated with reduced parent feelings of self-efficacy and increased parenting stress relative to parents of typically developing children (Hoffman, Sweeney, Hodge, Lopez-Wagner, & Looney, 2009) and parents of children with other developmental delays (Schieve et al., 2011). Moreover, having a child with ASD has been associated with general increase in parent mental health concerns, especially depression and anxiety (Singer & Floyd, 2006). Focusing more broadly on the family and marital systems, data indicate that the divorce rate among couples with a child with ASD is approximately two times greater than among couples who are parenting typically developing children (Hartley et al., 2010). High parenting stress can lead to increased externalizing of behavior problems over time in children with ASD (Baker et al., 2003). Similarly, family conflict is predictive of greater ASD symptom severity (Kelly, Garnett, Attwood, & Peterson, 2008), highlighting that children with ASD are susceptible to the negative effects of interparental conflict just as are typically developing children. As such, it is important to consider the entire family when developing a treatment plan.

Differential diagnosis of ASD and other disorders will continue to be a challenge. ADHD, in particular, is thought to be highly comorbid with ASD (Jang et al., 2013). Previously in the *DSM-IV-TR* ADHD and PDDs were rule-out diagnoses for each other; by definition, you could not meet criteria for both diagnoses (Jang et al., 2013). Interestingly, many children still received both diagnoses in clinical practice (Jang et al., 2013). The *DSM-5* represents an important change in that you now can receive both diagnoses. Still, it will be difficult (and important) for clinicians to determine the utility of a single primary diagnosis of ASD or ADHD versus a dual diagnosis. For example, what might appear to be inattention in an individual with ASD might be better characterized as sensitivity to sensory stimuli in certain circumstances. It will be important to understand the context and cause of the behavior in addition to the behavior itself.

Summary

At its core, ASD is a neurodevelopmental disorder that is defined by persistent impairment in reciprocal social communication and social interaction, and by restricted, repetitive patterns of behavior, interest, or activities that become apparent in the first two years of life. ASD consists of deficits in social communication or interaction, and of repetitive behaviors or stereotyped interests. Importantly, these behaviors vary widely in the ASD population. There is no singular cause of autism; multiple factors contribute to the risk of developing the disorder. Substantial changes in the diagnostic criteria between the *DSM-IV-TR* and the *DSM-5* exist, the most important being the establishment of a singular ASD classification that replaces previous diagnoses grouped under the category of Pervasive Developmental Disorders. Early diagnosis remains critical (albeit challenging) because early detection and early access to treatment are important predictors of positive outcomes in this population. The most successful treatments involve teaching and altering behavior. Treatment approaches using ABA strategies (e.g., discrete trial training, incidental teaching, and Verbal Behavior) have received the most empirical support. Importantly, there has been a recent movement to implement ABA intervention strategies within a developmental framework (e.g., Early Start Denver Model, TEACCH, and SCERTS) that changes foci as the children age. Important areas of future research and clinical attention involve identifying early cues to the disorder in infants and toddlers, understanding the manifestation of the disorder in females, and improving the speed and effectiveness of treatment. ASD has gone through substantial changes in how it is defined and understood over the past two decades, and it continues to evolve. It is crucial for clinicians to keep abreast of the latest in clinical research to ensure the highest quality of care. The References provide additional information relating to chapter topics.

References

Adelman, H. S., & Taylor, L. (1993). School-based mental health: Toward a comprehensive approach. *The Journal of Mental Health Administration, 20*(1), 32–45. doi:10.1007/BF02521401.

Allen, C., Silove, N., Williams, K., & Hutchins, P. (2007). Validity of the social communication questionnaire in assessing risk of autism in preschool children with developmental problems. *Journal of Autism and Developmental Disorders, 37*(7), 1272–1278. doi:10.1007/s10803-006-0279-7

American Psychiatric Association. (1952). *Diagnostic and statistical manual of mental disorders*. Washington, DC: Author.

American Psychiatric Association. (1968). *Diagnostic and statistical manual of mental disorders* (2nd ed.). Washington, DC: Author.

American Psychiatric Association. (1980). *Diagnostic and statistical manual of mental disorders* (3rd ed.). Washington, DC: Author.

American Psychiatric Association. (2000). *Diagnostic and statistical manual of mental disorders* (4th ed., text rev.). Washington, DC: Author.

American Psychiatric Association. (2013). *Diagnostic and statistical manual of mental disorders* (5th ed.). Arlington, VA: American Psychiatric Publishing.

Asperger, H. (1944). Die "autistischen psychopathen" im kindesalter. *Archive für Psychiatrie und Nervenkrankheiten, 117*, 76–136. doi:10.1007/BF01837709

Attwood, T. (2003). Understanding and managing circumscribed interests. In M. Prior (Ed.), *Learning and Behavior Problems in Asperger Syndrome* (pp. 126–147). New York, NY: Guilford Press.

Baker, B. L., McIntyre, L. L., Blacher, J., Crnic, K., Edelbrock, C., & Low, C. (2003). Pre-school children with and without developmental delay: Behaviour problems and parenting stress over time. *Journal of Intellectual Disability Research, 47*(4–5), 217–230. doi:10.1046/j.1365-2788.2003.00484.x

Barton, M. L., Dumont-Mathieu, T., & Fein, D. (2012). Screening young children for autism spectrum disorders in primary practice. *Journal of Autism and Developmental Disorders, 42*(6), 1165–1174. doi:10.1007/s10803-011-1343-5

Belmonte, M. K., & Bourgeron, T. (2006). Fragile X syndrome and autism at the intersection of genetic and neural networks. *Nature Neuroscience, 9*(10), 1221–1225. doi:10.1038/nn1765

Ben Itzchak, E., & Zachor, D. A. (2009). Change in autism classification with early intervention: Predictors and outcomes. *Research in Autism Spectrum Disorders, 3*(4), 967–976. doi:10.1016/j.rasd.2009.05.001

Blumberg, S. J., Bramlett, M. D., Kogan, M. D., Schieve, L. A., Jones, J. R., & Lu, M. C. (2013, March 20). Changes in prevalence of parent-reported autism spectrum disorder in school-aged US children: 2007 to 2011–2012. *National Health Statistics Reports, 65*, 1–11. Retrieved from http://www.sased.org/vimages/shared/vnews/stories/513f815505c21/AUTISM%20National%20Health%20Statistics%203%2020%2013.pdf

Bolte, E., & Diehl, J. J. (2013). Measurement tools and target symptoms/skills used to assess treatment response in individuals with autism spectrum disorder. *Journal of Autism and Developmental Disorders, 43*(11), 2491–2501. doi:10.1007/s10803-013-1798-7

Boyd, B. A., Baranek, G. T., Sideris, J., Poe, M. D., Watson, L. R., Patten, E., & Miller, H. (2010). Sensory features and repetitive behaviors in children with autism and developmental delays. *Autism Research, 3*(2), 78–87. doi:10.1002/aur.124

Braden, J. S., DiMarino-Linnen, E., & Good, T. L. (2001). Schools, society, and school psychologists: History and future directions. *Journal of School Psychology, 39*(2), 203–219. doi:10.1016/S0022-4405(01)00056-5

Carbone, V. J., Sweeney-Kerwin, E. J., Attanasio, V., & Kasper, T. (2010). Increasing the vocal responses of children with autism and developmental disabilities using manual since mand training and prompt delay. *Journal of Applied Behavior Analysis, 43*(4), 705–709. doi:10.1901/jaba.2010.43–705

Chavira, D. A. Shipon-Blum, E., Hitchcock, C., Cohan, S., & Stein, M. B. (2007). Selective mutism and social anxiety disorder: All in the family? *Journal of the American Academy of Child & Adolescent Psychiatry, 46*(11), 1464–1472. doi:10.1097/chi.0b013e318149366a

Cline, T., & Baldwin, S. (2004). *Selective mutism in children*. London, United Kingdom: Whurr.

Constantino, J. N., Todorov, A., Hilton, C., Law, P., Zhang, Y., Molloy, E., … Geschwind, D. (2013). Autism recurrence in half siblings: Strong support for genetic mechanisms of transmission in ASD. *Mol Psychiatry, 18*(2), 137–138. doi:10.1038/mp.2012.9

Dawson, G., Rogers, S., Munson, J., Smith, M., Winter, J., Greenson, J., ... Varley, J. (2010). Randomized, controlled trial of an intervention for toddlers with autism: The Early Start Denver Model. *Pediatrics*, *125*(1), e17-e23. doi:10.1542/peds.2009-0958

Dawson, G., Webb, S. J., & McPartland, J. (2005). Understanding the nature of face processing impairment in autism: Insights from behavioral and electrophysiological studies. *Developmental Neuropsychology*, *27*(3), 403–424. doi:10.1207/s15326942dn2703_6

Dietz, C., Swinkels, S., van Daalen, E., van Engeland, H., & Buitelaar, J. K. (2006). Screening for autistic spectrum disorder in children aged 14–15 months. II: Population screening with the Early Screening of Autistic Traits Questionnaire (ESAT). Design and general findings. *Journal of Autism and Developmental Disorders*, *36*(6), 713–722. doi:10.1007/s10803-006-0114-1

Eikeseth, S., Klintwall, L., Jahr, E., & Karlsson, P. (2012). Outcome for children with autism receiving early and intensive behavioral intervention in mainstream preschool and kindergarten settings. *Research in Autism Spectrum Disorders*, *6*(2), 829–835. doi:10.1016/j.rasd.2011.09.002

Elsabbagh, M., & Johnson, M. H. (2010). Infancy and autism: Progress, prospects, and challenges. *Progress in Brain Research*, *164*, 355–383. doi:10.1016/S0079-6123(07)64020-5

Esparza, N. (2009). Community factors influencing the prevalence of homeless youth services. *Children and Youth Services Review*, *31*(12), 1321–1329. doi:10.1016/j.childyouth.2009.06.010

Fein, D., Barton, M., Eigsti, I. M., Kelley, E., Naigles, L., Schultz, R. T., ... Tyson, K. (2013). Optimal outcome in individuals with a history of autism. *Journal of Child Psychology and Psychiatry*, *54*(2), 195–205. doi:10.1111/jcpp.12037

Flaherty, L. T., Weist, M. D., & Warner, B. S. (1996). School-based mental health services in the United States: History, current models and needs. *Community Mental Health Journal*, *32*(4), 341–352. doi:10.1007/BF02249452

Fombonne, E. (2005). The changing epidemiology of autism. *Journal of Applied Research in Intellectual Disabilities*, *18*(4), 281–294. doi:10.1111/j.1468-3148.2005.00266.x

Gernsbacher, M. A., Dawson, M., & Hill Goldsmith, H. (2005). Three reasons not to believe in an autism epidemic. *Current Directions in Psychological Science*, *14*(2), 55–58. doi:10.1111/j.0963-7214.2005.00334.x

Giarelli, E., Wiggins, L. D., Rice, C. E., Levy, S. E., Kirby, R. S., Pinto-Martin, J., & Mandell, D. (2010). Sex differences in the evaluation and diagnosis of autism spectrum disorders among children. *Disability and Health Journal*, *3*(2), 107–116. doi:10.1016/j.dhjo.2009.07.001

Gibson, J., Adams, C., Lockton, E., & Green J. (2013). Social communication disorder outside autism? A diagnostic classification approach to delineating pragmatic language impairment, high-functioning autism and specific language impairment. *Journal of Child Psychology and Psychiatry*, *54*(11), 1186–197. doi:10.1111/jcpp.12079

Gilliam, J. E. (2014). *The Gilliam Autism Rating Scale* (3rd ed.). Los Angeles, CA: Western Psychological Services.

Goldstein, S., & Schwebach, A. (2004). The comorbidity of pervasive developmental disorder and attention deficit hyperactivity disorder: Results of a retrospective chart review. *Journal of Autism and Developmental Disorders*, *34*(3), 329–339.

Gotham, K., Risi, S., Pickles, A., & Lord, C. (2007). The autism diagnostic observation schedule: Revised algorithms for improved diagnostic validity. *Journal of Autism and Developmental Disorders*, *37*(4), 613–627. doi:10.1023/B:JADD.0000029554.46570.68

Granpeesheh, D., Tarbox, J., Dixon, D. R., Carr, E., & Herbert, M. (2009). Retrospective analysis of clinical records in 38 cases of recovery from autism. *Annals of Clinical Psychiatry*, *21*(4), 195–204.

Greenspan, S. I., & Wieder, S. (1997). Developmental patterns and outcomes in infants and children with disorders in relating and communicating: A chart review of 200 cases of children with autistic spectrum diagnoses. *Journal of Developmental and Learning Disorders*, *1*(1), 87–142.

Guagliardo, M. F. (2004). Spatial accessibility of primary care: Concepts, methods and challenges. *International Journal of Health Geographics*, *3*(1), 3. doi:10.1186/1476-072X-3-3.

Guthrie, W., Swineford, L. B., Wetherby, A. M., & Lord C. (2013). Comparison of *DSM-IV* and *DSM-5* factor structure models for toddlers with autism spectrum disorder. *Journal of American Academy of Child & Adolescent Psychiatry*, *52*(8), 797–805. doi:10.1016/j.jaac.2013.05.004

Hansson, L. (2003). Inequality and inequity in use of mental health services. *Acta Psychiatrica Scandinavica*, *107*(3), 161–162. doi:10.1034/j.1600-0447.2003.00076.x

Happé, F. (1999). Autism: Cognitive deficit or cognitive style? *Trends in Cognitive Sciences*, *3*(6), 216–222. doi:10.1016/S1364-6613(99)01318-2

Hartley, S. L., Barker, E. T., Seltzer, M. M., Floyd, F., Greenberg, J., Orsmond, G., & Bolt, D. (2010). The relative risk and timing of divorce in families of children with an autism spectrum disorder. *Journal of Family Psychology*, *24*(4), 449. doi: 10.1037/a0019847

Helt, M., Kelley, E., Kinsbourne, M., Pandey, J., Boorstein, H., Herbert, M., & Fein, D. (2008). Can children with autism recover? If so, how? *Neuropsychology Review*, *18*(4), 339–366. doi: 10.1007/s11065-008-9075-9

Hoffman, C. D., Sweeney, D. P., Hodge, D., Lopez-Wagner, M. C., & Looney, L. (2009). Parenting stress and closeness: Mothers of typically developing children and mothers of children with autism. *Focus on Autism and Other Developmental Disabilities*, *24*(3), 178–187. doi:10.1177/1088357609338715

Howlin, P. A. (1981). The effectiveness of operant language training with autistic children. *Journal of Autism and Developmental Disorders*, *11*(1), 89–105. doi:10.1007/BF01531343

Howlin, P. (2013). Social disadvantage and exclusion: Adults with autism lag far behind in employment prospects. *Journal of the American Academy of Child & Adolescent Psychiatry*, *52*(9), 897–899. doi:10.1016/j.jaac.2013.06.010

Huerta, M., Bishop, S. L., Duncan, A., Hus, V., & Lord, C. (2012). Application of *DSM-5* criteria for autism spectrum disorder to three samples of children with DSM-IV diagnosis of pervasive developmental disorders. *American Journal of Psychiatry*, *169*(10), 1056–1064. doi:10.1176/appi.ajp.2012.12020276

Hus, V., Pickles, A., Cook, E. H., Risi, S., & Lord, C. (2007). Using the Autism Diagnostic Interview—Revised to increase phenotypic homogeneity in genetic studies of autism. *Biological Psychiatry*, *61*(4), 438–448. doi:10.1016/j.biopsych.2006.08.044

Hyman, S. E. (2010). The diagnosis of mental disorders: The problem of reification. *Annual Review of Clinical Psychology*, *6*, 155–179. doi:10.1146/annurev.clinpsy.3.022806.091532

Ingersoll, B., Dvortcsak, A., Whalen, C., & Sikora, D. (2005). The effects of a developmental, social-pragmatic language intervention on rate of expressive language production in young children with autistic spectrum disorders. *Focus on Autism and Other Developmental Disabilities*, *20*(4), 213–222. doi:10.1177/10883576050200040301

Jang, J., Matson, J. L., Williams, L. W., Tureck, K., Goldin, R. L., & Cervantes, P. E. (2013). Rates of comorbid symptoms in children with ASD, ADHD, and comorbid ASD and ADHD. *Research in Developmental Disabilities*, *34*(8), 2369–2378. doi:10.1016/j.ridd.2013.04.021

Kamp-Becker, I., Smidt, J., Ghahreman, M., Heinzel-Gutenbrunner, M., Becker, K., & Remschmidt, H. (2010). Categorical and dimensional structure of autism spectrum disorders: The nosologic validity of Asperger Syndrome. *Journal of Autism and Developmental Disorders*, *40*(8), 921–929. doi:10.1007/s10803-010-0939-5

Kanner, L. (1943). Autistic disturbances of affective contact. *Nervous Child*, *2*(3), 217–250.

Karst, J. S., & Van Hecke, A. V. (2012). Parent and family impact of autism spectrum disorders: A review and proposed model for intervention evaluation. *Clinical Child and Family Psychology Review*, *15*(3), 247–277. doi:10.1007/s10567-012-0119-6

Kelley, E., Naigles, L., & Fein, D. (2010). An in-depth examination of optimal outcome children with a history of autism spectrum disorders. *Research in Autism Spectrum Disorders*, *4*(3), 526–538. doi:10.1016/j.rasd.2009.12.001

Kelley, M. E., Shillingsburg, M. A., Castro, M. J., Addison, L. R., & LaRue, R. H. (2007). Further evaluation of emerging speech in children with developmental disabilities: Training verbal behavior. *Journal of Applied Behavior Analysis*, *40*(3), 431–445. doi:10.1901/jaba.2007.40–431

Kelly, A. B., Garnett, M. S., Attwood, T., & Peterson, C. (2008). Autism spectrum symptomatology in children: The impact of family and peer relationships. *Journal of Abnormal Child Psychology*, *36*(7), 1069–1081. doi:10.1007/s10802-008-9234-8

Koegel, L. K., Koegel, R. L., Harrower, J. K., & Carter, C. M. (1999). Pivotal response intervention I: Overview of approach. *Journal of the Association for Persons with Severe Handicaps*, *24*(3), 174–185. doi:10.2511/rpsd.24.3.174

Kogan, M. D., Blumberg, S. J., Schieve, L. A., Boyle, C. A., Perrin, J. M., Ghandour, R. M., ... van Dyck, P. C. (2009). Prevalence of parent-reported diagnosis of autism spectrum disorder among children in the US 2007. *Pediatrics*, *124*(5), 1395–1406. doi:10.1542/peds.2009-1522

Krantz, P. J., Zalenski, S., Hall, L. J., Fenske, E. C., & McClannahan, L. E. (1981). Teaching complex language to autistic children. *Analysis and Intervention in Developmental Disabilities*, *1*(3–4), 259–297. doi:10.1016/0270-4684(81)90003-3

Leekam, S. R., Prior, M. R., & Uljarevic, M. (2011). Restricted and repetitive behaviors in autism spectrum disorders: A review of research in the last decade. *Psychological Bulletin*, *137*(4), 562–593. doi:10.1037/a0023341

Leonard, H. L., & Dow, S. (1995). Selective mutism. In J. S. March (Ed.), *Anxiety disorders in children and adolescents* (pp. 235–250). New York, NY: Guilford Press.

Levy, A., & Perry, A. (2011). Outcomes in adolescents and adults with autism: A review of the literature. *Research in Autism Spectrum Disorders*, *5*(4), 1271–1282. doi:10.1016/j.rasd.2011.01.023

Lord, C., & Bishop, S. L. (2010). Autism spectrum disorders. *Social Policy Report*, *24*(2), 3–16.

Lord, C., & Jones, R. M. (2012). Annual research review: Re-thinking the classification of autism spectrum disorders. *Journal of Child Psychology and Psychiatry*, *53*(5), 490–509. doi:10.1111/j.1469–7610.2012.02547.x

Lord, C., & Richler, J. (2006). Early diagnosis of children with autism spectrum disorders. In T. Charman & W. L. Stone (Eds.), *Social and communication development in autism spectrum disorders: Early identification, diagnosis, and intervention.* (pp. 35–60). New York: Guilford Press.

Lord, C., & Risi, S. (1998). Frameworks and methods in diagnosing autism spectrum disorders. *Mental Retardation and Developmental Disabilities Research Reviews*, *4*(2), 90–96. doi:10.1002/(SICI)1098-2779(1998)4:2<90::AID-MRDD5>3.0.CO;2-0

Lord, C., Rutter, M., DiLavore, P. C., Risi, S., Gotham, K., & Bishop, S. L. (2012). *Autism Diagnostic Observation Schedule: ADOS-2*. Torrance, CA: Western Psychological Services.

Lovaas, O. I. (1977). *The autistic child: Language development through behavior modification*. Oxford, United Kingdom: Irvington.

Lovaas, O. I. (1981). *Teaching developmentally disabled children: The me book*. Austin, TX: PRO-ED.

Lovaas, O. I. (1987). Behavioral treatment and normal educational and intellectual functioning in young autistic children. *Journal of Consulting and Clinical Psychology*, *55*(1), 3–9.

Matson, J. L., Nebel-Schwalm, M., & Matson, M. L. (2007). A review of methodological issues in the differential diagnosis of autism spectrum disorders in children. *Research in Autism Spectrum Disorders*, *1*(1), 38–54. doi:10.1016/j.rasd.2006.07.004

Matson, J. L., & Shoemaker, M. (2009). Intellectual disability and its relationship to autism spectrum disorders. *Research in Developmental Disabilities*, *30*(6), 1107–1114. doi:10.1016/j.ridd.2009.06.003

Matson, J. L., & Sipes, M. (2010). Methods of early diagnosis and tracking for autism and pervasive developmental disorder not otherwise specified (PDDNOS). *Journal of Developmental and Physical Disabilities*, *22*(4), 343–358. doi:10.1007/s10882-009-9184-2

Matson, J. L., Wilkins, J., Sharp, B., Knight, C., Sevin, J. A., & Boisjoli, J. A. (2009). Sensitivity and specificity of the Baby and Infant Screen for Children with aUtIsm Traits (BISCUIT): Validity and cutoff scores for autism and PDD-NOS in toddlers. *Research in Autism Spectrum Disorders*, *3*(4), 924–930. doi:10.1016/j.rasd.2009.04.001

Mazefsky, C. A., McPartland, J. C., Gastgeb, H. Z., & Minshew, N. J. (2013). Brief report: Comparability of DSM-IV and DSM-5 ASD research samples. *Journal of Autism and Developmental Disorders*, *43*(5), 1236–1242. doi:10.1007/s10803-012-1665-y

McGee, G. G., Daly, T., Izeman, S. G., Mann, L. H., & Risley, T. (1991). Use of classroom materials to promote preschool engagement. *Teaching Exceptional Children*, *23*(4), 44–47.

Meindl, J. N., & Cannella-Malone, H. I. (2011). Initiating and responding to joint attention bids in children with autism: A review of the literature. *Research in Developmental Disabilities*, *32*(5), 1441–1454. doi:10.1016/j.ridd.2011.02.013

Mesibov, G. B., Shea, V., & Schopler, E. (2004). *The TEACCH approach to autism spectrum disorders*. New York, NY: Springer.

Odom, S. L., Boyd, B. A., Hall, L. J., & Hume, K. (2010). Evaluation of comprehensive treatment models for individuals with autism spectrum disorders. *Journal of Autism and Developmental Disorders*, *40*(4), 425–436. doi:10.1007/s10803-009-0825-1

Ozonoff, S. (2013). Editorial: Recovery from autism spectrum disorder (ASD) and the science of hope. *Journal of Child Psychology and Psychiatry*, *54*(2), 113–114. doi:10.1111/jcpp.12045

Ozonoff, S., Iosif, A., Baguio, F., Cook, I. C., Hill, M. M., Hutman, T., ... Young, G. S. (2010). A prospective study of the emergence of early behavioral signs of autism. *Journal of the American Academy of Child & Adolescent Psychiatry*, *49*(3), 256–266. doi:10.1097/00004583-201003000-00009

Prizant, B. M., Wetherby, A. M., Rubin, E., & Laurent, A. C. (2003). The SCERTS model: A transactional, family-centered approach to enhancing communication and socioemotional abilities of children with autism spectrum disorder. *Infants and Young Children*, *16*(4), 296–316.

Prizant, B. M., Wetherby, A. M., Rubin, E., Laurent, A. C., & Rydell, P. J. (2006). *The SCERTS model: A comprehensive educational approach for children with autism spectrum disorders*. Baltimore, MD: Paul H. Brookes.

Reisinger, L. M., Cornish, K. M., & Fombonne, É. (2011). Diagnostic differentiation of autism spectrum disorders and pragmatic language impairment. *Journal of Autism and Developmental Disorders*, *41*(12), 1694–704. doi:10.1007/s10803-011-1196-y

Robins, D. L., Fein, D., Barton, M. L., & Green, J. A. (2001). The Modified Checklist for Autism in Toddlers: An initial study investigating the early detection of autism and pervasive developmental disorders. *Journal of Autism and Developmental Disorders*, *31*(2), 131–144. doi:10.1023/A:1010738829569

Rogers, S. J. (2009). What are infant siblings teaching us about autism in infancy? *Autism Research*, *2*(3), 125–137. doi:10.1002/aur.81

Rogers, S. J., & Vismara, L. A. (2008). Evidence-based comprehensive treatments for early autism. *Journal of Clinical Child and Adolescent Psychology*, *37*(1), 8–38. doi:10.1080/15374410701817808

Ronzio, C. R., Guagliardo, M. F., & Persaud, N. (2006). Disparity in location of urban mental service providers. *American Journal of Orthopsychiatry*, *76*(1), 37–43. doi:10.1037/0002-9432.76.1.37

Rutter, M., Bailey, A., Berument, S. K., Lord, C., & Pickles, A. (2003a). *Social Communication Questionnaire (SCQ)*. Los Angeles, CA: Western Psychological Services.

Rutter, M., Le Couteur, A., & Lord, C. (2003b). *Autism Diagnostic Interview-Revised*. Los Angeles, CA: Western Psychological Services.

Scambler, D. J., Hepburn, S. L., & Rogers, S. J. (2006). A two-year follow-up on risk status identified by the checklist for autism in toddlers. *Journal of Developmental and Behavioral Pediatrics*, *27*(Suppl2), S104-S110. doi:10.1097/00004703-200604002-00008

Schieve, L. A., Boulet, S. L., Kogan, M. D., Yeargin-Allsopp, M., Boyle, C. A., Visser, S. N., … Rice, C. (2011). Parenting aggravation and autism spectrum disorders: 2007 National Survey of Children's Health. *Disability and Health Journal*, *4*(3), 143–152. doi:10.1016/j.dhjo.2010.09.002

Schopler, E., Mesibov, G., & Baker, A. (1982). Evaluation of treatment for autistic children and their parents. *Journal of the American Academy of Child Psychiatry*, *21*(3), 262–267. doi:10.1016/S0002-7138(09)60881-5

Schopler, E., & Van Bourgondien, M. E. (2010). *The Childhood Autism Rating Scale (CARS)*. Los Angeles, CA: Western Psychological Services.

Sheperis, C. J., Doggett, R. A., & Henington, C. (2005). Behavioral assessment: Principles and applications. In B. T. Erford (Ed.), *Counselor's guide to clinical, personality, and behavioral assessment* (pp. 105–123). Boston, MA: Lahaska Press.

Sheperis, C. J., Mohr, D., & Ammons, R. (2014). *Autism spectrum disorder*. Available from the American Counseling Association: http://www.counseling.org/knowledge-center/center-for-counseling-practice-policy-and-research/practice-briefs

Shumway, S., Thurm, A., Swedo, S., Deprey, L., Barnett, L., Amaral, D., … Ozonoff, S. (2011). Brief report: Symptom onset patterns and functional outcomes in young children with autism spectrum disorders. *Journal of Autism and Developmental Disorders*, *41*(12), 1727–1732. doi:10.1007/s10803-011-1203-3.

Simonoff, E., Pickles, A., Charman, T., Chandler, S., Loucas, T., & Baird, G. (2008). Psychiatric disorders in children with autism spectrum disorders: Prevalence, comorbidity, and associated factors in a population-derived sample. *Journal of the American Academy of Child & Adolescent Psychiatry* *47*(8), 921–929.

Singer, G. H., & Floyd, F. (2006). Meta-analysis of comparative studies of depression in mothers of children with and without developmental disabilities. *American Journal on Mental Retardation*, *111*(3), 155–169. doi:10.1352/0895-8017(2006)111[155:MOCSOD]2.0.CO;2

Smith, T. (2001). Discrete trial training in the treatment of autism. *Focus on Autism and Other Developmental Disabilities*, *16*(2), 86–92. doi:10.1177/108835760101600204

Snow, A. V., & Lecavalier, L. (2008). Sensitivity and specificity of the modified checklist for autism in toddlers and the Social Communication Questionnaire in preschoolers suspected of having pervasive developmental disorders. *Autism*, *12*(6), 627–644. doi:10.1177/1362361308097116

Sparrow, S., Balla, D., & Cicchetti, D. (2005). *Vinland adaptive behavior scales* (2nd ed.). Circle Pines, MN: American Guidance Services.

Sutera, S., Pandey, J., Esser, E. L., Rosenthal, M. A., Wilson, L. B., Barton, M., … Fein, D. (2007). Predictors of optimal outcome in toddlers diagnosed with autism spectrum disorders. *Journal of Autism and Developmental Disorders*, *37*(1), 98–107. doi:10.1007/s10803-006-0340-6

Taurines, R., Schwenck, C., Westerwald, E., Sachse, M., Siniatchkin, M., & Freitag, C. (2012). ADHD and autism: Differential diagnosis or overlapping traits? A selective review. *ADHD Attention Deficit and Hyperactivity Disorders*, *4*(3), 115–139. doi:10.1007/s12402-012-0086-2

Tsiouri, I., Simmons, E. S., & Paul, R. (2012). Enhancing the application and evaluation of a discrete trial intervention package for eliciting first words in preverbal preschoolers with ASD. *Journal of Autism and Developmental Disorders*, *42*(7), 1281–1293. doi:10.1007/s10803-011-1358-y

Vismara, L. A., & Bogin, J. (2009). *Steps for implementation: Pivotal response training*. Sacramento, CA: the National Professional Development Center on Autism Spectrum Disorders, the M.I.N.D. Institute, & the University of California at Davis School of Medicine.

Vismara, L. A., & Rogers, S. J. (2010). Behavioral treatments in autism spectrum disorder: What do we know? *Annual Review of Clinical Psychology*, *6*, 447–468. doi:10.1146/annurev.clinpsy .121208.131151

Volkmar, F. R., Klin, A., & Chawarska, K. (2008). Autism spectrum disorders in infants and toddlers:

An introduction. In K. Chawarska, A. Klin, & F. R. Volkmar (Eds.), *Autism spectrum disorders in infants and toddlers: Diagnosis, assessment, and intervention* (pp. 1–22). New York, NY: Guilford Press.

Volkmar, F. R., Lord, C., Bailey, A., Schultz, R. T., & Klin, A. (2004). Autism and pervasive developmental disorders. *Journal of Child Psychology and Psychiatry*, *45*(1), 135–170. doi:10.1046/j.0021 -9630.2003.00317.x

Wetherby, A. M., Woods, J., Allen, L., Cleary, J., Dickinson, H., & Lord, C. (2004). Early indicators of autism spectrum disorders in the second year of life. *Journal of Autism and Developmental Disorders*, *34*(5), 473–493. doi:10.1007/s10803-004-2544-y

Wetherby, A. M., & Woods, J. J. (2006). Early social interaction project for children with autism spectrum disorders beginning in the second year of life: A preliminary study. *Topics in Early Childhood Special Education*, *26*(2), 67–82. doi:10.1177/02711214060260020201

Wimpory, D. C., Hobson, R. P., Williams, J. M. G., & Nash, S. (2000). Are infants with autism socially engaged? A study of recent retrospective parental reports. *Journal of Autism and Developmental Disorders*, *30*(6), 525–536. doi:10.1023 /A:1005683209438

Yirmiya, N., & Charman, T. (2010). The prodrome of autism: Early behavioral and biological signs, regression, peri- and post-natal development and genetics. *Journal of Child Psychology and Psychiatry*, *51*(4), 432–458. doi:10.1111/j.1469-7610.2010.02214.x

Zwaigenbaum, L., Bryson, S., Rogers, T., Roberts, W., Brian, J., & Szatmari, P. (2005). Behavioral manifestations of autism in the first year of life. *International Journal of Developmental Neuroscience*, *23*(2–3), 143–152. doi:10.1016/j.ijdevneu.2004.05.001

Chapter 6

Attention-Deficit/Hyperactivity Disorder

Introduction

Attention-deficit/hyperactivity disorder (ADHD) affects nearly 5 percent of children and 2.5 percent of adults in population surveys of most cultures (American Psychiatric Association [APA], 2013), with slightly higher incidence rates in the United States, where nearly 11 percent of all children have had a diagnosis of ADHD at some point in their lives as of 2011 (Centers for Disease Control and Prevention, 2015). A parent, friend, teacher, or counselor who knows an individual with ADHD, or knows someone who has the symptoms of it, faces inherent challenges in settings where the behavioral manifestations of ADHD are most acute, such as in classrooms, social situations, workplaces, and the home (Tarver, Daley & Sayal, 2015). Because attention is so important in the process of acquiring new knowledge, and because all human behavior exists in the context where it takes place, the etiology and symptoms of ADHD are an educational and health concern nationally and internationally. ADHD can be complex, making it difficult for a counselor to remain up-to-date on current findings (Tarver, Daley, & Sayal, 2014). ADHD is a commonly known condition, and because the symptoms of it can be described even colloquially by people who do not have a clinical diagnosis, clinicians are cautioned to make a distinction between what is categorically a mental disorder and the symptoms of inattention or hyperactivity that everybody experiences at one time or another, depending upon his or her situation and environment (Hallowell & Ratey, 2011). In fact, according to Hallowell and Ratey (2011), ADHD is more impairing than depression or substance abuse, and 90 percent of adults who have ADHD do not even know it.

ADHD affects some 5.9 million children aged three to 17 in the United States (Centers for Disease Control and Prevention, 2013), and although it is not a learning disability by diagnostic classification, ADHD is often comorbid with specific learning disorder and autism spectrum disorder, making it difficult for parents and educators to distinguish between some of the specific characteristics of the differences between what might appear to be a learning disorder and the symptoms of hyperactivity and inattention. For example, nearly half of the population with a diagnosis of oppositional defiant disorder (ODD) have a co-occurring diagnosis of ADHD combined type while nearly one-quarter of people with ODD also have the primarily inattentive type of ADHD. Similarly, conduct disorder co-occurs in approximately 25 percent of children and adolescents with the combined inattention and hyperactivity type of ADHD. Unlike learning disabilities, which tend to have higher incidence of diagnosis in low-socioeconomic-status and minority populations by percentage, there is a higher degree of diagnosis of ADHD in non-Hispanic whites (12 percent) when compared with Hispanic children (6 percent) and African American children (9 percent) in the United States. ADHD also appears more frequently in single-parent families (12 percent) compared with two-parent families (7 percent), and ADHD appears nearly four times more often in children with a fair or poor health status compared with an excellent or very good health status, according to the 2012 National Health Interview Survey (Centers for Disease Control and Prevention, 2013). ADHD is also a condition that is diagnosed nearly three times more in males than in females, illustrating that, like other medical and psychological diagnoses, there is variance in incidence of ADHD by gender, race, ethnicity, and socioeconomic status, where counselors may look for the hyperactive and disruptive symptoms common in boys and are cautioned not to overlook the inattentive symptoms mostly found in females.

Although the symptoms of inattention and hyperactivity are important concerns for people of any age, they are of particular interest to children and adolescents from the elementary and secondary years. Symptoms of ADHD lay the foundation for problems that can become both learning and behavioral issues, and if left untreated the consequences can extend years beyond the time when an initial diagnosis of ADHD typically occurs, during elementary school. Some of the consequences include learning, social, behavioral, and developmental delays that can decrease the likelihood that a student will be successful throughout the schooling years and beyond into postsecondary education and careers. Because of the relatively high incidence of ADHD compared with all mental disorders and even those that are categorically related, such as specific learning disorders, practitioners need to have available to them a variety of treatment approaches that are safe, effective, and implementable to provide children and adolescents the opportunities earned and granted to those who do not have the symptoms of ADHD, because what is at stake is their potential for success in life.

HISTORICAL OVERVIEW

One of the many interesting characteristics about ADHD, which it has in common with a number of other mental disorders that are based upon a cluster of symptoms in the *Diagnostic and Statistical Manual of Mental Disorders* (*DSM*), is that there is no fast and easy way to determine whether somebody has ADHD. Historically, descriptions of a disorder related to what is today ADHD focused primarily on behavioral characteristics of hyperkinesis. Symptoms similar in description to ADHD appeared in eighteenth- and nineteenth-century literature by a number of authors, including a comical story by German psychiatrist Heinrich Hoffman in 1845, who, in describing fidgety Philip, told the story of a young boy who was unable to sit still at the dinner table and by rocking back and forth in his chair pulled a tablecloth and the entire dinner onto the floor, noting the behavioral context of the story. Other anecdotal accounts provided the basis for further scientific study later in the nineteenth century and came into full bloom in the research of the twentieth century (Lange, Reichl, Lange, Tucha, & Tucha, 2010).

In the early part of the twentieth century, hyperkinesis was broadly described as an inability to sit still, fidgety behavior, constant body movement, and a general inability for a person to control behavior. The condition primarily was described as a behavioral or somatic issue, because it predated the research into and knowledge of neurochemistry that would inform the literature and practice of the later part of the twentieth century and where we are today in the twenty-first century. Twentieth-century reports of hyperkinesis first appeared in the medical literature in 1902, with the publication of British physician George Frederick Still's account of symptoms that would today be similar to ADHD. In it, Still described behaviors that were defiant, aggressive, and resistant to discipline, the latter of which is most striking because this behavior illustrates that ADHD is not something that is inherently controllable, making ADHD distinctly different from other kinds of behaviors where a choices and consequences model would have a reasonable predictability of effectiveness. In today's modern medical context, though, the evolution of medical science offers much greater detail.

For most of the remainder of the twentieth century, ADHD continued to be described in the way of kinetic behavior from the 1930s to the 1950s: around a cluster of symptoms described from minimal brain dysfunction (Lange et al., 2010). But, as with the question and argument that goes on today, if it cannot be seen, does it exist? In essence, if there is brain damage, it would be revealed on a magnetic resonance imaging (MRI) scan or test of brain chemistry, or each person with it would present in the same way. However, that did not happen and does not happen, and the minimal brain dysfunction label discontinued. By the 1960s advances in psychopharmacology brought study of ADHD into the modern framework that today influences the description and treatment of ADHD. In the *DSM-II* (1968), hyperkinetic reaction in childhood appeared with the criteria of overactivity, restlessness, distractibility, and short attention span. The focus shifted to attention deficit with and without hyperactivity by the 1970s and into the publication of the *DSM-III* in 1980, where the disorder was described as attention deficit disorder with and without hyperactivity. After more research, coupled with the difficulty of separating hyperactivity and inattention, the *DSM-III-R* in 1987 renamed it attention-deficit/hyperactivity disorder. Later editions of the *DSM-IV* in 1994 and the *DSM-IV-TR* in 2000 continued with the ADHD label, and although the diagnostic criteria were not substantively changed, significant advancements in treatment strategies were made largely because of empirical studies of heritability and neurochemistry that addressed the symptoms to a greater degree than the causes. Although helpful in advancing the field, this conceptualization is still a matter of scientific debate.

Although there have not been fundamental changes in the *DSM-5* (APA, 2013) about the diagnostic criteria of ADHD compared to the *DSM-IV-TR* (2000), there have been some important updates to reflect the more global nature of the disorder to include a broader umbrella to classify it instead as a neurodevelopmental disorder over the prior categorization of a disruptive-behavior disorder type, in which it was grouped with other disorders diagnosed in infancy, childhood, or adolescence. ADHD continues to be divided into the broad presentations of inattention and hyperactivity-impulsivity, but whereas past interpretations of the disorder held that it is something that diminishes with age, today's view is that ADHD not only can be retroactively diagnosed during adulthood (only when several symptoms were manifest prior to age 12 because there is no symptom onset in adults) but also that the symptoms of ADHD do not necessarily recede once a person reaches adulthood. The onset of ADHD has been updated to include several symptoms manifest prior to age 12 versus the *DSM-IV-TR* requirement that some symptoms had to manifest prior to age seven. Because many people first diagnosed with ADHD or one of its related disorders are now adults, it is apparent the characteristics associated with the disorder persist into adulthood for many who live with the symptoms that began prior to age 12. Moreover, the related behavioral and pharmaceutical interventions often continue well into the adult years, providing symptom reduction in the later years. Finally, ADHD with onset prior to age 12 can be first diagnosed in adulthood, now defined as age 17 (APA, 2013), and does not necessitate a recollection of past events to make a diagnosis based on present functioning; although, according to the *DSM-5*, adult recall of childhood symptoms prior to age 12 tends to be unreliable (Klein et al., 2012; Mannuzza, Klein, Klein, Bessler, & Shrout, 2002), and it is beneficial to obtain ancillary information.

Description of the Disorder

Classified in the category of neurodevelopmental disorders, ADHD shares that category with intellectual disability, communication disorders, autism spectrum disorder, specific learning disorders, and motor disorders, among others. As is the case with all the disorders in this category, ADHD diagnosis is typically a matter of degree or severity of symptoms relative to what would be considered normal developmental behavior for any particular age. Specifically, to meet the diagnostic criteria of ADHD, symptoms of disorganization, hyperactivity-impulsivity, overactivity, inability to sit still or difficulty with waiting, impulsive behavior (such as blurting out or hitting or poking others because they are unable to control it), and other behaviors must be atypical given the child's or adolescent's age. In the area of attention deficits, symptoms can include but are not limited to an inability to pay attention to or stay on any specific task, seeming to have their head in the clouds, appearing to be unable to listen to or follow instructions, excessive loss of items, marked forgetfulness, and an inability to organize thoughts, items, and tasks to complete the learning and activities consistent with the developmental norms of the chronological age and level of functioning.

As is true of practically all mental disorders described in the *DSM-5*, ADHD manifests in different ways for different people, and the severity index also varies from person to person. Because of that variation, the utility of the diagnostic criteria is that they enable helping professionals to determine whether a diagnosis of ADHD is suitable given the symptoms with which the client presents. Moreover, in the past ADHD was excluded from a diagnosis of autism, but in the present diagnostic criteria in the *DSM-5*, this exclusion is no longer mandated. ADHD also often finds itself in a comorbid relationship with other attention- and behavior-related diagnoses, such as oppositional defiant disorder, specific learning disorder, and conduct disorder. Today's medical and helping professions' view of ADHD acknowledges that the symptoms for many people often continue into adulthood, and as with children in schools, treatment of adults with ADHD follows a similar pattern of cognitive, behavioral, psychoeducational, and pharmacological intervention. Sidebar 6.1 addresses a case teachers or counselors would be likely to observe. Read the case, and think about appropriate interventions and what might be ruled out.

SIDEBAR 6.1: RAMBUNCTIOUS RICHIE

Six-year-old Richie is in the fall term of his first-grade year. Seated near the door, he often gets up to see who's coming and going, always wants to use the bathroom, and interrupts the teacher when she's teaching challenging material. During rest time, he is unable to slow down; and in recess he has a difficult time following rules, so his classmates avoid him. What interventions should be tried? Is it ADHD? What should be ruled out?

DSM-5 Criteria

Published in 2013, the diagnostic criteria for ADHD in the *DSM-5* were developed by a team of medical and helping professionals whose goal was to provide a reliable, valid, ethical, and scientific approach to the diagnosis and understanding of ADHD in the context of global and culturally appropriate evidenced-based research since it first appeared in the *DSM* and, in particular, since the publication of the previous *DSM IV-TR* in 2000. What follows is a description of attention deficit and hyperactivity symptoms necessary to make an accurate diagnosis of ADHD, along with a description of other specified ADHD and unspecified ADHD.

In the current form of the diagnostic criteria of ADHD, clinicians need to understand that these two broad characteristics are joined together in the current diagnosis of ADHD and have been since 1987, even though there can be variations in the severity of inattention characteristics and hyperactivity-impulsivity characteristics. To make a diagnosis of ADHD, a pattern of inattention or hyperactivity-impulsivity has to interfere clearly with development or functioning, illustrated by six or more symptoms of inattention or hyperactivity-impulsivity present in two or more settings. The symptoms of ADHD cannot be explained by some other disorder even though they may have characteristics in common. For example, when diagnosing ADHD, clinicians would not include characteristics such as oppositional behavior, hostility, defiance, or failure to understand instructions, because some other type of information-processing disorder (such as intellectual disability) might better explain these behaviors. In addition, the diagnostic criteria need to be severe enough that they are related to impairment in functioning or development and have a negative relationship to social, academic, occupational, or vocational activities (APA, 2013).

To give clinicians more clarity, any six of the nine descriptors in the Inattention category, six of nine symptoms in the Hyperactivity-Impulsivity category, or a combination of six symptoms need to be present to make a diagnosis of ADHD, and for adults and adolescents 17 and older, the diagnostic criteria in the *DSM-5* require the presence of only five symptoms. Examples of inattention include failure to pay attention to details; difficulty maintaining focus; inability to pay attention in the absence of any obvious distraction; often leaving work incomplete; difficulty with organization or rule following; being easily sidetracked; avoiding activities that would require mental attention for a sustained period of time; frequently losing items, such as writing implements, personal computers, and education-related items, such as books, calculators, rulers, paperwork, or eyeglasses; being easily distracted by external stimuli or being unable to stay focused on a particular topic of conversation; and being forgetful of basic, routine chores (APA, 2013). See Sidebar 6.2 for commentary on accuracy in diagnosing.

SIDEBAR 6.2:   SELF-AWARENESS: THE CHALLENGE OF ACCURATE DIAGNOSIS

Many people work with adolescents and children who may present with a diagnosis of ADHD, including teachers, parents, day care workers, babysitters, and peers. Although some may assume that anybody who shows symptoms of inattention or hyperactivity-impulsivity must have ADHD, making an accurate diagnosis is more complex than simply observing somebody's behavior. What are some ways to increase an accurate diagnosis? What assessment instruments should one use? How can counseling professionals be a part of the conversation when children and adolescents (and their parents) present to their general practitioner doctor?

The Hyperactivity-Impulsivity category also requires six or more of the associated symptoms to be present for at least six months to a degree that age or developmental level could not otherwise explain. Likewise, another diagnosis, such as oppositional defiant disorder, conduct disorder, or specific learning disorder, cannot explain the symptoms. Like the Inattention category, the Hyperactivity–Impulsivity category includes nine symptoms, such as fidgeting, squirming, or tapping hands or feet; constantly moving around, getting up, or leaving the seat when it is not appropriate; showing restlessness by crawling or climbing where not appropriate; being unable to play quietly; being unable to sit for an extended period, such as during meetings or a meal in a restaurant; excessively talking; being unable to take turns in conversation; interrupting others; being unable to wait his or her turn; pushing others aside; or taking over activities in which others are obviously engaged (APA, 2013).

Clinicians will also note that several symptoms must have been present prior to the age of 12 in the *DSM-5* because many children have a more delayed onset or manifestation of ADHD symptoms, and when they do their clinical profile is very similar to those who have onset prior to age seven. The *DSM-5* specifies several symptoms must also be present in a variety of contexts, such as home, school, when playing with others, when playing independently, when trying to learn new tasks, and around friends and relatives. In addition, the symptoms have to cause apparent interference in academic, occupational, and social functioning, and the symptoms cannot be explained by some other diagnosis. Clinicians must understand that everybody in one situation or another may experience one or more of the symptoms, but the key difference for making a diagnosis is that the symptoms cause impairment, are obvious to others, and are atypical relative to expected human behavior for any given age or developmental level as a whole. Other specified ADHD and unspecified ADHD aim to address areas where, in the case of other specified, ADHD symptoms may be present but not in sufficient number to justify a full diagnosis, yet the assessing clinician is able to specify the key symptoms that make the diagnosis subclinical. The subclinical assessment is made by recording "other specified attention-deficit/hyperactivity disorder" followed by the specific reason (e.g., "with insufficient inattention symptoms"). Unspecified ADHD is used where the clinician chooses not to specify the reason he or she cannot make a diagnosis and includes presentations in which there is insufficient information to make a more specific diagnosis.

Using six months as the baseline to determine whether ADHD symptoms are not caused by some other environmental factor, clinicians need to specify whether the criteria for inattention and hyperactivity-impulsivity are both present, whether the presentation is predominantly inattentive, or whether the presentation is predominantly of the hyperactive-impulsive type. Partial remission would include the decrease in symptoms so as not to justify a full diagnosis of ADHD if symptoms were reduced for six months or longer (because of counseling or medication), and the symptoms would still result in impairment in social, academic, or occupational functioning. Severity levels can include mild, moderate, and severe. Mild severity indicates that few, if any, symptoms in excess of those required to make the diagnosis are present, and symptoms result in no more than minor impairments in social or occupational functioning and go largely unnoticed by others. Moderate severity includes symptoms between mild and severe, with alternating levels of severity either depending upon the context or an inability to control symptoms independently. Severe specification includes many symptoms in excess of those necessary to make an initial diagnosis; several symptoms that are particularly severe; or a marked impairment of academic, social, or occupational functioning because of the symptoms that are present. As noted in the *DSM-5*:

> The use of specifiers for the neurodevelopmental disorder diagnoses enriches the clinical description of the individual's clinical course and current symptomatology. In addition to specifiers that describe the clinical presentation,

such as age at onset or severity ratings, the neurodevelopmental disorders may include the specifier "associated with a known medical or genetic condition or environmental factor." This specifier gives clinicians an opportunity to document factors that may have played a role in the etiology of the disorder, as well as those that might affect the clinical course. Examples include genetic disorders, such as fragile X syndrome, tuberous sclerosis, and Rett syndrome; medical conditions such as epilepsy; and environmental factors, including very low birth weight and fetal alcohol exposure (even in the absence of stigmata of fetal alcohol syndrome). (APA, 2013, pp. 32–33)

Can a child's or adolescent's diet cause ADHD? See Sidebar 6.3 for more information.

SIDEBAR 6.3:   DIET AND ADHD

Kime is an 8-year-old boy who has an older sister who is 12 and a younger brother who is six in a single-parent home. Lately, he has been getting in trouble in school for talking out of turn, being aggressive with other students, and not completing his schoolwork or homework. Because his parent is very busy, he eats a lot of prepackaged foods, takeout food, pizza, and high-sugar items. This parent thinks that everything would be fine if he or she had the time to cook vegetables and well-rounded meals. Although certainly eating a balanced diet matters, there is no cause-and-effect relationship between diet and ADHD, and a high-sugar diet, while unhealthy, does not cause ADHD or result in a marked increase of symptoms. Although there is a popular belief that sugar causes ADHD, no empirical scientific evidence proves this claim.

Differential Diagnosis

Because all people can at one time or another experience symptoms of inattention or hyperactivity-impulsivity, helping professionals need to be mindful of whether a person truly meets the diagnostic criteria for ADHD. In fact, to meet the qualification for a diagnosis, a person has to rise to a relatively high level of severity of symptoms. Even though many people may present to a counselor, psychologist, social worker, or psychiatrist with some of the symptoms, most do not present with enough to justify making the diagnosis. Clinicians must also be mindful to be certain that ADHD, and not one of the other related disorders that can be comorbid or incorrectly diagnosed, is the appropriate diagnosis. The *DSM-5* lists other disorders that one might consider when constructing a differential diagnosis, such as oppositional defiant disorder, intermittent explosive disorder, specific learning disorder, autism spectrum disorder, reactive attachment disorder, anxiety disorders, depressive disorders (disruptive mood dysregulation disorder), bipolar-related disorders, substance use disorders, personality disorders, psychotic disorders, medication-induced symptoms of ADHD, or neurocognitive and other neurodevelopmental disorders. The value in following the diagnostic criteria in the *DSM* is that they help narrow the focus to the symptoms of attention deficit and hyperactivity-impulsivity.

A study by Gupta and Kar (2010) suggested there is a level of subjectivity in the empirical data used to generate a diagnosis of ADHD. For example, behavior rating scales, such as the Child Behavior Checklist and the Teacher's Report Form (TRF) of the Child Behavior Checklist, rely on parents, teachers, and other observers to make clinical judgments based upon what can be subjective opinions about behavior that are connected to emotion and other environmental factors. As others have noted, ADHD is a cluster of behavioral symptoms when it comes to formulating a diagnosis because no laboratory or set of physiological characteristics can test it.

According to Gupta and Kar (2010), differential diagnosis is important because ADHD shares characteristics with many of the related neurodevelopmental disorders and can, if not carefully ruled out, be confused with a bipolar-related disorder. Other researchers tend to use the same behavioral checklists that Gupta and Kar's study addressed to find differences. In a study by Bauermeister et al. (2007), the authors found that even in the case of using the same essential diagnostic criteria, boys were more often referred for school suspension than girls and that the presentation of symptoms, though objectively the same, can have discrete interpretations. Their study, based upon a Puerto Rican sample, lends some cross-cultural information to findings that are commonly held among the population in the United States. The researchers found similarity to the world statistics in that boys were nearly twice as likely as girls to be diagnosed with ADHD. Other research by Wåhlstedt, Thorell, and Bohlin (2009) supported the notion that cognitive deficits and learning disabilities can also explain the symptoms of ADHD. In particular, inattention was associated with poor academic achievement, and the defiance and behavioral issues are related to hyperactivity; in the end, they argued that ADHD is a heterogeneous disorder because of distinctions between attention deficit and hyperactivity, an argument others made in past descriptions and earlier editions of the *DSM*, where inattention and hyperactivity-impulsivity had distinct psychological and learning implications.

Assessment Strategies

ADHD is a unique psychological disorder to assess because it is both a heterogeneous disorder and a homogenous disorder at the same time. Attention deficits have unique characteristics that can delay learning and have compounding effects later in life because of the learning delays. Hyperactivity, which often correlates with learning delays, can be one of the symptoms of and reasons for attention deficits. Although it is important to understand that no single test can assess somebody for ADHD, most of the assessment strategies for ADHD include journals, behavior rating scales, observations, and questionnaires related to the symptoms of hyperactivity whereas symptoms related to inattention are often assessed with task performance scales, continuous performance tests, and visual and auditory assessments.

To establish ADHD, a baseline level of functioning assessment is the first step. An intelligence test, such as the Wechsler Intelligence Scale for Children or the Stanford-Binet Intelligence Scale, can provide normed scores to determine where the child or adolescent is relative to the population, and an achievement test, such as the Wechsler Individual Achievement Test for children, can assess grade-level functioning to rule out specific learning disabilities in reading, writing, or math. Apart from cognitive assessments, a comprehensive medical appraisal can help rule out other possible explanations. Tests of the thyroid, blood lead levels, hearing and vision, computed tomography (CT) scan for brain abnormalities, along with an analysis of proper levels of exercise and sleep and a healthy diet, are appropriate to exclude any competing explanations. A newer feature in the

DSM-5 is "emerging measures" of patient assessment instruments that one can adminis-ter at intake to clarify diagnostic impressions further. The *DSM-5* Parent/Guardian-Rated Level 1 Cross-Cutting Symptom Measure—Child Age 6–17 gives parents or guardians a list of symptoms to help narrow the clinical focus of attention. For ADHD, Domain III question 4 asks respondents whether the child "had problems paying attention when he/she was in class or doing his/her homework or reading a book or playing a game?" The *DSM-5* includes a similar measure called the Self-Rated Level 1 Cross-Cutting Symp-tom Measure—Child Age 11–17 that is a self-report measure children and adolescents aged 11–17 can complete to narrow symptoms from the list provided in the inventory. For ADHD, Domain III question 4 asks respondents whether they have "been bothered by not being able to pay attention when you were in class or doing homework or read-ing or playing a game?" The Likert-type scale of the Cross-Cutting Symptom Measure is coded numerically from 0 to 4, where 0 indicates "not at all," and 4 indicates problems "nearly every day." Finally, clinicians also need to take a biopsychosocial narrative of clients that addresses a family history of ADHD or related neurodevelopmental disorders, which are often among the best predictors of an accurate diagnosis of ADHD because it is a heritable disorder.

BEHAVIOR RATING SCALES

One of the most frequently used behavior rating scales for assessing ADHD is the Child Behavior Checklist (CBC), a battery of questions related to interests in the area of sports, hobbies, and academic subjects and questions about school problems, followed by a 113-item questionnaire that addresses behavioral and medical information. Developed along with the Achenbach System of Empirically Based Assessment (ASEBA), the Child Behavior Checklist items were designed to provide consistent assessment along the diagnostic criteria in the *DSM-5*. The Teacher Report Form is another commonly used part of the CBC where teachers evaluate behavior, adaptive functioning, and academic skills. The Conners' Parent and Teacher Rating Scales are questionnaires that assess behavior with a focus on ADHD and comorbid disorders. Like the CBC, the Conners' Scales are designed to provide users information for diagnostic validity with the *DSM-5* criteria for ADHD, and the Scales include versions for parents, teachers, and self-reporting. The Conners' Continuous Performance Test is a useful tool for children aged six and older, one that assesses inattention, impulsivity, sustained attention, and vigilance. The Conners' Auditory Test of Attention may be combined with other Conners tests to provide a complete profile. The current edition of the Conners matches its assessment to the *DSM-5* criteria for ADHD. The Diagnostic Interview Schedule for Children (DISC-IV) is a structured instrument that nonmedical and helping professionals can use to assess psychiatric and substance abuse disorders in children and adolescents. The Swanson, Nolan and Pelham Questionnaire (SNAP-IV-C) Teacher and Parent Rating Scale assesses ADHD symptoms while targeting other disorders commonly comorbid with ADHD to exclude non-ADHD symptoms in an effort to make a diagnosis more accurately. Available in short (18-question) and long (80-question) forms, the SNAP-IV-C includes items from the Conners' Index Scale. The Vanderbilt ADHD Diagnostic Teacher Rating Scale is a 55-item inventory that assesses ADHD and its subtypes, along with oppositional defiant disorder, conduct disorder, and anxiety or depression. The Vanderbilt ADHD Parent Rating Scale assesses ADHD and its subtypes, along with oppositional defiant disorder, conduct disorder, and anxiety or depression in a 55-question inventory similar to the Teacher Rating Scale but based on a home context. The Barkley Home and Barkley School Situations Questionnaire is another widely used instrument that includes assessments of level of severity and cross-situation attention problems.

The preceding assessment instruments, although not exhaustive in scope, represent some of the most commonly used behavior and inattention rating scales for children and adolescents. In addition to these scales, many others assess particular characteristics of ADHD and comorbid disorders, such as autism, oppositional defiant disorder, conduct disorder, and learning disabilities. Each of these assessments has also been normed on populations outside the United States and translated into other languages with the goal of attaining a global standard of ADHD symptoms, which increases the validity of the diagnosis and reduces variation in the incidence rates of ADHD in the United States when compared with other countries in the world (Centers for Disease Control and Prevention, 2013). Observational and behavioral checklists and questionnaires are far and away the most common assessment instruments used to determine a diagnosis of ADHD because there is little in the way of credible and consistent alternative explanations, such as differences in brain structure, the no-longer-considered-valid mild brain dysfunction, or explanations made by anecdotal reports of too much sugar in modern children's diet. Indeed, ADHD is a neurodevelopmental disorder characterized by a specific set of symptoms, but to date there is no neurochemical causal relationship that can be attributed strictly to diet or other environmental factors. See Table 6.1 for some distinctions between the *DSM-IV-TR* and the *DSM-5*.

Treatment Strategies and Interventions

Treatment for ADHD tends to fall into two broad categories: psychotherapy or behavioral approaches, and medication approaches. The two categories are often combined for children and adolescents. Behavioral interventions can help children and adolescents develop social skills, such as listening; turn taking; respecting boundaries; understanding how others feel, or to put it another way, empathy; sharing; and teamwork. Because the symptoms of hyperactivity-impulsivity can affect inattention, there is a relationship between the hyperactivity-impulsivity and the learning problems associated with inattention. Moreover, the inattention characteristics of ADHD are typically the associated symptoms that cause children to have behavioral problems in schools and social situations. Age-appropriate interventions for children and adolescents should always be used to maximize the ability for children and adolescents to learn strategies to help them regulate the symptoms of the disorder themselves. Behavioral approaches that counselors can use in counseling sessions include play therapy, role-playing, modeling appropriate behavior, and delayed-gratification exercises.

Adolescents with ADHD certainly are capable of learning, and in a study by Sibley et al. (2012), a summer treatment program that taught adolescents ages 12 to 16 academic and organizational skills important in secondary grades, such as note taking, planner use, study skills, writing skills, and life skills training (including avoidance of deviant-peer affiliation, substance use, and delinquency), found a modicum of success. Findings included a reduction in parental conflict with these adolescents, although in the absence of the treatment group, some of the participants regressed to earlier habits, illustrating that although adolescents were able to learn prosocial behaviors, some with a higher degree

TABLE 6.1   ADHD Changes between the *DSM-IV-TR* (2000) and the *DSM-5* (2013)

Clinical Formulation	DSM-IV-TR	DSM-5
Multiaxial/Categorical Diagnosis	Yes	No. The new manual uses a dimensional approach to communicate symptom intensity via *mild*, *moderate*, and *severe* specifiers
Adult Diagnosis	Yes. However, ADHD was underdiagnosed in adults because it was classified as a Disorder Usually First Diagnosed in Infancy, Childhood, and Adolescence Only 1 of the 18 diagnostic symptoms provided an adult example	Yes. Older adolescents and adults age 17 and older presenting with 5 of 18 symptoms (instead of 6 of 18 symptoms) Five of the 18 diagnostic symptoms provide examples for older adolescents and adults, and 15 of the 18 diagnostic symptom examples are significantly expanded
Autism Exclusion	Yes	No. ADHD can be comorbid with autism spectrum disorder because up to 30 percent of children manifest both disorders simultaneously. However, the social dysfunction and peer rejection seen in individuals with ADHD must be distinguished from the social disengagement, isolation, and indifference to facial and tonal communication cues seen in individuals with autism spectrum disorder; causal factors for tantrums also differ between the two disorders
Chapter Classification	Disorders Usually First Diagnosed in Infancy, Childhood, or Adolescence, subgrouped as a Disruptive Behavior Disorder. However, it was not meant to suggest that there is any clear distinction between "childhood" and "adult" disorders	Neurodevelopmental Disorders characterized by developmental deficits that produce impairments of personal, social, academic, or occupational functioning
Diagnostic Criteria	"Some" symptoms present before age 7 "Some" symptoms present in two or more settings (e.g., at school or work and at home). Criterion E did not list "substance-related disorders" regarding symptom exclusivity	"Several" symptoms present prior to age 12 "Several" symptoms present in two or more settings (e.g., at home, school, or work; with friends or relatives; in other activities) Criteria A.1 and A.2 have additional language: "and that negatively impacts directly on social and academic/occupational activities" Criterion A.2a. added the words "or taps" Criterion A.2c. removed the word "excessively" Criterion E lists "substance intoxication or withdrawal" regarding symptom exclusivity
Predominant Pattern	Use of the term "Type" for inattentive, hyperactive/impulsive, or combined clinical profiles	Use of the term "Presentation" for inattentive, hyperactive/impulsive, or combined clinical profiles

TABLE 6.2   ADHD Changes between the *DSM-IV-TR* (2000) and the *DSM-5* (2013)

Clinical Formulation	DSM-IV-TR	DSM-5
Course Specifier	No	Yes. "In Partial Remission" to indicate when full criteria were previously met, fewer than the full criteria have been met for the past six months, and the symptoms still result in impairment in social, academic, or occupational functioning
Suicide Risk	No	Yes. By early adulthood, ADHD is associated with an increased risk of suicide attempt, primarily when comorbid with mood, conduct, or substance use disorders
Risk and Prognostic Factors	No	Yes. The new manual summarizes current research on temperamental, environmental, genetic and physiological, and course modifiers
Functional Consequences	No	Yes. The new manual summarizes current research on the negative impacts ADHD has on social and academic or occupational activities
Differential Diagnosis	Yes. However, listing was limited	Yes. Listing is greatly expanded to include oppositional defiant disorder, intermittent explosive disorder, stereotypic movement disorder, Tourette's disorder, specific learning disorder, reactive attachment disorder, disruptive mood dysregulation disorder, and bipolar disorder

of impulsivity were unable to control their behavior for a prolonged period, suggesting the organic nature of the disorder. A successful approach in a study by Pfiffner, Villodas, Kaiser, Rooney, and McBurnett (2013) found relevant outcomes in a collaborative life skills program where parents and schools collaborated in symptom reduction to reduce the academic consequences associated with ADHD. Among the activities included were a daily report card, a homework plan, preferential seating, targeted use of praise, and providing compliance prompts for behavior for a sample of second to fifth graders with a mean age of eight. Nearly all mainstream approaches to nonmedication treatment of ADHD include elements related to regulation of executive functioning, consistency of parental behaviors, organizational skills, following prescribed methodologies of teaching and parenting, acknowledging differences in learning styles, time management, and self-regulation.

Although behavior treatment approaches remain the most popular of nonmedication treatments, most with a diagnosis of ADHD treat the symptoms with a combination of medication and psychotherapy. The present view of ADHD is that it is a long-term, chronic condition that one manages over time like other pervasive, lifelong disorders that are often treated with medication alone or a combination of medication and psychotherapy. The most widely prescribed class of medications for ADHD is stimulant medication. There is a seeming paradox in stimulant medication being prescribed to calm people down, but that is the nature of ADHD's effect on the human brain's chemistry, whereby stimulants actually calm the excitability and hyperactivity of those with ADHD. The most widely prescribed stimulant medications are of the methylphenidate type known by brand names such as Ritalin, Concerta, Metadate (pill form), and Daytrana (a patch). The other most common stimulants are the amphetamine medications, the most widely known of which is Adderall. Methylphenidate medications operate by increasing dopamine, an important neurotransmitter for cognitive functions related to attention and focus. Amphetamine medications operate by activating dopamine and norepinephrine, chemicals responsible for stimulation and alertness. Stimulant medications commonly prescribed for ADHD are scheduled medications of the U.S. Drug Enforcement Administration because of their high likelihood for dependence or addiction. Stimulant medications have also been prescribed for off-label uses in treating ADHD characteristics, a concern because of potential deleterious effects possible in the hands of people for whom they were not prescribed. Children, adolescents, and adults who have a stimulant prescription for ADHD symptoms still may experience the somatic side effects of increased heart rate, nervousness, restlessness, blood pressure elevation, excitability, and, in rare cases, tremors.

Because of the side effects of stimulant medication that are difficult to tolerate for some patients, nonstimulant medications, such as atomoxetine (Strattera), have been prescribed for symptom reduction. Atomoxetine functions as a serotonin and norepinephrine reuptake inhibitor (SNRI) that activates the amount of the chemical that is present in the brain that creates stimulation. As is the case with any psychotropic medication, children on these medications need to be closely monitored for adverse changes in behavior that can include suicidal ideation. Most of these stimulant and nonstimulant medications are available in extended-release formulations, and many are prescribed for children as young as six and in some cases are prescribed for off-label uses because they are not indicated for symptoms of distractibility that do not rise to the level of a clinical diagnosis of ADHD. In addition, stimulant medications have become drugs of abuse and recreational drugs for people seeking to achieve intoxication from them or other nonclinical purposes.

Though medication is far and away the most common initial intervention for ADHD, with 20 percent of high-school-age boys in the United States having an ADHD diagnosis at some point in their lives, and over 10 percent of high-school-age boys using an ADHD medication, controversy remains over the rapid increase in the past decade of the diagnosis of ADHD and the number of medications prescribed to treat it. Indeed, a disorder with a growth rate of 41 percent (Visser et al., 2014) in the past decade reasonably has parents, teachers, helping professionals, and the public concerned. A rational approach to treatment includes a combination of medication and psychotherapy with the knowledge that each person is unique and symptoms will manifest in slightly different ways for each person who has ADHD. The public-health concern is the sharp rise in the number of prescriptions of medication for ADHD, and in particular the abuse of prescription drugs for recreational purposes, and although there is some debate about the connection between the diagnostic criteria in the *DSM* and the availability of medication to treat it, helping professionals' best practice is to consider accurate diagnosis, individually tailored treatment, and empirically valid psychotherapeutic and pharmacological interventions.

Although substantial evidence exists for the efficacy of psychoeducation as an adjunct to pharmacological intervention in mental health disorders, such as schizophrenia and bipolar disorders, the literature for ADHD continues to be developed as more empirical studies are conducted and the results published. Positive outcomes for psychoeducational intervention was illustrated in a meta-analysis of studies of psychoeducation and ADHD for the period of 1980–2010 by Montoya, Colom, and Ferrin (2011). In the Montoya et al. study, psychoeducation included parent training, didactic and participatory classroom activities, and behavioral interventions, noting that there is no one definition of psychoeducation, which makes empirical measurements of its effectiveness in the absence of pharmacological intervention difficult. Hoffman and DuPaul (2000) argued for increased use of psychoeducational interventions in children, based in part upon their ability to increase successful functioning in academic areas in particular, because although psychostimulants decreased hyperactivity-impulsivity, medications alone did not increase academic achievement. Loe and Feldman (2007) echoed the Hoffman and DuPaul study in finding decreased reading and math achievement test scores and lower educational attainment rates in secondary and postsecondary education. Loe and Feldman (2007) recommended the following educational interventions: Section 504 plans, smaller class size, behavior management, combined (pharmacologic and behavioral) treatment, increased physical activity, and alternative methods of discipline; in essence, it is counterintuitive to punish students for behaviors (inattention, distraction, and disorganization) ADHD causes. Instead, Loe and Feldman (2007) suggested positive behavioral reinforcement to reward appropriate behaviors over out-of-school suspension, which is associated with decreased academic achievement and graduation rates.

Evaluation Strategies

Perhaps the most persistent challenge in evaluating the effectiveness of an ADHD intervention is whether the child or adolescent actually sticks to the prescribed course of treatment. Similar to other diagnoses, adhering to the treatment, whether medical, pharmaceutical, or behavioral, is vital to gain an effective and accurate evaluation of whether the intervention had any effect. Although it may seem counterintuitive to think that those prescribed a medication would not take it according to its prescribed course, the reality is that people with ADHD are particularly prone not to do so because of the nature of the disorder. As Ferrin et al. (2012) noted, what is important is to disentangle treatment adherence by determining what barriers are at play and addressing those barriers to increase the likelihood of following the course of intervention. With children, for example, a concern over preoccupations, insight, and self-concept emerged, whereas for parents, issues related to their children's personal attitudes, worries, social stigma, insight, side effects, and knowledge were revealed to be the salient features associated with treatment adherence. Other research by Cortese et al. (2013) noted that with respect to pharmacological intervention, practitioners need to be aware of and communicate with clients about adverse events that can happen with some portion of children and adolescents who take ADHD medication. Adverse events include cardiovascular events, loss of appetite, growth delay, increased blood pressure, suicidal thoughts, and psychotic symptoms, among others. The authors recommended a number of suggestions for managing adverse events, such as taking medication after a meal, monitoring blood pressure, and educating clients about appropriate reactions to potential side effects.

Does gender affect ADHD? See Sidebar 6.4 for some explanations.

SIDEBAR 6.4:   GIRLS AND ADHD

Girls and women can be diagnosed with ADHD; however, the diagnosis rate in the United States is less than half that of boys. The best evidence suggests that there are neurodevelopmental differences in boys and girls, and because ADHD is a disorder that is diagnosed by a cluster of symptoms (i.e., it cannot be detected by a blood test or other body fluid test), the reality is that boys, particularly in schools, have a much greater presentation of the symptoms—inattention, hyperactivity, constant movement, and aggression toward others—and because of the subjective nature of assessment, it may also be the case that girls' behavior is perceived differently. By the adolescent years, some 20 percent of boys have had at one time during their lives a diagnosis of ADHD, whereas only 7 percent of girls have, according to figures from the U.S. Centers for Disease Control and Prevention.

If children or adolescents have ADHD, illustrated by meeting six of the symptoms in one domain of the categories of inattention or hyperactivity-impulsivity required for diagnosis, then an age-appropriate dose of any number of the pharmacological products on the market for ADHD should show improvement in a relatively short time. If the medications are contraindicated for hyperactivity-impulsivity or inattention, the result would be an even greater animation of the symptoms because stimulants would cause a nonclinical population to behave with characteristics indicative of hyperactivity and inattention or typical effects of stimulants. The effects of medication typically are observed in presentations related to a decrease in inattention or in hyperactive-impulsive behaviors. Such evaluations can be completed by behavior observation, but more empirically based evaluations of the effectiveness of psychopharmacological and psychotherapeutic interventions are based upon the same behavioral and symptom checklists available to make an initial diagnosis. Outcome studies of the effectiveness of interventions are typically behaviorally based and can be assessed by reduction in problem behaviors, self-reports of greater levels of attention, behavioral observation, improvement in grades, and decrease of factors associated with externalizing behavior (hitting, poking, punching, blurting out, frequently getting up or leaving one's seat, disorganization, and low tolerance for sustained activity). Although the symptoms of ADHD persist throughout the life span, they are well managed with psychotherapeutic and pharmacological intervention. The current view is that adults can have ADHD and can be diagnosed with ADHD even though as a neurodevelopmental disorder, experts agree that the symptoms likely would have persisted over a life span and have presented prior to the age of 12. ADHD is a well-researched disorder that has had an increasing number of first-time diagnoses since the development of effective medication over the past 60 years, and in particular over the past 20 years since the Individuals with Disabilities Education Act (IDEA) was revised to include ADHD among the list of disorders that could qualify for intervention under the federal special education IDEA law of 1991. ADHD is also a disorder that is relatively well funded in the areas of research and development, as medications improve to target the specific symptoms without the sometimes-debilitating side effects of those medications and to quell some of the public perception that ADHD is relatively overdiagnosed because of the wide availability of medication for it, given the likely presence of the disorder in the global population, which varies around the world. Global diagnosis variation is purported to be a result of subjectivity in rating scales (Faraone, Sergeant, Gillberg, & Biederman, 2003). To address such public-perception concerns, the *DSM-5* revisions make the diagnosis more restrictive by replacing *some* with *several* symptoms and by including specific examples of symptoms within the diagnostic criteria.

Diagnostic Challenges

The primary diagnostic challenge with ADHD is that it shares characteristics of other disorders. Because ADHD, like many diagnoses, is a collection of symptoms, some controversy remains related to the subjectivity of those diagnoses. Self-reports of ADHD symptoms, observations by others, behavior rating scales, and reactions to medication are all potential roadblocks to accurate assessment, diagnosis, and treatment because they can be subjective. In addition, because ADHD can be comorbid with a number of other related disorders and can mimic the symptoms of other disorders, such as distractibility, impulsivity, loud or rapid speech, racing thoughts, and goal-driven behavior also associated with a diagnosis of a bipolar-related disorder, clinicians need to be thorough in their analysis and gain data from a variety of sources. After they rule out other explanations of behavior, they need to establish baseline data for normal behavior given developmental and chronological age. Pollak, Levy, and Breitholtz (1999) noted that neurodevelopmental disorders, a medical condition, can be misidentified as psychological disorders; for example, hyperthyroidism can be misidentified as generalized anxiety disorder, or ADHD can be misidentified as a bipolar-related disorder in the case of hyperactive symptoms, or as passive-aggressive personality disorder in the case of inattentive symptoms. Pollak et al. (1999) argued for a comprehensive medical and family history review to include information about mood disorders, autoimmune disease, degenerative brain disease, metabolic conditions, and other learning or speech-related conditions. To assess academic and vocational functioning, the authors recommended investigation of markedly uneven ability in verbal and quantitative skills, history of grade retention or special education, and ability and achievement discrepancies (brilliant underachiever or chronically stressed overachiever). For adolescents and adults, ruling out all other explanations is a function of accurate diagnosis of ADHD. Adolescents and adults, for example, would be asked to take a screen for alcohol or drug use, to have a full medical evaluation, and to undergo an assessment of social functioning. A study by Sibley et al. (2012) detailed some of the diagnostic challenges, and to mediate ADHD diagnosis concerns, the authors recommended establishing a diagnostic threshold that includes parent and teacher reports along with self-reports. For older clients, retrospective data are also included because symptoms should have appeared prior to the age of seven in the *DSM-IV-TR* diagnostic criteria used at the time of their study. Because some adolescents had clinically significant impairment but did not qualify for a diagnosis of ADHD, the authors recommended a combination of parent and teacher reports to get a more inclusive diagnosis on the sample. Teacher and self-reports are helpful because parent reports alone lead to many false negatives, whereby parents may be underestimating the level of symptom severity observed in their children, and the authors noted that the clinical sample studied may not be completely representative of the population of adolescents who may have ADHD (Sibley et al., 2012).

Several points of data are needed to make an accurate diagnosis. See Sidebar 6.5 for some of the people who should be involved.

SIDEBAR 6.5:   A HOLISTIC PERSPECTIVE

A reasonable concern about ADHD is that it may be diagnosed quickly based only on the description of symptoms by the child or adolescent and his or her parent(s). To get the best treatment for ADHD, information needs to be gathered by parents, teachers, doctors, and the child or adolescent. Every significant person in the child's or adolescent's life needs to be involved in providing support in a variety of contexts, including the school, the home, social situations, and later, the postsecondary school or workplace. Helping professionals should explain to parents that treatment approaches need to be adhered to consistently to maximize the benefit of psychotherapeutic or pharmacological intervention.

In addition, helping professionals must also evaluate children and adolescents for other potential contexts that can create a situation of having the appearance of symptoms that may be based on some other explanation. For example, Rinn and Reynolds (2012) explained that gifted students can present with symptoms of excitability that may appear to be ADHD but are not. Gifted students may also exhibit symptoms that may create a misdiagnosis because they may be bored with the activities or academic material presented to them. Other research by Shemmassian and Lee (2012) found that no one particular assessment, which included those by parents only, teachers only, or both parents and teachers using the Disruptive Behavior Disorder Rating Scale, was superior over another. But, in this context, the authors did find that teacher ratings were the most accurate in identifying children who were perceived negatively by their peers. Teachers and parents can have different interpretations of their student's or child's behavior, because they are observing their students or children in different contexts. Teachers are more likely to actually observe peer interactions with their students in a way that parents may not often observe their children's peer interactions, so there is an explanation for differences between parent and teacher ratings. The authors acknowledged that no one single assessment instrument can predict ADHD accurately every time, and they called for multiple informants to assess the likelihood of diagnosis accurately. Finally, because ADHD is diagnosed at higher rates than their comorbid counterparts, and other primary disorders can often explain the symptoms of ADHD, clinicians must rule out all other possible explanations for inattention or hyperactivity-impulsivity.

There are many relatively quick tools to assess ADHD on the market, and the assessment instruments used, in addition to observation, need to be understood in the context for which they were designed. No one single assessment instrument or one single observation of a child or adolescent can provide the opportunity for the comprehensive set of information required to make an accurate diagnosis of ADHD. Because ADHD is a highly heritable disease, a family history with medical and psychological records is a vital component of any complete appraisal. Finally, review of the *DSM-5* diagnostic criteria along with information from multiple sources provide the best opportunity for an accurate diagnosis that would lead to effective treatments, including psychotherapy, behavior modification, psychoeducation, and pharmacological intervention for ADHD.

Summary

ADHD is a neurodevelopmental disorder marked by inattention, hyperactivity, and impulsivity. Although the symptoms of ADHD can appear well into adulthood, the diagnostic criteria in the *DSM-5* require that symptoms be present prior to the age of 12, and even though adults may have symptoms of ADHD, recollection of those past events is helpful to contribute to an accurate diagnosis. As in the *DSM-IV-TR*, the *DSM-5* necessitates six symptoms in one or both of the two categories of inattention and hyperactivity-impulsivity. For older adolescents and adults (age 17 and older), at least five symptoms are required. Although there have been descriptions of people with the symptoms of ADHD for as long as narratives of human life have existed, ADHD in the clinical sense first appeared in the *DSM-II* in 1968, though it was then called hyperkinetic reaction of childhood. Since that time, volumes of research have been published about the etiology, symptoms, and treatment of this neurodevelopmental disorder. Today's formulation in the *DSM-5* (2013) joins the inattention and hyperactivity areas needed to make a diagnosis. Many diagnostic instruments to assess ADHD along the criteria in the *DSM-5* are available, and such assessment instruments, along with observations from parents, teachers, and clinicians, help provide the most accurate diagnosis, because a child or adolescent needs to be observed in a variety of settings to rule out other explanations and to evaluate ADHD independent of other comorbid disorders. ADHD is a well-known disorder around the world and, in particular, in the United States, where the rate of diagnosis and those prescribed medication for it is higher than the rest of the world. There is some controversy related to ADHD diagnosis because it is diagnosed more frequently for children receiving Medicaid benefits (Visser et al., 2014) and diagnosis is most frequent among Caucasian boys, with fewer Hispanic/Latino and African American children and adolescents diagnosed and far fewer Asian children diagnosed. Practitioners and the public need to evaluate the many stories in the popular media regarding ADHD carefully for sound scientific evidence about the causes of or new potential cures for ADHD. In conclusion, today there are many safe and effective treatments for ADHD that include empirically based psychotherapies, pharmacological intervention, psychoeducation, and combinations of medication and environmental intervention. The following References provide additional information relating to ADHD.

References

American Psychiatric Association. (2000). *Diagnostic and statistical manual of mental disorders* (4th ed., text rev.). Washington, DC: Author.

American Psychiatric Association. (2013). *Diagnostic and statistical manual of mental disorders* (5th ed.). Arlington, VA: American Psychiatric Publishing.

Bauermeister, J. J., Shrout, P.E., Chavez, L., Rubio-Stipec, M., Ramirez, R., Padilla, L., ... Canino, G. (2007). ADHD and gender: Are risks and sequel of ADHD the same for boys and girls? *Journal of Child Psychology and Psychiatry, 48*(8), 831–839.

Bloom, B., Jones L. I., Freeman G. (2013). Summary health statistics for U.S. children: National Health Interview Survey, 2012. *Vital and Health Statistics, 10*(258), 1–73.

Centers for Disease Control and Prevention (April 29, 2015). Key findings: Trends in the parent-report of health care provider-diagnosis and medication treatment for ADHD: United States, 2003-2011. Retrieved from: http://www.cdc.gov/ncbddd/adhd/features/key-findings-adhd72013.html

Cortese, S., Holtmann, M., Banaschewski, T., Buitelaar, J., Coghill, D., Danckaerts, M., ... Sergeant, J. (2013). Practitioner review: current best practice in the management of adverse events during treatment with ADHD medications in children and adolescents. *Journal of Child Psychology and Psychiatry, 54*(3), 227–246.

Faraone, S. V., Sergeant, J, Gillberg, C., & Biederman, J. (2003). The worldwide prevalence of ADHD: Is it an American condition? *World Psychiatry, 2*(2), 104–113.

Ferrin, M., Ruiz-Veguilla, M., Blanc-Betes, M., El Abd, S., Lax-Pericall, T., Sinclair, M., & Taylor, E. (2012). Evaluation of attitudes towards treatment in adolescents with attention deficit hyperactivity disorder (ADHD). *European Child & Adolescent Psychiatry, 21*(7), 387–401. doi:10.1007/s00787-012-0277-6

Gupta, R., & Kar, B. R. (2010). Specific cognitive deficits in ADHD: A diagnostic concern in differential diagnosis. *Journal of Child and Family Studies, 19*, 778–786.

Hallowell, E. M., & Ratey, J. J. (2011). *Driven to distraction: Recognizing and coping with attention deficit disorder from childhood through adulthood.* New York, NY: Random House.

Hoffman, J. B., & DuPaul, G. J. (2000). Psychoeducational interventions for children and adolescents with attention-deficit/hyperactivity disorder. *Child and Adolescent Psychiatric Clinics of North America, 9*(3), 647–61.

Klein, R. G., Mannuzza, S., Olazagasti, M. A., Roizen, E., Hutchison, J. A., Lashua, E. C., & Castellanos, F. X. (2012). Clinical and functional outcome of childhood attention-deficit/hyperactivity disorder 33 years later. *Archives of General Psychiatry, 69*(12), 1295–1303.

Lange, K. W., Reichl, S., Lange, K. M., Tucha, L., & Tucha, O. (2010). The history of attention deficit hyperactivity disorder. *Attention Deficit Hyperactivity Disorder, 2*(4), 241–255. doi:10.1007/s12402-010-0045-8

Loe, I. M., & Feldman, H. M. (2007). Academic and educational outcomes of children with ADHD. *Journal of Pediatric Psychology, 32*(6), 643–654. doi:10.1093/jpepsy/jsl054

Mannuzza, S., Klein, R. G., Klein, D. F., Bessler, A., & Shrout, P. (2002). Accuracy of adult recall of childhood attention deficit hyperactivity disorder. *American Journal of Psychiatry, 159*(11), 1882–1888.

Montoya, A., Colum, F., & Ferrin, M. (2011). Is psychoeducation for parents and teachers of children and adolescents with ADHD efficacious? A systematic literature review. *European Psychiatry, 26*(3), 166–175. doi:10.1016/j.eurpsy.2010.10.005

Pfiffner, L. J., Villodas, M., Kaiser, N., Rooney, M., & McBurnett, K. (2013). Educational outcomes of a collaborative school-home behavioral intervention for ADHD. *School Psychology Quarterly, 28*(1), 25–36. doi:10.1037/spq0000016

Pollak, J., Levy, S., & Breitholtz, T. (1999). Screening for medical and neurodevelopmental disorders for the professional counselor. *Journal of Counseling & Development, 77*(3), 350–358.

Rinn, A. N., & Reynolds, M. J. (2012). Overexcitabilities and ADHD in the gifted: An examination. *Roeper Review, 34*(1), 38–45. doi:0.1080/02783193.2012.627551

Shemmassian, S. K., & Lee, S. S. (2012). Comparing four methods of integrating parent and teacher symptom ratings of attention-deficit/hyperactivity disorder (ADHD). *Journal of Psychopathological Behavior Assessment, 34*(1), 1–10. doi:10.1007/s10862-011-9262-5

Sibley, M. H., Pelham, W. E., Molina, B. S. G., Gnagy, E. M., Waschbusch, D. A., Kuriyan, A. B., … Karch, K. M. (2012). Diagnosing ADHD in adolescence. *Journal of Consulting and Clinical Psychology, 80*(1), 139–150. doi:10.1037/a0026577

Still, G. F. (1902). On some abnormal psychical conditions in children: The Goulstonian lectures. *Lancet, 159*(4102), 1008–1012.

Tarver, J., Daley, D., & Sayal, K. (2014). Attention-deficit hyperactivity disorder (ADHD): An updated review of the essential facts. *Child: Care, health and development, 40*(6), 762–774.

Tarver, J., Daley, D., & Sayal, K. (2015). Beyond symptom control for attention-deficit hyperactivity disorder (ADHD): What can parents do to improve outcomes? *Child: Care, health and development, 41*(1), 1–14. doi:10.1111/cch.12159

Visser, S. N., Danielson, M. L., Bitsko, R. H., Holbrook, J. R., Kogan, M. D., Ghandour, R. M., … Blumberg, S. J. (2014). Trends in the parent-report of health care provider-diagnosed and medicated attention-deficit/hyperactivity disorder: United States, 2003–2011. *Journal of the American Academy of Child & Adolescent Psychiatry, 53*(1), 34–46.e.2.

Wåhlstedt, C., Thorell, L. B., & Bohlin G. (2009). Heterogeneity in ADHD: Neuropsychological pathways, comorbidity, and symptom domains. *Journal of Abnormal Child Psychology, 37*(4), 551–564. doi:10.1007/s10802-008-9286-9

Chapter 7

Schizophrenia Spectrum and Other Psychotic Disorders

Tara Chandrasekhar, Lindsey M. Hazzard, and Linmarie Sikich

Introduction

Psychosis is characterized by a loss of touch with reality. Psychotic symptoms are typically classified as positive or negative, referring to the presence or absence of features compared with what one sees in a typically developing child or adolescent. Positive symptoms consist of perceptual abnormalities in any sensory modality without an external stimulus (hallucinations), fixed beliefs that are not amenable to change (delusions), and disorganized speech or behavior. Disorganized behavior may present in myriad ways, including childlike regression, unpredictable agitation, or a lack of interaction with others. Negative symptoms include reduced expression of emotions or limited motivation to participate in typical activities. Catatonia is characterized by inappropriate interaction with the environment, including resistance to instructions, unusual posture or limb movements, or purposeless psychomotor activity (American Psychiatric Association [APA], 2013). See Table 7.1 for definitions of terms often used to describe psychotic symptoms.

Psychosis is a defining feature of several mental disorders, including schizophrenia, brief psychotic disorder, delusional disorder, and schizophreniform disorder. Psychosis may accompany bipolar disorder or a depressive disorder. It also may be induced by a medical illness, prescription medication, or drug of abuse. A child or adolescent with psychosis may suffer from a combination of symptoms, including impaired reality testing, perceptual abnormalities, disorganized thinking, inappropriate affect or behavior, and a disturbance of social relatedness.

When schizophrenia spectrum disorders occur in childhood or adolescence, they often derail normal development and cause significant morbidity and suffering to the child and family members. Youth may fail to achieve typical developmental milestones and are at higher risk for poor outcomes or reduced functioning (American Association of Child and Adolescent Psychiatry, 2012). For example, an adolescent may withdraw from social interactions, fail to graduate from high school, or struggle to work at a first job.

This chapter is organized based on the framework provided by the *Diagnostic and Statistical Manual of Mental Disorders, Fifth Edition* (*DSM-5*; APA, 2013), which lists psychotic disorders along a gradient of psychopathology. Emphasis will be placed on the aspects of these disorders most relevant to counselors who assess and treat children and adolescents.

148

TABLE 7.1   Definitions of Commonly Used Terms to Describe Psychosis

- Positive Symptoms:
  - Impaired reality testing: beliefs that do not reflect most youth's understanding of what is realistically possible or of the laws of nature
  - Hallucinations: perceptual experiences that do not reflect actual stimuli in the environment. Hallucinations may be auditory, visual, tactile, or olfactory. They may appear with no stimulus at all or may be a misinterpretation of something in the environment
  - Delusions: fixed, false beliefs that are extremely difficult or impossible to change despite conflicting evidence
  - Disorganized thinking: typically inferred from the form or content of speech. An examiner may notice the following:
    - Loose associations: switching from one topic to another
    - Tangentiality: Answers are minimally related or completely unrelated to the questions being asked
    - Word salad: Language may be incomprehensible
    - Thought latency or thought blocking: Responses to questions take a very long time or do not occur

- Negative symptoms:
  - Affective flattening: reductions in the expression of emotions in the face, eye contact, intonation of speech (prosody), and movements of the hand, head, and face that normally give an emotional emphasis to speech
  - Avolition: a decrease in motivated self-initiated purposeful activities
  - Anhedonia: decreased ability to experience pleasure from positive stimuli or a degradation in the recollection of pleasure previously experienced
  - Amotivation: a state of lacking any motivation to engage in an activity, characterized by a lack of perceived competence and/or a failure to value the activity or its outcomes
  - Alogia: diminished speech output
  - Apathy: absence or suppression of emotion, feeling, concern, or passion; an indifference to things generally found to be exciting or moving
  - Asociality: reduced initiative for interacting with other people

- Catatonia: abnormal movements or behavior, which range from stupor failure to move limbs voluntarily when positioned by others, repetitive movements, to agitated movements

Description of Disorder

SCHIZOTYPAL (PERSONALITY) DISORDER

Schizotypal personality disorder is considered within the schizophrenia spectrum, despite the fact that it is a personality disorder. Symptoms may emerge in early adolescence and adulthood and should be differentiated from other psychotic disorders. Features of the disorder include a pervasive pattern of social and interpersonal deficits, cognitive and perceptual distortions, and odd or eccentric behavior. A child or adolescent who is eventually diagnosed with schizotypal personality disorder may exhibit a preference for solitary activities, limited and strained peer relationships, low academic achievement, social anxiety, hypersensitivity, bizarre fantasies, and unusual thoughts or language.

Youth with this disorder do not meet the diagnostic criteria for another psychotic disorder, because abnormalities in beliefs, thinking and perception do not rise to the level seen in a schizophrenia spectrum disorder (APA, 2013).

Delusional Disorder

Delusional disorder is characterized by the presence of delusional thinking for at least one month in the absence of prominent hallucinations and significant deterioration in functioning. If hallucinations are present, they are related to the underlying theme of the client's delusions. The lifetime prevalence of delusional disorder is estimated to be 0.2 percent; this disorder is typically thought to have an adult onset, in the mid- to late 30s, though it may be rarely identified in adolescents (APA, 2013). Many affected individuals are likely not identified because they do not seek treatment for this condition (Sadock & Sadock, 2007). The low prevalence and infrequent identification of the disorder likely contributes to the lack of data on specific epidemiological factors and clinical features that may be unique to children and adolescents.

Delusions often involve situations that may occur in real life (infidelity, poisoning, or illness) but the affected individual cannot be persuaded that his or her beliefs are false, even when presented with convincing evidence otherwise. Affected individuals often have little to no insight into their condition. Negative outcomes tend to occur when an individual is unable to resist acting on a delusional belief. For example, an adolescent with a delusional belief that a celebrity is in love with her may not be identified unless she becomes extremely persistent or threatening in her pursuit of a relationship. Subtypes of delusional disorder include erotomanic, grandiose, jealous, persecutory, somatic, mixed, and unspecified types (see Table 7.2 for relevant clinical examples by subtype).

This disorder is differentiated from schizophrenia by the lack of functional impairment, obviously bizarre or odd behavior, and absence of negative symptoms. Cultural influences must be taken into account when evaluating a client for a delusional disorder; the context of the potential delusion should be considered within his or her cultural or religious background, and the potential delusion should be in disagreement with the values of the client's community.

Brief Psychotic Disorder

Psychotic symptoms (delusions, hallucinations, or disorganized speech) occur for more than one day and less than one month in brief psychotic disorder. Symptoms have sudden

TABLE 7.2   Clinical Examples of Delusional Disorder by Subtype

Erotomanic type—a teenage male becomes convinced that a prominent local female politician is in love with him.

Grandiose type—a 12-year-old female endorses a belief that she alone possesses the knowledge and ability needed to cure a rare medical disease.

Jealous type—an adolescent female is fixated on the belief that her boyfriend has been unfaithful, and uses information on social media to bolster her conviction.

Persecutory type—an individual repeatedly calls the police, reporting that her neighbors are following her, listening to her phone calls, and opening her mail.

Somatic type—a female youth visits the health department multiple times, requesting a pregnancy test, because she is convinced that she is expecting a baby.

onset (change from a nonpsychotic state to a psychotic state within two weeks, usually without a prodrome). After psychotic symptoms remit, there is an eventual return to the client's premorbid level of functioning. The illness should not be better explained by another psychiatric or medical disorder. Though lasting a brief period, symptoms may be severe enough to warrant close supervision, assistance with activities of daily living (e.g., hygiene and nutrition), and even potentially hospitalization for suicidal or aggressive behavior.

This illness may present across the life span, from adolescence to late adulthood, though the average age of onset is thought to be in the mid-30s (APA, 2013). Individuals who have undergone a major stressor may be at increased risk of the disorder (Sadock & Sadock, 2007). A brief psychotic disorder can occur with or without a marked stressor, with onset during pregnancy or the postpartum period, or with catatonic behavior. A culturally accepted response to a stressor should not be considered a psychotic symptom. For example, an adolescent from a family that strongly believes in the existence of spirits may report hearing the voice of a deceased grandmother saying "good-bye" immediately after her death. This is not felt to be a psychotic symptom if it aligns with the family's beliefs and doesn't cause functional impairment. Sidebar 7.1 provides a case example of this disorder.

SIDEBAR 7.1: CASE EXAMPLE—BRIEF PSYCHOTIC DISORDER

Mary is a 15-year-old female with no psychiatric or medical history. The summer before ninth grade her family moves, and her grandmother unexpectedly dies. Though Mary is very upset by this loss, her parents do not initially notice any changes in her behavior. However, for the month of August, Mary refuses to eat meals with her family, stating that her food is poisoned. She appears increasingly guarded. She hears a male voice narrating her actions and intermittently threatening her family members. She takes less interest in her personal hygiene and isolates herself from peers. However, after one month's duration, her symptoms appear to improve markedly. She reports that auditory hallucinations have ceased and begins eating meals with her family. She eventually begins to participate in social outings and joins the soccer team. Two years later there is no recurrence of psychotic symptoms.

SCHIZOPHRENIFORM DISORDER

Criteria for schizophreniform disorder are met if a child or adolescent displays at least two of the five symptoms of Criterion A for schizophrenia for longer than one month but less than six months. Though social or occupational functioning may be affected, individuals typically do not exhibit the degree of functional decline seen in schizophrenia (APA, 2013). The previous level of social or occupational functioning is regained after the symptoms go into remission. This disorder is uncommon in adolescents and young adults; its incidence is thought to be similar to that of schizophrenia (APA, 2013; Sadock & Sadock, 2007). Most estimates of progression to schizophrenia range between 60 to 80 percent (Sadock & Sadock, 2007); unfortunately this epidemiologic feature has not been well studied in children and adolescents. Because of differences between duration criteria for schizophrenia in the United States (six months) and Europe (one month, using *International Classification of Diseases, Tenth Revision [ICD-10]*, guidelines), it may be more appropriate to diagnosis individuals with less than six months of psychotic symptoms who do not ultimately develop schizophrenia with a brief psychotic disorder (Sadock & Sadock, 2007).

SCHIZOPHRENIA

Schizophrenia is a complex, potentially disabling illness, involving a multitude of deficits in the cognitive, behavioral, and emotional domains. Referred to as early-onset schizophrenia when diagnosed prior to the age of 18 (the peak age at onset for the first psychotic episode is in the early to mid-20s for males and in the late 20s for females; APA, 2013), it is diagnosed with the same criteria and considered the same illness as adult onset schizophrenia (American Association of Child and Adolescent Psychiatry, 2012; Kuniyoshi & McClellan, 2010). Although the worldwide prevalence of schizophrenia is 0.3 to 0.7 percent (APA, 2013), early-onset schizophrenia is estimated to occur in one to two per 1,000 adolescents. Onset in childhood appears to be quite rare, less than one of 10,000 children (American Association of Child and Adolescent Psychiatry, 2012; Sadock & Sadock, 2007).

Symptoms tend to occur more frequently in males than females; as age increases, males and females are affected at a one-to-one ratio. Males typically report onset of symptoms between 10 to 25 years, whereas females report onset at 25 to 35 years and a second peak after age 40 (Sadock & Sadock, 2007). The incidence of schizophrenia appears to be higher for children growing up in an urban environment and for some minority ethnic groups (APA, 2013).

Early-onset illness, particularly in children, appears to be associated with nonspecific emotional-behavioral disturbances, intellectual and language delays, and premorbid developmental abnormalities (APA, 2013; Sadock & Sadock, 2007). Because there are fewer cases of childhood-onset schizophrenia, the validity of the diagnostic criteria in children younger than 6 years has not been established (American Academy of Child and Adolescent Psychiatry, 2012). Rates of comorbid attention-deficit/hyperactivity disorder (ADHD), depressive disorder, and separation anxiety disorder are extremely high in children and adolescents (Sadock & Sadock, 2007). Schizophrenia is viewed as a multifactorial illness with no single cause; rather risk is increased by specific genetic and environmental factors.

Schizophrenia is characterized by one month of active phase symptoms (less if successfully treated), including delusions, hallucinations, disorganized speech, grossly disorganized or catatonic behavior, and negative symptoms. Continuous signs of disturbance must be present for at least six months, including one month of active phase symptoms. Symptoms should not be caused by a bipolar, depressive, or schizoaffective disorder, or by medical illness, medication, or drug abuse. A child with a preexisting autism spectrum disorder or communication disorder of childhood onset meets criteria for schizophrenia only if there are prominent delusions or hallucinations for at least one month (or less, if successfully treated), in addition to other features, such as social-communication deficits or restricted and repetitive behaviors. Youth must show evidence of a functional decline, such as failing school grades, withdrawal from social activities, or poor attention to personal hygiene. Youth also fail to achieve expected milestones based on age and developmental level. Often youth lack insight into their impairments.

Though not included in *DSM-5* diagnostic criteria, cognitive impairment is a well-established and disabling feature of schizophrenia. Cognitive deficits include diminished intellectual ability, impaired verbal memory, reduced learning and processing speed, reduced attentional reserve, and trouble with organization and problem solving (Frangou, 2013; Puetz, Günther, Kahraman-Lanzerath, Herpertz-Dahlmann, & Konrad, 2014). See Sidebar 7.2 for a case example of this disorder.

SIDEBAR 7.2: CASE EXAMPLE—EARLY-ONSET SCHIZOPHRENIA

John is a 12-year-old male with a family history of bipolar disorder and depression. At age 8 he begins to see shadows and "images" of spiders crawling on his walls. He expresses worried thoughts about "murder" and "problems in the world" and seems overly concerned about the safety of his family members. When his parents tell him that he is imagining things and shouldn't be scared, he stops reporting these experiences until a period of heightened family stress. Then he wakes his parents in the middle of the night, shaking because he sees spiders in his room trying to bite him. He expresses a fear that other people are watching him and believes that peers at school do not like him. A previously social child, he refuses to skateboard with his neighbors and avoids gatherings. He denies depression, substance use, suicidal ideation, or manic symptoms.

A counselor may obtain a history of attenuated psychosis syndrome or prodromal symptoms, characterized by mild and transient perceptual abnormalities, delusional interpretations, and disorganized speech. During the prodrome, one retains insight into his impairments but is at increased risk of developing schizophrenia over time. Although the majority of those with prodromal symptoms do not develop schizophrenia, they often develop other psychiatric problems. Hence, the prodromal phase is an important time for close monitoring and intervention to increase coping skills and social supports (Addington et al., 2011; Kuniyoshi & McClellan, 2010).

SCHIZOAFFECTIVE DISORDER

Schizoaffective disorder is characterized by the co-occurrence of a major depressive or manic episode concurrent with Criterion A of schizophrenia. This disorder is distinguished from bipolar disorder with psychotic features by the presence of delusions or hallucinations for at least two weeks in the absence of a major mood episode for the lifetime duration of the illness. The major depressive episode must include a pervasive depressed mood, rather than loss of interest or anhedonia (though this may also be present). An individual with schizoaffective disorder must manifest symptoms consistent with a major mood episode for the majority of the total duration of the illness, during either active or residual phases. Assessment of cognition, depression, and mania symptoms is extremely useful to differentiate schizoaffective disorder from other schizophrenia spectrum disorders.

Varied interpretations of previous criteria for schizoaffective disorder have affected the ability of researchers to study the incidence and prevalence of the disorder. Currently, the lifetime prevalence is estimated to be 0.3 percent (APA, 2013). The prevalence in youth less than 18 years of age has not been well studied, and the current diagnostic framework does not specify particular features unique to children and adolescents. The typical age of onset is early adulthood, though symptoms may present in adolescence or late in life. Schizoaffective disorder, bipolar type, may be more common in younger individuals, while schizoaffective disorder, depressive type, may be more common in older individuals (Sadock & Sadock, 2007).

Unlike schizophrenia, functional decline is often seen but is not required for the diagnosis, and Criteria B (social dysfunction) and F (exclusion of autism spectrum disorder or other communication disorder of childhood onset) for schizophrenia do not have to be met (APA, 2013). However, there is substantial variability in the severity of the illness within affected individuals. Those with more prominent psychotic symptoms are thought to have a worse prognosis compared with those with prominent mood symptoms (Sadock & Sadock, 2007). Sidebar 7.3 provides a case example of schizoaffective disorder.

SIDEBAR 7.3:   CASE EXAMPLE—SCHIZOAFFECTIVE DISORDER

Janice is a 17-year-old high-school senior who reported prominent hallucinations (a male voice narrating her daily actions) and a delusion that her science teacher was sabotaging her attempts to gain admission to a private university. These symptoms were present in isolation for two months before she also began to manifest symptoms consistent with a bipolar episode. She attempted to create several online businesses selling baked goods, reported that she was very wealthy and powerful, and had excessive energy despite very little sleep. The psychotic and manic symptoms lasted for about three months together before her bipolar symptoms abated. Her auditory hallucinations and paranoia continued for about another month before they also disappeared. She continued to report mood symptoms with intermittent psychotic symptoms over time.

SUBSTANCE/MEDICATION-INDUCED PSYCHOTIC DISORDER

A prescription medication (e.g., dexamethasone) or an illicit substance (e.g., cocaine, amphetamine, and cannabis) may cause a psychotic disorder. Symptoms, primarily prominent hallucinations or delusions, occur soon after exposure to the medication or substance intoxication. Psychotic symptoms may also occur during withdrawal from the substance. Symptoms are felt to be the direct physiologic effect of the offending agent and psychotic symptoms cease in a short amount of time (within one month or less) after the offending agent is stopped. The prevalence of substance-induced psychotic disorder in children and adolescents is not known. Table 7.3 provides an abbreviated list of common agents that may induce a psychotic disorder.

PSYCHOTIC DISORDER DUE TO ANOTHER MEDICAL CONDITION

A child or adolescent with a medical illness may present with psychotic symptoms. Symptoms occur during the course of the medical illness, cause functional impairment, and

TABLE 7.3 An Abbreviated List of Medications and Substances That May Elicit Psychotic Symptoms

Drugs of Abuse	Prescription Medications	Toxins
• Alcohol	• Anesthetic agents	• Insecticides
• Cannabis	• Anticonvulsants	• Nerve gas
• Cocaine	• Antihistamines	• Carbon monoxide
• Hallucinogens (phencyclidine, LSD)	• Corticosteroids	• Volatile substances (fuel, paint)
• Inhalant	• Psychostimulants	• Mercury
• Methamphetamine	• Sedative-hypnotics	

Source: APA, 2013; Kuniyoshi & McClellan, 2010.

are not because of an underlying mental disorder. This must be distinguished from the presence of both a medical illness and a psychiatric illness. A psychiatrist, primary care physician, and other appropriate medical specialists should evaluate an individual with this disorder. Often a medical workup is initiated in a hospital setting, though individuals may also be seen in ambulatory clinics. Identification of and treatment of the underlying medical illness may be lifesaving.

CATATONIA

An often puzzling and fascinating array of features characterizes catatonia, a constellation of psychomotor symptoms. Catatonia can occur with psychotic, autism spectrum, bipolar, and depressive disorders, as well as multiple medical conditions. An individual with catatonia may present with hyperactive behaviors (agitation, repetitive, or stereotypic movements) or hypoactive behaviors (stupor, mutism, negativism, or no response to instructions). Catalepsy (holding an unusual posture against gravity) and waxy flexibility (slight resistance to positioning by an examiner) may be elicited on a physical examination. An individual may grimace, repeat another's speech (echolalia), or mimic another's movements (echopraxia). In severe cases, an individual may require constant supervision for his or her safety or be at risk of malnutrition, exhaustion, or self-injury (APA, 2013).

OTHER SPECIFIED SCHIZOPHRENIA SPECTRUM AND OTHER PSYCHOTIC DISORDER

This category applies to individuals who present with characteristic symptoms of a schizophrenia spectrum or other psychotic disorder that cause distress but do not meet criteria for another disorder. A potential use of this disorder would be to identify the presence of attenuated psychosis syndrome, symptoms that are below a threshold for full psychosis. Another example would be a child or adolescent whose parent expresses delusional beliefs that the individual also endorses, but the delusions do not rise to the level of a delusional disorder. Over time an individual with this diagnosis may meet criteria for another psychotic disorder.

UNSPECIFIED SCHIZOPHRENIA SPECTRUM AND OTHER PSYCHOTIC DISORDER

This diagnosis applies to cases in which individuals report symptoms consistent with a schizophrenia spectrum disorder that causes distress and functional impairment but do not meet the full criteria for any of the other disorders in the schizophrenia spectrum. An example would be an evaluation in an emergency room setting in which insufficient information is available to make a more specific diagnosis.

DSM-5 Criteria

The *DSM-5* presents diagnostic criteria for schizophrenia spectrum and other psychotic disorders. The diagnostic criteria for a selected group of disorders are presented in this section, as well as a discussion of important changes from the *DSM-IV-TR* to the *DSM-5*. These criteria represent an important diagnostic framework to conceptualize signs and symptoms of psychotic disorders, but currently do not capture the underlying pathophysiology of these complex and heterogeneous illnesses.

In addition to utilizing the diagnostic criteria for a given disorder, counselors should apply course specifiers indicated in the *DSM-5* to communicate the age of disorder onset, timing of symptom remission, and duration of symptom expression. Used after a schizophrenia spectrum or other psychotic disorder has been present for one year, course specifiers provide counselors the ability to document first episodes, multiple episodes, and the stage of illness (acute episode, partial remission, or full remission; Heckers et al., 2013; Tandon et al., 2013). This may have important implications in the formulation of a treatment plan. For example, treatment may focus on crisis management and symptom stabilization (with medications and supportive therapy) during an acute first episode. Treatment may then shift to psychoeducation, monitoring of side effects of medications, and family support when the first episode is in partial remission. A client with continuous episodes may require services at an increased intensity compared with a client whose symptoms are in full or partial remission. Severity may be rated using the Clinician-Rated Dimensions of Psychosis Symptom Severity, which may be accessed on pages 742–744 of the *DSM-5* or online at http://www.psychiatry.org/practice/dsm/dsm5/online-assessment-measures.

This measure is a quantitative assessment of the symptoms, including hallucinations, delusions, disorganized speech, abnormal psychomotor behavior and negative symptoms, impaired cognition, depression, and mania. Further discussion of this rating scale follows discussion of *DSM-5* criteria.

DELUSIONAL DISORDER

DSM-5 diagnostic criteria specify that an individual with delusional disorder report one or more delusions for at least one month's duration without associated features that meet diagnostic criteria for schizophrenia. Hallucinations may be present, but they are not considered prominent. Functioning is not markedly impaired, and the individual's behavior is not obviously bizarre. If present, manic or depressive episodes have occurred for brief periods, relative to the duration of delusional periods. The disturbance cannot be better accounted for by another mental disorder (such as body dysmorphic disorder or obsessive-compulsive disorder), the direct effects of a substance, or an underlying medical problem (APA, 2013).

The delusional subtype, presence of bizarre content, and duration of the disorder may be specified. Subtypes of delusional disorder include erotomanic type, grandiose type, jealous type, persecutory type, somatic type, mixed type, and unspecified type. Delusions are considered bizarre if they are incomprehensible or not considered to be plausible based on common life experiences. An example includes an individual's belief that his small intestine is infested with maggots and requires surgical removal.

BRIEF PSYCHOTIC DISORDER

Diagnostic criteria for this disorder specify that an affected individual must present with one or more of the following symptoms: delusions, hallucinations, disorganized speech, and grossly disorganized or catatonic behavior. A behavioral disturbance alone without evidence of positive symptoms (delusions or hallucinations) is not sufficient to meet diagnostic criteria. Symptoms must be present for at least one day and less than one month. The individual must eventually return to his or her prior level of functioning. The disturbance cannot be better accounted for by another mental disorder (such as a major depressive or bipolar disorder with psychotic features or another psychotic disorder), the direct effects of a substance, or an underlying medical problem (APA, 2013).

Counselors may specify if the disturbance occurs with or without marked stressors, with peripartum onset, or with catatonia. To be considered related to a stressor, psychotic symptoms must occur in response to an event that would be considered markedly stressful to other individuals in a similar situation. Peripartum onset is considered if psychotic symptoms present during pregnancy or within four weeks following delivery (APA, 2013).

SCHIZOPHRENIFORM DISORDER

An individual affected by this disorder must report two or more of the following symptoms for a significant portion of time during a one-month period (less if successfully treated): delusions, hallucinations, disorganized behavior, grossly disorganized or catatonic behavior, and negative symptoms. Delusions or hallucinations must be present. The duration of the episode is less than six months (but greater than one month, distinguishing the illness from brief psychotic disorder). The individual should not meet criteria for schizoaffective, depressive, or bipolar disorders. The disturbance should not be better explained by the effects of a substance or an underlying medical condition (APA, 2013).

Counselors may specify if the affected individual's illness occurs with or without good prognostic features or with catatonia. Good prognostic features include a fairly rapid onset of prominent psychotic symptoms (within four weeks of the change in behavior or functioning), reported confusion about the symptoms, good premorbid functioning, and the absence of a blunted or flat affect (APA, 2013).

SCHIZOPHRENIA

Of the disorders listed in the *DSM-5*'s Schizophrenia Spectrum and Other Psychotic Disorders chapter, schizophrenia is the most studied in children and adolescents. There are

TABLE 7.4   *DSM-5* Criteria for Schizophrenia

A. Over the course of a one-month period, an individual must have at least two of the following symptoms. At least one of the symptoms must be (1), (2), or (3):
  1. Delusions
  2. Hallucinations
  3. Disorganized speech
  4. Grossly disorganized or catatonic behavior
  5. Negative symptoms

B. Level of functioning is significantly impaired since the illness started. An individual may show impaired functioning at work, in relationships, or in self-care. A child or adolescent may fail to achieve the expected level of functioning

C. Symptoms must persist for at least six months. An individual must have the symptoms of Criterion A for at least one month. There may be periods of negative symptoms, prodromal disturbance, or residual evidence of illness

D. The individual does not meet diagnostic criteria for schizoaffective disorder, depressive disorder, or bipolar illness with psychotic features

E. The individual does have an underlying medical condition, and symptoms cannot be directly attributed to a substance

F. Children with an autism spectrum disorder or a communication disorder of childhood onset must have prominent delusions or hallucinations in addition to the other required criteria for a diagnosis of schizophrenia

no separate diagnostic criteria for early-onset schizophrenia (symptoms presenting before age 18) or other early-onset psychotic disorders. See Table 7.4 for a summary of *DSM-5* diagnostic criteria for schizophrenia.

SCHIZOAFFECTIVE DISORDER

The *DSM-5* diagnostic criteria specify that an affected individual must present with symptoms that meet the criteria for a major mood episode (major depressive or manic) and Criterion A of schizophrenia for an uninterrupted period. Additionally, delusions or hallucinations must be present for two weeks in the absence of a major mood episode during the lifetime duration of the illness. The individual must report symptoms that meet criteria for a major mood episode during the active and residual portions of the illness, and the disorder is not better explained by the effects of a substance or an underlying medical condition (APA, 2013).

Counselors may specify if the individual's symptoms are primarily bipolar or depressive type, and identify the presence of catatonia. If a manic episode is part of the presentation, the bipolar subtype specifier is used. The presence of a major depressive episode on presentation warrants the use of the term depressive subtype (APA, 2013).

SUBSTANCE/MEDICATION INDUCED PSYCHOTIC DISORDER

Individuals with this disorder present with delusions and/or hallucinations that can be directly attributed to substance intoxication or withdrawal, or exposure to a medication based on the history, physical examination, or laboratory findings. The suspected substance or medication should be known to produce psychotic symptoms in other individuals, and the symptoms should not be better explained by another psychotic disorder or delirium. The affected individual must experience clinically significant distress or impairment in functioning.

PSYCHOTIC DISORDER DUE TO ANOTHER MEDICAL CONDITION

This disorder is characterized by the presence of prominent delusions or hallucinations that are the direct pathophysiological consequence of a medical condition based on history, physical examination, or laboratory findings. The symptoms are not because of another mental disorder and do not occur exclusively during the course of a delirium. Individuals show evidence of clinically significant distress or impairment in functioning. Counselors may specify if the predominant symptom is delusions or hallucinations (for example, psychotic disorder due to anti-N-methyl-D-aspartate [NMDA] receptor encephalitis, with hallucinations).

THE *DSM-IV-TR* VERSUS THE *DSM-5*

The *DSM-5* preserves much of the categorical framework of schizophrenia spectrum disorders captured in the *DSM-IV-TR*, though disorders are reorganized on a gradient of pathophysiology to emphasize the spectrum of illness. The *DSM-5* encourages diagnosticians to consider a more severe psychotic disorder (such as schizophrenia) after time-limited or less severe conditions are excluded (Heckers et al., 2013). Because current research efforts have not yet yielded the underlying mechanism of psychotic illnesses (Heckers, 2008), the descriptions in the *DSM-5* remain categorical, though important attempts have been made to clarify or better define the symptoms required for diagnosis. Sidebar 7.4 highlights changes from the *DSM-IV-TR* to the *DSM-5*.

SIDEBAR 7.4:   IMPORTANT CHANGES FROM THE *DSM-IV-TR* TO THE *DSM-5*

- Disorders are presented partly based on severity of illness. Schizophrenia is presented later in the chapter to reduce the likelihood that counselors would place a greater emphasis on schizophrenia when evaluating individuals with psychotic symptoms.
- Schizophrenia Spectrum Disorder retained the *DSM-IV-TR* requirements of at least two of five symptoms; however it removed the *DSM-IV-TR*'s exception that "Only one Criterion A symptom is required if delusions are bizarre or hallucinations consist of a voice keeping up a running commentary on the persons' behavior or thoughts, or two or more voices conversing with each other" (APA, 2000, p. 312).
- Removal of schizophrenia subtypes (e.g. paranoid type and undifferentiated type) that were not reliable descriptors of illness presentation and course.

- At least one of the two required symptoms of schizophrenia is delusions, hallucinations, or disorganized speech.
- Removal of the special emphasis on bizarre delusion as a pathognomonic sign of schizophrenia.
- Bizarre delusions are no longer exclusionary criteria for delusional disorder.
- Shared Psychotic Disorder (Folie a Deux) was removed and integrated into Delusional Disorder.
- The catatonia specifier is used in psychotic, bipolar, depressive, and autism spectrum disorders and medical conditions. It may be used as a diagnosis for cases where the medical and psychiatric etiology is unknown.
- Significant mood symptoms must be present for the majority of the illness for a diagnosis of schizoaffective disorder rather than schizophrenia.
- Clarification of Criterion F of schizophrenia to include other communication disorders of childhood onset.
- Attenuated psychosis syndrome is included in the diagnostic criteria for *other specified schizophrenia spectrum and other psychotic disorders* and in Section III as an area for future study.

Within the categorical framework, dimensional assessments are recommended to attempt to capture the considerable variability of symptom profiles, which may potentially predict illness course or functional impairments, influence treatment planning, and contribute to future research of psychotic disorders (Barch et al., 2013; Heckers et al., 2013). The severity of symptoms may predict important aspects of the illness, such as the degree of cognitive and neurobiological deficits (Barch et al., 2013) and contribute to development of a differential diagnosis. By tracking symptoms over time, counselors may be able to identify important patterns that influence the diagnosis and treatment plan.

Dimensional assessments evaluate the severity of the five domains that define a schizophrenia spectrum disorder (hallucinations, delusions, disorganized speech, abnormal psychomotor behavior, and negative symptoms) as well as cognition, depression, and mania. Using the Clinician-Rated Dimensions of Psychosis Symptom Severity (included in Section III of the *DSM-5* or online at http://www.psychiatry.org/practice/dsm/dsm5/online-assessment-measures), counselors assign a rating to the relative presence and impairment of these domains of a client's presentation using a five-point scale for the previous seven days (APA, 2013). Including an assessment of cognitive impairment may alert counselors to functional abilities and deficits. The scoring refers to cognitive function based on standard deviation from the mean, implying that the counselor has access to neuropsychological testing (Maj, 2013). However, cognition may also be assessed using the Folstein Mini-Mental Status Exam, which tests attention and concentration, orientation, language, memory, and abstract thinking, providing counselors with a relatively rapid assessment of cognitive function (Polanski & Hinkle, 2011). Ratings of mania and depression may alert a counselor to evidence of a mood component to the illness, further

TABLE 7.5 Sample Diagnosis Using *DSM-5* Criteria

295.90 Schizophrenia, first episode, acute episode	
Hallucinations	severe (auditory and visual)
Delusions	mild (persecutory)
Disorganized speech	moderate (speech is difficult to follow)
Abnormal psychomotor behavior	equivocal
Negative symptoms	moderate (decreased facial expressions and gestures)
Cognitive function	equivocal
Depression	not present
Mania	not present

refining the differential diagnosis. See Table 7.5 for a sample diagnosis informed by the Clinician-Rated Dimensions of Psychosis Symptom Severity per the *DSM-5*.

Differential Diagnosis

Counselors must consider psychiatric or neurodevelopmental etiologies, medical illness, or the effect of a substance or medication on a child or adolescent with psychotic symptoms. The following is a discussion of important components of the differential diagnosis. Table 7.6 provides further description of the differential diagnosis for schizophrenia spectrum and other psychotic disorders.

BIPOLAR DISORDER

Affective illnesses may present with psychotic symptoms. These symptoms occur in the context of a mood episode (depression or mania) and are not present during periods of euthymic mood. Negative symptoms in a teenager with schizophrenia may be mistaken for depression, especially since a first episode of psychosis may present with dysphoria. Mania may present with florid psychosis, delusions, and disorganized thought process. Often the symptom presentation over time (following the relative presence and temporal relationship between affective and psychotic symptoms) may help to differentiate a bipolar-related disorder from a schizophrenia spectrum disorder.

MAJOR DEPRESSIVE DISORDER WITH PSYCHOTIC FEATURES

Psychotic symptoms occurring during a major depressive disorder may appear similar to symptoms of schizophrenia. Hallucinations may be mood congruent or mood incongruent. For example, a youth with depression may hear a voice telling him that he should harm himself or that he is unworthy of affection. Apathy, anhedonia, and amotivation associated with depression may mimic negative symptoms of psychosis. Psychotic symptoms are not present during periods of euthymia or remission of depressive illness, differentiating a psychotic depression from a schizophrenia spectrum disorder.

TABLE 7.6   Schizophrenia Spectrum and Other Psychotic Disorders Differential Diagnosis

If the client ...	Then the diagnosis may be ...
Reports a pattern of social AND interpersonal deficits marked by acute discomfort with, AND reduced capacity for, close relationships, as well as by cognitive or perceptual distortions AND eccentricities of behavior	Schizotypal (Personality) Disorder
Reports the presence of one delusion with a duration of one month; AND HAS NEVER MANIFESTED prominent hallucinations, disorganized speech, or negative symptoms; AND functioning is NOT markedly impaired; AND behavior is NOT grossly bizarre, odd, disorganized, or catatonic behavior	Delusional Disorder
Reports the presence of delusions, hallucinations, or disorganized speech; WITH a duration of one day to one month; WITH eventual full return to premorbid level of functioning	Brief Psychotic Disorder, without/with marked stressors (brief reactive psychosis)
Reports the presence of delusions, hallucinations, or disorganized speech; WITH a duration of one day to one month; WITH grossly bizarre, odd, disorganized, or catatonic behavior; WITH eventual full return to premorbid level of functioning	Brief Psychotic Disorder, with catatonia
Reports the presence of delusions, hallucinations, or disorganized speech; WITH onset during pregnancy or within four weeks postpartum; WITH a duration of one day to one month; WITH eventual full return to premorbid level of functioning	Brief Psychotic Disorder, with peripartum onset
Reports the presence of delusions, and/or hallucinations, and/or disorganized speech for a SIGNIFICANT PORTION of time BUT LESS than six months; AND equivocal or no major depressive or manic episodes have occurred concurrently with the active-phase symptoms; BUT DOES NOT report marked functional impairment	Schizophreniform Disorder, with good prognostic features
Reports the presence of delusions, and/or hallucinations, and/or disorganized speech; AND negative grossly bizarre, odd, disorganized, or catatonic behavior; AND mild-moderate negative symptoms for a SIGNIFICANT PORTION of time during one month BUT LESS than six months; AND equivocal or no major depressive or manic episodes have occurred concurrently with the active-phase symptoms; and/or manifests onset of prominent psychotic symptoms within four weeks of the first noticeable change in usual behavior or functioning; and/or confusion or perplexity; and/or good premorbid social and occupational functioning; and/or absence of blunted/flat affect	Schizophreniform Disorder, without good prognostic features
Reports cognitive, emotional, and behavioral dysfunctions IN THE PRESENCE of delusions, and/or hallucinations, and/or disorganized speech; AND negative grossly bizarre, odd, disorganized, or catatonic behavior; AND moderate-severe negative symptoms for at least six months; AND equivocal or no major depressive or manic episodes have occurred concurrently with the active-phase symptoms; AND marked functional impairment	Schizophrenia
Reports an uninterrupted period of illness AND the presence of delusions, and/or hallucinations, and/or disorganized speech, and/or negative grossly bizarre, odd, disorganized, or catatonic behavior, and/or negative symptoms; AND delusions or hallucinations for two or more weeks IN THE ABSENCE of a major depressive episode, BUT WITH a manic episode present for the majority of the total duration of the active and residual portions of the illness	Schizoaffective Disorder, Bipolar Type

TABLE 7.6   (*continued*)

If the client ...	Then the diagnosis may be ...
Reports an uninterrupted period of illness AND the presence of delusions, and/or hallucinations, and/or disorganized speech, and/or negative grossly bizarre, odd, disorganized, or catatonic behavior, and/or negative symptoms; AND delusions or hallucinations for two or more weeks IN THE ABSENCE of a manic episode, BUT WITH a major depressive episode present for the majority of the total duration of the active and residual portions of the illness	Schizoaffective Disorder, Depressive Type
Reports MANIC episode (three or more symptoms; four if the mood is only irritable) lasting at least seven consecutive days AND present most of the day, nearly every day; AND delusions or hallucinations are present at any time in the episode	Bipolar I Disorder, with psychotic features
Reports major depressive episode (five or more symptoms) lasting at least 14 consecutive days AND present most of the day, nearly every day; AND delusions or hallucinations are present at any time in the episode	Major Depressive Disorder, with psychotic features
Reports INTRUSIVE hallucinations (visual or auditory) or NONBIZARRE delusions (persecutory or nihilistic) IN THE CONTEXT of flashbacks AND/OR dissociative symptoms (depersonalization/derealization) WITH a trauma stressor theme IN THE PRESENCE OF intact reality testing	Posttraumatic Stress Disorder, Acute Stress Disorder, Dissociative Identity Disorder, or Depersonalization/ Derealization Disorder
Reports ONSET IN LATER LIFE of nonbizarre delusions (usually persecutory) or simple hallucinations (usually visual) WITHOUT disorganized speech and disorganized behavior IN THE CONTEXT of an acquired etiological syndrome (e.g., Alzheimer's disease or Parkinson's disease), RESULTING in a primary clinical deficit in cognitive function (e.g., complex attention, executive function, learning and memory, language, perceptual-motor, or social cognition) CAUSING decline from a previously attained level of functioning	Major or Mild Neurocognitive Disorder, with behavioral disturbance
Reports TRANSIENT paranoid ideation MOST FREQUENTLY IN RESPONSE to real or imagined abandonment with the real or perceived return of the attachment figure, RESULTING in symptom remission	Borderline Personality Disorder

Source: King, 2014.

POSTTRAUMATIC STRESS DISORDER

Children or adolescents with a history of trauma or abuse may report *psychotic-like* symptoms. These symptoms may represent dissociation or anxiety, intrusive thoughts, derealization, or depersonalization (American Academy of Child and Adolescent Psychiatry, 2012). It may be difficult to differentiate psychotic-like symptoms from an underlying psychotic illness. Those with a history of abuse and adverse life events may be at higher risk for schizophrenia or other psychotic disorders when associated with family history, and a trauma- or stressor-related disorder may be comorbid with a psychotic disorder. Serial assessments over time in conjunction with treatment of target symptoms (e.g., anxiety and irritability) are often helpful to clarify the diagnosis.

AUTISM SPECTRUM DISORDER (ASD)

Impairments in social communication and the presence of restricted interests and repetitive behavior are characteristic of autism spectrum disorder (see Chapter 5). The earlier age of onset and lack of a period of normal development distinguish ASD from psychotic disorders. In addition, youth with ASD do not typically report overt hallucinations or delusions. However, social withdrawal and odd behavior associated with the prodromal phase of early-onset schizophrenia may be similar to the social aloofness characterized by high-functioning autism (Kuniyoshi & McClellan, 2010), and disorganized speech may be seen in both psychosis and autism (APA, 2013).

DELIRIUM

A sudden alteration in mental abilities and confused thinking accompanies delirium, a serious condition that may accompany a variety of medical illnesses or be due to medications or substances. Some features of delirium may mimic a primary psychotic disorder, such as dysphoria, hallucinations, lack of interaction, or agitation. However, disorientation, reduced ability to pay attention to the interview, or problems with cognitive tasks, in addition to the time frame of symptom onset, typically distinguish delirium from psychotic illness. The clinical history is often consistent with severe or chronic medical illness, medication use, infection, surgery, or drug or alcohol abuse. Because delirium is independently associated with increased mortality, identification and treatment of the underlying cause is vital (Kuniyoshi & McClellan, 2010).

MEDICAL ILLNESS

Multiple medical or neurological illnesses may present with psychotic symptoms, including brain tumors, seizure disorders, head injuries, meningitis, autoimmune encephalitis, cerebrovascular accidents, electrolyte abnormalities, blood glucose imbalance, or endocrine disorders. Inherited conditions, such as Wilson's disease and porphyria, may also present with psychotic symptoms (Kuniyoshi & McClellan, 2010; Sikich, 2013). Assessment of medical history, physical exam, neurological evaluation, and other appropriate medical workup is helpful to distinguish medical illness from a schizophrenia spectrum or other psychotic disorder.

OBSESSIVE-COMPULSIVE DISORDER

Severe obsessive-compulsive disorder may present with preoccupations that reach delusional proportions, as well as poor insight into impairments. For example, a child with obsessive-compulsive disorder might scrub her hands repeatedly until they are raw because of a belief that doing otherwise would cause her mother to die. However, this disorder is distinguished from schizophrenia by prominent obsessions and compulsions rather than hallucinations and delusions.

SUBSTANCE INTOXICATION OR WITHDRAWAL

Prescription medication and drugs of abuse may cause psychotic symptoms in youth. A history of psychotic symptoms during use of or withdrawal from a prescription medication or drug of abuse is often suggestive of substance-induced psychotic disorder rather than a schizophrenia spectrum disorder. It may be challenging to make this distinction clinically, especially given comorbid substance use with a primary psychiatric disorder. Removal of the offending agent and monitoring of symptoms over time helps with diagnostic clarification.

MALINGERING

An individual who intentionally produces false or exaggerated symptoms while seeking external incentives (for example to avoid legal charges or to obtain drugs) would be considered to be malingering. This is distinguished from a primary psychotic disorder by the presence of an external incentive, a significant discrepancy between the individual's claimed impairment and objective findings, limited cooperation with the diagnostic evaluation, and antisocial personality disorder (APA, 2013). Often, the time course of illness, collateral information from parents and other sources, and psychological testing helps distinguish a psychotic disorder from malingering.

Assessment Strategies

Youth with possible psychotic symptoms require a thorough psychiatric diagnostic assessment, including separate interviews with the child or adolescent and the parent or caregiver. The counselor should review any past records or information from other sources, such as teachers, therapists, or past providers, including nonpsychiatric medical personnel such as pediatricians or neurologists. A counselor must carefully assess the youth's symptom presentation, course of illness, medical and psychiatric history, current medications, family history, and level of functioning in his or her environment (e.g., school and home). Establish a timeline of symptom presentation, exploring which symptoms occur together or in isolation, and the influence of stressors or psychosocial factors.

Use developmentally appropriate questions to inquire about hallucinations, recognizing that a child may be reluctant or too paranoid to report frightening or confusing psychotic symptoms. Counselors may find differentiating normal childhood imagination or fantasy from psychotic symptoms difficult in an initial interview. Youth with psychotic symptoms tend to report multimodal hallucinations, in auditory, visual, and tactile domains. Children and adolescents often name their hallucinations by referencing their physical characteristics (e.g. "Jay, the man who wears a hat and a coat") or refer to them as culturally referenced phenomena (e.g., "monsters"). True hallucinations are often vivid but lack detail, and typically provoke an emotional or behavioral response from the child. Unlike imaginary companions, youths cannot make hallucinations disappear, though they may learn strategies to ignore them (American Association of Child and Adolescent Psychiatry,

2012; Sikich, 2013). Sidebar 7.5 provides guidance on screening a child or adolescent for psychotic symptoms.

SIDEBAR 7.5:   SCREENING A CHILD OR ADOLESCENT FOR PSYCHOTIC SYMPTOMS (SIKICH, 2013)

Youth frequently do not spontaneously volunteer psychotic symptoms, especially to mental health counselors they have just met. Avoid using jargon, such as "hearing voices," and attempt to normalize psychotic symptoms as much as possible, while ensuring that the child understands the question. Ask the child to describe experiences in detail. Counselors may find the following questions helpful in screening a child for psychosis:

"Do you ever feel like your mind is playing a trick on you?"

"Do you ever hear a voice but don't know who is talking? Do other people seem to hear it, too?"

"Do you ever see something that others do not see or react to?"

"Do these experiences ever happen when you are having strong feelings?"

Youth younger than 16 years rarely report complex or highly specific delusions, as are common in adults with schizophrenia (APA, 2013; Sikich, 2013). If present, delusions tend to be vague and related to the content of hallucinations. For example, a child may believe that a hallucinatory figure is trying to harm a sibling or parent. Delusions may also stem from real experiences; a child who was teased by peers may endorse a delusional belief that his classmates are turning his teachers against him.

Additional support for a schizophrenia spectrum disorder may be gained from a history of prodromal symptoms (social isolation, academic difficulties, odd or idiosyncratic preoccupations, or mood symptoms), evidence of negative symptoms, and cognitive decline (Kuniyoshi & McClellan, 2010). Descriptions of the child's behavior and findings on a mental status exam should provide evidence for overt signs of psychosis, in addition to subjective report of hallucinations. For example, a counselor may notice that the child is very guarded, has disorganized thinking, or is responding to internal stimuli.

Any life-threatening symptoms, such as suicidal behavior or serious aggression toward others, should take priority in the treatment plan. Hospitalization for safety and stabilization may be needed during the acute phase of the illness. Carefully assess for any comorbid psychiatric or developmental disorders, including substance use, mood disorders, developmental disabilities, cognitive or speech or language delays, trauma, and psychosocial stressors (American Association of Child and Adolescent Psychiatry, 2012). Youth with psychotic symptoms also require a thorough medical evaluation by a physician to rule out any underlying medical problems that may masquerade as early-onset schizophrenia. Youth with neurological deficits should undergo neuroimaging (preferably brain magnetic resonance imaging [MRI]) to rule out a brain lesion and electroencephalogram (EEG) monitoring to evaluate for a seizure disorder. Laboratory evaluation for metabolic, endocrine, infectious, inherited, or other medical causes of psychosis is also necessary. Drug intoxication or substance use should be evaluated with a urine or serum drug screen. Genetic testing is indicated if there are associated dysmorphic or syndromic features (Kuniyoshi & McClellan, 2010).

Carefully consider cultural or religious factors when assessing a patient for a psychotic disorder. These factors should influence a counselor's determination of whether a symptom is consistent with psychosis or should be considered a commonly held belief within the client's background. For example, in some cultures the experience of hearing God's voice or seeing "spirits" is considered part of one's religious experience. In certain cultures distress may present as hallucinations or pseudohallucinations, and overvalued ideas may appear similar to true psychosis but are considered normal in a client's community (APA, 2013). Hallucinations or delusions that are ego dystonic, are overtly distressing, or are in direct conflict with the beliefs and values of the individual's environment and culture should elicit greater concern (Kuniyoshi & McClellan, 2010). For example, a belief in God is often congruent with individual beliefs, but refusing to ingest food because of a command from God violates most societal norms and raises greater concern for psychosis.

A client's language, thought process, affect, eye contact, and even willingness to report symptoms may be influenced by his or her cultural background. For example, diminished eye contact may be a sign of respect for the counselor, or reduced emotional expression may be expected within a particular culture. Assessment of possible psychotic symptoms in clients who speak English as a second language or via an interpreter should be carefully done, ensuring not only that the client understands the examiner's questions, but also that translation by the interpreter is not interfering with the assessment of thought process or content. Look for collateral information or objective data to support a psychotic illness.

Neuropsychological testing may reveal cognitive deficits and provide important information for educational intervention. However, testing cannot be used in isolation to establish a diagnosis. Counselors may utilize screening instruments, such as the Child Behavior Checklist, Behavior Assessment System for Children (BASC), or Youth Self-Report to identify positive psychotic symptoms or behavioral problems. Structured diagnostic tools such as the Positive and Negative Syndrome Scale (PANSS) are useful in diagnosis and monitoring response to treatment (Sikich, 2013). Projective psychological testing, using a Rorschach or Thematic Apperception Test may reveal disorganized thinking, paranoia, or guardedness but should not be used in isolation to rule out a psychotic disorder. The Clinician-Rated Dimensions of Psychosis Symptom Severity (found online at http://www.psychiatry.org/practice/dsm/dsm5/online-assessment-measures), which is presented in the *DSM-5*, may be used at an initial evaluation and again at subsequent visits to track symptoms over time. Diagnosis should be revisited over time, because clinical presentation of symptoms may change, especially in the first few years of illness (Bromet et al., 2011).

Treatment Strategies and Interventions

Treatment of schizophrenia spectrum disorders is multimodal, comprising of medication management, psychoeducation, therapy, and psychosocial interventions. Youth with a suspected schizophrenia spectrum disorder should be referred to a child and adolescent psychiatrist for evaluation. Cognitive, behavioral, and social interventions should be developmentally appropriate, aimed at reducing symptoms and improving quality of life. Family issues and educational or job performance are relevant targets of treatment.

PHARMACOTHERAPY

Antipsychotic medications are the somatic treatment of choice for schizophrenia spectrum disorders. Controlled research trials in adults with schizophrenia demonstrate improvement in psychotic symptoms and reduced likelihood of symptom recurrence with both older and newer antipsychotics. Older medications, referred to as first-generation or typical antipsychotics, include haloperidol, loxapine, thioridazine, and thiothixene. Newer medications, termed second-generation or atypical antipsychotics, include risperidone, olanzapine, quetiapine, and aripiprazole. There are fewer research trials comparing the effectiveness and safety of using antipsychotics in youth; however the U.S. Food and Drug Administration (FDA) has approved the use of aripiprazole, olanzapine, quetiapine, and risperidone for youth ages 10 to 17 (olanzapine 13 to 17 years) with schizophrenia, schizoaffective disorder, and bipolar mania (Kranzler & Cohen, 2013; Kumra et al., 2008). Specific medication choice is often made based on current medication profile, past response to medication, patient or family preference, common side effects, and cost.

In research studies, compared with a placebo (e.g., sugar pill), aripiprazole, risperidone, quetiapine, paliperidone, and olanzapine have been shown to reduce symptoms of schizophrenia effectively in youth. Head-to-head trials comparing medications (including molindone, a typical antipsychotic, and atypical antipsychotics) showed no differences in effectiveness among antipsychotics, with the exception of clozapine (Kranzler & Cohen, 2013; Schimmelmann, Schmidt, Carbon, & Correll, 2013; Sikich et al., 2008). Dose should be titrated with careful attention to side effects. Youth should receive a trial of a medication for six weeks at an adequate dose before a different antipsychotic is tried.

Medications are often required in treatment of comorbid conditions, such as depression, anxiety, insomnia, agitation, explosive behaviors, and catatonia. Removal of the offending substance or prescription medication is a key component to treatment of a substance-induced psychotic disorder. Treatment of the underlying medical illness is necessary in a psychotic disorder due to a medical condition. Youth may benefit from medication to treat adverse effects of antipsychotic medications or to reduce weight gain. Comorbid substance abuse should be addressed with appropriate treatment strategies.

Antipsychotic Treatment Resistance

Many youth with schizophrenia spectrum disorders exhibit severe or persistent symptoms that are unresponsive to antipsychotic therapy (Kim, Kim, Cho, Kim, & Shin, 2008; Schneider, Corrigall, Hayes, Kyriakopoulos, & Frangou, 2014). Patients who have failed at least two antipsychotic regimens should receive a trial of clozapine, an atypical antipsychotic that is effective in adults with treatment-resistant schizophrenia. This medication may be prescribed to lower the risk of suicidal behavior in patients with psychotic illnesses (FDA, 2003). The only atypical agent shown to be clearly effective for the treatment of negative symptoms (Souza, Kayo, Tassell, Martins, & Elkis, 2013), clozapine has a number of side effects. Psychiatrists must follow guidelines to monitor for serious side effects.

Common Side Effects

Weight gain, diabetes, and hyperlipidemia are among potential adverse effects of atypical antipsychotics. Some youth experience significant weight gain, which may negatively

TABLE 7.7   Common Side Effects of Antipsychotic Medications

Agranulocytosis (highest risk with clozapine)	Movement disorders[b]
Akathisia (inner restlessness or trouble feeling comfortable in one's body)[a]	• Dystonias (persistent contraction of individual muscles)
Cardiovascular	• Parkinsonian symptoms (tremor, shuffling walk, stiffness, or decreased arm swing)
• Orthostatic hypotension	• Tardive dyksinesia (involuntary repetitive movements that may persist even after medication is stopped)
• Tachycardia	
• EKG abnormalities, risk of cardiac arrhythmias	• Withdrawal dyskinesia (involuntary movements that may occur when antipsychotic is abruptly reduced or stopped)
Metabolic[a]	
• Weight gain	• Neuroleptic Malignant Syndrome (rapid changes in pulse and blood pressure, fever, stiffness, disorientation, and agitation)
• Hyperlipidemia	
• Insulin resistance, diabetes	
Neuroendocrine[c]	Seizures
Prolactin elevation (increased risk of increased size of breasts, discharge from breasts, or absence of menses.)	
Sedation	

[a]Higher risk with atypical antipsychotics
[b]Higher risk with risperidone and high-potency typical antipsychotics
[c]Higher risk with typical antipsychotics

affect their self-esteem and reduce treatment adherence. Psychiatrists must monitor a patient's weight or body mass index (BMI), waist circumference, fasting lipids, and blood glucose according to recommended guidelines. Cardiovascular effects of antipsychotics include QTc prolongation, orthostatic hypotension, tachycardia, and pericarditis. Prolactin levels may rise with atypical antipsychotic administration. Neuroleptic malignant syndrome (NMS) is a rare, but potentially fatal, complication of antipsychotic treatment, consisting of autonomic instability, elevated temperature, rigidity, and elevated levels of muscle enzymes. Movement disorders, including tremor, tardive dyskinesia, and extrapyramidal effects, may occur with first-generation and less commonly with second-generation antipsychotics. Youth may be more susceptible to movement disorders than adults; abnormal movements are monitored at regular intervals and scored on the Abnormal Involuntary Movement Scale (American Association of Child and Adolescent Psychiatry, 2012; Kranzler et al., 2013). See Table 7.7 for side effects associated with antipsychotic medications.

Psychosocial Interventions

Psychosocial treatments aim to reduce the impact of early-onset psychosis on psychological development and restore a youth to his or her best possible level of functioning. Psychosocial therapies are an essential aspect of treatment, augmenting the benefits of medication in reducing symptoms and improving quality of life. Some level of insight into the illness and reality testing increases the success of these interventions and may help foster rapport between the youth and the counselor.

When appropriate and with proper consent, consider involving a member of a youth's religious or ethnic community in his recovery. Consider the role that cultural or religious factors may play in diagnosis and treatment. For example, youth with a particular cultural background may be ambivalent about medications or reluctant to report nonadherence to treatment. The stigma of mental illness may be more acute in minority or immigrant cultures, reducing help-seeking behaviors or adherence to therapy and medications.

Common goals of intervention include return to school or work, living in a stable environment, involvement in prosocial activities, adherence to medication, and accessing physical and mental health services (Killackey, Alvarez-Jimenez, Allott, Bendall, & McGorry, 2013; Patterson & Leeuwenkamp, 2008). Early intervention, focusing on collaboration with the youth and family, is associated with symptomatic and functional recovery. Psychosocial therapies include cognitive-behavioral therapy, family therapy, social skills therapy, and cognitive remediation. The severity of psychotic or affective symptoms and cognitive impairment will influence the choice of psychosocial intervention. Counselors may use an integrative approach, using different therapeutic modalities based on the needs of the individual.

Cognitive-Behavioral Therapy (CBT)

Goals of CBT in schizophrenia spectrum disorders include medication adherence, relapse prevention, psychoeducation, and enhanced functional capacity. A therapist works closely with the client to help him or her better understand and cope with distressing symptoms, recognize early signs of relapse, reframe distressing or delusional thoughts, and practice stress reduction techniques. There are few studies of CBT in early-onset schizophrenia, but current evidence supports reduced hallucinations, depression, and anxiety symptoms with this therapeutic modality (Schimmelmann et al., 2013). In adults with schizophrenia, CBT is associated with improved medication adherence, reduced positive symptoms, and fewer negative symptoms (Patterson & Leeuwenkamp, 2008).

Family Therapy

Schizophrenia spectrum disorders profoundly influence family members of those youth who are affected. Parents may be overwhelmed with the implications of a diagnosis of a psychotic disorder, struggling to navigate a complex mental health system, and grappling with the financial stress of caring for a child with a chronic illness. Family therapy seeks to support distressed family members by providing psychoeducation and strategies to improve problem-solving skills and communication within the family (Breitborde et al., 2011). Parents or caregivers learn about the symptoms of their child's illness, the role of medication, and the warning signs of illness relapse. Counselors may work with an individual family or with a group of families with similar treatment concerns. This therapeutic modality provides necessary support to family systems under stress, increasing the coping skills family members can use to support their loved one with schizophrenia (Patterson & Leeuwenkamp, 2008). More studies are needed to support the role of family therapy in early-onset psychosis; however this form of therapy may reduce the number of or length of hospitalizations and reduce rates of relapse (Breitborde et al, 2011; Schimmelmann et al., 2013).

Social Skills Training (SST)

Youth with schizophrenia spectrum disorders miss important opportunities to learn valuable life and self-care skills. Psychosis may derail the acquisition of normal social milestones, such as joining a peer group, having a first romantic relationship, or participating in extracurricular or leadership activities. Youth may lack assertiveness skills or struggle to initiate or maintain appropriate reciprocal conversations. Social skills therapy focuses on improving skills necessary for social functioning, including social cognition, social perception, and behavioral responding or expression (Chien, Leung, Yeung, & Wong, 2013). Techniques such as role-play, social stories, behaviorally based instruction, corrective feedback, and positive reinforcement may improve generalizability of skills to real-world situations (Chien et al., 2013; Patterson & Leeuwenkamp, 2008). This treatment modality has been studied in adults with schizophrenia but has important implications for youth with schizophrenia spectrum disorders. Social skills therapy may help youth with schizophrenia feel better equipped to manage life stressors and more engaged in the management of their illness.

Cognitive Remediation Therapy (CRT)

Cognitive deficits can significantly impair a client's ability to function in a school or work setting. Cognitive deficits are present in the prodromal phase and can worsen with the onset of psychosis. Medications alone have little positive effect on cognitive performance. Processing speed and verbal memory at first episode can predict community functioning years later (Fisher et al., 2014). Cognitive remediation therapy aims to improve attention, memory, cognitive flexibility, and executive function using repetitive supervised exercises, positive reinforcement, and active modeling of methods to reduce complex tasks into more manageable components. The difficulty of the tasks increases over the course of treatment (Patterson & Leeuwenkamp, 2008; Wykes et al., 2007). Youth may benefit from neuroplasticity-based cognitive training with a laptop computer to improve working memory, global cognition, and problem-solving skills (Fisher et al., 2014). In adults with schizophrenia, CRT consistently improves performance on neurocognitive tests, but its effects on overall functioning and psychopathology are less clear. More studies are needed to assess the effects of CRT on youth with schizophrenia spectrum disorders.

GROUP THERAPY

A therapeutic group comprising adolescents with a schizophrenia spectrum disorder may be helpful in both inpatient and outpatient settings. The group may allow individuals to practice social skills, benefit from shared experiences, and learn from interactions between their peers and therapists (Compton & Broussard, 2009). Although a group setting may not be appropriate for all individuals (particularly those with social anxiety), it may serve to promote recovery and reduce the stigma of illness. The focus of a group may be psychoeducation, coping skills, participation in structured activities, or development of job skills.

EDUCATIONAL SUPPORT

Collaboration with school personnel is a vital part of the youth's treatment plan. School attendance may be reduced or absent during periods of illness exacerbation. A counselor can assist by identifying a plan for reenrollment in school. Most often an Individual Education Plan (IEP) is developed to incorporate appropriate modifications to their educational environment. Modifications can include class restructuring, home-based schooling, or specific interventions during the school day to help youth be successful in their educational environment. A counselor should be made aware of the youth's IEP and be invited to contribute his or her expertise when creating and modifying the IEP. Some youth benefit from vocational training programs to address the cognitive and functional deficits associated with the disorder (American Association of Child and Adolescent Psychiatry, 2012). Treatment goals related to education or employment are outlined in Sidebar 7.6.

SIDEBAR 7.6:   EDUCATION AND EMPLOYMENT

Consider how important a job is for one's self-esteem, self-worth, and independence. Employment provides not only financial rewards but also a valued social role. Youth with schizophrenia spectrum and other psychotic disorders may lack important educational credentials or vocational skills to pursue employment. Important areas of focus for these youth include:

- High school graduation or obtaining an equivalent credential
- Job search and interview skills
- Vocational rehabilitation

Supported employment, an intervention that matches a client with a job on the open labor market, has been very successful in adults with schizophrenia. Youth and young adults may also benefit from structured programs to assist with obtaining and maintaining employment.

ASSERTIVE COMMUNITY TREATMENT (ACT)

This treatment model focuses on providing services to individuals in their natural living environments using a team-based approach. Team members often include a psychiatrist, nurses, therapists, and peer support specialists. A team member is available 24 hours per day, seven days a week, to provide support and emergency coverage. Medications may be delivered to the individual's home, to attempt to increase adherence. Caseloads are shared among team members, who closely monitor the client's symptoms and functioning by frequent contacts throughout the month. The ACT model is often used in adults with schizophrenia or other major mental illnesses that have a history of frequent hospitalizations, medication noncompliance, comorbid substance abuse or medical illness, and psychosocial stressors, including unstable housing or finances (Sadock & Sadock, 2007). This model may be of significant benefit in youth with early-onset psychosis, to facilitate functional recovery and achievement of developmental milestones while improving safety and reducing costly hospitalizations.

PARTIAL HOSPITALIZATION OR DAY TREATMENT

These facilities may serve as a step down from an inpatient hospitalization or as a more intensive intervention than traditional outpatient therapy in order to prevent psychiatric hospitalization (Compton & Broussard, 2009). The individual receives educational and psychosocial services in a facility during the day, in an environment tailored to treating children and adolescents with psychosis or other major mental illnesses. During evenings and weekends youth reside with family and are encouraged to participate in prosocial activities. Day treatment facilities may offer individual and group therapies as well as support from teachers who can provide individualized tutoring and assist the individual with achieving his or her academic goals. Day treatment staff coordinate services and treatment to promote an eventual return to the youth's school and outpatient team.

Evaluation Strategies

Counselors should incorporate a youth's subjective report, objective assessments (mental status exam, rating scales), and parent and teacher report into an assessment of response to treatment. Over time the counselor may track the relative presence or absence of positive, negative, and cognitive symptoms, substance use, depression, or mania. As previously discussed, the Clinician-Rated Dimensions of Psychosis Severity is one tool to track these symptoms efficiently over time. Ideally counselors are in close communication with the treating psychiatrist, to easily share information and updates on the client's status.

Ultimately, the focus of treatment should go beyond reduction in clinical symptoms and focus on improving functional status and promoting personal recovery. The focus of recovery may differ based on the individual's priorities, premorbid functioning, and cultural background. For example, a teenager may make participation in the football team a priority (and thus a focus of treatment) rather than the absence of auditory hallucinations. Counselors should work with clients to foster a positive self-identity, reframe their experience of mental illness, identify methods to self-manage appropriate aspects of the illness, and develop a valued role in society (Slade, 2013).

Schizophrenia spectrum disorders in youth are associated with higher morbidity and mortality than the adult onset disease. Often the majority of patients (72 to 74 percent) require long-term psychiatric treatment, though the course of illness varies by individual (Schneider et al., 2014). Long-term follow-up studies suggest moderate to severe impairment across the life span. A diagnosis of a schizophrenia spectrum disorder in childhood or adolescence is associated with lower educational achievement, higher rates of unemployment and disability, impaired relationships and reduced independence. Youth are at higher risk of physical illness, homelessness, and early death or suicide than the general community (Clemmensen, Vernal, & Steinhausen, 2012; Killackey et al. 2013). Early intervention is aimed at maximizing symptomatic and functional recovery and preventing or minimizing the impact of relapse.

Diagnostic Challenges

Misdiagnosis of schizophrenia spectrum disorders is common (American Association of Child an Adolescent Psychiatry, 2012). These disorders are rare, and counselors may not be comfortable making a diagnosis in a child or adolescent, given its prognostic implications. Schizophrenia spectrum disorders may be initially misdiagnosed as bipolar disorder, personality disorders, obsessive-compulsive disorders, anxiety or trauma disorders, or developmental delays. Additionally, most children who report hallucinations do not have a schizophrenia spectrum disorder or other psychotic disorder. Distinguishing between a formal thought disorder and developmental disorders impairing speech and language may be extremely challenging. A thorough evaluation, careful mental status exam, use of standardized diagnostic tools, and rigorous application of the diagnostic criteria will help improve accuracy of diagnosis. Reevaluation of diagnosis over time will provide further support for a client's diagnosis.

Summary

Schizophrenia spectrum disorders in children and adolescents are uncommon but serious illnesses, causing significant morbidity and distress to afflicted youth and their families. A thoughtful, comprehensive assessment is needed when assessing for a psychotic illness, with careful attention to potential medical or psychiatric comorbidities and cultural influences. Antipsychotic medications and psychosocial therapies are the treatments of choice. Early intervention shows promise in improving symptoms, functioning, and quality of life. The following References provide additional information relating to chapter topics.

References

Addington, J., Cornblatt, B. A., Cadenhead, K. S., Cannon, T. D., McGlashan, T. H., Perkins, D. O., ... Heinssen, R. (2011). At clinical high risk for psychosis: Outcome for nonconverters. *American Journal of Psychiatry, 168*(8), 800–805. doi:10.1176/appi.ajp.2011.10081191

American Academy of Child and Adolescent Psychiatry. (2012). Practice parameter for the assessment and treatment of children and adolescents with schizophrenia. Retrieved from http://www.aacap.org/App_Themes/AACAP/docs/practice_parameters/Schizophrenia_Web.pdf

American Psychiatric Association. (2000). *Diagnostic and statistical manual of mental disorders* (4th ed., text rev.). Washington, DC: Author.

American Psychiatric Association. (2013). *Diagnostic and statistical manual of mental disorders* (5th ed.). Arlington, VA: American Psychiatric Publishing.

Barch, D., Bustillo, J., Gaebel, W., Gur, R., Heckers, S., Malaspina, D., ... Carpenter, W. (2013). Logic and justification for dimensional assessment of symptoms and related clinical phenomena in psychosis: Relevance to DSM-5. *Schizophrenia Research, 150*(1), 15–20. doi:10.1016/j.schres.2013.04.027

Breitborde, N. J., Moreno, F. A., Mai-Dixon, N., Peterson, R., Durst, L., Bernstein, B., & McFarlane, W. R. (2011). Multifamily group psychoeducation and cognitive remediation for first-episode psychosis: A randomized controlled trial. *BMC Psychiatry, 11*, 9. doi: 10.1186/1471-244X-11-9

Bromet, E. J., Kotov, R., Fochtmann, L., J., Carlson, G. A., Tanenbert-Karant, M., Ruggero, C., & Chang, S., W. (2011). Diagnostic shifts during the decade following first admission for psychosis. *American Journal of Psychiatry, 168*(11), 1186–1194. doi:10.1176/appi.ajp.2011.11010048

Chien, W. T., Leung, S. F., Yeung, F. K., & Wong, W. K. (2013). Current approaches to treatments for schizophrenia spectrum disorders, part II: Psychosocial interventions and patient-focused perspectives in psychiatric care. *Neuropsychiatric Disease and Treatment 9*, 1463–1481. doi:10.2147/NDT.S49263

Clemmensen, L., Vernal, D. L., & Steinhausen, H. C. (2012). A systematic review of the long-term outcome of early onset schizophrenia. *BMC Psychiatry, 12*, 150. doi:10.1186/1471-244X-12-150

Compton, M. T., & Broussard, B. (2009). The first episode of psychosis: A guide for patients and their families. New York, NY: Oxford University Press.

Fisher, M., Loewy, R., Carter, C., Lee, A., Ragland, J. D., Niendam, T., ... Vinogradov, S. (2014). Neuroplasticity-based auditory training via laptop computer improves cognition in young individuals with recent onset schizophrenia. *Schizophrenia Bulletin*. Advance online publication. Retrieved from http://schizophreniabulletin.oxfordjournals.org/content/current

Frangou, S. (2013). Neurocognition in early-onset schizophrenia. *Child & Adolescent Psychiatric Clinics of North America, 22*(4), 715–726. doi:10.1016/j.chc.2013.04.007

Heckers, S. (2008). Making progress in schizophrenia research. *Schizophrenia Bulletin, 34*(4), 591–594. doi:10.1093/schbul/sbn046

Heckers, S., Barch, D. M., Bustillo, J., Gaebel, W., Gur, R., Malaspina, D., ... Carpenter, W. (2013). Structure of the psychotic disorders classification in DSM-5. *Schizophrenia Research, 150*(1), 11–14. doi:10.1016/j.schres.2013.04.039

Killackey, E., Alvarez-Jimenez, M., Allott, K., Bendall, S., & McGorry, P. (2013). Community rehabilitation and psychosocial interventions for psychotic disorders in youth. *Child & Adolescent Psychiatric Clinics of North America, 22*(4), 745–758. doi:10.1016/j.chc.2013.04.009

King, J. H. (2014). Using the DSM-5: Try It, You'll Like It. Retrieved from http://www.continuingedcourses.net/active/courses/course081.php

Kim, Y., Kim, B. N., Cho, S. C. Kim, J. W., & Shin, M. S. (2008). Long-term sustained benefits of clozapine treatment in refractory early onset schizophrenia: A retrospective study in Korean children and adolescents. *Human Psychopharmacology, 23*(8), 715–722. doi:10.1002/hup.982

Kranzler, H. N., & Cohen, S. D. (2013). Psychopharmacologic treatment of psychosis in children and adolescents: efficacy and management. *Child & Adolescent Psychiatric Clinics of North America, 22*(4), 727–744. doi:10.1016/j.chc.2013.06.002

Kumra, S., Oberstar, J. V., Sikich, L., Findling, R. L., McClellan, J. M., Vinogradov, S., & Schulz, S. C. (2008). Efficacy and tolerability of second-generation antipsychotics in children and adolescents with schizophrenia. *Schizophrenia Bulletin, 34*(1), 60–71. Retrieved from http://schizophreniabulletin.oxfordjournals.org/content/current

Kuniyoshi, J. S., & McClellan, J. M. (2010). Early-Onset schizophrenia. In M. K. Dulcan (Ed.), *Dulcan's textbook of child and adolescent psychiatry*. Arlington, VA: American Psychiatric Publishing. doi:10.1176/appi.books.9781585623921.461045

Maj, M. (2013). The DSM-5 approach to psychotic disorders: Is it possible to overcome the 'inherent conservative bias'? *Schizophrenia Research, 150*(1), 38–39. doi:10.1016/j.schres.2013.06.034

Patterson, T. L., & Leeuwenkamp, O. R. (2008). Adjunctive psychosocial therapies for the treatment of schizophrenia. *Schizophrenia Research, 100*(1–3), 108–119. doi:10.1016/j.schres.2007.12.468

Polanski, P. J., & Hinkle, J. S. (2011). The mental status examination: Its use by professional counselors. *Journal of Counseling & Development, 78*(3), 109–116. doi:10.1002/j.1556-6676.2000.tb01918.x

Puetz, V., Günther, T., Kahraman-Lanzerath, B., Herpertz-Dahlmann, B., & Konrad, K. (2014). Neuropsychological deficits in the prodromal phase and course of an early-onset schizophrenia. *Zeitschrift für Kinder- und Jugendpsychiatrie und Psychotherapie, 42*(3), 167–176. doi:10.1024/1422-4917/a000286

Sadock, B. J., & Sadock, V. A. (2007). *Kaplan and Sadock's synopsis of psychiatry: Behavioral sciences/clinical psychiatry* (10th ed.). Philadelphia, PA: Lippincott Williams & Wilkins.

Schimmelmann, B. G., Schmidt, S. J., Carbon, M. & Correll, C. U. (2013). Treatment of adolescents with early-onset schizophrenia spectrum disorders: In search of a rational, evidence-informed approach. *Current Opinion in Psychiatry, 26*(2), 219–230. doi:10.1097/YCO.0b013e32835dcc2a

Schneider, C., Corrigall, R., Hayes, D., Kyriakopoulos, M., & Frangou, S. (2014). Systematic review of the efficacy and tolerability of clozapine in the treatment of youth with early onset schizophrenia. *European Psychiatry, 29*(1), 1–10. doi:10.1016/j.eurpsy.2013.08.001

Sikich, L. (2013). Diagnosis and evaluation of hallucinations and other psychotic symptoms in children and adolescents. *Child & Adolescent Psychiatry Clinics of North America, 22*(4), 655–673. doi:10.1016/j.chc.2013.06.005

Sikich, L., Frazier, J. A., McClellan, J., Findling, R.L., Vitiello, B., Ritz, L., ... Lieberman, J. A. (2008). Double-blind comparison of first- and second-generation antipsychotics in early-onset schizophrenia and schizoaffective disorder: Findings from the treatment of early-onset schizophrenia spectrum disorders (TEOSS) study. *American Journal of Psychiatry, 165*(11), 1420–1431. doi:10.1176/appi.ajp.2008.08050756

Slade, M. (2013). *100 ways to support recovery* (2nd ed.). London, United Kingdom: Rethink Mental Illness.

Souza, J. S., Kayo, M., Tassell, I., Martins, C. B., Elkis, H. (2013). Efficacy of olanzapine in comparison with clozapine for treatment-resistant schizophrenia: Evidence from a systemic review and meta-analyses. *CNS Spectrums, 18*(2), 82–89. doi:10.1017/S1092852912000806

Tandon, R., Gaebel, W., Barch, D. M., Bustillo, J., Gur, R. E., Heckers, S., ... Carpenter, W. (2013). Definition and description of schizophrenia in the DSM-5. *Schizophrenia Research, 150*(1), 3–10. doi:10.1016/j.schres.2013.05.028

U.S. Food and Drug Administration. (2003). Clozaril approved for reducing risk of suicide. *FDA Consumer Reports, 37*(2), 5. Retrieved from http://www.fda.gov

Wykes, T., Newton, E., Landau, S., Rice, C., Thompson, N., & Frangou, S. (2007). Cognitive remediation therapy (CRT) for young early onset patients with schizophrenia: an exploratory randomized controlled trial. *Schizophrenia Research, 94*(1–3), 221–230. Retrieved from http://www.journals.elsevier.com/schizophrenia-research/

Chapter 8

Bipolar and Related Disorders

GREGORY T. HATCHETT AND NICOLE R. MOTLEY

Introduction

The symptom profile of irritability, aggression, and oppositional behavior continues to be among the top reasons that children and adolescents are referred to mental health care treatment in the United States (Bambauer & Connor, 2005). While these problems are nothing new, there has been a dramatic change over the past 20 years in how such problems are diagnosed and subsequently treated. Prior to the 1990s, children with this clinical profile would have likely been diagnosed with one or more *externalizing disorders*, such as oppositional defiant disorder (ODD), conduct disorder (CD), or attention-deficit/ hyperactivity disorder (ADHD). Irritability and belligerent behavior were considered to be associated features of these disorders, and as a result clinicians did not regard these symptoms as indicative of a bipolar spectrum disorder (Carlson, 1998). Furthermore, clinicians believed that bipolar disorder was relatively rare before early adulthood (Weckerly, 2002). Reflective of the thinking of this time, Bowring and Kovacs (1992) expressed concern that many clinicians might overlook cases of early-onset bipolar disorder because of its low prevalence and somewhat atypical symptom presentation. They wrote, "The consequence of the low base rate of mania in childhood is that most professionals may have only read about it" (p. 614).

The days of only reading about early-onset bipolar disorder seem long past because clinicians have found themselves working with a record number of children and adolescents who have—or at least have been diagnosed with—some variant of bipolar disorder. As one example of this trend, Moreno et al. (2007) reported that the number of outpatient office visits among children and adolescents for bipolar disorder increased nearly 400 percent between the periods of 1995–1996 and 2002–2003. Published that same year, Blader and Carlson (2007) reported that the percentage of youth diagnosed with bipolar disorder in the National Hospital Discharge Survey increased from 10 percent of all discharges in 1996 to 34 percent in 2004. Not surprisingly, this increased diagnosis of bipolar disorder has been accompanied by a corresponding increase in the number of children and adolescents prescribed mood stabilizers and atypical antipsychotics (Olfson, Blanco, Wang, Laje, & Correll, 2014), medications that often carry serious risks for developing children (Chung, Vesco, Resko, Schiman, & Fristad, 2012).

Yet, despite the dramatic increases in bipolar disorder diagnoses in clinical settings, there has not been an equivalent increase in the prevalence of the disorder in community samples of children and adolescents (Stringaris, Santosh, Leibenluft, & Goodman, 2010;

Van Meter, Moreira, & Youngstrom, 2011). This discrepancy may be explained by differences in how bipolar disorder has been operationalized across settings. In epidemiological studies, researchers typically adopt very strict definitions of bipolar disorder, based either on the *Diagnostic and Statistical Manual of Mental Disorders* (*DSM*) or on a set of narrow research criteria. In contrast, clinicians in practice settings typically have much more latitude in deciding what constitutes evidence for bipolar disorder. Many of the children and adolescents who have been diagnosed with bipolar disorder over the past 20 years have not met the official diagnostic criteria for either bipolar I or II disorder (Leibenluft, 2011; Van Meter et al., 2011). Because of this, clinicians often assigned diagnoses of bipolar disorder *not otherwise specified* (National Institute of Mental Health, 2001; Van Meter et al., 2011), a residual category in the *DSM, Fourth Edition* (*DSM-IV*; American Psychiatric Association [APA], 1994), and *DSM, Fourth Edition, Text Revision* (*DSM-IV-TR*; APA, 2000), under which many variations of emotional and behavioral instability could conceivably be made to fit.

Analogous to *off-label* prescribing, in which a physician prescribes a medication for a condition outside the Food and Drug Administration's (FDA) approved uses, some psychiatrists and other clinicians began using *off-label* diagnoses of bipolar disorder to categorize youth who presented with hypothesized developmental variations in the expression of bipolar disorder. Specifically, these proponents argued that many of the young people who develop bipolar disorder experience nonepisodic irritability and aggression rather than distinct episodes of mania/hypomania and depression (Faedda, Baldessarini, Glovinsky, & Austin, 2004). Though this hypothesized syndrome has been referred to by multiple names in the literature, we will refer to it as *pediatric bipolar disorder* to distinguish it from conventional cases of bipolar disorder I or II.

Not surprisingly, this expansion in both the conceptualization and diagnosis of bipolar disorder generated a great deal of controversy among both mental health professionals and the general public. As Weller, Calvert, and Weller (2003) observed, "while underdiagnosis may have been a problem in the past, overdiagnosis is now more prevalent and is exacerbated by the lack of agreement on diagnostic criteria" (p. 387). Critics of the *pediatric bipolar disorder* phenotype have argued that the hypothesized developmental differences in the expression of bipolar disorder have not been scientifically validated and, as a result, too many children and adolescents are being misdiagnosed with bipolar disorder and treated unnecessarily with potentially dangerous medications (Stringaris et al., 2010).

The debates over pediatric bipolar disorder eventually led to changes in the fifth edition of the *DSM* published in 2013; however, contrary to the diagnostic trends occurring in many community settings, the new *DSM* failed to recognize pediatric bipolar disorder as an official variant of bipolar disorder. In fact, the *DSM* actually went in the opposite direction by providing an even stronger description of bipolar disorder as an episodic disorder in which an individual experiences distinct *mood episodes* that differ from his or her typical functioning. As one example of this emphasis, Criterion A now requires the presence of "persistently increased goal-directed activity or energy" (APA, 2013, p. 124) in conjunction with the requisite mood changes (i.e., elation and expansive or irritable mood). However, the most monumental change in response to the bipolar disorder controversy was the addition of a new disorder—disruptive mood dysregulation disorder (DMDD)—to the Depressive Disorders chapter of the *DSM-5* (APA, 2013). This disorder was added to the *DSM-5* for the express purpose of reducing the number of children and adolescents misdiagnosed with bipolar disorder. DMDD refers to a syndrome in which a child or adolescent, ages 6 to 17, exhibits chronic irritability and temper outbursts that have occurred on a regular basis for a minimum of one year, with symptom onset prior to age 10 (APA, 2013). While DMDD is somewhat similar to the pediatric bipolar disorder phenotype described earlier, DMDD is conceptualized as a variant of (unipolar) depression, whereas pediatric bipolar disorder is conceptualized as being part of a bipolar spectrum.

As of this writing, it is too early to evaluate how the inclusion of DMDD in the *DSM-5* (APA, 2013) will affect diagnostic and treatment practices. However, there are several factors that might contribute to the continued (over)diagnosis of bipolar disorder in youth who present with chronic irritability and behavioral dyscontrol. First, as a new disorder, there are not any validated treatments for DMDD (Towbin, Axelson, Leibenluft, & Birmaher, 2013). Only two studies have evaluated the effectiveness of medication in treating youth with severe mood dysregulation (SMD), a syndrome from which DMDD was derived: Valle Krieger et al. (2011) reported some success for risperidone in an open-label trial, while Dickstein et al. (2009) reported that the results of a random clinical trial did not provide support for the use of lithium. Second, DMDD is a somewhat controversial addition to the *DSM-5* that the psychiatric community has not fully embraced. Morrison (2014) noted that DMDD is the only disorder that has ever been added to the *DSM* to intentionally prevent clinicians from overdiagnosing another disorder (i.e., bipolar disorder). In addition, Axelson et al. (2011) raised a number of criticisms about adding DMDD (in the revision process formerly called temper dysregulation disorder with dysphoria) to the *DSM-5*, such as a lack of research support and its poor discriminant validity from other disorders. Finally, clinicians will still have the opportunity to diagnose pediatric bipolar disorder through the *other specified* and *unspecified bipolar and related disorder* options available in the *DSM-5*:

> The recognition that many individuals, particularly children and, to a lesser extent, adolescents, experience bipolar-like phenomena that do not meet the criteria for bipolar I, bipolar II, or cyclothymic disorder is reflected in the availability of the other specified bipolar and related disorder category. (APA, 2013; p. 123)

Description of the Disorders

In the *DSM-IV* (APA, 1994) and *DSM-IV-TR* (APA, 2000), depressive and bipolar disorders were placed together into a single Mood Disorders chapter. In the *DSM-5* (APA, 2013), bipolar-related disorders are now organized into their own chapter so as to reflect their predominant elated mood and increased energy and behavior in contrast with the sad mood and decreased energy and behavior manifest in depressive disorders. Diagnoses in this chapter include bipolar I disorder, bipolar II disorder, cyclothymic disorder, substance- or medication-induced bipolar and related disorder, bipolar and related disorder due to another medical condition, other specified bipolar and related disorder, and unspecified bipolar and related disorder.

Bipolar-related disorders, whether in youth or adults, are associated with high levels of distress and substantial impairments in psychosocial functioning. As one example, the risk of suicide among individuals with bipolar disorder is estimated to be at least 15 times higher than that of the general population. In addition, about one-third of individuals with bipolar I or bipolar II disorder have a history of at least one suicide attempt (APA, 2013), and approximately 10 to 20 percent will eventually complete suicide (Goodwin, 2002). Bipolar disorders are also frequently accompanied by one or more additional mental disorders (APA, 2013). In children and adolescents, bipolar disorder tends to be comorbid with ADHD, ODD, CD, substance use disorders, anxiety disorders, and learning disabilities (American Academy of Child and Adolescent Psychiatry, 2010). In addition, a diagnosis of bipolar disorder carries a poor prognosis. The risk of relapse following a period of recovery is very high; even when on a careful medication regimen, about 40 percent of individuals with bipolar disorder experience a mood episode in a given year, 60 percent in two years, and 73 percent within five years (Gitlin, Swendsen, Heller, & Hammen, 1995). Among those who do not formally relapse, at least half experience some residual mood symptoms (Gitlin et al., 1995; Harrow, Goldberg, Grossman, & Meltzer, 1990).

The estimated prevalence rates for the most common bipolar disorders are 0.6 percent for bipolar I disorder, 0.8 percent for bipolar II disorder, and 0.4 to 1 percent for cyclothymic disorder (APA, 2013). Compared with other countries, higher rates of bipolar disorder have been reported in samples of children and adolescents in the United States, but these studies have included cases of subthreshold or broadband bipolar disorders in their prevalence estimates (Kessler et al., 2009; Van Meter et al., 2011).

DSM-5 Criteria

Sidebar 8.1 provides a brief overview of the major changes made in the diagnosis of bipolar disorder in the *DSM-5*.

SIDEBAR 8.1: MAJOR CHANGES FROM THE *DSM-IV/IV-TR* TO THE *DSM-5*

- The phenomenon of mixed episodes, in which an individual meets full diagnostic criteria for both a manic and a depressive episode, was not continued to the *DSM-5*. In its place, *with mixed features* has been added as a specifer to denote the presence of significant depressive symptoms during a manic or hypomanic episode or the presence of manic or hypomanic symptoms during a depressive episode. The *with mixed features* can also be added to the diagnosis of a depressive disorder as long as the individual has never met full criteria for a manic or hypomanic episode.
- Criterion A for a manic or hypomanic episode now requires *abnormally and persistently increased goal-directed activity or energy* in addition to the presence of an expansive, elevated, or irritable mood.
- Criterion B for a manic or hypomanic episode now requires that symptoms that persist during the period of mood disturbance *represent a noticeable change from usual behavior.*
- Clinicians can now add a *with anxious distress* specifier to a bipolar diagnosis to better describe clients who are exhibiting significant anxiety symptoms (minimum two of five) during a mood episode.

- The residual category of bipolar disorder not otherwise specified, available in prior editions of the *DSM*, was replaced with the *other specified bipolar and related disorder* and the *unspecified bipolar and elated disorder* options in the *DSM-5*. *Other specified* is used when a clinician chooses to describe why the presentation does not meet the full criteria for a specific bipolar disorder, whereas *unspecified* is used when a clinician chooses not to explain why the diagnostic criteria are not met for a specific bipolar disorder.

BIPOLAR I DISORDER

To qualify for a diagnosis of bipolar I disorder, a child or adolescent must have a history of at least one manic episode. Although it is common for individuals with bipolar I disorder to experience major depressive and hypomanic episodes as well, such episodes are not necessary for an initial diagnosis of bipolar I. A manic episode is characterized by a sustained period of excessively elevated, expansive, or irritable mood together with an abnormal increase in energy or goal-directed behavior. These symptoms should persist for at least one week—unless hospitalization is necessary—and these changes must be uncharacteristic for the person. In addition to noticeable mood changes, a child or adolescent must also concurrently exhibit at least three additional symptoms (four if the mood is exclusively irritable): (a) grandiosity, (b) reduced need for sleep, (c) increased talkativeness or pressured speech, (d) racing thoughts, (e) extreme distractibility, (f) increased activity, and (g) impulsive participation in activities that may lead to negative outcomes.

BIPOLAR II DISORDER

Bipolar II disorder was first introduced in the *DSM-IV* (APA, 1994) to provide a diagnostic home to individuals on the bipolar spectrum who had never experienced a full manic episode. Bipolar II disorder is lower than bipolar I on the diagnostic hierarchy and should *not* be diagnosed if a child or adolescent has any history of a manic episode; in this case, the correct diagnosis would be bipolar I disorder. Though once considered to be a less severe variant of bipolar I, individuals with bipolar II disorder are now recognized as having distress and disability that equal—if not exceed—those with bipolar I disorder. For example, those who meet criteria for bipolar II will likely have more severe and recurrent depressive episodes than those with bipolar I disorder (APA, 2013). The typical age of onset for bipolar II is in the mid-20s. This is similar to the typical age of onset for major depressive disorder but a few years later than that for bipolar I disorder, which typically begins in late adolescence (APA, 2013).

The defining feature of bipolar II disorder is a history of at least one hypomanic and one major depressive episode. Hypomanic episodes are similar to manic episodes, but differ in several important respects. First, to count toward a manic episode, the individual is only required to exhibit a symptom pattern that persists for four consecutive days instead of the week duration criterion required for mania. Second, the mood and behavioral changes that occur in a hypomanic episode must be out of character for the individual and clearly noticeable by others. Consequently, hypomania is not likely present if a child or adolescent exhibits inattention, irritability, hyperactivity, and impulsivity on a nonepisodic and consistent basis (APA, 2013). A major depressive episode occurs when a child or adolescent experiences a constellation of at least five depressive symptoms for a minimum of two weeks. This symptom presentation must include either a depressed mood (can be replaced by irritability in youth) or a significantly reduced interest or pleasure in previously enjoyed activities. Additional symptoms that count toward the identification of a depressive episode include significant changes in weight or appetite, insomnia or hypersomnia, observable restlessness or listlessness, persistent fatigue or loss of energy, inappropriate feelings of worthlessness or guilt, reduced ability to concentrate or make decisions, and recurrent thoughts or actions related to death or suicide (APA, 2013).

Individuals with bipolar II disorder are unlikely to seek treatment during a hypomanic episode because the hypomanic symptoms are typically not experienced as bothersome; instead, it is during a major depressive episode that most individuals with bipolar II disorder present for treatment (APA, 2013). As a result, clinicians should carefully assess for any previous hypomanic episodes in a child or adolescent who presents with symptoms of a major depressive episode.

To improve clinical description and treatment planning decisions, a number of specifiers are available in the *DSM-5* to provide more detailed information about the symptom presentation of an individual with bipolar I or II disorder. These specifiers include *with anxious distress* (new to the *DSM-5*), *with mixed features* (formerly an independent diagnosis in the *DSM-IV-TR*), *with rapid cycling, with melancholic features, with atypical features, with psychotic features* (mood-congruent or mood-incongruent), *with catatonia* (new to the *DSM-5*), *with peripartum onset* (formerly *postpartum onset* in the *DSM-IV-TR*), and *with seasonal pattern* (APA, 2013).

CYCLOTHYMIC DISORDER

Cyclothymic disorder is characterized by a chronic and sustained pattern of hypomanic- and depressive-like symptoms, during which the child or adolescent has never met the full criteria for either hypomanic or major depressive episodes. In a child or adolescent, this mood pattern must be present for at least one year; the duration requirement is increased to two years for adults. During the course of the disorder, depressive and hypomanic symptoms must be present at least half of the time and must not be absent for more than two consecutive months. Cyclothymic disorder is not diagnosed if a child or adolescent has previously met the full criteria for a hypomanic, manic, or major depressive episode. In the *DSM-IV/IV-TR* (APA, 1994, 2000), an individual with cyclothymic disorder who subsequently developed a manic/mixed or depressive episode would receive an additional diagnosis of bipolar I or II disorder, respectively, while retaining the original diagnosis of cyclothymic disorder. This diagnostic rule was discontinued in the *DSM-5*. Now, if an individual with cyclothymic disorder subsequently develops a manic, hypomanic, or depressive episode, the initial diagnosis of cyclothymic disorder is discontinued; in its place, the individual is given a diagnosis of bipolar I, other specified bipolar and related disorder, or major depressive disorder, respectively (APA, 2013).

Cyclothymic disorder tends to develop in adolescence or early adulthood, but when it develops before adulthood, the typical age of onset is about 6.5 years. Approximately 15 to 50 percent of the children who develop cyclothymic disorder will eventually meet full diagnostic criteria for either bipolar I or bipolar II disorder (APA, 2013). Cyclothymic disorder is considered low on the diagnostic hierarchy and should only be diagnosed when there is no history of psychosis or mood episodes. Relative to bipolar I or II disorder, much less is known about the course and treatment of cyclothymic disorder. It is infrequently diagnosed in clinical settings and has not been well represented in the research literature (Youngstrom, Freeman, & McKewon-Jenkins, 2009).

SUBSTANCE- OR MEDICATION-INDUCED BIPOLAR AND RELATED DISORDER

A diagnosis of a substance- or medication-induced bipolar and related disorder is appropriate when there is a strong presumption that a drug or medication is responsible for an individual's reported symptoms of mania or hypomania. To support this suspicion, the mood symptoms should develop close in time to the intoxication or withdrawal from a substance/medication that is known to be physiologically capable of producing the mood symptoms under investigation. Because substance use disorders are highly comorbid with bipolar disorders, it can be difficult for clinicians to differentiate cases in which bipolar disorder is comorbid with one or more substance use disorders from cases in which mood symptoms are due exclusively to medication or substance use (APA, 2013).

BIPOLAR AND RELATED DISORDER DUE TO ANOTHER MEDICAL CONDITION

A diagnosis of bipolar and related disorder due to another medical condition is the appropriate diagnosis when there is evidence that a medical condition is directly responsible for producing symptoms of mania/hypomania. Medical conditions that might produce such symptoms include, but are not limited to, multiple sclerosis and traumatic brain injuries (APA, 2013).

OTHER SPECIFIED/UNSPECIFIED BIPOLAR AND RELATED DISORDER

In the *DSM-III-R* and *DSM-IV/IV-TR*, clinicians could identify atypical cases of bipolar disorder through the bipolar disorder not otherwise specified (NOS) option. However, in the *DSM-5*, bipolar disorder NOS has been replaced with either the other specified or the unspecified bipolar and related disorder options. The other specified option is to be used when a clinician chooses to document the reason that a client's presentation does not meet full diagnostic criteria for a specific bipolar disorder, whereas the unspecified option is used when a clinician chooses not to describe why the presentation does not meet full diagnostic criteria for another bipolar disorder. In the *DSM-5*, the text includes examples of four conditions that might warrant a diagnosis of other specified bipolar and related disorder: (1) short-duration hypomanic episodes and major depressive episodes, (2) hypomanic episodes with insufficient symptoms and major depressive episodes, (3) hypomanic episode without prior major depressive episode, and (4) short-duration cyclothymia. Although none of these examples fits the description of pediatric bipolar disorder described earlier, the text of the *DSM-5* does include the caveat that the other specified bipolar and related disorder category may be appropriate for children and adolescents who exhibit atypical or broadband symptoms of bipolar disorder (APA, 2013). Thus, despite the recommendation in the *DSM-5* to use DMDD to describe children who exhibit chronic nonepisodic irritability and temper dysregulation, clinicians will still have the opportunity to diagnose bipolar and related disorders through the use of the other or unspecified specified bipolar and related disorder category options.

TABLE 8.1   Differential Diagnosis of Bipolar and Related Disorders

If the client ...	Then the diagnosis may be ...
Reports delusions or hallucinations for two or more weeks IN THE ABSENCE of a major mood episode (depressive or manic) during the lifetime duration of the illness	Schizoaffective Disorder, Bipolar Type
Reports MANIC episode (three or more symptoms; four if the mood is only irritable) lasting at least seven consecutive days and present most of the day, nearly every day	Bipolar I
Reports the mood disturbance IS sufficiently severe to cause marked IMPAIRMENT in social or occupational functioning, or to necessitate HOSPITALIZATION to prevent harm to self or others, or there are PSYCHOTIC features	Bipolar I
Reports HYPOMANIC episode (three or more symptoms; four if the mood is only irritable), lasting at least four consecutive days and present most of the day, nearly every day	Bipolar II
Reports the mood disturbance is NOT severe enough to cause marked IMPAIRMENT in social or occupational functioning, or to necessitate HOSPITALIZATION, or there is an absence of PSYCHOTIC features	Bipolar II
Reports a mood episode that is associated with an unequivocal change in functioning that is uncharacteristic of the individual when not symptomatic	Bipolar II
Reports for at least two years (at least one years for children and adolescents) criteria for a major depressive episode (five or more symptoms), a manic episode (three or more symptoms), or hypomanic episode (three or more symptoms) have NEVER BEEN MET	Cyclothymic Disorder

Source: King, 2014.

Table 8.1 consists of a series of algorithms clinicians can reference for differentiating bipolar-related disorders from one another (King, 2014).

Differential Diagnosis

Though clinicians should be mindful of alternative diagnostic possibilities throughout the various chapters of the *DSM-5*, they should pay closest attention to differentiating bipolar disorder from the following disorders or conditions: disruptive, impulse-control, and conduct disorders; disruptive mood dysregulation disorder (DMDD); depressive disorders; substance/medication-induced disorders; early-onset personality disorders; and normal variations in child or adolescent behavior.

NEURODEVELOPMENTAL AND DISRUPTIVE, IMPULSE-CONTROL, AND CONDUCT DISORDERS

As previously mentioned, several psychiatrists in the 1990s put forward the argument that many of the children and adolescents diagnosed with severe ADHD were actually experiencing an early-onset variant of bipolar disorder, in essence, pediatric bipolar disorder (Biederman & Jellinek, 1998). Though ADHD and mania/hypomania share some symptom overlap—distractibility, excessive talkativeness, and impulsivity—clinicians can improve diagnostic accuracy through both a close evaluation of a youth's specific symptoms and their persistence over time. Consistent with the model of bipolar disorder in the *DSM-5* (APA, 2013), empirical studies have found that it is the more traditional symptoms of mania/hypomania that best differentiate bipolar disorder from ADHD. In one such study, Geller et al. (2002) found that five symptoms—decreased need for sleep, grandiosity, racing thoughts, hypersexuality, and elation—best differentiated bipolar disorder from ADHD. They also found that many of the hypothesized symptoms of pediatric bipolar disorder, such as irritability, accelerated speech, and hyperarousal, were not useful in differentiating bipolar disorder from ADHD. In addition to symptom specificity, clinicians should also evaluate for symptom chronicity. Children with ADHD experience symptoms of hyperactivity and inattention on a relatively continuous basis in a minimum of two settings before the age of 10, whereas the same symptoms occur more intermittently in cases of bipolar disorder, which has a much later average age of onset at 18 years (Leibenluft et al., 2006).

Clinicians also need to distinguish the problematic behaviors that might occur during a manic/hypomanic episode from the more chronic behavioral and attitudinal problems associated with ODD or CD (APA, 2013; Sobanski et al., 2010). Similar to the differential diagnosis of bipolar disorder from ADHD, clinicians should carefully evaluate the specificity and chronicity of a youth's symptom presentation. In the case of a youth with bipolar disorder—absent an additional behavioral disorder (e.g., ODD, CD)—criminal or aggressive behavior will likely be limited to clear episodes of mania or hypomania. In contrast, youth who meet the diagnostic criteria for ODD or CD engage in noncompliant and disruptive behavior on a relatively ongoing basis. In sum, conduct problems that occur suddenly during noticeable mood changes and seem out of character suggest a diagnosis of bipolar disorder, whereas chronic aggressive and predatory behavior suggests a diagnosis of ODD or CD (Bowring & Kovacs, 1992).

The emotional and behavioral outbursts that may occur during a manic or hypomanic episode can also be difficult to differentiate from similar outbursts that occur in the context of intermittent explosive disorder (IED). IED is characterized by a failure to control impulsive verbal aggression (e.g., temper tantrums, tirades, verbal arguments, or fights) or impulsive physical aggression (e.g., toward property, animals, or other individuals), resulting in repeated aggressive outbursts (occurring twice weekly, on average, for a period of three months) that commonly occur in response to a minor provocation. These aggressive outbursts are, by definition, short lived (less than 30 minutes), whereas if the irritability occurs most of the day, nearly every day as part of a manic/hypomanic episode it must last at least one week and be accompanied by abnormally and persistently increased goal-directed activity or energy and four additional symptoms of mania/hypomania (e.g., grandiosity and decreased need for sleep). IED is fairly low on the diagnostic hierarchy, because it is superseded by bipolar disorder, DMDD, MDD, and psychotic disorders; and for children ages 6 to 18, aggressive behavior that occurs as part of an adjustment disorder should not be considered for this diagnosis (APA, 2013). Consequently, a diagnosis of IED should not be made if one of these other disorders is present and adequately explains a youth's symptoms.

DISRUPTIVE MOOD DYSREGULATION DISORDER

As already mentioned, DMDD was specifically added to the *DSM-5* to provide an alternative to bipolar disorder for categorizing children and adolescents who experience chronic irritability and aggression. A diagnosis of DMDD is appropriate for children and adolescents, ages 6 to 18, who exhibit chronically irritable moods punctuated by severe temper outbursts that occur, on average, at least three times per week. These symptoms should be present for a minimum of a year and begin before the age of 10. Although DMDD cannot be diagnosed simultaneously with ODD, IED, PTSD, ASD, or bipolar and related disorders, it can be diagnosed with major depressive disorder, ADHD, or CD (APA, 2013).

Similar to the strategies for differentiating bipolar disorder from the disruptive, impulse-control, and conduct disorders, clinicians should, again, evaluate for both symptom specificity and persistence. Though irritability is a shared symptom in both bipolar and related disorders and DMDD, the irritability exhibited by a child or adolescent with bipolar and related disorders is episodic, accompanied by additional symptoms of mania/hypomania, and differs from the youth's typical functioning. In contrast, the irritability that occurs as part of DMDD is relatively severe and continuous in two or more settings and is not accompanied by additional symptoms of mania/hypomania, such as grandiosity or elation (APA, 2013).

DEPRESSIVE DISORDERS

While irritability has been increasingly viewed as evidence for a bipolar disorder, it is important to remember that irritability has long been recognized as a common symptom of depression in children and adolescents. In fact, since at least the publication of the *DSM-III-R* in 1987 (APA, 1987), irritability can be substituted for a depressed mood in identifying a major depressive episode in a child or adolescent. Though no such accommodation is made for adults, irritability is also a common symptom experienced by adults with depressive disorders. In the National Comorbidity Survey Replication, Fava et al. (2010) reported that irritability occurred in about half of the adults with major depressive disorder. Compared with those with nonirritable depression, they found that those with irritable depression were more likely to have comorbid anxiety disorders as well as prior histories of ADHD, ODD, and IED. If a child or adolescent experiences irritability accompanied by additional symptoms of depression (e.g., low energy, insomnia, feelings of worthlessness), suspect a depressive disorder, whereas if the irritability is episodic and accompanied by additional symptoms of mania/hypomania (e.g., grandiosity, decreased need for sleep), suspect a bipolar disorder.

Table 8.2, courtesy of King (2014), is helpful for assisting clinicians in differentiating depressive and disruptive behavior disorders in children and adolescents.

SUBSTANCE- OR MEDICATION-INDUCED DISORDERS

Though a standard rule-out for nearly all mental disorders, clinicians should be especially sensitive to the possibility that substance or medication use is responsible for the symptoms of mania/hypomania reported by a youth or his or her parent(s). Many commonly used illicit drugs affect the dopamine system, which can produce such reactions as hyperarousal, decreased need for sleep, grandiosity, and irritability (Youngstrom et al., 2009).

TABLE 8.2 Differential Diagnoses between Depressive Disorders and Disruptive Disorders in Youth

	Disruptive Mood Dysregulation Disorder	*Persistent Depressive Disorder*	*Oppositional Defiant Disorder*	*Intermittent Explosive Disorder*
Profile	Presence of sad, empty, or irritable mood, accompanied by somatic and cognitive changes that significantly affect the individual's capacity to function	Presence of sad, empty, or irritable mood, accompanied by somatic and cognitive changes that significantly affect the individual's capacity to function	Problems in the self-control of emotions and behaviors that violate the rights of others (e.g., aggression, destruction of property) and/or that bring the individual into significant conflict with societal norms or authority figures	Problems in the self-control of emotions and behaviors that violate the rights of others (e.g., aggression, destruction of property) and/or that bring the individual into significant conflict with societal norms or authority figures
Onset	Prior to age 10. Common among children presenting to pediatric mental health clinics	Often early and insidious (i.e., in childhood, adolescence or early adult life)	The first symptoms usually appear during the preschool years and rarely later than early adolescence	Late childhood or adolescence and rarely begins for the first time after age 40 years
Age Limits	Restricted prior to age 6 and after age 18	None	None	Restricted prior to age 6.
Irritable Mood	Very severe persistent, chronic, nonepisodic irritability and anger	Persistent irritability	Persistent irritability/anger (e.g., loses temper, is touchy or easily annoyed, and is angry and resentful) However, common for individuals to show behavioral features without negative mood	None
Temper Outbursts	Severe recurrent behavioral temper outbursts that are grossly out of proportion and are inconsistent with developmental level	None	None	Severe damage or destruction of property and/or physical assault involving physical injury against animals or other individuals

(continued)

TABLE 8.2   (*continued*)

	Disruptive Mood Dysregulation Disorder	Persistent Depressive Disorder	Oppositional Defiant Disorder	Intermittent Explosive Disorder
Verbal Outbursts	Severe recurrent verbal outbursts that are grossly out of proportion and are inconsistent with developmental level	None	Argumentative/defiant behavior (e.g., argues with adults, actively defies or refuses to comply with requests from authority figures or with rules, deliberately annoys others, blames others for his or her mistakes or misbehavior)	Less severe verbal aggression (e.g., temper tantrums, tirades, verbal arguments or fights) Outbursts typically last for less than 30 minutes
Physical Aggression	Consistently against property, self, or others	None	None	Impulsive/anger-based toward property, animals, or other individuals
Settings Frequency	Two minimum Irritable mood most of the day, nearly every day Temper outbursts three or more times per week	One minimum. Irritable mood most of the day, for more days than not	One minimum. Children <5 years most days Children >5 years once per week	One minimum Twice weekly for verbal aggression or nondamaging, nondestructive, or noninjurious physical aggression Three damaging, destructive, or injurious behavioral outbursts within a 12-month period
Duration	12 months minimum	12 months minimum	6 months minimum	3 months for either verbal aggression or nondamaging, nondestructive, or noninjurious physical aggression 12 months for damaging, destructive, or injurious behavioral outbursts

TABLE 8.2 (*continued*)

	Disruptive Mood Dysregulation Disorder	Persistent Depressive Disorder	Oppositional Defiant Disorder	Intermittent Explosive Disorder
Chronicity	Characteristic of the child, being present most of the day, nearly every day, and noticeable by others in the child's environment. Approximately half of children continue to meet criteria for the condition one year later. Symptoms are likely to change as children mature (i.e., unipolar major depression w/comorbid anxiety)	Symptoms have become a part of the individual's day-to-day experience and have a chronic course	Commonly shows symptoms only at home and only with family members; often are part of a pattern of problematic interactions with others	May be episodic or chronic and persistent over many years
Diagnostic Criteria	11 (with 0 of 0 symptoms threshold)	8 (with 2 of 6 symptoms threshold)	3 (with 4 of 8 symptoms threshold)	6 (with 1 of 2 symptoms threshold)
Mutual Exclusivity	Autism spectrum disorder, bipolar disorder, persistent depressive disorder (dysthymia), posttraumatic stress disorder, separation anxiety disorder, oppositional defiant disorder, intermittent explosive disorder	Schizoaffective disorder, schizophrenia, delusional disorder, other specified or unspecified schizophrenia spectrum and other psychotic disorder, bipolar-related disorders	Psychotic disorder, bipolar disorder, disruptive mood dysregulation disorder and other depressive disorders, substance use disorders	Psychotic disorder, bipolar disorder, major depressive disorder, disruptive mood dysregulation disorder, antisocial personality disorder, borderline personality disorder; not attributable to another medical condition (e.g., head trauma, Alzheimer's disease) or to the physiological effects of a substance (e.g., a drug of abuse, a medication)

Source: King, 2014

As one example, methamphetamine intoxication is commonly associated with increased energy, euphoria, and hypersexuality, whereas methamphetamine withdrawal may produce symptoms of depression, irritability, suicidal ideation, and aggression (Meredith, Jaffe, Ang-Lee, & Saxton, 2005). Such a pattern may be misinterpreted as a switch from a manic or hypomanic to a depressive episode. Because many children and adolescents will not report or admit to illicit drug use, toxicology screens may be needed to rule out a substance-induced etiology. Further complicating the differential diagnostic process, substance use disorders are also highly comorbid with bipolar disorder (American Academy of Child and Adolescent Psychiatry, 2010). Thus, a clinician will need to evaluate whether symptoms of mania/hypomania should be attributed to bipolar disorder, substance use disorder, or both disorders.

In addition to illicit drug use, clinicians should also consider the possibility that a prescription medication, whether prescribed or obtained by other means, is responsible for reported symptoms of mania/hypomania. Several classes of medications may produce symptoms that mimic mania/hypomania, including antidepressants, antihypertensives, corticosteroids, opiates or opioids, and psychostimulants (Sinacola & Peters-Strickland, 2012). A great deal of controversy revolves around the diagnostic significance of agitation or maniclike symptoms following a trial of a selective serotonin reuptake inhibitor (SSRI), such as fluoxetine (Prozac). Many children and adolescents take these medications for a number of different mental disorders (Hunkeler et al., 2005), and these medications frequently produce *activating side effects*, such as increased agitation and insomnia (Stahl, 2006). While some clinicians have suggested that such reactions may foreshadow an eventual diagnosis of bipolar disorder (Akiskal & Pinto, 1999), such reactions, even if clinically noteworthy, would only warrant a diagnosis of a substance/medication-induced bipolar and related disorder. The text of the *DSM-5* clearly states that "the appearance of one or two nonspecific symptoms—irritability, edginess, or agitation during antidepressant treatment—in the absence of a full manic or hypomanic episode should not be taken to support a diagnosis of bipolar disorder" (p. 144). However, if symptoms of mania or hypomania persist for a significant period following antidepressant discontinuation, a diagnosis of bipolar disorder may then be warranted (APA, 2013).

EARLY-ONSET PERSONALITY DISORDERS

Many of the core symptoms exhibited by children and adolescents on the hypothesized bipolar spectrum—chronic affective instability, impulsivity, and anger control problems—are also essential features of borderline personality disorder. Hence, a diagnosis of borderline personality disorder should be added to one's differential diagnostic list in evaluating a youth, particularly an adolescent, who presents with such symptoms (Carlson & Meyer, 2006). However, a diagnosis of a personality disorder should not be made during an untreated mood episode, and cyclothymic disorder is the most likely of the bipolar and related disorders to coexist with borderline personality disorder (APA, 2013). Contrary to clinical lore, borderline personality disorder can be present and reliably diagnosed in adolescents (Miller, Muehlenkamp & Jacobson, 2008). With the exception of antisocial personality disorder, the most recent editions of the *DSM* have allowed for the diagnosis of a personality disorder in an individual under age 18 if the problematic personality characteristics are severe, chronic, developmentally inappropriate, and unaccounted for by another mental disorder.

NORMAL CHILDHOOD BEHAVIOR

Though often overlooked when searching for and expecting to find psychopathology, clinicians should also question whether the problems attributed to a child or adolescent fall within the realm of normal behavior. Many of the potential symptoms of mania or hypomania, such as irritability, restlessness, temper tantrums, and grandiose thinking, could be developmentally appropriate and not indicative of any mental disorder (Rich & Leibenluft, 2006; Towbin et al., 2013; Weckerly, 2002). For example, it is quite common for children to overestimate their abilities and to believe that they are superior to others in certain domains, such as sports or academic achievement; such unrealistic thinking commonly occurs among children with no known psychopathology (Bowring & Kovacs, 1992). Thus, clinicians should not just check for the mere presence of a symptom or behavior, but they also must evaluate whether these reported problems are developmentally inappropriate, accompanied by additional symptoms of mania or hypomania, and result in significant distress or psychosocial impairment (APA, 2013). Without the lens of a developmental perspective, there is a danger that normal variations in childhood behavior—though irritating to parents or teachers—may become pathologized.

Assessment Strategies

To facilitate the diagnostic process, Youngstrom et al. (2009) provided a three-step procedure for evaluating children and adolescents suspected of having bipolar disorder. At the first step of this process, Youngstrom et al. recommended that the clinician assess for both individual and family risk factors associated with bipolar disorder. Individual risk factors might include recurrent depressive symptoms that do not respond well to treatment and symptoms of ADHD that appear episodic rather than continuous (Youngstrom, Birmaher, & Findling, 2008). Family risk factors can be reliably assessed through administration of the Family Index of Risk for Mood Issues (FIRM; Algorta, Youngstrom, Phelps, Jenkins, & Youngstrom, 2013). Because bipolar disorder tends to be more common among first-degree biological relatives, any family history of bipolar disorder among close relatives should raise a clinician's suspicions (Youngstrom et al., 2008). Although the absence of a family history of bipolar disorder cannot conclusively rule the disorder out, a clinician should be very cautious about diagnosing bipolar disorder in any child or adolescent who does not have a positive family history of the disorder (Weckerly, 2002).

At the second step of the assessment process, Youngstrom et al. (2009) recommended that clinicians administer a general measure of childhood psychopathology to assess the youth's overall level of psychological impairment. Though several options are available, the Child Behavior Checklist (CBCL) is one of the most popular inventories for assessing both internalizing and externalizing problems in youth (Althoff, Ayer, Rettew, & Hudziak, 2010). Significant elevations on the CBCL's ADHD, aggressive behavior, and anxious/depressed scales have been found to be associated with early-onset bipolar disorder (Faraone, Althoff, Hudziak, Monuteaux, & Biderman, 2005; Mick, Biederman, Pandina, & Faraone, 2003), and as a result, this profile has been referred to as the CBCL-Pediatric/Juvenile Bipolar Disorder profile (Galanter et al., 2003; Hudziak, Althoff, Derks, Faraone, & Boomsma, 2005; Mick et al., 2003). Whereas low-to-normal scores on these scales are fairly useful in ruling bipolar disorder out, elevated scores are not definitive because such elevations also occur among youth with other common childhood disorders, such as ADHD.

Finally, if either family history or test data indicate an elevated risk for bipolar disorder, Youngstrom et al. (2009) recommended that clinicians assess for specific symptoms of mania/hypomania through the use of a validated inventory for this purpose. Specifically, they recommended the Parent General Behavior Inventory (Youngstrom, Findling, Danielson, & Calabrese, 2001), Parent Mood Disorder Questionnaire (Wagner et al., 2006), or the Child Mania Rating Scale (Pavuluri, Henry, Devineni, Carbray, & Birmaher, 2006).

As an alternative to the above-mentioned inventories, clinicians might use the cross-cutting measures described in Section III of the *DSM-5* (APA, 2013). The measures are based on the medical concept of *a review of symptoms* in which a clinician systematically assesses for problems across multiple domains. These cross-cutting measures are organized based on developmental age (children or adults), breadth or depth of symptom assessment (Level I or Level II), and informant perspective (self-report or parent or guardian ratings). There is also a brief list of *Disorder-Specific Severity Measures*, but none of these inventories assess specifically for bipolar disorder in either children or adults. Because of this, we will focus on the use of Level I and Level II measures with children and adolescents suspected of having a bipolar disorder.

The Level I Cross-Cutting Symptom Measures for children, both the self-report and parent/guardian-rating versions, contain 25 items that assess 12 common problem areas: anger, anxiety, depression, inattention, irritability, mania, psychosis, repetitive thoughts or behaviors, sleeping problems, somatic complaints, substance abuse, and suicidal ideation. If problem areas are identified through a Level I screening measure, a clinician might then use one or more Level II Cross-Cutting Measures to attain more detailed information about a youth's specific symptoms and their severity. Most pertinent to the differential diagnosis of bipolar disorder, Level II Cross-Cutting Measures are available for assessing symptoms of mania (hypomania), irritability, depression, and anger specifically in children and adolescents. These inventories are highlighted below:

- Mania (Hypomania): self-report (Level 2—Mania—Child Age 11–17 [Altman Self-Rating Mania Scale]) and parent/guardian ratings (Level 2—Mania—Parent/ Guardian of Child Age 11–17)
- Mania—Parent/Guardian of Child Age 6–17 (modified Altman Self-Rating Mania Scale).
- Irritability: self-report (Level 2—Irritability—Child Age 11–17 [Affective Reactivity Index]) and parent/guardian ratings (Level 2—Irritability—Parent/Guardian of Child Age 6–17 [Affective Reactivity Index]).
- Depression: self-report (Level 2—Depression—Child Age 11–17 [PROMIS Emotional Distress—Depression—Pediatric Item Blank]) and parent/guardian ratings (Level 2—Depression—Parent/Guardian of Child Age 6–17 [PROMIS Emotional Distress—Depression—Parent Item Blank]).
- Anger: self-report (Level 2—Anger—Child Age 11–17 [PROMIS Emotional Distress—Calibrated Anger Measure—Pediatric]) and parent/guardian ratings (Level 2—Anger—Parent/Guardian of Child Age 6–17 [PROMIS Emotional Distress—Calibrated Anger Measure—Parent]).

These inventories are available at no cost and easily accessible online via the APA's *DSM-5* website: http://www.psychiatry.org/practice/dsm/dsm5/online-assessment -measures. As a cautionary note, these inventories are described by the APA (2013) as *emerging* (i.e., experimental) *measures* that should not be used exclusively for making clinical diagnoses, yet they can facilitate the differential diagnostic process and assist with determining symptom severity to inform personalized treatment planning.

Treatment Strategies and Interventions

In addition to providing a three-step process for assessing bipolar disorder, Youngstrom et al. (2009) also provided three general treatment planning strategies based on a youth's risk of having bipolar disorder. For youth with a *low probability* of bipolar disorder, Youngstrom et al. recommended that treatment be directed to any nonbipolar disorders identified through the assessment process. For youth with a *medium probability* of bipolar disorder, they recommended that clinicians continue to monitor and assess for bipolar symptoms, while providing treatment for any nonbipolar disorders, along with preventive interventions, such as sleep hygiene, to improve general mood. Finally, for those in the *high probability* group, they recommended that clinicians begin standard pharmacotherapy for bipolar disorder and, if needed, pursue psychiatric hospitalization to achieve stabilization. (Readers should consult the original Youngstrom et al. [2009] article for more detailed information on their decision-making model.)

PHARMACOTHERAPY

Because pharmacotherapy is considered the first-line treatment for a child or adolescent with bipolar disorder (Chung, Vesco, Resko, Schiman, & Fristad, 2012; Rivas-Vazquez, Johnson, Rey, Blais, & Rivas-Vazquez, 2002), any youth who is identified as having bipolar disorder should be immediately referred to a physician—preferably a board-certified child and adolescent psychiatrist—for evaluation and treatment. While lithium was once considered the gold (or only) standard for treating bipolar disorder, the use of lithium has been gradually supplanted by newer atypical antipsychotics and mood stabilizers (Danielyan, Pathak, Kowatch, Arszman, & Johns, 2007). As of this writing, in addition to lithium, the following medications have FDA approval for treating symptoms of bipolar disorder in older children and adolescents: risperidone (Risperdal), aripiprazole (Abilify), quetiapine (Seroquel), and olanzapine (Zyprexa; American Academy of Child and Adolescent Psychiatry, 2010). However, this list is not exhaustive in delineating the medications that youth with bipolar disorder may be prescribed. Not only might physicians prescribe medications that carry FDA approval for adults with bipolar disorder, but they also may prescribe additional medications under the banner of *off-label* uses. For example, clozapine (Clozaril), which has FDA approval for treating schizophrenia, is also sometimes prescribed to individuals with treatment-resistant bipolar disorder as an off-label use (Stahl, 2006).

To assist physicians in what can become a complex decision-making process, an expert panel convened by the Child and Adolescent Bipolar Foundation created treatment guidelines for physicians to follow in treating children and adolescents with bipolar disorder (Kowatch et al., 2005). This panel developed several complex algorithms for reaching treatment decisions, two examples of which will be illustrated below. For children with a diagnosis of bipolar I, the panel recommended that monotherapy be tried first, either with a mood stabilizer (e.g., lithium or valproate acid) or an atypical antipsychotic (e.g., risperidone or olanzapine). If only a partial response is achieved, the panel recommended adding another mood stabilizer or antipsychotic. For children with a diagnosis of bipolar I with psychotic features, the panel recommended that treatment commence with both a mood stabilizer and an atypical antipsychotic. (Interested readers should consult the original article for a complete description of the algorithms developed for treatment planning decisions.)

PSYCHOSOCIAL INTERVENTIONS

Although pharmacotherapy is considered to be the essential treatment for bipolar disorder (Chung et al., 2012), psychosocial interventions also have complementary roles to play in bringing about both symptomatic and functional improvement. These psychosocial interventions can be divided into two general areas: (1) psychoeducation about bipolar disorder, and (2) psychotherapy for comorbid disorders.

Psychoeducation is the means by which youth and their families learn about the nature and impact of bipolar disorder, the need for consistent pharmacotherapy and medication monitoring, and strategies for preventing relapse (Frank et al., 1999; Swartz, Levenson, & Frank, 2012). Based on the standards for treatment efficacy developed by the Task Force on the Promotion and Dissemination of Psychological Procedures (Chambless & Hollon, 1998), Fristad and MacPherson (2014) identified two formal psychoeducation programs—Multi-Family Psychoeducational Psychotherapy (Fristad, 2006) and Family-Focused Treatment for Adolescents (FFT-A; Miklowitz, 2007; Miklowitz et al., 2008)—as *probably efficacious* in improving treatment outcomes for youth with bipolar disorders. In addition to these two specific models, they also reported that cognitive-behavior therapy also met the standard for a *probably efficacious* treatment as well. While these three programs differ, common components that cut across all three programs include family involvement, skills training (e.g., communication, problem-solving training), and relapse prevention.

Using the same treatment standards rubric (Chambless & Hollon, 1998), Fristad and MacPherson (2014) also identified two other interventions as *experimental* and in need of additional research support. One of these interventions, interpersonal and social rhythm therapy (IPSRT; Frank et al., 1999; Frank, Swartz, & Boland, 2007), is a therapy model that combines an interpersonal focus with behavioral and environmental interventions to help promote stability in the lives of children and adolescents with bipolar disorder. Through IPSRT, individuals learn strategies for medication adherence, stress management, relapse prevention, and how to manage daily social routines and circadian rhythms more effectively. Through IPSRT, individuals with bipolar disorder learn to monitor their routines and maintain a regular schedule, and this regularity helps prevent the onset and persistence of mood episodes. Also, similar to standard interpersonal therapy for depression (Bleiberg & Markowitz, 2008), an *interpersonal inventory* is conducted, from which the client and clinician identify an interpersonal issue focus for therapy: grief, role disputes, role transitions, or interpersonal deficits. Altogether, IPSRT is directed toward improving interpersonal and social role functioning in addition to mood stabilization. (Additional information and training opportunities are available through the IPSRT website: www.ipsrt.org.) The second experimental intervention, dialectical behavior therapy (DBT; Linehan, 1993), is a psychotherapy model originally developed for adults with borderline personality disorder that has shown some preliminary success with youth diagnosed with bipolar disorder (Goldstein, Axelson, Birmaher, & Brent, 2007). As an amalgamation of behavior therapy, Zen practice, and dialectical philosophy, DBT attempts to help individuals reach a balance between changing unhealthy behavioral patterns and accepting what cannot be changed. Clinicians use a number of varied interventions, such as skills training, exposure treatments, grief work, cognitive restructuring or reframing, and functional analyses of behavior, to work through the dialectical dilemmas encountered in the change process. DBT treatment goals are wide ranging and include, but are not limited to, reducing suicidality and nonsuicidal self-injury, resolving past traumas, and improving self-management and emotional regulation skills.

In addition to serving an auxiliary role to pharmacotherapy, counseling or psychotherapy is also recommended for the comorbid disorders that frequently accompany bipolar disorder (Pavuluri et al., 2005). A number of empirically supported interventions are available to clinicians for targeting the depressive, anxiety, and behavioral disorders that are frequently comorbid with bipolar disorder (see Christophersen & Mortweet, 2001; Weisz & Kazdin, 2010). In fact, in those cases in which a child's or adolescent's mood is relatively stable, Towbin et al. (2013) recommended that psychosocial treatments for these comorbid disorders take precedence over pharmacotherapy.

Evaluation Strategies

First, the good news! Prior to the 1990s, lithium was the only medication with FDA approval for treating bipolar disorder in youth, and there were not any evidence-based psychosocial interventions for this clinical population. Beginning in the 1990s, a number of new medications became available to physicians for treating the different symptoms and phases of bipolar disorder, including risperidone (Risperdal), aripiprazole (Abilify), quetiapine (Seroquel), and olanzapine (Zyprexa; American Academy of Child and Adolescent Psychiatry, 2010). In addition to these new medications, three psychosocial intervention models—multifamily psychoeducational psychotherapy, family-focused treatment for adolescents, and cognitive behavioral therapy—have been found to be effective in enhancing treatment outcomes for youth with bipolar disorders (Fristad & MacPherson, 2014). Thus, compared to 25 years ago, mental health providers now have a number of potentially effective treatment options for helping youth with bipolar disorder.

Now, the bad news! Despite the availability of these new treatment options, recovery from bipolar disorder continues to be difficult to obtain and even more difficult to sustain. One of the most common barriers to achieving symptomatic and functional recovery is noncompliance with treatment. Many of the children and adolescents who start treatment for bipolar disorder do not take their medications as prescribed, and many will eventually drop out of treatment altogether (DelBello, Hanseman, Adler, Fleck, & Strakowski, 2007; Drotar et al., 2007). For those who continue in treatment, vigilant monitoring is essential because many of the commonly prescribed medications cause numerous side effects, including extrapyramidal effects, excessive weight gain, nausea, sedation, and metabolic problems (Chung et al., 2012; Hamrin & Pachler, 2007); these side effects also contribute to medication noncompliance and premature termination. Yet, even when families conscientiously adhere to treatment recommendations, continued impairment and relapse are common phenomena (Danielyan et al., 2007). Furthermore, research indicates that individuals who first develop bipolar disorder during childhood or adolescence have more comorbid disorders and worse clinical outcomes than those who develop the disorder in adulthood (Carlson, Bromet, & Sievers, 2000; Goldstein & Levitt, 2006).

Diagnostic Challenges

Despite the contentious debates surrounding the validity of pediatric bipolar disorder, there seems to be near universal agreement on two key points. First, there appears to be a consensus that bipolar disorder—even clear-cut cases of bipolar I or II—occur more often in children and adolescents than was commonly believed in the past. Consequently, clinicians should be receptive to the possibility that a child or adolescent may be experiencing a legitimate manifestation of bipolar disorder. Second, there also seems to be a strong consensus that the children and adolescents who exhibit nonepisodic irritability and aggression are highly impaired and in great need of effective mental health treatment services (Leibenluft, 2011). The problem is that researchers and clinicians cannot agree on how such children and adolescents should be conceptualized (Masi et al., 2006).

Until when—or if—the debate over the diagnostic boundaries of bipolar disorder is resolved, we recommend that clinicians adopt a conservative approach to the diagnosis of bipolar disorder that errs on the side of diagnostic *sensitivity*. *Sensitivity*, also referred to as the *true positive rate*, refers to the proportion of cases that are correctly classified as having a condition, in this case bipolar disorder, based on a test result or decision rule. To maximize the *sensitivity* of bipolar disorder diagnoses, we advise that clinicians strictly adhere to the diagnostic criteria for bipolar disorder in the *DSM-5* (APA, 2013). Accordingly, a child or adolescent would *only* receive a diagnosis of bipolar disorder if all of the requisite diagnostic criteria were met for either bipolar disorder I or II. With regards to atypical or ambiguous cases, we agree with Towbin et al. (2013) that the specified or unspecified bipolar and related disorder options should only be used in those cases where a child and adolescent experiences brief episodes of mania or hypomania that do not meet the requisite duration criteria required for full episodes. These strategies will increase the likelihood that only youth with true cases of bipolar disorder receive the bipolar label and the standard pharmacotherapy that goes along with it.

Unfortunately, a decision model that puts a premium on *diagnostic sensitivity* will likely increase the number of *false negatives* (i.e., youth who are classified as not having bipolar disorder but who actually do have it). When such a mistake is made, a child or adolescent with bipolar disorder will not immediately receive needed pharmacotherapy, which will likely prolong distress and disability. Despite this risk, we believe that a diagnostic model that errs on the side of *diagnostic sensitivity* (i.e., true positives) over *diagnostic specificity* (i.e., true negatives) is the more prudent approach because of the serious consequences that can follow a child or adolescent with a false positive diagnosis of bipolar disorder. In addition to the danger of administering unnecessary pharmacotherapy, there is danger that a false positive diagnosis of bipolar disorder will become unfalsifiable because of confirmatory biases (Garb, 1998).

For example, consider the case of an adolescent client, Brian, a 14-year-old boy whose diagnosis is only oppositional defiant disorder (ODD). Consistent with such a diagnosis, Brian is exhibiting persistent anger, irritability, and belligerent behavior toward his parents and other authority figures. However, Brian's psychiatrist viewed these symptoms as evidence of a bipolar spectrum disorder (unspecified bipolar and related disorder), for which he prescribed a combination of risperidone (Risperdal) and olanzapine (Zyprexa). Given the dynamics associated with a confirmatory bias, there is a risk that any response that Brian has to these medications will be interpreted as confirmation for the original diagnosis of bipolar disorder. For example, if Brian's symptoms do not improve, this could mean that a new combination of medication needs to be tried or that Brian has a treatment-resistant variant of bipolar disorder. On the other hand, any positive response to pharmacotherapy could be interpreted as confirmation that the bipolar disorder diagnosis was correct all along. In addition, any symptomatic improvement exhibited by Brian might lead to a pattern of negative reinforcement in which medications are continued indefinitely to prevent a perceived, but false, risk of relapse. Because of these potential dynamics, Brian, his family, and the psychiatrist may miss the opportunity to explore an important *counterfactual*: How well would Brian be functioning if these medications were reduced or eliminated?

In a perfect world with perfect clinicians, we would all get our clients' diagnoses correct on the first visit. However, especially in working with children and adolescents, additional time is frequently needed to complete the diagnostic process, and diagnostic impressions commonly change as new information becomes available from other informants, prior treatment records, educational records, and psychological test data. Of course, there is a danger that a wait-and-see approach might result in some children and adolescents getting delayed treatment for bipolar disorder. However, that risk must be weighed against the risk of initiating risky and potentially unnecessary pharmacological treatments for youth who do not actually have bipolar disorder. A new diagnosis of bipolar disorder can always be added to a treatment record later as new information becomes available. However, because of confirmatory biases, a premature and incorrect diagnosis of bipolar disorder may be very difficult to take back.

Summary

Historically, bipolar disorder has been viewed as a rather infrequent disorder (1 to 2 percent prevalence rate) that typically first emerges during early adulthood. In this classical prototype of bipolar disorder, an individual experiences clear-cut episodes of mania/hypomania and depression that may be interrupted with periods of relative wellness or remission (APA, 1987; APA, 1994). Shortly after the publication of the *DSM-IV* in 1994, a number of articles appeared in the psychiatric literature in which researchers claimed this historical conceptualization of bipolar disorder was too strict and failed to account for many of the divergent manifestations of the disorder being treated in clinical settings (Akiskal & Pinto, 1999). As part of this movement, several groups of psychiatric researchers hypothesized that many of the children and adolescents diagnosed with severe AHDD or conduct problems were actually experiencing an early-onset phenotype of bipolar disorder, commonly referred to as *pediatric bipolar disorder* (Biederman, Mick, Faraone, & Wozniak, 2004; Wozniak et al., 1995). In place of distinct episodes of mania/hypomania and depression, youth who developed pediatric bipolar disorder were hypothesized to experience chronic (nonepisodic) irritability, aggression, and hyperarousal. During this same period, a number of new medications became available to physicians with FDA approval to treat symptoms of bipolar disorder in both youth and adults. As a result, a perfect storm developed in which physicians now had a number of new medications to treat a newly identified population of children and adolescents with bipolar disorder. By the end of the 2000s, both anecdotal reports and research studies had documented an exponential increase in the number of children and adolescents diagnosed with some variant of bipolar disorder (Blader & Carlson, 2007; Moreno et al., 2007).

Beginning in the early 2000s, another group of psychiatric researchers began closely investigating the divergent groups of children and adolescents who had been grouped together on this expanded bipolar disorder spectrum (Leibenluft et al., 2003). These researchers discovered that many of the youth diagnosed with bipolar disorder on the basis of nonepisodic irritability and aggression differed from youth with bipolar disorder I/II on a number of important dimensions, such as developmental course (Brotman et al., 2006), comorbidity (Dickstein et al., 2005), family aggregation (Brotman et al., 2007), and brain structure (Adleman et al., 2012). This research eventually led to the addition of a new depressive disorder—disruptive mood dysregulation disorder (DMDD)—to the *DSM-5* to provide an alternative to bipolar disorder for categorizing youth who experience chronic (nonepisodic) irritability and anger dysregulation.

In between clear-cut cases of DMDD and bipolar I or bipolar II disorder, clinicians are likely to encounter a number of children and adolescents who fall within an ambiguous borderland area. In such circumstances, a clinician might elect to use one of the *other specified* or *unspecified* options to communicate this lack of diagnostic certainty. Even when selecting this route, a clinician still must decide which general category or chapter of the *DSM-5*—bipolar or depressive—the child or adolescent should be placed in. This placement in the *DSM-5* should be done very cautiously because it will likely have a considerable impact on what treatment services a youth receives. For example, a diagnosis of other specified or unspecified depressive disorder may lead to a treatment plan that includes antidepressants or use of an evidence-based psychotherapy, such as interpersonal therapy (Mufson, 2010). On the other hand, a diagnosis of other specified or unspecified bipolar and related disorder would place the youth on a bipolar spectrum and may foreshadow the long-term use of atypical antipsychotics or mood stabilizers. As Findling et al. (2010) pointed out:

> The diagnosis of bipolar disorder implies a lifelong, heritable condition, with psychological and social sequelae for both the child and his/her family. Youth who are assigned a bipolar diagnosis in error may receive inappropriate treatments for years, particularly unnecessary psychotropic medications that carry with them significant risks. (p. 1665)

For these reasons, any diagnosis of bipolar disorder—even the other specified or unspecified options—should be made very cautiously.

References

Adleman, N. E., Fromm, S. J., Razdan, V., Kayser, R., Dickstein, D. P., Brotman, M. A., ... Leibenluft, E. (2012). Cross-sectional and longitudinal abnormalities in brain structure in children with severe mood dysregulation or bipolar disorder. *Journal of Child Psychology and Psychiatry*, *53*(11), 1149–1156. doi:10.1111/j.1469-7610.2012.02568.x

Akiskal, H. S., & Pinto, O. (1999). The evolving bipolar spectrum: Prototypes I, II, III and IV. *Psychiatric Clinics Of North America*, *22*(3), 517–534. doi:10.1016/S0193-953X(05)70093-9

Algorta, G. P., Youngstrom, E. A., Phelps, J., Jenkins, M. M., & Youngstrom, J. K. (2013). An inexpensive family index of risk for mood issues improves identification of pediatric bipolar disorder. *Psychological Assessment, 25*(1), 12–22. doi:10.1037/a0029225

Althoff, R. R., Ayer, L. A., Rettew, D. C., & Hudziak, J. J. (2010). Assessment of dysregulated children using the Child Behavior Checklist: A receiver operating characteristic curve analysis. *Psychological Assessment, 22*(3), 609–617. doi:10.1037/a0019699

American Academy of Child and Adolescent Psychiatry. (2010). *Bipolar disorder: Parents' medication guide for bipolar disorder in children and adolescents*. Retrieved from http://www.psychiatry.org/File%20Library/Mental%20Illness/Bipolar-parentes-med-guide.pdf

American Psychiatric Association. (1987). *Diagnostic and statistical manual of mental disorders* (3rd ed., text rev.). Washington, DC: Author.

American Psychiatric Association. (1994). *Diagnostic and statistical manual of mental disorders* (4th ed.). Washington, DC: Author.

American Psychiatric Association. (2000). *Diagnostic and statistical manual of mental disorders* (4th ed., text rev.). Washington, DC: Author.

American Psychiatric Association. (2013). *Diagnostic and statistical manual of mental disorders* (5th ed.). Arlington, VA: American Psychiatric Publishing.

Axelson, D. A., Birmaher, B., Findling, R. L., Fristad, M. A., Kowatch, R. A., Youngstrom, E. A., & ... Diler, R. S. (2011). Concerns regarding the inclusion of temper dysregulation disorder with dysphoria in the Diagnostic and Statistical Manual of Mental Disorders, Fifth Edition. *Journal of Clinical Psychiatry, 72*(9), 1257–1262. doi:10.4088/JCP.10com06220

Bambauer, K., & Connor, D. F. (2005). Characteristics of aggression in clinically referred children. *CNS Spectrums, 10*, 709–710.

Biederman, J., Faraone, S. V., Wozniak, J., Mick, E., Kwon, A., & Aleardi, M. (2004). Further evidence of unique developmental phenotypic correlates of pediatric bipolar disorder: findings from a large sample of clinically referred preadolescent children assessed over the last 7 years. *Journal of Affective Disorders, 82*(Suppl1), S45–S58. doi:10.1016/j.jad.2004.05.021

Biederman, J., & Jellinek, M. S. (1998). Resolved: Mania is mistaken for ADHD in prepubertal children. *Journal of the American Academy of Child & Adolescent Psychiatry, 37*(10), 1096–1098. doi:10.1097/00004583–199810000–00022

Blader, J. C., & Carlson, G. A. (2007). Increased rates of bipolar disorder diagnoses among U.S. child, adolescent, and adult inpatients, 1996–2004. *Biological Psychiatry, 62*(2), 107–114.

Bleiberg, K. L., & Markowitz, J. C. (2008). Interpersonal therapy for depression. In D. H. Barlow (Ed.), *Clinical handbook of psychological disorders: A step-by-step treatment manual* (pp. 306–327). New York, NY: Guilford Press.

Bowring, M. A., & Kovacs, M. (1992). Difficulties in diagnosing manic disorders among children and adolescents. *Journal of the American Academy of Child & Adolescent Psychiatry, 31*(4), 611–614. doi:10.1097/00004583–199207000–00006

Brotman, M. A., Kassem, L., Reising, M. M., Guyer, A. E., Dickstein, D. P., Rich, B. A. ... Leibenluft, E. (2007). Parental diagnoses in youth with narrow phenotype bipolar disorder or severe mood dysregulation. *American Journal of Psychiatry, 164*(8), 1238–1241.

Brotman, M. A., Schmajuk, M., Rich, B. A., Dickstein, D. P., Guyer, A. E., Costello, E., ... Leibenluft, E. (2006). Prevalence, clinical correlates, and longitudinal course of severe mood dysregulation in children. *Biological Psychiatry, 60*(9), 991–997. doi:10.1016/j.biopsych.2006.08.042

Carlson, G. A. (1998). Mania and ADHD: Comorbidity or confusion. *Journal of Affective Disorders, 51*(2), 177–187.

Carlson, G. A., Bromet, E. J., & Sievers, S. (2000). Phenomenology and outcome of subjects with early- and adult-onset psychotic mania. *The American*

Journal of Psychiatry, 157(2), 213–219. doi:10.1176/appi.ajp.157.2.213

Carlson, G. A., & Meyer, S. E. (2006). Phenomenology and diagnosis of bipolar disorder in children, adolescents, and adults: Complexities and developmental issues. *Development and Psychopathology, 18*(4), 939–969.

Chambless, D. L., & Hollon, S. D. (1998). Defining empirically supported therapies. *Journal of Consulting and Clinical Psychology, 66*(1), 7–18. doi:10.1037/0022-006X.66.1.7

Christopher, E. R., & Mortweet, S. L. (Eds.) (2001). *Treatments that work with children: Empirically supported strategies for managing childhood problems*. Washington DC: American Psychological Association.

Chung, W. W., Vesco, A. T., Resko, S., Schiman, N., & Fristad, M. A. (2012). Psychosocial interventions for youth with bipolar disorders: Combining clinicians' and caregivers' perspectives. *Professional Psychology: Research and Practice, 43*(6), 633–640. doi:10.1037/a0028754

Danielyan, A., Pathak, S., Kowatch, R. A., Arszman, S. P., & Johns, E. S. (2007). Clinical characteristics of bipolar disorder in very young children. *Journal of Affective Disorders, 97*(1–3), 51–59. doi:10.1016/j.jad.2006.05.028

DelBello, M. P., Hanseman, D., Adler, C. M., Fleck, D. E., & Strakowski, S. M. (2007). Twelve-month outcome of adolescents with bipolar disorder following first hospitalization for a manic or mixed episode. *American Journal of Psychiatry, 164*(4), 582–590.

Dickstein, D. P., Towbin, K. E., Van Der Veen, J., Rich, B. A., Brotman, M. A., Knopf, L., ... Leibenluft, E. (2009). Randomized double-blind placebo-controlled trial of lithium in youths with severe mood dysregulation. *Journal of Child and Adolescent Psychopharmacology, 19*(1), 61–73. doi:10.1089/cap.2008.044

Drotar, D., Greenley, R., Demeter, C. A., McNamara, N. K., Stansbrey, R. J., Calabrese, J. R., ... Findling, R. L. (2007). Adherence to pharmacological treatment for juvenile bipolar disorder. *Journal of the American Academy of Child & Adolescent Psychiatry, 46*(7), 831–839. doi:10.1097/chi.0b013e31805c7421

Faedda, G. L., Baldessarini, R. J., Glovinsky, I. P., & Austin, N. B. (2004). Pediatric bipolar disorder: phenomenology and course of illness. *Bipolar Disorders, 6*(4), 305–313. doi:10.1111/j.1399-5618.2004.00128.x

Faranoe, S. V., Althoff, R. R., Hudziak, J. J., Monuteaux, M., & Biederman, J. (2005). The CBCL predicts DSM bipolar disorder in children: A receiver operating characteristic curve analysis. *Bipolar Disorders, 7*(6), 518–524.

Fava, M. M., Hwang, I. I., Rush, A. J., Sampson, N. N., Walters, E. E., & Kessler, R. C. (2010). The importance of irritability as a symptom of major depressive disorder: Results from the National Comorbidity Survey Replication. *Molecular Psychiatry, 15*(8), 856–867. doi:10.1038/mp.2009.20

Findling, R. L., Youngstrom, E. A., Fristad, M. A., Birmaher, B., Kowatch, R. A., Arnold, L., ... Horwitz, S. (2010). Characteristics of children with elevated symptoms of mania: The Longitudinal Assessment of Manic Symptoms (LAMS) Study. *Journal of Clinical Psychiatry, 71*(12), 1664–1672. doi:10.4088/JCP.09m05859yel

Frank, E., Swartz, H. A., & Boland, E. (2007). Interpersonal and social rhythm therapy: An intervention addressing rhythm dysregulation in bipolar disorder. *Dialogues in Clinical Neuroscience, 9*(3), 325–332.

Frank, E., Swartz, H. A., Mallinger, A. G., Thase, M. E., Weaver, E. V., & Kupfer, D. J. (1999). Adjunctive psychotherapy for bipolar disorder: Effects of changing treatment modality. *Journal of Abnormal Psychology, 108*(4), 579–587.

Fristad, M. A. (2006). Psychoeducational treatment for school-aged children with bipolar disorder. *Development and Psychopathology, 18*(4), 1289–1306. doi:10.1017/S0954579406060627

Fristad, M. A., & MacPherson, H. A. (2014). Evidence-based psychosocial treatments for child and adolescent bipolar spectrum disorders. *Journal of Clinical Child & Adolescent Psychology, 43*(3), 339–355. doi:10.1080/15374416.2013.822309

Galanter, C. A., Carlson, G. A., Jensen, P. S., Greenhill, L. L., Davies, M., Li, W., ... Swanson, J. M. (2003). Response to methylphenidate in children with attention deficit hyperactivity disorder and manic symptoms in the multimodal treatment study of children with attention deficit hyperactivity disorder titration trial. *Journal of Child and Adolescent Psychopharmacology, 13*(2), 123–136.

Garb, H. N. (1998). *Studying the clinician: Judgment research and psychological assessment*. Washington DC: American Psychological Association.

Geller, B., Zimerman, B., Williams, M., Del Bello, M. P., Bolhofner, K., Craney, J. L., ... Nickelsburg, M. J. (2002). DSM-IV mania symptoms in a prepubertal and early adolescent bipolar disorder phenotype compared to attention-deficit hyperactive and normal controls. *Journal of Child and Adolescent Psychopharmacology, 12*(1), 11–25. doi:10.1089/10445460252943533

Gitlin, M. J., Swendsen, J., Heller, T. L., & Hammen, C. (1995). Relapse and impairment in bipolar disorder. *American Journal of Psychiatry, 152*(11), 1635–1640.

Goldstein, T. R., Axelson, D. A., Birmaher, B., & Brent, D. A. (2007). Dialectical behavior therapy for adolescents with bipolar disorder: A 1-year open trial. *Journal of the American Academy of Child & Adolescent Psychiatry, 46*(7), 820–830.

Goldstein, B. I., & Levitt, A. J. (2006). Further evidence for a developmental subtype of bipolar disorder defined by age at onset: Results from the National Epidemiologic Survey on Alcohol and Related Conditions. *American Journal of Psychiatry, 163*(9), 1633–1636. doi:10.1176/appi.ajp.163.9.1633

Goodwin, F. (2002). Rationale for long-term treatment of bipolar disorder and evidence for long-term lithium treatment. *Journal of Clinical Psychiatry, 63*(suppl 10), 5–12.

Hamrin, V., & Pachler, M. (2007). Pediatric bipolar disorder: Evidence-based psychopharmacological treatments. *Journal of Child and Adolescent Psychiatric Nursing, 20*(1), 40–58. doi:10.1111/j.1744-6171.2007.00083.x

Harrow, M., Goldberg, J. F., Grossman, L. S., & Meltzer, H. Y. (1990). Outcome in manic disorders: A naturalistic follow-up study. *Archives of General Psychiatry, 47*(7), 665–671.

Hudziak, J. J., Althoff, R. R., Derks, E. M., Faraone, S. V., & Boomsma, D. I. (2005). Prevalence and genetic architecture of Child Behavior Checklist—Juvenile Bipolar Disorder. *Biological Psychiatry, 58*(7), 562–568.

Hunkeler, E. M., Fireman, B., Lee, J., Diamond, R., Hamilton, J., He, C. X., … Hargreaves, W. A. (2005). Trends in use of antidepressants, lithium, and anticonvulsants in Kaiser Permanente-Insured youths, 1994–2003. *Journal of Child and Adolescent Psychopharmacology, 15*(1), 26–37. doi:10.1089/cap.2005.15.26

Kessler, R. C., Avenevoli, S., Green, J., Gruber, M. J., Guyer, M., He, Y., … Merikangas, K. R. (2009). National Comorbidity Survey Replication Adolescent Supplement (NCS-A): III. Concordance of DSM-IV/CIDI diagnoses with clinical reassessments. *Journal of the American Academy of Child & Adolescent Psychiatry, 48*(4), 386–399. doi:10.1097/CHI.0b013e31819a1cbc

King, J. H. (2014). *Using the DSM-5: Try it, you'll like it.* Retrieved from http://www.continuingedcourses.net/active/courses/course081.php

Kowatch, R. A., Fristad, M., Birmaher, B., Wagner, K., Findling, R. L., & Hellander, M. (2005). Treatment guidelines for children and adolescents with bipolar disorder. *Journal of the American Academy of Child & Adolescent Psychiatry, 44*(3), 213–235. doi:10.1097/00004583-200503000-00006

Leibenluft, E. (2011). Severe mood dysregulation, irritability, and the diagnostic boundaries of bipolar disorder in youths. *American Journal of Psychiatry, 168*(2), 129–142. doi:10.1176/appi.ajp.2010.10050766

Leibenluft, E., Charney, D. S., Towbin, K. E., Bhangoo, R. K., & Pine, D. S. (2003). Defining clinical phenotypes of juvenile mania. *American Journal of Psychiatry, 160*(3), 430–437.

Leibenluft, E., Cohen, P., Gorrindo, T., Brook, J. S., & Pine, D. S. (2006). Chronic versus episodic irritability in youth: A community-based, longitudinal study of clinical and diagnostic associations. *Journal of Child and Adolescent Psychopharmacology, 16*(4), 456–466.

Linehan, M. M. (1993). *Cognitive-behavioral treatment of borderline personality disorder.* New York, NY: Guilford Press.

Meredith, C. W., Jaffe, C., Ang-Lee, K., & Saxon, A. J. (2005). Implications of chronic methamphetamine use: A literature review. *Harvard Review of Psychiatry, 13*(3), 141–154. doi:10.1080/10673220591003605

Mick, E., Biederman, J., Pandina, G., & Faraone, S. V. (2003). A preliminary meta-analysis of the Child Behavior Checklist in pediatric bipolar disorder. *Biological Psychiatry, 53*(11), 1021–1027.

Miklowitz, D. J. (2007). The role of the family in the course and treatment of bipolar disorder. *Current Directions in Psychological Science, 16*(4), 192–196. doi:10.1111/j.1467–8721.2007.00502.x

Miklowitz, D. J., Axelson, D. A., Birmaher, B., George, E. L., Taylor, D. O., Schneck, C. D., … Brent, D. A. (2008). Family-focused treatment for adolescents with bipolar disorder: Results of a 2-year randomized trial. *Archives of General Psychiatry, 65*(9), 1053–1061. doi:10.1001/archpsyc.65.9.1053

Miller, A. L., Muehlenkamp, J. J., & Jacobson, C. M. (2008). Fact or fiction: Diagnosing borderline personality disorder in adolescents. *Clinical Psychology Review, 28*(6), 969–981. doi:10.1016/j.cpr.2008.02.004

Moreno, C., Laje, G., Blanco, C., Jiang, H. Schmidt, A. B., & Olfson, M. (2007). National trends in the outpatient diagnosis and treatment of bipolar disorder in youth. *Archives of General Psychiatry, 64*(9), 1032–1039.

Morrison, J. (2014). *DSM-5 made easy: The clinician's guide to diagnosis.* New York, NY: Guilford Press.

Mufson, L. (2010). Interpersonal psychotherapy for depressed adolescents (IPT- A): Extending the reach from academic to community settings. *Child and Adolescent Mental Health, 15*(2), 66–72.

National Institute of Mental Health. (2001). National Institute of Mental Health research roundtable on prepubertal bipolar disorder. *Journal of the American Academy of Child & Adolescent Psychiatry, 40*(8), 871–878.

Olfson, M., Blanco, C., Wang, S., Laje, G., & Correll, C. U. (2014). National trends in the mental health care of children, adolescents, and adults by office-based physicians. *JAMA Psychiatry, 71*(1), 81–90. doi:10.1001/jamapsychiatry.2013.3074

Pavuluri, M. N., Birmaher, B., & Naylor, M. W. (2005). Pediatric bipolar disorder: A review of the past 10 years. *Journal of the American Academy of Child & Adolescent Psychiatry, 44*(9), 846–871. doi:10.1097/01.chi.0000170554.23422.c1

Pavuluri, M. N., Henry, D. B., Devineni, B., Carbray, J. A., & Birmaher, B. (2006). Child Mania Rating Scale: Development, reliability, and validity. *Journal of the American Academy of Child & Adolescent Psychiatry, 45*(5), 550–560. doi:10.1097/01.chi.0000205700.40700.50

Rich, B. A., & Leibenluft, E. (2006). Irritability in pediatric mania. *Clinical Neuropsychiatry: Journal of Treatment Evaluation, 3*(3), 205–218.

Rivas-Vazquez, R. A., Johnson, S. L., Rey, G. J., Blais, M. A., & Rivas-Vazquez, A. (2002). Current treatments for bipolar disorder: A review and update for psychologists. *Professional Psychology: Research and Practice, 33*(2), 212–223. doi:10.1037//0735-7028.33.2.212

Sinacola, R. S., & Peters-Strickland, T. (2012). *Basic psychopharmacology for counselors and psychotherapists* (2nd ed.). Boston, MA: Allyn & Bacon.

Sobanski, E., Banaschewski, T., Asherson, P., Buitelaar, J., Chen, W., Franke, B., … Faraone, S. V. (2010). Emotional lability in children and adolescents with attention deficit hyperactivity disorder (ADHD): Clinical correlates and familial prevalence. *Journal of Child Psychology and Psychiatry, 51*(8), 915–923. doi:10.1111/j.1469-7610.2010.02217.x

Stahl, S. M. (2006). *Essential psychopharmacology: The prescriber's guide.* New York, NY: Cambridge University Press.

Stringaris, A., Santosh, P., Leibenluft, E., & Goodman, R. (2010). Youth meeting symptom and impairment criteria for mania-like episodes lasting less than four days: An epidemiological enquiry. *Journal of Child Psychology and Psychiatry, 51*(1), 31–38. doi:10.1111/j.1469-7610.2009.02129.x

Swartz, H. A., Levenson, J. C., & Frank, E. (2012). Psychotherapy for bipolar II disorder: The role of interpersonal and social rhythm therapy. *Professional Psychology: Research and Practice, 43*(2), 145–153. doi:10.1037/a0027671

Towbin, K., Axelson, D., Leibenluft, E., & Birmaher, B. (2013). Differentiating bipolar disorder–not otherwise specified and severe mood dysregulation. *Journal of the American Academy of Child & Adolescent Psychiatry, 52*(5), 466–481. doi:10.1016/j.jaac.2013.02.006

Valle Krieger, F., Pheula, G., Coelho, R., Zeni, T., Tramontina, S., Zeni, C., & Rohde, L. (2011). An open-label trial of risperidone in children and adolescents with severe mood dysregulation. *Journal of Child and Adolescent Psychopharmacology, 21*(3), 237–243. doi:10.1089/cap.2010.0123

Van Meter, A. R., Moreira, A. R., & Youngstrom, E. A. (2011). Meta-analysis of epidemiologic studies of pediatric bipolar disorder. *Journal of Clinical Psychiatry, 72*(9), 1250–1256. doi:10.4088/JCP.10m06290

Wagner, K., Hirschfeld, R. A., Emslie, G. J., Findling, R. L., Gracious, B. L., & Reed, M. L. (2006). Validation of the Mood Disorder Questionnaire for bipolar disorders in adolescents. *Journal of Clinical Psychiatry, 67*(5), 827–830. doi:10.4088/JCP.v67n0518

Weckerly, J. (2002). Pediatric bipolar mood disorder. *Developmental & Behavioral Pediatrics, 23*(1), 42–56.

Weisz, J. R., & Kazdin, A. E. (Eds.). (2010). *Evidence-based psychotherapies for children and adolescents* (2nd ed.). New York, NY: Guilford Press.

Weller, E. B., Calvert, S. M., & Weller, R. A. (2003). Bipolar disorder in children and adolescents: Diagnosis and treatment. *Current Opinion in Psychiatry, 16*(4), 383–388. doi:10.1097/00001504-200307000-00003

Wozniak, J., Biederman, J., Kiely, K., Ablon, J., Faraone, S. V., Mundy, E., & Mennin, D. (1995). Mania-like symptoms suggestive of childhood-onset bipolar disorder in clinically referred children. *Journal of the American Academy of Child & Adolescent Psychiatry, 34*(7), 867–876. doi:10.1097/00004583-199507000-00010

Youngstrom, E. A., Birmaher, B., & Findling, R. L. (2008). Pediatric bipolar disorder: Validity, phenomenology, and recommendations for diagnosis. *Bipolar Disorders, 10*(Suppl1 p2), 194–214. doi:10.1111/j.1399-5618.2007.00563.x

Youngstrom, E. A., Findling, R. L., Danielson, C., & Calabrese, J. R. (2001). Discriminative validity of parent report of hypomanic and depressive symptoms on the General Behavior Inventory. *Psychological Assessment, 13*(1), 267–276. doi:10.1037/1040-3590.13.2.267

Youngstrom, E. A., Freeman, A. J., & McKewon-Jenkins, M. (2009). The assessment of children and adolescents with bipolar disorder. *Child and Adolescent Psychiatric Clinics of North America, 18*(2), 353–390. doi:10.1016/j.chc.2008.12.002

Chapter 9

Depressive Disorders

CARLOS P. ZALAQUETT AND SERIASHIA CHATTERS-SMITH

Introduction

Childhood depressive disorders are frequent (Centers for Disease Control and Prevention [CDC], 2012; Kessler et al., 2005; Perou et al., 2013) and include major depressive disorder (MDD, also known as clinical depression or unipolar depression), persistent depressive disorder (PDD, includes former dysthymia diagnosis), disruptive mood dysregulation disorder (DMDD), premenstrual dysphoric disorder (PMDD), substance/medication-induced depressive disorder, depressive disorder due to another medical condition, other specified depressive disorder, and unspecified depressive disorder (American Psychiatric Association [APA], 2013). Sidebar 9.1 presents current data on children's mental health and related costs.

> ### SIDEBAR 9.1:   CDC 2013 REPORT
>
> - Childhood mental disorders are a public health issue because of high prevalence, early onset, and negative impact at all levels: child, family, and community.
> - Yearly, 13 to 20 percent of children in the United States experience a mental disorder.
> - Suicide is the second leading cause of death among children aged 12 to 17 in 2012.
> - The cost of mental disorders among persons aged 23 years old or younger per year is $247.
> - Children's mental disorders are among the most costly to treat.
>
> Adapted from Perou et al., 2013 and Sullivan, Annest, Simon, Luo, & Dahlberg, 2015.

Children and adolescents' depressive disorders are considered a public health issue because they are more frequent than expected, can be recurrent or chronic, produce significant impairment and mortality (Perou et al., 2013; Substance Abuse and Mental Health

Services Administration [SAMHSA], 2014), and have far-reaching effects on the functioning and adjustment of youngsters. Depressed students are at high risk of school failure, interpersonal difficulties, and high suicide rates (Perou et al., 2013).

In spite of their seriousness, depressive disorders, especially major depressive disorder and persistent depressive disorder (dysthymia), are frequently overlooked and undertreated (Gelaye et al., 2013; Hazler & Mellin, 2004; Kramer, Miller, Phillips, & Robbins, 2008; Thapar, Collishaw, Pine, Ajay, & Thapar, 2012; Zalaquett & Saunders, 2010), especially in low-income and ethnically diverse youth (Fox et al., 2007; Gudiño, Martinez, & Lau, 2012; Thomas, Temple, Perez, & Rupp, 2011). Mental health professionals tend to look at depressive symptoms as reflecting expected manifestations of biological maturation, or they lack specific training to diagnose depressive disorders; as a consequence, children are not referred to treatment or are referred and treated for symptoms other than their depression (Zalaquett & Saunders, 2010). This situation is unacceptable because depressive disorders are treatable and respond to psychosocial and biological interventions (Goldman, 2012; Zalaquett & Saunders, 2010). Childhood depressive disorders are pervasive and demand to be addressed actively within our society. Depression is a frequent disorder that starts early in life and affects children and adolescents' feelings, thoughts, activity level, and physical health (Allen, Chango, Szwedo, & Schad, 2014; Schwarz, 2009). The purpose of this chapter is to present current information regarding depressive disorders and describe their assessment, prevalence, and treatment. Relevant facts about depression are presented in Sidebar 9.2.

SIDEBAR 9.2:   FACTS ABOUT DEPRESSION

- Depression affects all people.
- Nearly twice as many women (12.0 percent) as men (6.6 percent) are affected.
- Depressive disorders often co-occur with anxiety disorders and substance abuse.
- Leading cause of disability in the United States for ages 15-44.
- About 2.5 percent of children in the United States suffer from depression.
- In 2012, suicide was the second leading cause of death of 10- to 24-year-olds and the third leading cause of death of 15 to 24 year olds. All too often suicide is the result of extended periods of depression.
- Early diagnosis can help children in their emotional, social, and behavioral development.
- Depression can be hard to detect or masked by other factors.
- Signs may be viewed as mood swings typical of children as they move through developmental stages, and this makes it difficult to diagnose a young person with depression accurately.

Adapted from APA, 2014, National Institute of Mental Health (NIMH) n.d.a, and Karch, Logan, McDaniel, Parks, & Patel 2012.

Treating depression and other disorders is a professional responsibility and matter of social justice for practitioners (Silver, Battin, & Rhodes, 2012; Royal College of Nursing, 2012) because untreated major depressive disorder can lead to adverse outcomes later in life (Allen et al., 2014; Fergusson, Boden, & Horwood, 2007); children may fail to thrive and depressed adolescents may become involved in the criminal justice system or attempt suicide later in life (Perou et al., 2013). More than seven percent of adolescents diagnosed with major depressive disorder may attempt suicide during their young adult years (Perou et al., 2013). Furthermore, adolescents who experience an episode of depression have a higher probability of becoming depressed again, failing in school, or using substances in early adulthood (Brière, Rohde, Seeley, Klein, & Lewinsohn, 2014; Melvina et al., 2013). Conversely, young adults (to age 24) who experience depression as adolescents have a higher probability to drop from college, have lower salaries, become single parents, and experience more stressful life events (Zima et al., 2013). Depression in adolescents is associated with an increased risk of suicidal behavior (Zima et al., 2013; Wolitzky-Taylor et al., 2010). Major depressive disorder represents one of the foremost risk factors for suicidal ideation and suicide in adolescents (Asarnow et al., 2011; Zakharov, Navratil, & Pelclova, 2013). The negative outcomes of depressive disorders make it essential to assess childhood depressive disorders, provide appropriate treatment, and implement preventative interventions (Neves & Leanza, 2014; NIMH, n.d.). Early identification, treatment, and prevention of depressive disorders can reduce or prevent negative consequences (Barbe, Bridge, Birmaher, Kolko, & Brent, 2004; David-Ferdon & Kaslow, 2008; NIMH, n.d.a; Zalaquett & Saunders, 2010; Zima et al., 2013). How children experience depression and the burden of this disorder are presented in Sidebar 9.3 and Sidebar 9.4, respectively.

SIDEBAR 9.3:   HOW DO CHILDREN AND TEENS EXPERIENCE DEPRESSION?

- Children who develop depression may continue to have episodes in adulthood.
- Children who develop depression are more likely to have more severe illnesses in adulthood.
- Young children may pretend to be sick, refuse to go to school, cling to a parent, or worry that a parent may die.
- Older children may sulk, get into trouble at school, be negative and irritable, and feel misunderstood.
- Before puberty, boys and girls are equally likely to develop depression. By age 15, however, girls are twice as likely as boys to have had a major depressive episode.
- Depression during the teen years comes at a time of great personal change—when boys and girls are forming an identity apart from their parents, grappling with gender issues and emerging sexuality, and making independent decisions for the first time in their lives. Depression in adolescence frequently co-occurs with other disorders such as anxiety, eating disorders, or substance abuse. It can also lead to increased risk for suicide.
- Childhood depression often persists, recurs, and continues into adulthood, especially if left untreated.

Adapted from NIMH, n.d.b.

SIDEBAR 9.4:   BURDEN OF DEPRESSION

- The World Health Organization (WHO) reports that unipolar depression was the third most important cause of disease burden worldwide in 2004.
- Unipolar depression ranked in "eighth place in low-income countries, but at first place in middle- and high-income countries" (WHO, 2008, as cited in CDC National Center for Chronic Disease Prevention and Health Promotion, 2013, para. 1).
- Ethnic differences reveal lifetime percentages of depression of 6.52 percent among whites and 4.57 percent among blacks and 5.17 percent among Hispanics.

Adapted from CDC National Center for Chronic Disease Prevention and Health Promotion, 2013

How to Distinguish between Childhood Moodiness and Depression

Childhood depressive disorders must be distinguished from normal grief, adjustment disorders, moodiness, sadness, and other affective reductions. Most children experience brief, sometimes intense, episodes of the blues, appetite changes, sleep disruptions, increments of reductions in activity level, reduced concentration, low self-worth, behavior problems at home or school, inattentiveness, unexplained drops in grades, skipping classes, avoiding activities, or withdrawing from friends. The question is: How do counselors distinguish the difference between a moody child and adolescent and one who may be suffering from depression? Differentiation between normal childhood mood and depressed mood is based on the observed persistence of symptoms (duration), the level of distress observed (intensity), and the degree of interference with normal functioning (dysfunction). Nosological systems, such as the *Diagnostic and Statistical Manual of Mental Disorders, Fifth Edition* (*DSM-5*; APA, 2013); the *International Classification of Diseases, Tenth Revision, Clinical Modification* (*ICD-10-CM*; WHO, 2010); or the National Center for Health Statistics (NCHS, 2014), exist with criteria to diminish the variability in the interpretation of symptoms and standardize diagnostic procedure. Specific disorders and diagnostic criteria are presented below.

Description of Depressive Disorders

DISRUPTIVE MOOD DYSREGULATION DISORDER (DMDD)

Over the past two decades, the diagnosis of bipolar disorder in children and adolescents rose exponentially in lieu of the development of new medications, especially atypical or second-generation antipsychotics. The rise in bipolar prevalence, especially when diagnosed solely as an irritable mood, became an issue because of the lack of established diagnostic criteria. Some researchers and practitioners proposed a modification of bipolar disorder diagnostic criteria that would allow the presence of a manic or hypomanic episode to include nonepisodic irritability, because they believed it was the simile of adult mania (Margulies, Weintraub, Basile, Grover, & Carlson, 2012; Ryan, 2013). This combination of events resulted in a 40-fold increase in the diagnosis of bipolar disorder in children and adolescents over the previous decade, causing significant concern in the mental health and medical communities (Eme & Mouritson, 2013; Moreno et al., 2007). The diagnosis of DMDD was added to address the concerns about overdiagnosis and treatment of bipolar disorder in children (APA, 2013; Ryan, 2013). The prevalence of DMDD is approximately 0.8 to 3.3 percent (Ryan, 2013). Children with this disorder are susceptible to developing symptoms of major depression and anxiety later in life, instead of bipolar disorder (Leibenluft, 2011).

To be diagnosed with DMDD, children must manifest symptoms before 10 years of age, and they must be at least chronologically 6 years old. Additionally, they must display severe recurrent temper outbursts three or more times a week, inconsistent with the child's developmental age, for a year or longer. Extreme dyscontrol and information-processing deficits (e.g., dangerous behavior, suicidal ideation or suicide attempts, severe aggression, and psychiatric hospitalization) are common. In between the verbal or behavioral temper outbursts, their mood, as described by parents, guardians, or teachers, is persistent, chronic, and severely irritable or angry most of the day, nearly every day, and in at least two different settings. Most important, the full symptom criteria, except duration, for a manic or hypomanic episode have never lasted more than one day. Rationale for the inclusion of this new disorder is presented in Sidebar 9.5. Differential diagnosis procedures are presented in Table 9.1.

TABLE 9.1 Differential Diagnosis of Disruptive Mood Dysregulation Disorder (DMDD)

If the client (or his or her parent or guardian) ...	Then the diagnosis may be ...
Reports nonsevere/nonchronic irritability or mood elevation that is episodic and distinctly different from the normal mood	Bipolar Disorder I or II
Reports temper outbursts without the presence of an irritable mood most of the day, every day	Oppositional Defiant Disorder
Reports irritability exclusively during a major depressive episode or during persistent depressive disorder	Major Depressive Disorder or Persistent Depressive Disorder
Reports irritability exclusively during the presence of an anxiety disorder	Specific Anxiety Disorder (e.g., Generalized Anxiety Disorder)
Reports symptoms of autism spectrum disorder and irritability or temper outbursts because of their routine being disturbed or changed	Autism Spectrum Disorder
Reports temper outbursts but DOES NOT report irritable mood between temper outbursts and reports symptoms over the past two months	Intermittent Explosive Disorder

Source: Chatters, 2014.

SIDEBAR 9.5: DMDD

The main reasons behind this new diagnosis were the alarming 40-fold increment in the diagnosis of bipolar disorder observed between 1994 and 2003 and the fact that the symptomatology was not consistent with that of adult bipolar diagnosis. Most children presenting this symptomatology develop depression and comorbid anxiety as adults.

MAJOR DEPRESSIVE DISORDER (AND EPISODE)

Major Depressive Disorder (MDD), or clinical depression, is characterized by an episode of persistent feelings of sadness, emptiness, hopelessness, crankiness, or irritability and by somatic and cognitive changes that significantly affect the child's capacity to function. To be classified as clinical depression, these episodes must occur without any history of independent episodes of mania, also known as mood elevation and increased energy (WHO, 2010). In addition to the previously mentioned symptoms, a major depressive episode must also include four or more of the following symptoms: marked diminished interest or pleasure, significant gain or loss in weight or appetite, difficulty or change in sleeping habits, excessive feelings of inappropriate guilt or worthlessness, fatigue, a decreased ability to think or concentrate, thoughts of death or suicidal ideation, and observed feelings of restlessness or appearance of being in "slow motion." In children and adolescents some of these psychological symptoms may manifest as physical symptoms such as stomachaches or discomfort and headaches that do not respond to treatment, unexplained crying and/or vocal outbursts, withdrawal from social activities, body aches and pains, and impaired ability to function in school, at home, and in extracurricular activities or hobbies.

Depressive episodes can range in severity from mild to severe, with mild episodes consisting of five to six symptoms, moderate episodes consisting of six to seven symptoms, and severe episodes consisting of eight to nine seriously distressing and unmanageable symptoms, resulting in substantial functional impairment (American Psychiatric Association, 2013). Severity of episodes is also defined by level of impairment of functioning. A child experiencing mild clinical depression may experience little to no impairment in functioning in day-to-day activities. Subsequently, a child experiencing severe clinical depression may experience significant impairment in functioning in many to all day-to-day activities. For example, a child with mild depression may experience sadness, increased boredom, or loss of interest in activities, however, this child will continue to attend school regularly, socialize with friends and family, and participate in daily activities. In contrast, a child experiencing severe depression may experience sadness, hopelessness, loss of interest in activities, and changes in appetite and sleep habits. A child who is severely depressed may also withdraw from social and family activities, have excessive absences from school, and express thoughts of self-harm and/or suicide. Clinicians are encouraged to use the *DSM-5* cross-cutting symptom measures to determine severity rating of depression in children. These assessments include the PROMIS Emotional Distress Depression Parent Item Bank (Level 2—Depression—Parent/Guardian of Child Age 6–17), PROMIS Emotional Distress Depression Pediatric Item Bank (Level 2—Depression—Child Age 11–17), and the PHQ-9 modified for Adolescents (PHQ-A) Adapted (Severity Measure for Depression—Child Age 11–17).

Children and adolescents typically experience variations in mood and affect that may be inherent to their developmental stage (McGorry, Purcell, Goldstone, & Amminger, 2011). For example, adolescent girls may experience emotional changes due to hormonal fluctuations during puberty. Symptoms of depression can be differentiated from *normal* changes in mood because depressed mood is usually minimally affected by circumstances and remains low throughout the day. Gradual improvements during the day are observed in some cases, but the low mood tends to return the following morning. For others, mood elevations observed in response to positive environmental changes do not last, and depressive feelings return soon thereafter (National Institute for Health and Care Excellence [NICE], 2015). Furthermore, in youngsters an irritable mood (e.g., easily annoyed by others, often losing temper, staying angry for a long time, or getting angry frequently) instead of a sad mood may be observed. Children may fail to gain expected weight, their grades may fall, and they may display separation anxiety (APA, 2013). Major depressive disorder in adolescence has been associated with impaired functioning in all areas and early pregnancy (Fergusson & Woodward, 2002; Han et al., 2012; Keenan-Miller, Hammen, & Brennan, 2007; Zima et al., 2013). Differential diagnosis is presented in Table 9.2.

Prevalence

MDD is experienced by approximately 8 percent of persons 12 years old or younger (6 percent of males; 10 percent of females; CDC, 2012). Prevalence increases with age and sharply rises around puberty. It also changes by gender, with preadolescent boys and girls affected equally, but the rate sharply increases 1.5- to three-fold among girls during adolescence (APA, 2013). The Substance Abuse and Mental Health Services Administration (2014) reported that in 2013, 10.7 percent of adolescents experienced at least one major depressive episode. Adolescents' major depressive episodes are longer in duration and present higher risk of relapse (Milin, Walker, & Chow, 2003; American Academy of Child and Adolescent Psychiatry [AACAP], 2007). Duration ranging from 12 to 16 weeks has been reported for clinical samples of adolescents (Kaminski & Garber, 2002). The longer

TABLE 9.2   Differential Diagnosis of Major Depressive Disorder (MDD)

If the client (or his or her parent or guardian) …	*Then the diagnosis may be …*
Reports irritability and mood elevation significantly different than normal mood in addition to depressive symptoms	Bipolar I or II
Reports depressive symptoms that occur only as a direct consequence of a medical condition	Depressive disorder due to another medical condition
Reports depressive symptoms or changes in mood that occur only as a direct consequence of a substance, such as alcohol or prescription or recreational drugs	Substance/Medication-Induced depressive or bipolar disorder
Reports distractibility and low frustration tolerance AND mood disturbance attributed primarily to irritability rather than sadness or loss of interest	Attention-Deficit/Hyperactivity Disorder, Inattentive Presentation
Reports depressed mood specifically attributed to a psychosocial stressor (e.g., parents' divorce); however, all criteria for MDD are not met	Adjustment Disorder with Depressed Mood
Reports sadness or low mood; however, all criteria for MDD or any other mental disorder are not met	Sadness

Source: Chatters, 2014.

the duration of the major depressive episode in adolescence, the higher the likelihood of symptoms persisting or returning in young adulthood (Patton et al., 2014).

Risk Factors

Potential risk factors include family history of depression, previous depressive episodes, adverse childhood experiences, current family conflict, low academic performance, doubts regarding sexual orientation, negative affect, negative life events, and comorbid conditions, such as dysthymia, anxiety disorders, and substance abuse disorders (APA, 2013; Kendler & Gardner, 2011). Exposure of adolescents to a peer's suicide is also a risk factor as it increments 28 times the risk of depression, which usually starts within a month after the event (Borowsky, Ireland, & Resnick, 2001).

Comorbidity

Clinical and epidemiologic studies show that 40 to 93 percent of adolescents with depression exhibit comorbid disorders (AACAP, 2007; Nock et al., 2013). Comorbidity includes the superimposition of persistent depressive disorder (dysthymia) and major depressive disorder (Comer, 2014). Other comorbid disorders include obsessive-compulsive and related disorders; panic disorder or panic attack specifier; disruptive, impulse-control, and conduct disorders; feeding and eating disorders; and substance use disorders (which frequently exacerbate depressive symptoms; AACAP, 2007; APA, 2013; Greenberg, Domitrovich, & Bumbarger, 2001). Depression can significantly affect children's functioning, disrupting daily life at home, at school, or in the community; one episode of depression increases by 50 percent the risk of experiencing additional episodes; and adolescent-onset depression increases the risk of attempted suicide fivefold (Zima et al., 2013).

PERSISTENT DEPRESSIVE DISORDER (PDD, DYSTHYMIA)

PDD is a depressive disorder like MDD, requiring a depressed mood for most of the day for more days than not; however, it is more chronic, and it requires a minimum two of six available symptoms to satisfy one criteria (whereas MDD requires a minimum five of nine available symptoms), along with six additional criteria needing to be satisfied. PDD (a consolidation of the *DSM-IV-TR* defined chronic major depressive disorder and dysthymic disorder) symptoms may include poor appetite, insomnia or hypersomnia, low energy or fatigue, low self-esteem, poor concentration or difficulty making decisions, or feeling hopeless (APA, 2013). These symptoms may persist for several years, without a manic episode or a hypomanic episode. Unlike MDD, recurrent thoughts of death (not just fear of dying), recurrent suicidal ideation without a specific plan, or a suicide attempt or a specific plan for committing suicide are not manifest in PDD. Moreover, children and adolescents with PDD differ from children and adolescents with MDD in that they manifest feelings of hopelessness instead of worthlessness or excessive guilt, they do not manifest psychomotor agitation or retardation, and they display poor appetite or overeating without resulting in significant weight loss or weight gain.

Sometimes children and adolescents are depressed for so long that they may not complain of feeling depressed because they do not recognize their mood as out of the ordinary (U.S. Department of Health and Human Services, 2012). Because of its tenacious nature, persistent depressive disorder (dysthymia) is especially likely to interfere with normal adjustment in social, occupational, or other important areas of functioning. Sidebar 9.6 explains the reason for dysthymic disorder reconceptualization. For an example of a *DSM-5* clinical formulation, see Sidebar 9.7.

SIDEBAR 9.6: DYSTHYMIA

Dysthymia was replaced with Persistent Depressive Disorder, which includes both DSM-IV chronic major depressive disorder and the previous dysthymic disorder. This change was motivated by the lack of scientific evidence supporting differences between the two conditions.

SIDEBAR 9.7:   EXAMPLE OF *DSM-5* CLINICAL FORMULATION

300.4 Moderate Persistent Depressive Disorder (Dysthymia), With Anxious Distress (feeling keyed up or tense, feeling unusually restless, and difficulty concentrating because of worry), With Atypical Features (mood reactivity, hypersomnia, and a long-standing pattern of extreme sensitivity at perceived interpersonal rejection), Early Onset, With Intermittent Major Depressive Episodes, Without Current Episode

---

The onset of PDD is usually in childhood or adolescence (U.S. Department of Health and Human Services, 2012). The prevalence of PDD is approximately 0.6 to 1.7 percent in children and 1.6 to 8 percent in adolescents (Rogers & Kraft, 2014). PDD is considered a "gateway" disorder because approximately 70 percent of children with PDD may develop experience a major depressive disorder within five years, also known as *double depression*. Children and adolescents diagnosed with PDD also are more likely to experience comorbid psychiatric disorders, such as anxiety disorders, conduct disorder, attention-deficit hyperactivity disorder (ADHD), cluster B and C personality disorders, and elimination disorders. Approximately 15 percent of pediatric patients with dysthymic disorder have two or more comorbid disorders (APA, 2013; Comer, 2014; Rogers & Kraft, 2014). Differential diagnosis procedures are presented in Table 9.3.

PREMENSTRUAL DYSPHORIC DISORDER

Premenstrual Dysphoric Disorder (PMDD) was previously in the section of the *DSM-IV-TR* (pp. 771–774) as a condition for further study and is qualitatively distinct from premenstrual syndrome (PMS). PMDD is a chronic condition of reproductive-aged women and is characterized by emotional, cognitive, behavioral, and physical symptoms consistently occurring during the menstrual cycle's luteal phase (the phase that begins with ovulation and ends with the onset of menses). As many as 80 percent of women in the United States experience emotional, behavioral, or physical premenstrual symptoms,

TABLE 9.3   Differential Diagnosis of Persistent Depressive Disorder (PDD)

If the client (or his or her parent or guardian) …	*Then the diagnosis may be …*
Has been diagnosed with PDD but reports symptoms that meet the full criteria for major depressive disorder, but there have been periods of at least eight weeks in at least the preceding two years with symptoms below the threshold for a full major depressive episode	Persistent Depressive Disorder with Intermittent Major Depressive Episodes, with current episode
Was diagnosed with PDD and reports symptoms that meet the full criteria for major depressive disorder that have persisted for at least two years	Persistent Depressive Disorder with persistent major depressive episode
Is diagnosed with PDD and DOES NOT CURRENTLY report symptoms that meet the full criteria for major depressive disorder BUT has experienced a major depressive episode with the past two years	Persistent Depressive Disorder with intermittent major depressive episodes, without current episode
Is diagnosed with PDD and HAS NOT reported symptoms that meet the full criteria for major depressive disorder over the past two years	Persistent Depressive Disorder with pure dysthymic syndrome
Reports symptoms of PDD that occur ONLY during a psychotic episode	Psychotic Disorder
Reports symptoms of PDD that can be directly connected to a period in which the client can report experiencing the physiological effects of a specific and/or chronic illness (through self-report or physician or laboratory reports	Depressive or bipolar and related disorder due to another medical condition
Reports symptoms of PDD that were experienced during their use of a substance (e.g., prescription or recreational drugs, alcohol)	Substance/medication-induced depressive or bipolar disorder
Reports symptoms of PDD and symptoms of a coexisting personality disorder	Both diagnoses are given

Source: Chatters, 2014.

with 3 to 8 percent meeting diagnostic criteria for this disorder (Epperson et al., 2012; Htay & Aung, 2014). Diagnosis of PMDD can be complicated by the high comorbidity with other psychiatric disorders in adults (Epperson et al., 2012). Although extensive studies have been conducted in adults, it is estimated that comorbidity is high in adolescents as well (Rapkin, & Mikacich, 2013). Comorbid disorders, such as unipolar depressive disorder, anxiety disorders, and obsessive-compulsive disorder are usually diagnosed within 10 years of the onset of menses. Beyond comorbidity, it is possible that some of these behaviors may possibly exacerbate menstrual cycle-linked disorders (Lee, Chen, Lee, & Kaur, 2006). Counselors serving children and adolescents must have the ability to conduct differential diagnosis to discern between the symptoms of pathological PMDD and normal PMS that is not diagnosable as a mental disorder.

Two of the most important aspects of the PMDD diagnosis are the time of onset and the time that symptoms subside. In PMDD, an adolescent may begin experiencing symptoms approximately one week prior to the onset of menses. Symptoms should begin to subside within a few days after the onset of menses and continue to improve or disappear approximately one week post menses (APA, 2013), and they should be confirmed by prospective daily ratings during at least two symptomatic cycles. Young women experiencing PMDD must report at least one or more of the following symptoms: marked emotional fluctuations (e.g., sensitivity, mood swings, and unexplained sadness or tear-fulness), marked irritability/anger or interpersonal conflict, marked depressed mood (e.g., hopelessness or self-deprecating thoughts), or marked anxiety, tension, or agitation. Additionally, the adolescent must report one or more of the following symptoms, to reach a total of five symptoms minimum when combined with symptoms listed above: decreased interest in normal activities (e.g., friends, hobbies, school, work, and family), difficulty concentrating, fatigue or sluggishness, significant change in appetite (e.g., specific food cravings) or overeating, excessive sleep or marked sleep disruption, feeling overwhelmed, or physical symptoms (e.g., breast tenderness, swelling or pain in joints or muscles, bloat-ing, or weight gain). In addition, symptoms were manifest for most of the previous year's menstruations and must cause clinically significant distress or marked functional impair-ment for the adolescent (APA, 2013). Differential diagnosis procedures are presented in Table 9.4.

DEPRESSIVE DISORDER DUE TO A MEDICAL CONDITION

Many children and adolescents, similar to adults, who suffer from chronic diseases may experience psychosocial issues as they adjust to the impact of the disease on their activities at home, at school, and with friends. The prevalence of depression and chronic diseases can be very high. Approximately 26 percent of patients suffering from juvenile diabetes reported experiencing depression (Holt, de Groot, & Golden, 2014; Jaser, 2010). An estimated 30 to 40 percent of young patients diagnosed with multiple sclerosis (Feinstein, 2011; Goretti et al., 2010) and approximately 25 percent of patients diag-nosed with cancer (Massie, 2004; Simon, Palmer, & Coyne, 2006) report experiencing symptoms of depression.

Children and adolescents experiencing depression due to a medical condition must expe-rience a definitive period of depressed mood, sadness, or irritability and loss of interest in almost all, or all activities. These symptoms differ from MDD and PDD because of their direct correlation with a physical examination, history, or information from medical records or a laboratory being the cause of the change in mood.

SUBSTANCE/MEDICATION INDUCED DEPRESSIVE DISORDER

Adolescence can be a difficult and awkward period in life. Although substance use in chil-dren and adolescents, including alcohol and tobacco, has steadily decreased over the past

TABLE 9.4   Differential Diagnosis of Premenstrual Dysphoric Disorder

If the client ...	Then the diagnosis may be ...
Does not report at least five of the symptoms of PMDD	Premenstrual Syndrome
Does not report the affective symptoms of PMDD	
Does not report the physical or behavioral symptoms of PMDD	
Reports painful periods without emotional changes	Dysmenorrhea
Reports pain that only begins on the first day of their period	
Reports premenstrual symptoms AND is currently on hormonal treatments; symptoms subside when hormonal treatment is discontinued	Due to hormonal treatments

Source: Chatters, 2014.

decade (National Institute of Drug Abuse, 2014), it is important to note that substance use is still prevalent among preteens and teens and can have a significant psychological impact. Furthermore, use of illegal drugs has increased, especially the use of marijuana (National Institute of Drug Abuse, 2014). Unfortunately it can be difficult for counselors to determine which of these issues developed first, substance use or the mood disorder. Mental health professionals should conduct a thorough evaluation to determine whether any symptoms of depression were present prior to substance use. If symptoms of depression were present, using differential diagnostic procedures is important to identify the specific depressive disorder present. If the depressive disorder can be directly connected to the use of a substance and/or medication, a diagnosis of Substance/Medication-Induced Depressive Disorder is warranted.

A diagnosis of substance/medication-induced depressive disorder requires the youth to be experiencing a significant and persistent shift in mood that is marked by a loss of interest in almost all or all activities in school and at home or depressed mood. Additionally, these symptoms must have developed during or immediately following the use of a substance (e.g., alcohol, hallucinogens, inhalants, sedatives, or stimulants) that is capable of causing depressive symptoms.

OTHER SPECIFIED DEPRESSIVE DISORDER

As previously discussed, depression can be difficult to diagnose in children and adolescents. This category is utilized when the client's symptoms do not meet the criteria of any other depressive disorder; however, the clinician deems it important to identify the reason criteria was not met. The clinician should record the diagnosis as Other Specified Depressive Disorder. It is also important to follow this diagnosis with the specific reason. Some of the specific reasons that may be applicable to child and adolescent populations are recurrent brief depression, short duration depressive episode, and depressive episode with insufficient symptoms. Both recurrent brief depression and short duration depressive episode are characterized by at least four symptoms of depression that are present for less than 14 days. In recurrent brief depression, symptoms must persist from two to 13 days at least once a month; however symptoms in short-duration depressive episodes must be present for at least four days. Finally, a client may meet the criteria for depressive episode with insufficient symptoms if they report experiencing at least one of the eight symptoms characterized in a Major Depressive Episode for 14 days or longer.

SPECIFIERS FOR DEPRESSIVE DISORDERS

The following descriptive specifiers for depressive disorders are included in the *DSM-5* (APA, 2013):

With Anxious Distress

This specifier communicates the comorbid presence of at least two of five anxiety-related symptoms (i.e., feeling keyed up or tense, feeling unusually restless, difficulty concentrating, fear that something awful may happen, and perceived loss of control) that uniquely manifest during a depressive disorder. Additional specifiers include mild, moderate, moderate-severe, and severe. This is important to determine because higher levels of anxiety are associated with higher suicide risk, longer illness duration, and poor treatment response; knowing this information would help treatment planning and monitoring of progress.

With Mixed Features

This specifier is a modification of the *DSM-IV-TR* mixed episode disorder in which the criteria are met both for a manic episode and for a major depressive episode nearly every day for at least one week, and it requires at least three of the seven manic or hypomanic symptoms to manifest during the majority of days for a major depressive episode. Presence of mixed symptoms increases the risk for developing bipolar I or bipolar II disorders, and should be noticed for treatment planning and monitoring.

With Melancholic Features

This specifier is indicated when at least four symptoms of a near-complete absence of the capacity for pleasure, not merely a diminution, are present. This clinical profile is less likely to occur in milder than in more severe major depressive episodes, and it is more likely to occur in those with psychotic features (APA, 2013).

With Atypical Features

This specifier can be applied when the current depressive episode mood improves in response to events and two of four symptoms are observed, such as somatic complaints and interpersonal rejection sensitivity.

With Psychotic Features

This specifier is used when delusions, hallucinations, or both are observed. This clinical profile can be further specified as *with mood-congruent psychotic features* or *with mood-incongruent psychotic features*. These specifiers are used when the content of the delusions or hallucinations do involve typical depressive themes or when it does not, respectively. When there is a mixture of both, the latter specifier is applied.

With Catatonia

This specifier indicates a state of neurogenic motor immobility and behavioral abnormality manifested by stupor that is present during most of the depressive episode (for a description of catatonia, see the *DSM-5* chapter "Schizophrenia Spectrum and Other Psychotic Disorders").

With Peripartum Onset

Formerly known as *with postpartum onset* in the *DSM-IV-TR*, this specifier can be applied to the current or most recent episode of major depression when the onset of mood episodes occur during pregnancy or within four weeks postdelivery. Distinguished from delirium (a fluctuating level of awareness or attention), counselors should be attentive to severe anxiety and even panic attacks and psychotic features (e.g., infanticide during command hallucinations) in this clinical profile.

With Seasonal Pattern

This specifier applies to recurrent and regular episodes during a two-year period related to a particular time of the year, such as fall or winter. There has been a regular temporal relationship between the onset of major depressive episodes in major depressive disorder and a particular time of the year (e.g., in the fall or winter). This clinical profile is often characterized by loss of energy, hypersomnia, overeating, weight gain, and a craving for carbohydrates (APA, 2013).

Remission Specifiers

In partial remission is used when symptoms of the immediately previous major depressive episode are present, but criteria for the disorder is not met or less than two months have elapsed without symptoms after the last episode. *In full remission* is used when no symptoms are present during the last two months after episode.

Differential Diagnosis

The symptomatology of depressive disorders may resemble the symptomatology of other disorders, especially somatic symptom disorders. Sidebar 9.8 provides a list of instruments listed online by the American Psychiatric Association to measure somatic symptoms. Depressive disorders must be distinguished from other mental disorders such as anxiety disorders, bipolar disorders, and adjustment disorders. Specific strategies were provided within the disorders presented above to facilitate differential diagnoses.

SIDEBAR 9.8:   APA ONLINE INSTRUMENTS TO ASSESS SOMATIC SYMPTOMS

DSM-5 online instruments to assess somatic symptoms:

Level 2—Somatic Symptom—Parent/Guardian of Child Age 6–17 (Patient Health Questionnaire 15 Somatic Symptom Severity Scale [PHQ-15]),

Level 2—Somatic Symptom—Child Age 11–17 (Patient Health Questionnaire 15 Somatic Symptom Severity Scale [PHQ-15])

From http://www.psychiatry.org/practice/dsm/dsm5/online-assessment-measures

---

Assessment Strategies

Assessment of depressive disorders in children and adolescents is conducted to achieve one or more of the following goals: (a) screening, (b) diagnosis, and (c) monitoring treatment (Gelenberg, 2010). Assessment procedures of childhood depression should consider that depressive symptoms are expressed differently in children than in adults, as children, especially younger children, have limited capacity to recognize and communicate emotions and thoughts. Children and adolescents may appear irritable, cranky, and/or angry, may fail to gain weight or meet milestones, may appear distracted, unable to concentrate in school, or may experience a drop in grades. These symptoms can disguise typical symptoms of depression often observed in adults. Obtaining information from different sources, such as parents or teachers, when possible, is essential to achieve a comprehensive and accurate diagnosis.

Depression questionnaires are commonly used to identify a specific disorder, obtain a comprehensive review of areas or dimensions affected (e.g., affective, behavioral, and physiological), or to determine the degree of severity or intensity of symptoms and to monitor symptom changes. Table 9.5 presents questionnaires used to assess depressive disorders. Sidebar 9.9 provides a list of online instruments to assess depression suggested by the APA.

When assessing depression, it is important to evaluate children and adolescents for suicide risk. Children and adolescents suffering from a major depressive episode may experience reoccurring thoughts of death, experience suicidal ideation, have a specific plan to commit suicide, or attempt suicide. A child or adolescent may be at risk for suicide during the entire period in which they are experiencing symptoms of depression (APA, 2013).

SIDEBAR 9.9:   APA ONLINE INSTRUMENTS TO ASSESS DEPRESSION

DSM-5 online instruments to assess depression symptoms and severity:

Level 2—Depression—Parent/Guardian of Child Age 6–17 (PROMIS Emotional Distress—Depression—Parent Item Bank)

Level 2—Depression—Child Age 11–17 (PROMIS Emotional Distress—Depression—Pediatric Item Bank)

Severity Measure for Depression—Child Age 11–17 (PHQ-9 modified for Adolescents [PHQ-A]—Adapted)

From http://www.psychiatry.org/practice/dsm/dsm5/online-assessment-measures

---

Interviews are used extensively, can be structured or semistructured, and allow information to be made uniform. These instruments offer a guide for asking questions and recording information obtained. This information is used to establish a diagnosis. Interviews may be used by mental health specialists and training for proficient use is required. A list of structured and semistructured interviews used for depression in children and adolescents is presented in Table 9.6.

The following symptom inventories are available to help assess premenstrual dysphoric disorder (PMDD): *Daily Record of Severity of Problems* (DRSP; includes the 11 symptoms from the PMDD criteria; has high test-retest reliability), *Calendar of Premenstrual Experiences* (COPE), the *Penn Daily Symptom Report* (DSR), and the *Premenstrual Symptoms Screening Tool* (PSST).

There are no specific questionnaires to assess the new diagnosis of disruptive mood dysregulation disorder (DMDD), but some researchers suggest that the Child Behavior Checklist dysregulation profile (CBCL-DP; Achenbach, 1991) may be a valuable tool to identify children and adolescents with severe mood dysregulation (Zepf & Holtmann, 2012). Other professionals suggest counselors can use the following from the *DSM-5* to

TABLE 9.5 Questionnaires to Assess Depressive Disorders

Screening Tool	Administered By	Age	Time to Administer	Assessment Time Frame	Languages Available	Scoring System	Website Address
Beck Depression Inventory for Youth (BDI-Y)*	Self-administered	7–14 years	5–10 minutes	Symptoms within the past two weeks	English Spanish	Scored using a 0–3 system with "never" a 0 and "always" a 3". Designed to reflect DSM-IV criteria for specific disorders	http://www.pearsonassessments.com/HAIWEB/Cultures/en-us/Productdetail.htm?Pid=015–8014–197
Beck Depression Inventory®–II (BDI®–II) (Beck, Steer, & Brown, 1996).	Administered by an experienced clinician	14 years to adult	5–10 minutes	Symptoms within the past two weeks	English Spanish	Each of the 21 inventory items corresponds to a specific category of depressive symptom or attitude according to the DSM-IV. The statements are rank ordered and weighted.	http://www.pearsonassessments.com/HAIWEB/Cultures/en-us/Productdetail.htm?Pid=015–8018–370&Mode=summary
Center for Epidemiological Studies Depression Scale Modified for Children (CES-DC) (Radloff, 1977; Weissman, Orvaschel, & Padian, 1980).	Self-administe red	6–17 years	5 minutes	Symptoms within past week	English Spanish	20-item self-report depression inventory with possible scores ranging from 0 to 60	Copies are available free at www.brightfutures.org/mentalhealth/.
Child Depression Inventory (CDI).	Self-administered	7–17 years	5–15 minutes	Symptoms within the past two weeks	English, Spanish	Derived from the Beck Depression Inventory. Parent's version includes 17 items, teacher's version contains 12 items, and youth self-report includes 27 items.	https://ecom.mhs.com/(S(2eage1bp42qhdiftqqdqv4i1))/inventory.aspx?gr=edu&prod=cdi&id=pricing&RptGrpID=cdi
Children's Depression Inventory (CDI, 3rd ed.) (Kovacs, 1992)	Self-administered	7–17 years	5–15 minutes	Symptoms within the past two weeks	English, French, Spanish	Combined scoring of child, parent and teacher. Scored using a 0–3 system (ranging from "all the time" to "once in a while").	https://ecom.mhs.com/(S(2eage1bp42qhdiftqqdqv4i1))/inventory.aspx?gr=edu&prod=cdi&id=pricing&RptGrpID=cdi

Instrument	Administration	Age	Time	Timeframe	Language	Description	Contact/URL
Columbia Depression Scale-Teen Version* (formerly known as the Columbia DISC Depression Scale) (Shaffer, Fisher, Lucas, Dulcan, & Schwab-Stone, 2000).	Self-administered	11–18 years	10–15 minutes	Symptoms within the past four weeks	English Spanish	Scored using 22 yes/no questions. "No" answers are scored as "0," and "yes" answers are scored as "1." Question 22 is not scored.	E-mail for permission: FisherP@childpsych.columbia.edu
Mood and Feelings Questionnaire (MFQ) (Wood, Kroll, Moore, & Harrington, 1995).	Self-administered	8–18 years	5–10 minutes		English, Spanish	Format for children and parents. Good diagnostic validity. With different cutoff points depending on whether it concerns adolescents or younger children. Number of items: 33 (long version), 13 (brief version)	
Multiscore Depression Inventory for Adolescents and Adults (MDI)	Self-administered	13 years or older	5–10 minutes		English, Spanish	Number of items: 118 (long version), 47 (shorter version). True/false items provide 10 depression indicators.	
Multiscore Inventory for Adolescents and Adults (MDI) and Multiscore Inventory for Children (MDI-C)	Self-administered	8–12 years	20 minutes		English, Spanish	Includes 79 true/false items regarding anxiety, self-esteem, sad mood, helplessness, social introversion, low energy, pessimism, and defiance.	
Kutcher Adolescent Depression Scale (LeBlanc, Almudevar, Brooks, & Kutcher, 2002)	Self-administered	12–17 years	5 minutes	Symptoms within the past one week	English, French, Chinese, German, Spanish, Portuguese, Korean, Polish	Scored using a 0–3 system with "hardly ever" scored as a 0 and "all of the time" scored as a 3. Number of items: 16 (long form), 6 (brief form)	http://teenmentalhealth.org/for-health-professionals/clinical-tools/

TABLE 9.5 (continued)

Screening Tool	Administered By	Age	Time to Administer	Assessment Time Frame	Languages Available	Scoring System	Website Address
Patient Health Questionnaire for Adolescents (PHQ-A) (Johnson, Harris, Spitzer, & Williams, 2002).	Self-administered	12–18 years	5 minutes	Symptoms within the past two weeks	English, Spanish	Modified version of PHQ-9 developed for adolescents. Scored using a 0–3 system with "not at all" a 0 and "nearly every day" a 3. Also positive if either suicide question is answered as "yes."	http://www.teenscreen.org/programs/primary-care/primary-care-screening/
Patient Health Questionnaire 2-Item (PHQ-2)	Self-administered	13 years to adult	<1 minute	Symptoms within the past two weeks	Multiple languages available	Uses the first two questions of the PHQ-9. Scored using a 0–3 system with "not at all" a 0 and "nearly every day" as a 3.	http://brightfutures.aap.org/tool_and_resource_kit.html
Patient Health Questionnaire 9-Item (PHQ-9)	Self-administered	Adult	5 minutes	Symptoms within the past two weeks	Multiple languages available	Scored using a 0–3 system with "not at all" scored as a 0 and "nearly every day" scored as a 3. Based on 9 DSM-IV criteria for the diagnosis of depression.	http://www.phqscreeners.com/
Revised Children's Anxiety and Depression Scale (RCADS) (parent version also available, RCADS-P)	Self-administered	8–18 years	10–15 minutes	Not specified	English, Spanish, Dutch, Danish	For overall score, each item is assigned a numerical value from 0 to 3. For each subscale add the numerical values for each item together. Conversion tables used for scoring, based on gender and age/grade level. Excel scoring program available.	http://www.childfirst.ucla.edu/resources.html

Instrument	Administration	Age	Time	Language	Description	Link
Reynolds Adolescent Depression Scale (RADS) (Reynolds, 1987).	Self-administered	13–17 years	30 minutes	English, Spanish		
Reynolds Child Depression Scale (RCDS) (Reynolds, 1987).	Self-administered	9–12 years	30 minutes	English, Spanish		
Preschool Symptom Self-Report (PRESS) (Martini, Strayhorn, & Puig-Antich, 1990)	Self-administered	3–7 years		English, Spanish		
Suicidal Ideation Questionnaire (SIQ and SIQ-JR) (Reynolds 1987, 1988; Reynolds & Mazza, 1999)	Self-administered	3–7 years		English, Spanish	30 items (questions) in the SIQ and 15 in the SIQ-JR, all focusing on suicidal ideation	http://www4.parinc.com/Products/Product.aspx?ProductID=SIQ
Suicidal Behaviors Questionnaire-Revised (SBQ-R) (Linehan 1996; Osman et al., 2001)	Self-administered	14–17 years	5 minutes	Two items refer to lifetime, one to this year, and one to the future	English, Spanish	The 14-item SBQ-R and the 4-item SBQ-R are used with adolescents. Youth check any of five responses to whether they have experienced thoughts about killing themselves, whether they have told anyone before about it, and how likely they believe it is that they will attempt suicide someday.	http://www.glaje.com/Scales/SuicidalBehQuestpreassessment.pdf
Weinberg Depression Scale for Children and Adolescents (WDSCA)	Self-administered	5–21 years	3–5 minutes	English, Spanish	Self-report instrument. • Can be used as an initial assessment scale and can be repeated to measure response to treatment. • 56 yes/no items.	

TABLE 9.6   **Interviews for Assessing Depression**

Name/Author, Year	Age (Years)	Characteristics	Languages
Kiddie Schedule for Affective Disorders and Schizophrenia for School-Age Children (K-SADS)/Kaufman et al., 1997	6–18	• Semistructured. • Reliable and valid procedure for the diagnostic assessment of depression. • It takes a long time; not ideal for daily use in a doctor's office.	English, Spanish
Diagnostic Interview Schedule for Children (DISC)/Costello, Edelbrock, & Costello, 1985.	6–17	• Structured. • Advantage: It can be completed by nonhealth personnel with brief training.	English, Spanish
Diagnostic Interview for Children and Adolescents–Revised (DICA-R)/Herjanic & Reich, 1982.	8–18	• Structured. • Version for parents and children. • Good validity in adolescents.	English
Child and Adolescent Psychiatric Assessment (CAPA)/Angold & Costello, 2000.	9–17	• Structured. • Version for parents and children. • Reliable at diagnosing depression. • Detailed glossary for interviewers.	English, Spanish
Development and Well-Being Assessment (DAWBA)/Goodman, Ford, Richards, Gatward, & Meltzer, 2000.	5–16	• Structured interview and open questions. • Set of questionnaires, interviews, and rating scales designed to generate psychiatric diagnoses based on the *ICD-10* and on the *DSM-IV* in children from 5–16 years.	English
Children's Depression Rating Scale, Revised (CDRS-R). Poznanski et al., 1984.	6–12 and a dolescents	• Semistructured • Assesses the level of severity of depression. • It scores verbal and nonverbal information (speaking time, hypoactivity, nonverbal expression of depressive affect). 17 symptoms, with most of these symptom areas rated on a 7-point scale—See more at: http://www.wpspublish.com/store/p/2703/childrens-depression-rating-scale-revised-cdrs-r#sthash.r3UETheL.dpuf	English, Dutch, Spanish

measure the key symptoms of DMDD, and to further differentiate between bipolar-related disorders (http://www.psychiatry.org/practice/dsm/dsm5/online-assessment-measures):

- Level 2—Anger—Parent/Guardian of Child Age 6–17 (PROMIS Emotional Distress—Calibrated Anger Measure—Parent)
- Level 2—Irritability—Parent/Guardian of Child Age 6–17 (Affective Reactivity Index [ARI])
- Level 2—Mania—Parent/Guardian of Child Age 6–17 (Adapted from the Altman Self-Rating Mania Scale [ASRM])
- Level 2—Anger—Child Age 11–17 (PROMIS Emotional Distress—Calibrated Anger Measure—Pediatric)
- Level 2—Irritability—Child Age 11–17 (Affective Reactivity Index [ARI])
- Level 2—Mania—Child Age 11–17 (Altman Self-Rating Mania Scale [ASRM])
- To assess for suicide risk, counselors and mental health professionals may use the Columbia Suicide Severity Rating Scale (C-SSRS; APA, 2013).

Treatment and Intervention Strategies

Research regarding empirically supported treatment interventions in children and adolescents is still in the development stage. Most therapeutic interventions used to treat mental health issues in children and adolescents were originally developed to treat adults and do not address the developmental needs of some children, especially prepubescent and preschool children (Coyle et al., 2003). Over the years, research has highlighted the importance of clinicians understanding that child, adolescent, and adult depression should not receive identical treatment; however, best practices, in the treatment of adolescent depression, remain controversial due to a large variation of accepted practices and guidelines across countries. Antidepressant use in children younger than 18 years of age remains controversial as well because of documented side effects, such as increased suicidal ideation (Thapar et al., 2012).

In spite of available treatments for depression, only one fourth to one third of depressed adolescents receive care (Zuckerbrot, Maxon, Pagar, Davies, Fisher, & Shaffer, 2007). More recently, pediatricians' and family physicians' perceptions of the screening and treatment of depression have changed. In a study conducted by Taliaferro and associates (2013), family physicians and pediatricians reported feeling prepared to screen for depression in adolescents and also indicated they felt they should be involved in the treatment of depression in conjunction with mental health professionals. Although perceptions have changed, unfortunately, another study found that only approximately 30 percent of diagnosable cases were identified by primary care providers (Richardson, Russo, Lozano, McCauley, & Katon, 2010). Despite these findings, parents are still encouraged to report their concerns regarding their child's psychosocial issues to the pediatrician or primary care provider. Therefore, when a child or adolescent is brought in for mental health treatment, it is important to conduct a thorough evaluation, parent interview, and history examination because the symptoms might have been present for some time.

Even after children and adolescents are brought in for treatment, researchers found that they may not be receiving adequate services. In past research studies, researchers found that 22 percent of adolescents received merely one to two sessions with about one quarter of adolescents receiving three to seven sessions (Lewinsohn, Clarke,

Seeley, & Rohde, 1994). More recently, Kramer and colleagues (2008) found that although approximately 40 percent of adolescents in their study had received at least eight sessions of outpatient counseling, they were still as likely to relapse as those who had not. These results indicate a need for further study in the treatment of children and adolescents and a need to tailor therapeutic interventions to the needs of the child.

Evidence-based therapies refer to those interventions for which there is scientific evidence supporting their effectiveness and safety (McClellan & Werry, 2003; Zalaquett & Saunders, 2010). Cognitive Behavioral Therapy (CBT) and Interpersonal Therapy (IPT) are two therapeutic approaches that have been heavily researched in randomized controlled trials (RCTs) and have been found to be effective in the treatment of depression in children and teens from different cultural or ethnic backgrounds (Brent et al., 2008; Klein, Jacobs, & Reinecke, 2007; Mufson et al., 2004; Thapar et al., 2012). However, both of these therapeutic interventions are recommended primarily for children 10 years of age or older by the American Association of Family Physicians (AAFP; Clark, Jansen, & Cloy, 2012). For children age 11 and under, play therapy is recommended as an effective therapeutic intervention, especially when compared to no treatment at all (Bratton, Ray, Rhine, & Jones, 2005). As for the use of psychotropic medication, an extensive meta-analysis comparing psychotherapy, combination therapy (psychotherapy and medication), and medication alone found none of the three options significantly more effective in the treatment of depression in children and adolescents and the prevention of relapse (Cox et al., 2012). It is important to note, however, that the use of SSRIs and other psychotropic medication has been found to be helpful in adolescents who are experiencing moderate to severe depression (Taurines, Gerlach, Warnke, Thome, & Wewetzer, 2011).

In the next section we provide a brief description of some of the recommended therapeutic interventions to be used in the treatment of children and adolescents. It is highly recommended that you seek additional resources and use collaboration and consultation to aid in the implementation of these therapeutic approaches.

COGNITIVE THERAPY (CT)

Cognitive therapy (CT), developed by Aaron Beck, is a time-limited, collaborative therapeutic approach in which the therapist aims to change thoughts, improve skills, and modify emotional states that contribute to depression (Beck, 1967). There are three primary models of cognitive behavioral therapy (CBT), including Beck's (Beck, 1967) cognitive therapy model, Albert Ellis's (Ellis, 1973; Ellis & Grieger, 1986) rational emotive behavioral therapy (REBT) model, and Meichenbaum's (Meichenbaum, 1977) cognitive behavioral modification (CBM) program. CBT treatment for clinical depression is efficacious and specific (Hollon & Ponniah, 2010; Zalaquett & Stens, 2006). One of the primary mechanisms of change in depressed adolescents is the reduction of negative cognitions. Reduction of negative cognitions remains constant across various modalities of CBT, including individual CBT (Kolko, Brent, Baugher, Bridge, & Birmaher, 2000), cognitive bibliotherapy (Ackerson, Scogin, McKendree-Smith, & Lyman, 1998), group CBT (Kaufman et al., 2005), and computerized CBT (Abeles et al., 2009).

BEHAVIOR THERAPY (BT)

Behavioral therapy interventions include contextual approaches based on functional analyses (contingency management and behavioral activation), problem-solving therapy, social skills training, and self-control therapy (SCT; David-Ferdon & Kaslow, 2008). Common behavioral therapeutic strategies include, but are not limited to, self-monitoring, self-reinforcement, graded task assignments, activity scheduling, and targeted improvements in social skills through assertiveness training, modeling, and role-playing (Zalaquett, 2012). BT treatment for clinical depression is efficacious and specific (Hollon & Ponniah, 2010; Zalaquett & Stens, 2006).

INTERPERSONAL PSYCHOTHERAPY (IPT)

Interpersonal psychotherapy (IPT) for depression is another time-limited approach to psychotherapy that focuses on how interpersonal roles and conflicts can maintain, prevent, or cause depression (Kennedy & Tanenbaum, 2000). The theory is rooted in the interpersonal theories of depression articulated by Harry Stack Sullivan (1953), Adolf Meyer (1957), and Bowlby's attachment theory (Bowlby, 2008). There are three phases of treatment in IPT in which clients receive education about depression, learn how their interpersonal relationships are impacted by depression, and how to apply skills learned in therapy to future depressive episodes. Some of the primary problem areas addressed by IPT are grief, interpersonal disputes, role transition, and interpersonal deficits. Short-term IPT usually involves up to 20 weekly hour-long sessions. IPT treatment for clinical depression is efficacious and specific (Hollon & Ponniah, 2010; Zalaquett & Sanders, 2010; Zalaquett & Stens, 2006).

PLAY THERAPY (PT)

For some time, play therapy has been used as a method to treat behavioral and emotional issues in children because of its responsiveness to each child's developmental needs. Many children, 11 years of age and under, are limited in their ability to participate in therapeutic interventions that require abstract thought (Piaget, 1962). In play therapy, play is utilized as the primary method of communication, and children are encouraged to use toys and other play materials to symbolically represent their thoughts, feelings, and experiences that they may otherwise be unable to communicate through words (Axline, 1947; Kottman, 2001; Landreth, 2002; O'Connor, 2001; Schaefer, 2001). Although play therapy has been criticized over the years because of a lack of empirical support, several meta-analyses have demonstrated significant effect sizes and therapeutic outcomes when compared to control groups (Bratton, Ray, Rhine, & Jones, 2005; LeBlanc & Ritchie, 2001).

ATTACHMENT-BASED FAMILY THERAPY (ABFT)

A therapeutic approach gaining popularity and empirical support is family therapy. Family therapy has been found to be effective in the treatment of a variety of mood, anxiety, and other psychological disorders as the sole treatment intervention and in conjunction with other treatment modalities (Kaslow, Broth, Smith, & Collins, 2012). ABFT provides a family systems approach to therapy that is primarily based on attachment theory (Diamond, Reis, Diamond, Siqueland, & Isaacs, 2002; Diamond, Siqueland, & Diamond, 2003). The primary focus of ABFT for adolescents is on motivation, self-concept, emotional regulations, and reframing relationships. Parents focus on identifying personal stressors, criticism, sources of disengagement, and improvement of parenting skills (Kaslow, Broth, Smith, & Collins, 2012).

Evaluation Strategies

Methods to evaluate depression may vary depending on the developmental stage of the child. Some important guidelines to follow regarding evaluation are as follows:

INTERVIEW THE ADULT AND CHILD SEPARATELY

Separate interviews will allow you to focus solely on the child and his or her account of symptoms. Additionally, some children, especially children from minority backgrounds, may not feel comfortable discussing personal issues with their parents present because they may feel they are being disrespectful or ungrateful.

REQUEST A PHYSICIAN'S EVALUATION

A physician's evaluation may aid in ruling out causes of physical symptoms. Young children tend to report physical symptoms more often than they do psychological symptoms.

BE AWARE OF DEVELOPMENTAL AGE

Infants and toddlers' symptoms of depression may be exacerbated by a failure to meet milestones or a failure to thrive, a failure to develop normal attachment with caregivers, or an inconsistent gaze. Preschool children may display reckless, aggressive, or destructive behavior, may suffer from comorbid enuresis or encopresis, and may engage in repetitive behavior. Additionally, their drawings or creative projects may display morbid or macabre themes. School-aged children may display issues in their social and academic skills. Absenteeism, antisocial behavior, frequent referrals to the office, and low self-esteem are additional issues often experienced by depressed children. Adolescents are usually able to communicate their feelings verbally and can be evaluated utilizing traditional *talk therapy* methods.

ENSURE TO ASK ABOUT PSYCHOSOCIAL STRESSORS

Asking about loss of relatives, changes in family or social structure, changes in school or home environment, or changes in friendships are important.

EVALUATE POSSIBLE SUBSTANCE USE

As discussed in the Substance/Medication-Induced Depressive Disorder section, although substance use among children and adolescents has declined, it is still a common issue. Recently, prescription medications have become more popular. Children and adolescents could be taking prescription medications that have not been prescribed for them. It is important to evaluate for substance use because it can be the cause of depression.

Overall, in the evaluation of depression, differential diagnosis is extremely important. The *DSM-5* (APA, 2013) also has a section for differential diagnosis provided for each disorder. These tools can improve the accuracy of the mental health evaluation and help mitigate diagnostic challenges.

Diagnostic Challenges

As important as it is to diagnose and treat depressive disorders, depression in children and adolescents is often undetected and undiagnosed (National Institute for Health Care Management Research and Educational Foundation [NIHCM], 2011; Zalaquett & Saunders, 2010). Sidebar 9.10 presents common misperceptions of depression in children.

SIDEBAR 9.10: MISCONCEPTIONS ABOUT CHILDREN AND DEPRESSION

A common response about a child who has depression is, "What would he or she be depressed about?"

Two common misconceptions about clinical depression:

1. Childhood is an easy, trouble-free, and all the way enjoyable journey from birth to adulthood.
2. Depression is a brief moodiness or blue mood occasionally observed and triggered by many factors, such as unhappiness with parents, schools, and friends.

When asked, many adults remember their struggles with their parents' acceptance, friendship formation, loving relationships, feelings of powerlessness, lack of control over things and events, fears, and frustration they experience growing up. What are your recollections?

Depressed children and adolescents are sometimes referred to mental health professionals and treated for symptoms other than their depression and may receive inadequate treatment (Bhardwaj & Goodyer, 2009). Parents, school personnel, mental health professionals, and pediatricians often have difficulties differentiating between a moody and a depressed youngster. Behavioral, hormonal, psychological, and social changes experienced during this developmental period make it difficult to distinguish depression from the effects of these changes (Christner, Stewart, & Freeman, 2007). Difficulties achieving diagnosis of depressive disorders are increased by lack of training in such diagnosis, shortened periods of time to interview clients due to cost reductions enforced by insurance providers, or both.

Many parents, relatives, and adults perceive depressive disorders as something children and adolescents will grow out of, when in reality this is not the case for many (Fritz, 2008). Furthermore, about one third of the parents who have concerns about the mental health of their children will not discuss these concerns with their physicians (Cassidy & Jellinek, 1998). When parents do initiate this discussion, only 40 percent of the pediatricians respond to their concerns. Additionally, teachers and school counselors also fail to identify depressive symptoms (Auger, 2004). All these factors result in many children and adolescents with depressive disorders not getting the care they need, a phenomenon observed worldwide (Bhardwaj & Goodyer, 2009).

Summary

Understanding symptoms of depression in childhood and adolescence may aid in improving accuracy of diagnosis and treatment outcomes. Early detection, intervention, and prevention should help reduce the painful consequences of these depressive disorders and the long-term negative impact these disorders pose for the lives of children, adolescents, and their families, if left untreated. Differential diagnostic skills may aid clinicians in distinguishing normal moodiness, emotional, and developmental changes from mental disorders. New additions to the *DSM-5* may provide health care professionals with additional options to use when considering the depressive disorders. For example, PMDD may help to bridge a gap for those adolescent girls experiencing significant affective symptoms in addition to many of the symptoms of premenstrual syndrome. DMDD will hopefully reduce the number of children being misdiagnosed with bipolar-related disorders. Additional specifiers will hopefully aid in diagnostic accuracy and allow the health care community to improve communication regarding mental health needs. Many strides are being made to improve mental health care for children and adolescents experiencing depression, and it is exciting to see what may come in the future.

References

Abeles, P., Verduyn, C, Robinson, A., Smith, P., Yule, W., & Proudfoot, J. (2009). Computerized CBT for adolescent depression (stressbusters) and its initial evaluation through an extended case series. *Behavioural and Cognitive Psychotherapy, 37*(2), 151–165.

Achenbach, T. M. (1991). *Manual for Child Behavior Checklist/4–18 and 1991 Profile*. Burlington: University of Vermont, Department of Psychiatry.

Ackerson, J., Scogin, F., McKendree-Smith, N., & Lyman, R. D. (1998). Cognitive bibliotherapy for mild and moderate adolescent depressive symptomatology. *Journal of Consulting and Clinical Psychology, 66*(4), 685–690.

Allen, J. P., Chango, J., Szwedo, D., & Schad, M. (2014). Long-term sequelae of subclinical depressive symptoms in early adolescence. *Development and Psychopathology, 26*(1), 171–180.

American Academy of Child and Adolescent Psychiatry. (2007). Practice parameter for the assessment and treatment of children and adolescents with depressive disorders. *Journal of the American Academy of Child & Adolescent Psychiatry, 45*(11), 1503–1526. doi: 10.1097/chi.0b013e318145ae1c.

American Psychiatric Association. (2013). *Diagnostic and statistical manual of mental disorders* (5th ed.). Arlington, VA: American Psychiatric Publishing.

American Psychological Association. (2014). *Data on behavioral health in the United States*. Retrieved from https://www.apa.org/helpcenter/data-behavioral-health.aspx

Angold, A., & Costello, E. J. The Child and Adolescent Psychiatric Assessment (CAPA). *Journal of the American Academy of Child & Adolescent Psychiatry, 39*(1), 39–48.

Asarnow, J. R., Porta, G., Spirito, A., Emslie, G., Clarke, G., Wagner. K. D., & Brent, D.A. (2011). Suicide attempts and nonsuicidal self-injury in the treatment of resistant depression in adolescents: Findings from the TORDIA study. *Journal of the American Academy of Child & Adolescent Psychiatry, 50*(8), 772–781. doi:10.1016/j.jaac.2011.04.003

Auger, R. W. (2004). The accuracy of teacher reports in the identification of middle school students with depressive symptomatology. *Psychology in the Schools, 41*, 379–389.

Axline, V. (1947). *Play therapy*. New York, NY: Ballantine Books.

Barbe, R. P., Bridge, J., Birmaher, B., Kolko, D., & Brent, D.A. (2004). Suicidality and its relationship to treatment outcome in depressed adolescents. *Suicide and Life-Threatening Behavior, 34*(1), 44–55.

Beck, A. T. (1967). Depression: Clinical, experimental, and theoretical aspects. New York, NY: Harper & Row.

Beck, A. T., Steer, R. A., & Brown, G. K. (1996). *Beck Depression Inventory – Second edition manual*. San Antonio, TX: The Psychological Corporation.

Bhardwaj, A., & Goodyer, I. M. (2009) Depression and allied illness in children and adolescents: Basic facts. *Psychoanalytic Psychotherapy, 23*(3), 176–184. doi:10.1080/02668730903227206

Borowsky, I. W., Ireland, M., & Resnick, M. D. (2001). Adolescent suicide attempts: Risks and protectors. *Pediatrics, 107*(3), 485–493.

Bowlby, J. (2008). *Attachment*. New York, NY: Basic Books.

Bratton, S. C., Ray, D., Rhine, T., & Jones, L. (2005). The efficacy of play therapy with children: A meta-analytic review of treatment outcomes. *Professional Psychology: Research and Practice, 36*(4), 376–390.

Brent, D., Emslie, G., Clarke, G., Wagner, K. D., Asarnow, J. R., Keller, M., & Zelazny, J. (2008). Switching to another SSRI or to venlafaxine with or without cognitive behavioral therapy for adolescents with SSRI-resistant depression: The TORDIA randomized controlled trial. *Journal of the American Medical Association, 299*, 901–913.

Brière, N.F., Rohde, P., Seeley, J. R., Klein, D., & Lewinsohn, P. M. (2014). Comorbidity between major depression and alcohol use disorder from adolescence to adulthood. *Comprehensive Psychiatry, 55*(3), 526–533. Doi:10.1016/j.comppsych.2013.10.007

Cassidy, L. J., & Jellinek, M. S. (1998). Approaches to recognition and management of childhood psychiatric disorders in pediatric primary care. *Pediatric Clinics of North America, 45*(5), 1037–1052.

Centers for Disease Control and Prevention. (2012). *National Health and Nutrition Examination Survey data, 2007–2010*. Retrieved from http://www.cdc

.gov/mmwr/preview/mmwrhtml/mm6051a7.htm?s_cid=mm6051a7_w

Centers for Disease Control and Prevention National Center for Chronic Disease Prevention and Health Promotion. (2013, October 4). *Burden of mental illness.* Retrieved from http://www.cdc.gov/mentalhealth/basics/burden.htm

Chatters, S. J. (2014, March 13). Differential diagnosis tables. In S.J. Chatters, & C.P. Zalaquett. (2014, March 13). *DSM-5 Update for School Counselors.* Archdiocese of Washington D.C.. Washington, DC.

Christner, R. W., Stewart, J. L., & Freeman, A. (Eds.). (2007). *Handbook of cognitive-behavior therapy (CBT) groups with children and adolescents: Specific settings and presenting problems.* New York, NY: Routledge.

Clark, M. S., Jansen, K. L., & Cloy, J. A. (2012). Treatment of childhood and adolescent depression. *American Family Physician, 86*(5), 442–448.

Comer, R. J. (2014). *Abnormal psychology* (8th ed.). New York, NY: Worth Publishers.

Costello, E. J., Edelbrock, C. S., & Costello, A. J. (1985). Validity of the NIMH Diagnostic Interview Schedule for Children: A comparison between psychiatric and pediatric referrals. *Journal of Abnormal Child Psychology, 13*(4), 579–595.

Cox, G. R., Callahan, P., Churchill, R., Hunot, V., Merry, S. N., Parker, A. G., & Hetrick, S. E. (2012). Psychological therapies versus antidepressant medication, alone and in combination for depression in children and adolescents. *Cochrane Database of Systematic Reviews, 11,* CD008324, doi:10.1002/14651858.CD008324.pub2.

Coyle, J. T., Pine, D. S., Charney, D. S., Lewis, L., Nemeroff, C. B., Carlson, G. A., & Joshi, P. T. (2003). Depression and bipolar support alliance consensus statement on the unmet needs in diagnosis and treatment of mood disorders in children and adolescents. *Journal of the American Academy of Child & Adolescent Psychiatry, 42*(12), 1494–1503.

David-Ferdon, C., & Kaslow, N. J. (2008). Evidence-based psychosocial treatments for child and adolescent depression. *Journal of Clinical Child & Adolescent Psychology, 37*(1), 62–104.

Diamond, G. S., Reis, B. F., Diamond, G. M., Siqueland, L., & Isaacs, L. (2002). Attachment-based family therapy for depressed adolescents: A treatment development study. *Journal of the American Academy of Child & Adolescent Psychiatry, 41*(10), 1190–1196.

Diamond, G. S., Siqueland, L., & Diamond, G. M. (2003). Attachment-based family therapy for depressed adolescents: Programmatic treatment development. *Clinical Child and Family Psychology Review, 6,* 107–127.

Ellis, A. (1973). *Humanistic psychotherapy: The rational-emotive approach.* New York, NY: Julian Press.

Ellis, A., & Grieger, R. (1986). *Handbook of rational-emotive therapy: Volume 2.* New York, NY: Springer.

Eme, R., & Mouritson, R. (2013). The addition of disruptive mood dysregulation disorder to DSM-5: Differential diagnosis and case examples. *The Practitioner Scholar: Journal of Counseling and Professional Psychology, 2*(1), 84–94.

Epperson, C. N., Steiner, M., Hartlage, A., Eriksson, E., Schmidt, P. J., Jones, I., & Yonkers, K.A. (2012). Premenstrual dysphoric disorder: Evidence for a new category for DSM-5. *American Journal of Psychiatry, 169*(5), 465–475. doi: 10.1176/appi.ajp.2012.11081302

Feinstein, A. (2011). Multiple sclerosis and depression. *Multiple Sclerosis Journal, 17*(11), 1276–1281.

Fergusson, D. M., & Woodward, L. J., (2002) Mental health, educational and social role outcomes of adolescents with depression. *Archives of General Psychiatry, 59,* 225–231.

Fergusson, D. M., Boden, J. M., & Horwood, L. J. (2007). Recurrence of major depression in adolescence and early adulthood, and later mental health, educational and economic outcomes. *British Journal of Psychiatry, 191,* 335–342.

Fox, H. B., McManus, M. A., Zarit, M., Fairbrother, G., Cassedy, A. E., Bethell, C. D., & Read, D. (2007). *Racial and ethnic disparities in adolescent health and access to care* (Fact Sheet No. 1) Washington, DC: The National Alliance to Advance Mental Health.

Fritz, G. K. (2008, July). Is your child depressed? A guide to recognizing and responding to depressive symptoms. *Brown University Child & Adolescent Behavior Letter, 24*(S7), 8–9.

Gelaye, B., Williams, M. A., Lemmac, S., Deyessad, N., Bahretibebd, Y., Shibred, T., … Xiao-Hua, A. Z. (2013). Validity of the Patient Health Questionnaire-9 for depression screening and diagnosis in East Africa. *Psychiatry Research, 210*(2), 653–661.

Gelenberg, A. J. (2009). Using assessment tools to screen for, diagnose, and treat major depressive disorder in clinical practice. *The Journal of Clinical Psychiatry, 71*(Suppl E1), e01.

Goldman, S. (2012). I: Development and depression: Developmental epidemiology of depressive disorders. *Child and Adolescent Psychiatric Clinics of*

North America, *21*(2), 217–235. doi:10.1016/j.chc .2011.12.002

Goodman, R., Ford, T., Richard, H. Gatward, R. & Meltzer, H. (2000). The Development and Well-Being Assessment: Description and initial validation of an integrated assessment of child and adolescent psychopathology. *Journal of Child Psychology and Psychiatry*, *41*(5), 645–650.

Goretti, B., Ghezzi, A., Portaccio, E., Lori, S., Zipoli, V., Razzolini, L., & Amato, M. P. (2010). Psychosocial issue in children and adolescents with multiple sclerosis. *Neurological Sciences*, *31*(4), 467–470.

Greenberg, M. T., Domitrovich, C., & Bumbarger, B. (2001). The prevention of mental disorders in school-aged children: Current state of the field. *Prevention & Treatment*, *4*, 1. Retrieved from http://journals.apa.org/prevention/volume4/pre0040001a .html#c107#c107

Gudiño, O. G., Martinez, J. I., & Lau, A. S. (2012). Mental health service use by youths in contact with child welfare: Racial disparities by problem type. *Psychiatric Services*, *63*(10), 1004–1010. doi: 10.1176/appi.ps.201100427

Han, G., Klimes-Dougan, B., Jepsen, S., Ballard, K., Nelson, M., Houri, A., …Cullen, K. (2012). Selective neurocognitive impairments in adolescents with major depressive disorder. *Journal of Adolescence*, *35*(1), 11–20. doi:10.1016/j.adolescence .2011.06.009

Hazler, R. J., & Mellin, E. A. (2004). The developmental origins and treatment needs of female adolescents with depression. *Journal of Counseling and Development*, *82*(1), 18–24.

Herjanic, B., & Reich, W. (1982) Development of a structured psychiatric interview for children: Agreement between child and parent on individual symptoms. *Journal of Abnormal Child Psychology*, *10*(3), 307–324.

Hollon, S. D., & Ponniah, K. (2010). A review of empirically supported psychological therapies for mood disorders in adults. *Depression and Anxiety*, *27*(10), 891–932. doi:10.1002/da.20741

Holt, R. I., de Groot, M., & Golden, S. H. (2014). Diabetes and depression. *Current Diabetes Reports*, *14*, 1–9.

Htay, T. T., & Aung, K. (2014). *Premenstrual dysphoric disorder*. Retrieved from http://emedicine.medscape .com/article/293257-overview#a5

Jaser, S. S. (2010). Psychological problems in adolescents with diabetes. *Adolescent Medicine: State of the Art Reviews*, *21*(1), 138–151.

Johnson, J. G., Harris, E. S., Spitzer, R. L., & Williams, J. B. (2002). The Patient Health Questionnaire for Adolescents: Validation of an instrument for the assessment of mental disorders among adolescent primary care patients. *Journal of Adolescent Health*, *30*(3), 196–204.

Kaminski, K. M., & Garber, J. (2002). Depressive spectrum disorders in high-risk adolescents: Episode duration and predictors of time to recovery. *Journal of the American Academy of Child & Adolescent Psychiatry*, *41*(4), 410–418.

Karch, D. L., Logan, J., McDaniel, D., Parks, S., & Patel, N. (2012). Surveillance for violent deaths—national violent death reporting system, 16 states, 2009. *MMWR surveillance summary*, *61*, 1–43. Available at: http://www.cdc.gov/mmwr/preview/ mmwrhtml/ss6106a1.htm?s_cid=ss6106a1_e#tab6.

Kaslow, N. J., Broth, M. R., Smith, C. O., & Collins, M. H. (2012). Family-based interventions for child and adolescent disorders. *Journal of Marital and Family Therapy*, *38*(1), 82–100.

Kaufman, J., Birmaher, B., Brent, D., Rao, U., Flynn, C., Moreci, P., . . . Ryan, N. (1997). Schedule for Affective Disorders and Schizophrenia for school-age children-Present and Lifetime version (K-SADS-PL): Initial reliability and validity data. *Journal of the American Academy of Child & Adolescent Psychiatry*, *36*(7), 980–988.

Kaufman, N. K., Rohde, P., Seeley, J. R., Clarke, G. N., & Stice, E. (2005). Potential mediators of cognitive-behavioral therapy for adolescents with comorbid major depression and conduct disorder. *Journal of Consulting and Clinical Psychology*, *73*(1), 38–46.

Keenan-Miller, D., Hammen, C. L., & Brennan, P. A. (2007). Health outcomes related to early adolescent depression. *Journal of Adolescent Health*, *41*(3), 256–262.

Kendler, K. S., & Gardner, C.O. (2011). A longitudinal etiologic model for symptoms of anxiety and depression in women. *Psychological Medicine*, *41*(10), 2035–2045.

Kennedy, G. J., & Tanenbaum, S. (2000). Psychotherapy with older adults. *American Journal of Psychotherapy*, *54*(3), 386–407.

Kessler, R. C., Berglund, P., Demler, O., Jin, R., Merikangas, K. R., & Walters, E. E. (2005). Lifetime prevalence and age-of-onset distributions of DSM-IV disorders in the National Comorbidity Survey Replication. *Archives of General Psychiatry*, *62*(6), 593–602. doi:10.1001/archpsyc.62.6.593

King, J. H. (2014). *Using the DSM-5: Try it, you'll like it*. Retrieved from http://www.continuingedcourses.net/active/courses/course081.php

Klein, J. B., Jacobs, R. H., & Reinecke, M. A. (2007). Cognitive-behavioral therapy for adolescent depression: A meta-analytic investigation of changes in effect-size estimates. *Journal of the American Academy of Child & Adolescent Psychiatry, 46*(11), 1403–1413.

Kolko, D. J., Brent, D. A., Baugher, M., Bridge, J., & Birmaher, B. (2000). Cognitive and family therapies for adolescent depression: Treatment specificity, mediation, and moderation. *Journal of Consulting and Clinical Psychology, 68*, 603–614.

Kottman, T. (2001). Adlerian play therapy. *International Journal of Play Therapy, 10*, 1–12.

Kovacs, M. *The Children's Depression Inventory manual*. New York: Multi-Health Systems.

Kramer, T. L., Miller, T. L., Phillips, S. D., & Robbins, J. M. (2008). Quality of mental health care for depressed adolescents. *American Journal of Medical Quality, 23*, 96–104.

Landreth, G. (2002). *Play therapy: The art of the relationship* (2nd ed.). New York, NY: Brunner-Routledge.

LeBlanc, J. C., Almudevar, A., Brooks, S. J., & Kutcher, S. (2002). Screening for adolescent depression: Comparison of the Kutcher Adolescent Scale with the Beck Depression Inventory. *Journal of Child and Adolescent Psychopharmacology, 12*(2), 113–126.

LeBlanc, M., & Ritchie, M. (2001). A meta-analysis of play therapy outcomes. *Counseling Psychology Quarterly, 14*(2), 149–163.

Lee, L. K., Chen, P. C., Lee K. K., & Kaur, J. (2006). Menstruation among adolescent girls in Malaysia: A cross-sectional school survey. *Singapore Medical Journal, 47*(10), 869–874.

Leibenluft, E. (2011). Severe mood dysregulation, irritability, and the diagnostic boundaries of bipolar disorder in youths. *American Journal of Psychiatry, 168*(2), 129–142.

Lewinsohn, P. M., Clarke, G. N., Seeley, J. R., & Rohde, P. (1994). Major depression in community adolescents: Age of onset, episode duration, and time to recurrence. *Journal of the American Academy of Child & Adolescent Psychiatry, 33*(6), 809–818.

Linehan, M. (1996). *The Suicidal Behaviors Questionnaire-14 (SBQ-14)*. Unpublished instrument: University of Washington. Retrieved from http://www.glaje.com/Scales/SuicidalBehQuest preassessment.pdf

Margulies, D. M., Weintraub, S., Basile, J., Grover, P. J., & Carlson, G. A. (2012). Will disruptive mood dysregulation disorder reduce false diagnosis of bipolar disorder in children? *Bipolar Disorders, 14*(5), 488–496.

Martini, D. R., Strayhorn, J. M., & Puig-Antich, J. (1990). A symptom self-report measure for preschool children. *Journal of the American Academy of Child & Adolescent Psychiatry, 29*(4), 594–600.

Massie, M. J. (2004). Prevalence of depression in patients with cancer. *Journal of the National Cancer Institute Monographs, 1*, 57–71.

McClellan, J. M., & Werry, J. S. (2003). Evidence-based treatments in child and adolescent psychiatry: An inventory. *Journal of the American Academy of Child & Adolescent Psychiatry, 42*(12), 1388–1400.

McGorry, P. D., Purcell, R., Goldstone, S., & Amminger, G. P. (2011). Age of onset and timing of treatment for mental and substance use disorders: implications for preventive intervention strategies and models of care. *Current Opinion in Psychiatry, 24*(4), 301–306.

Meichenbaum, D. (1977). *Cognitive behavior modification: An integrative approach*. New York, NY: Plenum.

Melvina, G. A., Dudleya, A. L., Gordon, M. S., Forda, S., Taffea, J., & Tongea. B. J. (2013). What happens to depressed adolescents? A follow-up study into early adulthood. *Journal of Affective Disorders, 151*(1), 298–305.

Meyer, A. (1957). *Psychobiology: A science of man*. Springfield, IL: Charles C. Thomas.

Milin, R., Walker, S., & Chow, J. (2003). Major depressive disorder in adolescence: A brief review of the recent treatment literature. *Canadian Journal of Psychiatry, 48*(9), 600–606.

Moreno, C., Laje, G., Blanco, C., Jiang, H., Schmidt, A. B., & Olfson, M. (2013). National trends in the outpatient diagnosis and treatment of bipolar disorder in youth. *Archives of General Psychiatry, 64*(9), 1032–1039.

Mufson, L., Dorta, K. P., Wickramaratne, P., Nomura, Y., Olfson, M., & Weissman, M. M. (2004). A randomized effectiveness trial of interpersonal psychotherapy for depressed adolescents. *Archives of General Psychiatry, 61* 577–584.

National Institute for Health Care Management Research and Educational Foundation. (2011). *Adolescent mental health issues brief*. Retrieved from http://www.nihcm.org/pdf/Adol_MH_Issue_Brief_FINAL.pdf

National Center for Health Statistics (NCHS, 2014), Retrieved from http://www.cdc.gov/nchs/icd/icd10cm.htm

National Institute of Drug Abuse. (2014). *Drug-Facts: Nationwide trends.* Retrieved from http://www.drugabuse.gov/publications/drugfacts/nationwide-trends

National Institute of Mental Health (n.d.a). *The numbers count: Mental disorders in America.* Retrieved from http://www.nimh.nih.gov/health/publications/the-numbers-count-mental-disorders-in-america/index.shtml

National Institute of Mental Health (n.d.b). *What is depression?* Retrieved from http://www.nimh.nih.gov/health/topics/depression/index.shtml

Neves, M. G., & Leanza, F. (2014). Mood disorders in adolescents: Diagnosis, treatment, and suicide assessment in the primary care setting. *Primary Care: Clinics in Office Practice, 41,* 587–606.

National Institute for Health and Care Excellence. (2015). *Depression in children and young people: Identification and management in primary, community and secondary care (update).* Retrieved from https://www.nice.org.uk/guidance/cg28

Nock, M. K., Green, J. G., Hwang, I., McLaughlin, K. A., Sampson, N. A., Zaslavsky, A. M., & Kessler, R. C. (2013). Prevalence, correlates, and treatment of lifetime suicidal behavior among adolescents: Results from the National Comorbidity Survey Replication Adolescent Supplement. *Journal of the American Medical Association Psychiatry, 70*(3), 300–310. doi:10.1001/2013.jamapsychiatry.55.

O'Connor, K. (2001). Ecosystemic play therapy. *International Journal of Play Therapy, 10*(2), 33–44.

Osman, A., Bagge, C.L., Gutierrez, P.M., Konick, L.C., Kopper, B.A., & Barrios, F.X.(2001). The Suicidal Behaviors Questionnaire-Revised (SBQ-R): Validation with clinical and nonclinical samples. *Assessment, 8*(4), 443–54.

Perou, R., Bitsko, R. H., Pastor, P., Ghandour, R. M., Gfroerer, J. C., Hedden, S. L.... Huang, L. N. (2013). Mental health surveillance among children—United States, 2005–2011. *Morbidity and Mortality Weekly Report 62*(2), 1–35.

Piaget, J. (1962). *Play, dreams, and imitation in childhood* (C. Gattengo & F. M. Hodgson, Trans.). New York, NY: Norton.

Poznanski, E. O., Grossman, J. A., Buchbaum, Y., Banegas, M., Freeman, L., & Gibbons, R. (1984). Preliminary studies of the reliability and validity of the Children's Depression Scale. *Journal of the*

American Academy of Child & Adolescent Psychiatry, 23*(2), 191–197.

Radloff, L. S. (1977). The CES-D Scale: A self-report depression scale for research in the general population. *Applied Psychological Measurement, 1*(3), 385–401.

Rapkin, A. J., & Mikacich, J. A. (2013). Premenstrual dysphoric disorder and severe premenstrual syndrome in adolescents: Diagnosis and pharmacological treatment. *Pediatric Drugs, 15*(3), 191–202. doi:10.1007/s40272-013-0018-4

Reynolds, W. M. (1987). *Reynolds Adolescent Depression Scale: Professor manual.* Odessa, FL: Psychological Assessment Resources.

Reynolds, W. M., & Mazza, J. J. (1999). Assessment of suicidal ideation in inner-city children and young adolescents: Reliability and validity of the Suicidal Ideation Questionnaire-JR. *School Psychology Review, 28,* 17–30.

Richardson, L. P., Russo, J. E., Lozano, P., McCauley, E., & Katon, W. (2010). Factors associated with detection and receipt of treatment for youth with depression and anxiety disorders. *Academic Pediatrics, 10*(1), 36–40.

Rogers, E. S., & Kraft, C. A. (2014, January 3). *Pediatric dysthymic disorder.* Retrieved from Medscape: http://emedicine.medscape.com/article/913941-overview#aw2aab6b2b4

Royal College of Nursing. (2012). *Health inequalities and the social determinants of health. Policy briefing #01/12.* Retrieved from http://www.rcn.org.uk/__data/assets/pdf_file/0007/438838/01.12_Health_inequalities_and_the_social_determinants_of_health.pdf

Ryan, N. D. (2013). Severe irritability in youths: Disruptive mood dysregulation disorder and associated brain circuit changes. *American Journal of Psychiatry, 170*(10), 1093–1096. doi:10.1176/appi.ajp.2013.13070934.

Schwarz, S. W. (2009). *Adolescent mental health in the United States: Facts for policymakers.* Retrieved from http://nccp.org/publications/pdf/text_878.pdf

Schaefer, C. (2001). Prescriptive play therapy. *International Journal of Play Therapy, 10*(2), 57–73.

Silver, A., Battin, M. P., & Rhodes, R. (2012). *Medicine and social justice: Essays on the distribution of health care.* New York, NY: Oxford University Press.

Simon, A. E., Palmer, S. C., & Coyne, J. C. (2006). Cancer and depression. In A. Steptoe (Ed.), *Depression and physical illness* (pp. 211–237). New York, NY: Cambridge University Press.

Substance Abuse and Mental Health Services Administration (2014). *Substance use and mental health estimates from the 2013 national survey on drug use and health: Overview of findings.* Retrieved from http://www.samhsa.gov/data/sites/default/files/NSDUH-SR200-RecoveryMonth-2014/NSDUH-SR200-RecoveryMonth-2014.htm

Sullivan, H. S. (1953). *The interpersonal theory of psychiatry.* New York, NY: W.W. Norton & Company.

Sullivan, E. M., Annest, J. L., Simon, T. R., Luo, F., & Dahlberg, L. L. (2015). Suicide trends among persons aged 10–24 years — United States, 1994–2012. *MMWR surveillance summary, 64,* 201–205. Available at: http://www.cdc.gov/mmwr/preview/mmwrhtml/mm6408a1.htm

Taliaferro, L. A., Hetler, J., Edwall, G., Wright, C., Edwards, A. R., & Borowsky, I. W. (2013). Depression screening and management among adolescents in primary care factors associated with best practice. *Clinical Pediatrics, 52*(6), 557–567.

Taurines, R., Gerlach, M., Warnke, A., Thome, J., & Wewetzer, C. (2011). Pharmacotherapy in depressed children and adolescents. *World Journal of Biological Psychiatry, 12*(S1), 11–15.

Thapar, A., Collishaw, S., Pine, D. S., & Thapar, A. K. (2012). Depression in adolescence. *The Lancet, 379*(9820), 1056–1067.

Thomas, J. F., Temple, J. R., Perez, N., & Rupp, R. (2011). Ethnic and gender disparities in needed adolescent mental health care. *Journal of Health Care for the Poor and Underserved, 22*(1), 101–110. doi:10.1353/hpu.2011.0029

U.S. Department of Health and Human Services. (2012). *Depression and high school students.* Retrieved from http://www.nimh.nih.gov/health/publications/depression-and-high-school-students/index.shtml

Weissman, M. M., Orvaschel, H., Padian N. 1980. Children's symptom and social functioning self-report scales: Comparison of mothers' and children's reports. *Journal of Nervous Mental Disorders, 168*(12), 736–740.

Wolitzky-Taylor, K. B., Ruggiero, K. J., Johnson, R. H., McCart, M. R., Smith, D. W., Hanson, R. F., & Kilpatrick, D.G. (2010). Has adolescent suicidality decreased in the United States? Data from two national samples of adolescents interviewed in 1995 and 2005. *Journal of Clinical Child & Adolescent Psychology, 39*(1), 64–76.

Wood, A., Kroll, L., Moore, A., & Harrington, R. (1995). Properties of the Mood and Feelings Questionnaire in adolescent psychiatric outpatients: A research note. *Journal of Child Psychology Psychiatry and Allied Disciplines, 36*(2), 327–334.

World Health Organization. (2010). *ICD-10, International Statistical Classification of Diseases and Related Health Problems.* Retrieved from http://apps.who.int/classifications/icd10/browse/2010/en

Zakharov, S., Navratil, T., & Pelclova, D. (2013). Suicide attempts by deliberate self-poisoning in children and adolescents. *Psychiatry Research, 210*(1), 302–307. doi:10.1016/j.psychres.2013.03.037

Zalaquett, C. P. (2013). *Clinical depression.* Available from the Knowledge Center of the American Counseling Association: http://www.counseling.org/knowledge-center/center-for-counseling-practice-policy-and-research/practice-briefs

Zalaquett, C. P., & Sanders, A. E. (2010). *Major depression and dysthymic disorder in adolescents: The critical role of school counselors.* Retrieved from http://counselingoutfitters.com/vistas/vistas10/Article_77.pdf

Zalaquett, C. P., & Stens, A. (2006). Psychosocial treatments for major depression and dysthymia in older adults: A review of the research literature. *Journal of Counseling & Development, 84*(2), 192–201.

Zepf, F. D., & Holtmann, M. (2012). Disruptive mood dysregulation disorder. In J. M. Rey (Ed.), *IACAPAP e-textbook of child and adolescent mental health* (3rd. ed., pp. 1–11). Geneva, Switzerland: International Association for Child and Adolescent Psychiatry and Allied Professions.

Zima, B. T., Murphy, J. M., Scholle, S. H., Hoagwood, K. E., Sachdeva, R.C., Mangione-Smith, R., … Jellinek, M. (2013). National quality measures for child mental health care: Background, progress, and next steps. *Pediatrics, 131*(S1), S38–S49.

Zuckerbrot, R. A., Maxon, L., Pagar, D., Davies, M., Fisher, P. W., & Shaffer, D. (2007). Adolescent depression screening in primary care: Feasibility and acceptability. *Pediatrics, 119,* 101–118.

Chapter 10

Anxiety Disorders

Dee C. Ray, Hayley L. Stulmaker, and Sue C. Bratton

Introduction

Children experience anxiety and fear as a normal part of development. When a child's anxiety response exceeds the level of threat in reality, there is a possibility that diagnosis of an anxiety disorder is warranted. Although between 10 and 20 percent of children experience heightened levels of anxiety (Compton et al., 2014; Kendall, Furr, & Podell, 2010), clinical levels of anxiety impair a child's ability to master developmentally appropriate tasks and manifest as dysfunction that can cause harm and suffering (Fonseca & Perrin, 2011). Children diagnosed with anxiety disorders display a greater intensity and frequency of negative emotions, as well as low ability to regulate emotions, which leads to overall functional impairment (Carthy, Horesh, Apter, & Gross, 2010). Prevalence rates of anxiety disorders (12.3 percent for 6- to 12-year-olds and 11 percent for 13- to 18-year-olds) indicate that many children experience excessive fears and worries that cause impairment along the expected developmental trajectory (Costello, Egger, Copeland, Erkanli, & Angold, 2011).

Children's anxiety symptoms encompass affective, physiological, behavioral, and cognitive components. Symptoms must interfere with educational or occupational achievement or with social interactions when manifested as excessive avoidance of everyday activities, interactions, and possible onset of panic attacks. As persistent worries, fears, and anxiety symptoms increase, children may experience a lack of support from their social environment or family system. If left untreated, children with anxiety disorders are at high risk for delays in social-emotional and cognitive development because of the high level of comorbidity and low levels of remission (Kendall et al., 2010; Paul & Barrett, 2010). As a result, children who have anxiety disorders often struggle with academic achievement, family cohesion, general happiness, self-esteem, and social and peer relationships (Kendall et al., 2010). They typically have an increased risk for future psychiatric disorders, substance-related disorders, and conduct problems (Levin-Decanini, Connolly, Simpson, Suarez, & Jacob, 2013). However, in general, all humans are subject to anxiety. Sidebar 10.1 offers the opportunity to take a moment to consider your experiences of anxiety.

SIDEBAR 10.1:   INCREASE AWARENESS—PREVALENCE

Anxiety disorders are extremely prevalent in children and adolescents. As clinicians, you have likely encountered clients who are anxious or you have experienced anxiety yourself. Some people's anxiety manifests through withdrawing. Others manifest through desperately seeking approval or being clingy. Some tend to try to find ways to control other aspects of their life that do not seem as frightening. What happens when you feel your own anxiety? How does your anxiety manifest? Do your feelings of anxiety match the actual level of the reality of threat involved? What is it like to be with someone else who is anxious? Do different manifestations produce different reactions within you? Does it feel different when you are with anxious children or adolescents versus anxious adults?

Description of Anxiety Disorders

The *Diagnostic and Statistical Manual of Mental Disorders, Fifth Edition* (*DSM-5*; American Psychiatric Association [APA], 2013), represents a reconceptualization of anxiety disorders, which now include those previously associated with other disorders usually first diagnosed in infancy, childhood, or adolescence (e.g., separation anxiety disorder and selective mutism) and exclusion of disorders that have been supported as distinct constructs through increased research and understanding of etiology and symptom expression (e.g., obsessive-compulsive disorder [OCD] and posttraumatic stress disorder [PTSD]). However, the sequencing of chapters on obsessive-compulsive and related disorders and trauma- and stressor-related disorders directly following the anxiety disorders chapter represents recognition that these disorders may be comorbid and share similar neurobiological underpinnings. The sequencing of anxiety disorders in the *DSM-5* is based on age of onset. For anxiety disorder (except for selective mutism), specific assessment measures can be used to determine symptom intensity over time, helping to define level of impairment and severity experienced by the child. The *DSM-5* anxiety disorder categories include separation anxiety disorder, selective mutism, specific phobia, social anxiety disorder, panic disorder, panic attack specifier, agoraphobia, generalized anxiety disorder, substance/medication-induced anxiety disorder, anxiety disorder due to another medical condition, other specified anxiety disorder, and unspecified anxiety disorder.

In regard to children, the most noticeable change in the *DSM-5* among anxiety disorders is the reconceptualization of childhood disorders, a *DSM-IV-TR* chapter that included separation anxiety disorder and selective mutism, resulting in their relocation to the anxiety disorders chapter. Cumulative research supports separation anxiety disorder and selective mutism as manifestations of anxiety, rather than as exclusively related to childhood neurodevelopment. Additional changes reflected in the *DSM-5* include separation of agoraphobia from panic disorder, previously categorized in relationship with each other (i.e., panic disorder without agoraphobia, panic disorder with agoraphobia, and agoraphobia without history of panic disorder). The distinct categories of agoraphobia and panic disorder signify that the disorders are discrete and one can be present without the

TABLE 10.1   *DSM-IV-TR* versus *DSM-5* Anxiety Disorders Chapter

DSM-IV-TR	*DSM-5*
• Includes OCD, PTSD, and Acute Stress Disorder • Client subjectively determines whether anxiety is unreasonable • Panic disorder with agoraphobia or panic disorder without agoraphobia • Social Phobia • Separation anxiety disorder and selective mutism as Disorders Usually First Diagnosed in Infancy, Childhood, or Adolescence	• Includes OCD, PTSD, and Acute Stress Disorder in a new chapter titled Trauma- and Stressor-Related Disorders sequenced after Anxiety Disorders chapter • Client uses level 1, level 2, and disorder-specific cross cutting symptom measures • Panic disorder and agoraphobia are unlinked • Social Phobia is now called Social Anxiety Disorder • Separation anxiety disorder and selective mutism as Anxiety Disorders

other. Another central difference in diagnosing anxiety disorders is the emphasis on the clinician's determination of whether an anxiety or fear response is excessive to the situation and to the sociocultural context (resulting in exclusion of a diagnosis) or is culture specific (resulting in justification of a diagnosis). Previously, specific phobia and social phobia required that an individual under age 18 manifest symptoms for six months minimum and were not required to recognize that the fear was excessive or unreasonable. However, this particular criterion was removed in the *DSM-5* based on evidence that individuals with such disorders often overestimate the danger in *phobic* situations. The determination of symptom severity can be aided by using the *DSM-5* disorder specific severity measures (see Chapter 2). Table 10.1 offers a side-by-side comparison of substantial changes from the *DSM-IV-TR* to the *DSM-5* regarding anxiety disorder chapters.

In a comprehensive meta-analysis, Costello et al. (2011) found that the most common anxiety disorders among children are specific phobia, followed by separation anxiety disorder, social phobia, and generalized anxiety disorder. There were too few panic disorder and agoraphobia studies from which to determine prevalence. The order of prevalence was similar among adolescents, with order of prevalence being specific phobia, social phobia, separation anxiety disorder, generalized anxiety, and panic disorder.

DSM-5 Criteria

SEPARATION ANXIETY DISORDER

Separation anxiety disorder is marked by persistent and excessive fear or anxiety in response to separation from a person who is perceived as a major attachment figure, usually a parent (Kossowsky et al., 2013). Developmentally inappropriate and excessive fear or anxiety is evidenced by the presence of three conditions among eight possibilities, including (a) visible distress when the child anticipates or experiences separation from an attachment figure, (b) excessive worry about losing an attachment figure, (c) excessive worry about a possible event that might cause separation, (d) refusal to leave home or place of safety, (e) excessive worry or hesitancy about being alone or without caretaker, (f) hesitancy or refusal to sleep away from attachment figure, (g) nightmares about separation, or (h) physical symptoms related to separation (APA, 2013). To diagnose separation anxiety disorder, excessive fear or avoidance must be present for at least four weeks in children or adolescents and six months or more in adults. Clinically significant impairment in social, academic, occupational, or other important areas of functioning must be observed, and the separation anxiety must not be better explained by another condition.

Excessive worry, a condition of separation anxiety disorder that is common among all anxiety disorders, is specific to separation from primary attachment figures. When the symptoms are severe enough to negatively affect a child's functioning in social, personal, or family settings, separation anxiety can be considered a clinical disorder (Huberty, 2012). Typically, separation anxiety disorder has an early and acute onset, which may result from a specific event, such as a move, entry into school, or death (Huberty, 2012). However, onset of separation anxiety disorder can occur at any age. Because separation anxiety is a common characteristic among children six months to 6 years of age, determination of a clinical diagnosis may be difficult. The presence of clinical levels of impairment, such as social withdrawal, apathy, sadness, or difficulty concentrating, along with excessive worries, is essential to the diagnosis. The most frequently reported symptoms are distress related to separation, reluctance to be alone or without an attachment figure, or refusal to sleep away from home (Kossowsky, Wilhelm, Roth, & Schneider, 2012). Kossowsky et al. (2012) found that children with a separation anxiety diagnosis demonstrated physiological responses to separation from their mothers, including hyperreactivity and negative cardiovascular and respiratory effects.

Separation anxiety disorder is one of the most frequently diagnosed disorders in children younger than 12 years old, with lifetime prevalence rates between 4.1 percent and 5.1 percent (Kossowsky et al., 2013; Santucci & Ehrenreich-May, 2013). For ages 2 through 8 years old, prevalence of separation anxiety disorder was reported between 2.4 percent and 3.6 percent and the disorder is cited as the earliest of anxiety disorders to begin with a mean age 6.5 at onset (Costello et al., 2011). The disorder appears to be diagnosed equally between girls and boys in clinical samples, but community samples reported a higher incidence of the diagnosis among girls (Huberty, 2012).

In examining the trajectory of separation anxiety disorder and its relationship to future disorders, Kossowsky et al. (2013) found that children with separation anxiety disorder were significantly more at risk to develop a future anxiety disorder. A diagnosis of separation anxiety disorder was also more likely to lead to panic disorder. However, there was no conclusive evidence that separation anxiety was linked to future diagnosis of major depressive disorder. A diagnosis of separation anxiety disorder was not predictive of future substance-related disorders. Researchers suggested exploration of the role of attachment as a mediator of separation anxiety disorder and its trajectory to subsequent disorders. Additional research on etiology linked separation anxiety disorder to genetic and environmental factors, with the identification of parents as a significant environmental influence on separation anxiety symptoms (Scaini, Ogliari, Eley, Zavos, & Battaglia, 2012). Authors suggested the inclusion of parents in treatment of separation anxiety disorder, specifically to manage parental levels of anxiety. Consider the case study in Sidebar 10.2 to explore the diagnosis of separation anxiety disorder.

SIDEBAR 10.2: CASE STUDY—SEPARATION ANXIETY DISORDER

Teddy is a 4-year-old child who struggles to leave his mother. In any situation where he will be separated from her, including mom putting his sister to bed, he has a complete meltdown. Teddy becomes inconsolable anytime he is forced to leave his mother's side, often becoming violent toward his mother in an attempt to demonstrate his anxiety. Teddy struggles through the day in preschool because he is unable to stop crying when his mother leaves. Teddy will recover from his distress in the presence of his mother or babysitter, who has been in his life since he was born. Teddy has experienced these symptoms for as long as his mother can remember. Has Teddy met the criteria for separation anxiety disorder? Would you feel comfortable diagnosing him? What would be your treatment plan for him, and how would you intervene, given his young age and lack of ability to separate from his mother?

SELECTIVE MUTISM

Selective mutism is the "consistent failure to speak in specific social situations in which there is an expectation for speaking" (APA, 2013, p. 195). This is the essential criteria for a diagnosis of selective mutism, specifically if the child speaks in other settings. As in all anxiety disorders, the failure to speak must interfere with school or occupational functioning. Failure to speak in specific settings must last at least one month and not be attributed to acquisition or familiarity with language. Notably, *DSM-5* criteria specify that the one month of symptoms is not limited to the first month of school, recognition of what would be developmentally appropriate for many children. Finally, the symptoms of selective mutism cannot be better accounted for by another condition or disorder.

Selective mutism tends to have an anxiety presentation with possible secondary features of oppositional attitude and is sometimes conceptualized as a type of social phobia (Freeman, Garcia, Miller, Dow, & Leonard, 2004). Onset of selective mutism is often correlated with starting school, specifically preschool, and may not be diagnosed until children enter elementary school (Hung, Spencer, & Dronamraju, 2012). Children with selective mutism are less likely to initiate conversation in social interactions or reciprocate when verbally approached. Impairment is typically related to lack of speech in school, which limits social and academic progress. It is common for children with selective mutism to communicate through nonverbal messages, such as using a series of signs or facial expressions. Children with selective mutism experience limited social interaction, delayed language skills, and restricted school and social activities (Hung et al., 2012). Anxiety features of selective mutism include shyness, fear of social embarrassment, isolation, withdrawal, clingy behavior, compulsive traits, negativism, temper tantrums, and controlling or oppositional behavior (Hung et al., 2012).

Prevalence rates of selective mutism are reported to be 0.7 to 0.8 percent in childhood, which indicates that the disorder is quite rare (Oerbeck, Stein, Wentzel-Larsen, Langsrud & Kristensen, 2014). Selective mutism is more frequently reported for girls than for boys. Because typical onset is early, between 3 and 5 years old, there is a misconception that children will outgrow the condition (Hung et al., 2012). However, selective mutism may progress into other pervasive anxiety diagnoses. Selective mutism is difficult to treat, and the longer the condition persists, the more resistant selective mutism is to intervention (Hung et al., 2012; Oerbeck et al., 2014). Sidebar 10.3 offers a case study scenario for further reflection on selective mutism.

SIDEBAR 10.3:   CASE STUDY—SELECTIVE MUTISM

Ashanti, a 14-year-old female, has been diagnosed with selective mutism. She would not speak outside of her home starting at age 5. Her parents attempted to help the issue by home schooling her and continue to do so to this day. One year ago, she experienced an incident with peers in an extracurricular activity, and afterward she stopped talking at home as well. Her parents are unaware of the incident that occurred and have not been successful in getting her to communicate with them ever since. How would you intervene with this client? What strategies could you try with her? Knowing that the more time has passed, the less likely it is for people who are selectively mute to improve, what would be your goals for this client?

SPECIFIC PHOBIA

The diagnosis of specific phobia is characterized by an excessive and marked fear regarding a specific object or situation. In children, the *DSM-5* (APA, 2013) specifies that the fear or anxiety may be demonstrated through crying, tantrums, freezing, or clinging. Several other criteria are required for specific phobia diagnosis, including that the phobic stimulus consistently provokes fear, phobic stimulus is avoided or endured with high levels of anxiety, fear regarding the stimulus is excessive in regard to reality of threat, and fear lasts for six months or more. Finally, the fear related to phobia or avoidance of phobic stimulus causes functional impairment in social, occupational, or other important areas of functioning. For a diagnosis of specific phobia, symptoms are not better accounted for by another condition or disorder. Specific phobia diagnosis is followed by specifiers intended to identify the nature of the phobic stimulus. Specifiers include animals, natural environment, blood-injection-injury, situational, and other. Specific phobia with *animal* specifier may indicate that children are fearful of spiders, dogs, or other animals. Specific phobia with *natural environment* specifier indicates the child is fearful of typical situations found in nature, such as storms, water, or heights. Specific phobia with *blood-injection-injury* specifier suggests that the child is fearful of anything related to blood, needles, or hospital procedures. Specific phobia with *situational* specifier marks a child's fear of certain situations that could occur, such as being in an airplane, an elevator, or other enclosed places. Specific phobia with *other* specifier gives the diagnostician freedom to identify more unique sources of phobia that are concerning to a child, such as costumed characters. Diagnosis of specific phobia can be formulated with one or more descriptive specifiers.

The identifying feature of specific phobia is that physiological arousal and excessive fear are a reaction to an identified phobic stimulus. Children may respond to the phobic stimulus by running away, clinging to others, crying, freezing, or possibly having panic attacks (Fonseca & Perrin, 2011; Huberty, 2012). Specific fears are common in childhood, such as fear of the dark, certain animals, or other beings, and typically follow a normal developmental trajectory of dissipation (Muris et al., 2009). When these fears interfere with normal functioning and become debilitating, specific phobia diagnosis may be justified. Specific phobia is distinct from other anxiety disorders because symptoms do not appear linked to internalized cognitive distortions yet appear as reactions to stimuli that can be identified by others (Huberty, 2012).

Specific phobia is the most common anxiety disorder in children and adolescents, with a stable prevalence rate of 6.7 percent among children and 6.7 percent among adolescents (Costello et al., 2011). Onset of specific phobia appears to be about the time children start school, and most are reported prior to age 10. Specific phobia is typically reported more among girls than boys. There is little to no evidence that links specific phobia to future anxiety disorders or depression (Huberty, 2012). Learning experiences, direct and indirect, appear to play a role in acquisitions of specific phobias, yet onset is rare past adolescence (Huberty, 2012; Muris et al., 2009). Although not restricted to children, the *DSM-5* (APA, 2013) reports that the average individual diagnosed with specific phobia fears three objects or situations, with approximately 75 percent of all diagnosed with specific phobia reporting fear of more than one stimulus.

Social Anxiety Disorder (Social Phobia)

Diagnosis of social anxiety disorder requires the presence and identification of multiple features. Individuals with social anxiety disorder experience fear or anxiety related to social situations in which they might be scrutinized. For children, these situations are peer based and not interactions with adults. Other criteria include that the child fears their behavior will result in a negative evaluation by others; the social situation provokes fear as evidenced by crying, tantruming, freezing, clinging, shrinking, or failing to speak; the social situation is avoided or approached with distress; fear is excessive to reality of threat; fear or avoidance of social situations lasts for six or more months; and fear or avoidance causes significant functional impairment. For a diagnosis of social anxiety disorder, fear or avoidance is not better accounted for by use of a substance, another mental disorder, or medical condition. Social anxiety disorder has one descriptive specifier of *performance only* that is included if the fear or avoidance behavior is restricted to public performance, such as dancing, speaking, playing music, and athletics. The *DSM-5* provides further examples of social anxiety presentations, including individuals that avoid fear of offending others through gazing or other contact, fear of blushing by avoiding public performance or bright lights, or fear of urinating in public, among others. However, these are not specific to children. In social anxiety disorder, the individual may fear showing a nervous reaction that would be humiliating or embarrassing, and the reaction is out of proportion to the reality of the situation and the social context.

Children with social anxiety disorder may be fearful of specific social situations or a wide range of social settings (Huberty, 2012). Historically, social anxiety has been marked by anxious solitary behaviors in early childhood, including onlooking behavior, shyness, social hesitancy, and hesitancy to speak among peers (Gazelle, Workman, & Allan, 2010). These children typically desire to interact with peers but resist because of fear that they will perform poorly or be perceived as performing poorly. Gazelle et al. (2010) found that 40 percent of third- and fourth-grade children in one sample who were identified by others as anxious solitary self-reported a clinical level of social anxiety symptoms.

Costello et al. (2011) reported a social anxiety disorder prevalence rate of 2.2 percent for six- to 12-year-olds and 5 percent for 13- to 18-year-olds. Mean age of onset was close to 10 years old. Social anxiety is rare in children under age 10, but prevalence increases during middle to late adolescence (Bokhorst & Westenberg, 2011). Social anxiety tends to remain stable or decrease following adolescence. Bokhorst and Westenberg (2011) suggested that social anxiety does not appear to be developmentally normal, as can often be detected in other anxiety disorders. As children reach adolescence, it appears that some become distressfully fearful of evaluative situations, yet response to other social situations remains unaffected by age.

Social anxiety disorder symptoms are often present early in life but remain undiagnosed for several years. When finally diagnosed in early adolescence, symptoms are often associated with chronic distress and dysfunction (Simon et al., 2009). Social anxiety disorder has been correlated with dropping out of school, decreased well-being, and poorer quality of life. Additionally problematic is that the severity of symptoms related to the high comorbidity between social anxiety disorder and generalized anxiety disorder (Whitmore, Kim-Spoon, & Ollendick, 2014).

PANIC DISORDER

In panic disorder, the child experiences recurrent and unexpected panic attacks that are accompanied by at least four identified symptoms that may include accelerated heart rate, sweating, trembling, feeling short of breath, feeling as if the person is being choked, chest pain, nausea, dizziness, feeling chilled or overheated, numbness, feelings of detachment, fear of losing control, or fear of dying (APA, 2013). If panic attacks are initiated because of cultural specificities or if symptoms are culture specific, such as tinnitus, neck soreness, and so forth, those symptoms do not meet criteria for panic disorder. For a panic disorder diagnosis, at least one of the panic attacks is followed by one month or more of worry about future panic attacks or maladjusted change in behavior related to the attack. Additionally, symptoms of panic disorder cannot be attributed to substance use or a medical condition or be better accounted for by another disorder.

Panic disorder is intensified by the level of worry that follows recurrent panic attacks regarding the possibility of future attacks. The fear of future attacks may become the debilitating factor (Huberty, 2012). This fear may be exacerbated by the presence of anxiety sensitivity, the belief that the physical symptoms of anxiety will be life threatening or result in substantial negative consequences, causing the child to become overly sensitive to such symptoms (Huberty, 2012; Noel & Francis, 2011). The interpretation of the physical symptoms related to panic attacks as severely consequential predisposes the child to fear of imminent attacks. In one sample of youth, Noel and Francis (2011) found higher levels of reported anxiety sensitivity in children diagnosed with panic disorder.

Panic disorder has low prevalence in children ages 6 to 12 years, with a reported 1.5 percent, and in adolescents ages 13 to 18 years, with a reported 1.1 percent (Costello et al., 2011). Age of onset for panic disorder is the latest of all anxiety disorders found in child populations, with panic disorders rarely reported before midadolescence. According to Ollendick, Birmaher, and Mattis (2004), some theorists hypothesize that panic disorder is found less frequently among children because they do not have the cognitive ability to make internal, catastrophic misinterpretations of physical symptoms related to panic attacks. However, the scarcity of research on panic disorder in children limits understanding of its etiology and trajectory.

Panic Attack Specifier

According to the APA (2013), a panic attack can be defined as a penetrating sense of fear or discomfort that occurs suddenly and with effects that rapidly peak. A panic attack includes symptoms such as accelerated heart rate, sweating, trembling, feeling short of breath, and numbness. Panic attacks are not conceptualized as a mental disorder and are only used to specify other *DSM-5* disorders, including anxiety disorder. The *DSM-5* identifies two types of panic attacks: expected and unexpected. Expected panic attacks are usually triggered by a specific and identified stimulus, whereas unexpected panic attacks appear spontaneously and without provocation. Although panic attacks can be unexpected or expected in most anxiety disorders, panic disorder requires only unexpected panic attacks.

A panic attack occurs as an excessive response to a stimulus that poses no real danger. The child may feel that something is wrong but is confused about what, when, where, and why events are occurring, which leads to intensification of fears about future attacks (Ollendick et al., 2004). Panic attacks are considered one of the most debilitating of psychiatric conditions, resulting in pursuit of mental health treatment (Mathyssek, Olino, Verhulst, & van Oort, 2012). Typical onset of panic attacks is late adolescence and prevalence rates range from 3.3 percent to 11.6 percent among children 9 to 17 years old, with the rate of prevalence increasing in adolescence (Mathyseek et al., 2012).

Agoraphobia

Children meeting criteria for agoraphobia fear two or more types of situations, including use of public transportation, being in open spaces, being in enclosed spaces, standing in line or with a crowd, and being outside the home alone (APA, 2013). For an agoraphobia diagnosis, the child fears these situations because they anticipate that they will not be able to escape or acquire help if they have panic symptoms. Other criteria include an anxiety response provoked by the agoraphobic situations, avoidance of the identified situations or endurance of situations with great anxiety, and presence of fear out of proportion to the actual threat. Diagnosis requires duration of fear of agoraphobic situations to be six or more months, with significant impairment in functioning. The fear must not be attributed to expectant fear related to a medical condition and must not be explained by another diagnosis. Costello et al. (2011) cited too few reports of agoraphobia to make reliable estimates on prevalence and comorbidity. However, they reported mean onset of agoraphobia is approximately 12 years old. Occurrence of agoraphobia is well documented in adolescence but not in childhood (Fonseca & Perrin, 2011).

Additionally, the identification of two or more agoraphobic situations represents a change in *DSM-5* criteria and allows for better differentiation between specific phobia and agoraphobia. Ollendick et al. (2004) noted children with agoraphobia begin to withdraw from unfamiliar people and situations to cope with their distress. Some experts theorized that agoraphobia is related to insecure attachment and is conceptually linked to separation anxiety disorder; yet no conclusive evidence supports this theory (Silverman & Dick-Niederhauser, 2004). Although diagnostically separated in the *DSM-5*, agoraphobia is often associated with panic attacks, and in such situations, addition of the panic attack specifier to the agoraphobia diagnosis is warranted.

GENERALIZED ANXIETY DISORDER

Generalized anxiety disorder is characterized by the presence of excessive and numerous worries occurring most days within a six-month or longer period. The clinician assesses the excessive nature and pervasiveness of worries, as well as the distress caused by the worries. A child with generalized anxiety disorder finds it difficult to control worries, which are associated with at least one of the following items: restlessness, being easily tired, difficulty concentrating, irritability, muscle tension, or sleep disturbance (APA, 2013). As true for all anxiety disorders, generalized anxiety disorder is marked by clinically significant impairment in social, occupational, or other important areas of functioning, and the anxiety symptoms are not better accounted for by substance use, medical condition, or another disorder. The *DSM-5* lists 11 other disorders that mimic the symptoms of generalized anxiety disorder and must be considered in differential diagnosis. The *DSM-5* reports that generalized anxiety disorder may also be accompanied by physical symptoms, such as trembling, and somatic symptoms such as sweating and nausea (APA, 2013).

The high level, prevalence, and frequency of reported worries are characteristic of generalized anxiety disorder. Worry is developmentally normal for all children and can be observed in children as young as 4 years old (Cartwright-Hatton, Reynolds, & Wilson, 2011). However, by age 7 or 8 years, children begin to access future possibilities cognitively and thus report more worries. Nonclinical children report the same number of worries as children with generalized anxiety disorder; however clinical children report greater intensity of worries (Huberty, 2012). Cartwright et al. (2011) found three specific factors associated with generalized anxiety disorder in children, including difficulty in controlling worry, impact of worry is significant on child's life, and presence of at least one physical symptom of anxiety. Moreover, worries indicative of generalized anxiety disorder are more pervasive, pronounced, and distressing, have longer duration, and frequency occur without precipitants (APA, 2013). Children and adolescents tend to worry most about performance at school or sporting events, even when they are not being evaluated (APA, 2013). Worries may be smaller, such as punctuality concerns, or much larger, such as fear of catastrophic events. Generalized anxiety disorder may manifest through perfectionistic tendencies, conformity, and constant need for reassurance.

Costello et al. (2011) reported a 1.7 percent prevalence of generalized anxiety disorder in children 6 to 12 years old and 1.9 percent in adolescents 13 to 18 years old, with reported age of onset at 8 years old (Fonseca & Perrin, 2011). Generalized anxiety disorder (GAD) has been studied less in childhood and early adolescence because of its reclassification from the *DSM-IV* (Fonseca & Perrin, 2011). In 1994, GAD was the new name for *DSM-III-R* Overanxious Disorder of Childhood. GAD occurs more than twice as often in adolescent girls and shows a persistent trajectory with low remission rate (Huberty, 2012).

GAD is reported to be highly comorbid with other diagnoses, most notably other anxiety disorders and depression, and may be overdiagnosed in children (APA, 2013).

Because of high comorbidity, GAD is questioned as a distinct disorder (Huberty, 2012). The presence of GAD along with at least one other diagnosis predicts greater levels of functional impairment. However, Alfano (2012) found that a singular diagnosis of GAD was correlated with global functional impairment.

SUBSTANCE/MEDICATION-INDUCED ANXIETY DISORDER

The diagnostic criteria for a substance/medication-induced anxiety disorder include the presence of panic attacks or excessive anxiety symptoms that develop during or directly after substance/medication use or withdrawal (APA, 2013). For the diagnosis, anxiety is not better explained by another anxiety disorder, does not occur during the course of delirium, and causes clinically significant impairment in functioning. This particular disorder requires the use of specifiers to indicate the substance, and subsequently the context of onset, including during intoxication, during withdrawal, and after medication use.

The diagnosis of substance/medication-induced anxiety disorder has not been considerably studied and hence has uncertain validity (Fonseca & Perrin, 2011). Substance use, which is more likely among adolescents, can cause symptoms that simulate anxiety, specifically physical symptoms (Huberty, 2012). Additionally, the widespread use of medication for children and adolescent behavioral and emotional issues may result in the development of anxiety symptoms. Prevalence rates among individuals are extremely small, approximately 0.002 percent, and rates are not reported for children and adolescents (APA, 2013).

ANXIETY DISORDER DUE TO ANOTHER MEDICAL CONDITION

Anxiety disorder due to another medical condition has been studied less among children and has questionable validity (Fonseca & Perrin, 2011). A criterion for this particular anxiety disorder is the presence of panic attacks or excessive anxiety. Evidence must link anxiety symptoms to an identifiable medical condition. Additionally, anxiety is not better accounted for by another disorder and does not occur during the course of a delirium. Finally, anxiety symptoms cause clinically significant impairment for a diagnosis.

Generally, chronic medical illness is a significant risk factor for the development of anxiety disorders among children (Pao & Bosk, 2011). Anxiety may relate to a specific medical illness, a response to being ill or in the hospital, or a response to other genetic and environmental factors. Children may become engaged in a vicious cycle in which chronic worry and anxiety may decrease immune function, making the child more susceptible to infections and increasing severity of physical illness, resulting in increased anxiety. Alternatively, clinicians note physical symptoms from various neurological, endocrine, cardiac, pulmonary, and metabolic disorders mimic anxiety symptoms (Pao & Bosk, 2011).

OTHER SPECIFIED AND UNSPECIFIED ANXIETY DISORDER

In the *DSM-5*, the two categories of other specified anxiety disorder and unspecified anxiety disorder replace the previous anxiety disorder not otherwise specified in the *DSM-IV-TR*. *Other specified anxiety disorder* is used by clinicians to diagnose a

presentation of symptoms that does not clearly meet criteria for any of the anxiety disorders. Counselors use *other specified anxiety disorder* when they prefer to communicate
the reason criteria was not met for another disorder (APA, 2013). The unspecified anxiety
disorder category allows counselors to diagnose presentation of symptoms that do not
meet criteria for another anxiety disorder and prefer not to specify the reason criteria
were not met. For both diagnoses, symptoms of the disorder should result in clinically
significant functional impairment to meet criteria for diagnosis.

Differential Diagnosis

The distinctive characteristic in the diagnosis of anxiety disorders is the presence of
intense feelings of worry or fear that seem out of proportion to the stimulus or situation.
Identification of prevalence, intensity, and frequency of fears helps the clinician conduct
differential diagnosis of anxiety in the context of other nonanxiety disorders. Perhaps, the
most difficult task in diagnosis of anxiety is differentiating between anxiety disorders,
as comorbidity is reported to be high among almost all anxiety disorders. Clinicians
should pay close attention to the distinguishing criteria for each anxiety disorder and
rule out the possibility of symptoms explained by another anxiety disorder or other
condition. For example, anxiety reactions common to separation anxiety disorder are in
response to being separated from or fearing the thought of being separated from a primary
attachment figure. Although children with separation anxiety disorder may also avoid
school (common in social anxiety) or fear leaving the house (common in agoraphobia),
the motivation for such fear is the separation from a primary caretaker.

Another example is the presentation of selective mutism versus social anxiety. Children
with social anxiety will fear situations where negative evaluation is anticipated, whether
speaking is required or not. The symptoms of selective mutism are specific to speaking
situations and need to be differentiated from normal developmental complications associated with language acquisition among children who do not speak the primary language
of the cultural setting (Freeman et al., 2004).

Clinicians should also be able to distinguish a case where children or adolescents fear
social situations that may involve a perceived negative evaluation by others (social anxiety
disorder) from fear about social situations that extend beyond performance (generalized
anxiety disorder) and those where a child fears separation from the primary caretaker (separation anxiety). Similarly, clinicians should differentiate cases where panic is unexpected
(panic disorder) versus those cases where panic occurs in response to a specific stimulus,
such as the presence of a dog (specific phobia).

Differential diagnosis in anxiety disorders also requires the consideration of cases in
which an individual experiences considerable anxiety and fears situations where they
believe that there will be an inability to escape or acquire help (e.g., agoraphobia). In these
cases, differential diagnosis is determined by identification of the cognitive motivation for
fear or avoidance of agoraphobic situations.

Due to the high level of comorbidity between generalized anxiety disorder and depressive disorders, differential diagnosis considerations are necessary. Typically, children with
generalized anxiety disorder show greater degree of worry, while children with depressive
disorders demonstrate an absence of positive affect and more negative affect (Huberty,
2012). Consider the case in Sidebar 10.4 to explore the nature of generalized anxiety
disorder further.

SIDEBAR 10.4: CASE STUDY—GENERALIZED ANXIETY DISORDER

Evie is an 8-year-old girl who seems to worry about many things. Worrying takes up a large portion of her life, ranging from inconsequential issues to larger world problems. She has frequent nightmares about catastrophic events occurring, and worries about these events throughout the day. Evie's teachers noticed the large amounts of pressure she seems to put on herself with her schoolwork and drive to succeed. She is looking for approval constantly and is striving for perfection. However, she seems to lack friends within her peer group. Would you diagnose Evie with generalized anxiety disorder? Why or why not? How would you work with Evie?

ADDITIONAL DIFFERENTIAL DIAGNOSIS CONSIDERATIONS

Special attention has been paid to the link between anxiety disorders and autism spectrum disorder. Results of meta-analysis revealed that 39.6 percent of children with autism spectrum disorders have at least one comorbid *DSM-IV-TR* anxiety disorder, including obsessive-compulsive disorder (Van Steensel, Bogels, & Perrin, 2011). Researchers reported the most frequent comorbid anxiety disorder as specific phobia (29.8 percent), followed by social phobia (16.6 percent). Because of the higher prevalence rates of anxiety disorders found for children with less severe autistic spectrum disorders, researchers concluded that criteria for autism spectrum disorders can be distinguished from criteria for anxiety disorders.

High comorbidity rates between children with attention-deficit/hyperactivity disorder (ADHD) and an anxiety disorder warrants attention to differential diagnosis. Levin-Decanini et al. (2013) reported comorbidity rates of 15 percent to 35 percent between ADHD and anxiety, signifying that ADHD is the most common externalizing disorder related to anxiety. Because of the common symptoms of distractibility and lack of focus associated with both ADHD and anxiety, counselors benefit from carefully scrutinizing the most fitting category for anxiety symptoms.

Assessment Strategies

Anxiety disorders are prevalent among children and can be assessed through informal and formal measures. The American Academy of Child and Adolescent Psychiatry (AACAP) created guidelines for assessing anxiety in children and adolescents based on the prevalence of anxiety. They suggested that in all mental health examinations, screening questions for anxiety symptoms should be used and followed up by a formal evaluation if needed. Because of the comorbidity of anxiety disorders, broader assessments for other mental health disorders should be considered after determining the duration and severity of the anxiety (Mohr & Schneider, 2013).

Mohr and Schneider (2013) discussed recommendations for most accurately assessing anxiety levels, including the selection of assessments that reliably differentiate age-appropriate anxiety from age-inappropriate anxiety and those that consider manifestations at various developmental levels. To assess appropriately, they suggested using multiple sources of information and multiple methods, not just a single anxiety measure that captures one perspective of the child's anxiety. They advocated for self-report measures as screening tools but also using a diagnostic interview to diagnose anxiety in children and adolescents. To assess young children, it is important to consider developmentally appropriate assessments, such as the Picture Anxiety Test for children 4 to 8 years of age or the Revised Children's Manifest Anxiety Scale (RCMAS-2; Reynolds & Richmond, 2008), which assesses children ages 6 to 17 years. Overall, we recommend a combination of child report measures, parent or teacher report measures, and diagnostic assessment instruments.

CHILD REPORT MEASURES

Self-report measures for anxiety capture children's experiences of their anxiety. They are directly administered to the child to assess for their perspective. Child report measures can be especially insightful given the internalizing nature of anxiety.

Multidimensional Anxiety Scale for Children

The Multidimensional Anxiety Scale for Children (MASC; March, Parker, Sullivan, Stallings, & Conners, 1997) measures four facets of anxiety in 8- to 19-year-olds. Through asking children to respond to 39 items, the MASC assesses physical symptoms, social anxiety, harm avoidance, and separation/panic.

Picture Anxiety Test

The Picture Anxiety Test (Dubi & Schneider, 2009) can be used for children as young as 4 until 8 years of age. The Picture Anxiety Test measures a range of anxieties and avoidance patterns using 21 hypothetical vignettes involving situations and objects that young children are likely to fear.

Revised Child Anxiety and Depression Scales

The Revised Child Anxiety and Depression Scales (Chorpita, Yim, Moffit, Umemoto, & Francis, 2000) is a 47-item assessment for children ages 6 to 19. This assessment examines separation anxiety disorder, social phobia, generalized anxiety disorder, panic disorder, obsessive-compulsive disorder, and major depressive disorder.

Revised Children's Manifest Anxiety Scale

The Revised Children's Manifest Anxiety Scale (RCMAS-2; Reynolds & Richmond, 2008) measures total anxiety, physiological anxiety, worry, and social anxiety in children ages 6 to 18.

State-Trait Anxiety Inventory for Children

The State-Trait Anxiety Inventory for Children (STAIC; Spielberger, 1973) assesses chronic symptoms of anxiety in 8- to 15-year-olds. The STAIC has 20 items, which create two subscales: Anxiety-Trait assesses chronic situational anxiety; A-State assesses acute, transitory anxiety.

PARENT/TEACHER REPORT

Parents and teachers also have valuable insight into children's experiences and their observations of children's behaviors. Parent and teacher reports help clinicians understand children's anxiety from multiple perspectives of people who spend a great amount of time with the child.

Behavior Assessment System for Children, Second Edition

The Behavior Assessment System for Children, Second Edition (BASC-2; Reynolds & Kamphaus, 2003), assesses behavior problems across a wide range of symptoms. The BASC-2 has both a teacher and a parent form to gather data on children from multiple perspectives.

Child Behavior Checklist

The Child Behavior Checklist (CBCL; Achenbach & Rescorla, 2001) is parent report assessment that assesses behaviors across a wide range of symptoms. The 118 items are distributed into subscales addressing many concerns, including anxious/depressed behaviors. The Teacher Report Form (TRF; Achenbach, & Rescorla, 2001) is the teacher companion assessment to the CBCL. The TRF has 120 items to assess behaviors across a wide range of symptoms, including anxious/depressed.

State-Trait Anxiety Inventory for Children—Parent Report—Trait Version

The State-Trait Anxiety Inventory for Children—Parent Report—Trait Version (Spielberger, 1973) is a parent companion assessment to the STAIC. This assessment comprises 26 items to assess parents' perceptions of the child's trait anxiety as defined in the STAIC.

DIAGNOSTIC ASSESSMENTS

Diagnostic assessments help clinicians provide accurate diagnoses. Diagnostic interviews tend to take much longer than screening assessments. The following diagnostic assessments can help diagnose children with anxiety; however, diagnostic assessments have yet to be created for the new *DSM-5*.

Diagnostic Interview Schedule for Children and Adolescents

The Diagnostic Interview Schedule for Children and Adolescents (DICA; Reich, 2000) is a semistructured interview to assess mental health disorders for children ages 6 to 17. The DICA has child, adolescent, and parent forms that assess for overanxious disorder, separation anxiety disorder, and social phobia.

Anxiety Disorders Interview Scale

The Anxiety Disorders Interview Scale (ADIS; Silverman, Saavedra, & Pina, 2001) is a semistructured diagnostic interview specifically designed to diagnose anxiety disorders. The ADIS has a parent and child version, with the child self-reporting and parents reporting on their child's behaviors. The ADIS can be used with 6- to 18-year-olds.

Schniering, Hudson, and Rapee (2000) investigated the validity of assessments for childhood anxiety. They concluded that there is validity for anxiety disorders in children based on the constructs measured with the assessments. However, the assessments seem to have weaknesses regarding the ability to differentiate between specific anxiety disorders. Additionally, the assessments seem to have poor discriminant validity, meaning the assessments are not able to demonstrate that the constructs are different from other constructs that should be different. Schniering et al. (2000) also commented on the lack of sensitivity to developmental levels across assessments. These findings should be considered when utilizing assessments, ensuring that clinical judgment on the part of the clinician should be enacted when providing specific anxiety diagnoses based on assessments.

ASSESSMENTS WITHIN THE *DSM-5*

The *DSM-5* recognizes emerging assessment measures to differentiate between disorders and most important to determine the severity level of disorder symptoms. Cross cutting symptom measures consider a more general review of overall symptoms that may spread across diagnoses. Childhood disorders can be assessed through the 25-item Level 1 Cross-Cutting Symptom Measures included in the *DSM-5* that screens 12 psychiatric domains, with three questions dedicated to anxiety symptoms. Each question is geared toward symptom frequency as expressed by the child or observed by parent/guardian.

Childhood anxiety frequency can also be measured through the Level 2 Anxiety— Parent/Guardian of Child Age 6–7 (Adapted from PROMIS Emotional Distress-Anxiety—Parent Item Bank) and the Anxiety—Child Age 11–17 (PROMIS Emotional Distress-Anxiety—Pediatric Item Bank). These assessment measures are drawn primarily from calibrated item banks (sets of well-defined and validated items) measuring concepts. There are also disorder specific severity measures. For anxiety, these assessments include: Severity Measure for Separation Anxiety Disorder—Child Age 11–17, Severity Measure for Specific Phobia—Child Age 11–17, Severity Measure for Social Anxiety Disorder (Social Phobia)—Child Age 11–17, Severity Measure for Panic Disorder—Child Age 11–17, Severity Measure for Agoraphobia—Child Age 11–17, and Severity Measure for Generalized Anxiety Disorder—Child Age 11–17. These assessment measures are considered emerging, with further data on the instruments' usefulness in characterizing child status and improving child care strongly recommended.

Treatment Strategies and Interventions

Huberty (2012) emphasized the importance of treating children with anxiety disorders early so that symptoms do not increase or intensify and cause greater resistance to intervention. In reviewing psychosocial treatments for children and adolescents with anxiety disorders, Silverman, Pina, and Viswesvaran (2008) found that no current treatments meet standards for well-established treatments; that is, treatments supported by multiple randomized controlled trials with rigorous guidelines. However, through the review process, they listed various forms of cognitive behavioral therapy (CBT) as probably efficacious. Several behavioral interventions were categorized as possibly efficacious. Medications are often used in the treatment of children with anxiety disorders. Finally, relational interventions, such as play therapy or family interventions have also been examined as possible treatments for anxiety in children.

For particularly young children, ages 2 to 7, treatment options are less clear. In a review of treatment effectiveness, Anticich, Barrett, Gillies, and Silverman (2012) found that most treatments for young children direct intervention toward parents, with only one treatment study focusing on child-only intervention. They preliminarily concluded that early intervention and prevention programs for child only and parent only and child and parent programs of different theoretical orientations were effective in reducing anxiety symptoms.

Treatments that target reduction of clinical levels of childhood worry are necessary and recommended for intervention with children (Silverman, La Greca, & Wasserstein, 1995). Other common goals for treatment of anxiety in children include increasing awareness of emotional reactivity, improving knowledge of the role of emotions in anxiety, improving tolerance to negative emotional experiences, increasing awareness of regulatory processes, and developing new strategies that help children cope and regulate in reaction to anxiety-provoking situations (Carthy, Horesh, Apter, & Gross, 2010).

COGNITIVE BEHAVIORAL THERAPY (CBT)

Currently, cognitive behavioral therapy (CBT) is the best-supported intervention for childhood anxiety disorders based on its research foundation (Compton, March, Brent, Albano, Weersing, & Curry, 2004; Silverman, Pina, & Viswesvaran, 2008). Multiple meta-analyses and systematic reviews confirm the use of CBT with anxious children (Compton et al., 2004; In-Albon & Schneider, 2007; Silverman et al., 2008). In CBT, children learn to identify situations and thoughts that produce fear, as well as learn to adopt alternative thoughts and behaviors that lead to a reduction in anxiety symptoms. Group CBT can also be effective in reducing symptoms of social anxiety disorder when intervention focuses on recognition of physiological symptoms and self-talk, as well as exposure techniques (Silverman et al., 2008).

The advanced cognitive processes involved in the success of CBT may limit its effectiveness with particularly young children (Rey et al., 2011). Grave and Blissett (2004) further noted that the foundation of CBT is that irrational beliefs, thoughts, and attitudes are the driving force behind problematic behavior, which requires a level of self-reflection, perspective taking, understanding causality, and reasoning. The egocentric nature of young children precludes the ability to take another's perspective or view themselves separate from their environment. Therefore, there is some debate regarding the appropriate developmental fit between CBT and children younger than 8 years old. Rey et al. (2011) concluded that CBT is more likely to be successful when children exhibit few symptoms, have a generally more positive mind-set, are struggling with anxiety only, have supportive environments, are willing to engage in treatment, and have strong connections with their therapists.

BEHAVIORAL INTERVENTIONS

Although CBT incorporates some behavioral interventions, evidence supports the effectiveness of behavioral strategies alone in treating children with anxiety disorders. Huberty (2012) theorized that behavioral therapy, rather than CBT, appears more effective for the diagnosis of separation anxiety when strategies are positively oriented and gradual reinforcement is offered for steps to separation. Specific phobia can be addressed through contingency management and self-control reinforcements (Silverman et al., 1999). For selective mutism, behavioral interventions are most frequently used (Oerbeck et al., 2014). Hung et al. (2012) listed contingency management, fading, systematic desensitization, positive reinforcement, and self-modeling as the most effective behavioral interventions for selective mutism. There is some evidence that exposure-based practice, versus contingency management, is most effective. Oerbeck et al. (2014) explored the use of defocused communication (creating focus on joint activity without focusing on child's verbal participation) and behavioral rewards with children who were selectively mute. They found intervention resulted in significant increases in verbal communication. Social effectiveness training has been shown to be effective for children with social anxiety disorder (Silverman et al., 2008). Designed as a behavioral treatment program, social effectiveness training integrates social skills training, peer group sessions, and exposure sessions to help reduce social anxiety symptoms.

To help children identify and cope with the phobic stimulus, Huberty (2012) noted that direct and indirect exposure techniques are beneficial in reducing symptoms associated with specific phobia. Ollendick et al. (2009) found that a one-session treatment originally designed for adults could be modified to effectively reduce phobia symptoms for children 7 to 11 years old. Treatment involved participant modeling, in vivo exposure, and reinforced practice.

PLAY THERAPY

Child-centered play therapy (CCPT; Landreth, 2012; Ray, 2011) is one possible treatment for childhood anxiety that is empirically supported (Bratton, Ray, Rhine, & Jones, 2005), specifically for young children. Using play as the child's natural medium of communication, CCPT provides an environment that allows the child to express emotions and thoughts through self-directed play. CCPT is based on the principles of person-centered therapy and recognizes the therapeutic relationship between counselor and child as the healing factor of change. CCPT works with the internal process of the child, as opposed to specific behavioral concerns, potentially addressing the physiological and cognitive components of anxiety that occur in young children. Hung et al. (2012) cited play therapy as a possible intervention for selective mutism because of its focus on nonverbal ways of communicating.

Research linking the impact of CCPT on children's anxiety levels indicates positive effects. Shen (2002) found that children who were earthquake victims and received 10 CCPT group sessions demonstrated significantly reduced levels of physiological anxiety and worry when compared with control counterparts. When examining trauma symptoms in sexually abused children, Reyes and Asbrand (2005) determined that sexually abused children who participated in play therapy over 18 months showed a statistically significant reduction in anxiety symptoms. As an intervention for elementary school-aged Hispanic children referred for school counseling, CCPT demonstrated a moderate treatment effect on anxiety symptoms, compared with a randomized comparison group (Garza & Bratton, 2005). Finally, Stulmaker and Ray (2015) found that young children who met criteria for increased levels of anxiety reported significantly less anxiety following 16 sessions of CCPT, as compared with a randomized active control group.

PARENT-CHILD INTERVENTIONS

Research reveals that parental factors, such as parent anxiety, stress, modeling, and response to child symptoms, are influential in the development and maintenance of anxiety disorders in children (Brendel & Maynard, 2014; Compton et al., 2014; Huberty, 2012; Silverman & Dick-Niederhauser, 2004). In a meta-analysis of parent-child interventions for childhood anxiety disorders, Brendel and Maynard (2014) found that parent-child family cognitive behavioral interventions appear to be more effective than child-focused individual and group CBT in reduction of childhood anxiety symptoms. In family CBT, parents are asked to examine factors associated with anxiety, and facilitate new opportunities with children to test distorted beliefs (Brendel & Maynard, 2014). Authors listed additional parent-child programs that might be beneficial for children with anxiety. In parent-child interaction therapy, parents learn to modify their own actions through child-directed and parent-directed play phases. Theraplay uses structuring, challenging, engagement, nurturing, and play to facilitate bonding and attunement in parent–child interactions. The child–parent psychotherapy model uses play as the primary medium of intervention, concentrating on the therapeutic effect of the parent–child relationship. Finally, child parent relationship therapy (CPRT), also referred to as filial therapy (Landreth & Bratton, 2006), uses the principles of child-centered play therapy to teach parent skills to use in weekly, supervised, child-directed play sessions. Designed to foster a secure, attuned relationship between parent and child, CPRT has been shown in controlled outcome studies to reduce anxiety significantly in child witnesses of domestic violence (Smith & Landreth, 2003), chronically ill children (Tew, Landreth, Joiner, & Solt (2002), and sexually abused children (Costas & Landreth, 1999).

MEDICATION

Childhood anxiety disorders are often treated through pharmacotherapy, use of medication to decrease symptoms of anxiety. Because there are few studies on the impact of medications and long-term effects on children, treatment of childhood anxiety through medication is controversial (Huberty, 2012). Yet, due to frequency of use, clinicians are obligated to maintain knowledge regarding current practices in prescription of anxiety-targeted medications. Compton et al. (2014) reported that selective serotonin reuptake inhibitor medications (SSRIs) are effective in decreasing anxiety symptoms and functional impairment. Mohr and Schneider (2013) also noted the benefit of medication, specifically SSRIs in the treatment of anxiety. Speaking specifically in regard to selective mutism, Hung et al. (2012) recognized the common use of SSRIs for anxiety treatment but said that no specific drugs have been approved by the U.S. Federal Drug Administration for use with children. All authors suggest the use of psychosocial treatment prior to initiation of medication and encourage caution in the use of medications for childhood anxiety because of lack of knowledge regarding their effects.

Evaluation Strategies

When left untreated, children with anxiety disorders continue to deteriorate in regard to symptom frequency, intensity, comorbidity, and global functioning. The presence of one anxiety disorder and lack of treatment in childhood increases risk of subsequent and multiple anxiety disorders, as well as other mental health conditions. In one study of 196 children first assessed between the ages of 4 and 9 (Broeren, Muris, Diamantopoulou, & Baker, 2013), most children belonged to low- or medium-level anxiety trajectories, which seemed to reflect the normative course of anxiety symptoms, whereas a small number of children were assigned to high or very high anxiety trajectories. The high-anxiety group continued to be more anxious, and the low-anxiety group continued to be less anxious. The authors concluded that behavioral inhibition and higher number of internalizing symptoms at first assessment predicted high social anxiety trajectories. Children diagnosed with anxiety experience greater impairments in school functioning, and those with comorbid diagnoses exhibit the greatest levels of impairment, including academic performance and the degree to which they are happy, working hard, or learning well (Mychailyszyn, Mendez, & Kendall, 2010).

Generalized anxiety disorder or social anxiety among first grade boys predicted earlier initiation of alcohol and tobacco use, as well as development of marijuana problems (Marmorstein, White, Loeber, & Stouthamer-Loeber, 2010). The authors theorized that once anxious youths overcome the anticipatory anxiety associated with trying marijuana, they discover that it helps them relax, and they begin to use it regularly. Girls with generalized anxiety disorder or separation anxiety were more likely to engage in smoking, drinking, or illicit drug use (Wu et al., 2010). Research seems to suggest that early signs of anxiety are stable indicators of continued problems.

In examining effectiveness of psychosocial treatments for childhood anxiety, Silverman et al. (2008) found that treatment effects ranged between 46 to 79 percent, indicating that approximately 46 to 79 percent of children in the examined studies reduced their diagnostic status for anxiety following treatment. Beneficial effects were found as a result of individual, group, and parent-involved treatments. Most treatments examined were identified as CBT or related to CBT. Follow-up data demonstrated a decrease in approximately 10 percent of the effect size, meaning that treatment gains began to decline with the passage of time (Silverman et al., 2008). CBT is not effective in reducing anxiety diagnoses for 20 to 40 percent of children who successfully complete treatment (Silverman et al., 2008; Rey et al., 2011). Compton et al. (2014) reported higher nonresponse rates between 40 to 50 percent. In examining mediators of treatment for childhood anxiety, Compton et al. (2014) concluded that severity and frequency of symptoms, greater caregiver stress, and a principal diagnosis of social phobia were predictive of resistance to treatment. Evaluation of treatment for childhood anxiety disorders indicates the need for treatment interventions that target the appropriate developmental level of children, contextual environment of those children struggling with anxiety, and the severity of overall functioning.

Diagnostic Challenges

Fear, distress, worry, and anxiety are normal responses to certain situations for most children. It is widely known that children exhibit fears throughout their development, such as anxiety related to separation from a parent within the first year of life, fears of monsters when they reach toddler age, and later fears regarding social situations as adolescents. Because fear is a normal part of child development, diagnosing an anxiety disorder may be challenging. The clinician is assigned the task of determining the proportional nature of the anxiety response to the stimulus, as well as the level of impairment associated with the anxiety response. The inability of a child to operate functionally in home and/or school settings is an essential feature necessary for diagnosis.

The *DSM-5* emphasizes the importance of understanding cultural context and individual differences for effective diagnosis and treatment. Culture, gender, race, and ethnicity of a child may affect the clinician's perspective on the diagnosis of an anxiety disorder. Typically, girls report more fears than boys, which may be a result of gender socialization from which girls learn that it is okay to express fear (Meltzer, Vostanis, Dogra, Doos, Ford, & Goodman, 2008). Because of environmental threats, girls may be taught more explicitly about possible dangers, creating a higher level of sensitivity. Meltzer et al. (2008) found that children from different ethnic groups manifest and express fear differently. Costello et al. (2011) reported meta-analysis findings on race, ethnic, and cultural differences in rates of anxiety disorders. Studies reporting the highest rates of any anxiety disorder were from Holland, Mexico, and the United States. Some studies have shown a lower prevalence rate of anxiety disorders among African American, Asian American, and Native American children when compared with White children, whereas other studies have shown no differences among these ethnicities (Costello et al., 2011; Lewis-Fernández et al., 2010).

Cultural values including religious beliefs also influence the types of fears experienced by children (Costello et al., 2011; Meltzer et al., 2008). Cultures that value conformity and compliance have been linked to higher levels of fear in children. Families that operate with heavy dependence and intrusiveness may contribute to more fears in children. To inform clinicians regarding cultural variance among anxiety disorders, the *DSM-5* provided specific culture-related diagnostic issues for the following disorders: separation anxiety, selective mutism, specific phobia, social anxiety, panic disorder, panic attack specifier, and generalized anxiety disorder. Because there is a lack of data regarding racial, cultural, and ethnic differences, the clinician is encouraged to utilize the Cultural Formulation Interview (CFI) included in the *DSM-5* as one tool to understand the impact of culture on the child's presentation of symptoms prior to assigning a diagnosis.

An additional challenge to the diagnosis of anxiety disorders is the lack of clear delineations between diagnoses (Fonseca & Perrin, 2011). In children and adolescents, the phenomenon of comorbidity is "the rule rather than the exception" (Fonseca & Perrin, 2011, p. 32). Although the *DSM-5* provides guidelines related to differential diagnosis, there is still a considerable symptom overlap between separation anxiety disorder, social anxiety disorder, panic disorder, and generalized anxiety disorder and depressive and bipolar-related disorders with anxious distress. The new *DSM-5* descriptive specifier, *with anxious distress*, communicates the presence of at least two of five anxiety symptoms (i.e., feeling tense, unusually restless, difficulty concentrating, fear that something awful will happen, and fear of loss of control) that are uniquely expressed during the depressive or manic episode and remit when the episode ends (APA, 2013). However, some research supports the distinct categories of separation anxiety disorder, social anxiety disorder, panic disorder, and generalized anxiety disorder (Langer, Wood, Bergman, & Piacentini, 2010). Hence, the clinician is often confronted with the daunting task of deciding what disorder best accounts for the demonstrated anxiety symptoms.

Summary

Anxiety disorders are prevalent in children and adolescents who may exhibit various levels of anxiety and associated symptoms that are in response to specific stimuli. Because of the comorbidity of anxiety disorders with depressive and bipolar-related disorders, and the overlap between many of the anxiety disorders, it is important to carefully consider clients' concerns and experiences when diagnosing. In addition, the use of valid and reliable assessments, as well as *DSM-5* cross cutting symptom measures (http://www.psychiatry.org/practice/dsm/dsm5/online-assessment-measures), is recommended for diagnostic precision. Understanding the trajectory of anxiety in developing children and adolescents is essential to discerning normal developmental concerns from diagnosable disorders. Counselors are given the responsibility to determine the level of impairment that the anxiety symptoms provide for children, which in turn should foster greater caution among clinicians as they are assessing and diagnosing children. After formulation of an anxiety disorder in children and adolescents, deciding upon developmentally appropriate and symptom-targeted treatments is imperative so as to mitigate the functional impairment they experience in family, school, social, and work settings.

References

Achenbach, T., & Rescorla, L. (2001). *Manual for the ASEBA school-age forms and profiles*. Burlington: University of Vermont Research Center for Children, Youth, & Families.

Alfano, C. A. (2012). Are children with "pure" generalized anxiety disorder impaired? A comparison with comorbid and healthy children. *Journal of Clinical Child & Adolescent Psychology, 41*(6), 739–745. doi:10.1080/15374416.2012.715367

American Psychiatric Association. (1994). *Diagnostic and statistical manual of mental disorders* (4th ed.). Washington, DC: American Psychiatric Association.

American Psychiatric Association. (2013). *Diagnostic and statistical manual of mental disorders* (5th ed.). Arlington, VA: American Psychiatric Publishing.

Anticich, S. A., Barrett, P. M., Gillies, R., & Silverman, W. (2012). Recent advances in intervention for early childhood anxiety. *Australian Journal of Guidance and Counselling, 22*(2), 157–172.

Bokhorst, C., & Westenberg, P. (2011). Social anxiety disorder: A normal fear gone awry? In W. K. Silverman and A. P. Field (Eds.), *Anxiety disorders in children and adolescents* (2nd ed., pp. 90–102). New York, NY: Cambridge University Press.

Bratton, S., Ray, D., Rhine, T., & Jones, L. (2005). The efficacy of play therapy with children: A meta-analytic review of treatment outcomes. *Professional Psychology: Research and Practice, 36*(4), 376–390.

Brendel, K., & Maynard, B. (2014). Child-parent interventions for childhood anxiety disorders: A systematic review and meta-analysis. *Research on Social Work Practice, 24*, 287–295. doi:10.1177/1049731513503713

Broeren, S., Muris, P., Diamantopoulou, S., & Baker, J. (2013). The course of childhood anxiety symptoms: Developmental trajectories and child-related factors in normal children. *Journal of Abnormal Child Psychology, 41*, 81–95. doi:10.1007/s10802-012-9669-9

Cartwright-Hatton, S., Reynolds, S., & Wilson, C. (2011). Adult models of anxiety and their application to children and adolescents. In W. K. Silverman and A. P. Field (Eds.), *Anxiety disorders in children and adolescents* (2nd ed., pp. 129–158). New York, NY: Cambridge University Press.

Carthy, T., Horesh, N., Apter, A., & Gross, J. (2010). Patterns of emotional reactivity and regulation in children with anxiety disorders. *Journal of Psychopathology & Behavioral Assessment, 32*, 23–36. doi:10.1007/s10862-009-9167-8

Chorpita, B. F., Yim, L., Moffitt, C., Umemoto, L. A., & Francis, S. E. (2000). Assessment of symptoms of DSM-IV anxiety and depression in children: A revised child anxiety and depression scale. *Behaviour Research and Therapy, 38*, 835–855.

Compton, S. N., March, J. S., Brent, D., Albano, A. M., Weersing, V. R., & Curry, J. (2004). Cognitive-behavioral psychotherapy for anxiety and depressive disorders in children and adolescents: An evidence-based medicine review. *Journal of the American Academy of Child & Adolescent Psychiatry, 43*(6), 930–950.

Compton, S. N., Peris, T. S., Almirall, D., Birmaher, B., Sherrill, J., Kendall, P. C., … Albano, A. M. (2014). Predictors and moderators of treatment response in childhood anxiety disorders: Results from the CAMS trial. *Journal of Consulting and Clinical Psychology, 82*(2), 212–224. doi:10.1037/a0035458

Costas, M., & Landreth, G. (1999). Filial therapy with nonoffending parents of children who have been sexually abused. *International Journal of Play Therapy, 8*(1), 43–66.

Costello, E. J., Egger, H., Copeland, W., Erkanli, A., & Angold, A. (2011). The developmental epidemiology of anxiety disorders: Phenomenology, prevalence, and comorbidity. In W. K. Silverman and A. P. Field (Eds.), *Anxiety disorders in children and adolescents* (2nd ed., pp. 56–75). New York, NY: Cambridge University Press.

Dubi, K., & Schneider, S. (2009). The Picture Anxiety Test (PAT): A new pictorial assessment of anxiety symptoms in young children. *Journal of Anxiety Disorders, 23*, 1148–1157.

Freeman, J. B., Garcia, A. M., Miller, L. M., Dow, S. P., & Leonard, H. L. (2004). Selective mutism. In T. L. Morris & J. S. March (Eds.), *Anxiety disorders in children and adolescents* (2nd ed., pp. 280–301). New York, NY: The Guilford Press.

Fonseca, A. C., & Perrin, S. (2011). The clinical phenomenology and classification of child and adolescent anxiety. In W. K. Silverman and A. P. Field (Eds.), *Anxiety disorders in children and adolescents* (2nd ed., pp. 25–55). New York, NY: Cambridge University Press.

Garza, Y., & Bratton, S. (2005). School-based child-centered play therapy with Hispanic children: Outcomes and cultural considerations. *International Journal of Play Therapy, 14*(1), 51–79.

Gazelle, H., Workman, J., & Allan, W. (2010). Anxious solitude and clinical disorder in middle childhood: Bridging developmental and clinical approaches to childhood social anxiety. *Journal of Abnormal Child Psychology, 38,* 1–17. doi:10.1007/s10802-009-9343-z

Grave, J., & Blissett, J. (2004). Is cognitive behavior therapy developmentally appropriate for young children: A critical review of the evidence. *Clinical Psychology Review, 24,* 399–420.

Huberty, T. (2012). *Anxiety and depression in children and adolescents: Assessment, intervention, and prevention.* New York, NY: Springer.

Hung, S., Spencer, M., & Dronamraju, R. (2012). Selective mutism: Practice and intervention strategies for children. *Children & Schools, 34,* 222–230. doi:10.1093/cs/cds006

In-Albon, T., & Schneider, S. (2007). Psychotherapy of childhood anxiety disorders: A meta-analysis. *Psychotherapy and Psychosomatics, 76,* 15–24.

Kendall, P. C., Furr, J. M., & Podell, J. L. (2010). Child-focused treatment of anxiety. In J. R. Weisz & A. E. Kazdin (Eds.), *Evidence-based psychotherapies for children and adolescents* (2nd ed., pp. 45–60). New York, NY: Guilford Press.

Kossowsky, J., Pfaltz, M., Schneider, S., Taeymans, J., Locher, C., & Gaab, J. (2013). The separation anxiety hypothesis of panic disorder revisited: A meta-analysis. *American Journal of Psychiatry, 170*(7), 768–781.

Kossowsky, J., Wilhelm, F. H., Roth, W. T., & Schneider, S. (2012). Separation anxiety disorder in children: Disorder specific responses to experimental separation from the mother. *Journal of Child Psychology and Psychiatry, 53*(2), 178–187. doi:10.1111/j.1469-7610.2011.02465.x

Landreth, G. (2012). *Play therapy: The art of the relationship* (3rd ed.). New York, NY: Routledge.

Landreth, G., & Bratton, S. (2006). *Child parent relationship therapy (CPRT): A 10-session filial therapy model.* New York, NY: Routledge.

Langer, D., Wood, J., Bergman, R., & Piacentini, J. (2010). A multi-trait-multimethod analysis of the construct validity of child anxiety disorders in a clinical sample. *Child Psychiatry & Human Development, 41,* 549–561. doi:10.1007/s10578-010-0187-0

Levin-Decanini, T., Connolly, S. D., Simpson, D., Suarez, L., & Jacob, S. (2013). Comparison of behavioral profiles for anxiety-related comorbidities including ADHD and selective mutism in children. *Depression and Anxiety, 30*(9), 857–864. doi:10.1002/da.22094

Lewis-Fernández, R., Hinton, D. E., Laria, A. J., Patterson, E. H., Hofmann, S. G., Craske, M. G., ...

Liao, B. (2010). Culture and the anxiety disorders: Recommendations for the DSM-V. *Depression and Anxiety, 27*(2), 212–229.

March, J. S., Parker, J. D. A., Sullivan, K., Stallings, P., & Conners, C. K. (1997). The Multidimensional Anxiety Scale for Children (MASC): Factor, structure, reliability, and validity. *Journal of the American Academy of Child & Adolescent Psychiatry, 36*(4), 554–565.

Marmorstein, N., White, H., Loeber, R., & Stouthamer-Loeber, M. (2010). Anxiety as a predictor of age at first use of substances and progression to substance use problems among boys. *Journal of Abnormal Psychology, 38,* 211–224. doi:10.1007/s10802-009-9360-y

Mathyssek, C., Olino, T., Verhulst, F., van Oort, F. (2012). Childhood internalizing and externalizing problems predict the onset of clinical panic attacks over adolescence: The TRAILS study. *PLoS One, 7,* 1–6. doi:10.1371/journal.pone.0051564

Meltzer, H., Vostanis, P., Dogra, N., Doos, L., Ford, T., & Goodman, R. (2008). Children's specific fears. *Child: Care, Health and Development, 35,* 781–789. doi:10.1111/j.1365-2214.2008.00908.x

Mohr, C., & Schneider, S. (2013). Anxiety disorders. *European Child and Adolescent Psychiatry, 22*(Suppl 1), S17–S22.

Muris, P., Huijding, J., Mayer, B., Leemreis, W., Passchier, S., & Bouwmeester, S. (2009). The effects of verbal disgust- and threat-related information about novel animals on disgust and fear beliefs and avoidance in children. *Journal of Clinical Child & Adolescent Psychology, 38*(4), 551–563. doi:10.1080/15374410902976379

Mychailyszyn, M., Mendez, J., & Kendall, P. (2010). School functioning in youth with and without anxiety disorders: Comparisons by diagnosis and comorbidity. *School Psychology Review, 39,* 106–121.

Noel, V., & Francis, S. (2011). A meta-analytic review of the role of child anxiety sensitivity in child anxiety. *Journal of Abnormal Child Psychology, 39,* 721–733.

Oerbeck, B., Stein, M., Wentzel-Larsen, T., Langsrud, O., & Kristensen, H. (2014). A randomized controlled trial of a home and school-based intervention for selective mutism – defocused communication and behavioral techniques. *Child and Adolescent Mental Health, 19,* 192–198. doi:10.1111/camh.12045

Ollendick, T. H., Birmaher, B., & Mattis, S. G. (2004). Panic disorder. In T. L. Morris & J. S. March (Eds.), *Anxiety disorders in children and adolescents* (2nd ed., pp. 189–211). New York, NY: Guilford Press.

Ollendick, T., Ost, L., Reuterskiold, L., Costa, N., Cederlund, R., Sirbu, C., Davis, T., & Jarrett, M. (2009). One-session treatment of specific phobias in youth: A randomized clinical trial in the United States and Sweden. *Journal of Consulting and Clinical Psychology, 77,* 504–516. doi:10.1037/a0015158

Pao, M., & Bosk, A. (2011). Anxiety in medically ill children/adolescents. *Depression and Anxiety, 28*(1), 40–49. doi:10.1002/da.20727

Paul, K. M., & Barrett, P. M. (2010). Interventions for anxiety disorders in children using group cognitive-behavioral therapy with family involvement. In J. R. Weisz & A. E. Kazdin (Eds.), *Evidence-based psychotherapies for children and adolescents* (2nd ed., pp. 61–79). New York, NY: Guilford Press.

Ray, D. (2011). *Advanced play therapy: Essential conditions, knowledge, and skills for child practice.* New York, NY: Routledge.

Reich, W. (2000). Diagnostic Interview for Children and Adolescents (DICA). *Journal of the American Academy of Child & Adolescent Psychiatry, 39*(1), 59–66.

Rey, Y., Marin, C. E., & Silverman, W. K. (2011). Failures in cognitive-behavior therapy for children. *Journal of Clinical Psychology, 67*(11), 1140–1150.

Reyes, C. J., & Asbrand, J. P. (2005). A longitudinal study assessing trauma symptoms in sexually abused children engaged in play therapy. *International Journal of Play Therapy, 14*(2), 25–27.

Reynolds, C. R., & Kamphaus, R. W. (2004). BASC-2: *Behavior assessment system for children, second edition manual.* Circle Pines, MN: American Guidance Service.

Reynolds, C. R., & Richmond, B. O. (2008). *Revised Children's Manifest Anxiety Scale, second edition, manual.* Los Angeles, CA: Western Psychological Services.

Santucci, L. C., & Ehrenreich-May, J. (2013). A randomized controlled trial of the child anxiety multi-day program (CAMP) for separation anxiety disorder. *Child Psychiatry and Human Development, 44*(3), 439–451. doi:10.1007/s10578-012-0338-6

Scaini, S. M., Ogliari, A., Eley, T. C., Zavos, H. M. S., & Battaglia, M. (2012). Genetic and environmental contributions to separation anxiety: A meta-analytic approach to twin data. *Depression and Anxiety, 29*(9), 754–761. doi:10.1002/da.21941

Schniering, C. A., Hudson, J. L., & Rapee, R. M. (2000). Issues in the diagnosis and assessment of anxiety disorders in children and adolescents. *Clinical Psychology Review, 20*(4), 453–478.

Shen, Y. (2002). Short-term group play therapy with Chinese earthquake victims: Effects on anxiety, depression, and adjustment. *International Journal of Play Therapy, 11*(1), 43–63.

Silverman, W. K., & Dick-Niederhauser, A. (2004). Separation anxiety disorder. In T. L. Morris & J. S. March (Eds.), *Anxiety disorders in children and adolescents* (2nd ed., pp. 164–188). New York, NY: Guilford Press.

Silverman, W. K., Kurtines, W. M., Ginsburg, G. S., Weems, C. F., Rabian, B., & Serafini, L. T. (1999). Contingency management, self-control, and education support in the treatment of childhood phobic disorders: A randomized clinical trial. *Journal of Consulting and Clinical Psychology, 67*(5), 675–687.

Silverman, W. K., La Greca, A. M., & Wasserstein, S. (1995). What do children worry about? Worries and their relation to anxiety. *Child Development, 66*, 671–68.

Silverman, W. K., Pina, A. A., & Viswesvaran, C. (2008). Evidence-based psychosocial treatments for phobic and anxiety disorders in children and adolescents. *Journal of Clinical Child and Adolescent Psychology, 37*(1), 105–130. doi:10.1080/15374410701817907

Silverman, W. K., Saavedra, L. M., & Pina, A. A. (2001). Test-retest reliability of anxiety symptoms and diagnoses using the Anxiety Disorders Interview Schedule for DSM-IV: Child and Parent Versions (ADIS for DSM-IV: C/P). *Journal of the American Academy of Child & Adolescent Psychiatry, 40*(8), 937–944.

Simon, N. M., Herlands, N. N., Marks, E. H., Mancini, C., Letamendi, A., Li, Z., ... Stein, M. B. (2009). Childhood maltreatment linked to greater symptom severity and poorer quality of life and function in social anxiety disorder. *Depression and Anxiety, 26*(11), 1027–1032. doi:10.1002/da.20604

Smith, N., & Landreth, G. (2003). Intensive filial therapy with child witnesses of domestic violence: A comparison with individual and sibling group play therapy. *International Journal of Play Therapy, 12*(1), 67–88.

Spielberger, C. D. (1973). *Manual for the State-Trait Anxiety Inventory for Children.* Palo Alto, CA: Consulting Psychologists Press.

Stulmaker, H. L., & Ray, D. C. (2015). *Child-centered play therapy with young children who are anxious: A controlled trial.* Manuscript submitted for publication.

Tew, K., Landreth, G., Joiner, K. D., & Solt, M. D. (2002). Filial therapy with parents of chronically ill children. *International Journal of Play Therapy, 11*(1), 79–100.

Van Steensel, F., Bogels, S., & Perrin, S. (2011). Anxiety disorders in children and adolescents with autistic spectrum disorders: A meta-analysis. *Clinical Child & Family Psychology Review, 14*, 302–317. doi:10.1007/s10567-011-0097-0

Whitmore, M. J., Kim-Spoon, J., & Ollendick, T. H. (2014). Generalized anxiety disorder and social anxiety disorder in youth: Are they distinguishable? *Child Psychiatry and Human Development, 45*(4), 456–463. doi:10.1007/s10578-013-0415-5

Wu, P., Goodwin, R. D., Fuller, C., Liu, X., Comer, J. S., Cohen, P., & Hoven, C. W. (2010). The relationship between anxiety disorders and substance use among adolescents in the community: Specificity and gender differences. *Journal of Youth & Adolescence, 39*(2), 177–188. doi:10.1007/s10964-008-9385-5

Chapter 11

Obsessive-Compulsive and Related Disorders

NICOLE R. HILL, TOREY PORTRIE-BETHKE, BROOKS BASTIAN HANKS, AND HOLLY H. WAGNER

Introduction

Obsessive-compulsive (OC) and related disorders, such as body dysmorphic disorder, trichotillomania (hair-pulling disorder), and excoriation (skin-picking) disorder, can affect the manner in which youth function at home, in school, and in the community, with potentially severe and chronic manifestations across their lifespans (Lewin et al., 2014). Further, clients with OC and related diagnoses tend to have high rates of comorbidity with other mental health disorders, including anxiety disorders, autism spectrum disorder, depressive disorders, attention-deficit/hyperactivity disorder, bipolar-related disorders, substance-use disorders, intellectual disability, and conduct/oppositional defiant disorders (Rapoport & Inoff-Germain, 2000), thereby complicating the diagnostic, clinical, and treatment decision-making process. Some researchers have found that 80 percent of youth diagnosed with OC disorder fulfill the requirements for other psychiatric diagnoses (Langley et al., 2010).

Prevalence of OCD in the pediatric population is typically reported between 1 and 4 percent, with the average age of onset for youth ranging from ages 7.5 to 12.5 (Boileau, 2011). Despite reports of high prevalence when juxtaposed to other psychiatric disorders, Sheppard et al. (2010) cautioned that the high incidence of comorbidity and misdiagnoses among children with OC disorder may lead to ongoing underestimates of the prevalence of pediatric OCD. Given the possibly debilitating impact that OC disorder symptomology can have on children and adolescents, it is imperative that counselors are well informed about diagnostic criteria and effective treatment strategies for youth who are diagnosed with OC and related disorders.

There are a multitude of potential contributors to the etiology of OC and related disorders, including genetic, neurobiological, social, personality, and psychological influences (Dembo, 2014). Family-based risk is established with early-onset OC and related disorders. Coskun, Zoroglu, and Ozturk (2012) explored family history rates with 25 preschoolers diagnosed with OC and related disorders. The researchers found that 68 percent of the preschoolers in the sample had at least one parent diagnosed with OC and related disorders. In addition to the genetic etiology, there are distinct neurobiological features associated with OC and related disorders. Current research focuses on the striatum, orbitofrontal context, and anterior cingulate cortex structures of the brain (American Psychiatric Association [APA], 2013; Millad & Rauch, 2012).

Further, there are data related to diagnosis and treatment of OC and related disorders to support the impact of children infected with group A beta-hemolytic streptococci (GABHS) on the development and intensification of OC and related disorder symptomatology (Martino, Defazio, & Giovanni, 2009). Youth impacted by this infection are classified in the subgroup termed PANDAS, which represents pediatric autoimmune neuropsychiatric disorders associated with streptococcal infections (Shulman, 2009). In addition to a correlation of GABHS with the onset or escalation of OC and related disorder symptoms, other clinical features that define this group include onset between age 3 and puberty and association with neurological impacts during symptom escalation.

Additional risk factors associated with the development of OC and related disorders in children and adolescents include a history of sexual or physical abuse, increased attribution of events to the internal self, and increased negative emotional expressiveness (Grisham et al., 2011). The multidimensional etiological context of OC and related disorders is coupled with a complex and challenging set of effects that OC and related disorders have on children and adolescents. Moreover, the impact of OC and related disorders on children and adolescents is multifaceted and multisystemic.

In 2012, the American Academy of Child and Adolescent Psychiatry (AACAP) released OC and related disorders treatment guidelines that identified negative outcomes for youth with such disorders, namely peer challenges for 50 to 100 percent and isolation for 45 percent of those identified. Pervasive preoccupations and compulsions can affect a child's ability to concentrate, attend to others, and complete tasks. The extensive use of mental energy required to manage OC and related disorder symptoms is correlated with increased exhaustion and psychosomatic symptoms. Further, engaging in compulsions can sometimes be observed by peers and become a source for being bullied. Increased suicidality is another risk factor of youth diagnosed with OC and related disorders (APA, 2013). The impact of OC and related disorders tends to emerge across contexts, including the family, school, community, and other systems. Exploring the degree and pervasiveness of symptoms is an essential function of counselors in the assessment, diagnosis, and treatment of youth with OC and related disorders.

This chapter describes OC and related disorders in pediatric populations, provides the *Diagnostic and Statistical Manual of Mental Disorders, Fifth Edition* (*DSM-5*), diagnostic criteria and differential diagnosis considerations, examines assessment strategies, and discusses diagnostic challenges. The chapter will also explore treatment strategies and their potential effectiveness with children and adolescents diagnosed with OC and related disorders. The developmental experience of children and adolescents will be highlighted to ensure counselors are engaged in developmentally appropriate diagnosis and responsive treatment.

Description of the Disorder

OBSESSIVE-COMPULSIVE DISORDER (OCD)

Children and adolescents with OCD may exhibit obsessions, compulsions, or both. More commonly, they will experience both criteria (APA, 2013). Obsessions are unwanted recurrent and persistent thoughts, urges, or images that continually intrude into consciousness, causing anxiety and stress. Common obsessions among children may include intrusive thoughts, urges, or images regarding contamination, orderliness, grooming, and disasters within the family, such as illness or death, as well as mental preoccupation with doubt, danger, sex, religion, violence, or physical symptomology (APA, 2013; Menon, 2013). Obsessions have developmental nuances when compared to adult reports of obsessions. For example, children and adolescents tend to manifest higher levels of harm-focused anxious thoughts compared to adults (Kalra & Swedo, 2009). Children may try to ignore, suppress, or neutralize the unwanted obsessive thoughts, urges, or images, but they inevitably return.

Within OCD, obsessions are coupled with compulsions. Compulsions are behaviors or mental acts the child is compelled to perform repeatedly, in a stereotypical fashion, although he or she may have no desire to do so. Common compulsions in children may include checking, washing, ordering, touching, counting, and repeating (Rapoport & Inoff-Germain, 2000), with cleaning being the most prevalent (Boileau, 2011). The specifics of the compulsion may be different with pediatric populations compared to adult populations in that the content may be more developmentally situated. Compulsions seem to ameliorate the anxiety and stress caused by the obsessions. Juxtaposed to obsessions, compulsions within pediatric populations are much more identifiable because they can be observed. Given that children and adolescents may not have the level of insight or cognitive complexity to recognize the irrationality of the accompanying thought, there is a decreased ability for them, and thus parents and counselors, to identify the obsessions. The thoughts, urges, or images and the associated behaviors or mental acts characteristic in OCD significantly restrict normal psychosocial functioning (Storch et al., 2007a) and lead to developmental, academic, and relational issues, independent living concerns, and family dysfunction (APA, 2013; Farrell et al., 2010). For example, children's development may be adversely affected if they cannot complete school tasks and assignments, avoid interacting with peers and developing social connections, refuse to go to the doctor or other health provider, struggle with leaving home and becoming independent adults, and isolate themselves from important familial and relational supports (APA, 2013). If a young child is obsessed with the idea of symmetry, tasks may not be completed in a timely fashion because something is "just off" or "not quite right." These consequences have developmental significance in that children and adolescents experiencing obsessions and compulsions may not meet expected developmental benchmarks. To gain experience in identifying obsessions and compulsions, please review the case study of Amaya, which is described in Sidebar 11.1.

SIDEBAR 11.1: CASE OF AMAYA—IDENTIFYING OBSESSIONS AND COMPULSIONS

Amaya is a 5-year-old girl who attends preschool. Her parents have brought her into counseling because they have noticed some odd behaviors. Amaya's parents have observed that when someone unfamiliar to Amaya comes to the home and Amaya sees the stranger, she immediately gathers up all of her dolls and starts lining the dolls into a single row in the front entryway. When the parents have tried to move the dolls out of the way before she has them all in a line, she will scream and tantrum for up to an hour. Her parents also report noticing that Amaya will do things to make sure that her body experiences sensations evenly. For example, when Amaya's mother kisses Amaya's right cheek, Amaya will turn her left cheek for her mother to kiss. Amaya will also sit on the edge of the bathtub and place her feet into the bathtub at the same time instead of one foot at a time. Amaya's parents describe Amaya as "quirky" and want you to help her with these odd behaviors before she starts kindergarten in the fall.

Questions for Reflection

1. As you consider the details of Amaya's case, what emerge as potential compulsions that she is exhibiting? What are potential obsessions that could be affecting Amaya's behaviors? How are they potentially affecting each other?

2. Given Amaya's behaviors, what are potential things that her parents could be doing to accommodate her actions? How might these contribute to Amaya's experiences?

3. What are potential ways that Amaya's behaviors could affect her at home, in school, and in the community?

The *DSM-5* specifiers include various levels of insight related to rationality of OCD symptomology (APA, 2013). Rapoport and Inoff-Germain (2000) differentiated OCD in children and adults by the absence of insight related to symptoms. Therefore, children may not understand that their obsessions are irrational. Furthermore, children may not be aware that their compulsions are aimed at decreasing their anxiety and stress (APA, 2013). Both insight-related differentiations may vary according to developmental stage and will influence courses of treatment in children and adolescents. Attending to the developmental level of the child and adolescent is critical for counselors to diagnose and treat the disorder accurately (APA, 2013). Evaluating cognitive complexity is necessary to contextualize the child's meaning-making of the obsession, as well as to gauge potential responsiveness to cognitively focused treatment interventions (Rapoport & Inoff-Germain, 2000). At times, it is developmentally appropriate for children and adolescents to experience normative fixations and compulsions. To differentiate normative thoughts and enactments from clinical symptomatology, counselors need to consider the developmental appropriateness of anxious thoughts, ritualized behaviors, or mental acts in the family and social context, as well as the degree of persistence, the level of negative impact on functioning, and the intensity of thoughts, behaviors, or mental acts (APA, 2013).

RELATED DISORDERS

Disorders related to OCD (because of similar neurobiological substrates, such as the basal ganglia, the frontal gyrus, and symptom manifestation) include body dysmorphic disorder, hoarding disorder, trichotillomania (hair-pulling disorder), excoriation (skin-picking) disorder, substance or medication induced OC and related disorder, OC and related disorder due to medical condition, and other specified and unspecified OC and related disorders (APA, 2013).

Body Dysmorphic Disorder

OCD co-occurs with 12 percent of people diagnosed with body dysmorphic disorder (BDD; Seligman & Reichenberg, 2007; Butcher, Mineka, & Hooley, 2006). This syndrome is associated with an intrusive, unwanted, and time-consuming preoccupation of a perceived defect or flaw in physical appearance that others do not perceive (APA, 2013). The individual's actions may result in excessive mental acts (e.g., comparing his or her appearance with that of others) or repetitive behaviors that are difficult to resist or control, such as mirror checking, dressing in concealing garments, skin picking, excessive grooming, camouflaging the defect, avoiding social situations, or improving appearance through cosmetic surgery (Dingemans, van Rood, de Groot, & van Furth, 2012). These perceptions of self are harmful and result in restriction of activity, inaccurate self-efficacy, and loss of pleasure because of the perceived abnormalities or flaws in their physical appearance (APA, 2013).

The median age of onset for BDD is 15 years, and the most common subclinical age of onset is 12 to 13 years (APA, 2013). Given the developmental perceptions of adolescents, mental health professionals can explore adolescents' high levels of anxiety, feelings of shame for their appearance, excessive disapproval of how they look, and belief that other people take special notice of their appearance (APA, 2013). However, adolescents with BDD are less likely to explore and address their symptoms and beliefs with others due to feeling ashamed and embarrassed (APA, 2013). Twenty percent of youth with this disorder are reported to drop out of school. Mental health professionals providing counseling services to youth with BDD need to be mindful of the adolescent's increased risk for suicide and that individuals with the onset before 18 years of age are more likely to attempt suicide.

Hoarding Disorder

Characteristics of hoarding disorder include: excessive acquisition of and persistent difficulty discarding or parting (including throwing away, selling, giving away, or recycling) with possessions (including animals), congested and cluttered active living areas in which their intended use becomes substantially compromised, and marked functional impairment in familial, social, or occupational areas. The occurrence of children with OCD and hoarding is 25 to 30 percent (Mataix-Cols & Pertusa, 2012). Although the majority of research regarding hoarding disorder has focused on adulthood manifestations and treatment of the disorder, Storch et al. (2011b) found notable variations between hoarding disorder in children and adults. These differences presented through (a) the clutter being limited to a smaller area (child's room) and (b) the content of hoarded materials being less varied because of the limited resources of the child. Furthermore, fewer assessment and treatment resources were available due to the dearth of research regarding hoarding in children. Items and materials commonly hoarded by children include books, bags, clothing, school-related items, toys, and food (Storch et al., 2011b).

Trichotillomania (Hair-Pulling Disorder)

Trichotillomania (hair-pulling disorder) is characterized by the recurrent pulling out of one's own hair, repeated attempts to reduce or stop hair pulling, and significant impairment and distress due to the hair pulling behavior (APA, 2013). The location of the hair pulling is most commonly the scalp, eyebrows, and eyelashes. Hair pulling from other regions of the body, such as the pubic, peri-rectal, axillary, and facial regions, occurs less frequently. The estimated prevalence of trichotillomania is between 1 percent and 2 percent of the public (APA, 2013). In terms of gender differences, males and females are equally represented within children, but the prevalence of trichotillomania (hair-pulling disorder) increases in females who are older (Panza, Pittenger, & Bloch, 2013). The age of onset for this disorder is typically early adolescence. (Duke et al., 2010). The etiology of trichotillomania has been associated with genetic, physiologic, and environmental factors, such as trauma (Snorrason, Belleau, & Woods, 2012).

Excoriation (Skin-Picking Disorder)

Excoriation (skin-picking disorder) is characterized by recurrent skin picking resulting in skin lesions, repeated attempts to reduce or stop skin picking, and experiencing significant impairment and distress due to the skin picking behavior (APA, 2013). Typically, individuals will pick at skin on their face, arms, and hands, but other areas of the body may occur as well. Often the individual will use his or her fingernails to pick at the skin, but some may use tweezers, pins, or other tools to pick at the skin as well. The age of onset of this disorder is most commonly connected to the developmental life stage of puberty (APA, 2013). The etiology of excoriation is similar to that of trichotillomania (hair-pulling disorder), with the association of genetic, physiologic, and environmental factors, such as trauma, resulting in a high level of co-occurrence (Snorrason et al., 2012).

Substance/Medication-Induced OC and Related Disorder and OC and Related Disorder Due to Another Medical Condition

Both substance/medication-induced OC and related disorder and OC and related disorder due to medical condition manifest similar symptoms as detailed in OC and related disorders, yet those symptoms are attributed to a substance, medication, or medical condition. Commensurate with etiological criteria, clients diagnosed with substance or medication induced OC and related disorder would manifest a significant decrease in symptomatology after the discontinuation of the medication or substance as expected on the half-life of the particular substance.

Other Specified OC and Related Disorder and Unspecified OC and Related Disorder

This diagnosis encompasses clients experiencing OC and related symptoms that generate clinical distress across multiple domains, yet their symptoms are not meeting the full criteria of other diagnostic categories (APA, 2013). The classification of Other Specified OC and Related Disorder provides a counselor with the ability to articulate the specific feature of the pediatric client's symptomatology and how it does not meet other categories. The specification component by the counselor is what differentiates it from the unspecified OC and related disorder diagnosis. In the context of unspecified OC and related disorder, counselors make a decision not to articulate the manner in which symptoms do not meet the full diagnostic criteria of OCD and related disorders.

DSM-5 Criteria

Within the *DSM-5*, OCD is classified as a diagnostic category distinct from anxiety disorders, thereby privileging the recognition that certain subpopulations, especially children and adolescents, evidence higher levels of comorbidity with development-focused disorders, rather than anxiety disorders (Thomsen, 2013). There are some noteworthy changes

TABLE 11.1   OCD Diagnostic Criteria Differences between the *DSM-IV-TR* and the *DSM*-5

DSM-TR-IV (APA, 2000)	*DSM-5 (APA, 2013)*
1. Language of "thoughts, impulses, or images"	1. Updated to be "thoughts, urges, or images"
Terminology of "impulses" was removed and revised to be "urges"	
2. Language of "intrusive and inappropriate"	2. Revised to be "intrusive and unwanted"
Terminology of "inappropriate" updated to be "unwanted"	
3. Criteria A2, A4, and B stipulated the following: "The thoughts, impulses, or images are not simply excessive worries about real life problems"; "The person recognizes that the obsessional thoughts, impulses, or images are a product of his or her own mind"; and "At some point during the course of the disorder, the person has recognized that the obsessions or compulsions are excessive or unreasonable."	3. Descriptive specifiers for the diagnosis communicate the following: "With good or fair insight," "With poor insight," and "With absent insight/delusional beliefs"

DSM IV-TR Criteria A.2, A.4, and B are removed from the diagnostic criteria and are framed descriptively from mild ("With good or fair insight"), to moderate ("With poor insight"), and to severe ("With absent insight/delusional belief")

moving from the *DSM-IV-TR* to the *DSM-5* in terms of the diagnostic criteria for OCD. Some terminology was updated to more accurately describe client symptoms. For a brief review of differences between the *DSM-IV-TR* and the *DSM-5*, please review Table 11.1.

Although OCD is not classified within the anxiety disorders, anxiety is a common and prominent symptom. Individuals diagnosed with anxiety disorders work hard to avoid or distance themselves from the anxiety-provoking stimuli. Juxtaposed to the anxiety disorders, individuals with OC and related disorders will engage in rituals or repetitive behaviors in response to the anxiety-inducing stimuli. For example, an individual diagnosed with the anxiety disorder agoraphobia avoids leaving his or her home. An individual diagnosed with OCD may be so obsessed with perfectionism that he or she will rewrite a paper multiple times until he or she perceives the paper to be perfect, thus engaging in the anxiety-provoking stimulus. In the first example, the person is avoiding the fear-inducing situation, and in the second example, the person is pursuing the anxiety-inducing situation.

Next in our discussion is a brief summary of the four diagnostic criteria and the two specifiers for OCD.

CRITERIA 1: PRESENCE OF PREOCCUPATION, URGE, OR BOTH EXHIBITED BY THE INDIVIDUAL

A preoccupation is defined as regular thoughts or images that are intrusive and unwanted and cause the child or adolescent to experience marked distress or anxiety. The child or adolescent may be aware of these preoccupations and work to subdue the thought or image by utilizing a different action or thought, such as an impulse. A compulsive urge is defined as repetitive behavior (mental or physical) children or adolescents think they must do to reduce anxiety or distress, or prevent some dreaded event or situation. Some examples of typical compulsive urges may include, but are not limited to, hand washing, checking locks, counting, organizing, and so forth. The purpose of the compulsive urges is to decrease the anxiety or discomfort the child or adolescent is feeling because of the unwanted preoccupation. The child or adolescent may also believe that by engaging in these compulsive urges, they are in some way preventing something bad from happening. However, these behaviors (mental or physical) are not viewed by others as actually preventing something from happening, or they may be done in excess. Young children may not have the insight to be able to express why they are engaging in these behaviors.

CRITERIA 2: FUNCTIONAL IMPACT OF OBSESSIONS AND COMPULSIONS

These mental preoccupations and compulsive urges take significant time during the day (more than one hour) and cause the child or adolescent significant discomfort or anxiety to the point of impairment within daily functioning. Some areas where the child or adolescent may be experiencing impairment may include at school, at home, with friends, and at work. An example of impairment at school may be a child who is not able to concentrate on what the teacher is saying until there is an even number of pencils located on the child's desk, thus resulting in the child missing important instructional information. Impairment at home may consist of a child who must order his/her stuffed animals from smallest to largest before leaving home. A child or adolescent who has been diagnosed with OCD may experience impairment socially because he or she may be so consumed by the obsession of even numbers that he or she is not able to go out with friends unless there is an even number of friends attending.

CRITERIA 3: NONPHYSIOLOGICAL CAUSE

Obsessive thoughts, urges, or images are not a result of substance use or exhibited as a side effect of a medication that the child or adolescent is currently taking.

CRITERIA 4: BEST EXPLAINED BY OCD DIAGNOSIS

The child's or adolescent's thoughts, urges, or images are not better suited for a different mental disorder. Some other mental disorders, such as autism spectrum disorder, eating disorders, body dysmorphic disorder, trichotillomania (hair-pulling disorder), major depressive disorder, and stereotypic movement disorder, may better explain the child's or adolescent's behaviors and should be considered before diagnosing a child with OCD.

SPECIFIERS FOR DIAGNOSIS: INSIGHT AND TIC-RELATED

DSM-5 criteria for OCD offer two descriptive specifiers to assist the counselor in creating a clear description of how the child or adolescent is experiencing the intrusive obsessions and recurrent compulsions. One focus of specification is on how much insight the child or adolescent may have regarding the accuracy or dysfunctionality of his or her preoccupation and urges. There are three potential designations, namely *with good or fair insight* (belief that the distressing outcome of the mental intrusion definitely will not, probably will not, or may or may not occur), *with poor insight* (belief that the distressing outcome of the mental intrusion will probably occur), and *with absent insight/delusional beliefs* (absolute conviction that the distressing outcome of the mental intrusion will occur). This specifier is especially relevant for counselors to consider with pediatric populations, given the limited development in children of the abstract cognitive abilities needed for self-reflection and self-analysis. The second specification indicates a current or past history of a tic disorder (i.e., sudden, rapid, recurrent, nonrhythmic motor movements or vocalizations manifest in Tourette's disorder and persistent [chronic] motor or vocal tic disorder). A comorbid tic disorder is most common in males with onset of OCD in childhood (APA, 2013).

Sidebar 11.2 provides a case study of a young child named Jacob. Please review the details about Jacob's experience, and consider the diagnostic data presented, developmental context, and potential functional impairments.

SIDEBAR 11.2:   CASE OF JACOB—DIAGNOSTIC IMPRESSIONS

Jacob is a 9-year-old boy who is enrolled in fourth grade. He lives with his mom and dad and older sister. Both of Jacob's parents work outside of the home, which leaves Jacob and his 12-year-old sister at home alone after school. Jacob presents with OCD and has no other diagnosis. Jacob presents with two preoccupations, which cause him great distress at home, at school, and socially. Jacob believes that when any food particle touches another food particle, the food then becomes contaminated. For example, if gravy is poured onto his mashed potatoes, it is now contaminated. If any of Jacob's food touches, his urge is to refuse to eat it, or he will go to the bathroom and make himself vomit if he does eat it. After refusing the food or making himself vomit, Jacob will then use bleach wipes to clean the plate until he feels it is sufficiently clean (sometimes this process requires an entire package of bleach wipes). Jacob reports that he has been able to use plates that have built-in divided sections, but he reports feeling more anxiety when using those types of plates.

Jacob also presents with a preoccupation to organize objects and routines into even numbers. For example, he will brush his teeth twice, walk up or down stairs two stairs at a time, keep two pencils on his desk at school, give his parents an even number of kisses on both cheeks, and wear only shirts that have an even number of buttons. If there is an odd number present, Jacob has an overwhelming urge to make it into an even number. For example, if his shirt has an odd number of buttons, he will cut off a button to make the number even.

Jacob's parents report that they do accommodate his urges. They do not prepare food in front of Jacob because it causes him anxiety to see the various ingredients mixed together to make the final food item (for example, a cookie). Jacob's parents will also dish up each item of food on individual plates for Jacob and send him to school with a sack lunch with each item in its own container and lid. They will also send Jacob to school with a new package of bleach wipes every day. They also purchase items in even numbers (four pairs of socks, 12-count pencil packets, and so forth). His parents stated Jacob's preoccupation with even numbers was taken into consideration when deciding to have only two children. Jacob's mother expressed sadness about not having at least one more child, but she reported that she knows having another baby would cause much distress for Jacob in every situation, and she does not want to do that to her son.

1. When considering Criteria 1 for obsessions, what are your initial diagnostic impressions? What preoccupations or urges, if any, are emergent in the case study?

2. Given Jacob's age, in what cognitive developmental level would you expect in him? How would that affect his level of insight into the irrationality of the obsessive thoughts, urges, or images, and his problematic repetitive behaviors?

3. What is the personal functional impact of Jacob's behaviors? What is the functional impact of his behaviors on his family?

Differential Diagnosis

OCD has a complex etiology relating both to environmental and genetic factors (Hanna et al., 2011). Gaining a historical perspective involves exploring the adverse environmental factors leading back to a child's early fetal development experiences that may be associated with an increased risk for developing OC symptoms in adulthood (Moreso et al., 2012). The limited knowledge of the interacting genes and pathophysiological pathways prevents researchers from ascribing specific candidate genes (Nestadt et al., 2010).

Over the past decade, the prevalence rate of OCD in children and adolescents has increased, resulting in more attention being given to OCD in this population than any other anxiety disorder in children (Moreso et al., 2013). Several reasons are reported for the increased rate of diagnosing OCD, namely the frequency and awareness of the disorder and the implication for testing approved new drugs for pediatric OCD (Rapoport & Inoff-Germain, 2000). Moreso and colleagues (2013) address the environmental implications of the disorder to be the leading cause of the prevalence and increase in psychiatric focus and diagnosing of OCD because of its deleterious impact on the child's or adolescent's quality of life in the areas of school, family, and social functioning. The increased prevalence of OCD directly speaks to the importance of understanding the relationships between OCD and other psychiatric conditions that are highly prevalent in children and adolescents (Moreso et al., 2013).

OCD is distinct from 13 other mental disorders (i.e., generalized anxiety disorder, body dysmorphic disorder, hoarding disorder, trichotillomania, excoriation, stereotypic movement disorder, eating disorders, substance-related and addictive disorders, illness anxiety disorder, paraphilic disorders, disruptive, impulse-control, and conduct disorders, major depressive disorder, schizophrenia spectrum and other psychotic disorders, and autism spectrum disorder; APA, 2013). Given that OCD is considered a heterogeneous psychiatric disorder, differentiating between OCD and MDD may pose a challenge (Hanna et al., 2011). MDD and OCD are considered to be the most common comorbid psychiatric disorders, with a prevalence ranging from 40 percent to 80 percent (Hanna et al., 2011). Persistent guilty ruminations characteristic of MDD are differentiated from intrusive or distressing thoughts, urges, or images characteristic of OCD because they are usually mood-congruent and not accompanied by compulsive rituals or routines intended to neutralize the persistent guilty ruminations (APA, 2013).

Other challenging diagnoses to explore with children diagnosed with OCD are anxiety disorders. These are characterized differently than OCD by the child's or adolescent's attempt to reduce the real life fear associated with a given thought, situation, or experience by engaging in active avoidance behaviors of the anxiety-provoking stimulus—rather than the possible strange, irrational, or potentially magical OCD response—along with rituals to reduce the distressing associations (APA, 2013). For illness anxiety disorder, preoccupations are limited to having or acquiring a disease, which is different from the more multidimensional and cumulative obsessions and compulsions characteristic of OCD. Children and adolescents are noted, at times, to have less insight into the irrationality of their OC symptoms. Their decreased understanding of the compulsions or obsessions does not contribute to the exhibition of hallucinations or delusions that a client with psychotic disorders would evidence (Rapoport, 2000). Other tempting compulsive-like behaviors less likely observed in children and adolescents, such as gambling, sexual behavior, and substance use, are considered pleasure seeking (ego-syntonic) and not resulting in the distressing intrusive experiences (ego-dystonic) of a person suffering from OCD (APA, 2013).

OCD symptomatology can be differentiated from the criteria for body dysmorphic disorder because the limited scope of body dysmorphic preoccupations on appearance (APA, 2013). Similarly, a key differentiation between OCD and eating disorders is that obsessions and compulsions are not limited in focus to weight and food, as is true when diagnosing eating disorders. When compared to hoarding disorder, OCD very rarely manifests in compulsions related to acquisitions, and if accumulating possessions is associated with alleviating the anxiety emergent from obsessions, then the acquisition of items does not bring any pleasure, as it would in criteria associated with hoarding disorder. For differentiating between trichotillomania, excoriation, and OCD, the etiology of behaviors needs to be closely considered. For example, if a client is picking at his or her skin, the counselor needs to consider what is motivating that behavior. If the compulsive behavior of hair pulling originates from a preoccupation with symmetry, then OCD would be the more appropriate diagnosis. Both excoriation and trichotillomania do not include obsessions as part of the diagnostic criteria (APA, 2013).

When diagnosing stereotypic movement disorder, counselors need to consider what is driving the motor behaviors. OCD criteria require compulsions to be driven by obsessions, whereas stereotypic movement criteria are more driven by sensory impulses. Counselors can specify tic disorder when diagnosing OCD if both features are present. This occurs in approximately 30 percent of cases, especially with men with early onset of OCD (APA, 2013). Similarly, autism spectrum disorder includes repetitive patterns of behavior, which could parallel the enactment of compulsions in OCD. The difference is that the repetitive behaviors in autism spectrum disorder must be coupled with an essential diagnostic feature of persistent social impairment in communication and interaction. Children may manifest compulsions that negatively affect their social interactions, yet the social impairment present in autism spectrum disorder is pervasive across multiple contexts and is not emergent from the singular desire to alleviate the anxiety generated by an obsession (APA, 2013). Further, obsessions are not present in the diagnostic criteria for autism spectrum disorder. Please review Sidebar 11.4, which provides a summary of differential diagnosis descriptors for client symptomatology.

After proper differential diagnosis from these other disorders, the *DSM*-5 requires counselors to measure the child's or adolescent's functional impact of symptomatology

(APA, 2013). Counselors need to consider the degree of marked distress on the child's or adolescent's intrapersonal and interpersonal development and functioning at school, at home, and in the community. Typical development in children and adolescents is described as routines that are not irrational and that do not create a disruption or interference with daily functioning, resulting in increased distress or discomfort (Rapoport & Inoff-Germain, 2000). Several of the differential diagnoses counselors must rule out cause physically noticeable distress in the child or adolescent identified with Tourette's/tic disorder, Sydenham's chorea, pediatric autoimmune neuropsychiatric disorder associated with streptococcal infection (PANDAS), or eating disorders (Rapoport & Inoff-Germain, 2000).

Diagnosis of OC and related disorders in children and adolescents is a complex process that necessitates systematic assessment of multiple facets of the individual and family system while examining the presence and severity of obsessions and compulsions. Situating the assessment process within a developmental perspective is essential, given the cognitive requirements to meet the *DSM-5* criteria for OC and related disorders. Identify the differential diagnoses that Jacob's counselor must consider during the assessment process by tackling the questions listed in Sidebar 11.3.

SIDEBAR 11.3:   CASE OF JACOB—DIFFERENTIAL DIAGNOSIS EXAMINATION

1. Which OC and related disorders, if any, would you need to rule out in diagnosing Jacob?
2. What additional clinical information would you need to rule out autism spectrum disorder, major depressive disorder, and anxiety disorders?
3. What are the developmentally normative behaviors for a child the age of Jacob? How would you explain your diagnostic decisions to Jacob's parents while contextualizing them in a developmental framework?

Assessment Strategies

With an increased need for understanding and diagnosing OCD in children and adolescents, researchers are moving from conventional assessment, which has focused on systematic categorization using interviews and questionnaires, to evidence-based assessment in child psychiatry to provide evidence-based mental health treatment (Lewin & Piacentini, 2010). Evidence-based assessment involves the use of instruments that have undergone rigorous empirical examination to ensure their utility in assessing and diagnosing OCD and related disorders. The clinical validity of the assessment protocols is enhanced by the ongoing research correlating the assessment functions to clinically relevant diagnostic outcomes.

When conducting assessments for a potential OC and related disorder diagnosis in pediatric populations, it is important that counselors interact with parents or caregivers and consult with early professional contacts (Thomsen, 2013). Many parents or caregivers struggle to discriminate between clinically relevant behaviors of their child and actions that are developmentally appropriate. Children themselves may not understand the existence of obsessions or be able to express their experiences and how they are experiencing distress. Engaging early professional contacts, parents or caregivers, and the child in the assessment protocol can bridge potential gaps in insight, recognition, identification, and expression. To best understand the process for establishing diagnosis of OC or a related disorder, previsit screening (Lewin & Piacentini, 2010), clinician-administered diagnostic interviews, behavioral observations, and evidence-based assessments will be explored.

PREVISIT SCREENING

Attending mental health services for the first time may be experienced as challenging to fit into an already complicated schedule and difficult for parents and children alike to discuss personal experiences. The previsit screening process may ease parents and children into the counseling experience and is an opportunity for parents to receive the necessary informed consent related to assessments, diagnostic testing, interviews, observations, and parent/child checklists (Lewin & Piacentini, 2010). Prior to the visit, the mental health counselor will generate the tentative diagnosis of the presenting problems informed by the information gather in the previsit, professional knowledge, and expertise (Lewin & Piacentini, 2010). The four questions (i.e., thoughts that something bad would happen, the need to check on certain things over and over again, excessive worry, and doing things in a certain way), contained in the Repetitive Thoughts and Behaviors domain of the *DSM-5* Self-Rated Level 1 Cross-Cutting Symptom Measure—Child Age 11–17 and the *DSM-5* Parent/Guardian-Rated Level 1 Cross-Cutting Symptom Measure—Child Age 6–17 are essential to the assessment process (APA, 2013). Responses to these four questions may indicate the need for further inquiry by using the *DSM-5* Level 2-Repetitive Thoughts and Behaviors—Child Age 11–17 (adapted from the Children's Florida Obsessive-Compulsive Inventory [C-FOCI] Severity Scale) assessment measure.

Lewin and colleagues (2010) strongly encouraged comprehensively evaluating a child's and adolescent's family, academic, and social environments. Integrating assessment measures into this protocol can be very helpful. One measure used to evaluate the degree to which family members of individuals with OC and related disorders have accommodated the individuals' repetitive rituals over the previous month is the Family Accommodation Scale (FAS; Calvocoressi et al., 1995; Lewin & Piacentini, 2010). Another instrument to consider during the prescreening visit is the Family Environmental Scale (FES; Moos & Moos, 1994), which is another valuable measurement assessing the overall social environment within the individual's family. Both the FAS and FES are detailed in the Evidenced-Based Assessment section. Formal questionnaires, self-report measures, and checklists offer an important supplement to the diagnostic interview process.

DIAGNOSTIC INTERVIEWS

A structured clinical interview (SCI) for *DSM-5* disorders helps mental health professionals determine an accurate diagnosis for OC and related disorders. A SCI uses standardized questions to ensure that each person is offered the same experience to explore OC and related symptoms. Interviewing children and adolescents regarding OC and related symptoms poses many challenges because of the youth's potentially limited insight into the repetitive behaviors or mental acts and their reluctance to share their experiences (Moreso et al., 2013). Children and adolescents may perceive their rituals and symptoms to be experienced by all people and not unique to them. Empathy and multiple perspective taking have yet to be crystallized. Therefore, the expected cognitive developmental feature for youth may exacerbate the challenge to diagnose and treat OC symptoms. For children to assess whether their symptoms are unreasonable, they must have the cognitive skills and life experiences to make this judgment (Lewin & Piacentini, 2010). A child's inability to differentiate the self from the other, as correlated to egocentrism, hinders his or her ability to assess the reasonableness of symptoms.

Interviewing children requires questions to be developmentally appropriate and considerate of their cognitive and language abilities. For example, the question "What are the specific details of your compulsions and obsessions?" may be too abstract for a child or adolescent to comprehend because of his or her developmentally normative concrete thinking style. Another question that may challenge a child's or adolescent's cognitive abilities may be "Did your symptoms start after beginning a new medication or drug or after you were diagnosed with a new illness?" In contrast, asking a child or adolescent to describe unwanted, recurrent, and persistent thoughts, urges, or images may promote greater awareness of their symptoms. For example, stating, "Describe a behavior that you feel a strong desire to repeat, and may be hard to control, that bothers your parents or siblings" may help a child or adolescent understand that compulsively washing his or her hands to the extent that skin lesions occur is not common. The child's or adolescent's candor involves overcoming fears to address challenges and embarrassing routines that may adversely affect his or her positive sense of self. Counselors need to be mindful of these overwhelming challenges and offer genuine empathy and compassion when assessing clients for mental illness.

BEHAVIORAL OBSERVATIONS

Given the presence of rigidly applied compulsions that interfere with the child's or adolescent's school, social life, family life, or job to meet the diagnostic criteria of OCD, counselors can request that parents and teachers conduct behavioral observations. Because others frequently observe the child's or adolescent's compulsions, this assessment strategy can yield important diagnostic data. One important system to engage is the school because of the high level of functional impairment that can manifest for youth presenting with OC and related symptoms. One example of such a behavioral observation rating form is the Child Behavior Checklist (see Chapter 2) (Achenbach, 1994).

Engaging caregivers and teachers in the process of observing and tracking behaviors can provide a wealth of assessment data. The impact of OC and related disorders is multisystemic, and understanding how compulsions manifest across settings would be therapeutically beneficial. Harnessing data from behavioral observations expands the counselor's assessment process. It is recommended that behavioral observations be conducted at multiple points across the therapeutic intervention because assessment is an ongoing process that can contextualize treatment progress.

EVIDENCE-BASED ASSESSMENTS

There are many evidence-based assessments that are used routinely for assessing and measuring treatment effectiveness for youth diagnosed with OCD. This section provides an introduction and overview to 11 common assessment instruments that counselors utilize when working with children and adolescents. The instruments range from self-report to counselor administered.

Children's Yale-Brown Obsessive-Compulsive Scale (CY-BOCS)

The CY-BOCS is the most well established and most frequently used instrument to assess the level of severity of OCD symptomology (Scahill et al., 1997). It has served as the primary screening and outcome measurement for psychotherapeutic and psychopharmacology studies (POTS Team, 2004). In addition to a global severity score, CY-BOCS provides severity data across five subscales: (1) time occupied with symptoms, (2) level of interference, (3) distress, (4) resistance, and (5) level of symptom control. It is a semistructured interview clinicians complete.

The CY-BOCS measures OCD symptomology across the past week, with scores ranging from 0 to 40. Higher scores correlate with higher levels of symptom severity. One important facet of the CY-BOCS is that it does provide assessment data related to a child's level of insight. Assessing insight level is important for diagnostic and treatment reasons (Storch et al., 2007b).

Recently, Lewin et al. (2014) established a severity scores benchmark that can be used to designate clinically relevant differentiation across severity levels of OCD. Treatment outcomes are optimized if interventions are selected to meet the individual needs of the clients. Symptom severity is the clinical feature most closely correlated to treatment outcome. Developing severity thresholds across severe, moderate, and mild provides counselors with a tool to identify the most appropriate treatment approach. Lewin et al.'s research provides a foundation for using the CY-BOCS as a measure to translate individual scores into different levels of symptom severity.

Children's Florida Obsessive-Compulsive Inventory (C-FOCI)

The C-FOCI is a self-report instrument that consists of 17 symptoms on a yes/no checklist and five items that measure symptom severity and impact on functioning (Storch et al., 2009). The five items assess the level of control, amount of time, degree of interference, level of distress, and extent of control of the symptoms in the past month. The C-FOCI was developed to be administered in clinical settings and in the community. Initial psychometric property findings suggest an adequate level of validity and reliability (Storch et al., 2009).

The Level 2-Repetitive Thoughts and Behavior–Child Age 11–17 is a modified version of the Children's Florida Obsessive-Compulsive Inventory [C-FOCI] Severity Scale. The C-FOCI severity scale has been tested in only children and adolescents ages 11 to 17 in the *DSM-5* field trails, as opposed to the original purpose of the assessment, which was to test children ranging from 7 to 17 years of age (APA, 2013; Goodman & Storch, 1994). The increased age range offers clients an opportunity to complete the inventory independently prior to the first counseling session. The measure provides counselors' insights into the clients' perceived severity of repetitive behaviors and thoughts in the past seven days (Goodman & Storch, 1994).

CHILDREN'S OBSESSIONAL COMPULSIVE INVENTORY

The first version, Maudsley Obsessional Compulsive Inventory (MOCI), was a self-report instrument for measuring observable obsessive compulsive symptoms. The initial version was updated to include an assessment of compulsions, avoidance behaviors, range of obsessions, and personality characteristics observed in OCD (Thordarson, Radomsky, Shafran, Sawchuk, & Hakstian, 2004). The revised version is the Vancouver Obsessional Compulsive Inventory (VOCI). The VOCI rates the 55-items on a five-point Likert-type scale to attend to therapeutic change by exploring the following subscales: hoarding, obsessions, contamination, and checking (Thordarson et al., 2004). The VOCI highlights a thorough measurement of the range of OCD symptoms.

Child OCD Impact Scale Revised-Child/Adolescent Report and Parent Report (COIS-R)

The Child OCD Impact Scale Revised assesses the level of functional impairment across three contexts, namely family/home, school, and social. The COIS-R includes 33 items, which are rated on three-point Likert-type measures. It is a self-report survey that captures perceptions of both the youth and the parents. The child and parent forms display good internal consistency, test-retest reliability, and concurrent validity (Piancentini et al., 2011).

Clinical Global Impression Scale—Severity (CGI-S)

The CGI-S is a single-item rating of global OCD severity based on a rating scale ranging from 0, "no illness," to 6, "serious illness" (Guy, 1976). Counselors using the assessment scale are encouraged to consider a global level of psychosocial functioning of a client compared to other youth who have been diagnosed with OCD. The comprehensive focus of the CGI-S requires counselors to consider functioning and severity beyond specific symptoms. Because it requires a clinical comparison to other cases, counselors are recommended to have adequate clinical experience prior to relying on this scale to determine treatment protocols.

Family Accommodation Scale (FAS)

The FAS measures the extent to which family members have accommodated compulsions across the most recent month (Calvocoressi et al., 1995). Because of the negative correlation between level of family accommodation and treatment efficacy, gaining an understanding of how the family does or does not accommodate the rituals of the child or adolescent can provide significant clinical information. The FAS has been revised to be a relative/self-report measure (Pinto, Van Noppen, & Calvocoressi, in press). The FAS assesses the presence of eight obsessions and seven compulsions in a family member across the past week. It concludes with frequency rating of behaviors that the relative engaged in across the last week to respond to the youth's symptoms.

Family Environmental Scale (FES)

The FES (Moos & Moos, 1994) is administered to the individual's primary caregivers and the individual herself or himself (depending on the age and benefits gained from administering the assessment to the child). The FES explores the overall functioning of the family's social environment and the interpersonal relationships (Moos & Moos, 1994). The FES benefits the assessment process by the self-report measurement and as a tool to observe the perceived effect of the family environment on the individuals (Moos & Moos, 1994). The self-report measurement assesses three dimensions of the family environment: directions of personal growth, basic organization and structure, and interpersonal relationships (Moos & Moos, 1994). Three scales that were developed to assess the effect on the family environment include control, conflict, and moral-religious emphasis (Moos & Moos, 1994).

Leyton Obsessional Inventory-Child Version (LOI-CV)

The LOI-CV was created for children as an adaption from the Leyton Obsessive Inventory for adults (Bamber, Tamplin, Park, Kyte, & Goodyer, 2002). The LOI-CV is a 20-item self-report questionnaire for children and adolescents that explores three factors, namely obsessions/incompleteness, compulsions, and a concern with cleanliness. The Short LOI-CV was developed to screen for present (within the past two weeks) OCD symptoms by offering more developmentally suitable questions for children's cognitive and language development. The short LOI-CV may be administered by counselors and nonclinical providers. The short version is manageable for children and their attention spans as the assessment takes one to two minutes to complete (Bamber et al., 2002). It should be noted that there are equivocal findings related to the usefulness of the LOI-CV in assessing obsessive-compulsive disorder in pediatric populations, with some researchers, such as Storch et al. (2011a), cautioning about its psychometric properties.

National Institute of Mental Health Global Obsessive-Compulsive Scale (NIMH-GOCS)

To complete the NIMH GOCS, clinicians complete a single item that assesses global diagnostic severity. The scale for the single item ranges from 1 ("minimal symptoms, within normal range") to 15 ("very severe"). Researchers have reported good test-retest reliability and adequate convergent validity with the CY-BOCS (Storch et al., 2010b).

Obsessive Compulsive Inventory—Child Version (OCI-CV)

The OCI-CV has 21 items, completed by the child or adolescent, concerning his or her symptoms across the past month (Foa et al., 2010). The OCI-CV is appropriate for youth ranging from seven to 17. The OCI-CV was adapted from the Obsessive-Compulsive Inventory-Revised (Foa et al., 2002) to provide a measure of symptom presence and dimensionality for youth. It comprises six subscales, namely doubting/checking, obsessions, hoarding, washing, ordering, and neutralizing, that have been verified through a confirmatory factor analysis (Jones et al., 2012). These subscales are totaled to generate an overall OCI-CV score. Convergent validity has been evidenced through correlations of the OCI-CV to the CY-BOCS, NIMH-COGS, and reports of anxiety and depression (Jones et al., 2013; Scahill et al., 1997).

Because of the criticality of treatment being aligned with a client's needs and symptom severity (Lewin et al., 2014), assessing for OCD in youth needs to be conducted in a multidimensional manner that incorporates information from the client, family, teacher (if applicable), and other professionals. Completing a comprehensive, multisystemic, and accurate assessment optimizes the client's opportunity to receive effective treatment, thereby minimizing chronic OCD symptomology into adulthood. Determining an accurate diagnosis is necessary for providing the most effective evidence-based treatment options and for assessing the treatments' effectiveness for treating OCD. Counselors must also focus on engaging in assessment in an ongoing way that highlights how clients are responding to treatment interventions. Sidebar 11.4 provides some reflection questions about the assessment process in the case of Jacob.

SIDEBAR 11.4:   CASE OF JACOB—ASSESSMENT STRATEGIES

1. To conduct a comprehensive assessment, who in Jacob's life do you want to include as a source of information? Which systems do you want to consult as part of your assessment protocol?

2. What would be effective and meaningful questions to ask during the previsit screening process?

3. Given Jacob's age, what would be some developmentally appropriate questions you could ask during the structured clinical interview?

4. Which, if any, evidence-based assessments would you want to complete? Provide a rationale for why the data provided would be helpful in your assessment and diagnosis process.

Treatment Strategies and Interventions

Treatment of children and adolescents with OC and related disorders requires a comprehensive assessment of *DSM-5* criteria, symptom severity, comorbidity, developmental stages, and systemic context. Because of the high level of impact of the family system on the client, treatment interventions need to include family education at the onset of counseling. To meet best practice guidelines, intervention needs to align with an individual client's needs (Lewin et al., 2014). Early diagnosis and treatment of OC symptoms may reduce the severity and chronicity into adulthood (Moreso et al., 2013). Epidemiology data reports that one-third to one-half of adults with OCD develop the disorder during early childhood or adolescence. Given that one in 200 youth have OCD, researchers and counselors are charged with developing interventions that reduce the severe disruption in social, academic, and family functioning (Franklin, Harrison, & Benavides, 2012).

For pediatric clients, severity is the threshold on which treatment decisions are made. Interventions vary based on whether the counselor perceives the OCD symptomatology to be severe, moderate, or mild (Geller & March, 2012). For mild severity, psychoeducation, coping skill development, and increased self-awareness are recommended interventions. For moderate to severe functional impact, cognitive behavioral therapy can be combined with psychopharmacological management if needed (Thomsen, 2013).

Researchers overwhelmingly conclude that there are two evidence-based treatments for pediatric populations diagnosed with OC and related disorders, namely pharmacotherapy with selective serotonin reuptake inhibitors (SSRIs) and CBT with exposure/response prevention (Lewin et al., 2014; Thomsen, 2013). The pediatric literature concurs with the adult research reporting that the efficacy of pharmacotherapy with SSRI for pediatric OCD has been established for fluvoxamine, fluoxetine, clomipramine, and sertraline (March, 2004). Additional treatment options include behavioral therapy, cognitive therapy, family therapy, and play therapy. Children and adolescents may not have reached the cognitive and emotional developmental milestones that are necessary to understand and navigate their preoccupations and compulsions. Therefore, all treatment approaches need to involve the parents or caregivers as coaches and to minimize family accommodation of compulsions as much as possible (Lewin & Piacentini, 2010).

COUNSELING THERAPIES

Counseling is an effective way to assist children and adolescents in navigating OC and related disorders. Counseling techniques may vary from individual, group, or family counseling interventions. Rapoport and Inoff-Germain (2000) discuss the importance of initiating treatment with a focus on family education about the disorder and how the family can assist in the child's treatment of OC and related disorders by recommending helpful responses to the child's behaviors. Once engaged in counseling, counselors may use a variety of therapies to address the cognitions and behaviors associated with this disorder. Some of the flagship therapies associated with the treatment of OCD in children and adolescents are behavioral therapy, cognitive therapy, and cognitive behavioral therapy (CBT) (Hill & Crews, 2013).

Behavioral Therapy

The process of behavioral therapy typically involves first identifying the maladaptive behaviors the client desires to be addressed. For children who have been diagnosed with OC and certain related disorders, the counselor may choose to have the client and his and her parents rank the compulsive behaviors, with the least distressing or debilitating behavior being the focus of counseling first and then focusing on the other behaviors as they are ordered in terms of distress. By focusing on the least distressing or debilitating behavior, the client is able to see success and be more willing to experience the discomfort of not engaging in their compulsive behavior. Second, a type of contract is formed regarding the treatment of the behavior, and treatment options are addressed. Then treatment ensues, with the focus of treatment being on the present and changing the behaviors that are currently causing the client distress or impairment. Under the umbrella of behavior therapy, a technique that has been shown to be effective in OC and related disorders treatment studies is exposure and response prevention (ERP; Duke et al., 2010).

ERP consists of daily exposure to stimuli typically avoided by the child or adolescent. Exposure to the stimulus is coupled with response prevention. Behavioral coping strategies such as relaxation and mindfulness are utilized to increase the client's ability to maintain exposure without engaging in avoidance or a ritualized behavior. Children and adolescents engaged in ERP need to understand the treatment and tolerate the increasing exposure to stimuli (Rapoport & Inoff-Germain, 2000). Positive treatment outcomes are maximized if children and adolescents are empowered to collaborate on deciding the gradients of exposure to relevant stimuli. Researchers have found that ERP tends to be the most helpful with symmetry rituals, hoarding, counting, repeating, aggressive urges, and contamination fears, whereas ERP is less effective when guilt or doubt are components of the obsessive criteria (Rapoport & Inoff-Germain, 2000). Engaging in ERP with young children needs to be done with caution, given their inability to identify the irrationality of the obsession and its corresponding anxiety, fear, and distress.

Cognitive Therapy

As a treatment for OCD, cognitive therapy is efficacious alone (Beck & Dozois, 2010) but is more effective when paired with another technique (Rapoport & Inoff-Germain, 2000), such as medication, relaxation techniques, or behavioral experiments. Multiple studies have identified cognitive therapy as effective in regards to the treatment of clients who have been diagnosed with OC and related disorders (Rapoport & Inoff-Germain, 2000; Turner, 2006). A limitation to utilizing this type of therapy with children is the focus placed on the child's ability to self-assess or identify faulty thoughts. Dependent upon the child's current developmental level, the child may not have the ability to explore his or her thought process or gain insight into his or her own thoughts. Therefore, cognitive therapy may be more appropriate with older adolescent clients.

Cognitive Behavioral Therapy

CBT has been researched and found to be effective in treating individuals, including children and adolescents, diagnosed with OC and related disorders (Gelinas & Gagnon, 2013). Bolton et al. (2011) examined the benefits of CBT in children and adolescents and found that CBT interventions were effective in treating OCD even with a lower counselor intensity delivery with the use of counselor-guided workbooks. Storch et al. (2007b) also researched the effectiveness of CBT treatment for pediatric OCD and found that intensive treatment, defined as individual CBT 90-minute sessions five days a week, was as effective as individual CBT 90-minute sessions one day a week after a three-month follow-up. Results of studies like these listed suggest that CBT is an effective treatment therapy for children and adolescents who have been diagnosed with OC and related disorders.

Within the CBT framework CBT, exposure and response prevention (ERP) is a technique that is commonly found. ERP consists of confronting the anxiety provoking triggers, either by *in vivo* exposure or mental imagery, while consciously not engaging in compulsions that would reduce the client's anxiety or distress (Turner, 2006). ERP is arguably one of the more successful techniques found within CBT treatment and has been researched to be effective with children and adolescents (Rapoport & Inoff-Germain, 2000). Effect sizes from controlled CBT trials are large, thereby generating the recommendation that CBT should be provided as the initial treatment protocol with children and adolescents diagnosed with OCD (Storch et al., 2007b).

Through funding by the National Institute of Mental Health (NIMH), March et al. (2004) evaluated the efficacy of medication management with the SSRI sertraline, CBT, or a combined treatment consisting of CBT and sertraline as an initial treatment for children and adolescents (March et al., 2004). March et al. randomly assigned 112 youths ages 7 to 17 years of age to three academic centers in the United States to receive CBT alone, combined CBT and sertraline, or pill placebo for 12 weeks (March et al., 2004). The CBT treatment regimen entailed 14 visits over 12 weeks to complete four components of the treatment. The CBT regimen involved adapting developmentally appropriate interventions that included mapping OCD, psychoeducation, exposure and response ritual prevention, and cognitive training (March et al., 2004). In the first two weeks, participants experienced two visits each week lasting one hour. The remaining weeks participants met for approximately one hour to address the statement of goals, review of previous treatment experiences, the details of the new information for the treatment, counselor-assisted practice, homework for the future week, and monitoring procedures (March et al., 2004). Three of the sessions involved the parents in the session to address maladaptive parent–child interactions as a result of the OCD symptoms (March et al., 2004).

The individuals who received the combined treatment, CBT, and medication management followed procedures for treatment in the pharmacotherapy manuals, and the CBT visits were timed to meet parents' scheduling needs (March et al., 2004). The medication group alone met independently with one child or adolescent psychiatrist throughout the study. The psychiatrist offered support and encouragement to resist OCD but provided no formal psychotherapy procedures for OCD (March et al., 2004).

March et al. (2004) concluded that children and adolescents diagnosed with OCD benefited significantly from a combination of SSRI and CBT treatment or CBT alone. One caution the authors presented was that the participants were provided state-of-the-art mental health counseling services and strict psychopharmacology supports to adhere to the study's regimen (March et al., 2004). Given this concern, counselors are charged with training and creating portable CBT treatments. Future research may benefit youth diagnosed with OCD by focusing on the efficacy of the dissemination of training CBT models for OCD specialists and the treatment outcomes. Creating reliable CBT treatment services for individuals with OCD is one aspect of providing effective treatment. Another important consideration is that providing counseling services for youth largely depends on the family's support and commitment to the process.

Family-Focused Therapy

For many families in which there is a child or adolescent diagnosed with OCD, parents/caregivers can feel overwhelmed, engage in accommodation behaviors that can exacerbate OCD symptomatology, be asked to serve as therapeutic coaches, and manifest anxiety that can increase OCD symptomatology (Ginsburg, Burstein, Becker, & Drake, 2011; Storch et al., 2007a). Higher levels of family accommodation have been correlated to resistance in treatment and ongoing severity of symptoms (Storch et al., 2007a). The developmental stage of a youth impacted by OC and related disorders can mean that involving the parents/caregivers in treatment is a necessary process. Attending to family-oriented issues within treatment is critical to optimize outcomes in OCD reduction of symptom severity (Ginsburg, Burstein, Becker, & Drake, 2011).

Psychopharmacology

Empirical evidence consistently supports the positive impact of pharmacotherapy with SSRIs, either independently or coupled with CBT with exposure/response prevention, on reducing OCD symptomatology and increasing client functioning at home and school (Farrell et al., 2010; Lewin et al., 2014; Reynolds et al., 2013; Thomsen, 2013). Support for the effectiveness of psychopharmacology has also been established for treating excoriation (skin-picking disorder), trichotillomania (hair-pulling disorder), hoarding disorder, and body dysmorphic disorder (Duke et al., 2010; Gelinas & Gagnon, 2013). The most common SSRIs used to treat pediatric OCD are sertraline, fluoxetine, clomipramine, and fluvoxamine (March et al., 2004). A recent randomized controlled clinical study highlighted the treatment efficacy of citalopram at the same level of fluoxetine in 29 children and adolescents diagnosed with OCD.

Recently, Ercan et al. (2012) examined the use of fluoxetine with preschool-age children diagnosed with OCD who were not responsive to initial treatment protocols of CBT and hydroxyzine. The Food and Drug Administration sets age-based parameters for the use of psychotropic drugs with children. Based on this, fluoxetine was recommended for children ages 7 and higher, whereas sertraline and fluvoxamine were recommended for children ages 8 and higher and 6 and higher, respectively. Despite these recommendations, Ercan et al. (2012) explored the safety and efficacy of fluoxetine with four preschoolers ranging in ages from 31 months to 5 years old. The SSRI was administered at a 5 mg/day dosage initially in each case and then titrated up. For three of the four preschoolers, a period of behavioral activation emerged as dosages increased. The symptomology disappeared when dosage was decreased. OCD symptomatology significantly decreased and maintenance was provided at 5 mg/day level. Discontinuation is recommended after six to eight months of symptom relief, and this recommendation was effective for three of the four preschoolers.

Sidebar 11.7 encourages you to consider the treatment protocol for Jacob. Consider the effectiveness of behavioral, cognitive, CBT, family-based, play, and psychopharmacology interventions when working with Jacob by reflecting on the questions in Sidebar 11.5.

SIDEBAR 11.5:   CASE OF JACOB—EFFECTIVE TREATMENT STRATEGIES

1. Which counseling therapies do you think would be most helpful in the case of Jacob? What would be your initial treatment plan?

2. Which interventions from behavioral, cognitive, CBT, family-based therapy, and play therapy seem the most helpful? How might you apply these specific interventions with Jacob and his family?

3. How would you approach issues of family accommodation? How would you integrate treatment strategies related to family accommodation?

4. How beneficial would psychopharmacology be for Jacob? When, if ever, would you consider recommending it to the family?

Evaluation Strategies

According to the American Psychiatric Association (2013), if OCD is not treated, the rate of remission is low (20 percent). When left untreated, children and adolescents diagnosed with OCD may display symptoms throughout their lifetimes (Storch et al., 2007b). However, with treatment strategies including individual, group, and family-based cognitive behavioral therapy (CBT), family psychoeducation, and serotonergic medication (SSRIs; Ercan et al., 2012; Ginsburg et al., 2011; Hill & Crews, 2013; Olino et al., 2011; Rapoport & Inoff- Germain, 2000; Storch et. al., 2010a; Turner, 2006), researchers have found that as many as 40 percent of pediatric OCD cases can be remitted by adulthood (APA, 2013).

CBT, specifically exposure and response prevention (ERP), can be delivered within clinical and community settings and has proven to be efficacious in the treatment of OCD and related disorders in children and adolescents (Olino et al., 2011). Rapoport and Inoff-Germain (2000) stressed the importance of family involvement and education with successful treatment outcomes. In more severe cases of childhood OCD, psychotropic drugs, such as fluoxetine, citalopram, and sertraline, along with augmenting agents, such as haloperidol may be utilized (Ercan et al., 2012; Gelinas & Gagnon, 2013; Rapoport & Inoff-Germain, 2000).

In regard to treatment evaluation and effectiveness, it is important to consider the impact that individual factors have in determining treatment response. Olino et al. (2011) found treatment response varied based on the presence of certain clinical symptoms as well as comorbidity of other disorders (APA, 2013). Furthermore, Storch et al. (2010a) ascertained the significance of establishing treatment efficacy through consensus regarding what determined treatment response and remission. Specifically, clarity was needed in determining what scores on the CY-BOCS indicated that treatment had been efficacious as defined by these terms. A method called signal detection analysis was utilized to discover that a 25 percent decrease on the CY-BOCS was associated with treatment response, while a 45 to 50 percent decrease was correlated with remission (Storch et al., 2010a).

Diagnostic Challenges

As discussed previously, the high rates of comorbidity, developmental matters, and increased variability of symptoms in the pediatric population complicate diagnosis of OC and related disorders in children and adolescents. Therefore, counselors must be cognizant of the likelihood that youth may need to be dually or poly diagnosed (APA, 2013) if comprehensive and systematic assessment procedures clearly identify distinct clinical syndromes. For example, a triad of OCD, tic disorder, and attention-deficit/hyperactivity disorder can also be seen in children (APA, 2013). Further, when diagnoses such as body dysmorphic disorder, hoarding disorder, trichotillomania (hair-pulling disorder), and excoriation (skin-picking) disorder are identified within children and adolescents, it is paramount that counselors also screen for the presence of OCD. Increased levels of comorbidity among children and adolescents can engender challenges in appropriately diagnosing and effectively treating clients.

Diagnosing OCD is also complicated by the developmental level of children and adolescents. Even at the age-expected cognitive development level, children and adolescents may not be capable of the level of insight required to differentiate the irrationality of the obsessions from normative thinking patterns. Lack of insight into the irrationality of obsessions has been correlated with decreased treatment responsiveness (APA, 2013). Also, the identification of obsessions is increasingly difficult with children and adolescents because they tend to be concrete and egocentric thinkers. However, because compulsions are observable, they are more easily diagnosed in children than obsessions (APA, 2013).

A final issue that contributes to diagnostic challenges is the higher variability of symptom patterns in children compared to adults. This variability of symptom patterns may be connected to the variability of developmental stages of children and adolescents. For example, children and adolescents may display higher rates of obsessions related to death and illness to self or loved ones than adults (APA, 2013). Adolescents tend to manifest higher incidents of sexual and religious obsession (APA, 2013). Increased variability can complicate assessment processes while hindering treatment effectiveness.

Counselors must be aware of the child's and adolescent's developmental level and must recognize that the course of symptomatology may be more erratic than expected with adult clients. Clinical judgment is required to ensure appropriate diagnosis and efficacious treatment (Rapoport & Inoff-Germain, 2000). When using one's clinical judgment, the counselor should consider his/her familiarity with the disorder and diagnostic criteria. The counselor should also consider the severity of the symptoms of the client, the developmental level of the client, and the level of disturbance the client is experiencing. Given the complexity of differential diagnosis, counselors need to evaluate not only the manifesting behaviors, explicitly stated and implied cognitive facets, and level of impairment, but also the origination and intention behind behaviors. Framing clinical judgment in terms of developmental analysis, diagnostic conceptualization, sociocultural and familial systems, and severity indices will prepare counselors to be more effective and accurate in their diagnosis and treatment decisions.

Summary

OC and related disorders in children and adolescents may impact them in multiple contexts, with potentially severe, pervasive consequences related to all aspects of living (Rapoport & Inoff-Germain, 2000). The rate of comorbidity with other childhood disorders is high (80 percent), which presents challenges with diagnosis and treatment (Langley et al., 2010). Utilizing established assessment procedures and understanding the complexity involved in differential diagnosis are imperative in the process of accurate diagnosis of this disorder. Successful treatment approaches may include individual, group, and family-based cognitive behavioral therapy (CBT), parent education, and in some cases, medication (SSRIs) (Ercan et al., 2012; Ginsburg et al., 2011; Hill & Crews, 2013; Olino et al., 2011; Rapoport & Inoff-Germain, 2000; Storch et. al., 2010a; Turner, 2006).

Accurate diagnosis and successful treatment of OC and related disorders in children and adolescents necessitate the careful consideration of their developmental level. Issues related to normative and nonnormative development need to be differentiated in order to ascertain that the child's or adolescent's recurrent and persistent thoughts, urges, or images are intrusive, unwanted—resulting in marked anxiety or distress; and that their excessive, ritualistic, and repetitive behaviors or mental acts are abnormal (APA, 2013). Children's and adolescent's cognitive development, insight, and awareness must be considered when assessing, diagnosing, and treating OC and related disorders.

References

Achenbach, T. M. (1994). Child behavior checklist and related instruments. In M. E. Maruish (Ed.), *The use of psychological testing for treatment planning and outcome assessment* (pp. 517–549). Hillsdale, NJ: Lawrence Erlbaum Associates.

American Psychiatric Association. (2000). *Diagnostic and statistical manual of mental disorders IV-TR* (4th ed.). Washington, DC: Author.

American Psychiatric Association. (2013). *Diagnostic and statistical manual of mental disorders* (5th ed.). Arlington, VA: American Psychiatric Publishing.

Bamber, D., Tamplin, A., Park, R. J., Kyte, Z. A., Goodyer, I. M. (2002). Development of a short Leyton Obsessional Inventory for children and adolescents. *Journal of the American Association of Child & Adolescent Psychiatry, 41*(10), 1246–1252. doi:10.1097/01.CHI.0000020265.43550.25

Beck, A. T., & Dozois, D. J. A. (2010). Cognitive therapy: Current status and future directions. *Annual Review of Medicine, 62,* 397–409. doi:10.1146/annurev-med-052209-100032

Boileau, B. (2011). A review of obsessive-compulsive disorder in children and adolescents. *Dialogues in Clinical Neuroscience, 13*(4), 401–411.

Bolton, D., Williams, T., Perrin, S., Atkinson, L., Gallop, C., Waite, P., & Salkovskis, P. (2011). Randomized controlled trial of full and brief cognitive-behavior therapy and wait-list for pediatric obsessive-compulsive disorder. *Journal of Child Psychology and Psychiatry, 52*(12), 1269–1278. doi:10.1111/j.1469-7610.2011.02419.x

Butcher, J. N., Mineka, S., & Hooley, J. M. (2006). *Abnormal psychology* (13th ed.). Boston, MA: Pearson Education.

Calvocoressi, L., Lewis, B., Harris, M., Trufan, S. J., Goodman, W. K., McDougle, C. J., & Price, L. H. (1995). Family accommodation in obsessive-compulsive disorder. *American Journal of Psychiatry, 152*(3), 441–443.

Coskun, M., Zoroglu, S., & Ozturk, M. (2012). Phenomenology, psychiatric comorbidity and family history in referred preschool children with obsessive-compulsive disorder. *Child and Adolescent Psychiatry and Mental Health, 6,* 36.

Dembo, J. S. (2014). "The ickiness factor:" Case study of an unconventional psychotherapeutic approach to pediatric OCD. *American Journal of Psychotherapy, 68,* 57–79.

Dingemans, A. E., van Rood, Y. R., de Groot, I., & van Furth, E. F. (2012). Body dysmorphic disorder in patients with an eating disorder: Prevalence and characteristics. *International Journal of Eating Disorders, 45*(4), 562–569.

Duke, D. C., Keeley, M. L., Geffken, G. R., & Storch, E. A. (2010). Trichotillomania: A current review. *Clinical Psychology Review, 30*(2), 181–193. doi:10.1016j.cpr.2009.10.008

Ercan, E. S., Kandulu, R., & Ardic, U. A. (2012). Preschool children with obsessive-compulsive disorder and fluoxetine treatment. *European Child and Adolescent Psychiatry, 21,* 169–172. doi:10.1007/s00787-012-0244-2

Farrell, L. J., Schlup, B., & Boschen, M. J. (2010). Cognitive-behavioral treatment of childhood obsessive-compulsive disorder in community-based clinical practice: Clinical significance and benchmarking against efficacy. *Behavior Research and Therapy, 48,* 409–417. doi:10.1016/j.brat.2010.01.004

Foa, E. B., Coles, M., Huppert, J. D., Pasupuleti, R. V., Franklin, M. E., & March, J. (2010). Development and validation of a child version of the obsessive compulsive inventory. *Behavior Therapies, 41,* 121–132.

Foa, E. B., Huppert, J. D., Leiberg, S., Langner, R., Kichic, R., Hajack, G., & Salkovskis, P. M. (2002). The obsessive-compulsive inventory: Development and validation of a short version. *Psychological Assessment, 14,* 485–496.

Franklin, M. E., Harrison, J. P., & Benavides, K. L. (2012). Obsessive-compulsive and tic-related disorders. *Child and Adolescent Psychiatric Clinics of North America, 21*(3), 555.

Gelinas, B. L. & Gagnon, M. M. (2013). Pharmacological and psychological treatments of pathological skin-picking: A preliminary meta-analysis. *Journal of Obsessive-Compulsive and Related Disorders, 2,* 167–175. doi:10.1016/j.jocrd.2013.02.003

Geller, D. A., & March, J. (2012). Practice parameter for the assessment and treatment of children and adolescents with obsessive-compulsive disorder. *Journal of the American Academy of Child & Adolescent Psychiatry, 51,* 98–113. doi:10.1016/j.jaac.2011.09.019

Ginsburg, G. S., Burstein, M., Becker, K. D., & Drake, K. L. (2011). Treatment of obsessive-compulsive disorder in young children: An intervention model and case series. *Child and Family Behavior Therapy, 33*, 97–122. doi:10.1080/07317107.2011.571130

Goodman, W. K., & Storch, E. (1994). *Level 2-Repetitive thoughts and behaviors-Child Age 11–17 (adapted from the Children's Florida Obsessive–Compulsive Inventory [C-FOCI] Severity Scale).* Arlington, VA: American Psychiatric Association.

Grisham, J. R., Fullana, M. A., Mataix-Cols, D., Moffitt, T. E., Caspi, A. & Poulton, R. (2011). Risk factors prospectively associated with adult obsessive-compulsive symptom dimensions and obsessive-compulsive disorder. *Psychological Medicine, 41*, 2495–2506. doi: 10.1017/S0033291711000894.

Guy, W. (1976). Clinical global impressions. In W. Guy (Ed.), *ECDEU assessment manual for psychopharmacology* (pp. 218–222). Rockville, MD: National Institute of Mental Health.

Hanna, G. L., Himle, J. A., Hanna, B. S., Gold, K. J., & Gillespie, B. W. (2011). Major depressive disorder in family study of obsessive-compulsive disorder with pediatric probands. *Depression and Anxiety, 28*(6), 501–508.

Hill, N. R., & Crews, J. A. (2013). *ACA Practice Brief: Obsessive-Compulsive Disorder.* Alexandria, VA: American Counseling Association.

Jones, A. M., De Nadai, A. S., Arnold, E. B., McGuire, J. F., Lewin, A. B., Murphy, T. K., et al. (2012). Psychometric properties of the obsessive compulsive inventory: Child version in children and adolescents with obsessive-compulsive disorder. *Child Psychiatry and Human Development, 43*, 1–15.

Kalra, S. K., & Swedo, S. E. (2009). Children with obsessive-compulsive disorder: Are they just "little adults"? *Journal of Clinical Investigation, 119*, 737–746.

Langley, A. K., Lewin, A. B., Bergman, R. L., Lee, J. C., & Piacentini, J. (2010). Correlates of comorbid anxiety and externalizing disorders in childhood obsessive compulsive disorder. *European Child and Adolescent Psychiatry, 19*, 637–645.

Lewin, A. B., & Piacentini, J. (2010). Evidence-based assessment of child obsessive compulsive disorder: Recommendations for clinical practice and treatment research. *Child Youth Care Forum, 39*, 73–89.

Lewin, A. B., Piacentini, J., De Nadai, A. S., Jones, A. M., Peris, T. S., Geffken, G. R., ... Storch, E. A. (2014). Defining clinical severity in pediatric obsessive-compulsive disorder. *Psychological Assessment, 26*, 679–684. doi:10.1037/a0035174

Mataix-Cols, D., & Pertusa, A. (2012). Annual Research Review: Hoarding disorder: Potential benefits and pitfalls of a new mental disorder. *Journal of Child Psychology and Psychiatry, 53*(5), 608–618. doi:10.1111/j.1469-7610.2011.02464.x

March, J. S., Foa, E., Gammon, P., Chrisman, A., Curry, J., Fitzgerald, D., ... Tu, X. (2004). Cognitive-behavioral therapy, sertraline, and their combination for children and adolescents with obsessive-compulsive disorder: The pediatric OCD treatment study (POTS) randomized controlled trial. *Journal of American Medical Association, 292*(16), 1969–1976.

Martino, D., Defazio, G., & Giovannoni, G. (2009). The PANDAS subgroup of tic disorders and child-onset obsessive-compulsive disorder. *Journal of Psychosomatic Research, 67*, 547–557.

Menon, V. (2014). Juvenile obsessive-compulsive disorder: A case report. *Industrial Psychiatry Journal, 22*(2), 155–156. doi:10.4103/0972-6748.132932.

Millad, M. R., & Rauch, S. L. (2012). Obsessive-compulsive disorder: Beyond segregated corticostriatal pathways. *Trends in Cognitive Sciences, 16*, 43–51.

Moos, R. H., & Moos, B. S. (1994). *Family environment scale manual.* Consulting Psychologists Press.

Moreso, N. V., Hernaandez-Martinez, C., Val, V., & Sans, J. (2013). Socio-demographic and psychopathological risk factors in obsessive-compulsive disorder: Epidemiologic study of school population. *International Journal of Clinical and Health Psychology, 13*, 118–126.

Nakatani, E., Krebs, G., Micali, N., Turner, C., Heyman, I., & Mataix-Cols, D. (2011). Children with very early onset obsessive-compulsive disorder: clinical features and treatment outcome. *Journal of Child Psychology & Psychiatry, 52*(12), 1261–1268. doi:10.1111/j.1469-7610.2011.02434.x.

Nestadt, G., Grados, M., Samuels, J. F. (2010). Genetics of OCD. *Psychiatry Clinics of North America, 33*(1): 141–158. doi:10.1016/j.psc.2009.11.001.

Olino, T.M., Gillo, S., Rowe, D., Palermo, S., Nuhfer, E.C., Birmaher, B., & Gilbert, A.R. (2011). Evidence for successful implementation of exposure and response prevention in a naturalistic group format for pediatric OCD. Depression and Anxiety, 28, 342–348.

Panza, K. E., Pittenger, C., & Bloch, M. H. (2013). Age and gender correlates of pulling in pediatric trichotillomania. *Journal of the American Academy of Child & Adolescent Psychiatry, 52*(3), 241–249.

Pediatric OCD Treatment Study Team. (2004). Cognitive-behavior therapy, sertraline, and their combination for children and adolescents with obsessive-compulsive disorder: The Pediatric OCD Treatment Study (POTS) randomized controlled trial. *Journal of the American Medical Association, 292*, 1969–1976. doi:10.1001/jama.292.16.1969

Piacentini, J., Bergman, R. L., Chang, S., Langley, A., Peris, T., Wood, J. J., & McCracken, J. (2011). Controlled comparison of family cognitive behavioral therapy and psychoeducation/relaxation training for child obsessive-compulsive disorder. *Journal of the American Academy of Child & Adolescent Psychiatry, 50*(11), 1149–1161.

Pinto, A., Van Noppen, B., & Calvocoressi, L. (in press). Development and preliminary psychometric evaluation of a self-rated version of the Family Accommodation Scale for Obsessive-Compulsive Disorder. *Journal of Obsessive-Compulsive and Related Disorders.*

Rapoport, J. L., & Inoff-Germain, G. (2000). Practitioner review: Treatment of obsessive-compulsive disorder in children and adolescents. *Journal of Child Psychiatry, 41*(4), 419–431.

Reynolds, S. A., Clark, S., Smith, H., Langdon, P. E., Payne, R., Bowers, G., Norton, E., ... McIlwham, H. (2013), Randomized controlled trial of parent-enhanced CBT compared with individual CBT for obsessive-compulsive disorder in young people. *Journal of Counseling and Clinical Psychology, 81*(6), 1021–1026. doi:10.1037/a0034429

Scahill, L., Riddle, M. A., McSwiggin-Hardin, M., Ort, S. I., King, R. A., Goodman, W. K., & Leckman, J. F. (1997). Children's Yale-Brown Obsessive Compulsive Scale: Reliability and validity. *Journal of the American Academy of Child & Adolescent Psychiatry, 36*, 844–852. doi:10.1097/00004583-199706000-00023

Seligman, L., & Reichenberg, L. W. (2007). *Selecting effective treatments: A comprehensive, systematic guide to treating mental disorders* (3rd ed.). San Francisco, CA: Jossey-Bass.

Sheppard, B., Chavira, D., Azzam, A., Grados, M. A., Umaña, P., Garrido, H., & Mathews, C. A. (2010). ADHD prevalence and association with hoarding behaviors in childhood-onset OCD. *Depression and Anxiety, 27*(7), 667–674.

Shulman, S. T. (2009). Pediatric autoimmune neuropsychiatric disorders associated with streptococci (PANDAS): Update. *Current Opinions in Pediatrics, 21*, 127–130.

Snorrason, Í., Belleau, E., & Woods, D. W. (2012). How related are hair pulling disorder (trichotillomania) and skin picking disorder? A review of evidence for comorbidity, similarities and shared etiology. *Clinical Psychology Review, 32*(7), 618–629.

Storch, E. A., Geffken, G. R., Merlo, L. J., Jacob, M. L., Murphy, T. K., Goodman, W. K., ... Grabill, K. (2007a). Family accommodation in pediatric obsessive-compulsive disorder. *Journal of Clinical Child & Adolescent Psychology, 36*(2), 207–216.

Storch, E. A., Geffken, G. R., Merlo, L. J., Mann, G., Duke, D., Munson, M., ... Goodman, W. K. (2007b). Family-based cognitive behavioral therapy for pediatric obsessive-compulsive disorder: Comparison of intensive and weekly approaches. *Journal of the American Academy of Child & Adolescent Psychiatry, 46*(4), 469–478.

Storch, E. A., Khanna, M., Merlo, L. J., Loew, B.A., Franklin, M., Reid, J. M., ... Murphy, T. K. (2009). Children's Florida Obsessive Compulsive Inventory: Psychometric properties and feasibility of a self-report measure of obsessive-compulsive symptoms in youth. *Child Psychiatry and Human Development, 40*(3), 467–483. doi:10.1007/s10578-009-0138-9

Storch, E. A., Lewin, A. B., De Nadai, A. S., & Murphy, T. K. (2010a). Defining treatment response and remission in obsessive-compulsive disorder: A signal detection analysis of the Children's Yale-Brown Obsessive-Compulsive Scale. *Journal of the Academy of Child & Adolescent Psychiatry, 49*(7), 708–717.

Storch, E. A., Rasmussen, S. A., Price, L. H., Larson, M. J., Murphy, T. K., & Goodman, W. K. (2010b). Development and psychometric evaluation of the Yale–Brown Obsessive-Compulsive Scale—Second Edition. *Psychological Assessment, 22*(2), 223.

Storch, E. A., Park, J. M., Lewin, A. B., Morgan, J. R., Jones, A. M., & Murphy, T. K. (2011a). The Leyton Obsessional Inventory-Child Version Survey Form does not demonstrate adequate psychometric properties in American youth with pediatric obsessive-compulsive disorder. *Journal of Anxiety Disorders, 25*(4), 574–578.

Storch, E. A., Rahman, O., Park, J. M., Reid, J., Murphy, T. K., & Lewin, A. B. (2011b). Compulsive hoarding in children. *Journal of Clinical Psychology, 67*(5), 507–516. doi:10.1002/jclp.20794

Thomsen, P. H. (2013). Obsessive-compulsive disorders. *European Child and Adolescent Psychiatry, 22*(Suppl 1), S23–S28. doi:10.1007/s00787-012-0357-7.

Thordarson D. S., Radomsky, A. S., Shafran, R., Sawchuk, C. N., & Hakstian, R. (2004). The Vancouver Obsessional Compulsive Inventory (VOCI). *Behaviour Research and Therapy, 42*, 1289–1314. doi:10.1016/j.brat.2003.08.007

Turner, C. (2006). Cognitive-behavioural therapy for obsessive-compulsive disorder in children and adolescents: Current status and future directions. *Clinical Psychology Review, 29*, 912–938. doi:10.1016/j.cpr.2005.10.004

Chapter 12

Trauma- and Stressor-Related Disorders

GERARD LAWSON, RYAN M. COOK, AND CLAUDIA E. HOWELL

Introduction

This chapter addresses diagnoses within the *DSM-5* that have their origins in traumatic or stressful experiences. Traumas and other stressors are especially common, with nearly 85% percent of Americans experiencing a trauma that would qualify them for posttraumatic stress disorder (PTSD) at some point in their lifetime (Pietrzak, Goldstein, Southwick, & Grant, 2011). Pietrzak et al. (2011) found that 6.4 percent of individuals will meet some criteria of PTSD and 6.6 percent of individuals will develop PTSD during their lifetime. Some of the stressor-related disorders in this chapter have their roots not in a discrete traumatic event, but in the chronic lack of care that the individual received as a young child. In this chapter, we will explore each of the trauma- and stressor-related disorders, beginning with reactive attachment disorder, disinhibited social engagement disorder, posttraumatic stress disorder, acute stress disorder, and adjustment disorders as they relate to trauma and stress related disorders.

Description of the Disorders

The *Diagnostic and Statistical Manual of Mental Disorders, Fifth Edition* (*DSM-5*), includes a new section on trauma- and stressor-related disorders, which has not existed in previous versions of the manual. One of the significant changes in the *DSM-5* involved moving posttraumatic stress disorder (PTSD) out of the anxiety disorders section and into this newly formed Trauma- and Stressor-Related Disorders chapter. Trauma- and stressor-related diagnoses have seen a significant evolution over the years up to and including the *DSM-5*, and that has resulted in new diagnostic categories and fine-tuning of existing categories. This enhanced focus also recognizes the fact that individuals regularly encounter traumas and other stressors, which may include exposure to natural or human caused disasters, significant threats to one's health or well-being, challenges to the normal caregiving required for children, and more. In addition, this new section of the *DSM-5* recognizes that how individuals respond to traumas and stressors can be quite varied. Individuals may respond with fear and anxiety (which is why PTSD was previously included the *DSM-IV-TR*'s Anxiety Disorders chapter), but individuals may also experience anhedonia, anger, aggression, or dissociative symptoms. As such, trauma- and stressor-related disorders required specific classification and receive that designation in the *DSM-5*.

Reactive attachment disorder has undergone significant revisions in the *DSM-5*. What used to be seen as one disorder, based on pathogenic care resulting in avoidant social interactions or diffuse attachments, was separated into two disorders, which better reflect the clinical presentation of children who have experienced severe social neglect, recurrent changes of their primary caregivers, or have lived in unusual settings where caregiver attachment was severely limited. Reactive attachment disorder (RAD) was first described in the *DSM-III*, though the behavioral characteristics of the disorders have been observed in the literature as far back as 1945 (Goldfarb, 1945). In previous editions of the *DSM* (American Psychiatric Association [APA], 2000), RAD had distinct subtypes: inhibited type (excessively reticent, hypervigilant, or highly ambivalent and contradictory responses) and disinhibited type (indiscriminate sociability with marked inability to exhibit appropriate selective attachments). In the *DSM-5* these subtypes are divided into two disorders: reactive attachment disorder and disinhibited social engagement disorder—which is the approach the *International Classification of Diseases, Tenth Revision (ICD-10)*, took when it was published in 1992 (world Health Organization [WHO], 1992). Gleason et al. (2011)) set about validating this separation of the two manifestations of RAD into what they categorized as the indiscriminately social/disinhibited and emotionally withdrawn/inhibited types. Their thorough investigation of RAD concluded that indiscriminately social/disinhibited and emotionally withdrawn/inhibited types should be viewed as clinically distinct disorders.

Although both disorders are rooted in pathological attachment, disinhibited social engagement disorder (DSED) is manifest by externalizing behaviors, whereas RAD is manifest by internalizing behaviors. Both disorders can develop in children who have had insufficient opportunities for attachments due to social neglect, repeated changes of primary caregivers, or institutionalization. Children who exhibit RAD tend not to respond to others socially or emotionally, or they demonstrate a restricted range of emotion (especially positive emotion) and yet may have "episodes of unexplained irritability, sadness, or fearfulness that are evident even during nonthreatening interactions with adult caregivers" (APA, 2013a, p. 265). Children with DSED display excessive, clingy, or overly familiar behaviors and inappropriate interactions with caregivers, new acquaintances, or strangers.

PTSD is the oldest and most well-researched diagnosis in this section of the *DSM*. PTSD has also undergone a significant evolution since the *DSM-I*, when Gross Stress Reaction, the precursor to PTSD, was used primarily for those who had seen horrific events during war (Friedman et al., 2011). The *DSM-III* brought the advent of the modern PTSD, which provided clinicians an opportunity to assess how traumatic experiences could affect individual's cognitions, emotions, behaviors, and psychological arousal long after resolution of the traumatic event. The *DSM-5* brings changes in both the diagnostic criteria and the list of traumatic experiences that can cause PTSD. There is a new subset of PTSD in preschool-aged children, which is a reflection of the emerging evidence that even young children are affected by traumatic experiences (e.g., abuse, witnessing violence to parent or caregiving figure, natural disasters, etc.) and those experiences are different enough from adult presentation to require developmentally sensitive criteria.

PTSD and acute stress disorder (ASD) are related but distinct conditions. Both require exposure to "actual or threatened death, serious injury, or sexual violence/violation" (APA,

2013a; pp. 271, 280), and resulting symptoms that cause clinically significant distress or impairment. One of the significant distinguishing factors between PTSD and ASD is the amount of time the individual has experienced the distressing symptoms. The symptoms associated with ASD are restricted to three days minimum to one month maximum, whereas the symptoms of PTSD must persist for over one month.

Adjustment Disorders

Individuals can experience an adjustment disorder based on their response to a stressor, which can be single or multiple events, and which may be recurring or continuous. Some stressors may be predictable developmental markers, such as becoming a parent or going off to school for the first time. Alternatively, natural disasters, bullying, or the end of an intimate relationship are unexpected and unpredictable stressors that can also underlie an adjustment disorder. Individuals with an adjustment disorder will experience marked distress that is out of proportion to the stressful events, and significant impairments in functioning across domains. The symptoms must begin within three months of the onset of the stressor and last no more than six months after the stressor, or its consequences, have resolved. That distinction is an important one because the consequences of an ongoing stressful experience (e.g., bullying, child abuse, intimate partner violence) will recur after each incident. This means that the adjustment disorder diagnosis would be available as long as the individual is experiencing the stressful events.

DSM-5 Criteria

In this section the diagnostic criteria for each trauma- and stressor-related disorder are discussed.

REACTIVE ATTACHMENT DISORDER (RAD)

For a diagnosis of RAD to be considered, the clinician must rule out autism spectrum disorder, as some of the features with regard to social interaction and emotional expression in particular can appear similar. The characteristic behaviors of RAD must be evident before the child is 5 years old and the child must have a developmental age of at least nine months, the point at which children are able to make selective attachments. The central behavioral features of RAD are the child's disinclination to seek out, or even to respond to, comfort from an adult caregiver when the child is distressed. RAD is experienced by children who have had insufficient opportunities for attachments because of social neglect, repeated changes of primary caregivers, or institutionalization; the clinician must determine that the distressing behaviors are results of the neglect in the child's experience.

DISINHIBITED SOCIAL ENGAGEMENT DISORDER (DSED)

To diagnose DSED, the child must be a developmental age of at least nine months. Clinicians making this diagnosis will look for a pattern of behavior whereby the child will approach and engage with adults they do not know with little or no hesitation, they will be overly familiar with those adults, even willing to go off with the unfamiliar adult, and they do not check back in with their adult caregivers. These difficult behaviors appear as socially disinhibited but are not merely the result of impulsivity that would typically be seen with attention-deficit/hyperactivity disorder (ADHD).

As with RAD, children diagnosed with DSED have histories of extreme neglect. Their basic emotional needs have not been met because their primary caregivers did not comfort them, pay attention to them, or interact with them to provide stimulation. Children might have had several primary caregivers in a series (e.g., multiple foster homes) without the ability to form stable attachments or might have lived in a situation where there was no opportunity to form stable attachments. The clinician must determine that the challenging behaviors are the result of the neglect the child has experienced. The disorder is descriptively specified as *persistent* if the emotionally withdrawn behaviors and the social disturbances have been present for more than 12 months, and the clinician can communicate intensity with use of the *severe* specifier when a child exhibits each of the eight available symptoms at relatively high levels. RAD and DSED have the same underlying contributing factors (i.e., a pattern of extremes of insufficient care), but the emotional disturbance and the behavioral manifestations differ significantly between them. Table 12.1 highlights the criteria differences between RAD and DSED.

Posttraumatic Stress Disorder (PTSD)

Children Older than Seven, Adolescents, and Adults

In order to diagnose a child 7 years or older with PTSD, the clinician will need to establish that the individual meets the criteria for trauma exposure, intrusive symptoms, persistent avoidant symptoms, negative changes in cognitions and mood, and marked alterations in arousal and reactivity associated with actual or threatened trauma. The essential features of PTSD include the individual's exposure to actual or threatened death, serious injury, or sexual violence. The specific mention of sexual trauma in Criterion A is new for the *DSM-5* and reflects that childhood sexual violation may include developmentally inappropriate sexual experiences without physical violence or injury (e.g., forced sexual penetration, alcohol/drug-facilitated sexual penetration, abusive sexual contact, noncontact sexual abuse, sexual trafficking). The trauma exposure can be direct (experiencing the trauma), witnessing it live, or learning of a traumatic experience of a close family member or friend. In addition, the trauma criterion was expanded somewhat from the *DSM-IV-TR*, and that expansion should be of special interest to counselors who work with trauma survivors. Now individuals who are repeatedly exposed to aversive traumatic details in a professional capacity qualify for a diagnosis of PTSD. This would appear to allow for counselors who are secondarily exposed to trauma-saturated life narratives from their clients to be diagnosed with primary PTSD (APA, 2013a), as opposed to vicarious traumatization, which is a phenomenon that was not included in prior editions of the *DSM*.

Beyond the exposure itself, individuals must experience intrusive symptoms such as distressing involuntary memories or dreams, dissociative reactions (with new language that such reactions occur on a continuum) where the individual feels they are reexperiencing the trauma, or intense psychological distress or physiological reactions when exposed to reminders of the trauma. Individuals with PTSD will often avoid external reminders of the traumatic experience, which cause distressing memories, thoughts or feelings about the traumatic event. This may include avoiding people, places, or situations that bring up

TABLE 12.1   Comparison of RAD and DSED Criteria A-C

Reactive Attachment Disorder and Disinhibited Social Engagement Disorder Differential Diagnosis

	RAD	DSED
Profile	*Inhibited*—a pattern of markedly disturbed and developmentally inappropriate behavior, in which a child rarely or minimally turns preferentially to an attachment figure for comfort, support, protection, and nurturance	*Disinhibited*—a pattern of markedly disturbed and developmentally inappropriate behavior, in which the child displays overly familiar attachment that actively violates the social and cultural boundaries with relative strangers
Expression	*Internalizing* disorder with depressive symptoms and withdrawn/avoidant behavior	*Externalizing* disorder with impulsive symptoms and approaching/attention-seeking behavior
Etiology	Persistent social neglect—a pattern of extremes of insufficient care or deprivation by caregiving adults	Persistent social neglect—a pattern of extremes of insufficient care or deprivation by caregiving adults
Onset	> age 9 months and < age 5 years	> age 9 months
Developmental delays	Cognition and language	Cognition and language
Associated features	• Stereotypies and other signs of severe neglect (e.g., malnutrition or signs of poor care)	• Stereotypies and other signs of severe neglect (e.g., malnutrition or signs of poor care)
Emotional aberrance	• Diminished or absent expression of positive emotions • Emotion regulation capacity is compromised; display episodes of negative emotions of fear, sadness, or irritability that are not readily explained	None
Disturbed behavior	Threshold: two of two • Rarely or minimally *seeks* comfort when distressed • Rarely or minimally *responds* to comfort when distressed	Threshold: two of four • Reduced or absent reticence in approaching and interacting with unfamiliar adults • Overly familiar verbal or physical behavior • Diminished or absent checking back with adult caregiver after venturing away, even in unfamiliar settings • Willingness to go off with an unfamiliar adult with minimal or no hesitation
Social and emotional disturbance	Threshold: two of three • Minimal social and emotional responsiveness to others • Limited positive affect • Episodes of unexplained irritability, sadness, or fearfulness that are evident even during nonthreatening interactions with adult caregivers	None

TABLE 12.1 (*continued*)

Reactive Attachment Disorder and Disinhibited Social Engagement Disorder Differential Diagnosis

	RAD	DSED
Chronicity	Evident in young children; may persist for several years—yet rarely evident in older children	Early childhood through adolescence; has not been described in adults
Diagnostic criteria	Seven (with five of eight symptoms minimum)	Five (with three of seven symptoms minimum)
Mutual exclusivity	Autism spectrum disorder	None. Cautiously codiagnose attention-deficit/hyperactivity disorder

Source: King, 2014.

memories associated with the trauma. In a new symptom cluster for *DSM-5*, the individual's cognitions and mood undergo negative alterations, resulting in inability to remember details of the trauma (typically due to dissociative amnesia and not to other factors, such as head injury, alcohol, or drugs); changes in schema (e.g., beginning to see the world as a dangerous place); internalized guilt regarding the traumatic events; persistent negative beliefs about self, others, or the world; persistent distorted cognitions that lead to blaming oneself or others for the trauma; and anhedonia.

Finally, individuals experiencing PTSD will often have irritable behavior, angry outbursts, concentration deficits, participate in reckless or self-destructive behavior (a new symptom for the *DSM-5*), or have difficulty with concentration, and sleep disturbances. These individuals are also prone to hypervigilance and an exaggerated startle response, even in situations when they know cognitively that there is no risk. These symptoms must present a level of clinical distress in various domains of functioning for the individual, and the symptoms must persist for more than one month. The clinician must also rule out that the symptoms are better accounted for by substance use or medical condition.

There are specifiers associated with PTSD, and in particular the clinician may designate the presentation is with dissociative symptoms. Dissociative symptoms may alternatively or inclusively manifest depersonalization (an internal phenomena), whereby an individual feels persistently disconnected, or detached, from their body, as if they were observing from the outside. Depersonalization experiences could include one's mental processes, such as feeling as though one were in a dream, feeling a sense of unreality of self or body, or as if time is moving slowly. Dissociative symptoms may alternatively or inclusively manifest derealization (an external phenomena) whereby the individual feels persistent experiences of unreality of surroundings as if the world and their surroundings are distorted somehow (e.g., dreamlike, removed, unreal). Table 12.2 summarizes changes made to criteria for PTSD from the *DSM-IV-TR* to the *DSM-5*. Notice the changes in terminology, symptoms, and specifiers between the two editions.

PTSD for Children 6 Years and Younger

The new diagnostic criteria for PTSD in children 6 years and younger mirror many of the criteria for older individuals but include possibilities for how younger children may experience exposure, intrusive symptoms, avoidant behaviors, and arousal. For young children, the arousal associated with PTSD can appear as outbursts of unprovoked anger and irritable behavior (such as extreme temper tantrums), and this feature is unique to the pediatric form of PTSD. In addition to directly experiencing a traumatic event or witnessing it live as it occurred to others (such as experience of co-occurring traumas, reexposure to

TABLE 12.2   Changes for PTSD Criteria from the *DSM-IV-TR* to the *DSM-5*

	DSM-IV TR	*DSM-5*
Exposure	Requires both: 1. Experienced, witnessed, or confronted with actual or threatened death or serious injury, or a threat to the physical integrity of self or others. 2. The individual's response involved intense fear, helplessness, or horror.	Requires actual or threatened death, serious injury, or sexual violation in one of the following ways: 1. Direct experience. 2. Witnessed in person. 3. Learned of trauma event(s). to a close family member or close friend. 4. Experienced repeated or extreme exposure to aversive details of traumatic event(s).
Intrusion Symptoms	Requires one or more of the following: 1. Recurrent and intrusive distressing memories of the event. 2. Recurrent distressing dreams of the event. 3. Acting or feeling as if the event were recurring. 4. Intense psychological distress when exposed to cues representing the event. 5. Physiological reactivity when exposed to cues that represent the event.	Requires one or more of the following: 1. Recurrent, involuntary, and intrusive memories of the traumatic event(s). 2. Recurrent distressing dreams related to the trauma. 3. Dissociative reactions in which the individual feels as if the traumatic event(s) are occurring again. 4. Psychological distress and exposure to cues representing the traumatic event(s). 5. Physiological reactions to cues that represent the traumatic event(s).
Avoidance Symptoms	Requires three or more of the following: 1. Efforts to avoid thoughts, feelings, or conversations regarding the trauma. 2. Efforts to avoid people, places, or activities that recall the trauma. 3. Inability to remember an important aspect of the trauma. 4. Diminished interest or participation in important activities. 5. Feeling detached or estranged from others. 6. A restricted range of affect. 7. Feelings of a foreshortened future.	Requires one or both of the following: 1. Avoidance of distressing memories, thoughts, or feelings associated with the traumatic event(s). 2. Avoidance of external reminders that arouse distressing memories thoughts or feelings of the traumatic event(s).

TABLE 12.2   *(continued)*

	DSM-IV TR	*DSM-5*
Negative Alterations of Cognitions and Mood		Requires two or more of the following:
		1. Inability to remember an important aspect of the traumatic event(s).
		2. Exaggerated and persistent negative beliefs about self, others, and/or the world.
		3. Persistent distorted beliefs, causing the individual to blame themselves for the traumatic event(s).
		4. Persistent negative emotional state.
		5. Diminished interest or participation in important activities.
		6. Feeling detached or estranged from others.
		7. Persistent inability to experience positive emotions.
Arousal Symptoms	Requires two or more of the following:	Requires two or more of the following:
	1. Difficulty falling asleep or staying asleep.	1. Irritable behavior and angry outbursts.
	2. Irritability or anger.	2. Reckless or self-destructive behavior.
	3. Difficulty concentrating.	3. Hypervigilance.
	4. Hypervigilance.	4. Exaggerated startle response.
	5. Exaggerated startle response.	5. Problems with concentration.
		6. Sleep disturbance.

DSM-IV-TR Source: APA, 2000, pp. 467–468
DSM-5 Source: APA, 2013a, pp. 271–272

trauma, or childhood adversity), children 6 years or younger may be vulnerable to PTSD when they learn of a traumatic event that happened to a parent or caregiver. As with adults, children may experience intrusive distressing memories or dreams of the events, although it may be difficult to determine whether the frightening content of the dreams is actually related to the trauma. Similarly, intrusive memories may not be expressed verbally but may be acted out through play (e.g., developmental regression or trauma-specific play reenactment). Children may have the same sort of dissociative reactions as adults, feeling as if the traumatic event is reoccurring, but they may also experience intense psychological or physiological distress when exposed to reminders of the trauma. Children could experience either avoidance of stimuli or negative alterations in cognitions.

The negative changes in cognitions for children may appear as them being more, or more frequently, fearful, confused, or sad; they may withdraw from social situations, including play, and there may be a marked decrease in the positive emotions that they are experiencing or expressing. Avoidance behaviors include efforts to evade situations, settings, and people that bring up memories of the traumatic events. The arousal symptoms in young children look very similar to those in older individuals. Children may become angry or irritable without provocation, they may be hypervigilant or experience an increased startle response, and they may experience difficulty with sleep and concentration. As with adults, the disturbing symptoms must be present for at least one month and cause significant impairment in relationships with family, caregivers, and friends, or with school behavior. The clinician must make the same determination as to whether there are sufficient dissociative experiences present to specify with dissociative symptoms, and must specify if there is a delayed expression when the full criteria are not met until at least six months after the traumatic event. Read Sidebar 12.1, the case of Jane the counselor, and consider the questions at the end.

SIDEBAR 12.1

Jane is a seasoned counselor, and over the past few years, she has begun working more with traumatized individuals. She initially enjoyed the challenge of helping people find relief from the stress and trauma they have experienced, but over the last several months she has been finding less enjoyment and reward in her work. In fact, she finds that she thinks about her clients more and more, and often cannot stop thinking about the traumatic stories they have shared with her in sessions, even dreaming about experiences. She has stopped socializing with friends, has begun avoiding certain clients, and just cannot seem to find enjoyment in things that she used to do. Jane isn't sleeping well, she is angry and irritable with her family, and when she goes to work, she finds she just can't concentrate. What do you think Jane is experiencing? Can she be diagnosed, even though she has never experienced these traumas firsthand?

ACUTE STRESS DISORDER (ASD)

As with PTSD, for an individual to be diagnosed with ASD, he or she must have directly experienced or witnessed a traumatic event that involved death, threats of death, grave injury, or sexual violation. Other exposure possibilities include learning of violent or accidental events that occurred to a close family member or friend, or repeated exposure to traumatic events in a professional capacity. ASD requires any nine of the 14 potential symptoms that are clustered into the five categories of intrusion symptoms, negative mood, dissociative symptoms, avoidance symptoms, and arousal symptoms. The symptoms must cause significant distress or impairment in social, occupational, or other important areas of functioning. The presentation of ASD in children may feature the traumatic events being expressed through repetitive play and frightening dreams, though the child may be unable to describe the content.

ADJUSTMENT DISORDERS

An adjustment disorder requires a determination that the individual has developed specific emotional or behavioral symptoms in response to an identifiable stressor. The individual may experience marked distress, which is significantly more intense than one would expect, considering the severity of the stressor, or the individual may experience significant impairments at work, in relationships, or in other significant areas of functioning. It is important to determine that these disturbances are not merely a preexisting disorder that has exacerbated as a result of the stressor, that the disturbance is not better accounted for by another disorder, and that it does not represent normal bereavement. After the stressor and the associated consequences have ended, the disturbance may not persist for longer than six months, though clinicians need to consider cultural factors and other contexts that may affect symptom severity or presentation. Clinicians should specify whether the adjustment disorder exists with depressed mood, anxiety, mixed anxiety and depressed mood, a disturbance of conduct, mixed disturbance of emotions and conduct, or unspecified.

OTHER SPECIFIED TRAUMA- AND STRESSOR-RELATED DISORDER

The category of Other Specified Trauma- and Stressor-Related Disorder is designated for when there are distressing symptoms that are similar to the other trauma- and stressor-related disorders in this chapter, but which do not meet the full criteria for a diagnosis. When using the *other specified* designation, the clinician chooses to identify and communicate the reason why a specific diagnosis is not met. The *DSM-5* offers examples of presentations that can be identified when using the *other specified* designation. This can include adjustment-like disorders, which either have a delayed onset of symptoms more than three months after the stressor, or have a duration of symptoms longer than six months without a persistent stressor. One example is the *ataque de nervios* ("attack of nerves"), which is referenced in the *DSM-5* Glossary of Cultural Concepts of Distress as a syndrome among individuals of Latino descent, which manifests with intense emotional upset, dissociative experiences, and the sense of being out of control. Finally, when appropriate, persistent complex bereavement disorder, which is a category included in the section for Conditions for Further Study, can be used in situations in which the clinician chooses to communicate the specific reason that the individual's presentation does not meet the criteria for any specific trauma- and stressor-related disorder.

UNSPECIFIED TRAUMA- AND STRESSOR-RELATED DISORDER

The category for *unspecified* can be used when there are distressing symptoms that are similar to the other trauma- and stressor-related disorders in this chapter, but which do not meet the full criteria for a diagnosis. In these instances the clinician may choose not to specify the reason why the criteria for another diagnosis are not met. This can include situations when there is insufficient information for a more specific diagnosis (e.g., in a hospital emergency department). The culture of an individual can play a significant role in how grief, loss, or trauma manifest. Sidebar 12.2 has you consider the role of culture in grief, loss, and trauma.

SIDEBAR 12.2

You have read about how some cultural manifestations of grief and loss could be misinterpreted as characteristic of a mental disorder. *Ataque de nervios* ("attack of nerves") is just one example provided of how a counselor needs to be careful in not rushing to diagnose. Some cultures have specified mourning periods that can last months, others encourage the tearing of clothes by the bereaved. Based on your own personal and professional experiences, what are some other ways of experiencing grief that may look out of the norm in your community? How will you remain culturally competent in working with those experiencing grief?

Differential Diagnosis

Because some of the autism spectrum disorder behavioral features are similar to those of RAD, it is essential that the counselor rule out autism spectrum disorder. The most significant distinguishing feature of RAD is the history of severe social neglect, which must precede the behaviors associated with RAD, but not those typical of autism spectrum disorder. In addition, children with autism spectrum disorder tend to display repetitive behaviors (e.g. checking and strict routines) and restricted interests, and those features are not typical of RAD. The other important distinguishing feature is that children with autism spectrum disorder demonstrate attachment behaviors that are appropriate to their developmental level whereas children with RAD engage in those attachment behaviors infrequently and inconsistently. Clinicians also need to differentiate RAD from children who have intellectual disability (intellectual developmental disorder) as those children typically demonstrate developmentally appropriate positive affect and emotion regulation, along with selective attachment behaviors, unlike children with RAD. Finally, clinicians should carefully differentiate between children who have depressive disorders from those who have RAD. There may be a similar presentation in terms of emotional and social interactions, but again, the most salient feature, the ability to form secure attachments, is not typically impaired among children with depressive disorders. These children are still able to seek out and respond to adults who will comfort them when they are distressed—especially when experiencing a sad, down, or irritable mood.

With regard to DSED, children with ADHD will occasionally demonstrate impulsivity that may appear similar to DSED. However, the underlying feature of DSED is poor attachment and social neglect, and children with DSED do not show difficulties with either attention or hyperactivity, which are the salient features of ADHD.

The *DSM-5* identifies 10 disorders that should be considered for a differential diagnosis of PTSD. Most significant among them are ASD and adjustment disorders, which are also discussed in this chapter. With ASD the symptom pattern is very similar to PTSD, but the timeframe is less (three days to one month). Other disorders to differentiate from PTSD include anxiety disorders, obsessive-compulsive disorders, major depressive disorders, dissociative disorders, and psychotic disorders. The critical component of each of these is that PTSD requires the symptomatology to result from a traumatic experience. One especially challenging differential diagnosis is traumatic brain injury (TBI). This new classification for the *DSM-5* is a merging of the *DSM-IV-TR*'s Dementia Due to Head Trauma and Postconcussional Disorder and is one of the 10 etiological specifiers among the new Neurocognitive Disorders classification. TBI induces headaches, dizziness, sensitivity to light or sound, irritability, and concentration deficits like PTSD; however, persistent disorientation and confusion are manifest exclusively in TBI. Neuropsychological testing is critical to differentiate between these two disorders.

Because adjustment disorders can present with depressed mood, anxiety, mixed anxiety and depressed mood, disturbance of conduct, or mixed disturbance of emotions and conduct, care must be taken with regard to a differential diagnosis. There are several differential diagnoses to consider, including major depressive disorder, PTSD or ASD, and personality disorders. If an individual experiences major depressive episode symptoms following a stressful event, major depressive disorder is the more appropriate diagnosis. Similarly, the intensity of the experiences following the stressful events required to meet criteria for adjustment disorder does not typically rise to the level required for PTSD or ASD. With regard to personality disorders, responses to stressors may seem out of proportion with individuals who have a history of characterlogical abnormalities. Counselors should clarify whether the stressful event is exacerbating an existing personality disorder or whether it is a clinically distinct adjustment disorder. Table 12.2 is a helpful table for assisting clinicians in differentiating trauma- and stressor-related disorders in children and adolescents.

Assessment Strategies

Table 12.3 summarizes types of trauma assessments for children.

CHILDREN AGES 0–12

PTSD Semi-Structured Interview and Observation (Sheeringa & Zeanah, 1994)

The PTSD Semi-Structured Interview and Observation is a measure designed to assess for the presence of PTSD symptoms in children ages 0 to 6 (Stover & Berkowitz, 2005). In an interview format, a caregiver is asked if a child has been exposed to 11 different traumas (Stover, 2014). Information about duration and frequency of the trauma experience is also collected (Stover, 2014). If a caregiver reports that a child has been exposed to a trauma-related experience, the interviewer then asks questions to assess for the presence of PTSD related symptoms that align with the *DSM-IV-TR* criteria (Stover & Berkowitz, 2005). Additional questions are asked for each symptom the caregiver endorses in order to understand the level of impairment the symptoms are having on the child (Stover & Berkowitz, 2005). A score can be calculated that corresponds to the *DSM-IV-TR* criteria that is more "developmentally sensitive" (Stover, 2014, n.p.). A unique feature of this assessment is that while the interviewer is asking questions of the parent, he or she is also observing the child for evidence of clinically significant information (Stover & Berkowitz, 2005). The assessment is 29 questions and takes approximately 45 minutes to complete (Stover, 2014).

Stover and Berkowitz (2005) noted that the PTSD Semi-Structured Interview and Observation is one of the more complete assessments for PTSD in young children because an interviewer gathers information from the caregiver while observing the child. Additionally, the measure was developed specifically for young children, an area that has been lacking (Stover & Berkowitz, 2005). This measure is free (Stover, 2014). However, it is recommended for an experienced clinician to administer this assessment due to the challenges of observing a child while asking a caregiver questions (Stover & Berkowitz, 2005). Another concern is that this assessment can take a long time to administer (Stover, 2014). Overall, if an experienced clinician who is familiar with the presentation of PTSD symptoms in young children is interested in using a formal assessment, then the PTSD Semi-Structured Interview and Observation would be an appropriate measure.

Trauma Symptom Checklist for Young Children (TSCYC, Briere, 2005)

The Trauma Symptom Checklist for Young Children (TSCYC) is a 90-item measure designed to be administered to caretakers of a child (ages three to 12) to assess for the presence of PTSD symptoms (U.S. Department of Veteran Affairs [VA], 2014e). The TSCYC comprises two validity scores (response level and atypical response) and eight clinical scales (anxiety, depression, anger/aggression, posttraumatic stress-intrusion,

TABLE 12.3   Trauma- and Stressor-Related Disorders Differential Diagnosis

	PTSD: < Age 7	*PTSD: > Age 6*	*Acute Stress Disorder*	*Adjustment Disorders*
Profile	Development of characteristic symptoms (e.g., fear-based reexperiencing, emotional, behavioral, anhedonic or dysphoric mood states, negative cognitions, arousal and reactive-externalizing, or dissociative) following exposure to one or more traumatic events	Development of characteristic symptoms (e.g., fear-based reexperiencing, emotional, behavioral, anhedonic or dysphoric mood states, negative cognitions, arousal and reactive-externalizing, or dissociative) following exposure to one or more traumatic events	Development of characteristic symptoms (e.g., reactive anxiety, dissociative or detached presentation, strong emotional or physiological reactivity, strong anger response/irritable or aggressive response)	Presence of marked emotional (e.g., depressed mood and/or anxiety) or behavioral symptoms (e.g., suicide attempts or disturbance of conduct) exceeding what would normally be expected in response to an identifiable stressor
Onset	Exposure to actual or threatened death, serious injury, or sexual violence	Exposure to actual or threatened death, serious injury, or sexual violence	Exposure to actual or threatened death, serious injury, or sexual violation	Identifiable stressor
Sources	• *Direct* recipient • *Witnessing* to others, especially primary caregivers (excludes electronic media, television, movies, or pictures) • *Learning* of events to a parent or caregiving figure	• *Direct* recipient • *Witnessing* to others • *Learning* of events, violent or accidental, to a family member or friend • *Exposure*, repeated or extreme, to aversive details (excludes non-work-related electronic media, television, movies, or pictures)	• *Direct* recipient • *Witnessing* to others • *Learning* of events, violent or accidental, to a family member or friend • *Exposure*, repeated or extreme, to aversive details (excludes non-work-related electronic media, television, movies, or pictures)	Identifiable stressor (e.g., single, multiple, recurrent, continuous, acute, or developmental)
Intrusion Symptoms	• Threshold: one of four • Psychological distress • Distressing memories • Distressing dreams • Dissociative reactions • Physiological reactions	• Threshold: one of four • Psychological distress • Distressing memories (*repetitive play with traumatic themes*) • Distressing dreams (*may be frightening without recognizable content*) • Dissociative reactions (trauma-specific reenactment in play) • Physiological reactions (... *to internal or external cues that symbolize or resemble an aspect ...*)	• Threshold: zero of four • Psychological distress or physiological reactions • Distressing memories (*repetitive play with traumatic themes*) • Distressing dreams (*may be frightening without recognizable content*) • Dissociative reactions (trauma-specific reenactment in play) • Physiological reactions (... *to internal or external cues that symbolize or resemble an aspect ...*)	None

TABLE 12.3 *(continued)*

	PTSD: < Age 7	PTSD: > Age 6	Acute Stress Disorder	Adjustment Disorders
Persistent Avoidance	Threshold: zero or one of two Activities, places, or physical reminders that arouse recollections of the traumatic event(s)	Threshold: one of two Memories, thoughts, or feelings about or closely associated with the traumatic event(s)	Threshold: zero of two Memories, thoughts, or feelings about or closely associated with the traumatic event(s)	None
Alterations in Cognitions and Mood	Threshold: zero or one of four • Significantly increased frequency of negative emotional states • Socially withdrawn behavior • Markedly diminished interest or participation in significant activities, *including constriction of play* • Persistent reduction in expression of positive emotions	Threshold: two of seven • Persistent negative emotional state • Feelings of detachment or estrangement from others • Markedly diminished interest or participation in significant activities • Persistent inability to experience positive emotions • Inability to remember an important aspect of the traumatic event(s) • Persistent and exaggerated negative beliefs or expectations about oneself, others, or the world • Persistent, distorted cognitions about the cause or consequences of the traumatic event(s) that lead the individual to blame himself/herself or others	Threshold: zero of one • Persistent inability to experience positive emotions	None
Alterations in Arousal and Reactivity	Threshold: two of five • Hypervigilance • Exaggerated startle response • Problems with concentration • Sleep disturbance • Irritable behavior and angry outbursts *(including extreme temper tantrums)*	Threshold: one of six • Hypervigilance • Exaggerated startle response • Problems with concentration • Sleep disturbance • Irritable behavior and angry outbursts • Reckless or self-destructive behavior	Threshold: zero of five • Hypervigilance • Exaggerated startle response • Problems with concentration • Sleep disturbance • Irritable behavior and angry outbursts	None

TABLE 12.3   (*continued*)

	PTSD: < Age 7	*PTSD: > Age 6*	*Acute Stress Disorder*	*Adjustment Disorders*
Dissociative Symptoms	None. Specify PTSD as depersonalization/ derealization	None. Specify PTSD as depersonalization/ derealization	Threshold: zero of two • Altered sense of the reality of one's surroundings or oneself (depersonalization/ derealization) • Inability to remember an important aspect of the trauma (amnesia)	None
Duration	> one month after trauma exposure	> one month after trauma exposure	> three days and < one month after trauma exposure	< three months of the stressor onset and < six months after the stressor cessation
Distress or Impairment	Relationships with parents, siblings, peers, or other caregivers or with school behavior	Social, occupational, or other important areas of functioning	Social, occupational, or other important areas of functioning	Social, occupational, or other important areas of functioning
Diagnostic Criteria	Seven (with three symptom clusters requiring four of 18 symptoms minimum)	Eight (with four symptom clusters requiring six of 20 symptoms minimum)	Five (with five symptom clusters requiring nine of 14 symptoms minimum)	Five (with one of two symptoms minimum)
Mutual Exclusivity	Acute stress disorder, physiological effects of a substance, and another medical condition	Acute stress disorder, physiological effects of a substance, and another medical condition	Posttraumatic stress disorder, brief psychotic disorder, physiological effects of a substance, and another medical condition	Normative stress reactions, another mental disorder, exacerbation of a preexisting mental disorder, and normal bereavement

Source: King, 2014.

posttraumatic stress-avoidance, posttraumatic stress-arousal, dissociation, and sexual concerns) measured using a Likert-type scale (Mackler, 2007). Caretakers are asked to report how often they have observed a particular symptom in the past month ranging from 1 (*not at all*) to 4 (*very often*; Stinnett, 2007). There is also a total score that is calculated (posttraumatic stress-total). Scores of each subscale are converted to t-scores and are compared to cutoffs in the TYCYC manual (Stinnett, 2007). These scores can be compared to a posttraumatic score worksheet to note the possibility of a PTSD diagnosis in children five or older (VA, 2014e). The TSYCYC is written at a 6.8 reading level

(Mackler, 2007). The TSCYC can be administered by anyone, but the results should be interpreted only by a trained mental health professional (Mackler, 2007).

A major positive of this measure is there is a short amount of time needed to administer the assessment (15 minutes on average; Gilbert & Acker, 2014). Additionally, both the validity and reliability of this measure are strong. However, there is a monetary cost to use the TSCYC. Additionally, while the measure is designed for young children, it does not include questions about symptomatology in young children specifically (Gilbert & Acker, 2014).

CHILDREN AGES 6–18

The Early Development and Home Background Measures

The Early Development and Home Background (EDHB) forms may be useful for clinicians who are interested in better understanding the home life, both past and present, of a child with whom they are working (APA, 2014). We include brief descriptions of the two EDHB forms: one designed for a parent or guardian of a child ages 6 to 17 and one for clinicians. The Early Development and Home Background-Parent/Guardian (EDHB) form is a 19-item measure across three domains (early development, early communication, and home environment; APA, 2013d). The clinician then completes the EDHB-Clinician, which is an eight-item measure across three domains (early CNS problems, early disturbance of home environment: early abuse or neglect, and home environment; APA, 2013b). The items in each domain correspond to the items in the domains for the EDHB-Parent/Guardian (APA, 2013b). Clinicians can read the general instructions for each measure, and they are both accessible for no cost at www.psychiatry.org/practice/dsm/dsm5/online-assessment-measures.

DSM-5 SEVERITY MEASURES

The *DSM-5* disorder-specific severity measures are designed to assess the extent to which an individual is bothered by problems becoming worse after a trauma- or stressor-related event. These measures are useful for clients who have experienced extremely stressful events and therefore may be administered over time to assess changes in symptomology (APA, 2013). To determine client prognosis, develop individualized treatment plans, and monitor outcomes, clinicians may choose from three *DSM-5* trauma- and stressor-related emerging assessment measures: Severity of Posttraumatic Stress Symptoms—Child Age 11–17, Severity of Acute Stress Symptoms—Child Age 11–17, and Severity of Dissociative Symptoms—Child Age 11–17. These measures are available at no cost at www.psychiatry.org/practice/dsm/dsm5/online-assessment-measures and are reviewed below.

Severity of Posttraumatic Stress Symptoms—Child Age 11–17—National Stressful Events Survey PTSD Short Scale (NSESSS; APA, 2013d)

This nine-item questionnaire assesses the presence of PTSD-related cognitive, affective, behavioral, and physiological symptoms in children ages 11 to 17 (APA, 2013d). Using a five-point Likert-type scale ranging (0 = not at all to 4 = extremely), children are asked to answer questions about the presence of symptoms over the past seven days (APA, 2013d). There are also two additional narrative questions where children are asked to "list the traumatic event you experienced" and the date of the traumatic experience (APA, 2013d, n.p.). A total score is computed by adding the child's score for each item (maximum of 36). A larger score is interpreted as the "greater severity of posttraumatic stress disorder" (APA, 2013d, n.p.).

Severity of Acute Stress Symptoms—Child Age 11–17—National Stressful Events Survey Acute Stress Disorder Short Scale (NSESSS; APA, 2013b)

Children are asked to answer "how bothered" they have been by symptoms over the past seven days related to a stressful or traumatic experience (APA, 2013b, n.p.). This seven-item questionnaire measures on a five-point Likert-type scale (0 = not at all to 4 = extremely; APA, 2013b). To score the results, the test administer added up the child's score on each question to get a total score (maximum = 28). This total score can be interpreted as the "greater severity of acute stress disorder" (APA, 2013b, n.p.).

Severity of Dissociative Symptoms—Child Age 11–17—Brief Dissociative Experiences Scale—Modified (DES-B, APA, 2013c)

This measure assess the presence of dissociative symptoms in children ages 11–17 (APA, 2013c). Children are asked to answer eight questions using a five-point Likert-type scale (0 = not at all to 4 = more than once a day; APA, 2013c) and they report how often "things" have happened in the past seven days (APA, 2013c, n.p.). To score the results, the clinician adds the rating for each of the seven items to get a total score (maximum = 28, APA, 2013c). The test administrator interprets this score (the larger the number, the more "dissociative experiences"; APA, 2013c, n.p.).

Trauma Symptom Checklist for Children (TSCC, Briere, 1996)

The Trauma Symptoms Checklist for Children (TSCC) is 54-item self-report item used to measure the presence of PTSD-related symptoms in children 8 to 16 years of age (VA, 2014d). The TSCC contains two validity scales (that measure over reporting and under-reporting), six clinical scales (anxiety, depression, posttraumatic stress, sexual concerns, dissociation, and anger) and four subscales (sexual preoccupation, sexual distress, dissociation fantasy, and overt dissociation; Boyle, 2003). There is another form of the TSCC that does not include the sexual concern questions if there are apprehensions about question appropriateness (Viswesvaran, 2003). The TSCC is written at an 8-year-old's reading level (VA, 2014d). It typically takes 15 to 20 minutes to complete the TSCC, though it can take longer in children who have experienced high levels of trauma (Boyle, 2003). The TSCC is a Likert-type assessment where children are asked about the presence or absence of symptoms (0 = never to 3 = almost all the time; VA, 2014d).

Children's PTSD Inventory (CPTSD-I, Saigh, 2004)

The Children's PTSD Inventory (CPTSD-I) is a structured interview designed to assess PTSD symptoms in children ages 6 to 18. The items in the CPTSD-I are divided into five sections, which correspond to the categories of the *DSM-IV-TR*: Exposure and Situational Reactivity, Reexperiencing, Avoidance and Numbing, Increased Arousal, and Significant Distress or Impairment (Christopher, 2007). If a child's experiences meet the criteria of a traumatic event, then symptomology is further assessed, which leads to a longer assessment time (VA, 2014a). It takes between 15 and 20 minutes for children who have experienced a trauma event, but much less for children who have not (Christopher, 2007). The assessment is 50 questions, and children answer yes or no to each question

(Ghosh Ippen & Alley, 2014). The instrument administrator continues to the next question if the child answers yes (Doll & Osborn, 2007).

Child PTSD Symptoms Scale (CPSS; Foa, Johnson, Fenny, & Treadwell, 2001)

The Child PTSD Symptoms Scale (CPSS) was developed from the PTSD Diagnostic Scale (Foa, Johnson, Feeny, & Treadwell, 2001), which was designed for adults. The language of the PTSD Diagnostic Scale was changed to be more appropriate for children to measure functional impairment (Foa et al, 2001). The CPSS is designed to assess symptoms of PTSD in children related to the *DSM-IV-TR* and is available at no cost. The CPSS is a paper-and-pencil, self-report measure designed for children ages 8 to 18 who have experienced a traumatic event (Foa et al., 2001). It averages 15 to 20 minutes to complete the CPSS and can be scored in five minutes (Smith, 2014). The CPSS is a 26-item measure scored using a four-point Likert scale asking children to answer how often have symptoms occurred over the past month (0 = not at all to 3 = 5 or more times a week; Foa et al., 2001). The instrument comprises three separate scales: two event items, 17 symptom items, and seven functional impairment items. Each question in the 17 symptoms item scale relate to the 17 diagnostic features of PTSD in the *DSM-IV-TR*. This scale produces a total score ranging 0–51 to rate the severity of symptoms and three subscale scores: reexperiencing, avoidance, and arousal. The seven-item functional impairment score assesses the impairment of daily functioning in the child caused by the severity of symptoms (Foa et al., 2001).

Clinician-Administered PTSD Scale for Children (CAPS-CA, Nader et al., 2004; Newman et al., 2004)

The Clinician-Administered PTSD Scale for Children (CAPS-CA) was developed from The Clinician-Administered PTSD Scale (CAPS), which is considered the gold standard of trauma assessments for individuals ages 15 and older (VA, 2014c). The CAPS-CA is a 33-item measure that is administered by a trained mental health professional. The CAPS-CA can be administered to children ages 8 to 18 to assess for PTSD symptoms (VA, 2014c). The average time of completion is 52 minutes, though it can range between 30 and 120 minutes to administer (Ghosh Ippen, Augenbraun, & DioGuardi, 2014; VA, 2014c). Should a child have experienced multiple trauma-related events, the CAPS-CA can account for that.

To administer the CAPS-CA, an interviewer asks a child questions about symptoms over the past month and the child answers using a Likert-type scale (0 = none at this time to 4 = most of the time, daily or almost every day; Ghosh Ippen et al., 2014). There is also a scale that measures the intensity of symptoms, which is also scored using a Likert-type scale (0 = not a problem, none to 3 = a lot, severe, considerable distress, difficulty dismissing). Children also have the option to select their answers using pictures that correspond to the frequency and intensity (Ghosh Ippen et al., 2014). A total score is then derived that is related to the *DSM-IV-TR* criteria (a version of the CAPS-CA corresponding to the *DSM-5* is being developed) and subscale scores for reexperiencing, avoidance and numbing, and arousal.

The CAPS-CA is a well-researched measure that has applications for numerous trauma experiences, including traffic accidents and sexual abuse (Ghosh Ippen et al., 2014). The CAPS-CA is an instrument that provides a comprehensive amount of information regarding trauma symptoms, including frequency and intensity. The CAPS-CA can take a long time to administer, and there is a cost associated with administering the assessment. It is also important to note that the CAPS-CA requires a child to have endorsed experiencing a traumatic event and therefore would not be useful if a child denies a history of trauma (Ghosh Ippen et al., 2014).

My Worst Experiences Scale (MWES; Hyman & Snook, 2002)

The My Worst Experiences Scale (MWES) is a self-report measure designed for children ages 9 to 18 (VA, 2014b). The MWES asks children about the worst trauma-related experience they have experienced and then assesses for symptoms related to that experience. The MWES comprises two separate sections. In Section One, children are asked to check the worst experience they have had from 21 options that are likely to cause stress or trauma (e.g., abuse, disaster, and family problems; VA, 2014b). Children are also asked to include information about the experience (e.g., age of the experience and whether this is still worrisome, Medway, 2005). In Section Two, children are asked to answer 105 Likert-type scale questions (0 = not at all to 5 = all the time) about their thoughts, feelings, and behaviors in the past month related to the worst experience (VA, 2014b). For any child who can read at a third-grade reading level or better, the test can be completed in 20 to 30 minutes (Moore, 2005).

The MWES can be administered on a computer that yields two important scores (Medway, 2005). The first score is an Inconsistent Responding Index, which measures the consistency (reliability and accuracy) of the child's answers. The second score, derived from t-scores, is a total score and subscale score (impact of the event, reexperience of the trauma, avoidance and numbing, and increased arousal) related to the *DSM-IV-TR* criteria for the diagnosis of PTSD (VA, 2014b). These subscales are scored ranging 4–24 (Medway, 2005). Within the subscales there are additional factors: depression, hopelessness, somatic symptoms, oppositional conduct, hypervigilance, dissociation/dreams, and general maladjustment. These subscales are used for differential diagnosis and possible need for further psychological assessment (Medway, 2005).

Overall, the MWES provides a significant amount of information for a clinician in a relatively limited amount of time. The MWES is computer based, meaning scoring is completed in a short amount of time and insures accuracy of the score. The test can be administered to an individual or to a group and is a useful screening tool. The Inconsistent Responding Index helps identify items that may be insignificant to the child (Medway, 2005). There is concern, however, that the MWES elicits trauma or a stress-related event that may or may not be stress related at all to the child (Medway, 2005). Similarly, events that may be a part of normal development are included, whereas events that many would find traumatic are not (Medway, 2005). The measure is available to any trained mental health professional (VA, 2014b). In conclusion, the MWES has strong reliability and has use in both community and school settings. However, there is a need for additional data on usefulness in younger children and underrepresented populations (Medway, 2005).

Trauma and Attachment Belief Scale (TABS, Pearlman, 2003)

The Trauma and Attachment Belief Scale is an 84-item self-report assessment designed to the cognitive beliefs related to experiencing a trauma (Garro, 2005). The TABS is scored using a six-point Likert-type scale on five major areas across 10 subscales (Ghosh Ippen & Kulkarni, 2014). The test will likely take between 10 to 20 minutes to complete (Garro, 2005). The TABS was developed from trauma theory (Ghosh Ippen & Kulkarni, 2014). However, there are concerns with the lack of the validity of the measure (Aidman, 2005).

Therefore it may not be useful as a clinical assessment if used independently without other measures (Garro, 2005). There is also a monetary cost to use this measure (Ghosh Ippen & Kulkarni, 2014). However, a clinician may find the TABS useful in clinical practice (Garro, 2005).

Treatment Strategies and Interventions

REACTIVE ATTACHMENT DISORDER AND DISINHIBITED SOCIAL ENGAGEMENT DISORDER

Seligman and Reichenberg (2012) have identified the treatments and interventions for RAD to also be appropriate for children with DSED; thus, the treatments and interventions for these disorders will be included together. Because children who exhibit symptoms of RAD and DSED often lack trust in a caregiver as a result of previous neglect or abuse, the treatment of the disorder is based on the principles of attachment theory (Horner, 2008). Using those tenets as the foundation of therapy, counselors can then choose between three empirically supported methods of treatment modalities: therapy through the caregiver, dyadic therapy, and therapy with the child alone. Prior to choosing a modality for treatment, the American Academy of Child and Adolescent Psychiatry (AACAP) has identified observation as a minimal standard of care. Specifically, the AACAP states the minimal standard for observation should include evidence from serial observations of the child interacting with the primary caregiver as well as unfamiliar adults, a history of the child's pattern of attachment behaviors with the caregivers and a history of the child's early caregiving environment (American Academy of Child and Adolescent Psychiatry, 1997 as cited in Boris & Zeaneh, 2005). Once these histories have been gathered and observations have taken place, the clinician can then choose which modality, or combination of modalities, to use in treatment.

Working through the Caregiver

Attachment patterns between caregivers and children with RAD and DSED are often sources of stress for caregivers, and it is common that they experience negative emotions toward the children because of this stress. When stress levels in a caregiver are high, it may benefit the caregiver to work through his or her own negative emotions before attempting to engage with the child. Working one-on-one with the caregiver encourages examination of the person's own perceptions and feelings about the child and allows room for exploration around the ways in which the caregiver's feelings about the child may be affecting his or her parenting choices (Boris & Zeanah, 2005). For example, adults who may be feeling disconnected from a child because of the child's disinterest in affection may become withdrawn in parenting style, which further impacts the child's attachment pattern. Through a narrative dialogue between clinician and caregiver, distortions or adjustments in parenting style can be examined with the intention of altering behaviors to diminish any disruptions in attachment that the caregiver may be contributing through defective parenting choices (Boris & Zeanah, 2005). Once a caregiver has examined his or her perceptions of the relationship with the child, a clinician can work with the caregiver to help him or her learn ways to establish a secure connection with the child and manage a child's behavior (Boris & Zeanah, 2005).

Dyad or Family System

A second modality for the treatment of these disorders involves working with the primary caregiver(s) and child in a dyad or family system. The basic principle in working with the dyad is to highlight the parenting strengths of the caregiver while the caregiver engages with the child. By establishing trust between caregiver and counselor through this strength-based approach, the clinician can then begin to challenge caregivers in moments when harmful emotional reactions to the child's behavior impact the engagement and establish alternative behaviors that facilitate healthy attachment (Shreeve, 2012). There are several empirically supported interventions that can be used within the dyad, specifically the Circle of Security, play therapy, and homework.

Circle of Security

The Circle of Security is a 20-week intervention that contains both educational and therapeutic components and originates from the dynamics of secure and insecure attachments (Marvin, Cooper, Hoffman, & Powell, 2002). Hoffman, Marvin, Cooper, and Powell (2006) outlined the five goals of the Circle of Security as:

1. Establish the therapist and the group as a secure base from which the caregiver can explore his or her relationship with the child
2. Increase caregiver sensitivity and appropriate responsiveness by providing caregivers a map of children's basic attachment needs
3. Increase caregivers' capacity to recognize and understand both the obvious and subtler verbal and nonverbal cues that children use to signal their internal states and needs when using the caregiver as a secure base for exploration and as a haven of safety
4. Increase caregiver empathy by supporting reflection about the caregiver's and the child's behaviors, thoughts, and feelings regarding attachment-oriented interactions
5. Increase caregiver reflection about how his or her own developmental history affects current caregiving behavior. (p. 1018)

In conjunction with the educational and therapeutic components, this intervention uses a group approach. Through videotaped sessions that are edited for use by the therapist, caregivers review their interactions with their children and discuss ways in which those interactions can be modified to promote healthier attachment patterns. While receiving feedback from other caregivers in the group and engaging with the educational and therapeutic components of this intervention, caregivers ultimately learn ways to repair disruptions in interactions, which is the core of secure attachment (Marvin et al., 2002).

Play Therapy

Play therapy is another intervention that can be used in the dyad/family system to address symptoms of RAD. Integrative play therapy approaches have demonstrated effectiveness in improving the relationship between caregivers and children (Weir, 2008). Before employing play therapy techniques, it may be beneficial for a clinician to assess the needs of the family from a family structure lens. By examining the family structure, patterns of interactions may emerge that aid a clinician in choosing play therapy techniques that will most benefit the child (Weir, 2008). The premise for use of play therapy is to create an environment of trust and security between caregiver and child and to replicate healthy caregiver–child interactions through play. The clinician may take on various roles when using play therapy within a family unit, such as coordinating and passively observing games, actively participating in games, and modeling healthy behaviors for parents (Weir, 2008).

At-Home Practice

Additionally, therapists working with a family unit may find activities that can be used at home to be a useful intervention (Weir, 2008). Asking families to practice new skills or purposefully engage in new behaviors outside of the counseling room encourages caregivers and children to experiment with new patterns of healthy interaction. For example, a family unit that is engaged in play therapy may be introduced to a game or activity in session, then asked to play that game together one time before the next session. As counseling progresses, choosing games that focus on the caregiver–child relationship that is experiencing the more severe attachment issues may offer additional benefit to the family unit (Weir, 2008).

Child Alone

Dyadic intervention is the preferred method of treatment for a child with RAD. Working with a child without the primary caregiver present should be considered an augmentation of the dyadic work that is being done. When working individually with a child, the therapist seeks to establish a trusting relationship with the child, with the intent of reducing behaviors that are interfering with the dyadic work. For the individual work to be successful, consistent collaboration with the caregivers is needed (Boris & Zeanah, 2005).

POSTTRAUMATIC STRESS DISORDER (PTSD)

Cognitive Model of PTSD

The most widely recognized model for conceptualizing PTSD is through a cognitive lens, and effective treatment for PTSD using a cognitive approach has been empirically supported (Smith et al., 2013). Recently, studies have modified the cognitive-behavioral approach to better meet the needs of children and adolescents by teaching anxiety management techniques as well as including the family in treatment (Nixon, Sterk, & Pearce, 2012). As with many interventions, developmental level must be taken into account when using CBT interventions with children (Cohen, Mannarino & Deblinger, 2012).

Cognitive-Behavioral Therapy (CBT)

PTSD can be viewed from a cognitive-behavioral lens because it results from stressful trigger events that have already taken place. Following these events, Ehlers and Clark (2000) stated that people begin to appraise these events negatively, and these appraisals affect current functioning. For example, if a child is involved in a car accident, that child may overgeneralize and appraise the situation to be that cars are no longer safe. These internal beliefs may lead to the child refusing to ride in a car or an unrealistic fear of another accident occurring. Emotional reactions result from these appraisals, and many children experience a range of negative emotions at various times, depending on the appraisal that the children encounter in any given situation (Ehlers & Clark, 2000). Using this model of appraisals, or distorted cognitions, followed by emotional reactions, cognitive-behavioral approach to PTSD can then be applied by working to uncover appraisals and correct distorted thought patterns that will ultimately decrease the emotional reactions that clients experience related to the traumatic event.

Anxiety Management Components

One aspect of using CBT to treat symptoms of PTSD in children is psychoeducational training in anxiety management techniques, such as controlled breathing and muscle relaxation (Saunders, Berliner, & Hanson, 2004). The anxiety management techniques are intended to enable the child to decrease the physiological symptoms that the child may encounter when thinking about or discussing the traumatic event. Focusing on relaxation techniques early in the therapeutic relationship facilitates later success for the child as he or she begins discussing the traumatic event (American Academy of Child and Adolescent Psychiatry, 2010). Additionally, a counselor can encourage a child to use the anxiety management techniques outside of the session if the child experiences physiological symptoms in daily life.

Trauma Narrative

Once relaxation techniques have been mastered, children and counselors can then begin to discuss the traumatic event. The National Crime Victims Research and Treatment Center (n.d.) stated that through gradual exposure and trauma narratives, counselors and children can explore the traumatic event, as well as cognitive distortions that arise. The counselor can facilitate the telling of the trauma narrative through drawings or verbally and remains mindful of the needs of the child, including the pace with which the trauma narrative unfolds (National Crime Victims Research and Treatment Center, n.d.).

Cognitive Restructuring

After the child has told his or her trauma narrative, the counselor then employs the basic cognitive-behavioral principles of teaching a child about cognitive distortions and identifying those distortions within the trauma narrative. Children and counselors can work together to identify not only cognitive distortions that occurred during the trauma but also those that children continue to experience as a result of it (Cohen et al., 2012). In some cases, the trauma narrative and subsequent restructuring is not sufficient to change avoidant behaviors in a child. In these cases, in vivo exposure may be indicated. In vivo situations promote cognitive restructuring by demonstrating to the child that the internal dialogue that is experienced during the feared situation is not rational. Cohen et al. (2012) cautioned counselors that the goal of in vivo exposure is not to overwhelm the child but to introduce the child to the feared situation in a gradual manner that allows the child to become increasingly comfortable.

Caregivers

An additional treatment component to working with children who are experiencing symptoms of PTSD is the inclusion of the parents or caregivers. Parents whose children have experienced trauma may find parenting effectively to be a difficult task, given the child's new emerging behavior patterns or avoidance techniques. Offering caregivers new skills to aid in effective parenting may, in turn, benefit the child. Cohen et al. (2012) suggested that counselors offer caregivers psychoeducation about trauma and trauma responses, role-play various situations with caregivers to identify or correct parenting skills, remind parents of the importance of praise, and discuss disciplinary options, such as time out. Additionally, parents can be included in the treatment of a child by having the child teach them the skills that they learn in sessions, such as breathing and muscle relaxation. Parents and children can read the trauma narrative together to encourage children to speak directly with parents about the trauma (Cohen et al., 2012).

Acute Stress Disorder

ASD shares similar criteria to PTSD but differs in the duration of symptoms. ASD is often considered a precursor to PTSD, with symptom presentation occurring anywhere between two days and four weeks post trauma, whereas PTSD is diagnosed from four weeks (Bryant, Friedman, Spiegel, Ursano, & Strain, 2011). Because the disorders are similar in presentation, studies have shown that cognitive-behavioral interventions are effective in reducing the likelihood of a subsequent diagnosis of PTSD (Bryant et al., 2011). Specifically, the in vivo techniques mentioned combined with prolonged exposure to the traumatic event, such as developing a trauma narrative over several counseling sessions, are interventions that can be used together to treat ASD (Cohen et al., 2012; Bryant et al., 2011). As with PTSD, Bryant and Harvey (2000) stressed the importance of psychoeducation with regard to the effects of trauma on cognitive processes, and the need to restructure cognitive processes remains important (Cohen et al., 2012). Diagnosing a trauma-related disorder is not easy and, as you have read, such a disorder can present in many different ways.

ADJUSTMENT DISORDERS

Adjustment disorders, by diagnostic criteria, are time-limited disorders and have not been as well researched as some of the other trauma- and stressor-related disorders, both with regard to pharmacological and psychological interventions. Because of the time specifier of this disorder, brief therapies are generally recommended, although there is not one specific treatment modality that has been found most effective (Casey, 2014). Effective treatment interventions have been identified to address various characteristics of the within the specifiers of adjustment disorder, such as cognitive-behavioral interventions for those who present with disturbance of conduct and for those presenting with anxiety, but not for the disorder itself (James, James, Cowdry, Soler, & Choke, 2015).

Evaluation Strategies

There is growing research and support for early interventions for trauma- and stressor-related disorders that promote prevention and identification of risk factors. Early intervention, especially with children and adolescents, may decrease the risk of chronic trauma responses. However, some researchers have found that individuals may develop other mental disorders because of trauma, including major depressive disorder, specific phobias, personality disorders, and panic disorder (Karam et al, 2014). Cognitive-behavioral treatment interventions are the most empirically supported treatments, and prognosis is good when the relief of trauma- and stressor-related symptomology is the focus of treatment (Forbes et al., 2010).

With regard to the evaluation of treatment, the remediation of trauma- and stressor-related symptomology is the goal. The specific remediation of symptoms varies by individual, as children who experience symptoms of RAD will not exhibit the same hallmark symptoms of those who are being treated for PTSD. Because daily functioning is commonly impaired in individuals who have experienced trauma, evaluation of the effectiveness of treatment may commonly be measured by decrease impairment in daily functioning.

Diagnostic Challenges

Adding a new chapter to the *DSM-5* on trauma- and stressor-related disorders provides clarity to diagnoses that have their roots in some of the most challenging experiences an individual can face. However, there are still numerous challenges in reaching a diagnosis. The presentation within disorders (e.g., PTSD) can vary significantly between children and adults. For example, many children have nightmares. It is often difficult to discern when a nonspecific nightmare (the PTSD criteria) is related to PTSD versus a normal childhood issue. Similarly, many differential diagnoses must be considered for adults and children. The behaviors associated with RAD can look very similar to behaviors found on the autism spectrum to the casual observer. TBI is another diagnostic challenge, because the roots are in a traumatic experience, but the underlying issues may be neurological, and not apparent in a traditional screening. Counselors need to take care in conducting a thorough assessment, including one or more of the instruments described above, and constantly seek verification that the behaviors being seen are in fact related to a trauma or other stressor.

TABLE 12.4 Types of Trauma Assessments for Children

Measure	Age	Respondent	Number of Items	Time to Complete	Cost
PTSD Semi-Structured Interview and Observation	0–6	Caregiver while observing Child	29	45 Minutes	No
TSCYC	3–12	Caregiver	90	15 Minutes	Yes
TSCC	8–16	Child	54	15–20 Minutes	Yes
CPTSD-I	6–18	Child	50	15–20 Minutes	Yes
CPSS	8–18	Child	26	15–20 Minutes	No
CAP-CA	8–18	Child	33	30–120 Minutes	Yes
MWES	9–18	Child	21 Scenarios 105 Questions	20–30 Minutes	No
TABS	9 and up	Child or Adult	84	10–20 Minutes	Yes
NSESS (PTSD)	11–17	Child	9	Unknown	No
NSESS (Acute Stress)	11–17	Child	7	Unknown	No
DES-B	11–17	Child	8	Unknown	No

TSCYC = Trauma Symptom Checklist for Young Children, TSCC = Trauma Symptom Checklist for Children, CPTSD-I = Children PTSD Inventory, CPSS = PTSD Symptom Scale, CAP-CA = Clinician-Administered PTSD Scale for Children and Adolescents, MWES = My Worst Experience Scale, TABS = Trauma and Attachment Belief Scale, NSESSS(PTSD) = Severity of Posttraumatic Stress Symptoms—Child Age 11–17—National Stressful Events Survey PTSD Short Scale, NSESSS(Acute Stress) = Severity of Posttraumatic Stress Symptoms—Child Age 11–17—National Stressful Events Survey PTSD Short Scale, DES-B = Severity of Dissociative Symptoms—Child Age 11–17—Brief Dissociative Experiences Scale—Modified

Summary

Trauma- and stressor-related disorders originate from distressing or demanding events and include reactive attachment disorder, disinhibited social engagement disorder, post-traumatic stress disorder, acute stress disorder, and adjustment disorders. The *DSM-5* introduces this new cluster of disorders and relocates PTSD from the *DSM-IV-TR* anxiety disorders. An additional significant change from the *DSM-IV-TR* to the *DSM-5* in this cluster of disorders is the creation of DSED, which originally was a subtype within RAD. Time is an important factor when considering diagnoses with these disorders, including the chronological and developmental stage of a child and the amount of elapsed time since the occurrence of a traumatic event. The most effective treatments for trauma- and stressor-related disorders center on cognitive behavioral techniques, especially for PTSD, so as to work through the child's distorted thought patterns stemming from the traumatic event(s). Regarding DSED and RAD, the use of play therapy techniques to foster trust and healthy attachments patterns between caregiver and child is an empirically supported method of treatment. Adjustment disorders is an area for future research because this disorder is not well understood, and treatment methods have not been well researched. Table 12.4 lists the types of assessments for children.

References

Aidman, E. (2005). Trauma and Attachment Belief Scale. In *The Sixteenth Measurements Yearbook*. Lincoln: University of Nebraska Press.

American Academy for Child and Adolescent Psychiatry (2010). Practice parameter for the assessment and treatment for children and adolescents with posttraumatic stress disorder. *Journal of American Academy for Child and Adolescent Psychiatry, 49*(4), 414-430.

American Psychiatric Association. (2000). *Diagnostic and Statistical Manual of Mental Disorders* (4th ed., text rev.). Washington, DC: Author.

American Psychiatric Association. (2013a). *Diagnostic and Statistical Manual of Mental Disorders* (5th ed.). Arlington, VA: American Psychiatric Publishing.

American Psychiatric Association (2013b). *Severity of Acute Stress Symptoms—Child Age 11–17-National Stressful Events Survey Acute Stress Disorder Short Scale*. Retrieved from http://www.psychiatry.org/practice/dsm/dsm5/online-assessment-measures

American Psychiatric Association (2013c). *Severity of Dissociative Symptoms—Child Age 11–17-Brief Dissociative Experiences Scale—Modified*. Retrieved from http://www.psychiatry.org/practice/dsm/dsm5/online-assessment-measures

American Psychiatric Association (2013d). *Severity of Posttraumatic Stress Symptoms—Child Age 11–17—National Stressful Events Survey PTSD Short Scale* . Retrieved from http://www.psychiatry.org/practice/dsm/dsm5/online-assessment-measures

American Psychiatric Association. (2014). *Online assessment measures*. Retrieved from http://www.psychiatry.org/practice/dsm/dsm5/online-assessment-measures

Boris, N. W., & Zeanah, M. D. (2005). Practice parameter for the assessment and treatment of children and adolescents with reactive attachment disorder of infancy and early childhood. *Journal of the American Academy of Child & Adolescent Psychiatry, 44*(11), 1206–1219. doi:10.1097/01.chi.0000177056.41655.ce

Boyle, G. (2003). Trauma Symptoms Checklist for Children. In *The Fifteenth Mental Measurements Yearbook*. Lincoln: University of Nebraska Press.

Briere, J. (1996). *Trauma Symptom Checklist for Children (TSCC): Professional manual*. Odessa, FL: Psychological Assessment Resources.

Briere, J. (2005). *Trauma Symptom Checklist for Young Children (TSCYC): professional manual*. Odessa, FL: Psychological Assessment Resources.

Bryant, R. A., Friedman, M. J., Spiegel, D., Ursano, R., & Strain, J. (2011). A review of acute stress disorder in DSM-5. *Depression and Anxiety, 28*(9), 802–817.

Bryant, R. A., & Harvey, A. G. (2000). *Acute stress disorder: A handbook of theory, assessment, and treatment*. Washington, DC: American Psychiatric Association.

Casey, P. (2014). Adjustment disorder: New developments. *Current Psychiatric Reports, 16*(6), 1–8. doi:10.1007/s11920–014–0451–2

Christopher, R. (2007). Children's PTSD Inventory. In *The Seventeenth Mental Measurements Yearbook*. Lincoln: University of Nebraska Press.

Cohen, J. A., Mannarino, A. P., & Deblinger, E., (2012). *Trauma-focused CBT for children and adolescents: Treatment Applications*. New York, NY: Guilford Press.

Doll, B., & Osborn, A. (2007). Children's PTSD Inventory. In *The Seventeenth Mental Measurements Yearbook*. Lincoln: University of Nebraska Press.

Ehlers, A., & Clark, D. M. (2000). A cognitive model of posttraumatic stress disorder. *Behaviour Research and Therapy, 38*, 319–345.

Foa, E. B., Johnson, K. M., Feeny, N. C., & Treadwell, K. R. (2001). The Child PTSD Symptom Scale: A preliminary examination of its psychometric properties. *Journal of Clinical Child Psychology, 30*(3), 376–384. doi:10.1207/S15374424JCCP3003_9

Forbes, D., Creamer, M., Bisson, J. I., Cohen, J. A., Crow, B. E., Foa, E. B., ... Ursano, R. J. (2010). A guide to guidelines for the treatment of PTSD and related conditions. *Journal of Traumatic Stress, 23*(5), 537–552. doi:10.1002/jts.20565

Friedman, M. J., Resick, P. A., Bryant, R. A., Strain, J., Horowitz, M., & Spiegel, D. (2011). Classification of trauma and stressor-related disorders in *DSM-5*. *Depression and Anxiety, 28*(9), 737–749. 10.1002/da.20845

Garro, A. (2005). Trauma and Attachment Belief Scale. In *The Sixteenth Measurements Yearbook*. Lincoln: University of Nebraska Press.

Ghosh Ippen, C., & Alley, A. (2014). *The Children's PTSD Inventory*. In C. Ghosh Ippen &

M. Kulkarni (Eds.), National Child Traumatic Stress Network Measure Review Database. Retrieved May 8, 2014, from http://www.nctsnet.org/resources/online-research/measures-review

Ghosh Ippen, C., Augenbraun, D., & DioGuardi, R. J. (2014). *Clinician-Administered PTSD Scale for Children and Adolescents (CAPS-CA)*. In C. Ghosh Ippen (Ed.), National Child Traumatic Stress Network Measure Review Database. Retrieved May 8, 2014, from http://www.nctsnet.org/resources/online-research/measures-review

Ghosh Ippen, C., & Kulkarni, M. (2014). *Trauma and Attachment Belief Scale*. In C. Ghosh Ippen (Ed.), National Child Traumatic Stress Network Measure Review Database. Retrieved May 12, 2014, from http://www.nctsnet.org/resources/online-research/measures-review

Gilbert, A., & Acker, M. (2014). *Trauma symptoms checklist for young children*. In N. Taylor, R. Igelman, M. Kulkarni, & C. Ghosh Ippen (Eds.), National Child Traumatic Stress Network Measure Review Database. Retrieved May 12, 2014, from http://www.nctsnet.org/resources/online-research/measures-review

Gleason, M. M., Fox, N. A., Drury, S., Smyke, A. T., Egger, H. L., Nelson, C. A., ... Zeanah, C. H. (2011). The validity of evidence-derived criteria for reactive attachment disorder: Indiscriminately social/disinhibited and emotionally withdrawn/inhibited types. *Journal of the American Academy of Child & Adolescent Psychiatry, 50*, 216–231. doi:10.1016/j.jaac.2010.12.012

Goldfarb, W. (1945). Effects of psychological deprivation in infancy and subsequent stimulation. *American Journal of Psychiatry, 102*(1), 18–33.

Hoffman, K. T., Marvin, R. S., Cooper, G., & Powell, B. (2006). Changing toddlers' and preschoolers' attachment classifications: The Circle of Security intervention. *Journal of Consulting and Clinical Psychology, 74*(6), 1017–1026. doi:10.1037/0022-006X.74.6.1017

Horner, G. (2008). Reactive attachment disorder. *Journal of Pediatric Health Care, 22*(4), 234–239. doi:10.1016/j.pedhc.2007.07.003

Hyman, I. A., & Snook, P. A. (2002). *My Worst Experience Scale (MWES): Manual*. Los Angeles, CA: Western Psychological Services.

James, A. C., James, G., Cowdrey, F. A., Soler, A., & Choke, A. (2015). Cognitive behavioral therapy for anxiety disorders in children and adolescents. *Cochrane Database of Systematic Reviews, 2*. doi:10.1002/14651858.CD004690.pub3

Karam, E., Fayyad, J., Karam, A., Melham, N., Mneimneh, Z., Dimassi, H., & Tabet, C. C. (2014). Outcome of depression and anxiety after war: A prospective epidemiologic study of children and adolescents. *Journal of Traumatic Stress, 27*(2), 192–199. doi:10.1002/jts.21895

King, J. H. (2014). *Using the DSM-5: Try it, you'll like it*. Retrieved from http://www.continuingedcourses.net/active/courses/course081.php

Mackler, K. (2007). Trauma Symptoms Checklist for Young Children. In *The Seventeenth Measurements Yearbook*. Lincoln: University of Nebraska Press.

Marvin, R. S., Cooper, G., Hoffman, K., & Powell, B. (2002). The Circle of Security project: Attachment-based intervention with caregiver-preschool child dyads. *Attachment & Human Development, 4*(1), 107–124. doi:10.1080/14616730252982491

Medway, F. (2005). *Mental My Worst Experience Scale*. In *The Sixteenth Mental Measurements Yearbook*. Lincoln, NE: University of Nebraska Press.

Moore, H. (2005). *My Worst Experience Scale*. In *The Sixteenth Mental Measurements Yearbook*. Lincoln: University of Nebraska Press.

Nader, K. O., Newman, E., Weathers, F. W., Kaloupek, D. G., Kriegler, J. A., & Blake, D. D. (2004). *National Center for PTSD Clinician-Administered PTSD Scale for Children and Adolescents (CAPS-CA) interview booklet*. Los Angeles, CA: Western Psychological Services.

National Crime Victims Research and Treatment Center. (2005). *TF-CBT Web: A Web-based learning course for trauma-focused cognitive behavioral therapy*. Retrieved from http://tfcbt.musc.edu/resources.php?p05

Newman, E., Weathers, F. W., Nader, K., Kaloupek, D. G., Pynoos, R. S., Blake, D. D., & Kriegler, J. A. (2004). *Clinician-Administered PTSD Scale for Children and Adolescents (CAPSCA) interviewer's guide*. Los Angeles, CA: Western Psychological Services.

Nixon, R. D. V., Sterk, J., & Pearce, A. (2012). A randomized trial of cognitive behaviour therapy and cognitive therapy for children with posttraumatic stress disorder following single-incident trauma. *Journal of Abnormal Child Psychology, 40*(3), 327–337.

Pearlman, L. A. (2003). *Trauma and Attachment Belief Scale*. Los Angeles, CA: Western Psychological Services.

Pietrzak, R. H., Goldstein, R. B., Southwick, S. M., & Grant, B. F. (2011). Prevalence and axis I comorbidity of full and partial posttraumatic stress disorder in the United States: Results from wave 2 of the National Epidemiologic Survey on Alcohol and Related Conditions. *Journal of Anxiety Disorders*, *25*(3), 456–465.

Saigh, P.A. (2004). *A structured interview for diagnosing Posttraumatic Stress Disorder: Children's PTSD Inventory*. San Antonio, TX: PsychCorp.

Saunders, B. E., Berliner, L., & Hanson, R. F. (Eds.). (2004, April 26). *Child Physical and Sexual Abuse: Guidelines for Treatment (Revised Report: April 26, 2004)*. Charleston, SC: National Crime Victims Research and Treatment Center.

Seligman, L., & Reichenberg, L. W. (2012). *Selecting effective treatments: A comprehensive, systematic guide to treating mental disorders* (4th ed.). Hoboken, NJ: John Wiley & Sons.

Sheeringa, M. S., & Zeanah, C. H. (1994). *PTSD semi-structured interview and observation record for infants and young children*. New Orleans, LA: Department of Psychiatry and Neurology, Tulane University Health Sciences Center.

Shreeve, D. F. (2012). *Reactive attachment disorder: A case-based approach*. New York, NY: Springer.

Smith, P., Perrin, S., Dalgleish, T., Meiser-Stedman, R., Clark, D. M., & Yule, W. (2013). Treatment of posttraumatic stress disorder in children and adolescents. *Current Opinion in Psychiatry*, *26*(1), 66–72.

Smith, S. (2014). *Review of the Child PTSD Symptom Scale (CPSS)*. In C. Ghosh Ippen (Ed.), National Child Traumatic Stress Network Measure Review Database. Retrieved May 8, 2014, from http://www.nctsnet.org/resources/online-research/measures-review

Stinnett, T. (2007). Trauma symptoms checklist for young children. In *The Seventeenth Mental Measurements Yearbook*. Lincoln: University of Nebraska Press.

Stover, C. (2014). *Review of the Posttraumatic Stress Disorder Semi-Structured Interview and Observational Record*. In C. Ghosh Ippen & M. Kulkarni (Eds.), National Child Traumatic Stress Network Measure Review Database. Retrieved May 13, 2014, from http://www.nctsnet.org/resources/online-research/measures-review

Stover, C. S., & Berkowitz, S. (2005). Assessing violence exposure and trauma symptoms in young children: A critical review of measures. *Journal of Traumatic Stress*, *18*(6), 707–717. doi:10.1002/jts.20079

U.S. Department of Veterans Affairs (2014a). *Children's PTSD inventory*. Retrieved from http://www.ptsd.va.gov/professional/assessment/child/index.asp

U.S. Department of Veterans Affairs (2014b). *My Worst Experience Survey*. Retrieved from http://www.ptsd.va.gov/professional/assessment/child/index.asp

U.S. Department of Veterans Affairs (2014c). *The Child PTSD Symptom Scale (CPSS)*. Retrieved from http://www.ptsd.va.gov/professional/assessment/child/index.asp

U.S. Department of Veterans Affairs (2014d). *Trauma symptoms checklist for children*. Retrieved from http://www.ptsd.va.gov/professional/assessment/child/index.asp

U.S. Department of Veterans Affairs (2014e). *Trauma symptoms checklist for young children*. Retrieved from http://www.ptsd.va.gov/professional/assessment/child/index.asp

Viswesvaran, C. (2003). Trauma symptoms checklist for children. In *The Fifteenth Mental Measurements Yearbook*. Lincoln: University of Nebraska Press.

Weir, K. (2008). Using integrative play therapy with adoptive families to treat reactive attachment disorder. *Journal of Family Psychotherapy, 18*(4), 1–16. doi:10.1300/J085v18n04_01

World Health Organization. (1992). *The ICD-10 classification of mental and behavioural disorders: Clinical descriptions and diagnostic guidelines*. Geneva, Switzerland: Author.

Chapter 13

Feeding and Eating Disorders

Laura H. Choate and Gary G. Gintner

Introduction

There is a high prevalence of disordered eating practices in children and especially adolescents, including eating disorder symptoms such as binge eating, dieting, weight concerns, and diagnosable eating disorders (Eaton et al., 2010; Hudson, Hiripi, Pope, & Kessler 2007). In fact, early adolescence is considered a high-risk period for the development of eating disorders, as the median age of onset for them is between 12 and 13 years of age (Swanson, Crow, LeGrange, Swensen, & Merikangas, 2011). In total, a recent large-scale study of adolescents (Swanson et al., 2011) indicated that the prevalence rates for eating disorders is .03 percent (anorexia nervosa, [AN]), 0.9 percent (bulimia nervosa [BN]), and 1.6 percent (binge eating disorder, [BED]).

Although eating-related problems were once considered a concern primarily for Caucasian, middle-class girls and women, research now indicates that disordered eating is increasingly prevalent among members of all Westernized racial and ethnic groups (Commission on Adolescent Eating Disorders, 2005; Tallyrand, 2013), and it is now recognized that a sizable minority of males experiences disordered eating (Maine & Bunnell, 2013). Even though boys and men have greater levels of eating-related problems than was previously recognized, the gender disparity in eating disorders is still much larger than with most diagnoses; AN and BN are 10 times more prevalent among females than males, and BED is up to three times more common (Treasure, 2007).

Although there has been much study regarding the diagnosis and treatment of eating disorders over the past several decades, questions have remained regarding the accuracy of the *Diagnostic and Statistical Manual of Mental Disorders* (*DSM*) system in classifying these disorders. To address some of these concerns, the *DSM-5*'s Eating Disorders Work Group sought to revise this section of the *DSM* so that it would include: (a) infusion of a developmental perspective and (b) coverage of diagnostic gaps and clinically significant eating disorder problems (Orenstein et al., 2013).

The first conceptual change of the *DSM-5* is the infusion of a developmental perspective throughout the manual (American Psychiatric Association [APA], 2013). Each chapter is arranged developmentally so that disorders that appear early in life are listed first, followed by those that typically emerge in adolescence or adulthood. Feeding disorders from the *DSM-IV* (APA, 1994) chapter on Disorders Usually First Diagnosed in Infancy, Childhood, or Adolescence have been moved into this chapter. Because these feeding disorders appear early developmentally, they are listed first (see Table 1). Of these, pica

315

and rumination disorder are essentially unchanged, but the former feeding disorder of infancy or early childhood has undergone significant changes and is renamed avoidant restrictive food intake disorder (ARFID).

Second, a major charge to the *DSM-5*'s Work Group on Eating Disorders was to decrease the use of Eating Disorder Not Otherwise Specified (EDNOS). There were concerns over data indicating that in clinical settings this diagnosis accounted for approximately 50 percent or more of eating disorder diagnoses (Fairburn et al., 2007; Turner & Bryant-Waugh, 2004), suggesting that the *DSM-IV*'s categories provided poor coverage of clinically significant eating disorder problems. Evidence suggested that many of these EDNOS cases shared similarities to either AN or BN and were associated with significant impairment, even though they did not meet the full diagnostic requirements (Thomas, Vartanian, & Brownell, 2009). Because of these types of data, the *DSM-5* tried to address the EDNOS problem in two ways. First, it modified and at times lowered diagnostic requirements to better capture clinically significant subthreshold presentations. Second, it added Binge-Eating Disorder (BED) and ARFID to also reduce reliance on EDNOS.

Description of Disorders

The essential feature of feeding and eating disorders is some sort of disturbance in eating or eating-related behavior that leads to significant distress or impairment in health status or psychosocial functioning (APA, 2013). These disorders encompass a range of eating-related problems that include eating too little, eating too much, and unusual eating-related behaviors. The *DSM-5* (APA, 2013) and the *International Classification of Diseases, Tenth revision* ([*ICD-10*]; World Health Organization [WHO], 2010) classify a similar group of disorders in this area, but there are some disparities between the two systems (see Table 13.1). Note that *DSM-5* code numbers are derived from their closest ICD counterpart.

Feeding disorders typically first appear during infancy or early childhood and involve problems such as food refusal, highly selective eating, eating nonnutritive foods (pica), and rechewing and regurgitation of food (rumination). Although the *ICD-10* (WHO, 2010) limits the diagnosis of feeding disorders to those who are 17 or younger, the *DSM-5* does not have a maximum age limit.

AN is the prototypical disorder that characterizes eating too little. In both the *DSM-5* and the *ICD-10*, the disorder has three main features: restricted food intake resulting in significantly low body weight, disturbance in body image, and intense fear of gaining weight. A less severe manifestation, referred to as atypical anorexia, includes all these features except that body weight is not significantly low (APA, 2013; WHO, 2010).

Disorders that involve eating too much must include bouts of overeating with a sense of lack of control (APA, 2013; WHO, 2010). If these episodes are accompanied by compensatory behaviors (e.g., vomiting and use of laxatives) designed to neutralize weight gain, then the presentation is characteristic of BN. On the other hand, binge eating in the absence of these compensatory behaviors exemplifies the *DSM-5*'s BED (APA, 2013). In contrast, the *ICD-10* classifies BED as form of BN. Both systems do not consider obesity a codable mental disorder.

TABLE 13.1 *DSM-5* Feeding and Eating Disorders and *ICD-10* Codes and Disorders

DSM-5 Disorder	CD-10 *Code*	ICD-10 *Disorder*
Pica	(In children) F98.3	Pica (0–17 years)
	(In adults) F50.8	Other Eating Disorder
Rumination Disorder	F98.21	Rumination Disorder of Infancy (0–17 years)
Avoidant/Restrictive Food Intake Disorder	F50.8	Other Eating Disorder
Anorexia nervosa		Anorexia nervosa
Restricting type	F50.1	Restricting Type
Binge-eating/purging type	F50.02	Binge eating/purging type
	F50.00	Unspecified
Bulimia Nervosa	F50.2	Bulimia nervosa
Binge-Eating Disorder	F50.2	Bulimia nervosa
Other Specified Feeding and Eating Disorder	F50.8	Other Eating Disorder
Unspecified Feeding and Eating Disorder	F50.9	Eating Disorder, Unspecified

Note: See WHO (2010) for *ICD-10* code numbers and disorders.

DSM-5 Criteria

In this section, the essential features and major diagnostic criteria for each of the disorders are discussed, with particular attention paid to the *DSM-5* changes. An overview of the major changes from the *DSM-IV-TR* to the *DSM-5* is described in Sidebar 13.1. The discussion also highlights identified diagnostic markers and risk factors that can inform the diagnosis. A diagnostic marker is a measurable quality that increases the confidence that the disorder is present (APA, 2013). It should be noted that the feeding disorder descriptions are brief because these are less common clinical presentations that do not typically fall within counselors' scope of practice.

SIDEBAR 13.1: MAJOR CHANGES FOR THE FEEDING AND EATING DISORDERS IN THE *DSM-5*

- New chapter title
- Includes the *DSM-IV-TR's* feeding disorders that were in the chapter Disorders Usually First Diagnosed in Infancy, Childhood, and Adolescence
- The *DSM-IV-TR's* Feeding Disorder of Early Childhood has been renamed Avoidant/Restrictive Food Intake Disorder and the criteria have been expanded
- Anorexia Nervosa:
  ◦ Amenorrhea is no longer required

- A new severity specifier has been added based upon body mass index
- Bulimia Nervosa:
  - The purging and nonpurging subtypes have been discontinued
  - A new severity specifier has been added based upon frequency of compensatory behaviors per week
- Binge Eating Disorder has been added as a new disorder
- Eating Disorder Not Otherwise Specified is replaced by two options: Other Specified Feeding and Eating Disorder, and Other Feeding and Eating Disorder

PICA

Essential Diagnostic Criteria

Pica involves the eating of nonnutritive, nonfood substances over a period of at least a month (APA, 2013). Examples of nonnutritive foods include dirt, paint, wood, cloth, and clay. The *DSM-5* suggests a minimum age of onset of at least 2 years to differentiate it from more normative mouthing of objects common in infants. A major exclusion criterion is culturally sanctioned eating behavior. If the eating of nonnutritive foods is associated with another mental disorder, such as an intellectual disability (ID), autism spectrum disorder (ASD), or schizophrenia, or with a medical condition (e.g., pregnancy), the pica behavior must be severe enough to require additional clinical attention in the treatment plan.

Developmental Considerations

Most cases of pica emerge prior to the age of 5 years, most commonly between age 2 and 3, and with incidence of cases decreasing with age. However, it may also present in adolescence or adulthood, especially in the context of an ID or ASD (Blinder, 2008; Ellis & Schnoer, 2014).

Diagnostic Markers and Risk Factors

The *DSM-5* mentions the following diagnostic marker: Medical scanning methods, such as ultrasound and laboratory work, can be used to detect common complications associated with pica, such as abdominal obstructions, accidental poisoning, vitamin and mineral deficiencies, and infections (APA, 2013). An ID, ASD, and other developmental delays increase the risk for pica. Environmental factors that increase risk include neglect, inadequate supervision, and a disorganized and impoverished family situation (APA, 2013, First & Tasman, 2004).

RUMINATION DISORDER

Essential Diagnostic Criteria

This disorder involves the repeated regurgitation of food, which is then rechewed, swallowed, or spit out. These behaviors must persist for at least a month and typically occur several times a week or even daily (APA, 2013). Rule-outs include medical conditions that can cause reflux and vomiting (e.g., esophageal reflux and hiatal hernia). A separate diagnosis of rumination disorder is not given if the symptoms occur exclusively during the course of AN, BN, or BED. On the other hand, while rumination disorder can co-occur with an ID, ASD or other developmental problem, it is not separately coded unless it requires clinical attention in the treatment plan.

Developmental Considerations

The onset of this disorder is commonly during the first year of life (First & Tasman, 2004). The infant may be observed arching the back, inserting fingers into the mouth, or sucking on the tongue to induce vomiting. The food is then rechewed and swallowed, or spit out. One proposed etiological mechanism is that this type of eating behavior is reinforcing because of its self-soothing or self-stimulating effects (APA, 2013). It also may be reinforced by eliciting attention and comfort from a caregiver (First & Tasman, 2004). While much less common, adolescents and adults may engage in regurgitation behaviors that include rechewing and spitting out of food. However, if the behaviors are associated with a desire to reduce calories or a distorted body image, AN, BN, or BED should be considered first.

Diagnostic Markers and Risk Factors

The *DSM-5* does not list any diagnostic markers that are reliable indicators of rumination disorder. Risk factors include an ID, ASD, and other developmental delays. An acute medical condition that is associated with regurgitation may be a predisposing factor. Environmental risks include stress, especially when it disrupts the infant–caregiver relationship.

Avoidant/Restrictive Food Intake Disorder (ARFID)

Essential Diagnostic Criteria

This disorder is characterized by either avoidance of eating or restriction in the types of foods that are consumed. This disturbed eating behavior needs to result in clinically significant adverse health outcomes or impair psychosocial functioning, as indicated by at least one of the following: significant weight loss or failure to meet growth milestones, a nutritional deficiency (e.g., iron, vitamin A), reliance on enteral feeding or other food supplements, or marked impairment in psychosocial functioning (e.g., eating behaviors disrupt family relationships). There are two major exclusion criteria or rule-outs in making a diagnosis. First, the eating disturbance does not occur exclusively during the course of either AN or BN, and, unlike these disorders, there is no evidence of disturbed body image. A second issue to rule out is whether the symptoms are because of underlying medical conditions that either affect eating (e.g., loss of appetite due to chemotherapy) or cause adverse reactions (e.g., food allergies).

   Avoidance of food intake can present in two major ways. First, there may be little interest in eating. An important rule-out for this variant is depression, some acute stress response (e.g., separation from a parent), or trauma, all of which can be associated with loss of appetite. However, more commonly, the food avoidance emerges following an adverse medical condition associated with feeding or eating. For example, a child may have had a particularly serious case of the flu in which nausea and vomiting were significant. Afterward, the child may avoid eating, even though there are no longer any medical symptoms or risk of vomiting.

The other manifestation of ARFID is a clinically significant restriction in type of food that is consumed. Typically, this restriction is based upon some sensory quality of the food such as its color, texture, smell, or temperature. For example, an 8-year-old child presented with a history of only eating plain noodles and refusing to eat any other types of food. While periods of picky eating are not unusual developmentally, an ARFID is more persistent and clinically significant in its impairment. In this case, for example, the restricted food preference not only interfered with family eating time but also adversely affected the child's socializing with other children, if food was involved.

An important rule-out is ASD, in which highly routinized eating behaviors or marked sensory sensitivity to stimuli including foods are not uncommon (APA, 2013). ARFID would be additionally diagnosed only if it met full criteria and was clinically significant to address in the treatment plan of the ASD. In a survey of seven eating disorder clinics nationally, Fisher et al. (2014) found that ARFIDs were a surprisingly common eating disorder. An ARFID accounted for about 14 percent of the eating disorder diagnoses in this sample of 8- to 18-year-olds. In comparison with AN or BN, those diagnosed with an ARFID were more likely to be younger, be male, have a longer duration of illness, and have a history of a medical disorder or anxiety disorder. Interestingly, a history of a mood disorder was less common, relative to those with AN or BN. The data indicated that ARFID appeared to be distinct in terms of course as well as demographics.

Developmental Considerations

Typically, ARFID appears in infancy or early childhood and can persist into adulthood (APA, 2013). Available estimates indicate that up to 25 percent of normal developing infants and 75 percent of those with a significant developmental disability experience avoidant or restrictive feeding and eating problems (First & Tasman, 2004). Aversion to food can occur after a negative event such as choking, in response to emotional difficulties, or to the actual sensory characteristics of food. Those with avoidance or restriction based upon sensory characteristics typically have a more stable course that can persist into adulthood. At this point, the relatively limited database is inconclusive relative to whether an ARFID converts to another eating disorder later in life. In adolescence and adulthood, a highly restricted diet is the most common presentation. The clinical significance is more commonly because of its psychosocial impact, versus acute medical issues, such as malnutrition. For example, a 13-year-old limited his diet to plain rice. He would avoid lunches at school as well as family and social events in which food was served.

Diagnostic Markers and Risk Factors

The key diagnostic markers are indicators of malnutrition (e.g., weight loss, mineral deficiency) and growth delays (APA, 2013). Risk factors include a history of gastrointestinal medical conditions and an anxious temperament. Environmental contributing factors include anxious caregivers, a parent with an eating disorder, and traumatic life events that disrupt attachment or family relationships (APA, 2013).

ANOREXIA NERVOSA (AN)

Essential Diagnostic Criteria

AN is a complex, potentially life-threatening disorder with significant impact on both the client and her entire family (Hurst & Read, 2013). AN is characterized by three major criteria: significant curtailment in energy intake leading to significantly low weight, fear of gaining weight or presence of behaviors that interfere with weight gain, and disturbance in perceived weight or shape (e.g., overestimation of body weight; APA, 2013).

The *DSM-5* has introduced four major changes to the criteria. First, "Restriction of energy intake ... leading to *significantly low weight*" (APA, 2013, p. 338) replaces the *DSM-IV*'s Criteria A of "Refusal to maintain body weight" leading to body weight "less than 85 percent of expected" (APA, 2000, p. 589). The rationale for this change is that clinicians found it difficult to use the 85 percent criteria. In addition, the terminology "refusal to maintain body weight" has been removed because it was seen as pejorative. The text of the *DSM-5* recommends that "significantly low weight" should be interpreted as a body mass index (BMI) of less than 18.5 kg/m^2 in adults and a BMI at the tenth to fifth percentile or below in children and adolescents (see the children and adolescent BMI calculator at the Centers for Disease Control site, http://apps.ncccd.cdc.gov/dnpabmi/).

A second change is that *DSM-5* criteria allow for a broader range of reasons for why the individual maintains a low weight (Brown, Holland, & Keel, 2014). Criteria B has been expanded to include self-reports of weight phobia or intense fear of gaining weight, as well as persistent behaviors that interfere with weight gain, despite low body weight (APA, 2013). A subset of individuals and especially children do not report weight phobia but nevertheless engage in behaviors that limit weight gain. For example, the individual may eat small meals, go hours between eating, and engage in excessive exercise. The modification in criteria is hoped to capture individuals who might have been diagnosed with EDNOS (Brown et al., 2014) and to identify presentations in children who may not have the cognitive capacity to report weight phobia (Knoll, Bulk, & Heberand, 2011).

A third change in the *DSM-5* is that amenorrhea is no longer a required criteria. There were two major reasons for this change. First, it was not applicable to premenarcheal and postmenarcheal females, women on oral contraceptives, and males. Second, while amenorrhea was a marker for greater severity and medical complications, those who met criteria otherwise also showed significant impairment. Thus, the change would enhance diagnostic sensitivity or the identification of true cases and reduce reliance on EDNOS.

The *DSM-5* further allows for three specifiers. Like the *DSM-IV-TR*, AN can be sub-typed as either binge-eating/purging type or restrictive type (e.g., absence of binging or purging behaviors). Because crossover between subtypes is common over the course of the disorder, the *DSM-5* has specified that the subtyping should reflect the pattern in the past three months (APA, 2013). The binge-eating/purging type is more common and is associated with greater severity, comorbidity and restrictive behaviors (APA, 2013; De Young et al., 2013).

AN can also be specified relative to remission status (partial or full) and severity. The *DSM-5* has quantified severity based upon BMI ranging from mild (BMI less than or equal to 17) to extreme (BMI less than 15). This may increase reliability but may make the diagnostic process more cumbersome for clinicians.

Brown and colleagues (2014) found that the *DSM-5*'s changes to AN increased lifetime prevalence by including milder cases. However, identified cases were associated with significant impairment, and the changes resulted in less reliance on EDNOS.

Developmental Considerations

The most common period of onset is early adolescence. Children who present with the disorder usually have the restrictive type and less commonly report weight phobia (Knoll et al., 2011). The course of the disorder is highly variable, ranging from a single episode to a chronic course with episodes of crossovers to BN (APA, 2013).

Diagnostic Markers and Risk Factors

The *DSM-5* lists a number of medical markers that are consistent with the diagnosis of AN. These include lab and physical exam measures of factors related to malnutrition and starvation syndrome, such as bone mineral density, dehydration, bradycardia, and hypotension. Risk factors include anxiety problems and obsessional traits in childhood. As stated previously, gender is highly associated with the development of AN: Females are far more likely to experience AN than males are. Those with a family history of AN, bipolar disorder, or depressive disorders are also at increased risk. Risk factors also include living in a wealthy postindustrialized country that emphasizes the importance of thinness. It should be noted that in the US, AN is less common in those from African American, Latino, and Asian backgrounds than it is in Caucasian individuals. It should be noted, however, that AN can occur in both males and females and among members of every racial and ethnic population.

BULIMIA NERVOSA (BN)

Essential Diagnostic Criteria

BN consists of three major features: binge-eating episodes, compensatory behaviors designed to prevent weight gain, and self evaluation that is disproportionately influenced by body weight and shape (APA, 2013). A binge is defined as a discrete period (e.g., two hours) in which the individual consumes an inordinately large amount of food, relative to what most individuals would eat under similar circumstances and time. This has been defined more objectively as consuming at least three times the typical portion size and can often be in the range of 3,000 or more calories (Craighead, Martinez, & Klump, 2013). There must be a sense of loss of control during the eating episode. Compensatory behaviors include purging, excessive exercise, fasting, and misuse of substances, such as laxatives, diuretics, or medications. The major exclusion criteria is that this pattern of behavior cannot occur during an episode of AN, in which case the diagnosis would be AN, binge-eating/purging type.

The *DSM-5* introduces three major changes relative to the *DSM-IV-TR*. First, the required frequency of binging-eating and compensatory behaviors has been reduced from two times a week to at least one time a week over a three-month period. This change was prompted by research that questioned the validity of the twice a week criteria (Wilson & Sysko, 2009). A second change is that purging and nonpurging subtypes have been discontinued. There were no clear data supporting the validity of this subtyping (APA, 2013). Third, the *DSM-5* has added a new severity specifier based upon the frequency of compensatory behaviors per week, ranging from mild (one to three compensatory behaviors) to extreme (14 or more compensatory behaviors). Data have indicated that most individuals with BN use more than one compensatory behavior and that frequency is related to severity and medical complications (APA, 2013).

Developmental Considerations

BN typically begins in adolescence or early adulthood, often triggered by a period of significant dieting or a marked stressful event (e.g., leaving home for college; APA, 2013). In others, there may first be an episode of binge-eating disorder that develops during the middle-school years and develops into BN in later adolescence. The course can be either chronic or intermittent with periods of remission. About 15 percent of the cases migrate to AN and have a course of crossovers between the two disorders (APA, 2013). Those who have a serious comorbid disorder (e.g., bipolar disorder, major depressive disorder) have a poorer long-term prognosis (APA, 2013).

Diagnostic Markers and Risk Factors

While there is no medical or laboratory test that is a specific marker for BN, laboratory tests and physical examination indicators can support the presence of BN. Excessive purging may result in electrolyte abnormalities and metabolic acidosis due to loss of gastric acid. Metabolic acidosis can also be caused by the abuse of laxatives and diuretics. Physical exam indicators include loss of tooth enamel, especially on the inner side of the teeth, enlarged salivary glands, and scarred fingers resulting from self-induced vomiting. Risk factors include childhood obesity, early pubertal maturation (in females), and a family history of BN (APA, 2013). Psychological factors such as low self-esteem, anxiety, and depression are also associated with increased risk. Like AN, BN is more common in females, and incidence is higher in industrialized countries that culturally value thinness. For a case example describing a client experiencing BN, see Sidebar 13.2.

SIDEBAR 13.2: BULIMIA NERVOSA CASE EXAMPLE

Caroline is a 14-year-old Caucasian girl who has become highly concerned about her weight after she gained a few pounds during her transition to puberty. While she is not medically overweight, she believes that she needs to lose 15 pounds and frequently compares her body shape and weight with other girls and with models she sees in the media. She has started to weigh herself every morning, and bases how she feels about herself on whether her weight has gone up or down. Because she wants to lose weight, she has developed a list of food-related rules that she believes she must follow, including no carbohydrates and no fats. Due to her highly restrictive diet, she is very hungry in the evenings but will not allow herself to eat anything beyond a small dinner. One evening in a moment of hunger, she samples a cookie from a plate of fresh cookies her mother has made. Afterward, she thinks, "I have blown my rule. I'm going to gain weight today anyway, so I might as well have all the cookies I want!" She begins to eat the cookies quickly, as if she can't stop, until she has finished the entire batch of cookies. Horrified at what she has done, she goes to the bathroom to try to force herself to vomit. She has read about this on the Internet, so she knows how to try it. Afterward, she feels weak and exhausted, and vows to begin her diet again in earnest the next day. The cycle continues the next day and in the days to follow. She feels trapped within this cycle but doesn't see a way out of it.

BINGE-EATING DISORDER (BED)

Essential Diagnostic Criteria

BED is characterized by episodes of binge eating without the presence of compensatory behaviors discussed above for BN. These binge-eating episodes must occur at least once a week for at least three months. The binge-eating episodes must be associated with marked distress and at least three of the following: eating more rapidly than normal, eating until uncomfortably full, eating large amounts when not hungry, eating alone because of embarrassment, and feeling negative afterward. Like BN, binge-eating episodes must be discrete periods of overeating and not merely snacking throughout the day (APA, 2013; Craighead et al., 2013).

While BED appeared as a disorder requiring further study in the *DSM-IV* (APA, 1994), the *DSM-5* has made three modifications. First, the criteria thresholds for the binge-eating episodes have been lowered from at least two times a week to at least one time per week for at least three months (versus six months). The available data suggest that the *DSM-5*'s lowered thresholds increase prevalence by 1 to 3 percent, but the additional cases identified are associated with clinically significant impairment that warrants clinical attention (Marek, Ben-Porath, Ashton, & Heinberg, 2014; Stice, Marti, & Rohde, 2012). A second change is that partial or full remission can be noted as a specifier. Third, the *DSM-5* adds a severity specifier based upon the number of binge episodes in the past week ranging from mild (one to three episodes) to extreme (14 or more). Severity is associated with greater impairment, comorbidity, and associated medical complications related to overweight (Craighead et al., 2013).

Common comorbid conditions include depression, anxiety disorders, and substance use. Medical complications associated with obesity, such as metabolic syndrome, are not uncommon (Craighead et al., 2013).

Developmental Considerations

The typical age of onset is in late adolescence or early adulthood, but onset in later adulthood is not uncommon. When BED appears in early adolescence, it is at greater likelihood to convert to BN (Allen, Byrne, Oddy, & Crosby, 2013) than if it begins in young adulthood or later (APA, 2013; Stice, Marti, & Rohnde, 2012). On average, adolescents with BED are average to overweight and tend to have higher BMI than those with BN (Wonderlich, Gordon, Mitchell, Crosby, & Enger, 2009). In comparison with AN and BN, those with BED are more likely to remit naturally over the course of the disorder (APA, 2013).

Diagnostic Markers and Risk Factors

The *DSM-5* does not list any diagnostic markers for BED per se. Risk factors include a family history of BED, of being overweight, and of body dissatisfaction. Environmental factors include sociocultural pressure for thinness and family factors that may either promote poor eating habits or exert undue pressures for thinness (Craighead et al., 2013; Wonderlich et al, 2009). The disorder is more common in industrialized countries. In comparison to AN and BN, BED is more demographically diverse, being more equally represented among males, individuals of color, and those in older age groups (APA, 2013; Wonderlich et al., 2009).

OTHER SPECIFIED AND UNSPECIFIED FEEDING OR EATING DISORDER

Essential Diagnostic Criteria

The *DSM-5* has discontinued the use of the Not Otherwise Specified (NOS) category throughout the manual in favor of an approach that requires more specific documentation of diagnoses that are clinically significant but do not fit the options available. Other

Specified ... (e.g., Feeding and Eating Disorder) replaces NOS and requires the additional narrative documentation of the clinically significant presentation. In the case of feeding and eating disorders, the *DSM-5* lists five presentations that can be noted: atypical AN (e.g., all criteria are met for AN but weight is not unusually low), low-frequency or limited duration BN (e.g., duration less than three months), low-frequency or limited duration BED, purging disorder (purging behaviors in the absence of any binge eating), and night eating syndrome (e.g., consuming 25 percent or more of daily calories after the evening meal). As an example of coding, a teen with only recurrent self-induced vomiting episodes because of body image concerns would be diagnosed as follows: 307.59 Other Specified Feeding and Eating Disorder, Purging Disorder. It was hoped that this approach would be more descriptive and aid professional communication and treatment planning. An Unspecified Feeding and Eating Disorder option is also available for situations in which the clinician does not chose to specify a clinically significant atypical presentation.

Differential Diagnosis

Diagnostically, the feeding and eating disorders are ordered hierarchically. At the top of the hierarchy, and the first disorder to rule out, is AN. If the clinical picture meets criteria for AN, other eating disorders, such as BN, BED, ARFID, and rumination disorder cannot be additionally coded. Next in the hierarchy is BN. If criteria are met, BED, ARFID, and rumination disorder cannot be additionally coded. If only binge-eating behaviors are present, then BED should be considered. An essential feature of all three of these disorders is the presence of dissatisfaction with body shape or weight. When this feature is not present and there is some type of disordered eating or feeding, the remaining eating disorders (ARFID, pica, and rumination disorder) can be considered.

Assessment Strategies

Berg and Peterson (2013) recommended that all clients, regardless of age, gender, race or ethnicity, or weight status, be assessed for feeding and eating disorders. They recommended that counselors first conduct a screen for symptoms and then follow up with a more comprehensive assessment if necessary. Depending upon the age of the child, the assessment should be conducted in conjunction with the parents or caregivers. During an intake session, counselors can easily integrate screening questions into typical questions about self-care. For example, the counselor can ask questions to ascertain restricting behaviors (e.g., "What is your general eating pattern?" "Do you ever skip meals?" "Are there any foods you like that you avoid eating?" "Do you follow any rules about eating?" "Do you ever feel like you exercise beyond what is physically healthy for you?") Other questions can focus on binge eating and general feelings about weight, body shape, and size (e.g., "Have you ever felt a loss of control over eating?" "How do you feel about yourself as a person?" "How does your weight influence how you feel about yourself overall?").

Certain physical characteristics and behaviors should always be indicators for follow-up assessment (see Sidebar 13.3). Depending on answers to initial screening queries, more comprehensive assessment is warranted. A biopsychosocial assessment should ideally be conducted by a multidisciplinary treatment team, comprised of a physician or nurse practitioner to evaluate ongoing medical issues, a dietician to collaborate with nutritional education and counseling, and possibly a psychiatrist to monitor the need for medication if appropriate (APA, 2006).

SIDEBAR 13.3:   EATING AND WEIGHT-RELATED BEHAVIORS THAT REQUIRE FURTHER ASSESSMENT

Eating and weight-related behaviors that require further assessment:

a. Pica or rumination in younger children;
b. Abrupt changes in food preferences;
c. Low body weight for age and height;
d. Substantial weight changes;
e. Recurrent binge eating that involves a loss of control, eating in secret, eating in the absence of hunger, and emotional eating;
f. Compensatory behaviors, including vomiting, diuretic use, laxative abuse, regular fasting or extreme restriction, or excessive exercise that is primarily motivated by weight or shape concerns; and
g. Cognitive symptoms such as extreme body dissatisfaction, overvaluation of shape or weight, or extreme fear of weight gain (Berg & Peterson, 2013).

Feeding Disorders Assessment

The feeding disorders in particular require a thorough medical evaluation prior to diagnosis. For pica, the assessment should include a full medical evaluation not only to identify acute complications but also to uncover potential underlying etiologies, such as malnutrition or vitamin or mineral deficiencies. Additional assessment areas include attainment of developmental milestones, intellectual functioning, family functioning, and parent-child interactions. Rumination disorder also necessitates a medical examination to rule out medical etiologies and to assess for medical complications such as malnutrition. The psychosocial assessment should determine whether the regurgitation related-behaviors are episodic or more pervasive (First & Tasman, 2004). The infant–caregiver relationship as well as family atmosphere should be assessed. Finally, ARFID also requires a medical evaluation to rule out any underlying medical etiology as well as medical sequelae of the avoidant or restrictive eating. For infants and young children, it is important to assess caregiver–child attachment and behaviors surrounding feeding and eating. For older children, adolescents, and adults, it is also important to assess the role of maladaptive cognitions; comorbid mental disorders, such as anxiety and obsessive-compulsive disorder; and social functioning. Self-monitoring of instances of avoidant and restrictive behaviors helps to identify key internal and external triggers and perpetuating factors, such as avoiding food because of anxiety (see Sidebar 13.4).

SIDEBAR 13.4:   SCREENING QUESTIONS TO ASSESS FOR ARFID SYMPTOMS

1. What is his or her current food intake? This ascertains whether the current intake represents an adequate, age-appropriate amount or range (is the diet sufficient in terms of energy, and does it include major food groups and essential micronutrients?).

2. Is his or her diet supplemented by oral nutritional supplements or enteral feeding? This helps ascertain whether the individual is dependent on these other means of feeding.

3. Is the avoidance or restriction persistent? This helps determine whether the condition is an established rather than transient problem.

4. What are the individual's weight and height? This allows calculation of body mass index or body mass index percentile, comparison of the individual's previous weight and height percentiles, assessment of whether growth is faltering and whether weight has been lost or is static when it should be increasing.

5. Does the individual present with clinical or laboratory signs and symptoms of nutritional deficiency or malnutrition? For example, is there lethargy secondary to iron deficiency anemia or delayed bone age as a consequence of chronic restricted intake?

6. Is there evidence of any significant distress or impairment to the individual's social and emotional development or functioning associated with the eating disturbance?

7. Is the avoidance or restriction associated with a lack of interest in food or eating, or a failure to recognize hunger?

8. Is the avoidance or restriction based on sensory aspects of food such as appearance (including color), taste, texture, smell, or temperature?

9. Does the avoidance or restriction follow an aversive experience associated with intense distress, such as a choking incident, an episode of vomiting or diarrhea, or complications from a medical procedure such as an esophagoscopy?

Adapted from Bryant-Waugh, Markham, Kreipe, & Walsh, 2010

Eating Disorders Assessment

Eating disorders assessment can involve a clinical interview as well as the use of self-report questionnaires and structured interviews (for a list, see Berg & Peterson, 2013). One self-report instrument, the Eating Disorders Inventory-3 (EDI-3, Garner, 2004), is commonly used to make an accurate assessment of symptoms to determine issues such as level of treatment, as well as to identify core issues to include in the treatment plan. The Eating Disorders Examination Questionnaire (Fairburn & Beglin,

2008) can also be used to assess for the severity of a wide range of eating disorder (ED) symptoms. Assessment should also include screening for the presence of comorbidity, including mood or anxiety disorders, substance abuse, self-injury, clinical perfectionism, core low self-esteem, and personality traits or disorders, because all are problems that frequently co-occur with clients with EDs and can interfere with treatment outcome (APA, 2006; Fairburn, 2008).

Treatment Strategies and Interventions

Once an accurate diagnosis has been established, the counselor will need to determine the appropriate level of care for treatment: outpatient, intensive outpatient, partial day treatment, inpatient, or residential. Determining level of care is both an initial as well as an ongoing process that takes into account multiple factors such as severity of feeding and eating disorder symptoms, co-occurring psychiatric symptoms, medical risk, the presence of self-injury, or suicidal ideation.

According to APA treatment guidelines, a client should start at the least restrictive level of care and should remain in that setting unless she refuses to comply with treatment, her weight continues to drop below a medically safe level, or her health is at risk. If she generally refuses to comply with current treatment recommendations, the guidelines recommend that more intensive services can be infused into the current level of treatment (e.g., adding more frequent sessions, family sessions, nutritional counseling) before moving to the next level of care (APA, 2006).

TREATMENTS FOR FEEDING DISORDERS

Counselors do not generally provide treatments for these childhood disorders. Therefore, only a brief summary highlighting these treatment approaches is included here:

Pica

Treatment recommendations include:

- Psychoeducation for the parent (e.g., childproofing home from objects that might be ingested)
- Behavior therapy (time out, overcorrection) to decrease pica behaviors and to increase more normative adaptive behaviors.
- Environmental enrichment interventions, such as play therapy, may be an adjunctive treatment (First & Tasman, 2004)

Rumination

Treatment recommendations include:

- Psychoeducation for the parent
- Behavioral treatments that include activities that are incompatible with regurgitation behaviors at high-risk times (e.g., following feeding)
- Enhancement of caregiver–infant relationship
- Stabilization of family stressors

ARFID

Treatment recommendations include:

- Behavioral interventions to help caregivers normalize eating and increasing the range of foods consumed
- Psychoeducation for parents, including creating a calm eating environment and avoiding coercive techniques, such as forcing the child to eat everything that is on the plate
- Use of counter conditioning by introducing a novel food in combination with a preferred food as a way of broadening the eating repertoire (First & Tasman, 2004)
- Cognitive behavioral therapy approaches are recommended for older children, adolescents, and adults, including techniques such as exposure, cognitive restructuring, and systematic desensitization (First & Tasman, 2004)

Anorexia Nervosa

Conceptualization. Family-based treatment (FBT) is recommended as the most effective intervention for children and adolescents who experience AN, with the most research support of any treatment studied to date (APA, 2006; Hurst & Read, 2013). Originally termed the Maudsley approach (so named because of its development at the Maudsley Hospital in London in the 1980s), FBT was translated into manual form (Lock, LeGrange, Agras, & Dare, 2001) and was updated to its second edition in 2012 (Lock & LeGrange, 2012). For further reading about this treatment, the reader is referred to the Lock and LeGrange (2012) treatment manual.

FBT is an intensive outpatient treatment that includes all family members. The treatment is family centered and all members are expected to participate in the treatment. Rather than focus on the factors that contributed to the development of AN, the FBT model conceptualizes treatment in terms of how to empower the family as an essential resource for helping to restore their daughter's health. This means that the parents or caregivers will temporarily take control of their daughter's eating until she has regained her target weight and her health. It is assumed that no matter her age, she has regressed developmentally in terms of food and eating choices, so therefore her parents must assume control over her eating, much as they did when she was much younger. Many parents fear that if they force their daughter to eat, then it will only make the problem worse, or cause her to cut off her relationship with them. Instead, the counselor helps the parents take charge of the client's eating by assuming an executive role, at least until she is thinking more clearly and can maintain healthier functioning. Once she has gained sufficient weight, the parents can hand control back over to her, and therapy can change focus from eating-related issues toward the developmental tasks of adolescence (Hurst & Read, 2013).

Another important issue in conceptualization is that AN is externalized; that is, it is not viewed as a part of the daughter's core identity. It is discussed objectively, as a third party that the family can unite against. This type of externalization, a narrative therapy technique, is helpful for reducing criticism and blame within the family (White & Epston, 1990). The counselor might say something like: "So the AN keeps tricking Annabeth, trying to make her think she needs to lose more weight, but everyone in the family, including Annabeth, wants to work hard to help her be healthy again." Three phases are included in the therapy process.

Treatment Phase One. Goals of this phase are as follows: (a) encouraging all family members to increase motivation for treatment, (b) providing a referral for medical monitoring and agreeing upon a weight that must be maintained if the client is to stay in outpatient treatment, (c) placing an emphasis on the seriousness and potential morbidity of the disorder, (d) providing a thorough rationale as to why the parents will be temporarily taking control over their child's eating, and (e) keeping a focus on weight gain as the primary goal in counseling during Phase One. In Session Two, a family meal is conducted where the counselor can provide actual coaching for the parents as they instruct their daughter to eat one more mouthful than the AN wants her to (Lock & LeGrange, 2006). The counselor can also provide positive support for this difficult and stressful time in parents' lives as they stay committed to doing what needs to be done in order to monitor their daughter's eating (Hurst & Read, 2013). For example, they may need to take time off from work or other activities for a time so that they can be home with their daughter to prevent her from skipping meals or engaging in secret purges.

Treatment Phase Two. This phase begins when the client has gained weight and the parents no longer struggle with having to force their daughter to eat nutritious meals and snacks on a regular basis. Now that parents have confidence in their daughter's willingness to eat, Phase Two includes experiments in which the parents slowly give her back her autonomy over eating choices. They may start with only one unsupervised meal or snack, and based on these results, they can make decisions about relinquishing additional control over her eating choices.

Treatment Phase Three. In this phase, the focus begins to turn away from eating and weight gain, and more toward normal adolescent developmental issues, such as dating, peers, academics, and increasing independence. The counselor can also help the family prepare for termination and for a return to normal family life—the time before the AN developed—so that the family can focus on life outside of her recovery.

Bulimia Nervosa (BN)

Conceptualization. Cognitive behavioral therapy (CBT) is the recommended treatment for BN in older children and adolescents (Commission on Adolescent Eating Disorders, 2005). CBT for BN (Fairburn, Marcus, & Wilson, 1993), a manualized form of CBT, shows higher rates of treatment effectiveness when compared with medication and other psychosocial approaches, including interpersonal therapy (IPT), behavioral therapy, supportive counseling, and nutritional counseling (APA, 2006; Shapiro et al., 2007; Wilson, Grilo, & Vitousek, 2007). Although CBT for BN has been well studied in adults, there is a comparative lack of research to support its effectiveness with children and adolescents specifically. However, because CBT is so effective in adolescents for disorders such as mood and anxiety disorders (Campbell & Schmidt, 2011), it remains the first-line treatment for child and adolescent BN. Fairburn (2008) recently updated CBT for BN so that it is now termed CBT-Enhanced (CBT-E). CBT-E has demonstrated initial effectiveness in both a randomized controlled trial (Fairburn et al., 2009) as well as in a community setting (Byrne, Fursland, Allen, & Watson, 2011).

According to the CBT-E model for understanding the development and maintenance of BN, when a child comes to equate her worth as a person with attractiveness and thinness, she may learn to center her identity on her weight, shape, and appearance. When she internalizes the current cultural ideal for thinness as her own standard of worth, she is likely to develop body dissatisfaction as a result. In response, she will begin to diet and use other weight loss strategies to control her weight and shape. Adhering to a strict diet then places her at risk for the development of binge eating (Stice, Presnell, & Spangler, 2002; Stice, Davis, Miller, & Marti, 2008). This occurs because when the body experiences deprivation, drives to maintain the body's physical needs are put in motion so that she is primed to lose control of her diet and to overeat or binge. In addition, her beliefs about the *abstinence violation effect* are triggered (i.e., she believes that once she has violated even one rule of her diet plan, she might as well go ahead and eat everything she wants).

Therefore, dieting creates a sense of deprivation and eventual loss of control, which then places her at risk for a binge-eating episode. Because her goal in the first place was to obtain thinness, she is highly driven after a binge to then rid her body of the unwanted calories she has consumed through purging. After a purge, she feels failure and guilt over the episode, and vows to work even harder at her diet (which then sets her up for repeated binge-eating episodes). Ultimately she begins to feel increasingly trapped in a vicious cycle of dieting, bingeing, purging, and feelings of failure. CBT-E is designed to inter-rupt this cycle through helping her normalize her eating (instead of dieting), reduce her overvaluation of weight and shape to her overall identity, and to enhance motivation for cognitive and behavioral change (Fairburn, 2008).

In the treatment manual, Fairburn (2008) described 20 sessions over four treatment phases. These are described briefly below:

Treatment Phase One. The goals of phase one (generally eight twice-weekly sessions) include: (a) building a relationship with the client so that she is motivated and commit-ted to treatment; (b) providing psychoeducation about the CBT model, the consequences of extreme dieting, and the ineffectiveness of purging methods such as vomiting, laxa-tive, and diuretic abuse; and (c) establishing weekly weighing procedures so that she will realize she is not gaining weight as she begins to eat on a more normal basis. She is also instructed to reduce weighing to once weekly because of the body weight fluctuations that occur daily and to establish an agreed-upon weight range that she must stay within if she is to continue in outpatient counseling.

Another important goal of Phase One is the introduction of regular eating patterns so that the client (with the assistance of her family) begins to plan and eat three meals per day and two snacks, with no more than a four-hour interval between eating. Eating on a normal basis rather than dieting might be new to some clients, so the client and her family should recognize that this type of eating routine will take dedication and planning to put into place effectively. Finally, the counselor and client can develop a list that outlines situations that place her at high risk for binge eating (e.g., immediately after school) and develop coping strategies for each situation (e.g., keep high-risk foods out of the house and stay at a friend's house after school).

Treatment Phase Two. The goals of Phase Two (two sessions) are to review client progress and to determine whether she is ready for Phase Three. If she is not making progress, the counselor may need to spend additional time on the client's motivation and commitment to change, or to determine whether she is following her eating plan. It is typ-ical that once she begins eating on a regular schedule, her binges will be reduced because she is no longer experiencing feelings of hunger or deprivation. If this is not the case, obstacles can be identified and goals from Phase One can be revisited before moving on to the next phase.

Treatment Phase Three.   The goal of Phase Three is to begin to help the client change her attitudes and behaviors that stem from her overvaluation of weight and shape concerns. Counselors can use cognitive restructuring exercises to help her changing belief patterns about the importance of weight and shape them in determining her success or worth as a person. In so doing, she can begin to recognize her strengths in multiple life dimensions that are not dependent upon physical appearance. The counselor can also ask her to try certain behavioral experiments, such as refraining from comparing herself with others or checking her appearance in the mirror less often (Fairburn, 2008).

A second goal of Phase Three is to reduce dietary restraint. Whereas in Phase One the client learned to eat on a regular schedule, the purpose in Phase Three is to continue the regular eating pattern but to also include a focus on the type and amount of food eaten. She can first identify any *forbidden foods* she will not allow herself to eat (e.g., chocolate), as well as any diet rules she has constructed for herself ("I will never eat anything past 7 PM"). She can then gradually begin to intentionally incorporate each forbidden food one at a time into her diet, and can challenge herself to slowly break each of her self-imposed rules. The purpose of this is so that she will not be triggered to binge again if she happens to eat a particular food or break a particular rule about eating. Without *forbidden foods* and strict rules, she will have more flexibility in her eating and will be less prone to binge and purge.

A third goal is to help her learn new ways for managing negative moods and stressful events. As we will discuss further in the section on treatments for binge eating, these stressors often serve as triggers for binges and subsequent purging behaviors. Instead of coping directly with the situation or her feelings, she might have learned instead to use binges or purges as a way to avoid or reduce her negative emotional states (Waller et al., 2007). During this phase, she can learn to implement problem-solving steps and active coping strategies for managing stressors more directly and effectively.

Treatment Phase Four.   The goal of this three-session phase, scheduled once every other week, is to explore the idea of termination so that the client can maintain her improvements without the support of a counselor. She can renew her commitment to regularly scheduled, nutritionally sound eating patterns, to refrain from dieting because this will set her up for binges, to identify areas needing continued improvement, and to plan for how she might cope with certain triggers or a relapse.

Binge Eating Disorder (BED)

Conceptualization.   Binge eating is generally conceptualized through a dietary restraint model (Stice et al., 2008) and an emotion dysregulation model (Polivy & Herman, 2002). Some clients binge eat either as a response to dietary restraint (as described in the previous section on CBT treatment for BN) or as an attempt to regulate emotions, whereas others are influenced by both factors.

CBT Treatment.   CBT is recommended as the first line of treatment for adolescents who are immersed in a cycle of dieting and binge eating and who tend to overvalue weight and shape in determining their self-worth (Fairburn, 2008). As with CBT-E for BN, the goal is to eliminate dieting by normalizing eating and to decrease the importance of weight and shape. The self-help manual *Overcoming Binge Eating*, now in its second edition (Fairburn, 2013), is often recommended as a supplement to treatment. For adolescents who binge eat for emotional reasons but do not diet or who are not overly focused on weight and shape concerns, interpersonal therapy (IPT) and dialectical behavior therapy (DBT) are recommended as promising treatment approaches (APA, 2006; Craighead et al., 2013; Hilbert et al., 2012). Both CBT and IPT in particular have been studied extensively and show improvement rates in the range of 80 percent (Craighead et al., 2013), with treatment gains being maintained up to four years (Hilbert et al., 2012).

Interpersonal Therapy (IPT).   While CBT has a treatment focus on changing eating and weight-related behaviors and thoughts, counselors using IPT do not discuss diets, food, or weight, and instead target relationship enhancement. IPT is a treatment originally developed for the treatment of depression, and focuses on helping clients to make improvements in their interpersonal relationships (Klerman, Weissman, Rounsaville, & Chevron, 1984). IPT is generally recommended for clients who have significant impairment in their relationships, lack adequate social support, and lack skills to effectively express feelings with others (Wilfley, MacKenzie, Welch, Ayers, & Weissman, 2000). IPT focuses on four major problem areas: grief, interpersonal role disputes, role transitions, and interpersonal deficits. Because interpersonal role disputes and transitions are most commonly experienced by clients with binge eating, only these two areas are discussed in the sections to follow.

Interpersonal Role Disputes.   It is well recognized that adolescents experience increasing disputes in their relationships with parents, peers, and authority figures as they negotiate new roles during this period in their lives. In the IPT approach, the counselor can assist the client in first creating a history of her relationship conflicts. She can explore such questions as:

• What are the expectations for each of the important relationships in her life?
• How does she typically communicate her needs?
• How effective are her communication patterns with significant others?
• How has she already tried to resolve conflicts?

The counselor then helps her assess the particular stage of the conflict: negotiation (relationship is still open to improvements), impasse (relationship is stuck with neither person being willing to change), or dissolution (relationship is considered beyond repair). The treatment plan can then be based upon the stage of the dispute. If the relationship is in the negotiation stage, the counselor and client can work toward generating ideas for resolving the particular conflict. For example, if the adolescent is having continued conflicts with her family, the family members might be invited to come to a joint therapy session. The client can be prepared in advance for ways to more effectively express her needs to her family members, and family members can be encouraged to offer her feedback in a way that validates her feelings.

If the relationship is in the impasse stage, the counselor and client work to determine whether the relationship has the potential to move forward (toward negotiation) or whether it needs to move to the dissolution stage. If she wants the relationship to move forward, she might need to invest more energy into the relationship, to assess her expectations of the relationship, and to take a risk to express her needs more openly. If the relationship needs to move toward dissolution, she can learn ways to disconnect from the relationship and grieve the loss of the relationship if necessary. For many adolescents, learning skills such as effective communication and assertiveness may become necessary pieces of this process.

Interpersonal Role Transitions.   Clients who have problems with role transitions are those who have difficulties in letting go of one role and stepping into a new one. Adolescents undergo many transitions during this period, including the transition to puberty, changing schools, the onset of dating, peer pressures, and negotiating new roles with parents. Recommended strategies for improving her transitions include:

- *Define the previous role.* What are her feelings about the previous role? How can she begin to mourn the loss of the role? How will this loss affect her sense of identity?
- *Fully examine the new role.* What is it that is causing ambivalence about the new role? What are her expectations for role? What are the good things about the new role?
- *Realistically explore what the new role requires.* What does she need to do to be successful in this new role? What does she need to change? Are there any new skills she needs to learn? Who can she count on for support as she makes this transition?

In sum, the goals in IPT for BED are for a client to (a) identify her specific role disputes or transitions, (b) explore her own thoughts and feelings about the direction of her relationships and the transitions she is facing, (c) develop skills for expressing her emotions and needs to others more effectively, (d) strengthen her support system, and (e) commit to investing time and effort into enhancing her relationships. As she expresses her needs more openly and her relationships improve, it is assumed that she will have a decreased need to turn to binges as a way to cope with her interpersonal difficulties (Wilfley et al., 2000).

Dialectical Behavior Therapy (DBT).   Like IPT, DBT does not focus on eating, weight, or shape directly, but rather emphasizes the need for building skills for identifying, accepting, tolerating, and regulating emotional reactions to daily life stressors (Safer, Telch, & Chen, 2009). Clients are taught these skills through learning core mindfulness skills, emotion regulation skills, and distress tolerance skills (Linehan, 1993a). It is assumed that with the use of more effective regulatory strategies, the need for binge eating will be decreased. Because a full description of DBT is beyond the scope of this chapter, a DBT treatment manual for binge eating (see Safer et al., 2009) and the original treatment manual and skills workbook by Linehan (1993a, 1993b) are recommended for further reading.

Evaluation Strategies

The prognosis for EDs is poor, because these disorders can be chronic and include high rates of relapse, distress, and functional impairment (Shaw & Stice, 2013). Feeding disorders, while often remitting spontaneously in childhood, may persist into adolescence and adulthood, especially in those clients with an ID or with ASD (Ellis & Schnoer, 2014). Clients who experience EDs are at risk for future obesity, depression, anxiety, suicide attempts, substance abuse, and morbidity risk (Stice, Marti, Shaw, & Jaconis, 2009; Swanson et al., 2011). AN in particular has the highest mortality rate of any psychiatric disorder (Arcelus, Mitchell, Wales, & Nielsen, 2011). A recent study by Swanson and colleagues

(2011) indicated that eating disorders among children and adolescents were associated with significant impairment, including high rates of suicide plans and attempts. Overall, Swanson and colleagues found that crude mortality rates for children and adolescents with EDs were concerning, at 4 percent for AN, 3.9 percent for BN, and 5.2 percent for EDNOS.

Given the chronicity and morbidity rates of these disorders, it is also of concern that although best practice treatments are effective, only about 35 to 45 percent of clients who receive treatment experience lasting symptom remission (Shaw & Stice, 2013). Because eating disorders are chronic and difficult to treat, scholars in the field of eating disorders emphasize the importance of prevention programs, particularly in the early adolescent years (Stice, Rohde, & Shaw, 2013). According to Shaw and Stice (2013), because of the serious nature of eating disorders, the implementation of effective prevention programs should be a public health priority.

Diagnostic Challenges

The assessment and diagnosis of feeding and eating disorders in children and adolescents can be challenging and may require several modifications to the standard procedures used with adult clients. In general, the *DSM-5* symptoms for AN, BN, and BED are better matched to the clinical presentations of adults and adolescents and are not as sensitive to the way the disorders are expressed in childhood (Knoll et al., 2011).

One particular challenge to diagnosis is the determination of weight status. Because of individual differences in growth rates (which can vary widely by gender, age, and pubertal status), it is difficult to determine whether a child is truly underweight or overweight (Berg & Peterson, 2013). It is also difficult to determine the extent of true weight gains that occur as a result of treatment, as children continue to grow in height throughout the course of treatment. There are also limitations to a child and adolescent's ability to self-report symptoms during the assessment process. This can occur because of lack of awareness and understanding or because of deliberate misreporting of symptom severity due to fears that the treatment will require forced weight gains.

Because of the cognitive developmental level of children and some adolescents, reporting of cognitive criteria for EDs can also be a challenge, as these require a level of abstract reasoning that younger individuals do not possess. Without abstract reasoning abilities, a client will have difficulty understanding what actually constitutes a binge (recalling the type of quantity of food consumed during binge-eating episodes, and whether or not it was an especially large amount) or understanding the concept of loss of control over eating. It is recommended that rather than focusing on actual foods consumed, it is more clinically useful to assess for episodes in which loss of control over eating actually occurred. Finally, asking about behaviors such as self-induced vomiting and laxative abuse may be inappropriate topics to introduce to children and adolescents. Berg and Peterson (2013) recommended asking more general questions, such as "When was the last time you threw up?" This may help a child to disclose purging behaviors if they are already occurring. Due to these developmental limitations, it is useful to incorporate behavioral indicators reported by parents or caregivers, rather than placing undue emphasis on client self-report.

A final diagnostic challenge stems from the biopsychosocial nature of feeding and eating disorders. Because multiple providers are likely involved in the assessment and treatment process, the counselor may need to coordinate information gained from a medical professional, nutritionist, the parent or caregiver, and sometimes the child's teacher. Obtaining information from multiple sources, although critical to understanding the client's concerns, can be challenging to collect and coordinate in actual practice.

Summary

In sum, there have been major changes to the *DSM-5* regarding eating disorders, including the renaming of the chapters to Feeding and Eating Disorders, the inclusion of the feeding disorders (pica, rumination disorder, and ARFID), the addition of binge eating disorder, and the elimination of EDNOS. We reviewed each of the feeding and eating disorders, including their essential features, diagnostic considerations, diagnostic markers, and risk factors. In addition, we briefly described treatments for the feeding disorders and then provided information regarding best practice treatments for eating disorders: CBT, IPT, and DBT. Assessment strategies and challenges to accurate diagnosis and treatment were also discussed. The following References provide additional information relating to eating disorders in children and adolescents.

References

American Psychiatric Association. (1994). *Diagnostic and statistical manual of mental disorders* (4th ed.). Washington DC: American Psychiatric Association.

American Psychiatric Association. (2006). Practice guidelines for the treatment of patients with eating disorders (revision). *American Journal of Psychiatry, 157*, 1–39.

American Psychiatric Association. (2013). *Diagnostic and statistical manual of mental disorders* (5th ed.). Arlington, VA: American Psychiatric Publishing.

Allen, K. L., Byrne, S. M., Oddy, W. H., & Crosby, R. D. (2013). DSM-IV-TR and DSM-5 eating disorders in adolescents: Prevalence, stability, and psychosocial correlates in a population-based sample of male and female adolescents. *Journal of Abnormal Psychology, 122*(3), 720–732. doi:10.1037/a0034004

Arcelus, J., Mitchell, A. J., Wales, J., & Nielsen, S. (2011). Mortality rates in patients with anorexia nervosa and other eating disorders: A meta-analysis of 37 studies. *Archives of General Psychiatry, 68*(7), 724–731. doi:10.1001/archgenpsychiatry.2011.74

Berg, K. C., & Peterson, C. B. (2013). Assessment and diagnosis of eating disorders. In L. Choate (Ed.), *Eating disorders and obesity: A counselor's guide to prevention and treatment* (pp. 193–231). Alexandria, VA: American Counseling Association Press.

Blinder, B. J. (2008). An update on Pica: Prevalence, contributing causes and treatment. *Psychiatric Times.* Retrieved from http://www.psychiatrictimes.com/articles/update-pica-prevalence-contributing-causes-and-treatment/page/0/4

Brown, T. A., Holland, L. A., & Keel, P. K. (2013). Comparing operational definitions of DSM-5 anorexia nervosa for research contexts. *International Journal of Eating Disorders, 47*(1), 76–84. doi:10.1002/eat.22184

Bryant-Waugh, R., Markham, L, Kriepe, R. E., & Walsh, B. T. (2010). Feeding and eating disorders in childhood. *International Journal of Eating Disorders, 43*(2), 98–111. doi:10.1002/eat.20795

Byrne, S. M., Fursland, A., Allen, K. L., & Watson, H. (2011). The effectiveness of enhanced cognitive behavioural therapy for eating disorders: An open trial. *Behaviour Research and Therapy, 49*(4), 219–226. doi:10.1016/j.brat.2011.01.006

Campbell, M., & Schmidt, U. (2011). Cognitive-behavioral therapy for adolescent bulimia nervosa. In D. LeGrange & J. Lock (Eds.), *Eating disorders in children and adolescents: A clinical handbook* (pp. 305–318). New York, NY: Guilford Press.

Castellini, G., Carolina, L. S., Mannucci, E., Rivaldi, C., Rotella, C. M., Faravelli, C., & Ricca, V. (2011). Diagnostic crossover and outcome predictors in eating disorders according to DSM-IV and DSM-V proposed criteria: A 6-year follow-up study. *Psychosomatic Medicine, 73*, 270–279. doi:10.1097/PSY.0b013e3120a1838

Commission on Adolescent Eating Disorders (2005). *Treatment of Eating Disorders.* In D. L. Evans, E. B. Foa, R. E. Gur, et al. (Eds.), *Treating and preventing adolescent mental health disorders: What we know and what we don't know: A research agenda for improving the mental health of our youth* (pp. 445–481). New York: Oxford University Press.

Craighead, L. W., Martinez, M. A., & Klump, K. L. (2013). Bulimia nervosa and binge eating disorder. In W. E. Craighead, D. J. Miklowitz, & L. W. Craighead (Eds.), *Psychopathology: History, diagnosis, and empirical foundations* (pp. 445–481). Hoboken, NJ: John Wiley & Sons.

De Young, K. P., Lavender, J. M., Steffen, K., Wonderlich, S. A., Engel, S. G., Mitchell, J. E., … Crosby, R. D. (2013). Restrictive eating behaviors are a nonweight-based marker of severity in anorexia nervosa. *International Journal of Eating Disorders, 46*(8), 849–854.

Eaton, D. K, Kann, L., Kinchen, S., Shanklin, S., Ross, J., Hawkins, J., … Wechsler, H. (2010). Youth risk behavior surveillance—United States, 2009. *MMWR Surveillance Summaries, 59*(SS05), 1–142.

Ellis, C. R., & Schnoer, C. J. (2014, September). Pica. *Medscape.* Retrieved from http://emedicine.medscape.com/article/914765-overview

First, M. B., & Tasman, A. (2004). *DSM-IV-TR mental disorders: Diagnosis, etiology & treatment.* Washington DC: American Psychiatric Association.

Fisher, M. M., Rosen, D. S., Ornstein, R. M., Mammel, K. A., Katzman, D. K., Rome, E. S., … Walsh, B. T. (2014). Characteristics of avoidant/restrictive food intake disorder in children and adolescents: A "new disorder" in DSM-5. *Journal of Adolescent Health, 53*(3), 307–310. doi:10.1016/j.jadohealth.2013.11.013

Fairburn, C. G. (2008). *Cognitive behavior therapy and eating disorders.* New York, NY: Guilford Press.

Fairburn, C. G. (2013). *Overcoming binge eating: The proven program to learn why you binge and how you can stop* (2nd ed.). New York, NY: Guilford Press.

Fairburn, C. G., & Belgin, S. (2008). Eating Disorder Examination Questionnaire. In C. G. Fairburn (Ed.), *Cognitive behavior therapy and eating disorders* (pp. 309–317). New York, NY: Guilford Press.

Fairburn, C. G., Cooper, Z., Bohn, K., O'Connor, M. E., Doll, H. A., & Palmer, R. L. (2007). The severity and status of eating disorder NOS: Implications for DSM-V. *Behaviour Research and Therapy, 45*(8), 1705–1715. doi:10.1016/j.brat.2007.01.010

Fairburn, C. G., Cooper, Z., Doll, H. A., O'Connor, M. E., Bohn, K., Hawker, D. M., ... Palmer, R. L. (2009). Transdiagnostic cognitive-behavioral therapy for patients with eating disorders: A two-site trial with 60-week follow-up. *American Journal of Psychiatry, 166*(3), 311–319. doi:10.1176/appi.ajp.2008.08040608

Fairburn, C. G., Marcus, M. D., & Wilson, G. T. (1993). Cognitive-behavioral therapy for binge eating and bulimia nervosa: A comprehensive treatment manual. In C. G. Fairburn & G. T. Wilsons (Eds.), *Binge eating: Nature, assessment, and treatment* (pp. 361–404). New York, NY: Guilford Press.

Garner, D. (2004). *Eating Disorder Inventory-3.* Torrance, CA: Western Psychological Services.

Grilo, C. M., Masheb, R. M., & Crosby, R. D. (2012). Predictors and moderators of response to cognitive behavioral therapy and medication for the treatment of binge eating disorder. *Journal of Consulting and Clinical Psychology, 80*(5), 897–906. doi:10.1037/a0027001

Guerdjikova, A. I., McElroy, S. L., Winstanley, E. L., Nelson, E. B., Mori, N., McCoy, J., ... & Hudson, J. I. (2012). Duloxetine in the treatment of binge eating disorder with depressive disorders: A placebo-controlled trial. *International Journal of Eating Disorders, 45*(2), 281–289. doi:10.1002/eat.20946

Hilbert, A., Bishop, M. E., Stein, R. I., Tanofsky-Kraff, M., Swenson, A. K., Welch, R. R., & Wilfley, D. E. (2012). Long-term efficacy of psychological treatments for binge eating disorder. *The British Journal of Psychiatry, 200*(3), 232–237. doi:10.1192/bjp.bp.110.089664

Hudson, J. I., Hiripi, E., Pope, H. G., & Kessler, R. C. (2007). The prevalence and correlates of eating disorders in the national comorbidity survey replication. *Biological Psychiatry, 61*(3), 348–358. doi:10.1016/j.biopsych.2006.03.040

Hurst, K., & Read, S. (2013). Family-based therapy for children and adolescents with anorexia. In L. Choate (Ed.), *Eating disorders and obesity: A counselor's guide to prevention and treatment* (pp. 193–231). Alexandria, VA: American Counseling Association Press.

Klerman, G. L., Weissman, M. M., Rounsaville, B. J., & Chevron, E. S. (1984). *Interpersonal psychotherapy of depression.* New York, NY: Basic Books.

Knoll, S., Bulik, C. M., & Heberand, J. (2011). Do the currently proposed DSM-5 criteria for anorexia nervosa adequately consider developmental aspects in children and adolescents? *European Child and Adolescent Psychiatry, 20,* 95–101. doi:10.1007/s00787-010-0141-5

Linehan, M. M. (1993a). *Cognitive behavioral treatment of borderline personality disorder.* New York, NY: Guilford Press.

Linehan, M. M. (1993b). *Skills training manual for treating borderline personality disorder.* New York, NY: Guilford Press.

Lock, J., & LeGrange, D. (2006). Eating disorders. In D. A. Wolfe & E. J. Mash (Eds.), *Behavioral and emotional disorders in adolescence* (pp. 485–504). New York, NY: Guilford Press.

Lock, J., & LeGrange, D. (2012). *Treatment manual for anorexia nervosa: A family-based approach* (2nd ed.). New York, NY: Guilford Press.

Lock, J., LeGrange, D., Agras, W. S., & Dare, C. (2001). *Treatment manual for anorexia nervosa: A family-based approach.* New York, NY: Guilford Press.

Maine, M., & Bunnell, D. (2013). Gendered considerations in the treatment and prevention of eating disorders. In L. Choate (Ed.), *Eating disorders and obesity: A counselor's guide to prevention and treatment* (pp. 193–231). Alexandria, VA: American Counseling Association Press.

Marek, R. J., Ben-Porath, Y. S., Ashton, K., & Heinberg, L. J. (2014). Impact of using DSM-5 criteria for diagnosing binge eating disorder in bariatric surgery candidates: Change in prevalence rate, demographic characteristics, and scores on the Minnesota multiphasic personality inventory—2 restructured form (MMPI-2-RF). *International Journal of Eating Disorders, 47*(5), 553–557. doi:10.002/eat.22268

Ornstein, R. M., Rosen, D. S., Mammel, K. A., Callahan, S. T., Forman, S., Jay, M. S., ... Walsh, B. T. (2013). Distribution of eating disorders in children and adolescents using the proposed DSM-5 criteria for feeding and eating disorders. *Journal of Adolescent Health, 53*(2), 303–305.

Polivy, J., & Herman, C. P. (2002). Causes of eating disorders. *Annual Review of Psychology, 53*, 187–213. doi:10.1146/annurev.psych.53.100901.135103

Safer, D. L., Telch, C. F., & Chen, E. Y. (2009). *Dialectical behavior therapy for binge eating and bulimia.* New York, NY: Guilford Press.

Shapiro, J. R., Woolson, S. L., Hamer, R. M., Kalarchian, M. A., Marcus, M. D., & Bulik, C. M. (2007). Evaluating binge eating disorder in children: Development of the children's binge eating disorder scale (C-BEDS). *International Journal of Eating Disorders, 40*(1), 82–89. doi:10.1002/eat.20318

Shaw, H. & Stice, E. (2013). Eating disorders prevention with adolescents and young adults. In L. Choate (Ed.), *Eating disorders and obesity: A counselor's guide to prevention and treatment* (pp. 396–428). Alexandria, VA: American Counseling Association Press.

Stice, E., Davis, K., Miller, N. P., & Marti, C. N. (2008). Fasting increases risk for onset of binge eating and bulimic pathology: A 5-year prospective study. *Journal of Abnormal Psychology, 117*(4), 941–946. doi:10.1037/a0013644

Stice, E., Marti, C. N., & Rohde, P. (2012). Prevalence, incidence, impairment, and course of the proposed DSM-5 eating disorder diagnoses in an 8-year prospective community study of young women. *Journal of Abnormal Psychology, 122*(2), 445–457. doi:10.1037/a0030679

Stice, E., Marti, C. N., Shaw, H., & Jaconis, M. (2009). An 8-year longitudinal study of the natural history of threshold, subthreshold, and partial eating disorders from a community sample of adolescents. *Journal of Abnormal Psychology, 118*(3), 587–597. doi:10.1037/a0016481

Stice, E., Presnell, K. & Spangler, D. (2002). Risk factors for binge eating onset in adolescent girls: A 2-year prospective investigation. *Health Psychology, 21*(2), 131–138. doi:10.1037/0278–6133.21.2.131

Stice, E., Rohde, P., & Shaw, H. (2013). *The Body Project: A dissonance-based eating disorder prevention program.* New York, NY: Oxford University Press.

Swanson, S. A., Crow, S. J., LeGrange, D., Swendsen, J., & Merikangas, K. R. (2011). Prevalence and correlates of eating disorders in adolescents: Results from the national comorbidity survey replication adolescent supplement. *Archives of General Psychiatry, 68*(7), 714–723. doi:10.1001/archgenpsychiatry.2011.22

Tallyrand, R. M. (2013). Clients of color and eating disorders: Cultural Considerations. In L. Choate (Ed.), *Eating disorders and obesity: A counselor's guide to prevention and treatment* (pp. 45–68). Alexandria, VA: American Counseling Association Press.

Thomas, J. J., Vartanian, L. R., & Brownell, K. D. (2009). The relationship between eating disorder not otherwise specified (EDNOS) and officially recognized eating disorders: A meta-analysis and implications for DSM. *Psychological Bulletin, 135*(3), 407–433. doi:10.1037/a0015326

Treasure, J. (2007). The trauma of self-starvation: Eating disorders and body image. In M. Nasser, K., Baistow, & J. Treasure (Eds.), *The female body in mind: The interface between the female body and mental health* (pp. 57–71). London, England: Routledge.

Turner, H., & Bryant-Waugh, R. (2004). Eating disorder not otherwise specified (EDNOS): Profile of clients presenting at a community eating disorder service. *European Eating Disorder Review, 12*(1), 18.

Waller, G., Cordery, H., Corstorphine, E., Hinrichsen, H., Lawson, R., Mountford, V., & Russell, K. (2007). *Cognitive behavioral therapy for eating disorders: A comprehensive treatment guide.* Cambridge, NY: Cambridge University Press.

White, M., & Epston, D. (1990). *Narrative means to therapeutic ends.* New York, NY: W.W. Norton.

Wilfley, D. E., MacKenzie, K. R., Welch, R. R., Ayers, V. E., & Weissman, M. M. (2000). *Interpersonal psychotherapy for group.* New York, NY: Basic Books.

Wilson, G. T., Grilo, C. M., & Vitousek, K. M. (2007). Psychological treatment of eating disorders. *American Psychologist, 62*(3), 199–216. doi:10.1037/0003-066X.62.3.199

Wilson, G. T., & Sysko, R. (2009). Frequency of binge eating episodes in bulimia nervosa and binge eating disorder: Diagnostic considerations. *International Journal of Eating Disorders, 42*(7), 603–610. doi:10.1002/eat.20726

World Health Organization. (1992). *International classification of diseases* (9th ed.). Geneva, Switzerland: Author.

World Health Organization. (2010). International statistical classification of diseases and related health problems (10th rev.). Retrieved from http://apps.who.int/classifications/icd10/browse/2010/en

Wonderlich, S. A., Gordon, K. H., Mitchell, J. E., Crosby, R. D., & Engel, S. G. (2009). The validity and clinical utility of binge eating disorder. *International Journal of Eating Disorders, 42*(8), 687–705. doi:10.1002/eat.20719

Chapter 14

Sleep-Wake Disorders

CARL J. SHEPERIS, TRACY K. CALLEY, KATHLEEN JONES-TREBATOSKI, AND LISA A. Wines

Introduction

Sleep is an essential component of healthy functioning, and as a result researchers examine all facets of sleep and its relationship to human behavior (e.g., Adams, Matson, & Jang, 2014; Chase & Pincus, 2011; Feige et al., 2013; O'Brien, 2011; Tan, Healey, Schaughency, Dawes, & Galland, 2014). Problems with sleep often begin during early childhood and can increase in severity over time (Jenni & Carskadon, 2012). Sleep problems often begin with behavioral compliance issues related to nighttime routines and ensuing postbedtime behavioral disruptions (e.g., crying, getting out of bed, leaving the bedroom, and playing in bed) and then develop into more severe problems (Jin, Hanley, & Beaulieu, 2013). When sleep problems become severe enough to create ongoing disruption of typical functioning, a sleep disorder may be present.

Sleep-wake disorders are an official classification in the *Diagnostic and Statistical Manual of Mental Disorders, Fifth Edition* (*DSM-5*), and clinicians should be conscious of the various comorbid conditions that may be present with sleep problems (e.g., depression, anxiety, and other neurocognitive issues). Sleep-wake disorders are serious conditions, and related symptomology, such as insomnia and excessive sleepiness, have been shown to be clear pathways to mental illness and substance abuse. It is estimated that over 40 percent of children have experienced sleep problems to some degree (Leahy & Gradisar, 2012). Although sleep disruption is common, many sleep problems are resolved without professional intervention. When sleep issues persist, the outlook is disconcerting. Researchers have demonstrated that ongoing sleep disturbances are highly correlated with a variety of issues, such as obesity, anxiety, depression, poor academic performance, seasonal affective disorder, suicidal behavior, and other neurocognitive issues (Abe & de Kernier, 2013; Adams et al., 2014; Chen et al., 2014; de Freitas Araújo & de Almondes, 2014; Kaplan, Ali, Simpson, Britt, & McCall, 2014; Maski & Kothare, 2013). Sleep-wake disorders affect 50 million to 70 million individuals in the United States. Regardless of the age of onset, sleep-wake disorders can lead to significant health complications and chronic illness (National Center for Chronic Disease and Prevention and Health Promotion, 2013).

It is important for clinicians to understand the typical sleep patterns of children and adolescents to place symptoms of sleep-wake disorders in context. Research by the National Sleep Foundation (2013) supported the notion that typically developing children need larger amounts of sleep than adults in order to function optimally. According to Mezter, Alvis, Reynolds, Crabtree, and Bevens (2013), adolescents under the age of 18 generally sleep about 40 percent of their life. Lack of proper sleep, particularly in adolescents, can lead to high-risk behaviors, poorer academic performance, moodiness, and anxiety (Berk, 2014; Marhefka, 2011). Interruptions in sleep-wake patterns by various factors, such as social media and technology, also can cause serious physical and mental health issues. Interestingly, there is often a discrepancy between adolescent and parental reporting of sleep-wake disorders (Short, Gradisar, Gill, & Camfferman, 2013). According to the study Short et al. (2013) did, 14.1 percent of parents believed their child had a sleep problem versus 21 percent of the self-reporting adolescents. With conflicting reports between parental and adolescent reporting, it is clear that various methods must be used for an accurate diagnosis of sleep-wake disorders.

Sleep-wake disorder has a spectrum of severity and, in the United States as much as 20 percent of the general population experiences a sleep-wake disorder to some degree. The prevalence rates are similar among children and adolescents. According to the *DSM-5* (American Psychiatric Association [APA], 2013), 65 percent of children report suffering sleep problems at least once per week. As is the case with all prevalence estimates, there is a range within the population who may be affected. The quality of studies, sample sizes, and other variables result in differences among sleep researchers in identifying the portion of the population who experiences the disorder. There also are subcategories of sleep problems and sleep disorders, and the prevalence may vary across each subcategory. According to the National Sleep Foundation (2013), sleep disorders are categorized as sleep-related movement disorders, sleep-related breathing disorders, circadian rhythm sleep disorders, excessive daytime sleepiness disorders, insomnia, sleep and disease, and abnormal sleep behavior disorders. Sleep problems may stem from a variety of comorbid issues ranging from common allergies to complex issues, such as pain, trauma, and fibromyalgia. Like many other disorders, sleep problems vary in severity and duration. It is important to note that sleep problems are common and that only a small portion will require medical attention and meet the criteria for a diagnosis.

The National Center for Chronic Disease and Prevention and Health Promotion (2013) identified sleep-wake disorders as a public health concern that requires accurate identification and effective management. The *DSM-5* includes sleep-wake disorder as an established diagnosis with specific criteria. In the present iteration of the *DSM*, clinicians are encouraged to use multidimensional methodology to rule out coexisting medical, mental health, substance abuse, and neurological conditions. It is important to note that many of the multidimensional measures contained in the *DSM-5* lack psychometric data to support their use. As such, clinicians should use best practices in assessment to determine the diagnosis of sleep-wake disorder.

Sleep problems are a common occurrence, and clinicians must be able to differentiate between typical sleep problems and an established disorder. According to the *DSM-5* (APA, 2013), as much as 20 percent of the general population struggles with some form of sleep-wake disorder. Interestingly, this percentage appears to increase with children. Researchers have discovered that over 65 percent of children report experiences of sleep disruption at least once per week (APA, 2013). For mental health providers to comprehend sleep-wake disorders accurately, there is a need to understand accompanying symptoms and treatment methods. In this chapter we explore various sleep disorders in adolescents, assessment tools, treatment strategies, and intervention methods. With sleep-wake disorders becoming more prevalent within our society and the possibility of adolescents suffering long-term health effects of this disorder, it is vital for mental health professionals to be educated on all the factors associated with this category of disorders.

Description of the Disorders

The normal sleep-wake cycle is a neurological process that involves cyclical alternating patterns (CAP) of nonrapid eye movement (NREM) and rapid eye movement (REM; D'Cruz & Vaughn, 2009). The sleep process can be mapped through various brain scan technologies, such as magnetic resonance imaging (MRI), functional MRI (fMRI), and electroencephalograms (EEGs). The EEG topography of slow-wave activity during non-REM sleep among children and adolescents has been found to be a predictable process across multiple regions of the brain that changes across maturational stages (Ringli, Kurth, Huber, & Jenni, 2013). The EEG topography also changes when sleep is disrupted, and clinicians can evaluate slow-wave activity patterns to determine potential problems that may be associated with sleep disruption. For example, sleep difficulties have been associated with behavioral issues and school performances. Novelli, Ferri, and Bruni (2013) discovered through an analysis of CAP that disruptions in sleep affect cognitive performance during the school day by. When the EEG topography of sleep varies dramatically from typical patterns by age and gender, a number of symptoms can occur during the waking period. When these patterns and symptoms are chronic, a sleep-wake disorder may be present.

The *DSM-5* (APA, 2013) is the primary tool mental health clinicians use to diagnose a sleep-wake disorder. Historically, sleep disturbances were categorized as Pickwickian syndrome (Jung & Kuhlo, 1965). However, today sleep-wake disorders can be subcategorized, but patients often experience symptoms across the subcategories that don't fit neatly into a single area. In these cases, clinicians often use lumping strategies to categorize the symptoms under a general sleep-wake disorder (e.g., insomnia). However, some individuals experience very specific symptomology, and clinicians can then split the subcategories and identify a more specific aspect of sleep-wake disorder that has a variety of substantiated validators, such as narcolepsy (APA, 2013). Although there are several types of sleep-wake disorders, the categories in the *DSM-5* are as follows: insomnia disorder, hypersomnolence disorder, narcolepsy, breathing-related sleep disorders, circadian rhythm sleep-wake disorder, nonrapid eye movement (NREM) sleep arousal disorders, nightmare disorder, rapid eye movement (REM) sleep behavior disorder, restless legs syndrome, and substance/medication-induced sleep disorder.

There are specific differences between each of the 10 sleep-wake disorder classifications. Although brain mapping could provide a clear answer to the presence of a sleep-wake disorder, the cost is often prohibitive. Given this, clinicians may use a set of key questions to differentiate the various subcategories and determine whether the diagnostic criteria for one or more have been met. Examples of key clinical questions D'Cruz and Vaughn (2009) reported are: (a) What is the quality of sleep, and is the child refreshed and rested? (b) Are there any related injuries that result from the sleep disruption? (c) How does the sleep disruption affect others in the home? The initial question is designed to assess the presence of restorative sleep. If restorative sleep is occurring, then the clinician can likely rule out a sleep-wake disorder. Before ruling out the disorder, be sure to investigate child functioning and determine whether the sleep disruption is affecting child behavior. If it is, then the sleep may not be as restorative as reported. The next question is used to screen for violent nocturnal behavior, seizures, sleepwalking, and obstructive sleep apnea syndrome. The presence of these types of symptoms is problematic, and more comprehensive assessment is warranted. The final question inquires about family predisposition and the impact of child or adolescent sleep disruption on caregivers (D'Cruz & Vaughn, 2009). Because sleep disruption in a child or adolescent can affect an entire family system, there may be enough related effects to warrant intervention from a professional. Finally, clinicians should explore the relationship of sleep disruption to various waking behavioral changes. Simply asking a caregiver whether he or she has noticed the onset of or increase in emotional, cognitive, or physical symptoms that appear to align with self-reported sleep issues may be enough to elicit the information needed to clarify the diagnostic process. The use of a clinical interview that involves specific questions about sleep behavior is a critical component in a multidimensional evaluation for the presence of a sleep-wake disorder.

As part of the assessment of sleep-wake disorders, clinicians should pay attention to the disruption of sleep. However, the primary diagnostic process is related to dissatisfaction with the quality or quantity of sleep. When evaluating satisfaction with the sleep process, clinicians should thoroughly explore the initiation of sleep (e.g., bedtime rituals, time to falling asleep, and behavior at bedtime), maintaining sleep (e.g., disruptions of sleep and severity of disruption), nonrestorative sleep (ongoing fatigue throughout the day), and any issues related to a combination of the various aspects identified (Hill, 2011). To assist with the assessment process, the *DSM-5* includes several emerging measures to clarify symptom severity and to inform treatment planning. It is important to note that these instruments require further research and should not be used as a primary tool for making a diagnosis. Some of the instruments included are the *DSM-5* Parent/Guardian-Rated Level 1 Cross-Cutting Symptom Measure—Child Age 6–17 (also available in a print book) and the *DSM-5* Self-Rated Level 1 Cross-Cutting Symptom Measure—Child Age 11–17 located at http://www.psychiatry.org/practice/dsm/dsm5/online-assessment-measures.

Arriving at an accurate diagnosis is critical. According to the *DSM-5*, individuals who experience sleep deprivation have an increased propensity for medical and mental-related illness (APA, 2013). Proportionately, mental illnesses, such as depression and anxiety, usually accompany sleep disorders (National Center for Chronic Disease and Prevention and Health Promotion, 2013; APA, 2013). Many of these conditions can be somatic in nature, in which physical pain operates in many parts of the body. Thus, the identification of a sleep-wake disorder should prompt a clinician to evaluate for medically related issues as well as mental illness. To diagnose a sleep-wake disorder, clinicians should establish that the symptoms cause significant distress and that a coexisting medical or psychological condition does not explain them (APA, 2013).

UNDERSTANDING SLEEP PATTERNS AND SLEEP-WAKE DISORDER

Identification of disrupted sleep patterns is a difficult process among young children. Younger children tend to require more sleep and frequent naps, which are developmentally appropriate. However, it is not always possible for them to relate the quality of that sleep directly to a clinician. For children who are verbal and can report sleep patterns, the perception may be discounted or undervalued (Dosi et al., 2013). For children who are nonverbal, clinicians must rely on parental reports. Regardless of age of the child, it is important to recognize that at least one-fourth of all children have experienced some form of sleep disruption (Dosi et al., 2013).

TABLE 14.1   Sleep-Wake 24-Hour Cycle from Infancy to Adolescence

Stage of Development	Approximate Developmental Period	Brief Sleep Descriptions	Approximate Sleep Duration
Neonatal	Birth to 5 weeks	Short periods alternating with wakefulness; differentiated	Indeterminate and not established
Infants	6 weeks to 3 months	Longer nocturnal periods	10 to 19 hours and not established
Early Childhood	1 year to 4 years	Decrease in daytime naps	Minimum of 10 hours; well established
School Aged	5 years to 11 years	Excellent with sustained nocturnal sleep; daytime naps are unusual	Maximum of 10 to 11 hours; well established
Adolescence	12 years to 18 years	Sleep affected by multifactorial origins	9 to 10 hours

Clinicians should conduct a developmental assessment and inquire about sleep patterns over time. According to Ringli et al. (2013), sleep patterns are usually developed in infancy and have predictable patterns through adolescence. By understanding developmental sleep patterns, clinicians can better interpret irregular occurrences within the sleep cycle. Clinicians should be cognizant of the potential for parent conditioning of sleep-related symptoms and should rule out the potential of a conditioned behavior before arriving at a diagnosis. For example, excessive attachment patterns on the part of the parent may lead to a child not being able to fall asleep without the parent present. In contrast, when parents fail to provide structure or bedtime rituals, a child may not develop appropriate sleep hygiene. Clinicians also should consider that insomnia in adolescence can be tied to poor sleep hygiene, such as erratic sleep schedules that create phase delay. Before diagnosing insomnia disorder, clinicians should take a full account of the psychological and medical factors that may be affecting the presence of symptoms. One example of a common explanation for sleep disruption may be overstimulation from electronic devices. Many adolescents now use iPads for reading and game play. Researchers have shown that the blue light from self-luminous tablets can have a negative effect on natural melatonin production and thus disrupt sleep (Wood, Rea, Plitnick, & Figueiro, 2013). Thus, before diagnosing a sleep-wake disorder, clinicians should take a full account of the psychological and medical factors that may be contributing to the presence of symptoms.

Table 14.1 provides information adapted from D'Cruz and Vaughn (2009) that explains the stages of development, sleep patterns, and the relationship to sleep-wake disorders.

DSM-5 Criteria

Criteria in the *DSM-5* encompass contemporary, evidence-based neurobiological research conducted since the publication of the *DSM-IV-TR* (APA, 2013). In addition to the *DSM-5*, clinicians should consider the information provided in the *International Classification of Sleep Disorders, Second Edition* (*ICSD-2*), which was created by the American Academy of Sleep Medicine (2005). The *ICSD-2* focuses heavily on the multidimensional aspect of sleep-wake disorders. Despite some similarities, the sleep-wake disorders in the *DSM-5* are more general compared with those in the *ICSD-2*. In contrast, the *ICSD-2* contains an expanded view of diagnostic subtypes. The *ICSD-2* may be a more appropriate resource when evaluating for the potential of a sleep-wake disorder because it was specifically developed for this purpose and reflects the science and opinions of the sleep specialist community (American Academy of Sleep Medicine, 2005). Although the *ICSD-2* may be a more specific resource, the *DSM-5* is a more common classification system for mental health professionals. As we indicated earlier in this chapter, sleep-wake disorders in the *DSM-5* have 10 subcategories: insomnia disorder, hypersomnolence disorder, narcolepsy, breathing-related disorders, circadian rhythm sleep-wake disorders, nonrapid eye movement (NREM) sleep arousal disorders, nightmare disorder, rapid eye movement (REM) sleep behavior disorder, restless legs syndrome, and substance/medication-induced sleep disorder. Because the *DSM-5* is a more common diagnostic classification system, we review each of the subcategories. Some of the categories are more common among children and adolescents than others are. As such, those categories specific to children and adolescents receive greater attention.

INSOMNIA DISORDER

Insomnia disorder has a typical onset in early adulthood but can occur at any age. Like other sleep-wake disorders, insomnia disorder is directly related to reported satisfaction with the amount and quality of sleep. To consider a diagnosis of insomnia disorder, an individual must manifest difficulty initiating sleep, maintaining sleep, or early-morning awakening without the ability to return to sleep. In the case of children, the criteria must manifest without caregiver attention. Difficulty maintaining sleep is the most common single symptom of insomnia, followed by difficulty falling asleep, although a combination of these symptoms is the most common presentation overall (Morin, Bootzin, Buysse, Edinger, Espie, & Lichstein 2006; Johnson, Roth, Schultz, & Breslau 2006).

Researchers suggest that 20 percent of children and preadolescents have insomnia indicators even without the presence of sleep-disordered breathing issues, such as apnea (Calhoun, Fernandez-Mendoza, Vgontzas, Liao, & Bixler, 2014). It is important to note that the occurrence of insomnia symptoms peaks in girls ages 11 to 12 and may be linked to hormonal fluctuations related to the start of puberty rather than depression and anxiety (Calhoun et al., 2014). The prevalence of sleep-wake disorders is particularly elevated among children with autism spectrum disorder (ASD), with rates ranging between 40 and 80 percent of children. Insomnia is the most frequently occurring diagnosis with this population (Miano & Fern, 2010).

Other essential insomnia disorder features include clinically significant life distress or impairment in daily functions, such as academic or relationship areas, resulting from impairment in cognitive performance with attention, concentration, and memory (APA, 2013). One of the criteria for a sleep-wake diagnosis of insomnia is frequency of disturbance. To be classified as insomnia, the sleep disturbance must occur with a minimum frequency of three days per week and duration of three months, despite adequate sleep opportunities (APA, 2013). During the diagnostic assessment, it is essential to ensure that the reported insomnia is not ascribed to the physiological effects of a substance (e.g., a drug of abuse or a medication) or better explained by coexisting mental disorder, medical condition, or another sleep-wake disorder (e.g., narcolepsy, a circadian rhythm sleep-wake disorder, a breathing-related sleep disorder, or a parasomnia).

A diagnosis of insomnia disorder should be reserved for those individuals with significant daytime distress or impairment related to their nighttime sleep difficulties

(APA, 2013). If a diagnosis is warranted, then clinicians should also attempt to quantify the severity of the disorder. According to Ohayon, Riemann, Morin, and Reynolds (2012), use of a classification tree allows for a hierarchical organization of symptoms. A hierarchical organization can be accomplished through quantifying symptom manifestation. For example, for a diagnosis of insomnia to be levied, the symptoms must be present at least three nights per week for a period of at least three months. However, it would also be important to know whether the individual being diagnosed experiences repeated symptoms, such as difficulty falling asleep that lasts for more than 20 to 30 minutes, difficulty maintaining sleep (e.g., when an individual experiences sleep, wakes up, and then has a delayed sleep onset for more than 20 to 30 minutes), or early-morning awakening 30 minutes prior to the scheduled time and before 6.5 hours of total sleep (Lineberger, Carney, Edinger, & Means, 2006). Please note that it is essential to take into account not only the final awakening time but also the bedtime on the previous evening. Awakening at 4 AM does not have the same clinical significance in those who go to bed at 9 PM as in those who go to bed at 11 PM. Such a symptom may also reflect an age-dependent decrease in the ability to sustain sleep or an age-dependent shift in the timing of the main sleep period.

When considering a diagnosis of insomnia disorder, clinicians must determine any specifiers that would help clarify understanding of the condition (e.g., medical comorbidity). However, the diagnostic process can be difficult because the symptoms of insomnia may change over time and the pattern can be situational, persistent, or recurrent (APA, 2013). Best practices in assessment for mental health diagnoses requires clinicians to rule out medical explanations for symptomology (Katon, Sullivan, & Walker, 2001). In the case of sleep-wake disorders such as insomnia, it is important to refer patients for sleep studies (e.g., polysomnography) to determine the level of sleep disruption or impairment. However, even though the results of polysomnography or electroencephalographic topography mapping may indicate impairment, the patient's subjective perception of sleep quality may not match qualitatively. In addition to insomnia disorder, clinicians will want to familiarize themselves with Other Specified Insomnia Disorder and Unspecified Insomnia Disorder in the *DSM-5*.

See Sidebar 14.1 for a case study. The case of Tamara describes a late adolescent with possible manifestations of insomnia. The discussion is about whether she meets *DSM-5* criteria for this disorder.

SIDEBAR 14.1:   CASE EXAMPLE—DIAGNOSING TAMARA

Tamara is a 16-year-old honors student who is highly concerned about obtaining a college scholarship based on her academic performance and American College Test (ACT) scores. Tamara is scheduled to take the ACT in one month and is spending considerable time studying. To help extend her study time, Tamara begins to consume energy drinks and caffeine pills daily. Within days of her new routine, Tamara's sleep schedule declines dramatically, and she is not able to maintain her sleep for any length of time. Within one week, Tamara begins to experience disorientation, and she is not able to concentrate during the day at all. Her studying efforts become increasingly frustrating. Consider the diagnostic criteria for insomnia disorder, and make a determination about Tamara's presenting symptomology.

Hypersomnolence Disorder

According to the APA (2013), hypersomnolence disorder involves disproportionate amounts of sleep and typically manifests from late adolescence to early adulthood. It is difficult to arrive at an accurate prevalence rate for hypersomnolence disorder because it has a gradual onset, with indicators starting between ages of 15 and 25, with a steady symptom development over weeks to months. Because of the gradual onset, patients may not seek help for a number of years after initial manifestation of symptoms. As a result, hypersomnolence disorder is not typically diagnosed until at least 10 years after the appearance of the first symptoms (APA, 2013). Because of the delay in help seeking, it is atypical for pediatric mental health providers to see patients with this disorder.

Hypersomnolence is often identified through sleep studies rather than pediatric mental health providers. Between 5 percent and 10 percent of people who participate in polysomnography or EEG studies meet the criteria for hypersomnolence. The excessive sleep patterns associated with hypersomnolence can include involuntary, nonrestorative daytime sleep that occurs, despite at least seven hours of primary sleep, and excessive nighttime (primary) sleep that lasts for more than nine hours but does not produce a restorative effect. It may also include impaired ability to initiate alertness upon awakening. Approximately 80 percent of people with hypersomnolence describe their sleep as nonrestrictive, though 36–50 percent experience sleep inertia. For example, an adolescent may report that although he or she is sleeping 12 hours per day, the behavior is not having any negative consequences. However, the parents of the adolescent may report that the adolescent seems in a daze after waking up and doesn't seem to have the ability to concentrate.

Although pediatric cases of hypersomnolence infrequently present in mental health settings, practitioners should be conscious of ruling out the disorder because of the potential for functional consequences, neurological impairments, and breathing-related disorders (Vinay et al., 2010). It is also important to consider that adolescent mental health issues can increase the potential for experience of hypersomnolence (Kotagai, 2009).

Clinicians can consider a diagnosis of hypersomnolence disorder when individuals are reporting unrefreshing, excessive sleepiness regardless of experiencing at least seven hours of sleep as well as a difficult time staying awake after being abruptly aroused (APA, 2013). Though criteria differ from an insomnia disorder diagnosis, the following criteria reflect those formerly examined. To meet the criteria, the symptoms must be persistent (e.g., three times per week over three months) and must cause significant distress.

Hypersomnolence disorder is also accompanied with the following specifiers to indicate comorbidity, frequency, and severity. Whereas comorbidity specifiers are identical to those for insomnia, stipulations for frequency are (a) *acute* to signify duration of less than one month, (b) *subacute* to signify duration of one to three months, and (c) *persistent* to signify duration of more than three months. Indicators for severity relate to the degree of maintaining wakefulness within the daytime period. This specifier can be (a) *mild*, perceiving reduced alertness one to two days per week; (b) *moderate*, perceiving reduced alertness three to four days per week; and (c) *severe*, perceiving reduced alertness five to seven days per week. In cases where individuals do not meet the full criteria for hypersomnolence disorder but experience significant distress, they may be diagnosed with an Other Specified Insomnia Disorder or an Unspecified Insomnia Disorder. Other specified insomnia disorder requires the clinician to specify the reason the individual doesn't meet the criteria (APA, 2013).

NARCOLEPSY

Narcolepsy is a sleep-wake disorder that may be underdiagnosed during childhood and adolescence (Nevsimalova, 2009). Typified by a disproportionate amount of daytime sleepiness (e.g., an abnormal need to sleep, drifting into a sleep state throughout the day, or frequent napping), narcolepsy is a lifelong, nonprogressive disorder that has bimodal peak onset between the ages of 15 to 25 or 30 to 35 (APA, 2013). The prevalence of narcolepsy appears in 0.02 to 0.04 percent of the general population, and like hypersomnolence, individuals typically delay seeking help for at least 10 years (Nevsimalova, 2009). Thus, child or adolescent cases of narcolepsy are rare in pediatric behavioral health care settings. For a diagnosis of narcolepsy to be established, sleep disturbance must occur, on average, at least three times a week over a three-month period. In addition to sleep disturbance, a patient must also experience at least one of the following: (a) cataplexy, (b) hypocretin deficiency, or (c) abnormal REM sleep phenomena specific to latency periods (APA, 2013). When children or adolescents present with narcolepsy, the chances are that a familial history of the disorder can be established, the symptoms are more severe, and that cataplexy is likely an associated feature (Inocente et al., 2014).

According to Mignot (2012), the most common presenting symptom in pediatric cases is cataplexy (i.e., a deficiency of hypocretin, which is characterized by brief occurrences of sudden bilateral loss of muscle tone while maintaining consciousness). Because child and adolescent cases of narcolepsy rarely present for treatment in behavioral health care, the cataplexy is often a secondary concern to other abnormal behavioral manifestations and is misdiagnosed as a seizure (Mignot, 2012). Cataplexy will manifest differently if tied to an emotional trigger (Nussbaum, 2013). When activated by joking or laughter, the patient may experience a sudden bilateral loss of muscle tone. Conversely, when cataplexy is activated without an emotional trigger, the presentation can be similar to tardive dyskinesia, with involuntary facial contortion, jaw-opening episodes with tongue thrusting, or a global decrease in muscle tone (i.e., hypotonia; APA, 2013).

Like other sleep-wake disorders with hypersomnolence features, narcolepsy is typically identified through polysomnography, and clinicians attempt to rule out sleep-disordered breathing (Nevsimalova, 2009). Narcolepsy is neurological in nature and is seen as a dysfunction in REM sleep patterns. Individuals with narcolepsy have been shown to have a significant reduction in hypocretin, which may be related to an autoimmune basis for the disorder (Kornum, Faraco, & Mignot, 2011).

As is the case with other disorders, clinicians should review sleep studies and other medical records to specify the subtypes of narcolepsy (e.g., narcolepsy without cataplexy but with hypocretin deficiency). It is also important to examine the possibility of comorbid conditions, such as other mental health issues or substance abuse. Finally, the clinician should specify the severity of the disorder from mild to severe.

BREATHING-RELATED SLEEP DISORDERS

Central sleep apnea, obstructive sleep apnea hypopnea, and sleep-related hypoventilation are the three breathing-related disorders identified in the *DSM-5*. Like other sleep-wake disorders, breathing-related sleep disorders have both neurological and psychological components, and the diagnosis is completed through polysomnography. Obstructive sleep apnea with partial or complete upper airway obstruction has significant neurocognitive and pulmonary implications (Brockmann, Schaefer, Poets, Poets, & Urschitz, 2013).

According to the APA (2013), the most common breathing-related sleep disorder is obstructive sleep apnea hypopnea. Like some of the hypersomnolence disorders, sleep apnea hypopnea has been a relatively rare condition among children—affecting 1 percent to 2 percent of the child and adolescent population. However, because the disorder is highly correlated with childhood obesity, Brockmann et al. (2013) hypothesized that the prevalence rate may be up to 10.3 percent of children and adolescents. Upper airway obstruction is often imperceptible to a behavioral health care provider. More often, children with sleep apnea hypopnea (SAH) will present with significant behavioral sleep disturbances (BSD), such as nocturnal enuresis. Children and adolescents may also present with a range of waking symptomology (e.g., open-mouth breathing, poor speech articulation, and difficulty swallowing) as well as issues such as behavioral disruption, developmental delays, or failure to thrive (APA, 2013).

Central sleep apnea and sleep-related hypoventilation are sleep-wake disorders that are comorbid with either substance abuse or adult pulmonary medical conditions. Both disorders are rare in children and adolescents. Central sleep apnea is tied to changes in neuromuscular respiration control subsequent to medication or other substance use. Sleep-related hypoventilation is associated with pulmonary dysfunction, chest wall disorder, or substance abuse (APA, 2013).

Circadian Rhythm Sleep-Wake Disorders

Occurring in more than 7 percent of the adolescent population, circadian rhythm sleep-wake disorder is a result of a persistent disruption in the endogenous sleep cycle because of issues with the physical environment or social or work-related schedule demands (APA, 2013). The *DSM-5* (APA, 2013) indicates that a clinician diagnosing circadian rhythm disorder should specify one of six types (i.e., delayed sleep phase, advanced sleep phase, irregular sleep-wake type, non-24-hour sleep-wake, shift work type, or unspecified type). This disorder is often comorbid with other mental health diagnoses and is correlated with the future development of a number of problems, such as insomnia, obesity, substance abuse, anxiety, and disrupted executive functioning (Gradisar & Crowley, 2013; Hahn et al., 2012; Harvey, 2011; Hasler & Clark, 2013; Hasler, Soehner, & Clark, 2014). The irregular sleep-wake type of the disorder is often comorbid with other neurodevelopmental disorders in children (APA, 2013).

Parasomnias

A number of sleep-wake disorders involve interplay between waking and nonrapid eye movement (NREM) sleep states and are characterized by a range of undesirable presenting issues (e.g., abnormal movements, incomplete arousal behaviors, or physiological or autonomic activation) at sleep onset, during stage transition, or throughout the various stages (National Sleep Foundation, 2013). Parasomnias are some of the more commonly experienced sleep-wake disorders among children and adolescents and can be considered nonthreatening conditions that have little impact on the quality and quantity of sleep (Tinuper, Bisulli, & Provini, 2012). Although typically brief in nature, the presentation of parasomnias can be more disruptive to family members than to the child or adolescent experiencing the disorder (Eckerberg, 2004). The primary parasomnias include nonrapid eye movement sleep arousal disorder, nightmare disorder, and rapid eye movement sleep behavior disorder.

The symptoms of NREM sleep arousal disorder include repeated episodes of sleep-walking or sleep terror that occur during the first third of primary sleep and typically last from one to 10 minutes. As is the case for other parasomnias, the repeated episodes have little impact on the quantity or quality of sleep, and the individual experiences amnesia related to the event. Clinicians diagnosing the disorder must specify whether disorder is the sleepwalking or sleep terror type.

Sleepwalking is a common phenomenon, with up to 30 percent of children experiencing at least one episode and 2 to 3 percent of children experiencing recurrent sleepwalking (Hoban, 2010). As it is termed, sleepwalking involves complex motor movement (e.g., rising from bed, walking, eating, or engaging in sexual activity) while maintaining a sleep state (Nevsimalova, Prihodova, Kemlink, & Skibova, 2013). Children who sleep-walk operate in a state of reduced alertness and may not be responsive to others. If awak-ened during the sleepwalking episode, the child may be somewhat disoriented but regains full functioning after a brief period (Fisher et al., 2014). The major concern related to sleepwalking is that the individual is operating with impaired judgment and may be at risk for injury (Tinuper et al., 2012).

The sleepwalking type of NREM sleep arousal disorder can be subcategorized as involv-ing either sleep-related eating behavior or sleep-related sexual behaviors (sexsomnia). With sleep-related eating, children engage in recurrent eating episodes, including inap-propriate food consumption, while in a sleep state. With sexsomnia, individuals (typically adult males) participate in complex sexual activities while maintaining a sleep state.

The sleep terror type of NREM sleep arousal disorder is characterized by an over-whelming sense of dread accompanied by extreme terror and biological responses, such as sweating or rapid breathing. The child also may appear to be fully awake and afraid and may be crying or screaming. Childhood sleep terrors typically occur during primary sleep and in a single episode per night pattern. Untreated, the disorder may dissipate over time with maturation (Jain, 2013). Sleep terrors are a common occurrence among infants and toddlers, with up to 40 percent of the infant and toddler population experiencing at least one episode (Hoban, 2010). However, the prevalence rate decreases dramatically over time, and only 2.2 percent of adults experience sleep terror episodes (APA, 2013).

NIGHTMARE DISORDER

Unlike sleep terrors, nightmare disorder involves disquieting or frightening experiences during sleep that arouse the individual and are recalled upon awakening (Langston, Davis, & Swopes, 2010). In contrast with sleepwalking and sleep terrors, nightmares typically occur during the second portion of the sleep cycle, and the manifestation can be acute, sub-acute, or persistent (APA, 2013). The frequency of nightmares can be classified as mild, moderate, or severe. To be classified as nightmare disorder, the individual must experi-ence significant distress or impairment in one or more areas of functioning. According to the APA (2013), nightmares are more prevalent during childhood (1.3 to 3.9 percent) but dissipate with age. Nightmares are a more common phenomenon for females and may be precipitated by some form of psychological stressor (Jain, 2013). It is important to note that nightmares can be comorbid with other *DSM-5* disorders (e.g., posttraumatic stress disorder [PTSD] or an acute stress disorder). Clinicians should determine whether an independent nightmare disorder exists (e.g., the symptoms occurred at a significantly distressing level prior to any trauma) or the symptoms occurred becuase of the trauma (APA, 2013).

Rapid Eye Movement Sleep Behavior Disorder

An additional parasomnia, rapid eye movement sleep behavior disorder (REMSBD), involves more complex behavioral patterns (e.g., vocalizations or motor movements) that occur later in the sleep period. Like other parasomnias, there is little impact on functioning during waking periods. REMSBD occurs in a very small portion of the population, with only 0.38 to 0.5 percent affected (APA, 2013). The primary population affected by REMSBD is males over age 50. As a result, this disorder is not a common occurrence for children. REMSBD is highly correlated with neurodegenerative disorders (e.g., Parkinson's disease) and is progressive in nature.

Restless Legs Syndrome

Restless legs syndrome (RLS) is a sensorimotor, neurological disorder that typically has an onset between ages 20 and 40 (APA, 2013). When children experience the symptoms of RLS, the condition is often comorbid with other neurological issues, such as attention-deficit/hyperactivity disorder (ADHD), kidney disease, and migraines (Amos et al., 2014; Arbuckle et al., 2010; Picchietti et al., 2013; Riar et al., 2013; Seidel et al., 2012). To be diagnosed with RLS, individuals must experience significant distress from a consistent and repetitive urge to move their legs. The diagnosis of RLS can be difficult with children because of their inability to relate to the term *urge* and its role in the diagnostic criteria (Picchietti et al., 2013). Because of the difficulty with adult criteria, Picchietti and colleagues developed a specific set of pediatric criteria for RLS. Although these criteria are not included in the *DSM-5*, they may be useful in identifying the disorder among children. The basic difference between the adult and child criteria is that the practitioner should take a developmental approach to the diagnostic and assessment process. The clinician should allow the child to describe the symptoms in his or her own words and should be familiar with children's terminology and vernacular. Like the other sleep-wake disorders, polysomnography can be a useful diagnostic tool with regard to pediatric RLS. Although the category of sleep disorders in the *DSM-IV-TR* and sleep-wake disorders in the *DSM-5* share various commonalities, there are a number of significant changes. Table 14.2 will help outline these differences.

Substance/Medication-Induced Sleep Disorder

A substance/medication-induced sleep disorder develops because of the pharmacological effects of a substance (i.e., a drug of abuse, a medication, or a toxin) and thus is more likely to develop during adolescence or beyond (APA, 2013). The primary criterion of this sleep disorder is that it develops somewhere between the onset of substance use and withdrawal from a substance. For the diagnosis to be considered, any experienced sleep disruption must be severe enough to merit clinical care but should not be better explained by another sleep disorder (APA, 2013). The symptoms from the sleep disruption can mimic the symptomology of other sleep disorders and thus can be classified as the insomnia type, daytime sleepiness type, parasomnia type, or the mixed type sleep disturbance (APA, 2013).

It is important to note that females have a much higher potential for development of a substance/medication-induced sleep disorder because of gender-specific differences in hepatic functioning (APA, 2013). Because the onset of substance use often occurs during

TABLE 14.2   Key Points: Changes in the *DSM-5*

DSM-IV TR	*DSM-5*
Sleep Disorders	Sleep-Wake Disorders
<ul><li>Four categories of disorders</li><li>One-dimensional assessments</li><li>Sleep disorders related to another mental health disorder and secondary sleep disorders related to a physical health issue categories of disorders</li></ul>	<ul><li>Ten disorders or disorder groups</li><li>Multidimensional and categorical assessments</li><li>Focus on the need for independent clinical attention of coexisting disorders through the elimination of sleep disorders related to mental health or medical condition</li></ul>
Lack of pediatric-related information for diagnoses:<ul><li>Primary Insomnia</li><li>Primary Hypersomnia</li><li>Sleepwalking Disorder and Sleep Terror Disorder</li><li>Parasomnia, Not Otherwise Specified (NOS)</li><li>Dyssomnia, NOS</li></ul>	Pediatric information added to many diagnoses:<ul><li>Insomnia Disorder</li><li>Hypersomnolence Disorder</li><li>Non-rapid Eye Movement Sleep Arousal Disorder</li><li>Rapid Eye Movement Sleep Behavior Disorder</li><li>Restless Legs Syndrome</li></ul>

adolescence, it is important for clinicians who work with children and adolescents to be able to identify substance/medication-induced sleep disorder as a separate clinical issue when necessary (APA, 2013). When cases of this nature are presented in clinical settings, caregivers may be a more reliable reporting source.

Differential Diagnosis

Diagnosis of a sleep-wake disorder involves a detailed neurocognitive, psychophysiological process, typically with the support of results from polysomnography. Because the sleep-wake disorders can be comorbid with other medical and psychological conditions, the separation of symptomology can be difficult for the clinician; thus a sleep study is paramount to accurate diagnosis. As stated throughout this chapter, many of the sleep-wake disorders do not present for behavioral services until after numerous years of distress. In those cases that do present, the reporting of symptomology may be difficult. To arrive at an accurate diagnosis, the clinician should use a multidimensional assessment process and rule out other medical or psychological disorders that may explain presenting symptoms. Of course, the clinician should always rule out malingering (e.g., faking) when reaching a diagnosis.

Because sleep affects cognitive functioning, the dopaminergic system, executive functioning, and emotional responses, clinicians should be prepared to address a range of issues when sleep disorders are present. Differential diagnosis is complicated because each of the 10 sleep-wake disorder groups involves impaired sleep that causes distress during waking hours. From the standpoint of a diagnostic decision tree, sleep-wake disorders can be separated into three categories: (a) normative sleep variations (ranging from the need for little sleep to a need for greater-than-average amounts of sleep),

(b) breathing-related sleep disorders, and (c) parasomnias. One example of differential diagnosis is determining whether a child is experiencing a nightmare disorder or a sleep terror disorder. Although both disorders are fairly similar with regard to presenting symptomology, they can be differentiated. A sleep study would be able to determine whether the experiences occur during NREM (sleep terrors) or REM (nightmares) cycles. However, a more simple differentiation could be that individuals typically recall nightmares whereas sleep terrors typically result in amnesia for the event (APA, 2013).

Although each of the sleep-wake disorders has symptomology that cuts across other sleep-wake disorders, medical conditions, and psychological disorders, narcolepsy has the most overlapping symptoms (e.g., hypersomnia, sleep deprivation, major depression, conversion disorder, ADHD, seizures, chorea, and schizophrenia). NREM sleep arousal disorders are the most prevalent parasomnia and have the highest degree of overlapping symptoms under that category (e.g., sleep-related and nocturnal seizures, alcohol-induced blackouts, dissociative amnesia, panic disorder, and sleep eating syndrome). Restless leg syndrome (RLS) is the sleep-wake disorder that, in addition to less intrusive symptoms, such as excessive foot tapping, has the greatest number of physiological implications (e.g., arthralgias or arthritis, myalgias, positional ischemia, leg edema, peripheral neuropathy, and radiculopathy).

As part of the differential diagnostic process, clinicians should work closely with the medical community and rule out neurological and medical disorders through comprehensive metabolic panels, polysomnography, and other neuroimaging. In addition to the assessment procedures the medical community conducts, behavioral health professionals should consider a range of assessment procedures to arrive at a diagnosis. The *DSM-5 Handbook of Differential Diagnosis* (2013) helps the clinician navigate the diagnostic decision tree and arrive at a clear diagnosis. In many instances of behavioral health, practitioners rely on clinical expertise and experience in the diagnostic process. However, in cases with a neurological basis, it is important to use a more thorough assessment process.

Assessment Strategies

Best practices in assessment require information from multiple informants that includes multiple data points across multiple settings (Drummond, Sheperis, & Jones, 2015). As indicated in this chapter, many sleep-wake disorders are rare among pediatric populations. As such, the disorders can be misdiagnosed or may go untreated for 10 years or more. Thus, when evaluating a patient for a possible sleep-wake disorder, a wide range of assessment data is essential.

MEDICAL AND NEUROPSYCHOLOGICAL TESTS

Diagnostic testing is essential when evaluating sleep-wake disorders. Clinicians should either have internal resources within a behavioral health care system or have a network of external referral sources to work with in gathering appropriate test data. Testing for sleep-wake disorders can be conducted through neuropsychological tests, actigraphy, polysomnography, and multiple sleep latency tests.

Neuropsychological Assessments

Neuropsychology is a specialized field of psychology that examines the interplay of brain and behavior. Based on neuropsychological assessment, interventions can be developed to address behaviors that develop because of challenges in neurological processes. Neuropsychologists have specialized training in the assessment and treatment of issues related to normal and abnormal functioning of the central nervous system (Association of Neuropsychology Students in Training, n.d.). Neuropsychologists may use a range of standardized assessment procedures to diagnose a sleep-wake disorder and rule out traumatic brain injuries, PTSD, and neuropsychological conditions (Dodzik, 2013; Ferini-Strambi et al., 2004; Koyama et al., 2012; Tanev, Pentel, Kredlow, & Charney, 2014; Wiseman-Hakes, 2013).

Polysomnography

Considered the gold standard in sleep assessment, polysomnography provides an objective analysis of wake time, sleep time, and sleep architecture (McCall & McCall, 2012). When compared with standardized neuropsychological assessment and other sleep evaluation medical procedures, polysomnography has proved to be a more reliable measure of disorders of consciousness (de Biase et al., 2014). A polysomnography is part of a behavioral medicine sleep study and measures REM, NREM, general sleep patterns, brain waves, breathing, and body movement (de Biase et al., 2014).

Actigraphy

Behavioral medical professionals often look for cost-effective and nonintrusive objective approaches to identify disorders. Actigraphy is a low-cost objective procedure used to measure body movement through a watchlike device (McCall & McCall, 2012). Actigraphy has developed as a popular assessment process because it can monitor sleep behavior in both home or lab settings (Martin & Hakim, 2011). In contrast with a sleep study that involves polysomnography, actigraphy can be used to collect data over longer periods. Although actigraphy can provide reliable data, it has less sensitivity than polysomnography and should be used in conjunction with a thorough laboratory sleep study (McCall & McCall, 2012).

Multiple Sleep Latency Test

A multiple sleep latency test (MLST) is a common assessment behavioral medical professionals use to measure the relationships among sleepiness, REM, NREM, and sleep latency (time to fall asleep; Insana, Glowacki, & Montgomery-Downs, 2011). The MSLT is an expensive process because it must be conducted in a laboratory setting or sleep clinic and a medical professional must interpret the data. The MLST is used in conjunction with other medical and neuropsychological measures (Wiebe, Carrier, Frenette, & Gruber, 2013).

BEHAVIORAL HEALTH CARE ASSESSMENT

Although medical and neuropsychological assessments are critical elements in the accurate diagnosis of sleep-wake disorders, behavioral health professionals can also collect meaningful data to aid in the diagnostic process. Some of the common assessments used in behavioral health care include sleep diaries (journals), self-report instruments, parental report instruments, and other standardized measures.

Sleep Diaries

Behavioral health care clinicians often ask patients to maintain sleep journals in an effort to track sleep, sleep latency, behavioral disruptions during sleep, the impact of sleep on

TABLE 14.3   Rating Sleep Quality

	Never	Sometimes	Often	Always
1. I typically fall asleep within 30 minutes of going to bed.				
2. I wake up in the middle of the night.				
3. I have trouble staying awake during the day.				
4. I have trouble sleeping.				

wake periods, and any other sleep-related phenomena that a patient can report. Sleep diaries have been shown to have some impact on sleep hygiene but are more often used for data tracking (Todd & Mullan, 2014). Clinicians interested in prescribing sleep journals should consider tracking bedtimes, sleepiness, sleep latency, hours of continuous sleep, total hours of sleep, number of sleep disruptions, nightmares, and mood (Schäfer & Bader, 2013). In some cases, patients also rate the elements of their sleep patterns. For example, a clinician may ask a patient to use a Likert scale to rate the quality of sleep from 1 to 5. Table 14.3 presents a sample rating scale.

Self-Assessment Questionnaires and Parental Assessments

Self-report instruments have limited reliability but can provide some useful information in conjunction with other assessment procedures (Drummond et al., 2015). A number of assessment instruments can used in the process of diagnosing sleep and wake disorders. When considering child reporting versus parent reporting, there are often discrepancies in data. For example, adolescents may report fewer hours of sleep per night than what their parents realize, and parents may not recognize the level of sleep hygiene for their children (Short, Gradisar, Lack, Wright, & Chatburn, 2013). The two primary parent report instruments are the Children's Sleep Habit Questionnaire and the Sleep Disturbance Scale for Children. Sidebar 14.2 provides a review of the Children's Sleep Habit Questionnaire.

SIDEBAR 14.2:   CHILDREN'S SLEEP HABIT QUESTIONNAIRE

Owens, Spirito, and McGuinn (2000) developed the Children's Sleep Habit Questionnaire (CSHQ) as a means to identify sleep disturbances in toddlers and children. The CSHQ results in a total score and eight subscale scores related to (a) bedtime resistance, (b) sleep onset delay, (c) sleep duration, (d), sleep anxiety, (e) night wakings, (f) parasomnias, (g) sleep-disordered breathing, and (h) daytime sleepiness. This rating scale was normed on over 600 parents of school-age children between the ages of 4 and 10. The psychometric properties of the CSHQ support its use in screening for sleep-related disturbance. Internal consistency for the instrument ranges between 0.68 for the community sample and 0.78 for the clinical sample. Reliability estimates were calculated using Cronbach's Alpha and ranged from 0.36 to 0.79 for the subscales. The parasomnia subscale demonstrated the least reliability (0.36) and may not be an adequate measure for those specific issues. Test-retest reliability ranged between 0.62 and 0.79. Overall, the CSHQ is a valid and reliable instrument for identifying sleep disturbance among children and adolescents.

TABLE 14.4   Assessment Instruments for Sleep-Wake Disorders

Name of Instrument	Diagnostic Purpose	Number of Items	Format	Target Population	Citation
Children's Report of Sleep Patterns	RLS and behavioral sleep problems	60	Likert	Children ages 8 and above	Meltzer et al., 2012
School Sleep Habits Survey	Identification of sleep cycles, waking performance, and psychological functioning	63	Likert	Ages 13 to 17	Sleep for Science, Sleep Research Lab, 2014
Patient-Reported Outcomes Measurement Information System	Various forms of sleep and wake functioning	8	Likert	Child Form – 6–17 and Adult Form	Yu et al., 2012
Sleep Disturbance Scale for Children	Evaluation and rating of nighttime behaviors on a scale between 1 (never) and 5 (always)	27	Likert	Parent Report	Bruni et al., 1996
Children's Sleep Habits Questionnaire	Sleep habits and behaviors in young children—used as a screener	45	Questionnaire	Parent Report	Owens, Spirito, & McGuinn, 2000

Specific Assessment Instruments

In addition to the Children's Sleep Habit Questionnaire and the Sleep Disturbance Scale for Children, behavioral health clinicians can use a number of specific assessment instruments to identify the symptoms of a sleep-wake disorder. The Children's Report of Sleep Patterns (CRSP), Children's Report of Sleep Patterns—Sleepiness Scale (CRSP-S), School Sleep Habits Survey (SSHS), and Promis—Sleep Disturbance Short Form are some of the other commonly used instruments. Each of these instruments has limitations because of the self or other report nature of the data. As a result, all of the instruments should be used in conjunction with behavioral medicine assessments. Please see Table 14.4 for a list of assessment instruments for assessing sleep-wake disorders in children and adolescents.

Treatment Strategies and Interventions

Treatment planning for a patient with a sleep-wake disorder should involve a wraparound approach, with close communication among behavioral health providers, physicians, medical staff, the individual, and family members (Moss, Lachowski, & Carney, 2013). A behavioral health care clinician can use a variety of behavioral interventions to address the symptoms of sleep-wake disorders. However, the interventions should be in conjunction with prescribed interventions by medical staff. Because pharmacological intervention is common in sleep-wake disorder treatment, behavioral health care clinicians should be familiar with commonly used prescriptions and mechanisms of action.

Behavioral Health Care Interventions

In some cases, sleep-wake symptomology is a result of environmental factors. In those cases, behavioral interventions can be the best option for making adjustments to the environment (Hall, Scher, Zaidman-Zait, Espezel, and Warnock, 2012). As is the case in other areas of mental health, behavioral or cognitive-behavioral interventions have the most evidence to support their use in treating sleep-wake disorders. The interventions used can be categorized within three specific types of behavioral techniques: (a) exercise and diet changes, (b) sleep hygiene, and (c) behavioral techniques. Prior to initiating any behavioral intervention, clinicians should conduct a functional analysis of the presenting sleep-wake symptoms. A functional analysis may include (a) an analysis of the ecology of the child and the presenting issue, (b) a specific analysis of the antecedent and consequent events that have a functional relationship with the presenting sleep issue, and (c) an analysis of the communicative functions of the child's sleep behavior (Anderson, Goldsmith, & Gardiner, 2014; Byars & Simon, 2014).

Sleep Hygiene

Intervention related to sleep hygiene is often psychoeducational in nature. Sleep hygiene training programs should include didactic instruction that focuses on the interplay between positive health practices and environmental factors. The clinician helps the patient understand the role of health and environment in quality sleep practices. A best practice approach includes teaching patients to engage in self-monitoring of sleep behaviors and helping them understand the impact of waking behaviors (e.g., food and caffeine consumption, playing games on an iPad, and stress) on sleep functioning (Saeedi, Shamsikhani, Varvani Farahani, & Haghverdi, 2014).

Sleep quality and duration link to a variety of psychosocial and neuropsychological outcomes in children and adolescents, but public understanding of this is low. Díaz-Morales, Delgado Prieto, Escribano, José Collado Mateo, and Randler (2012) noted improved quality of sleep and increased awareness of appropriate sleep habits among younger adolescents who attended sleep hygiene psychoeducational classes. Sidebar 14.3 illustrates the extent of difficulty in establishing a childhood diagnosis. When considering a diagnosis, the therapist should account for environmental changes as well as reported behaviors and sensations.

SIDEBAR 14.3:   SUDDEN SLEEP DISRUPTION

Lincoln is a 3-year-old who has had consistent quality sleep patterns since infancy. In the past two months, she has been waking in the middle of the night several times and crying out for her father. After being soothed by her father, Lincoln generally falls back to sleep. Within about an hour, Lincoln is awake; the cycle begins again. Both Lincoln and her father are experiencing significant distress as a result. What types of questions would you ask when interviewing Lincoln's father? What types of changes in environment might account for such a dramatic shift in sleep patterns? Try to generate several hypotheses related to developmental milestones, family functioning, and nutrition. What could Lincoln's father do to address the sleep disruption?

Extinction

Extinction procedures are used to weaken or eliminate objectionable conduct and are frequently employed with reinforcement procedures to intensify a preferred behavior (Todd, Vurbic, & Bouton, 2014). Extinction approaches are often used for parents to train infants to adapt to independent sleep. A controversial sleep behavior approach has been the Ferber method, which encourages the parent to avoid interaction with babies while they are crying (Johnson & Mindell, 2011) The Ferber method also encourages parents to establish a sleep time routine (e.g., a comforting bath, swaddling, and placing the child in bed at the same time every evening). Upon putting the child in the bed, the caregiver then departs the bedroom. Only when the youth becomes extremely distraught does the caregiver provide brief comfort and return the child to the bed. Because the pattern of behavior is predictable, the child learns to self-soothe and learns independent sleep (Synnott & Preyde, 2009). Extinction-based techniques can be seen as cruel. As such, Taylor and Roane (2010) developed a procedure for extinction with parental attendance. This approach provides for caregivers to remain in the bedroom to relieve any apprehensions regarding their child's welfare. Even though the caregivers are in the infant's bedroom, they will attempt to reduce the frequency of crying by delaying their response.

Bedtime Fading

An important factor to consider with the initial development of a healthy sleep-wake behavior would be controlling the youth's bedtime routines. The capability to target behavioral sleep-wake problems through various techniques empowers caregivers to find a method that best meets the child's distinct need. Extinction methods frequently lead to frustration, agitation, and conflict (Hill, 2011). Bedtime fading may be a possible substitute for extinction approaches. Bedtime fading is the procedure where the caregiver puts the infant to bed later in the evening, yet wakes the child up on time. As the child initiates sleep quicker upon being placed in bed, the caregiver moves up the bedtime schedule (Taylor & Roane, 2010). By regulating the sleep-wake schedule, the caregiver is able to enforce the developmental sleep pattern that is needed for the youth.

Scheduled Awakening

A significant factor that is essential for the effectiveness of both fading approaches and extinction is caregiver consistency is scheduled awakening. Scheduled awakenings are the third behavioral method and may be introduced with childhood nightmares that are accompanied by nighttime awakenings. This method necessitates the caregiver wake up the child 15 to 20 minutes before the time he or she usually would have the nightmare experience (Taylor & Roane, 2010). These behavioral sleep-wake approaches require psychoeducational tools for the caregivers to ensure consistency of strategies.

Other Behavioral Techniques

In spite of the research revealing the cost-effectiveness and efficiency in treating adults with sleep-wake disorders, there has been little investigation on the effectiveness of other behavioral methods with children (Sharma & Andrade, 2012). Taylor and Roane (2010) provided a review of some techniques that have been researched, including progressive muscle relaxation, sleep restriction therapy, paradoxical intention, biofeedback, and cognitive-behavioral therapy. Regardless of this review, there is a dearth of research on the effectiveness of relaxation techniques for childhood sleep-wake patterns. Hence, more research is needed to examine behavioral sleep-wake techniques for infants, children, and adolescents.

Diet and Exercise

Diet and exercise are intricate components of adolescent sleep hygiene. It is important for clinicians to ask children with sleep-wake disorders to document diet and exercise habits. Having a healthier lifestyle can improve more than just sleep quality. It can also enhance the adolescent's mood, increase alertness, and improve academic performance. Researchers have discovered a positive correlation between sleep quality and exercise (Ekstedt, Nyberg, Ingre, Ekblom, & Marcus, 2013; Lytle, Pasch, & Farbakhsh, 2011). In addition to increasing overall health and mood, a proper diet and increased exercise have been shown to improve breathing-related disorders, such as sleep apnea (Van Hoorenbeeck et al., 2012).

MEDICATIONS AND SUPPLEMENTS

Once behavioral and cognitive methods have been employed, diet and exercise have been investigated, and there are no improvements noted, medication and sleep supplements might be used to enhance sleep quality and duration (Van Hoorenbeeck et al., 2012). Behavioral health care clinicians work in conjunction with medical staff to address sleep-wake disorders. They typically conduct initial mental health assessments and make referrals to physicians to begin the treatment process. Licensed physicians evaluate for pharmacological needs and prescribe medication or sleep supplements. As with the other treatment methods, supplemental and psychopharmacological treatments that address sleep-wake disorders must be individually adapted for effective results. Subsequently, clinicians work with patients to address the behavioral aspects of the sleep-wake disorder and monitor for pharmacological compliance.

Melatonin, a hormone created in the brain, is a common over-the-counter supplement prescribed for individuals who have difficulty sleeping or who have irregular sleep cycles. Melatonin has been useful in treating childhood seizures, insomnia, and poor sleep quality of children diagnosed with autism spectrum disorder and ADHD (Malow et al., 2012; Damiani, Sweet, & Sohoni, 2014).

Clonidine is a regulated drug that reduces the body's heart rate and diminishes pressure in the blood vessels. It has been shown to be effective in the management of childhood sleep-wake syndromes (Nguyen, Tharani, Rahmani, & Shapiro, 2014). Additional medications, such as Singulair and Flonase, also have shown some effectiveness in the treatment of mild types of sleep-wake disorders (Moturi & Avis, 2010).

Other pharmacological approaches commonly used when treating adults for sleep-wake disorders are generally not used to treat children. The following medications are frequently avoided in children because of intensified hyperactivity. These medications include antihistamines, benzodiazepines, and sedating antidepressants (Moturi & Avis, 2010). If these medications are used in the treatment of childhood sleep-wake disorders, it is conceivable for an increase of behavioral problems and diminished academic functioning to occur. Consequently, medication education is a vital tool for the family as a means to recognize and monitor possible prescribed medication side effects that a child may experience.

Medical Devices

Specific medical equipment can alleviate the symptoms of some breathing-related sleep disorders. Continuous positive airway pressure (CPAP) machines and bilevel postulate airway pressure (BPAP) machines are two devices that have been proved to be successful in treating childhood breathing disorders (Aurora et al., 2012; Roux & Kryger, 2010).

Whereas the CPAP device delivers constant air to individuals wearing a sleep mask, the BPAP delivers variable-pressure air, rendering it more appropriate for individuals with neurological syndromes. Given the recognized effectiveness and absence of related side effects, these machines may be used pending conceivable future solutions.

One of the areas of advancement is smartphone-based devices and applications (SBDAs) with price value and distant detection, which are capable and applicable methods of bringing transportable health care. Numerous SBDAs have been commercialized for the customized management or monitoring of essential biological limits, such as electrocardiograph, weight, body analysis, blood pressure, pulse rate, blood glucose, physical activity, and sleep (Vashist, Schneider, & Luong, 2014).

Surgery

In general, medical operation choices apply only to the category of breathing-related sleep disorders. The common surgical procedures for this category involve removing the tonsils, adenoids, or both. As Moturi and Avis (2010) stated, these operations have been proved to have positive results on respiration-associated childhood sleep-wake disorders. Because breathing-related disorders are often associated with obesity, bariatric surgery is also becoming a more frequently used intervention (Hofmann, 2013).

Evaluation Strategies

Outcome evaluation can be conducted in various ways, including tracking various treatment outcomes (e.g., improvement in sleep hygiene, changes in sleep quality, quantity of sleep, sleep latency, mood changes, and other variables). The prognosis is generally good for improving sleep-wake related issues (Moturi & Avis, 2010). It is important to note that the prognosis is correlated with the types of treatment strategies used and the level of severity of symptoms. Counselors should consider using a multidimensional approach to diagnosing and treating sleep-wake disorders in adolescence.

Summary

Sleep-wake disorders are complex and difficult to diagnose accurately. Because many sleep-wake disorders are comorbid with other conditions, clinicians should be careful to use rule-out procedures during the assessment process. Aside from the comorbid medical conditions that are often associated with sleep-wake disorders, a number of psychiatric disorders commonly present with a sleep-wake disturbance. Psychiatric comorbidity is especially common when sleep-wake disorders are diagnosed in children and adolescents (Dosi et al., 2013; Murray, Murphy, Palermo, & Clarke, 2012). These co-occurring diagnoses make treatment difficult, causing clinicians or practitioners to decide whether to focus on issues concurrently or separately.

There are numerous challenges for the behavioral health care provider who works with children and adolescents who present with sleep-wake disorders. The clinician must be familiar with developmental issues and must be able to provide education to parents and patients. The lack of education regarding normal sleep and sleep hygiene may present diagnostic challenges in identifying children or adolescents with a sleep-wake disorder (Blythe et al., 2009; D'Cruz & Vaughn, 2009). Sleep quality or hygiene may change the outcome of a potential diagnosis and promote adherence to recommended sleep strategies, which are conducive to an increase in the quality and quantity of obtained sleep.

References

Abe, Y., & de Kernier, N. (2013). Sleep disturbances from the viewpoint of suicidality: Implications for future psychosocial interventions for youngsters. *International Medical Journal, 20*(5), 544–551.

Adams, H. L., Matson, J. L., & Jang, J. (2014). The relationship between sleep problems and challenging behavior among children and adolescents with autism spectrum disorder. *Research in Autism Spectrum Disorders, 8*(9), 1024–1030.

American Academy of Sleep Medicine. (2005). *International classification of sleep disorders: Diagnostic & coding manual* (2nd ed.). Darien, IL: Author.

American Psychiatric Association. (2013). *Diagnostic and statistical manual of mental disorders* (5th ed.). Arlington, VA: American Psychiatric Publishing.

Amos, L. B., Grekowicz, M. L., Kuhn, E. M., Olstad, J. D., Collins, M. M., Norins, N. A., & D'Andrea, L. A. (2014). Treatment of Pediatric Restless Legs Syndrome. *Clinical Pediatrics, 53*(4), 331–336. doi:10.1177/0009922813507997

Anderson, K. N., Goldsmith, P., & Gardiner, A. (2014). A pilot evaluation of an online cognitive behavioral therapy for insomnia disorder—Targeted screening and interactive Web design lead to improved sleep in a community population. *Nature and Science of Sleep, 6*, 43–49.

Arbuckle, R., Abetz, L., Durmer, J. S., Ivanenko, A., Owens, J. A., Croenlein, J., … Picchietti, D. L. (2010). Development of the Pediatric Restless Legs Syndrome Severity Scale (P-RLS-SS): A patient-reported outcome measure of pediatric RLS symptoms and impact. *Sleep Medicine, 11*(9), 897–906. doi:10.1016/j.sleep.2010.03.016

Association of Neuropsychology Students in Training (n.d.). *Professional definitions: Defining the field of clinical neuropsychology and the necessary training & education.* Retrieved from http://www.div40-anst.com/professional-definitions.html

Aurora, R. N., Chowdhuri, S., Ramar, K., Bista, S. R., Casey, K. R., Lamm, C. I., … Tracy, S. L. (2012). The treatment of central sleep apnea syndromes in adults: Practice parameters with an evidence-based literature review and meta-analyses. *SLEEP, 35*(1), 17–40.

Berk, L.E. (2014). *Development through the lifespan* (6th ed.). Boston: Pearson/Allyn and Bacon.

Blythe, J., Doghramji, P. P., Jungquist, C. R., Landau, M. B., Valerio, T. D., Ancoli-Israel, S., & Auerbach, S. H. (2009, December). Screening & treating patients with sleep/wake disorders. Retrieved from http://www.bu.edu/cme/iGiveTest_files/E.SLEEP HAYM08%20FINAL%20MONOGRAPH.pdf

Brockmann, P. E., Schaefer, C., Poets, A., Poets, C. F., & Urschitz, M. S. (2013). Diagnosis of obstructive sleep apnea in children: A systematic review. *Sleep Medicine Reviews, 17*(5), 331–340.

Bruni, O., Ottaviano, S., Guidetti, V., Romoli, N., Innocenzi, M., Cortesi, F., & Giannotti, F. (1996). The Sleep Disturbance Scale for Children (SDSC). Construction and validation of an instrument to evaluate sleep disturbances in childhood and adolescence. *Journal of Sleep Research, 5*(4), 251–261.

Byars, K., & Simon, S. (2014). Practice patterns and insomnia treatment outcomes from an evidence-based pediatric behavioral sleep medicine clinic. *Clinical Practice in Pediatric Psychology, 2*(3), 337–349.

Calhoun, S. L., Fernandez-Mendoza, J., Vgontzas, A. N., Liao, D., & Bixler, E. O. (2014). Prevalence of insomnia symptoms in a general population sample of young children and preadolescents: Gender effects. *Sleep Medicine, 15*(1), 91–95.

Chase, R. M., & Pincus, D. B. (2011). Sleep-related problems in children and adolescents with anxiety disorders. *Behavioral Sleep Medicine, 9*(4), 224–236.

Chen, G., Ratcliffe, J., Olds, T., Magarey, A., Jones, M., & Leslie, E. (2014). BMI, health behaviors, and quality of life in children and adolescents: A school-based study. *Pediatrics, 133*(4), e868–e874.

Damiani, J. M., Sweet, B. V., & Sohoni, P. (2014). Melatonin: An option for managing sleep disorders in children with autism spectrum disorder. *American Journal of Health-System Pharmacy, 71*(2), 95–101.

D'Cruz, O. F., & Vaughn, B. V. (2009). Sleep disorders. In R. B. David, J. B. Bodensteiner, D. E. Mandelbaum, & B. Olson (Eds.), *Clinical Pediatric Neurology* (3rd ed., pp. 541–548). New York, NY: Demos Medical.

de Biase, S., Gigli, G. L., Lorenzut, S., Bianconi, C., Sfreddo, P., Rossato, G., … Valente, M. (2014). The importance of polysomnography in the evaluation of prolonged disorders of consciousness: Sleep recordings more adequately correlate than stimulus-related evoked potentials with patients' clinical status. *Sleep Medicine, 15*(4), 393–400. 10.1016/j.sleep.2013.09.026

de Freitas Araújo, D., & Moraes de Almondes, K. (2014). Sleep and cognitive performance in children and pre-adolescents: A review. *Biological Rhythm Research, 45*(2), 193–207.

Díaz-Morales, J., Delgado Prieto, P. Escribano, C., José Collado Mateo, M., and Randler C. (2012). Sleep beliefs and chronotype among adolescents: The effect of a sleep education program. *Biological Rhythm Research, 43*, 397–412.

Dodzik, P. A. (2013). Cognitive disorders: Sleep disorders. In A. S. Davis (Ed.), *Psychopathology of childhood and adolescence: A neuropsychological approach* (pp. 793–820). New York, NY: Springer.

Dosi, C., Riccioni, A., della Corte, M., Novelli, L., Ferri, R., & Bruni, O. (2013). Comorbidities of sleep disorder in childhood and adolescence: Focus on migraine. *Nature and Science of Sleep, 5*, 77–85.

Drummond, R. J., Sheperis, C. J., & Jones, K. D. (2015). *Assessment Procedures for counselors and helping professionals* (8th ed.). Upper Saddle River, NJ: Pearson.

Eckerberg, B. (2004). Treatment of sleep problems in families with young children: Effects of treatment on family well-being. *Acta Paediatrica, 93*(1), 126–134.

Ekstedt, M., Nyberg, G., Ingre, M., Ekblom, Ö., & Marcus, C. (2013). Sleep, physical activity and BMI in six to ten-year-old children measured by accelerometry: A cross-sectional study. *International Journal of Behavioral Nutrition and Physical Activity, 10*, 82.

Feige, B., Baglioni, C., Spiegelhalder, K., Hirscher, V., Nissen, C., & Riemann, D. (2013). The microstructure of sleep in primary insomnia: An overview and extension. *International Journal of Psychophysiology, 89*(2), 171–180.

Ferini-Strambi, L., Di Gioia, M. R., Castronovo, V., Oldani, A., Zucconi, M., & Cappa, S. F. (2004). Neuropsychological assessment in idiopathic REM sleep behavior disorder (RBD): Does the idiopathic form of RBD really exist? *Neurology, 62*(1), 41–45.

Fisher, H. L., Lereya, S. T., Thompson, A., Lewis, G., Zammit, S., & Wolke, D. (2014). Childhood parasomnias and psychotic experiences at age 12 years in a United Kingdom birth cohort. *Sleep: Journal of Sleep and Sleep Disorders Research, 37*(3), 475–482.

Gradisar, M., & Crowley, S. J. (2013). Delayed sleep phase disorder in youth. *Current Opinion in Psychiatry, 26*(6), 580–585.

Hahn, C., Cowell, J. M., Wiprzycka, U. J., Goldstein, D., Ralph, M., Hasher, L., & Zelazo, P. D. (2012). Circadian rhythms in executive function during the transition to adolescence: The effect of synchrony between chronotype and time of day. *Developmental Science, 15*(3), 408–416.

Hall, W. A., Scher, A., Zaidman-Zait, A., Espezel, H., & Warnock, F. (2012). A community-base study of sleep and behavioural problems in 12- to 36-month-old children. Child: Care, Health & Development, *38*(3), 379–389. doi:10.1111/j.1365-2214.2011.01252.x

Harvey, A. G. (2011). Sleep and circadian functioning: Critical mechanisms in the mood disorders? *Annual Review of Clinical Psychology, 7*, 297–319.

Hasler, B. P., & Clark, D. B. (2013). Circadian misalignment, reward-related brain function, and adolescent alcohol involvement. *Alcoholism: Clinical and Experimental Research, 37*(4), 558–565.

Hasler, B. P., Soehner, A. M., & Clark, D. B. (2014). Sleep and circadian contributions to adolescent alcohol use disorder. *Alcohol.* 10.1016/j.alcohol.2014.06.010

Hill, C. (2011). Practitioner review: Effective treatment of behavioural insomnia in children. *Journal of Child Psychology and Psychiatry and Allied Disciplines, 52*(7), 731–740. doi:10.1111/j.1469-7610.2011.02396.

Hoban, T. F. (2010). Sleep disorders in children. *Annals of the New York Academy of Sciences, 1184*(2), 1–14. doi:10.1111/j.1749-6632.2009.05112.x

Hofmann, B. (2013). Bariatric surgery for obese children and adolescents: A review of the moral challenges. *BMC Medical Ethics, 14* (1), 1–13.

Inocente, C. O., Gustin, M. P., Lavault, S., Guignard-Perret, A., Raoux, A., Christol, N., ... Franco, P. (2014). Quality of life in children with narcolepsy. *CNS Neuroscience & Therapeutics.*

Insana, S. P., Glowacki, S. S., & Montgomery-Downs, H. E. (2011). Assessing the efficacy to conduct the multiple sleep latency test with actigraphy. *Behavioral Sleep Medicine, 9*(4), 257–265. doi:10.1080/15402002.2011.607018

Jain, S. V. (2013). Sleep terrors and confusional arousals in children and adolescents. In S. V. Kothare & A. Ivanenko (Eds.), *Parasomnias: Clinical characteristics and treatment* (pp. 123–136). New York, NY: Springer Science + Business Media.

Jenni, O. G., & Carskadon, M. A. (2012). Sleep behavior and sleep regulation from infancy through adolescence: Normative aspects. *Sleep Medicine Clinics, 7*(3), 529–538.

Johnson, E., Roth, T., Schultz, L., & Breslau, N. (2006). Epidemiology of DSM-IV insomnia in adolescence: Lifetime prevalence, chronicity, and an emergent gender difference. *Pediatrics, 117*(2), 247–56.

Jin, C. S., Hanley, G. P., & Beaulieu, L. (2013). An individualized and comprehensive approach to treating sleep problems in young children. *Journal of Applied Behavior Analysis, 46*(1), 161–180. doi:10.1002/jaba.16

Johnson, C., & Mindell, J. A. (2011). Family-based interventions for sleep problems of infants and children. In M. El-Sheikh (Ed.), *Sleep and development: Familial and socio-cultural considerations* (pp. 375–402). New York, NY: Oxford University Press.

Jung, R., & Kuhlo, W. (1965). Neurophysiological studies of abnormal night sleep and the Pickwickian syndrome. In K. Akert, C. Bally, & J. P. Schadé (Eds.), *Progress in Brain Research* (vol. 18, pp. 140–159). Amsterdam, Netherlands: Elsevier.

Kaplan, S. G., Ali, S. K., Simpson, B., Britt, V., & McCall, W. V. (2014). Associations between sleep disturbance and suicidal ideation in adolescents admitted to an inpatient psychiatric unit. *International Journal of Adolescent Medicine and Health, 26*(3), 411–416.

Katon, W., Sullivan, M., & Walker, E. (2001). Medical symptoms without identified pathology: Relationship to psychiatric disorders, childhood and adult trauma, and personality traits. *Annals of Internal Medicine, 134*(9, Part 2), 917–925.

Kornum, B. R., Faraco, J., & Mignot, E. (2011). Narcolepsy with hypocretin/orexin deficiency, infections and autoimmunity of the brain. *Current Opinion in Neurobiology, 21*(6), 897–903.

Kotagai, S. (2009). Hypersomnia in children: Interface with psychiatric disorders. *Child and Adolescent Psychiatric Clinics of North America, 18*(4), 967–977.

Koyama, S., Kobayakawa, M., Tachibana, N., Masaoka, Y., Homma, I., Ishii, K., & Kawamura, M. (2012). Neuropsychological and radiological assessments of two cases with apparent idiopathic rapid eye movement sleep behaviour disorder. *European Neurology, 67*(1), 18–25.

Langston, T. J., Davis, J. L., & Swopes, R. M. (2010). Idiopathic and posttrauma nightmares in a clinical sample of children and adolescents: Characteristics and related pathology. *Journal of Child & Adolescent Trauma, 3*(4), 344–356. doi:10.1080/19361521.2010.523064

Leahy, E., & Gradisar, M. (2012). Dismantling the bidirectional relationship between paediatric sleep and anxiety. *Clinical Psychologist, 16*(1), 44–56.

Lineberger, M. D., Carney, C. E., Edinger, J. D., & Means, M. K. (2006). Defining insomnia: Quantitative criteria for insomnia severity and frequency. *SLEEP, 29*(4), 479–485.

Lytle, L. A., Pasch, K. E., & Farbakhsh, K. (2011). The relationship between sleep and weight in a sample of adolescents. *Obesity, 19*(2), 324–331.

Malow, B., Adkins, K. W., McGrew, S. G., Wang, L., Goldman, S. E., Fawkes, D., and Burnette, C. (2012). Melatonin for sleep in children with autism: A controlled trial examining dose, tolerability, and outcomes. *Journal of Autism and Developmental Disorders, 42*(8), 1729–1737.

Marhefka, J. K. (2011). Sleep deprivation: Consequences for students. *Journal of Psychosocial Nursing and Mental Health Services, 49*(9), 20–25.

Martin, J. L., & Hakim, A. D. (2011). Wrist actigraphy. *Chest, 139*(6), 1514–1527.

Maski, K. P., & Kothare, S. V. (2013). Sleep deprivation and neurobehavioral functioning in children. *International Journal of Psychophysiology, 89*(2), 259–264.

McCall, C., & McCall, W. V. (2012). Comparison of actigraphy with polysomnography and sleep logs in depressed insomniacs. *Journal of Sleep Research, 21*(1), 122–127. doi:10.1111/j.1365-2869.2011.00917.x

Meltzer, L. J., Avis, K. T., Biggs, S., Reynolds, A. C., Crabtree V. M., & Bevans, K. B. (2013). The Children's Report of Sleep Patterns (CRSP): A self-report measure of sleep for school-aged children. *Journal of Clinical Sleep Medicine, 9*(3), 235–245. doi:10.5664/jcsm.2486.

Meltzer, L. J., Biggs, S., Reynolds, A., Avis, K. T., Crabtree, V. M., & Bevans, K. E. (2012). The Children's Report of Sleep Patterns—Sleepiness Scale: A self-report measure for school-aged children. *Sleep Medicine, 13*, 385–389.

Miano, S., & Fern, R. (2010). Epidemiology and management of insomnia in children with autistic spectrum disorders. *Pediatric Drugs, 12*(2), 75–84.

Mignot, E. J. M. (2012). A practical guide to the therapy of narcolepsy and hypersomnia syndromes. *Neurotherapeutics, 9*(4), 739–752.

Morin, C., Bootzin, R., Buysse, D., Edinger, J., Espie, C., Lichstein, K. (2006). Psychological and behavioral treatment of insomnia: Update of the recent evidence (1998-2004), *29*(11),1398–414.

Moss, T. G., Lachowski, A. M., & Carney, C. E. (2013). What all treatment providers should know about sleep hygiene recommendations. *The Behavior Therapist, 36*(4), 76–83.

Moturi, S., & Avis, K. (2010). Assessment and treatment of common pediatric sleep disorders. *Psychiatry, 7*(6), 24–37.

Murray, C. B., Murphy, L. K., Palermo, T. M., & Clarke, G. M. (2012). Pain and sleep-wake disturbances in adolescents with depressive disorders. *Journal of Clinical Child & Adolescent Psychology, 41*(4), 482–490.

National Center for Chronic Disease and Prevention and Health Promotion, Division of Adult and Community Health. (2014, January 13). *Insufficient sleep is a public health epidemic.* Retrieved from http://www.cdc.gov/features/dssleep/

National Sleep Foundation, (2013). *Sleep disorders.* Retrieved from http://sleepdisorders.sleepfoundation.org/

Nevsimalova, S. (2009). Narcolepsy in childhood. *Sleep Medicine Reviews, 13*(2), 169–180. 10.1016/j.smrv.2008.04.007

Nevsimalova, S., Prihodova, I., Kemlink, D., & Skibova, J. (2013). Childhood parasomnia–A disorder of sleep maturation? *European Journal of Paediatric Neurology, 17*(6), 615–619. doi:10.1016/j.ejpn.2013.05.004

Nguyen, M., Tharani, S., Rahmani, M., & Shapiro, M. (2014). A review of the use of Clonidine as a sleep aid in the child and adolescent population. *Clinical Pediatrics, 53*(3), 211–216.

Novelli, L., Ferri, R., & Bruni, O. (2013). Sleep cyclic alternating pattern and cognition in children: A review. *International Journal of Psychophysiology, 89*(2), 246–251.

Nussbaum, A. M. (2013). The pocket guide to the DSM-5 diagnostic exam. Arlington, VA: American Psychiatric Publishing.

O'Brien, L. M. (2011). The neurocognitive effects of sleep disruption in children and adolescents. *Sleep Medicine Clinics, 6*(1), 109–116.

Ohayon, M. M., Riemann, D., Morin, C., & Reynolds, C. F. (2012). Hierarchy of insomnia criteria based on daytime consequences. *Sleep Medicine, 13*(1), 52–57.

Owens, J. A., Spirito, A., & McGuinn, M. (2000). The Children's Sleep Habits Questionnaire (CSHQ): Psychometric properties of a survey instrument for school-aged children. *SLEEP, 23*(8), 1043–1051.

Parisi, P., Verrotti, A., Paolino, M. C., Ferretti, A., Raucci, U., Moavero, R., ... Curatolo, P. (2014). Headache and attention deficit and hyperactivity disorder in children: Common condition with complex relation and disabling consequences. *Epilepsy & Behavior, 32*, 72–75. doi:10.1016/j.yebeh.2013.12.028

Picchietti, D. L., Bruni, O., de Weerd, A., Durmer, J. S., Kotagal, S., Owens, J. A., & Simakajornboon, N. (2013). Pediatric restless legs syndrome diagnostic criteria: an update by the International Restless Legs Syndrome Study Group. *Sleep Medicine, 14*(12), 1253–1259. doi:10.1016/j.sleep.2013.08.778

Riar, S. K., Leu, R. M., Turner-Green, T. C, Rye, D. B., Kendrick-Allwood, S. R., McCracken, C., ... Greenbaum, L. A. (2013). Restless legs syndrome in children with chronic kidney disease. *Pediatric Nephrology, 28*(5), 773–795. doi:10.1007/s00467-013-2408-9

Ringli, M., Kurth, S., Huber, R., & Jenni, O. G. (2013). The sleep EEG topography in children and adolescents shows sex differences in language areas. *International Journal of Psychophysiology, 89*(2), 241–245.

Roux, F. J., & Kryger, M. H. (2010). Therapeutics for sleep-disordered breathing. *Sleep Medicine Clinics, 5*(4), 647–657.

Saeedi, M., Shamsikhani, S., Varvani Farahani, P., & Haghverdi, F. (2014). Sleep hygiene training program for patients on hemodialysis. *Iranian Journal of Kidney Diseases, 8*(1), 65–69.

Schäfer, V., & Bader, K. (2013). Relationship between early-life stress load and sleep in psychiatric outpatients: A sleep diary and actigraphy study. *Stress and Health: Journal of the International Society for the Investigation of Stress, 29*(3), 177–189. doi:10.1002/smi.2438

Seidel, S., Böck, A., Schlegel, W., Kilic, A., Wagner, G., Gelbmann, G., ... Wöber-Bingöl, Ç. (2012). Increased RLS prevalence in children and adolescents with migraine: A case-control study. *Cephalalgia, 32*(9), 693–699.

Sharma, M. P., & Andrade, C. (2012). Behavioral interventions for insomnia: Theory and practice. *Indian Journal of Psychiatry, 54*(4), 359–366. doi:10.4103/0019-5545.104825

Short, M. A., Gradisar, M., Gill, J., & Camfferman, D. (2013). *Identifying adolescent sleep problems.* PLoS One, 8(9), e75301.

Short, M. A., Gradisar, M., Lack, L. C., Wright, H. R., & Chatburn, A. (2013). Estimating adolescent sleep patterns: Parent reports versus adolescent self-report surveys, sleep diaries, and actigraphy. *Nature of Science and Sleep, 5*, 23–26.

Sleep for Science, Sleep Research Lab. (2014). *School Sleep Habits Survey.* Retrieved from http://www.sleepforscience.org/contentmgr/showdetails.php/id/93.

Synnott, E., & Preyde, M. (2009). Understanding infant sleep: A review of two distinctive setting strategies. *Canadian Children, 34*(1), 37–44.

Tan, E., Healey, D., Schaughency, E., Dawes, P., & Galland, B. (2014). Neurobehavioural correlates in older children and adolescents with obesity and obstructive sleep apnoea. *Journal of Paediatrics and Child Health, 50*(1), 16–23.

Tanev, K. S., Pentel, K. Z., Kredlow, M. A., & Charney, M. E. (2014). PTSD and TBI co-morbidity: Scope, clinical presentation and treatment options. *Brain Injury, 28*(3), 261–270. doi:10.3109/02699052 .2013.873821

Taylor, D. J., & Roane, B. M. (2010). Treatment of insomnia in adults and children: A practice-friendly review of research. *Journal of Clinical Psychology, 66*(11), 1137–1147.

Tinuper, P., Bisulli, F., & Provini, F. (2012). The parasomnias: Mechanisms and treatment. *Epilepsia (Series 4), 53*, 12–19. doi: 10.1111/j.1528-1167.2012 .03710.x

Todd, J., & Mullan, B. (2014). The role of self-monitoring and response inhibition in improving sleep behaviours. *International Journal of Behavioral Medicine, 21*(3), 470–477. doi:10.1007/ s12529-013-9328-8

Todd, T. P., Vurbic, D., & Bouton, M. E. (2014). Behavioral and neurobiological mechanisms of extinction in Pavlovian and instrumental learning. *Neurobiology of Learning and Memory, 108*, 52–64.

Van Hoorenbeeck, K., Franckx, H., Debode, P., Aerts, P., Ramet, J., Van Gaal, L. F., … Verhulst, S. L. (2013). Metabolic disregulation in obese adolescents with sleep-disordered breathing before and after weight loss. *Obesity, 21*(7), 1446–1450.

Vashist, S. K., Schneider, E. M., & Luong, J. H. T. (2014). Commercial smartphone-based devices and smart applications for personalized healthcare monitoring and management. *Diagnostics, 4*(3), 104–128.

Vinay, H. R., Danivas, V., Kutty, B. M., Kandasamy, P., Golhar, T. S., Palaniappan, P., … Srinath, S. (2010). Case series of three children and adolescents with periodic hypersomnia. *Journal of Indian Association for Child and Adolescent Mental Health, 6*(4), 120–124.

Wiebe, S., Carrier, J., Frenette, S., & Gruber, R. (2013). Sleep and sleepiness in children with attention deficit/hyperactivity disorder and controls. *Journal of Sleep Research, 22*(1), 41–49.

Wiseman-Hakes, C., Murray, B., Moineddin, R., Rochon, E., Cullen, N., Gargaro, J., & Colantonio, A. (2013). Evaluating the impact of treatment for sleep/wake disorders on recovery of cognition and communication in adults with chronic TBI. *Brain Injury, 27*(12), 1364–1376. doi:10.3109/02699052 .2013.823663

Wood, B., Rea, M. S., Plitnick, B., & Figueiro, M. G. (2013). Light level and duration of exposure determine the impact of self-luminous tablets on melatonin suppression. *Applied Ergonomics, 44*(2), 237–240. doi:10.1016/j.apergo.2012.07.008

Yu, L., Buysse, D. J., Moul, D. E., Germain, A., Stover, A. M., Dodds, N. E., … Pilkonis, P. A. (2012). Development of short forms from the PROMIS Sleep Disturbance and Sleep-Related Impairment Item Banks. *Behavioral Sleep Medicine, 10*(1), 6–24.

Chapter 15

Gender Dysphoria

ANNELIESE A. SINGH AND VARUNEE FAII SANGGANJANAVANICH

Introduction

As information and resources increase about transgender and gender nonconforming (TGNC) people, counselors will increasingly work with gender nonconforming children and will need to understand issues of diagnosis and assessment of gender dysphoria. The term *transgender* has historically been used to refer to individuals whose sex assigned at birth (typically male or female) may not be in alignment with their gender identity (typically boy or girl in children) or gender expression (American Counseling Association [ACA], 2010). *Gender identity* is a term that refers to a person's internal sense of gender, whereas *gender expression* denotes how an individual may express one's gender in behavior, dress, and other ways. When working with children, counselors will often use the term *gender nonconforming* to reflect a child's identity that does not fit into the gender binary of male or female (American Psychological Association [APA], 2015). *Cisgender* is a term that denotes people whose sex assigned at birth is in alignment with their gender identity, and *cisgender privilege* refers to the unearned advantages that are ascribed to a non-TGNC gender identity (ACA, 2010). There are many terms that counselors should know to have the foundational knowledge required for working with TGNC children who are discussed throughout this chapter. We use the phrase *sex assigned at birth* or some variation as opposed to the word *natal* to refer to TGNC children and their lifespans in recognition of the societal role of sex, gender identity, and gender expression assignment. Therefore, a TGNC boy, for instance, refers to a child who was assigned a female sex at birth and may identify as a boy (for a TGNC girl, assigned male at birth and identifying as a girl) in terms of gender identity or have gender nonconforming behaviors according to societal norms of gender.

In this chapter, the authors review the major considerations that counselors should be aware of when diagnosing and assessing gender dysphoria in children. In doing so, the authors detail the history of TGNC people and provide a description of the *Diagnostic Statistical Manual of Mental Disorders, Fifth Edition* (*DSM-5*; APA, 2013a) gender dysphoria diagnosis and related criteria. The authors then review differential diagnoses of which counselors should be aware, as well as assessment and treatment strategies and interventions. The chapter concludes with a discussion of common challenges and opportunities in the evaluation and counseling of TGNC children. See Sidebar 15.1 for information on differentiating sex and gender.

SIDEBAR 15.1: DIFFERENTIATING BETWEEN SEX AND GENDER

People often use the terms *sex* and *gender* interchangeably, and both are social constructs. Sex is assigned at birth based on a binary understanding (i.e., male or female). Sex is a biological construct that genetics, hormones, gonads, or genitalia can define. In contrast, gender, a sociocultural construct, refers to one's internal sense of gender (gender identity) and the ways that one expresses gender through behaviors, dress, activities, and other ways (gender expression). Practitioners should understand the difference between these terms and seek to understand evolving TGNC-affirmative language in the field. For instance, the phrase *gender affirmation surgery* or *gender confirmation surgery* is used as more TGNC-affirming than the dated *sex reassignment surgery* or what the *DSM-5* terms *gender reassignment surgery*. Also, it is well documented that not all TGNC people will want body modifications; therefore the phrases *social transition* and *medical transition* are used to denote these as separate processes.

TGNC Children and the History of Gender Dysphoria

To understand diagnosis of gender dysphoria in TGNC children, counselors should have knowledge of the history of TGNC people across countries and cultures around the world (Roberts & Singh, 2014). Gender fluidity and TGNC identities have been present across cultures, yet often this history of gender variance beyond the gender binary has been obscured by histories of colonization and transgender oppression (Nanda, 1998; Roberts & Singh, 2014). An additional important component of foundational knowledge when working with TGNC children includes the knowledge that gender is a social construct. Since birth, children receive strong, consistent, culturally informed messages about what it means to be a *girl* or a *boy* (Brill & Pepper, 2008). People often use the terms *sex* and *gender* interchangeably. Sex is assigned at birth based on a binary understanding (i.e., male or female). Gender refers to one's internal sense of gender (gender identity) and the ways that one expresses gender through behaviors, dress, activities, and other ways (gender expression). For TGNC children, these gendered messages can be quite confusing—and even traumatic—depending on how much TGNC-affirming information their families and communities have about TGNC people (Gonzalez & McNulty, 2010; Slesaransky-Poe, Ruzzi, Dimedio, & Stanley, 2013). In addition to understanding the impact of these gendered messages on TGNC children, counselors should also be familiar with the research base on gender identity development in childhood (Edwards-Leeper & Spack, 2012; Kohlberg, 1966).

The history of the *DSM* classification of TGNC children has evolved over time in several ways. Counselors should be aware that diagnosis related to TGNC children, adolescents, and adults has been a hotly contested and debated concern of TGNC advocates and counselors (Bryant, 2006). A diagnosis of gender dysphoria in childhood first appeared in the *DSM-III* (APA, 1980) and was termed *Gender Identity Disorder in Children*. Many feminists, amongst other advocates, critiqued the initial diagnosis because of the conflation of gender identity and gender role, and these concerns were addressed in the *DSM-IV-TR*

(Bryant, 2006). However, many TGNC advocates for diagnostic reform (Winters, 2008) expressed concern over the broadening of the diagnostic criteria from the *DSM-III* to the *DSM-IV* (1994) in Criteria A and Criteria B in this diagnosis.

One of the major concerns included that a non-TGNC child could potentially fall under the Gender Identity Disorder Diagnosis in Children, even if the child had not expressed being TGNC, if the child exhibited four out of five of Criteria A and any of Criteria B (Winters, 2008). Advocates for gender identity disorder (GID) reform also questioned these overarching criteria based on the *DSM*'s own assertions that a minimal number of children diagnosed with GID would persist in a TGNC identity into adolescence and adulthood (APA, 1994). In addition to pathologizing normative fluidity of gender identity and gender expression (e.g., toys, play, and clothing), the GID reform advocates noted the significantly different and gender-stereotyped criteria for those children who were assigned male or female at birth but identified with another gender. For instance, in Criteria A, the second characteristic required that assigned males had to demonstrate a "preference for cross-dressing or simulating female attire" whereas assigned females were required to have "insistence on wearing only stereotypical masculine clothing" (APA, 1994, p. 452).

In the *DSM-5*, Gender Identity Disorder is now titled Gender Dysphoria. A major focus in this shift is a recognition that some TGNC people living with gender dysphoria experience related mood effects because of gender incongruence with body phenotype. For instance, the term *gender dysphoria* denotes gender incongruence as opposed to referring to *cross-gender identification* (APA, 2013b, p. 14). The revision also shifted language ("repeatedly stated desire" to "strong desire to be of the other gender") to include TGNC children who may not be allowed to express their gender identity or gender expression in their environments or who may not verbally express their gender identity or gender expression.

The *DSM-5* asserts that gender dysphoria in adolescents may be diagnosed when two criteria are present. The first criterion requires a difference between an individual's experienced gender and assigned gender. With this first criterion, two of the following six symptoms are manifest for at least six months' duration. First, there is a marked incongruence between the primary sex characteristics an adolescent was assigned at birth and the adolescent's experienced gender identity. Dysphoria related to anticipated secondary sex characteristics may be manifest in young adolescents. Second, there is a strong desire to be rid of primary or secondary sex characteristics because of the marked incongruence the adolescent experiences with experienced gender. A desire to prevent the development of anticipated secondary sex characteristics may be manifest in young adolescents. Third, there is a strong desire to acquire the primary or secondary sex characteristics of the other gender. Fourth, there is a strong desire to be a gender other than the one assigned to the adolescent. Fifth, there is a strong desire to be treated as another gender. Sixth, there is a strong conviction of experiencing feelings or reactions of the other gender. The second criterion requires clinically significant distress or impairment in the adolescent's important areas of functioning (e.g., school, family, social, and work).

Because diagnosing is a controversial issue of concern within the counseling and psychological community, with many practitioners asserting that the disorder should be considered a medical condition and not a mental health disorder (Edwards-Leeper & Spack, 2012), it is important that counselors working with TGNC children are knowledgeable about the major professional documents guiding diagnosis. The seventh version of the *Standards of Care* (Coleman et al., 2011) provides guidelines on the diagnosis, assessment, and treatment of TGNC children. The American Counseling Association (2010) has outlined training and counseling competencies for counselors working with TGNC people, including a specific section on assessment concerns (termed *Appraisal* in the document). The American Psychiatric Association is developing guidelines for practice with TGNC people and has written a position paper that summarizes some of the major debates, challenges, and opportunities that counselors face when working with TGNC people with reference to TGNC children (Byne et al., 2012). Counselors should also be aware of the Endocrine Society guidelines for hormone therapy (Hembree et al., 2009) because working with TGNC children and their families often entails interdisciplinary care and extensive consultation and collaboration among health providers. These major professional documents will be discussed in detail in subsequent related sections in this chapter (e.g., Assessment Strategies and Treatment Strategies). See Sidebar 15.2 for information helpful for understanding competencies, guidelines, and standards of care related to working with TGNC children. Also, engage in the self-reflection activity on your own gender identity in Sidebar 15.3.

SIDEBAR 15.2:   UNDERSTANDING THE COMPETENCIES AND GUIDELINES FRAMING TGNC DIAGNOSIS AND COUNSELING

Select one of the major professional documents guiding TGNC diagnosis and counseling, such as the WPATH *Standards of Care* (Coleman et al., 2012), ACA Competencies for Counseling Transgender Clients (2010), or the APA Guidelines for Psychological Practice with Transgender and Gender Non-Conforming Clients (in progress), and discuss the following:

1. What are the major considerations the document contains related to diagnosis and counseling with TGNC children?

2. Based on this document, what should you keep in mind when diagnosing and counseling TGNC children?

SIDEBAR 15.3:   COUNSELOR SELF-REFLECTION ON GENDER

Take a moment to answer the following questions about your own gender journey:

1. When did you first realize your gender identity?

2. What were the gendered messages you received based on your assigned sex?

3. How do your answers to the two questions above influence your attitudes and beliefs about TGNC children and their families?

4. What are specific examples of how you will address issues of cisgender privilege when counseling TGNC children and their families?

Description of Gender Dysphoria

Although the majority of individuals feel a sense of congruence between their gender identity—femininity or masculinity—and physical anatomy, some do not experience such feelings. Gender dysphoria refers to a condition in which one experiences a marked incongruence between one's expressed and assigned gender (e.g., a child who was assigned female at birth but who identifies his gender as a boy). It is estimated that 0.005 percent to 0.014 percent of biological men and 0.002 percent to 0.003 percent of biological women experience gender dysphoria (APA, 2013a). There are no accurate statistics. Gender dysphoria typically has early onset, which begins during childhood. Although less common, the late onset in adolescence or adulthood is also presented.

There are different theories surrounding what causes gender dysphoria—atypical gender development. Although some scholars believe psychological factors (e.g., upbringing and mental disorders) significantly contribute to gender dysphoria (Cohen-Kettenis, Owen, Kaijser, Bradley, & Zucker, 2003; de Vries, Doreleijers, Steensma, & Cohen-Kettenis, 2011), others speculate that biological factors (e.g., brain structure and genetics) play an important role in the development of gender dysphoria (Carrillo et al., 2010; Meyer-Bahlburg, 2010). To date, however, there is no conclusive evidence as to what causes gender dysphoria. The plausible etiological explanation of gender dysphoria is "most likely a multifactorial condition in which psychological as well as biological aspects play some role" (de Vries & Cohen-Kettenis, 2012, p. 304).

The clinical presentation of gender dysphoria in children differs from the clinical presentation in adolescents and adults (see Table 15.1). In adolescents and adults, gender dysphoria is characterized by a strong and persistent desire to become a gender not assigned at birth (e.g., adopting mannerisms and gender roles of the desired gender) and to be free of one's primary and secondary sex characteristics. In children, although gender dysphoria is characterized by a strong and persistent desire to identify as another gender (e.g., a wish to dress like another gender and dislike of one's own physical anatomy), it is rare that children express a strong and persistent desire to eliminate their primary and secondary sex characteristics. As previously discussed, only a small number of children (ranging from 12 percent to 27 percent) diagnosed with gender dysphoria progress to having gender dysphoria in adolescence and adulthood, based on statistics derived from children referred to gender clinics (de Vries & Cohen-Kettenis, 2012).

Table 15.2 provides gender dysphoria–related terminology over the lifespan trajectory. Take a moment to answer the questions found in Sidebar 15.4. Use your answers to the questions to reflect on your ideas of stereotypical behaviors associated with gender.

SIDEBAR 15.4: GENDER STEREOTYPICAL BEHAVIORS

When thinking about gender nonconforming behaviors, what comes to your mind? List at least five behaviors of gender nonconforming behaviors (create a separate list for girls and boys). Once you have your list, reflect on why you think these behaviors are nonconforming. Pay attention to issues of privilege and oppression related to sexism and heterosexism that inform your responses (Dermer et al., 2010).

TABLE 15.1 Criterion Comparison between Gender Dysphoria Diagnostic Criteria in Children and in Adults and Adolescents

Early Onset: Children (Approximate Ages 2 to 10)— Requires 6 of 8 Symptoms	*Late Onset:* Adolescents (Approximate Ages 11 to 17) and Adults (Age 18+)— Requires 2 of 6 Symptoms
Strong Desire … A.1. To be of the other gender A.8. For the sex characteristics that match one's experienced gender Strong Preference for … A.2. Cross-dressing A.3. Cross-gender roles in play A.4. Cross-gender activities A.5. Cross-gender playmates Strong Rejection of … A.6. Stereotypical toys, games, and activities Strong Dislike of … A.7. One's sexual anatomy	Marked Incongruence … A.1. Between gender and sex characteristics Strong Desire … A.2. To be rid of one's sex characteristics A.3. For sex characteristics of the other gender A.4. To be of the other gender A.5. To be treated as the other gender Strong Conviction … A.6. That one has the typical feelings and reactions of the other gender

Source: King, 2014, Gender Dysphoria section, paras. 6–7.

GENDER DYSPHORIA WITHOUT A DISORDER OF SEX DEVELOPMENT

In children, cross-gender behaviors may begin between the ages of 2 and 4 years and some of these young children could articulate a desire to be the opposite gender. In some cases, children may even refer to themselves as a member of a gender other than the one they were assigned at birth. On the other hand, for some children, the feelings of being another gender may not be expressed until they start school. A small number of these children also report feeling uncomfortable with their sex organs or wishing for the sexual anatomy of another gender (*anatomic dysphoria*) (APA, 2013a).

Gender dysphoria tends to persist at different rates for girls and boys. For instance, for TGNC girls (assigned male at birth), persistence percentages range from 2.2 to 30, while in TGNC boys (assigned female at birth), they range from 12 to 50 percent. When gender dysphoria persists into adolescence, both TGNC girls and boys tend to be sexually attracted to people of their biological sex. However, when the negative feelings do not persist, most TGNC girls are androphilic (sexually attracted to males) and often identify as gay (ranging from 63 to 100 percent), while TGNC boys are usually gynephilic (sexually attracted to females) and they identify as lesbian at a much lower rate than girls (APA, 2013a).

In TGNC girls and women, there are two main courses for the development of the disorder: early onset and late onset. Early-onset gender dysphoria normally begins in childhood and continues into adolescence and adulthood. While there may be times when the symptoms remit and the individuals develop a gay identity, the dysphoria typically recurs. In contract, late-onset gender dysphoria does not typically manifest until puberty, at the earliest. Some individuals with this onset pattern often report that they experienced times

TABLE 15.2   Gender Dysphoria–Related Terminology Over the Life Span Trajectory

Disorder of sex development	Refers to a congenital condition in which development of chromosomal, gonadal, or anatomical sex does not fit into a designated binary sex systems
Gender or sex assignment	Refers to the initial sex assignment as male or female, usually at birth
Gender identity	Refers to an individual's identification as male, female, neither, or some category other than male or female
Gender role	Refers to the public (and usually legally recognized) lived role as boy or girl, man or woman
Gender dysphoria	Refers to the affective or cognitive discontent or distress that may accompany the incongruence between one's experienced or expressed gender and one's assigned gender
Gender-atypical/Gender-nonconforming	Refers to somatic features or behaviors that are not typical (in a statistical sense) of individuals with the same assigned gender in a given society and historical era
Transgender	Refers to the broad spectrum of individuals who transiently or persistently identify with a gender different from their sex assigned at birth
Sex reassignment or confirmation surgery	Refers to somatic transition by cross-sex hormone treatment and genital surgery
Transsexual	Refers to an individual who seeks, or has undergone, a social and medical transition (e.g., male to female or female to male)

Source: APA (2013a); King, 2014, Gender Dysphoria section, paras. 1 & 3.

during their childhoods when they wanted to be the other gender, but that they never expressed their desire to anyone else, whereas others note that they do not remember experiencing any symptoms during childhood (APA, 2013a).

TGNC females with the early-onset type usually report a sexual attraction to men (androphilic) and the majority of them are either gynephilic or attracted to other TGNC women. Among adult TGNC women with gender dysphoria, an earlier onset of symptoms predicts a tendency to seek out hormone therapy and gender affirmation surgery quicker than those with a later onset. However, the late-onset group may experience more fluctuations in the intensity of negative feelings, may be more unsure about gender affirmation surgery, and may be less satisfied after gender affirmation surgery than those who experience an earlier onset.

In TGNC male adolescents and men, the normal course is the early-onset form of gender dysphoria and these individuals are usually gynephilic. The late-onset form is much more rare in TGNC men as compared to TGNC women, but, when it occurs, these people tend to be androphiliac and identify as gay after the transition. As in TGNC women with gender dysphoria, there may have been a period in which the dysphoria remitted and the TGNC men identified as lesbian; however, when the symptoms recur, treatment is often sought, with the desire for hormone therapy and gender affirmation surgery.

GENDER DYSPHORIA IN ASSOCIATION WITH A DISORDER OF SEX DEVELOPMENT

A disorder of sex development refers to a condition in which multiple anatomical secondary sex characteristics that are societally assigned to female and male internal and external reproductive organs are present, previously called intersex or hermaphrodite (the latter is a dated and pathologizing term). There are various types of disorders of sex development, with congenital adrenal hyperplasia and androgen insensitivity syndrome as the most common forms. Congenital adrenal hyperplasia refers to a condition where an individual with assigned female sex chromosomes displays secondary sex characteristics typically assigned to males, whereas androgen insensitivity syndrome refers to a condition where an individual with assigned male sex chromosomes displays a societally normed feminine appearance.

Individuals with a disorder of sex development receive medical attention since birth. Particularly, those with gender dysphoria typically seek treatment related to their gender identity such as hormone therapy and genital reconstruction during their childhood and adolescence. Unlike in other cases of gender nonconforming children or adolescents who experience gender dysphoria without a disorder of sex development, health care professionals approach their situation without much consideration regarding their gender identity and tend to provide medical treatment early on in their lives to promote gender congruence of such individuals.

It is common that individuals with disorders of sex development present may at times experience uncertainty and confusion regarding their gender identity even though they successfully adopt their gender assignment. This situation is largely influenced by knowledge of their medical history. However, in this case, it is important to note that unlike individuals with true gender dysphoria, most individuals with a disorder of sex development may not pursue gender transition. In addition, different clinical manifestations of disorders of sex development inform health care providers' decisions regarding treatment of gender dysphoria and gender transition.

In many cases, parents and caregivers are the first to observe or become aware of gender-variant behaviors through their interactions with the child, interactions that are a major reason for referral. They may notice that the child demonstrates a pattern of behaviors surrounding gender discomfort. For instance, parents may notice that a girl refuses to wear skirts or dresses and that a boy avoids rough-and-tumble play with similar gender playmates. Later in this chapter, you will learn more about helping parents and caregivers understand gender dysphoria in children as well as working with parents and caregivers of children with gender dysphoria.

As mentioned earlier in this chapter, in the *DSM-5*, gender dysphoria is an independent classification rather than being included among the sexual dysfunctions and paraphilias in the *DSM-IV-TR*. Although some advocates prefer the removal of gender dysphoria from the *DSM* altogether and that counselors take a nonpathologizing stand when working with gender nonconforming children, the retention of gender dysphoria in the *DSM-5* may help TGNC clients with health insurance obtain access to quality medical procedures because third-party reimbursement is ensured. In the next section, you will learn the *DSM-5* criteria of gender dysphoria in children.

DSM-5 Criteria

The APA (2013a) defined gender dysphoria as "the distress that may accompany the incongruence between one's experienced or expressed gender and one's assigned gender" (p. 451). In children, gender incongruence is characterized by a strong and persistent desire to become another gender (e.g., wish to dress like another gender and dislike of one's physical anatomy). It is essential that the gender incongruence be accompanied with clinically significant distress or impairment in important areas of functioning, including social and school environments. Clinicians should keep in mind that if a disorder of sex development (e.g., a congenital adrenogenital disorder) causes gender dysphoria, they will need to identify a type of disorder of sex development. The *DSM-5* also denotes that some children experiencing gender dysphoria may not experience the diagnostic criteria persisting, because there is a large variation of gender fluidity in childhood. Those children who do not persist with gender nonconforming behaviors may eventually identify as gay (androphilic), lesbian (gynephilic), or straight.

TGNC children in this situation may experience challenges at school (e.g., peer rejection from both girls and boys). See the *DSM-5* for the diagnostic criteria for Gender Dysphoria in Children. Although the *DSM-5* provides criteria for children that are separate from adolescents and adults, it does not provide any guidelines regarding age ranges to distinguish between childhood and adolescence. Therefore, to assess whether an individual meets diagnostic criteria for Gender Dysphoria in Children or Adolescents and Adults, counselors are required to consider various factors, including physical growth, upbringing environment, and cultural norms.

The clinical threshold for children is higher compared with adolescents in that they must meet six symptoms out of the eight possible to avoid classification of developmentally normative cross-gender attitudes and behaviors. Children rarely voice their strong desire to become the other gender. Rather, they generally show their strong desire to become the other gender by expressing themselves like one of its members (e.g., playing only with toys that belong to the desired gender) or by avoiding expressing themselves based on their assigned gender (e.g., refusing to wear clothes that belong to their assigned gender).

Many child advocates (e.g., Ehrensaft, 2012) have commented that gender development is complex and varies from one child to another. Gender stereotypes dictate how children should behave, and a variation of gender-related behaviors often presents challenges to children and their families. It is possible that children may demonstrate gender-variant behaviors at some point in their development; however, this does not mean that those behaviors will continue to develop into gender dysphoria. Therefore, when approaching children who may present symptoms of gender dysphoria, counselors should take the development aspect into account and understand that gender-variant behaviors can be a part of typical gender development. Gender stability is proposed to be established between the ages of 2 to 4 years, and gender consistency forms between the ages of 4 and 7 years (Siegal & Robinson, 1987). These gender identity development markers are, however, general ones, and gender fluidity is quite common in childhood (American Academy of Child and Adolescent Psychiatry [AACAP], 2012). In addition, when children demonstrate gender dysphoric–like behaviors, it may not mean that children can or should be diagnosed with gender dysphoria. It is important for counselors to understand differential diagnoses related to gender dysphoria. Therefore, in the next section, you will learn about various differential diagnoses of gender dysphoria.

Differential Diagnosis

When the child presents with extreme or severe gender-dysphoric behaviors, the diagnostic process is much simpler for counselors. However, at times, clinical presentations of a gender-dysphoric condition are unclear and can potentially lead to an inaccurate diagnosis. This is because gender dysphoria is a multifaceted condition that requires counselors to attend to the biopsychosocial aspects of the child's life. Questions presented in Sidebar 15.5 can help you begin generating potential differential diagnosis of gender dysphoria in children.

SIDEBAR 15.5: DIFFERENTIAL DIAGNOSIS OF GENDER DYSPHORIA IN CHILDREN

1. Develop a list of potential differential diagnoses of gender dysphoria in children.
2. Provide a rationale for each potential different diagnosis (e.g., why do you believe so?).
3. Generate ways to rule out each of potential different diagnoses.

At times, children demonstrate temporary gender-variant behaviors; however, gender dysphoria does not cause these behavioral manifestations. First, it is important for counselors to understand that not all gender-variant behaviors lead to a gender dysphoria diagnosis (de Vries & Cohen-Kettenis, 2012). In addition to gender-variant behaviors shown in typical gender development, gender-variant behaviors can sometimes be situation specific. For example, a girl may start playing primarily with aggressive toys because of a birth of a younger brother. In this sense, gender dysphoria does not cause gender-variant behavior. Rather, the child may display this behavior as a way to ask for more parent attention or to let parents know that she experiences some adjustment issues, not mental disorders. Second, in rare instances, counselors should rule out differential diagnoses of gender dysphoria to provide accurate diagnosis of the condition. Differential diagnoses of gender dysphoria may include intersex, anxiety disorders, autism spectrum disorder (ASD), trauma-related disorders, psychotic disorders, body dysmorphic disorder, and transvestic disorder.

Intersex refers to a condition that an individual is born with sex organs or a genetic assignment that does not fit the societal sex binary of male and female (e.g., a person has a penis and ovaries, or a person has both XX and XY chromosomes). When this condition is presented, individuals may display a range of gender identities and expressions. Therefore, intersex is different from gender dysphoria where a person is assigned one of two of the sex binary options—female or male; a TGNC person feels that his or her sex assignment does not match with his or her expressed gender identity or expression.

Children with severe separation anxiety may develop gender-dysphoric behaviors as an attempt to feel attached to their caregivers. Ruble, Martin, and Berenbaum (2006) suggested that young children, before the ages of 5 to 7 years, had not yet developed gender constancy—one's cognitive understanding that the assigned gender is a never-changing part of the self. Therefore, some children who experience severe separation anxiety may develop gender-variant behaviors to substitute their parents or caregivers (e.g., a boy begins to dress like his mother when learning that he will enter kindergarten). In this case, gender dysphoria does not cause gender-variant behaviors.

Although more evidence suggests that ASD, especially the higher-functioning end of the spectrum, is co-occurring with gender dysphoria in children (de Vries,

Noens, Cohen-Kettenis, van Berckelaer-Onnes, & Doreleijers, 2010), it is possible that gender-variant behaviors of children diagnosed with ASD are not caused by gender dysphoria. For example, a boy has obsessional interests in playing with dolls and shows signs of distress (e.g., excessive crying and aggression) when the dolls are taken away. Counselors should assess whether ASD, gender dysphoria, or both cause this rigid obsession.

Trauma can be a co-occurring or differential diagnosis of gender dysphoria. Many gender-variant children experience traumas because of their gender-variant behaviors (e.g., social ostracism, bullying, and abuse). In contrast, it is possible that children who experience trauma may develop symptoms of gender dysphoria. For example, a girl who experiences pervasive sexual abuse may adopt masculine characteristics and a masculine personality as a safeguard against sexual abuse.

Symptoms of psychotic-related disorders (e.g., hallucinations and delusions) may at times appear similar to symptoms of gender dysphoria. Counselors should screen out and treat symptoms of psychotic disorders prior to conducting assessment of gender dysphoria. For example, a woman who experiences hallucination believes that she has a penis or a man with delusional thoughts may believe that he is a woman, and these are unrelated to gender dysphoria. A counselor then needs to treat these symptoms before beginning to examine a presence of gender dysphoria. Examples such as these are quite rare.

In addition, counselors should consider ruling out body dysmorphic disorder and transvestic disorder when assessing gender dysphoria. Children with body dysmorphic disorder may display symptoms that are not characteristic of gender dysphoria. For instance, a girl verbalizes that she dislikes her breast when disliking her breast is caused by a thought that the structure of her breast is malformed, not by wanting to get rid of her primary sex characteristics. Transvestic disorder is a very controversial diagnosis that remains in the *DSM-5*, as many TGNC scholars and advocates have argued for the removal of transvestic disorder because of its pathologization of sexuality and gender identity. Practitioners may find themselves working with families who are ask questions related to transvestic disorder and gender dysphoria. According to the *DSM-5*, individuals assessed with transvestic disorder display behaviors societally assigned to a different gender because of the needs for sexual arousal, whereas ones with gender dysphoria display such behaviors to achieve gender congruence. Many scholars have criticized the *DSM-5* for retaining a diagnosis of transvestic disorder.

As noted earlier, ruling out differential diagnoses is critical. Counselors should screen out gender-dysphoric-like symptoms that are not rooted in gender dysphoria to diagnose and treat gender dysphoria accurately in children. In addition to screening out differential diagnosis and other mental health concerns, counselors are responsible for conducting a thorough and comprehensive assessment of gender dysphoria. In the next section, you will learn about assessment strategies of gender dysphoria with both children and parents or caregivers.

Assessment Strategies

Some children experiencing gender dysphoria and their parents or caregivers find ways to manage their sense of unhappiness and gender discomfort on their own, whereas others seek treatment to alleviate this condition. Assessment is the first step of the treatment and can lead to appropriate clinical treatment. The goal of the assessment process is to determine whether gender dysphoria criteria have been met. As previously noted, differential diagnosis of gender dysphoria should be carefully examined to rule out gender-variant behaviors that are not caused by gender dysphoria. Counselors should take the biopsychosocial approach to assessment. It is important that a physical examination (e.g., sexual organs' development and hormones) is conducted to determine the biological development of a child. Psychological and social environment evaluations, through clinical interview or standardized assessments, assist counselors in achieving an understanding of a child's psychological state (e.g., severity of gender dysphoria and co-occurring mental health concerns) and environment (e.g., family and school). Counselors use clinical interviews, standardized assessments, or both in assessing gender dysphoria. Regardless of the chosen assessment methods, counselors should take a comprehensive approach to assessment of gender dysphoria by considering biological, psychological, and sociocultural aspects of a child's life. Take a moment to reflect on the questions indicated in Sidebar 15.6 in relation to assessment of gender dysphoria in children.

SIDEBAR 15.6:   ASSESSMENT OF GENDER DYSPHORIA IN CHILDREN

Reflect on the following questions:

- What can counselors do to provide comfort to and reduce anxiety of parents or caregivers and the child during the initial assessment? List behaviors, and provide a rationale for each behavior listed.
- What are possible questions to ask parents or caregivers about their child's gender dysphoria–related behaviors?
- What are possible questions to ask the child to describe his or her feelings and thoughts about his or her assigned and expressed gender?

CLINICAL INTERVIEW

To obtain a comprehensive assessment of the child, de Vries and Cohen-Kettenis (2012) recommended that counselors conduct a clinical interview with the child and parents or caregivers to understand gender dysphoria development and management strategies, as well as emotional and behavioral struggles that the child and parents or caregivers experience. Ideally, interviewing the child and parents or caregivers together may give counselors more information through observing their pattern of interactions and how they may contribute to the development of the child's gender dysphoria.

PSYCHOLOGICAL ASSESSMENT

When assessing gender dysphoria, it is critical that counselors understand normal gender development. In typical gender development, children may display gender-variant behaviors at times during their development. For example, a male-assigned toddler may love wearing his mom's high heels. This behavior may be influenced by gender curiosity and gender role exploration, not gender dysphoria. Counselors need to assess the child's understanding of her or his assigned gender and to gather information (e.g., emotions and behaviors) that indicate a child's desire to become the expressed gender. Clinical presentations of gender dysphoria vary by age. For example, a very young boy is extremely upset when learning that girls do not have a penis, whereas an older boy before entering the prepubertal period wishes he would grow breasts when he is older. In addition to assessment of the gender-dysphoric condition, counselors need to assess co-occurring mental health concerns (e.g., anxiety and depressive disorders, trauma history, and suicide risk) to understand the role gender dysphoria plays in the child's mental health and well-being (Coleman et al., 2012). The *DSM-5* notes that TGNC children may experience increased suicide risk because of a variety of factors (e.g., gender incongruence and bullying) and that suicidal risk may persist beyond a gender transition. Therefore, thorough and ongoing suicide assessment must be an integral aspect of diagnosis and clinical work with TGNC children.

In most cases, parents and caregivers are the reason for referral because they struggle with gender-variant behaviors of their children more than children do. Parents and caregivers may experience negative emotions, such as confusion, self-blame, isolation, and anger, because of their children's gender-dysphoric condition. They may not have accurate facts and understandings of gender dysphoria (e.g., every child will eventually need gender reassignment surgery to resolve gender-dysphoric conditions). It is important that counselors assess and validate these emotions and provide accurate information regarding gender dysphoria to parents and caregivers. Although some clinical researchers (e.g., de Vries & Cohen-Kettenis, 2012) recommend parents, caregivers, and counselors carefully observe the continued development of gender dysphoria in children before adolescence, there are no clear diagnostic guidelines of how counselors can assess the development and continuation of gender dysphoria as well as coexisting mental health symptoms because of gender discomfort.

SOCIOCULTURAL AND ENVIRONMENTAL ASSESSMENT

In addition to a thorough psychological evaluation, counselors should assess the sociocultural and environment contexts of the child. Culture plays an important role in conceptualizing gender dysphoria. Gender fixity and fluidity in gender development are more flexible in some cultures than in others. Although some cultural contexts have a higher degree of tolerance to gender nonconforming behaviors, others may view such behaviors as needing immediate intervention. These cultural beliefs and expectations influence families' and children's view of gender dysphoria and atypical gender development. Therefore, it is essential that counselors are culturally sensitive and take the cultural context of the child into account when assessing gender dysphoria (Newman, 2002). For instance, counselors should conduct a thorough cultural assessment of gender norms influencing a family's understandings and expectations of gender roles for their child.

A comprehensive picture of family, school, interpersonal relationships, and support of the child is important for counselors. For example, counselors should assess the child's home and school environment and how those affect a child's gender-dysphoric behaviors (e.g., punishment methods used to stop gender-dysphoric behaviors at home, conflicts with siblings, facing academic suspension because of gender behaviors, and poor peer relationships; Slesaransky-Poe et al., 2013). This is to help counselors determine safety issues of the child's current environment and perhaps history of the child's traumas. The information from assessments of social and environmental contexts of the child can be helpful during treatment planning and implementation.

STANDARDIZED ASSESSMENTS

Counselors may use standardized assessments with the child and parents or caregivers in conjunction with a clinical interview to get a more comprehensive picture of gender-dysphoric symptoms that a child experiences. Implementing valid and reliable assessments in evaluating the child's gender discomfort and displayed behaviors is critical for counselors. For children, direct observations of the child's behaviors, whether alone, with peers, or with parents, can be helpful for counselors to understand the child's behaviors better. Standardized assessments, symptom checklists, or questionnaires may also be used with older children who can read and understand the language in the assessment. For parents, in addition to the clinical interview, counselors can gather information through parent report by implementing standardized assessments, symptom checklists, or questionnaires (e.g., the Gender Identity Questionnaire by Johnson et al., 2004). For a comprehensive list of psychological assessments used in evaluating gender dysphoria in childhood, see Zucker, Wood, Singh, and Bradley (2012).

Assessment is an integral part of gender dysphoria treatment. Accurate diagnosis of gender dysphoria can help both the child and the parents or caregivers learn about treatment options. There is no doubt that gender-variant children face multiple challenges in various settings, including family, school, and community. Stigmatization associated with gender dysphoria creates psychological and social impacts on gender-variant children. In the next section, you will learn about treatment strategies and interventions to alleviate gender dysphoria.

Treatment Strategies and Interventions

A starting point for treatment strategies and interventions with TGNC children is specifically to develop a TGNC-affirmative approach. The ACA Competencies for Counseling with Transgender Clients (2010) detail many ways to develop this competence in terms of the self of the counselor, the interaction with TGNC people, and the counseling environment. Counselors should have an active, ongoing self-reflection on their gender journeys and related cultural contexts and worldviews that have shaped their gender identity; in addition, counselors should use this self-reflection to identify how these experiences and worldviews of gender influence their work with TGNC children.

To ensure TGNC-affirmative interactions with TGNC children, counselors educate themselves about TGNC-affirmative language, use of pronouns, and use of names. For instance, counselors may often work with TGNC children who use names or pronouns that are not in alignment with their assigned sex but are in alignment with their sense of gender identity or gender expression, and these TGNC children may have family members who refuse to use these terms or do not have TGNC-affirming attitudes and knowledge about the needs of TGNC children. In these instances, it is critical that counselors use the pronouns and names that the TGNC child uses, as well as provide active, ongoing psychoeducation and exploration of TGNC attitudes and knowledge with family members. In many instances, this psychoeducation will occur either inside a family counseling session or in separate sessions with the parents or other family members. In addition, counselor interventions also include helping family members who have little to no information about TGNC children to access online and offline resources (e.g., websites and books), support groups, and family members of TGNC children. A common reaction of family members of TGNC children can include grief and loss, which counselors are uniquely trained to explore.

When working with the TGNC child, counselors explore gender identity and gender expression in a variety of ways. Play therapy and expressive arts are helpful modalities to help TGNC children identify and express their gender with no restrictions (Brill & Pepper, 2008). Counselors should have access to a wide variety of toys and clothing for TGNC children to select from as they are in counseling. Noting the type of toys and clothing TGNC children select, however, should not be a major determinant of gender identity, but rather counselors should note patterns, likes, and dislikes that TGNC children have to support family understanding of TGNC needs in the home and school environments.

Another intervention area for counselors is their involvement in interdisciplinary care. The field of mental and physical health care with TGNC children is changing rapidly, so rapidly sometimes that mental and physical health care providers are not aware of revisions of major documents, such as the WPATH (2011) *Standards of Care*. The major documents (ACA, 2010; APA, 2015; Byne et al., 2012; Hembree et al., 2009) guiding counseling with TGNC children emphasize the important role of advocacy and education when working with other providers. An example is that a TGNC child may not have access to a pediatrician who is TGNC affirming and uses the correct pronouns and names with the TGNC child. In this instance, the counselor may need to facilitate education of a pediatrician who was not trained in TGNC-affirmative medicine. Ideally, the counselor should have TGNC-affirmative resources of providers working with TGNC children; however, there may be a shortage of these providers in the client's geographical area (Edwards-Leeper & Spack, 2012).

In addition, counselors working with TGNC children may use the ACA Advocacy Competencies (Lewis, Arnold, House, & Toporek, 2003) to guide their counseling interventions. The ACA Advocacy Competency domains include microlevel, mesolevel, and macrolevel opportunities for interventions, and each of these three domains is differentiated by activities a counselor engages in *with* clients through empowerment interventions or *on behalf* of clients through advocacy interventions. At the microlevel, counselors may act with TGNC children collaboratively to identify strengths in terms of their gender identity and gender expression, while teaching self-advocacy skills for TGNC children (e.g., how to select a public bathroom and how to speak with teachers or school counselors if bullied). When acting on behalf of TGNC children at the microlevel, the counselor may advocate for necessary health care and school-based needs that TGNC children have, as well as identify TGNC-affirming allies in their support networks. At the mesolevel, counselors may act with TGNC children to identify people in their settings whom they feel safe with and who affirm their gender, while acting on behalf of TGNC children through developing school and community collaborations and providing research and information on how best to support a TGNC child (e.g., use of correct names and pronouns, refraining from dividing up groups by gender, and supporting TGNC children in playing with gendered toys or wearing gendered clothing that they feel is right for their gender identity and gender expression). When working at the macrolevel, counselors will typically be advocating on behalf of TGNC children through, for example, developing TGNC-affirmative materials for schools and communities so that they can better meet TGNC children's needs, as well as lobbying for TGNC-affirming policy and legal changes. Counselors may be working simultaneously across the three levels as well. Many insurance companies may deny coverage to TGNC children for necessary medical care and base this denial on gender dysphoria being a mental health disorder excluding medical treatment (Edwards-Leeper & Spack, 2012). In these cases, counselors may be advocating with the insurance company specifically, as well as considering connecting with TGNC reform advocates working on policy and legal change (Gonzalez & McNulty, 2010).

A summary list of the six major counselor roles guiding interventions with TGNC children follows (WPATH, 2011).

Counselor Roles When Working with TGNC Children (WPATH, 2011, p. 14)

1. Directly assess gender dysphoria in children and adolescents ...

2. Provide family counseling and supportive psychotherapy to assist children and adolescents with exploring their gender identity, alleviating distress related to their gender dysphoria, and ameliorating any other psychosocial difficulties.

3. Assess and treat any coexisting mental health concerns of children or adolescents (or refer to another mental health professional for treatment). Such concerns should be addressed as part of the overall treatment plan.

4. Refer adolescents for additional physical interventions (such as puberty-suppressing hormones) to alleviate gender dysphoria. The referral should include documentation of an assessment of gender dysphoria and mental health, the adolescent's eligibility for physical interventions ... , the mental health professional's relevant expertise, and any other information pertinent to the youth's health and referral for specific treatments.

5. Educate and advocate on behalf of gender dysphoric children, adolescents, and their families in their community (e.g., day care centers, schools, camps, other organizations). This is particularly important in light of evidence that children and adolescents who do not conform to socially prescribed gender norms may experience harassment in school (Grossman, D'Augelli, & Salter, 2006; Grossman, D'Augelli, Howell, & Hubbard, 2006; Sausa, 2005), putting them at risk for social isolation, depression, and other negative sequelae (Nuttbrock et al., 2010).

6. Provide children, youth, and their families with information and referral for peer support, such as support groups for parents of gender-nonconforming and transgender children (Gold & MacNish, 2011; Pleak, 1999; Rosenberg, 2002).

Evaluation Strategies

Counselors should have an understanding of how they may evaluate diagnosis and treatment with TGNC children, including developing the knowledge and skills required to explain issues of prognosis and the effect counseling will have to TGNC children. Existing research suggests that a small percentage of children with a TGNC identity will have this identity persist until later in life (Edwards-Leeper & Spack, 2012; Zucker et al., 2012). Evaluation should support TGNC children in alleviating the distress they may feel because of gender dysphoria (WPATH, 2011). This evaluation should include attention to whether a social transition might be helpful for the TGNC child (Brill & Pepper, 2008). This social transition may involve selecting among the following avenues according to concerns of timing and safety: (a) supporting TGNC children expressing their gender identity within the home, for example using names and pronouns in alignment with the child's gender identity; (b) finding longer periods to be able to support the TGNC child in expressing his or her gender identity, for instance on vacations or in public spaces that may be more TGNC affirmative than a family's current neighborhood or community; and (c) collaborating with school personnel to support a TGNC child's full social transition in terms of name, pronouns, dress, and other matters related to his or her identified gender (Hembree et al., 2009; WPATH, 2011).

Diagnostic Challenges and Other Specified and Unspecified Designations

A common diagnostic challenge that counselors will encounter when working with TGNC children is the tension between the gender binary that some TGNC children will identify within and the gender fluidity that many TGNC children demonstrate (Wallace & Russell, 2013). Some TGNC children will assert their identified gender clearly verbally and through their desire in clothing and toy selection, for instance. Other TGNC children, however, may not use words that align with social constructs of the gender binary—such as asserting, "I am not a boy or a girl." It is important in these situations to provide ongoing information and education to family members and to the TGNC children themselves that the gender binary is limited and by its very nature does not comprehensively include the multitude of gender identities. In addition, some TGNC children will self-identify strictly within the gender binary ("I am a girl," or "I am a boy") but over time may also move away from a TGNC gender to a cisgender identity where their assigned sex is in alignment with their identified gender (Edwards-Leeper & Spack, 2012; Steensma, McGuire, Kreukels, Beekman, & Cohen-Kettenis, 2013). In these cases, family members—who often have invested significant energy into understanding and supporting their child's TGNC identity – may have difficulty accepting that their child is now identifying as cisgender. This is one of the reasons the counselor role of educating family members about the fluidity of gender identity development and gender expression is so important throughout the counseling process.

An additional challenge involves educating other providers on how to diagnose gender dysphoria appropriately in childhood. Mental health and other health care providers may lack education on the recent changes in diagnosing TGNC children, or they may be using alternate diagnostic criteria, such as the most recent *International Statistical Classification of Diseases and Related Health Problems, Tenth Revision (ICD-10)*, or previous version of the *ICD* because of health insurance requirements. The challenge with this use of the *ICD-10* and its earlier versions is that the diagnostic criteria in the *DSM-5* and *ICD-10* are not in alignment, with the *ICD-10* retaining Gender Identity Disorder of Childhood. The diagnostic criteria of this disorder reflect earlier, more restrictive conceptions of gender dysphoria in childhood. In these situations, counselors may endeavor to provide the most accurate and up-to-date information on best diagnostic practices with TGNC children (e.g., providing professional documents from the ACA, APA, WPATH, and others).

Another major diagnostic challenge when working with TGNC children preparing the child and family members for the transition from childhood into early adolescence. As discussed previously, researchers have suggested that the number of TGNC children who persist into a TGNC-identified adolescence and adulthood is small (Zucker et al., 2012). In addition, adolescence is a time of extraordinary developmental change (Edwards-Leeper & Spack, 2012); therefore, TGNC children and families may or may not have the information and resources they need for potential future health care decisions. The Tanner Stages describe the physical changes that occur in puberty (e.g., hair growth and secondary sex characteristic development), and pediatric endocrinologists use the Tanner Stages to guide medical interventions with TGNC adolescents. Early to midway in puberty, Tanner Stage 2–3, TGNC adolescents typically are treated with puberty suppression hormones, such as GnRH analog (Edwards-Leeper & Spack, 2012). This medical intervention allows TGNC adolescents to continue to explore their gender identity and gender expression, while not experiencing secondary sex characteristic development that can be quite traumatic for them and also not having irreversible effects of sex-specific hormones. If a TGNC adolescent identity continues by age 16 and if parental consent is secured, endocrinologists may begin to treat TGNC adolescents with sex-specific hormones (e.g., testosterone and estrogen; WPATH, 2011). Throughout the transition to adolescence from childhood, counselors continue the six major roles outlined in the WPATH *Standards of Care* (2011) discussed earlier in this chapter.

Summary

This chapter provided an overview of the major considerations counselors should keep in mind when providing TGNC-affirming diagnosis, assessment, treatment, intervention, and evaluation. The authors also reviewed common diagnostic challenges and opportunities counselors working with TGNC children encounter. Considering the pathology-focused history the field of TGNC mental health care has had and the extensive societal oppression TGNC children may face, the authors also highlighted the critical role of counselor advocacy in counseling TGNC children. The following References provide additional information relating to the chapter topics.

References

Adelson, S. L., & American Academy of Child and Adolescent Psychiatry Committee on Quality Issues. (2012). Practice parameter on gay, lesbian, or bisexual sexual orientation, gender nonconformity, and gender discordance in children and adolescents. *Journal of the American Academy of Child & Adolescent Psychiatry, 51*(9), 957–974. Retrieved from http://download.journals.elsevierhealth.com/pdfs/journals/0890–8567/PIIS089085671200500X.pdf

American Counseling Association. (2010). American Counseling Association competencies for counseling with transgender clients. *Journal of LGBT Issues in Counseling, 4*(3–4), 135–159. doi:10.1080/15538605.2010.524839

American Psychiatric Association. (1980). *Diagnostic and statistical manual of mental disorders* (3rd ed.). Washington, DC: Author.

American Psychiatric Association. (1994). *Diagnostic and statistical manual of mental disorders* (4th ed.). Washington, DC: Author.

American Psychiatric Association. (2000). *Diagnostic and statistical manual of mental disorders* (4th ed., text revision). Washington, DC: Author.

American Psychiatric Association. (2013a). *Diagnostic and statistical manual of mental disorders* (5th ed.). Arlington, VA: American Psychiatric Publishing.

American Psychiatric Association. (2013b). Highlights of changes from DSM-IV TR to DSM 5. Retrieved from http://www.dsm5.org/Documents/changes%20from%20dsm-iv-tr%20to%20dsm-5.pdf

American Psychological Association. (2015). *Guidelines for psychological practice with transgender and gender non-conforming clients*. Manuscript in preparation.

Brill, S. A., & Pepper, R. (2008). *The transgender child: A handbook for families and professionals*. San Francisco, CA: Cleis Press.

Bryant, K. (2006). Making gender identity disorder of childhood: Historical lessons for contemporary debates. *Sexuality Research and Social Policy, 3*(3), 23–39.

Byne, W., Bradley, S. J., Coleman, E., Eyler, A. E., Green, R., Menvielle, E. J ... Tompkins, D. A. (2012). Report of the American Psychiatric Association Task Force on the treatment of Gender Identity Disorder. *Archives of Sexual Behavior, 41*(4), 759–796. doi:10.1007/s10508-012-9975-x

Carrillo, B., Gómez-Gil, E., Rametti, G., Junque, C., Gomez, Á., Karadi, K., ... Guillamon, A. (2010). Cortical activation during mental rotation in male-to-female and female-to-male transsexuals under hormonal treatment. *Psychoneuroendocrinology, 35*(8), 1213–1222.

Cohen-Kettenis, P. T., Owen, A., Kaijser, V. G., Bradley, S. J., & Zucker, K. J. (2003). Demographic characteristics, social competence, and behavior problems in children with gender identity disorder: A cross-national, cross-clinic comparative analysis. *Journal of Abnormal Child Psychology, 31*(1), 41–53.

Coleman, E., Bockting, W., Botzer, M., Cohen-Kettenis, P., DeCuypere, G., Feldman, J., ... Zucker, K. (2011). Standards of care for the health of transsexual, transgender and gender non-conforming people, version 7. *International Journal of Transgenderism, 13*, 165–232. doi:10.1080/15532739.2011.700873

Coleman, E., Bockting, W., Botzer, M., Cohen-Kettenis, P., DeCuypere, G., Feldman, J., ... Zucker, K. (2012). Standards of care for the health of transsexual, transgender, and gender-nonconforming people, Version 7. *International Journal of Transgenderism, 13*(4), 165–232.

Dermer, S. B., Smith, S. D., & Barto, K. K. (2010). Identifying and correctly labeling sexual prejudice, discrimination, and oppression. *Journal of Counseling & Development, 88*(3), 325–331. doi:10.1002/j.1556-6678.2010.tb00029.x

de Vries, A. L. C., & Cohen-Kettenis, P. T. (2012). Clinical management of gender dysphoria in children and adolescents: The Dutch approach. *Journal of Homosexuality, 59*(3), 301–320. doi:10.1080/00918369.2012.653300

de Vries, A. L. C., Doreleijers, T. A. H., Steensma, T. D., & Cohen-Kettenis, P. T. (2011). Psychiatric comorbidity in gender dysphoric adolescents. *Journal of Child Psychology and Psychiatry, 52*(11), 1195–1202.

de Vries, A. L. C., Noens, I. L. J., Cohen-Kettenis, P. T., van Berckelaer-Onnes, I. A., & Doreleijers, T. A. (2010). Autism spectrum disorders in gender dysphoric children and adolescents. *Journal of Autism and Developmental Disorders, 40*(8), 930–936.

Edwards-Leeper, L., & Spack, N. P. (2012). Psychological evaluation and medical treatment of transgender youth in an interdisciplinary "Gender Management Service" (GeMS) in a major pediatric center. *Journal of Homosexuality, 59*(3), 321–336. doi:10.1080/00918369.2012.653302

Ehrensaft, D. (2012). From gender identity disorder to gender identity creativity: True gender self child therapy. *Journal of Homosexuality, 59*(3), 337–356. doi:10.1080/00918369.2012.653303

Elizabeth, P. H., & Green, R. (1984). Childhood sex-role behaviors: Similarities and differences in twins. *Acta Geneticae Medicae et Gemellologiae, 33,* 173–179.

Gonzalez, M., & McNulty, J. (2010). Achieving competency with transgender youth: School counselors as collaborative advocates. *Journal of LGBT Issues in Counseling, 4*(3–4), 176–186. doi:10.1080/15538605.2010.524841

Hembree, W. C., Cohen-Kettenis, P., Delemarre-van de Waal, H. A., Gooren, L. J., Meyer, W. J., Spack, N. P., ... Montori, V. M. (2009). Endocrine treatment of transsexual persons: An Endocrine Society clinical practice guideline. *Journal of Clinical Endocrinology & Metabolism, 94*(9), 3132–3154. doi:10.1210/jc.2009-0345

Johnson, L. L., Bradley, S. J., Birkenfeld-Adams, A. S., Kuksis, M. A., Maing, D. M., Mitchell, J. N, & Zucker, K. J. (2004). A parent-report Gender Identity Questionnaire for Children. *Archives of Sexual Behavior, 33*(2), 105–116.

King, J. H. (2014). *Using the DSM-5: Try it, you'll like it.* Retrieved from http://www.continuingedcourses.net/active/courses/course081.php

Kohlberg, L. (1966). A cognitive-developmental analysis of children's sex-role concepts and attitudes. In E. E. Maccoby (Ed.), *The development of sex differences* (pp. 82–173). Stanford, CA: Stanford University.

Lewis, J. A., Arnold, M. S., House, R., & Toporek, R. L. (2003). *Advocacy competencies.* Retrieved from http://www.counseling.org/docs/competencies/advocacy_competencies.pdf?sfvrsn=3

Meyer-Bahlburg, H. F. L. (2010). From mental disorder to iatrogenic hypogonadism: Dilemmas in conceptualizing gender identity variants as psychiatric conditions. *Archives of Sexual Behavior, 39*(2), 461–476.

Nanda, S. (1998). *Neither man nor woman: The Hijras of India* (2nd ed). Belmont, CA: Wadsworth Cengage Learning.

Newman, L. K. (2002). Sex, gender, and culture: Issues in the definition, assessment, and treatment of gender identity disorder. *Clinical Child Psychology and Psychiatry, 7*(3), 352–359.

Roberts, J., & Singh, A. (2014). Trans and gender non-conforming global leaders. In L. Erickson-Schroth (Ed.), *Trans bodies, trans selves: A resource for the transgender community.* New York, NY: Oxford Press.

Ruble, D. N., Martin, C. L., & Berenbaum, S. A. (2006). Gender development. In W. Damon & R. M. Lerner (Series Eds.) & N. Eisenberg (Vol. Ed.), *Handbook of Child Psychology: Volume 3: Social, emotional, and personality development* (6th ed., pp. 858–932). Hoboken, NJ: John Wiley & Sons.

Siegal, M., & Robinson, J. (1987). Order effects in children's gender-constancy responses. *Developmental Psychology, 23*(2), 283–286. doi:10.1037/0012-1649.23.2.283

Slesaransky-Poe, G., Ruzzi, L., Dimedio, C., & Stanley, J. (2013). Is this the right elementary school for my gender nonconforming child? *Journal of LGBT Youth, 10*(1–2), 29–44. doi:10.1080/19361653.2012.718521

Steensma, T. D., McGuire, J. K., Kreukels, B. P., Beekman, A. J., & Cohen-Kettenis, P. T. (2013). Factors associated with desistence and persistence of childhood gender dysphoria: A quantitative follow-up study. *Journal of the American Academy of Child & Adolescent Psychiatry, 52*(6), 582–590. doi:10.1016/j.jaac.2013.03.016

Wallace, R., & Russell, H. (2013). Attachment and shame in gender-nonconforming children and their families: Toward a theoretical framework for evaluating clinical interventions. *International Journal of Transgenderism, 14*(3), 113–126. 10.1080/15532739.2013.824845

Wallien, M. S. C., & Cohen-Kettenis, P. T. (2008). Psychosexual outcome of gender-dysphoric children. *Journal of the American Academy of Child & Adolescent Psychiatry, 47*(12), 1413–1423. doi:10.1097/CHI.0b013e31818956b9

White, T., & Ettner, R. (2004). Disclosure, risks and protective factors for children whose parents are undergoing a gender transition. *Journal of Gay & Lesbian Psychotherapy, 8*(1/2), 129–147.

Winters, K. (2008). *Issues of psychiatric diagnosis for gender non-conforming youth.* Retrieved from http://www.gidreform.org/gid3026.html

Zucker, K. J., Wood, H., Singh, D., & Bradley, S. J. (2012). A developmental, biopsychosocial model for the treatment of children with gender identity disorder. *Journal of Homosexuality, 59*(3), 369–397. doi:10.1080/00918369.2012.653309

Chapter 16

Disruptive, Impulse-Control, and Conduct Disorders

A. STEPHEN LENZ AND CHLOE LANCASTER

Introduction

This chapter will discuss a new cluster of diagnosable disorders within the *Diagnostic and Statistical Manual of Mental Disorders, Fifth Edition* (*DSM*-5), that counselors may encounter when working with children and adolescents who are disruptive, who lack effective impulse control, or whose conduct violates the rights or safety of themselves or others (see Sidebar 16.1). Of course, all children and adolescents experience some deficits and manifestations of these characteristics throughout normal development; however, when these activities become the usual mode of activity, a referral for counseling may help prevent negative life outcomes. Thus, it is critical that the frequency, persistence, pervasiveness across situations, and impairment associated with the behaviors indicative of the diagnosis be considered relative to what is normative for a person's age, gender, and culture when determining whether he or she is symptomatic of a disorder. Specifically, the diagnoses included within the broad category of disruptive, impulse-control, and conduct disorders include (a) oppositional defiant disorder (ODD), (b) intermittent explosive disorder (IED), (c) conduct disorder (CD), (d) antisocial personality disorder (ASP), (e) pyromania, (f) kleptomania, and (g) other specified and unspecified disruptive, impulse-control, and conduct disorders.

Each of the disorders discussed in this chapter is demarked by different combinations of problems related to self-control characterized by emotional (anger and irritation) and behavioral (argumentativeness and defiance) dysregulation. Although pyromania and kleptomania represent unique expressions of these characteristics, ODD, IED, CD, and ASP are at the heart of this diagnostic category and may be conceptualized along a continuum in which personal functioning and symptom severity are affected to different degrees. A visual depiction of this relationship that has been helpful to our students and colleagues is illustrated in Figure 16.1.

As a result, the symptoms discussed within this chapter are common causes of referrals to counselors across settings and specializations. Given the social consequences associated with disruptive, impulse-control, and conduct disorders, it is prudent for counselors to become familiar with the best practices for recognizing and treating these disorders. Furthermore, Sidebar 16.1 will support understanding of the differences from previous conceptualizations of these disorders and how they have evolved over time.

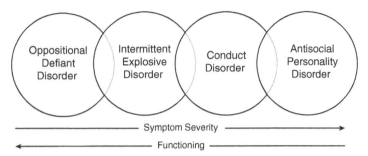

FIGURE 16.1 Continuum of Personal Functioning and Symptom Severity among Oppositional Defiant Disorder, Intermittent Explosive Disorder, Conduct Disorder, and Antisocial Personality Disorder

After reading this chapter, you will be able to identify and discuss (a) characteristics of these disorders, (b) strategies for assessment and intervention, and (c) considerations for evaluating progress.

SIDEBAR 16.1: EMERGENCE OF THIS DIAGNOSTIC CATEGORY WITHIN THE *DSM-5*

The inclusion of a chapter that characterized symptom clusters within the scope of disruptive, impulse-control, and conduct disorders is a new addition to this iteration of the *DSM*. The included disorders were previously presented across multiple chapters but consolidated based on problems related to behaviors that violate the rights of others (e.g., aggression and destruction of property) or that bring the individual into significant conflict with societal norms or authority figures. Within the composite disorders, oppositional defiant disorder criteria were equivocally refined by the grouping of common symptoms, an emphasis on frequency of problem behavior, and clarification using a severity specifier based on the prevalence of problems across settings. Intermittent explosive disorder also underwent significant restrictions and now requires counselors to be much more precise when describing symptoms and related impairments to promote more accurate diagnosis of the disorder. Finally, although the criteria for conduct disorder were unaltered, increased specification of limited prosocial emotions were included following a review of research findings.

Oppositional Defiant Disorder

Children and adolescents presenting with oppositional defiant disorder (ODD) typically display a negativistic pattern of behaviors that limit social and academic development. Although all children will exhibit bouts of stubbornness, disobedience, and tantrums, the frequency, severity, pervasiveness, and degree of impairment in functioning distinguishes ODD from what is reasonable within typical growth. The challenge presented to parents and teachers for managing the vacillating emotions and behavior among children with ODD can be quite difficult to manage, which is why ODD is a common referral issue among counselors working with this population treat.

DSM-5 Criteria

ODD is characterized by "a pattern of angry/irritable mood, argumentative/defiant behavior, or vindictiveness lasting at least 6 months" (American Psychiatric Association [APA], 2013, p. 462). To meet criteria for ODD, children must exhibit at least four symptoms within these three domains with someone who is not their sibling. The criteria include an angry/irritable mood (e.g., frequently loses temper or demonstrates intense bouts of aggression in response to annoyance), argumentative/defiant behavior (e.g., frequently engages in disrespectful conflict with people in positions of authority or adults in general), and vindictiveness (e.g., has been unpleasant, malicious, or vindictive at least two times within the past six months). Among children who are younger than 5 years, a diagnosis of ODD is indicated only when symptoms are manifest most days during the requisite six-month period; unless otherwise noted (Criterion A.8.), once children reach 5 years and older, symptoms need only be observed once per week for six months for ODD to be indicated.

In addition to meeting four symptom criteria over a six-month period, a diagnosis of ODD is indicated only when the observed emotional and behavioral dysregulation causes distinctive distress in the child or others within important social contexts, such as home, school, or recreational programs. The emotional and behavioral dysregulation manifests in decreased functioning or ability to achieve at age-appropriate levels within typical contexts. For example, children may become determined to win disputes with a teacher to the point that they are excused from class or to a degree that their academic development becomes impaired. In another example, a child with ODD may demonstrate a distinct intolerance or impatience with peers that results in social isolation and stymied social skills development. Counselors indicate the pervasiveness of impaired functioning across contexts using the specifiers *mild*, *moderate*, and *severe*. *Mild* indicates the symptoms are limited to one setting, *moderate* reflects the presence of symptoms in two settings, and *severe* notes that symptoms are present in three or more settings.

Differential Diagnosis

Oppositional and negativistic disposition are common among several other disorders (e.g., psychotic, bipolar, depressive, trauma- and stressor-related, and autism spectrum) and may even indicate high risk factor for development of later conduct disorder, anxiety, and depression (Copeland, Shanahan, Costello, & Angold, 2009; Quy & Stringaris, 2012). When determining the appropriateness of a diagnosis of ODD, counselors should rule out the presence of related disruptive, impulse-control, and conduct disorders (CD and IED), depressive disorders, bipolar and related disorders, impairments in abilities to comprehend information from the environment (intellectual disability or language disorder), fears related to evaluations by others (social anxiety disorder), and substance use disorders (APA, 2013; Quy & Stringaris, 2012).

Assessment Strategies

Prudent determination of an ODD diagnosis and related severity relies predominately on assessment of important psychosocial domains, review of formal assessment data, and direct observation. In each case, the presenting symptoms should be considered across contexts and in reference to situational variables. Therefore, collateral reports may be warranted from teachers or others who spend considerable time with the child or adolescent.

A rich psychosocial interview should include data related to (a) developmental issues that may present similarly to ODD, (b) history of abuse or neglect, (c) history of problematic substance use, (d) family dynamics and parenting style, and (e) the degree that the child's activities have endangered self or others. Several formal assessments of varying length are available for counselors. Longer, more comprehensive assessments may be completed using the *DSM-5* Cross-Cutting Symptom Measures, the Eyberg Child Behavior Inventory (CBI; Eyberg & Pincus, 1999), and Child Behavior Checklist (CBCL; Achenbach & Rescorla, 2001). Observations of child behavior can implement assessment protocols such as the Disruptive Behaviour Diagnostic Observation Schedule (DB-DOS; Wakschlag et al., 2008a; Wakschlag et al., 2008b) and may be completed in a number of settings, depending on the availability and background of counselors. Relevant contexts may include the office, a playroom, a school, the community, and the family home. Sidebar 16.2 provides an opportunity for you practice making diagnostic impressions given knowledge of diagnostic criteria and information yielded from a psychosocial assessment.

SIDEBAR 16.2: CASE STUDY—DOES MICHAEL HAVE OPPOSITIONAL DEFIANT DISORDER?

Michael was referred recently to his high-school counselor after repeated instances of being generally irritable and a number of anger outbursts toward other students. When discussing the referral with Michael's parents, his school counselor discovers that they also have been experiencing difficulties with him cleaning his room, talking back, and not taking responsibility for his actions. Does Michael meet the criteria for ODD? How would your initial impression be changed if you discovered that his parents were getting divorced or that he was questioning his sexual identity?

TREATMENT STRATEGIES AND INTERVENTIONS

In some cases, untreated ODD may remit as merely a pronounced period of defiant behavior. Although medication, such as antidepressants or mood stabilizers, may be included in treatment protocols to manage some symptoms of ODD, it is generally regarded as an adjunct to one or a combination of individual, group, or family counseling approaches (American Academy of Child and Adolescent Psychiatry [AACAP], 2009). Regardless of modality, a strong working alliance with both the child and parents or guardians may promote treatment adherence and, thus, effectiveness. Substantial evidence has supported the use of parent management training programs (Kaminski, Valle, Filene, & Boyle, 2008), parent–child interaction therapy (Querido & Eyberg, 2005), family therapy (Carr, 2009), cognitive problem-solving skills training (Lochman, Powell, Boxmeyer, & Jimenez-Camargo, 2011), and social skills training (Joseph & Strain, 2003) for treating ODD.

Parent Management Training Programs

These strategies are based on social learning theory and teach parents how to use basic behavioral interventions with children, such as identifying prosocial or problematic behaviors, implementing positive and negative reinforcement, and increasing desired behaviors. Although many strategies are available for counselors to access, Kazdin's (2005) parent management training protocol provides detailed descriptions of in-session procedures, supportive materials, and a review of empirical studies that support the education, modeling, and practice of behavioral principles to manage ODD symptoms.

Parent–Child Interaction Therapy

This is a therapeutic approach integrating aspects of social learning theory, traditional play therapy, and attachment theory intended to enhance the quality of interactions within the parent–child relationship. This strategy may be indicated when ODD symptoms are contextually associated with parent–child interactions.

Family Therapy

This approach is intended to promote developmental change and well-being through changing family dynamics and includes interventions such as psychoeducation, communication skills training, systems coaching, and related strategies. This strategy may be indicated when ODD symptoms occur with multiple family members or in other systems that resemble the family structure. Some family therapy approaches indicated for treatment of ODD include functional family therapy (Alexander & Parsons, 1982) which focuses on multiple aspects of functioning (i.e., cognitive, affective, and behavioral) across multiple aspects of a family system. Another popular approach, brief strategic family therapy (Szapocznik, Scopetta, & King, 1978), focuses on decreasing unhelpful family interactions, family alliances that cause difficulties, overly rigid or permeable boundaries between family members, and the blaming of one person for the family's troubles.

Cognitive Problem-Solving Skills Training

This approach educates, models, and practices systematic strategies for finding adaptive approaches to solving everyday problems within the social environment that is associated with ODD symptoms. This approach may be indicated when clients demonstrate a low threshold for distress tolerance that is accompanied by ODD symptoms.

Social Skills Training

Social skills training engages clients in the intentional learning and practice of basic to advanced social interaction behaviors associated with actively contributing to conversations, collaborating with others, and helping behaviors. These skills are intended to promote social reinforcement for peers and important others and may be indicated in the absence of such behaviors within the regular behavioral repertoire. One example of social skills training is aggression replacement training (Glick & Gibbs, 2011), which integrates strategies intended to promote use of positive social skills, anger management, and moral reasoning rather than oppositional or aggressive alternatives.

EVALUATION STRATEGIES

Although the course and severity of ODD symptoms has been closely linked to parent factors, especially early in development (APA, 2013), research regarding the effectiveness of counseling interventions for ODD is promising. Successful treatment of ODD symptoms is contextually referenced to the goals of individual families, but in cases effective treatment may represent nearly complete symptom remission; in other cases, successful treatment may be as lofty as changes in the family system that improve overall systemic functioning or as simple as keeping a child in the classroom so that he or she may stay academically on track. Some experts have suggested that, if unmitigated, children who meet the criteria for ODD may subsequently present with symptoms of conduct disorder (Connor, 2002; Diamantopoulou, Verhulst, & van der Ende, 2011). Therefore, evaluation of ODD symptoms should occur regularly by using *DSM-5* cross-cutting symptom measures and disorder specific severity measures and engaging the same collateral reports used to make the diagnosis. By assessing changes in psychosocial variables, scores on formal assessments completed by significant others (parents and teachers), and follow-up observations, a more accurate evaluation of treatment response can be noted. Many packaged programs developed to treat ODD (e.g., the Adolescent Transitions Program) come with their own measures related to specific treatment goals.

DIAGNOSTIC CHALLENGES

One of the most daunting challenges when determining a diagnosis of ODD is distinguishing the degree that presenting behaviors and attitudes are part of the typical developmental process or warrant clinical attention. This distinction is particularly complicated by the myriad expressions that cultural groups may endorse as suitable means for expressing discontent or asserting one's will. Furthermore, the symptoms of ODD are shared with numerous other clinical syndromes, so special attention should be given to differential diagnoses.

Intermittent Explosive Disorder

DESCRIPTION OF THE DISORDER

Children and adolescents with intermittent explosive disorder (IED) are distinguished by an inability to control their anger or temper, frequently resulting in discrete acts of aggression directed at individuals, objects, or animals. Intermittent explosive disorder first appeared in the third edition of the *Diagnostic and Statistical Manual of Mental Disorders* (APA, 1980), and although definitions have evolved with each subsequent edition, the most salient characteristic of this disorder is the tendency for individuals to exhibit levels of aggressive behavior disproportionate to the psychosocial stressor (Olvera et al., 2001). The typical onset of diagnosis is likely to occur in late childhood or adolescence, with very few new cases originating after middle adulthood (APA, 2013).

DSM-5 CRITERIA

Children with IED are prone to unprovoked acts of aggression, including verbal aggression, but also can be observed making behavioral outbursts characterized by the absence of provocation. Diagnosis can be made when children reach the chronological age of 6, or equivalent developmental level. The taxonomy of symptoms includes a frequent loss of emotional and behavioral control manifested through aggressive outbursts. IED is characterized by disproportionate verbal or physical aggression toward a person, an animal, or property that does not result in bodily injury or property damage and occurs twice weekly, on average, for a period of three months. Persistent aggression is not premeditated or motivated by personal gain (e.g., as manifested in conduct disorder or antisocial personality disorder). Persistent aggression significantly impairs social functioning and can cause financial and legal problems. Aggressive outbursts are not better explained by another mental disorder. Children with IED exhibit two clinical patterns: Most frequent are nonviolent outbursts consisting of tantrums, arguments, and verbal tirades. These non-physical episodes are often accompanied by infrequent, yet violent, rages that result in physical harm to the child, other individuals, or property (Coccaro, 2012).

The level of fury that children exhibit during episodic rages can damage social relationships, and consequently children with IED often struggle to sustain friendships, develop low self-esteem, and are at greater risk for noncompletion of school and legal issues (APA, 2013). As expected, children's volatility places a strain on family life, particularly as they tend to overreact to discipline and exhibit aggression toward family members, and inconsistent explosions jeopardize common family activities.

DIFFERENTIAL DIAGNOSIS

IED is the only disorder that describes maladaptive, anger-based, aggressive outbursts in the absence of a mood disorder, psychosis, or another disruptive behavior disorder associated with predatory aggression. Accurate diagnosis of IED is imperative for developing treatment plans that specifically target nonpreempted episodic aggression. Physical and verbal tirades are central diagnostic criteria to other disorders, and a diagnosis of IED should be made only following the exclusion of other disorders (Coccaro, 2012). Most notably, the severe temper tantrums, tirades, verbal arguments, or impulsive, aggressive outbursts that characterize IED present almost identical symptomology to children with disruptive mood dysregulation disorder (DMDD). However, IED does not require children to manifest a persistent and severe irritable mood between temper tantrums or aggressive outbursts that occur in a minimum of two settings (e.g., home and school). IED is further distinguished from DMDD by a timeline that permits diagnosis at a three-month period following the presentation of symptoms. By contrast, DMDD cannot be diagnosed earlier than 12 months after the onset of symptoms. Both disorders are mutually exclusive, and if children present with aggression associated with severe and ongoing irritability, a diagnosis of DMDD would better explain the symptomology (APA, 2013).

There are also important neurobiological differences between IED and DMDD. Children with chronic irritability typically exhibit complicated psychiatric histories. There is also evidence for disorder-specific dysfunction, such as during tasks assessing attention deployment in response to emotional stimuli, which has demonstrated unique signs of dysfunction in children with chronic irritability (Brotman et al., 2010; Rich et al., 2007; Rich et al., 2011). Researchers have provided neurobiological support for the presence of serotonergic abnormalities, globally (Coccaro et al., 2010) and in the brain, specifically in areas of the limbic system (New et al., 2002) and orbitofrontal cortex (Siever et al., 1999) in individuals with IED.

The family of disruptive, impulse-control, and conduct disorders involves problems in emotional or behavioral regulation that violate the rights of others or that bring the individual into significant conflict with societal norms or authority figures. Therefore, IED diagnoses tend to have a high rate of co-occurrence with CD (19.3 percent), attention-deficit/hyperactivity disorder (ADHD; 17.2 percent), and other disruptive behavior disorders (37.9 percent; Coccaro, 2012). Because aggression and destruction of property can occur in the context of many other disorders (e.g., major depressive disorder, bipolar disorder, DMDD, a psychotic disorder, antisocial personality disorder, and borderline personality disorder), the *DSM-5* suggests that IED should be considered only when none of these other disorders better explains presenting symptoms. Despite the overlap, the context for aggression in CD is an intention to cause harm, gain control, or leverage power. By contrast, the recurrent aggressive outbursts associated with IED are not premeditated, serve no purposeful gain for the child or adolescent, and often weaken their relationship in social groups. Furthermore, the hallmark of CD is an absence of remorse following an act of aggression, whereas children and adolescents with IED are apt to demonstrate contrition upon their return to a calm state (Olvera, 2002). IED is more readily differentiated from ADHD, because although both share impulsivity as a critical diagnostic feature, verbal aggression and behavioral outbursts are not diagnostically associated with ADHD.

ASSESSMENT STRATEGIES

Researchers have suggested that restrictive criterion in previous *DSM* classifications most likely led to an underdiagnosing of IED among children and adolescents, who were diagnosed with a disorder that could account, in part, for unmitigated loss of emotional control (Coccaro, 2012). Furthermore, few valid and reliable psychometric assessments are normed with child and adolescent populations, hampering precision in the diagnosis of IED. The tool most frequently used in the assessment of IED is Coccaro's (1998) Interview Module for Intermittent Explosive Disorder (M-IED) revised. Although Coccaro originally designed the instrument for the diagnosis of adult populations, Olvera and colleagues (2001) found promising results in its use for children and adolescents, modified by having a parent or guardian completing the survey on behalf of younger children. The M-IED consists of a structured clinical interview that assesses the frequency of outbursts, level of aggression, and level of social impairment. To screen for other disorders that may better explain the underlying cause of the outburst, the M-IED includes items related to drug use, psychosis, depression, and medications. The limited availability of instrumentation requires assessment of IED to be a process of exclusion, wherein professionals rule out other disorders before considering an IED diagnosis. In this respect thorough clinical interviewing that identifies symptom onset, intensity, frequency, and duration is imperative to the process, as are a full medical and neurological examination and a careful examination of child's medical records. Garnering information from family members and significant adults, with whom the child interacts across different contexts, such as school personnel, coaches, and after school care providers, is also central to a prudent diagnostic process. Because children cannot readily explain the triggers and precise nature of their aggressive outbursts, soliciting information from a variety of informants (e.g., parents, siblings, teachers, and religious leaders) helps reduce bias and assists practitioners in determining whether the child's anger-based outburst is impulsive versus premeditated. Some authors have noted that it may be helpful to construct a graphic timeline, consisting of age, diagnosis, and significant life events on the X axis and corresponding severity of symptomology on the Y axis (Olvera, 2002). Comprehensive diagnostic approaches, such as these, oblige practitioners to consider underlying contextual factors (e.g., age, gender, and culture), including the effects of child development, trauma, abuse, or neglect that might have triggered the onset of behaviors consistent with an IED diagnosis.

TREATMENT STRATEGIES AND INTERVENTIONS

Although causative factors of IED have not been clearly established, advancements in neuroimaging have provided preliminary evidence to indicate that individuals with IED demonstrate amygdala overreactivity associated with poor inhibitory control. These findings have helped mental health practitioners understand children with IED's diminished emotional regulation and anger control relative to nonthreatening provocations (Coccaro, 2012). Nonetheless, knowledge of effective treatment options has not kept pace with neuropsychology because few clinical studies have been published over the past five years. In this respect the treatment options presented in the following section provide a comprehensive overview yet reflect limitations of current knowledge.

Medication

Children and adolescents with IED often have co-occurring mental health conditions, which complicate treatment options. Currently there is neither a cure for IED nor a medication or therapy modality designed specifically to militate associated symptoms. Central to treatment goals is aggression reduction, which according to researchers is best achieved through combining medication with counseling and psychotherapy (Olvera, 2002). Medications that have been found to promote anger regulation in both adult and child populations include antidepressants (namely, selective serotonin reuptake inhibitors, or SSRIs), mood stabilizers (lithium and anticonvulsants), antipsychotic drugs, and antiepileptic drugs (Stanford, Anderson, Lake, & Baldridge, 2009). Evidentiary support of the ameliorative effects of medication upon episodic anger has been demonstrated from research conducted with adults with IED and youth with aggressive CD. To date few clinically controlled trials have been conducted children and youth with IED, limiting knowledge of effective psychopharmacological options (Stanford et al., 2009; Olvera et al., 2001).

Cognitive Behavior Therapy

Cognitive behavior therapy (CBT) is the most widely recognized therapy for treating IED in child, youth, and adult populations. CBT procedures reportedly used by mental health professionals in the treatment of their clients with IED include modeling, relaxation training, cognitive restructuring, teaching coping skills, behavior rehearsal, and strategies to resist aggressive impulses (Del Vecchio & O'Leary, 2004). Support for this approach can be found from studies that report positive results for adult populations following participation in a CBT-oriented program (McCloskey, Noblett, Deffenbacher, Gollan, & Coccaro, 2008). Once again efficacious treatment planning is mired by the lack of clinical trials conducted specifically with child populations. Merit for the application of CBT procedures for children and adolescents with IED can be found in research conducted with children with generalized disruptive anger and mood disorders. Results from a meta-analysis indicated that children and youth who participate in CBT therapy programs that include components of modeling, cognitive coping skills, behavior modification, behavior rehearsal, and affective education markedly improved their anger regulation and emotional control (Sukhodolsky, Kassinove, Bernard, & Gorman, 2004). Although positive effects were noted for children of all ages, children under 10 demonstrated fewer gains than adolescents following participation in CBT programs. Furthermore, children with moderate anger disorders were more responsive to treatment than children with mild or severe anger disorders.

Play Therapy

Play therapy is a developmentally informed approach that uses play as a therapeutic medium for children to overcome developmental hurdles and achieve optimum growth and development. Play therapy is most often used with children 12 and under, who have not reached a stage of cognitive development that would permit them to engage in talk therapy as a means to verbalize conflicts and resolve issues in their lives effectively (Kottman, 2011). The ameliorative effects of play therapy for children with IED are not well documented; however, extensive clinical case studies have reported on the benefits of play therapy for reducing anger and promoting emotional control for children with diagnosed and undiagnosed aggressive disorders (Schaefer & Mattei, 2005). Structured play therapy may be a more prudent approach for children with more severe behavior disorders (Kottman, 2011). For instance, Theraplay, a mode of intervention that integrates games and other forms of play as a featured component of treatment, has been found to decrease anger in children, through procedures that blend play with social skills training. This directive approach also includes parents in the therapeutic process, which can assist children in transferring learning to environments outside the therapy setting. Although traditional play therapy and Theraplay offer a viable alternative to CBT in the reduction of aggression in younger children, empirical studies are needed to further examine structural aspects of play therapy that may promote positive change for children with IED. Sidebar 16.3 illustrates the case of Sofía and provides practice with evaluating some considerations that counselors address when selecting the types of treatments associated with IED.

SIDEBAR 16.3:   CASE ILLUSTRATION—WHAT TREATMENT WOULD YOU RECOMMEND?

Sofía, an 11-year-old girl from the Southwestern region of the United States, was brought in to a community-based counseling agency after her parents had difficulty managing quickly precipitating tantrums, arguments, and verbal tirades of others. After reviewing the family psychosocial history, conducting a clinical interview, and reviewing assessment data, a diagnosis of IED was assigned. What treatments would you recommend for Sofía? How important is her age in determining your selection of a treatment protocol?

EVALUATION STRATEGIES

IED appears to follow a chronic and persistent course over many years that may be episodic, with recurrent periods of impulsive, aggressive outbursts (Kessler & Üstün, 2008). Determining the effect of treatment on long-term outcomes for children with IED is obscured by high rates of comorbidity with other mood, impulsive, and disruptive disorders (Coccaro, 2012). Poorer outcomes have been detected among those youth with dual or multiple diagnoses. Youth with diagnoses that include combinations of IED, CD, and ADHD are at greater risk for delinquency, recidivism, and incarceration. Although researchers have not confidently determined which disorder primarily accounts for the manifestation of these outcomes, those youth who demonstrate a subtype of reactive-hostile aggression, paired with impulsivity, have been found to have poorer outcomes into adulthood (Coccaro, 2012). Nonetheless, all children with an IED diagnosis face challenges that impair their social functioning, particularly because their eruptive tempers can isolate them from peers and lead to the development of low self-esteem (Coccaro, 2012). Over time children and adolescents with IED are at greater risk for engaging in self-harm and elevated risk for suicide during adolescence and young adulthood (Olvera et al., 2001). Depending on the frequency, duration, and intensity of externalizing behaviors, children with IED can also experience patterns of school failure. Children's proclivity toward unprovoked outbursts and low frustration tolerance interfere with their learning and can result in disciplinary consequences that remove them from the classroom, which further jeopardizes their academic achievement.

Balancing medication with therapy appears integral to managing the disorder and promoting optimal outcomes (Olvera, 2002). The length of time that children can expect to experience positive gains in the context of counseling depends on the therapeutic modality. Researchers have found promising treatment effects for children and adolescents with anger dysregulation who participate in CBT programs ranging from 10 to 18 weeks (McCloskey et al., 2008); however, follow-up research is needed to determine the maintenance of treatment effects following program completion. Play therapy offers an alternative approach for younger children for whom talk therapy may be unsuitable.

DIAGNOSTIC CHALLENGES

Recent estimates indicate that lifetime prevalence rates of IED occur in 3 percent of the total U.S. population (APA, 2013). Although there is no single known cause for IED, prevalence rates are markedly lower in certain Asian countries and Eastern Europe, leading some researchers to conclude that there may be a cultural dimension to the disorder related to socially permissible aggression (Kessler et al., 2006). This section discussed several diagnostic challenges related to coexisting conditions that interfere with precision in the diagnostic process. Nonetheless, it is worth noting that researchers have found that IED is not triggered by other disorders, because it often precedes the onset of disruptive behavior disorders or mood disorders (Kessler et al., 2006). In this respect, the loss of social functioning, academic declines, and anxiety that accompany IED symptomology may actuate the development of other mental health disorders in late adolescence and into adulthood, particularly depression and substance abuse disorders.

Conduct Disorder

Children and adolescents presenting with conduct disorder (CD) are often viewed by others as being negligent and offending to a degree that interferes with the rights and functioning of others. Whereas IED is characterized by impulsive (or anger-based), aggressive outbursts, CD represents repetitive and persistent behaviors that bring the individual into significant conflict with societal norms or authority figures (AACAP, 2013; APA, 2013). For this reason, adolescents with CD may be at risk for expulsion from school, problems adjusting to work environments, and legal adjudication. Some evidence indicates that, if untreated, the persistence of CD into early adulthood may predict deleterious psychosocial outcomes related to academic underachievement, incarceration, substance use, co-occurring mental health symptoms, and troubled interpersonal relationships (Castellanos-Ryan & Conrad, 2011; Fergusson, Horwood, & Ridde, 2005). For most individuals the symptoms of CD tend to wane by adulthood as part of the developmental process (APA, 2013), with a more promising prognosis for individuals with later onset of symptoms (e.g., after age 10) when compared with those with an earlier indication of symptoms (e.g., prior to age 10). Although counselors in many contexts may assist clients with CD, those professionals working in forensic or correctional settings may encounter individuals presenting with this diagnosis with regularity.

DSM-5 CRITERIA

CD represents a repetitive and persistent set of behaviors that either violate the rights of others or demonstrate disregard for major age-appropriate standards (AACAP, 2013; APA, 2013). To meet criteria for CD, children must exhibit at least three symptom criteria from any of the available four categories in the past 12 months, with at least one symptom occurring in the past six months. The criteria are specific to categories of aggression to people (e.g., often bullies or intimidates others, has stolen while confronting a victim, or has forced someone into sexual activity) and animals (e.g., has been physically cruel to animals), destruction of property (e.g., has deliberately engaged in setting a fire with the intent to cause notable damage), deceitfulness or theft (e.g., has stolen items of nontrivial value without confronting a victim), and serious violations of rules (e.g., has run away from home at least twice or once if the time gone was substantial).

In addition to meeting criteria across these four symptom categories during a 12-month period, a diagnosis of CD is indicated only when the persistent pattern of behavioral dysregulation is associated with marked impairments in academic, social, or occupational functioning. For example, a child's behaviors may be connected to expulsion from school, incarceration in a juvenile detention facility, or prohibition from age-appropriate social settings, such as after school programs, community centers, or sports teams.

When making a diagnosis of CD, counselors should also clarify the presentation of symptoms using three categories of specifiers related to age of onset, degree of prosocial emotions, and severity. Onset specifiers include *childhood-onset type* when symptoms present prior to age 10, *adolescent-onset type* when no symptoms are present prior to age 10, or *unspecified-onset type* when there is not enough information available to determine when symptoms began. Next, a specifier of *with limited prosocial emotions* is indicated only when youth persistently demonstrate at least two of the following characteristics: lack of remorse or guilt, lack of empathy, lack of concern for their performance, or scarce affect across multiple settings with multiple individuals for a 12-month period. It should be noted that at least two of these characteristics must be present and that these features must represent the typical pattern of relating for the individual. Thus, to assess the criteria for the specifier, multiple information sources are necessary. In addition to the individual's self-report, it is necessary to consider reports by others who have known the individual for extended periods (e.g., parents, teachers, coworkers, extended family members, and peers). Finally, counselors should indicate the pervasiveness of impaired functioning and effect on others using the specifiers *mild*, *moderate*, and *severe*. *Mild* indicates the symptoms barely meet criteria and are associated with negligible harm to others, such as lying, truancy, staying out after dark without permission, and other rule breaking. *Moderate* reflects the presence of symptoms between mild and severe, including stealing without confronting the victim and vandalism. The *severe* specifier notes cases in which symptoms notably exceed the minimum required to make a diagnosis and when symptoms are associated with significant harm to others through activities such as forced sex, physical cruelty, use of a weapon, stealing while confronting the victim, and breaking and entering.

DIFFERENTIAL DIAGNOSIS

Among typically developing children and adolescents, isolated or recurrent acting-out behaviors may be transitory reactions to external stressors, such as family discord, the loss of a family member, geographic relocation, or changing schools (Seawright, Rottnek, & Abby, 2001). Therefore, it is important for counselors not only to determine whether presenting symptoms are associated with an external stressor, but also to rule out the presence of a more appropriate diagnosis. Specifically, prudent assessment practices will rule out the presence of related disruptive, impulse-control, and conduct disorders (ODD and IED), depressive disorders, bipolar and related disorders, the presence of recent psychosocial stressors (adjustment disorder), and substance use disorders (APA, 2013; Seawright et al., 2001).

ASSESSMENT STRATEGIES

Judicious determination of a CD diagnosis and degree of implicated functioning should rely on assessment of psychosocial domains, review of formal assessment data, and direct observation. Like related disorders within this chapter (e.g., ODD and IED), the presenting symptoms should be considered across multiple settings, using data collected from a number of collaterals (parents, teachers, school counselor, and probation officer) and using multiple methods.

A comprehensive psychosocial interview should include data related to (a) developmental issues that may present similarly to ODD, (b) history of abuse or neglect, (c) history of problematic substance use, (d) family dynamics and parenting style, (e) history of legal problems and adjudication, and (f) the degree that the child's activities have endangered self or others. Many formal assessment options are similar to those used to assess ODD and thus can be a great resource to rule out ODD when investigating the hypothesis of a CD diagnosis. Formal comprehensive assessment may be completed using the *DSM-5* Level 1 Cross-Cutting Symptom Measures, the Conners Comprehensive Behavior Rating Scales (CBRS; Conners, 2008), the Conduct Disorder Scale (CDS; Gillum, 2002), Eyberg Child Behavior Inventory (CBI; Eyberg & Pincus, 1999), and Child Behavior Checklist (CBCL; Achenbach & Rescorla, 2001). Observations of child behavior can implement assessment protocols, such as the Disruptive Behavior Diagnostic Observation Schedule (DB-DOS; Wakschlag et al., 2008a; Wakschlag et al., 2008b), and may be completed in a number of settings, depending on the availability and background of counselors. Relevant contexts may include the office, a playroom, a school, the community, and the family home. Sidebar 16.4 provides a scenario similar to what some counselors face; practice determining what assessments to use when suspecting a case of CD.

SIDEBAR 16.4: CASE APPLICATION—SELECTING AN ASSESSMENT PROTOCOL

Dandre has been selected for a formal evaluation following his third incarceration in a juvenile detainment facility. Your review of his arrest history indicates a violent assault in his school cafeteria, vandalism of school property, chronic truancy, and providing false identification to police officers within the past 12 months. You suspect that Dandre may have a diagnosis of CD, but the juvenile court is requesting a formal evaluation. What assessment protocol would you select to administer? How may compensation limitations influence your selection of assessments and subsequent reporting?

TREATMENT STRATEGIES AND INTERVENTIONS

Medication

A review by Scott (2008) indicated that although there are not any medications presently developed to treat CD specifically, several psychopharmacological interventions are commonplace for treating associated co-occurring or associated symptoms and thus supporting counseling interventions. Among children with co-occurring ADHD, some studies have supported the use of psychostimulant medications (Gerardin et al., 2002; Harty, Ivanov, Newcorn, & Halperin, 2011); other medical professionals may advocate for the use of mood stabilizers, such as lithium (Masi et al., 2009); atypical antipsychotics, such as risperidone (Snyder et al., 2002); and drugs that mitigate affect dysregulation, such as buspirone and clonidine (Scott, 2008).

Multisystemic Therapy

Multisystemic therapy (MST) is an intensive approach to treatment that engages the youth and important family members in community-based settings. Treatment is intended to address externalizing behaviors that are characteristic of antisocial behavior, such as fighting, running away, and substance use. Counseling interventions that engage the family members to develop their personal strengths that promote success in relationships, interactions, and use of life skills have been demonstrated as highly efficacious (Klietz, Borduin, & Schaeffer, 2010; Schaeffer & Borduin, 2005).

Parent Management Training

As with ODD, parent management training (PMT) has been indicated for the treatment of CD. This approach, which integrates aspects of social learning theory, traditional play therapy, and attachment theory, can be helpful for developing parent–child relationships, teaching parents to give clear instructions and rewards, reorganizing activities to prevent problems, and promoting prosocial play (Scott, 2008). Examples of PMT curricula with a substantial evidentiary support include the helping the noncompliant child program (McMahon & Forehand, 2003) and parent–child interaction therapy (McNeil & Hembree-Kigin, 2010).

Functional Family Therapy

Functional family therapy (FFT) interventions with youth who have CD engage the family in understanding the underlying dynamics that promote undesirable behaviors and evaluation of the function that they serve (Kazdin, 2002). During FFT, family members evaluate how their behaviors influence the actions of others in an effort to promote reciprocal and reinforcing interactions while decreasing harmful manipulation and intimidation in the home. Several FFT programs are available for counselors to reference that provide guidelines for practice and summaries of supportive research (Alexander & Parsons, 1982; Sexton & Alexander, 2004).

Brief Strategic Family Therapy

Brief strategic family therapy (BSFT; Szapocznik, et al., 1978) tends to view the undesired behaviors of youth with CD as a product of unhealthy, dysfunctional family dynamics. Counselors implementing this approach to treatment focus on increasing helpful family interactions, cooperation among family members to meet mutually beneficial goals, reasonable boundaries among family members, and being accountable for one's role within the family's status. Because of the considerable amount of federal funding associated with treating youth with CD, several open-source counseling curricula are available for review (see Szapocznik, Hervis, & Schwartz, 2003).

Cognitive Behavioral Skills Training

Many approaches to treating CD using cognitive behavioral skills training (CBST) are intended to teach adaptive thinking and behaviors across five domains: (a) social interactions, (b) emotions, (c) thinking style, (d) behaviors, and (e) parent or family interactions (Barclay, 2012; Bloomquist & Schnell, 2002). Like other counseling interventions for CD, CBST is most effective when completed through engagement with family members and requires that the family system make changes in relations while teaching coping skills to both the youth and their parents or guardians (Dowell & Ogles, 2010). During treatment, youth and parents will receive education, modeling, and practice of skills such as problem solving, communication and negotiation, emotional expression, monitoring self-talk, response prevention, and pleasant activities engagement (Barclay, 2012; Bloomquist & Schnell, 2002).

EVALUATION STRATEGIES

The symptom constellation that constitutes CD represents a long, pervasive pattern of interacting with others that is characterized by marked behavior dysregulation (i.e., for at least 12 months). Counselors should be aware that the prognosis for youth with CD is less promising when their home life is characterized by poor parental monitoring or supervision, substance use, a history of criminal behavior, low amounts of affection and support, or harsh punishment styles. With this in mind, counselors should approach their evaluation of treatment outcomes with a realistic perspective that accounts for changes in formal assessment scores, decreases in the frequency of problematic behaviors as reported by meaningful collaterals, and observations of effective coping skill use by the youth and parents or guardians (APA, 2013; Kazdin, 2002). It is also important to consider that many of the evidence-based treatment interventions for CD that we discussed involve using moderately lengthy treatment protocols (e.g., 18 to 24 sessions during a four- to five-month period), so patience with the process and maintaining motivation for change are imperative. Without effective treatment, youth with CD are at risk for developing antisocial personality disorder, which can have a notably deleterious effect on individual functioning and communities at large.

DIAGNOSTIC CHALLENGES

Although the criteria for CD are predominantly behavioral and therefore readily qualified, some diagnostic challenges should be considered. Foremost, collateral reports can contradict with information received from the youth, so a review of formal assessment data may be indicated. When reviewing formal assessment data, youth with CD may have an incentive to *fake good*, and therefore it could be prudent to use formal assessments that yield a scale to evaluate faking good, inconsistency, and random responding phenomena, such as the Minnesota Multiphasic Personality Inventory-Adolescent (MMPI-A). Parents may also underreport the presence of family-related factors, such as parental absenteeism, overly harsh consequences for behavior, or inconsistent emotional availability that could contribute to development of conduct disorder, making diagnostic impressions more discreet. Finally, CD shares symptoms with several related disorders discussed within this chapter, so care should be taken to identify the degree of emotional versus behavioral dysregulation and rule out the presence of other possible clinical explanations of client behavior.

Antisocial Personality Disorder

Antisocial personality disorder (ASP) is more fully discussed in the chapter on personality disorders; however, it is cross-listed within this chapter because of the extreme nature of impulse control without consideration for generally accepted rules, laws, and social norms (APA, 2013). Among adolescents whose symptoms meet criteria for ASP, a pervasive pattern of callous indifference is noted as remorse for actions that harm others appears to be largely absent. However, it is important to clarify that an individual must be age 18 and have exhibited some evidence of CD before age 15 to receive this diagnosis. Assessment and treatment may be complicated by the tendency of individuals with this disorder to be dishonest, be overly aggressive, be involved with gangs or related criminal activities, and engage in alcohol or narcotic use (Glenn, Johnson, & Raine, 2013; Kerridge, Saha, & Hasin, 2014). When providing treatment to individuals who meet the criteria for ASP, we recommend that counselors consult the literature and experienced colleagues to promote optimal potential for positive outcomes.

Pyromania

Pyromania is a rare disorder that occurs in less than 1 percent of the population and is characterized by a compulsion to set fires for purposes of pleasure and affective relief. Although pyromania is uncommon, fire setting is a serious social problem that costs society nearly 2 billion dollars per year and results in over 6,000 deaths and 30,000 injuries. Pyromania is a relatively difficult disorder to diagnose and treat because clinicians are challenged to distinguish pyromania from other fire setting resultant from delinquency, inadequate supervision, or psychopathology. Fire setting in younger children is often ascribed to developmental curiosity, whereas fires started by juveniles are often perceived as committed for purposes of criminal intent or as results of other psychiatric diagnoses.

DSM-5 CRITERIA

Pyromania is an impulse-control disorder denoted by deliberate setting of fires for pleasure and release of tension. According to the *DSM-5* (APA, 2013), pyromania has six distinct diagnostic criteria related to fire setting, including multiple episodes of fire setting; affective arousal from the planning, preparation, and execution of a fire; and a fascination with fire and fire setting paraphernalia.

DIFFERENTIAL DIAGNOSIS

Over 40 percent of deliberate fire setting incidents in the United States are carried out by juveniles, yet few children and youth would meet the diagnostic criteria for pyromania (Grant & Odlaug, 2011). Children between the ages of 5 and 10 are thought to start fires out of curiosity or experimentation. In a study conducted with elementary-school boys, over 45 percent admitted to playing with matches (Grant & Odlaug, 2011). Adolescents are motivated to start fires for more complex psychopathological, individual, and environmental reasons (Ceylan, Durukan, Türkbay, Akca, & Kara, 2011). At the psychopathological level, fire setting is primarily associated with CD and antisocial symptomology. Other individual factors include attention and sensation seeking, social skill deficits, and a lack of knowledge in regard to fire safety. At the environmental level fire setting can indicate a lack of parental supervision and involvement, parent pathology, peer influence, or a maladaptive response to stress (Ceylan et al., 2011). Researchers have also found high rates of fire setting in youth diagnosed with bipolar disorder (14.3 percent), personality disorder (9.5 percent), substance abuse disorder (33.3 percent), and psychosis (38.9 percent; Grant & Odlaug, 2011). In most cases of psychiatric fire setting, the behavior is often best explained in the context of the primary diagnosis and does not merit a secondary diagnosis of pyromania. Sidebar 16.5 provides an opportunity to apply the diagnostic criteria for pyromania based on the information discussed in this section.

SIDEBAR 16.5:   CASE STUDY—DOES JING HAVE PYROMANIA?

Jing's family recently relocated to the United States because of her parents' career endeavors. Five months after moving into their new home, Jing's parents received a call from the neighbors that Jing was at their home because the fire department had responded to a small fire at their residence that destroyed the bathroom and a small section of the kitchen. Upon interviewing the teenager, Jing reports that she was playing with some candles, melting wax and pouring it on her hands to peel off, when she left them unattended. Her assessment data do not reveal any hostility or interpersonal sensitivity that is concerning. Does Jing meet the criteria for pyromania? Is there any additional information that you would like to consider before making a diagnosis?

ASSESSMENT STRATEGIES

The rarity of pyromania in adolescents and children is reflected in the dearth of assessment tools. Currently, the Minnesota Impulse Disorder Interview is the only commercially available protocol that screens for pyromania and has been found reliable with juvenile populations (sensitivity, 85.7 percent; specificity, 98.9 percent; Grant, 2008). To assess for pyromania, clinicians should follow comprehensive procedures that include a full structured interview to screen for other disorders that may better account for fire setting. In addition to formal measures, clinicians should interview parents and significant adults to glean a rich understanding of factors in the child's world that may provide a motive, or, as in the case of psychopathology, a possible contributing factor to the fire setting (Ceylan et al., 2011).

TREATMENT STRATEGIES AND INTERVENTIONS

Identifying effective treatments for juveniles with pyromania is limited by the absence of clinically controlled studies and time-dated research. Much of the research of treatment protocols for juvenile fire starters has been conducted by the nation's fire department as part of a broad-based effort to manage juvenile arson. To date, results of psychoeducational programs operated by fire departments have yielded mixed results: Reports of a protocol developed by the English national fire department intended to assist juvenile fire starters in understanding triggers to arson was found unsuccessful in quelling recidivism over a two-year period (less than 7 percent; Palmer, Caulfield, & Hollin, 2007). Another youth education initiative designed and operated by a fire department reported a 100 percent success rate among a juvenile population, all of whom had been court referred for fire setting (Bennett, Gamelli, Duchene, Atkocaitis, & Plunkett, 2004). Mixed results are most likely indicative of critical differences related to intervention protocols, recidivism indicators, and the timing of posttest intervals (short-term versus long-term follow-up).

Within clinical settings group counseling has been found somewhat effective to reduce fire setting. One longitudinal study conducted in a high-security psychiatric setting found that 90 percent of patients who completed an anger management and assertion training group reported no further fire setting 18 months after program completion (Rice & Quinsey, 1980). Cognitive behavioral group therapy has also been found to restructure attitudes, thoughts, and beliefs about fire setting effectively among youth incarcerated for arson (Taylor, Thorne, Robertson, & Avery, 2002). Although these studies present viable data on potential treatment options for youth with histories of fire setting, the studies were small, and none controlled for participants' clinical diagnosis. Because of these limitations in the research, clinicians are reliant on knowledge derived from populations of fire starters who seldom meet the diagnostic criteria for pyromania, and this limitation continues to hamper the construction of empirically informed treatment plans.

EVALUATION STRATEGIES

Pyromania is a largely unrecognized disorder, with little empirical knowledge existing regarding its origins or life cycle. It is thought to emerge during adolescence, which would account, in part, for the unprecedented spike in acts of fire setting among teenagers; however, prevalence rates following adolescence are unknown. It is estimated that pyromania presents in less than 1 percent of the total population and 3 percent of clinical populations (Palmer et al., 2007). Clinicians' attempts to establish a typical case prognosis are thwarted by the few individuals who have pure pyromania and the elevated rate of co-occurring disorders. Current understandings suggest that if pyromania persists through adolescence and into adulthood, rehabilitation becomes increasingly ineffective (Grant & Odlaug, 2011).

Although pyromania is rare, fire setting is relatively common among juveniles. The prognosis for recovery from fire setting among children and adolescents is contingent on the extent and severity of psychological and environmental factors. Children and adolescents who set fires for attention seeking, lack of knowledge, or lack of adult supervision have been found to benefit from therapy and psychoeducation. Nonetheless juveniles with CD and other psychopathology that predisposes them to delinquency have a more guarded outlook (Palmer et al., 2007).

DIAGNOSTIC CHALLENGES

Several challenges have been detected in the diagnosis of pyromania. Pyromania is a viable diagnosis only when the primary motive for persistent fire setting is affective release with an absence of criminal intent or personal gain. The rarity of these cases has led some clinicians to dispute the legitimacy of pyromania as an independent disorder, especially because co-occurring diagnoses often better explain the fire setting behavior (Grant & Odlaug, 2011). Pyromania's designation in the family of impulse-control disorders has also been questioned, because an act of fire setting can involve careful planning and execution, which may appear inconsistent with an act driven by impulsive tendencies. Finally, misdiagnosis of pyromania is purportedly common, resulting from lack of clinician knowledge and training (Grant & Odlaug, 2011).

Kleptomania

Kleptomania is an impulse-control disorder characterized by a compulsive desire to steal items not needed for one's survival, personal use, or monetary gain. Individuals with kleptomania do not steal items for a particular purpose, and they often give them away, discard them, or surreptitiously attempt to return the stolen property (Grant, Odlaug, & Kim, 2011). Prior to the theft, individuals with kleptomania report feeling intense tension or stress; these feelings are followed immediately after conducting the theft by feelings of relief, elation, and gratification. Because thievery is associated with a cycle of tension and release, kleptomania has been identified as a form of stress relief for individuals who meet the diagnostic criteria (Grant, Kim, & Grosz, 2003). By contrast to other disorders within the family of disruptive, impulse-control, and conduct disorders, girls are diagnosed more frequently than boys at a rate of three to one. The average age of onset is adolescence; however, kleptomania may begin in childhood or not emerge until adulthood (Grant et al., 2011). Kleptomania occurs in three clinically noted patterns: sporadic with brief episodes and long periods of remission, episodic with protracted periods of stealing and periods of remission, and chronic with some degree of fluctuation (APA, 2013).

DSM-5 CRITERIA

To be identified with kleptomania, individuals must manifest five distinct diagnostic criteria as described in the *DSM-5* (APA, 2013):

- Persistent impulse to steal objects not needed for personal use or gain
- Experience of increased tension before carrying out a theft

- Pleasure, gratification, or relief at the time of the theft
- The impulse to steal does not result from ulterior motives, such as revenge or anger or a response to a hallucination or delusion
- The act of stealing is not better explained by another disorder.

Differential Diagnosis

Distinguishing kleptomania from shoplifting and other forms of theft compels practitioners to consider the meaning individuals ascribe to the act of stealing. At some juncture in their development, children will most likely take something that does not belong to them, yet it is rare that children steal in a manner consistent with a kleptomania diagnosis (National Association of Shoplifting Prevention, 2014). The act of stealing in early and middle childhood is often linked to the challenges of achieving mastery relative to a developmental task. Between the ages of 5 to 8 children know the rules for property ownership, and an act of theft usually represents an attempt to test boundaries, gain something needed for survival, or to overcome a sense of powerlessness. Children who steal for power may engage in symbolic theft, a more complex form of thievery that can indicate underlying problems (Grant et al., 2011). For instance, an angry child may steal a beloved item from someone who they feel has mistreated him or her, or a child struggling in school may steal something from the top student to whom he or she feels inferior. As children enter adolescence, stealing may represent an attempt to forge an identity, either through stealing items they perceive help them fit in or through trying to prove themselves to a peer group. Of greater concern is that stealing among adolescents is frequently indicative of substance abuse problems and a gateway to adult criminality (Grant et al, 2011). Thus, although theft is prevalent among the teenage population, seldom would a kleptomania diagnosis be appropriate, because teenagers are typically not motivated to steal for intrinsic pleasure or stress relief. Proclivity for stealing can also be symptomatic of other mental health disorders that may better account for the behavior. For instance, theft conducted by children and adolescents with CD or antisocial behavior disorder frequently signifies a blatant disregard for the rules or a conscious attempt to violate the rights of others. Children in a state of psychosis or delusion may be driven to steal for reasons that can be understood only in the context of a manic episode (Grant et al., 2011).

Assessment Strategies

Few valid and reliable assessment tools screen exclusively for kleptomania in children and adolescents. The Kleptomania Symptom Assessment Scale (K-SAS) has been used to identify kleptomania in adult populations (Grant, 2004), yet no clinically controlled studies have been conducted using this assessment with children and adolescents. Clinicians should consider a diagnosis of kleptomania only upon completion of Diagnostic Interview Schedule for Children, Version 4 (DISC-IV; Shaffer et al., 2000) to comprehensively screen for other disorders that present in childhood, including personality disorder, disruptive behavior disorders, anxiety disorders, and psychosis (Grant et al., 2003). Parents and closely related adults are imperative for accurate diagnosis, especially because adult informants can provide pertinent information regarding transitions, stressors, and other life-altering events that might have contributed to a child acting out through stealing.

TREATMENT STRATEGIES AND INTERVENTIONS

Recommended treatment modalities for adults with kleptomania include behavioral and cognitive behavioral therapy (CBT; Kohn, 2006). Behavioral therapists contend that kleptomania can be understood through applying the principles of operant conditioning: The stress preceding theft is the antecedent, or the presentation stimulus, and the stress relief that accompanies the theft functions to reinforce the behavior positively and strengthen it over time. Although empirical studies are lacking, CBT appears to reduce stealing effectively among individuals diagnosed with kleptomania. Strategies that have been reported in case studies as effective include covert sensitization, exposure and response prevention, and imaginable desensitization (Kohn, 2006). Despite the purported benefit of behavioral approaches in reducing instances of stealing, the absence of research specifically with children and adolescents limits knowledge of optimum therapies for treating minors diagnosed with kleptomania. It would seem reasonable to infer that adolescents at the formal operational stage would be responsive to approaches that have been proven beneficial with adults; however, younger children lack the cognitive ability to address problems abstractly though talk therapy (Kottman, 2011). When working with younger children, therapists may want to consider using family therapy to identify aspects of the family dynamic that might have contributed to a child developing behaviors consistent with a kleptomania diagnosis (APA, 2013). Play therapy and Theraplay may also provide younger children an avenue to develop a sense of self-efficacy and mastery through a developmentally appropriate medium, especially if the act of theft represents an attempt to retrieve power lost in other aspects of their lives.

EVALUATION STRATEGIES

Few studies have reported on the life cycle of kleptomania, and given this limitation outcomes for children and adolescents with kleptomania are unclear. Extant knowledge is further limited because individuals with kleptomania often feel ashamed and embarrassed to self-report or bring up symptoms within therapy (Grant et al., 2011). Although most cases of kleptomania begin in adolescence, prevalence rates are highest among middle-class women in their 30s (Kohn, 2006). There is no known cause of kleptomania, yet family studies have revealed that individuals with kleptomania are more likely to have a first-degree relative with a substance abuse, personality, or mood disorder and to have weak parental attachment (Grant et al., 2011). These findings augment the notion that kleptomania functions as a discrete outlet for stress release, especially because many individuals with kleptomania often give no indication of pathology outside the context of stealing. Despite the secrecy that surrounds the disorder, if individuals with kleptomania fail to seek treatment, the disorder can become chronic (Kohn, 2006). Cases of kleptomania are often referred for treatment only when an individual is caught stealing, yet punishment has not been found to provide a long-term solution. For instance, individuals often return to theft once sanctions are rescinded, and the humiliation that accompanies being caught can create anxiety that can increase an individual's desire to steal (Grant et al., 2011).

DIAGNOSTIC CHALLENGES

Individuals with kleptomania conduct the majority of theft in retail environments, yet out of the total population arrested for theft, less than 8 percent fit the diagnostic criteria for kleptomania (Grant et al., 2011). Assessing prevalence rates of kleptomania is further limited to statistics based upon individuals who are caught as opposed to the entire population who engage in regular shoplifting. Furthermore, individuals who are caught for theft are processed through the justice system and are unlikely to be evaluated for psychopathology. Over 40 percent of individuals arrested for shoplifting are adolescents between the ages of 14 and 16 (National Association of Shoplifting Prevention, 2014). Researchers have hypothesized that theft among this population is demonstrative of their increased freedom, immaturity, inability to obtain desired items through legitimate means, and thrill seeking (Grant et al., 2011). In this respect, youth who steal are unlikely to meet diagnostic criteria for kleptomania. Evidence supporting this developmental perspective can be found in statistics indicating that rates of shoplifting peak at the tenth grade and decline quickly thereafter (Black, 2007).

Other Specified Disruptive, Impulse-Control, and Conduct Disorder

Other Specified Disruptive, Impulse-Control, and Conduct Disorder is a closely related diagnosis; however, clinicians include a specification as to why the child's symptoms do not fit criteria for CD, ODD, IED, or another disorder within this diagnostic class. This diagnosis should be considered when the presentation of symptoms is consistent with disorders in this category and substantially impairs individual functioning across major life domains, yet does not meet diagnostic criteria for any single diagnosis (APA, 2013).

Unspecified Disruptive, Impulse-Control, and Conduct Disorder

Children's symptomology may not always meet full diagnostic criteria even though the presentation of symptoms is clinically associated with a particular disorder or class of disorders (Brown, 2010). The application of an Unspecified Disruptive, Impulse-Control, and Conduct Disorder diagnosis is pertinent when a child or adolescent presents multiple symptoms that are both consistent with and anomalous to disorders within this category. An unspecified designation is given when a clinician determines that the presentation of a disorder does not merit a traditional diagnosis and chooses not to specify why criteria were not met.

Considerations for Assessment and Treatment

There are limited guidelines for Other Specified and Unspecified Disruptive, Impulse-Control, and Conduct Disorder. Nonetheless it is worth noting the clinical utility of this diagnostic set. Diagnoses are useful for younger populations when it is unclear whether behaviors are symptomatic of delayed or atypical developmental or psychopathology. Clinicians should adhere to prudent assessment practices when identifying a child with a specified or unspecified disorder, and determinations should follow methodical procedures to rule out the presence of other disorders (Taylor, Weiss, Ferretti, Belin, & Hollander, 2014). Clinicians are encouraged to exercise caution in identifying children with Other Specified and Unspecified Disruptive, Impulse-Control, and Conduct Disorder because the inherent ambiguity of these diagnoses can complicate treatment planning. Furthermore, children may be overlooked as candidates for a particular medication or therapy, and untreated symptoms can render children vulnerable to developing more severe disorders, especially with the onset of adolescence (Brown, 2010).

Summary

This chapter discussed disorders among children and adolescents who are disruptive, who lack effective impulse control, or whose conduct has violated the rights or safety of themselves or others. By now, you may have noted some similarities and differences between diagnosis and treatment strategies for this cluster of disorders. Although many children and adolescents will experience some related deficits and setbacks throughout normal development, there are a number of assessment and interventions available to counselors that may help prevent negative life outcomes. In addition to receiving training, practice, and supervision working with this population, counselors are encouraged to stay abreast of relevant research, best practice activities, and informational materials. Despite the challenges that may occur for counselors, clients, and client families when treating disruptive, impulse-control, and conduct disorders, positive outcomes can have a promising impact on individuals and society at large.

References

Achenbach, T. M., & Rescorla, L. A. (2001). *Manual for the ASEBA School-Age Forms and Profiles.* Burlington: University of Vermont Center for Children, Youth, and Families.

Alexander, J. F., & Parsons, B. V. (1982). *Functional family therapy: Principles and procedures.* Carmel, CA: Brooks & Cole.

American Academy of Child and Adolescent Psychiatry. (2009). ODD: A guide for families. Retrieved from https://www.aacap.org/App_Themes/AACAP/docs/resource_centers/odd/odd_resource_center_odd_guide.pdf

American Academy of Child and Adolescent Psychiatry. (2013, July). *Conduct disorder resource center.* Retrieved from https://www.aacap.org/AACAP/Families_and_Youth/Resource_Centers/Conduct_Disorder_Resource_Center/Home.aspx

American Psychiatric Association. (1980). *Diagnostic and statistical manual of mental disorders* (3rd ed.). Washington, DC: Author.

American Psychiatric Association. (2013). *Diagnostic and statistical manual of mental disorders* (5th ed.). Arlington, VA: American Psychiatric Publishing.

Barclay, R. A. (2012). *Defiant children: A clinician's manual for assessment and parent training.* New York, NY: Guilford Press.

Bennett, B. K., Gamelli, R. L., Duchene, R. C. Atkocaitis, D., & Plunkett, J.A. (2004). Burn Education Awareness Recognition and Support (BEARS): A community-based juvenile firesetters assessment and treatment program. *Journal of Burn Care & Rehabilitation, 25*(3), 324–327.

Black, D. W. (2007). A review of compulsive buying disorder. *World Psychiatry, 6*(1), 14–18.

Bloomquist, M. L., & Schnell, S. (2002). *Helping children with aggression and conduct problems: Best practices for intervention.* New York, NY: Guilford Press.

Brotman, M. A, Rich, B. A., Guyer, A. E., Lunsford, J. R., Horsey, S.E., Reising, M. M., Thomas, L. A., Fromm, S. J., Towbin, K., Pine, D. S., & Leibenluft, E. (2010). Amygdala activation during emotion processing of neutral faces in children with severe mood dysregulation versus ADHD or bipolar disorder. *American Journal of Psychiatry, 167*, 61–69.

Brown, J. D. (2010). Pediatric primary care as a component of systems of care. *Evaluation and Program Planning, 33*(1), 36–38.

Carr, A. (2009). The effectiveness of family therapy and systemic interventions for child-focused problems. *Journal of Family Therapy, 31*(1), 3–45. doi:10.1111/j.1467-6427.2008.00451.x

Castellanos-Ryan, N., & Conrad, P. J. (2011). Personality correlates of the common and unique variance across conduct disorder and substance misuse symptoms in adolescence. *Journal of Abnormal Child Psychology, 39*(4), 563–576.

Ceylan, M. F., Durukan, İ., Türkbay, T., Akca, O. F., & Kara, K. (2011). Pyromania associated with Escitalopram in a child. *Journal of Child and Adolescent Psychopharmacology, 21*(4), 381–382. doi:10.1089/cap.2010.0141

Coccaro, E. F. (2010). A family history study of intermittent explosive disorder. *Journal of Psychiatric Research, 44*, 1101–1105. doi:10.1016/j.jpsychires.2010.04.006

Coccaro, E. F. (2012). Intermittent explosive disorder as a disorder of impulsive aggression for DSM-5. *American Journal of Psychiatry, 169*(6), 577–588.

Conners, C. K. (2008). *Conners Comprehensive Behavior Rating Scales manual.* Toronto, Ontario, Canada: Multi-Health Systems.

Connor, D. F. (2002). *Aggression and antisocial behavior in children and adolescents: Research and treatment.* New York, NY: Guilford Press.

Copeland, W. E., Shanahan, L., Costello, E. J., & Angold, A. (2009). Childhood and adolescent psychiatric disorders as predictors of young adult disorders. *Archives of General Psychiatry, 66*(7), 764–772.

Del Vecchio, T., & O'Leary, K. D. (2004). Effectiveness of anger treatments for specific anger problems: A meta-analytic review. *Clinical Psychology Review, 24*(1), 15–34.

Diamantopoulou, S., Verhulst, F. C., & van der Ende, J. (2011). The parallel development of ODD and CD symptoms from early childhood to adolescence. *European Child and Adolescent Psychiatry, 20*, 301–309. doi:10.1007/s00787-011-0175-3

Dowell, K. A., & Ogles, B. M. (2010). The effects of parent participation on child psychotherapy outcome: A meta-analytic review. *Journal of Clinical Child and Adolescent Psychology, 39*(2), 151–62. doi:10.1080/15374410903532585

Eyberg, S. M., & Pincus, D. (1999). *Eyberg Child Behavior Inventory and Sutter-Eyberg Student*

Behavior Inventory-Revised: Professional manual. Odessa, FL: Psychological Assessment Resources.

Fergusson, D. M., Horwood, L. J., & Ridde, E. M. (2005). Show me the child at seven: The consequences of conduct problems in childhood for psychosocial functioning in adulthood. *Journal of Child Psychology and Psychiatry, 46*(8), 837–849. doi:10.1111/j.1469-7610.2004.00387.x

Gerardin, P., Cohen, D., Mazet, P., & Flament, M. F. (2002). Drug treatment of conduct disorder in young people. *European Neuropsychopharmacology, 12,* 361–370.

Gillum, J. E. (2002). *Conduct Disorder Scale: Examiner's manual.* Austin, TX: PRO-ED.

Glick, B., & Gibbs, J. C. (2011). *Aggression replacement training: A comprehensive intervention for aggressive youth* (3rd ed.). Champagne, IL: Research Press.

Glenn, A. L., Johnson, A. K., & Raine, A. (2013). Antisocial personality disorder: A current review. *Current Psychiatry Reports, 15,* 427–433. doi:10.1007/s11920-013-0427-7

Grant, J. E. (2004). Co-ocurrence of personality disorders in persons with kleptomania; A preliminary investigation. *American Academy of Psychiatry Law, 32*(4), 395–403.

Grant, J. E. (2008). *Impulse control disorders: A clinician's guide to understanding and treating behavioral addictions.* New York, NY: W. W. Norton and Company.

Grant, J. E., Kim, S. W., & Grosz, R. L. (2003). Perceived stress in kleptomania. *Psychiatric Quarterly, 74*(3), 251–258.

Grant, J. E., & Odlaug, B. L. (2011). Assessment and treatment of pyromania. In J. E. Grant & M. N. Potenza (Vol. Eds.) & P. E. Nathan (Series Ed.), *The Oxford library of psychology: Oxford handbook of impulse control disorders* (pp. 353–359). Oxford, United Kingdom: Oxford University Press.

Grant, J. E., Odlaug, B. L., & Kim, S. W. (2011). Assessment and treatment of kleptomania. In J. E. Grant & M. N. Potenza (Vol. Eds.) & P. E. Nathan (Series Ed.), *The Oxford Library of Psychology: Oxford handbook of impulse control disorders* (pp. 334–343). Oxford, United Kingdom: Oxford University Press.

Harty, S. C., Ivanov, I., Newcorn, J. H., & Halperin, J. M. (2011). The impact of conduct disorder and stimulant medication on later substance use in an ethnically diverse sample of individuals with attention-deficit/hyperactivity disorder in childhood.

Journal of Child and Adolescent Psychopharmacology, 21(4), 331–339.

Joseph, G. E., & Strain, P. S. (2003). Comprehensive evidence-based social-emotional curricula for young children: An analysis of efficacious adoption. *Topics in Early Childhood Special Education, 23*(2), 62–73. doi:10.1177/02711214030230020201

Kaminski, J. W., Valle, L. A., Filene, J. H., & Boyle, C. L. (2008). A meta-analytic review of components associated with parent training program effectiveness. *Journal of Abnormal Child Psychology, 36*(4), 567–589. doi:10.1007/s10802-007-9201-9

Kazdin, A. E. (2002). Psychosocial treatments for conduct disorder in children and adolescents. In P. E. Nathan & J. M. Gorman (Eds.). *A guide to treatments that work* (2nd ed.). New York, NY: Oxford University Press.

Kazdin, A. E. (2005). *Parent management training: Treatment for oppositional, aggressive, and anti-social behavior in adolescents.* New York, NY: Oxford University Press.

Kerridge, B., Saha, T. D., & Hasin, D. S. (2014). DSM-IV antisocial personality disorder and conduct disorder: Evidence for taxonic structures among individuals with and without substance use disorders in the general population. *Journal of Studies on Alcohol and Drugs, 75*(3), 496–509.

Kessler, R. C., Coccaro, E. F., Fava, M., Jaeger, S., Jin, R., & Walters, E. (2006). The prevalence and correlates of DSM-IV intermittent explosive disorder in the National Comorbidity Survey Replication. *Archives of General Psychiatry, 63*(6), 669–678.

Kessler, R. C., & Üstün, T. B. (2008). The World Health Organization Composite International Diagnostic Interview. In R. C. Kessler & T. B. Üstün (Eds.), *The WHO World Mental Health Surveys* (pp. 58–90). New York, NY: Cambridge University Press.

Klietz, S. J., Borduin, C. M., & Schaeffer, C. M. (2010). Cost-benefit analysis of multisystemic therapy with serious and violent juvenile offenders. *Journal of Family Psychology, 24*(5), 657–666.

Kohn, C. S. (2006). Conceptualization and treatment of kleptomania behaviors using cognitive and behavioral strategies. *International Journal of Behavioral Consultation and Therapy, 2*(4), 553–559.

Kottman, T. (2011). *Play therapy: Basics and beyond* (2nd ed.). Alexandria, VA: American Counseling Association.

Lochman, J. E., Powell, N. P., Boxmeyer, C. L., & Jimenez-Camargo, L. (2011). Cognitive-Behavioral therapy for externalizing disorders in children and adolescents. *Child and Adolescent Psychiatric Clinics of North America, 20*(2), 305–318.

Masi, G., Milone, A., Manfredi, A., Pari, C., Paziente, A., & Millepiedi, S. (2009). Effectiveness of lithium in children and adolescents with conduct disorder. *CNS Drugs, 23*(1), 59–69.

McCloskey, M. S., Noblett, K. L., Deffenbacher, J. L., Gollan, J. K., & Coccaro, E. F. (2008). Cognitive-behavioral therapy for intermittent explosive disorder: A pilot randomized clinical trial. *Journal of Consulting and Clinical Psychology, 76*(5), 876–886.

McMahon, R. J., & Forehand, R. L. (2003). *Helping the noncompliant child: Family-based treatment for oppositional behavior* (2nd ed.). New York, NY: Guilford Press.

McNeil, C. B., & Hembree-Kigin, T. L. (2010). *Parent-child interaction therapy*. New York, NY: Springer.

National Association of Shoplifting Prevention. (2014). *The shoplifting problem in the nation*. Retrieved from http://www.shopliftingprevention.org/what-we-do/learning-resource-center/

New, A. S., Hazlett, E. A., Buchsbaum, M. S., Goodman, M., Reynolds, D., Mitropoulou, V., ... Siever, L. (2002). Blunted prefrontal cortical 18fluorodeoxyglucose positron emission tomography response to meta-chlorophenylpiperazine in impulsive aggression. *Archives of General Psychiatry, 59* 621–629.

Olvera, R. L. (2002). Intermittent explosive disorder: Epidemiology, diagnosis and management. *CNS Drugs, 16*(8), 517–526.

Olvera, R., L., Pliszka, S. R., Konyecsni, W. M., Hernandez, Y., Farnum, S., & Tripp, R. F. (2001). Validation of the Interview Module for Intermittent Explosive Disorder (M-IED) in children and adolescents: A pilot study. *Psychiatry Research, 101*(3), 259–267.

Palmer, E. J., Caulfield, L. S., & Hollin, C. R. (2007). Interventions with arsonists and young fire setters: A survey of the national picture in England and Wales. *Legal and Criminological Psychology, 12*(1), 101–116.

Querido, J.G., & Eyberg, S.M. (2005). Parent-child interaction therapy: Maintaining treatment gains of preschoolers with disruptive behavior disorders. In E. Hibbs & P. Jensen (Eds.). *Psychosocial treatments for child and adolescent disorders: Empirically based strategies for clinical practice*. Washington, DC: American Psychiatric Publishing.

Quy, K., & Stringaris, A. (2012). Oppositional defiant disorder. In J. M. Rey (Ed.), *IACAPAP e- textbook of child and adolescent mental health*. Geneva, Switzerland: International Association for Child and Adolescent Psychiatry and Allied Professions.

Rice, M. E., & Quinsey, V. C. (1980). Assessment and training of social competence in dangerous psychiatric patients. *International Journal of Law and Psychiatry, 3*(4), 371–390.

Rich, B. A., Carver, F. W., Holroyd, T., Rosen, H. R., Mendoza, J. K., Cornwell, B. R., & Leibenluft, E. (2011). Different neural pathways to negative affect in youth with pediatric bipolar disorder and severe mood dysregulation. *Journal of Psychiatric Research, 45*, 1283–1294.

Rich, B. A., Schmajuk, M. Perez-Edgar, K. E., Fox, N. A., Pine, D. S., & Leibenluft, E. (2007). Different psychophysiological and behavioural responses elicited by frustration in pediatric bipolar disorder and severe mood dysregulation. *American Journal of Psychiatry, 164*, 309–317.

Schaeffer, C. M., & Borduin, C. M. (2005). Long-term follow-up to a randomized clinical trial of multisystemic therapy with serious and violent juvenile offenders. *Journal of Consulting and Clinical Psychology, 73*(3), 445–453.

Scott, S. (2008). An update on interventions for conduct disorder. *Advances in Psychiatric Treatment, 14*(1), 61–70. doi:10.1192/apt.bp.106.002626

Seawright, H. R., Rottnek, F., & Abby, S. (2001). Conduct disorder: Diagnosis and treatment in primary care. *American Family Physician, 63*(8), 1579–1588.

Sexton, T. L., & Alexander, J. (2004). *Functional family therapy clinical training manual*. Baltimore, MD: Annie E. Casey Foundation.

Schaefer, C. E., & Mattei, D. (2005). Catharsis: Effectiveness in children's aggression. *International Journal of Play Therapy, 14*(2), 103–109.

Shaffer, D., Fisher, P., Lucas, C. P., Dulcan, M. K., & Schwab-Stone, M. E. (2000). NIMH Diagnostic Interview Schedule for Children Version IV (NIMH DISC-IV): Description, differences from previous versions, and reliability of some common diagnoses. *Journal of the American Academy of Child & Adolescent Psychiatry, 39*(1), 28–38.

Siever, L. J., Buchsbaum, M. S., New, A. S., Spiegel-Cohen, J., Wei, T., Hazlett, E. A., ... Nunn, M. (1999). d,l-fenfluramine response in impulsive personality disorder assessed with [18F] fluorodeoxyglucose positron emission tomography. *Neuropsychopharmacology, 20*, 413–423. doi:10.1016/S0893-133X(98)00111-0

Snyder, R., Turgay, A., Aman, M., Binder, C., Fisman, S., & Carroll, A. (2002). Effects of risperidone on conduct and disruptive behavior disorders in children with subaverage IQs. *Journal of the Academy of Child & Adolescent Psychiatry, 41*(9), 1026–1036.

Stanford, M. S., Anderson, N. E., Lake, S.L., & Baldridge, R. M. (2009). Pharmacologic treatment impulsive aggression with antiepileptic drugs. *Current Treatment Options in Neurology, 11*(5), 383–390.

Sukhodolsky, D. G., Kassinove, H., Bernard S., & Gorman, B. S. (2004). Cognitive-behavioral therapy for anger in children and adolescents: A meta-analysis. *Aggression and Violent Behavior, 9*(3), 247–269.

Szapocznik, J., Hervis, O., & Schwartz, S. (2003). *Brief strategic family therapy for adolescent drug abuse*. Bethesda, MD: U.S. Department of Health and Human Services.

Szapocznik, J., Scopetta, M. A., & King, O. E. (1978). Theory and practice in matching treatment to the special characteristics and problems of Cuban immigrants. *Journal of Community Psychology, 6*(2), 112–122.

Taylor, J. L., Thorne, I., Robertson, A., & Avery, G. (2002). Evaluation of a group intervention for convicted arsonists with mild and borderline disabilities. *Criminal Behaviour and Mental Health, 12*(4), 282–293.

Taylor, B., Weiss, M., Ferretti, C. J., Berlin, G., & Hollander, E. (2014). Disruptive, impulse-control, and conduct disorders. In R. Hales, S. T. Yudofsky, L. Weiss, & D. J. Kupfer (Eds.), *The American Psychiatric Publishing textbook of psychiatry* (6th ed., pp. 703–735). Arlington, VA: American Psychiatric Publishing.

Wakschlag, L. S., Briggs-Gowan, M. J., Hill, C., Danis, B., Leventhal, B. L., Keenan, K., … Carter, A. S. (2008a). Observational assessment of preschool disruptive behavior, part II: Validity of the Disruptive Behavior Diagnostic Observation Schedule (DB-DOS). *Journal of the American Academy of Child and Adolescent Psychiatry, 47*(6), 632–641. doi:10.1097/CHI.0b013e31816c5c10

Wakschlag, L. S., Hill, C., Carter, A. S., Danis, B., Egger, H. L., Keenan, K., … Briggs-Gowan, M. J. (2008b). Observational assessment of preschool disruptive behavior, part I: Reliability of the Disruptive Behavior Diagnostic Observation Schedule (DB-DOS). *Journal of the American Academy of Child and Adolescent Psychiatry, 47*(6), 622–631. doi:10.1097/CHI.0b013e31816c5bdb

Chapter 17

Substance-Related Disorders

CARL J. SHEPERIS, TIMOTHY M. LIONETTI, AND JOY-DEL SNOOK

Introduction

Substance use is a significant area of knowledge for counselors and other behavioral health care clinicians because substance use among children and adolescents leads to a variety of problems in school, family, social, and health areas (Becker, 2013). In serious cases of intoxication or withdrawal, an adolescent can die from complications related to substance use. Thus, in comparison to some of the other disorders in this textbook, substance use is one of the most critical for clinicians to understand. Researchers have shown that early exposure to alcohol and drugs is associated with increased rates of addiction, increased length of use, and increased difficulty of recovery (Vaiserman, 2013). Thus, clinicians should also understand prevention strategies and be able to work with adolescent clients to stave off the potential for continued substance-related issues in adulthood. In this chapter, we review the primary substance use disorders covered in the *Diagnostic and Statistical Manual of Mental Disorders, Fifth Edition* (*DSM-5*), and provide information about the symptoms, intoxication, potential for withdrawal, treatment strategies, and differential diagnosis. The chapter reflects contemporary research on substance use issues among children and adolescents and is a framework for understanding the disorders listed in the *DSM-5*. By reading the material in this chapter, counselors and behavioral health care clinicians will have a better understanding of substance-related disorders, potential risk factors, assessment strategies, and intervention.

Description of the Disorders

Substance-related disorders are the most common disorders to present at behavioral health care facilities (Vaiserman, 2013). Within the *DSM-5* classification system, substance-related disorders are organized into two categories: substance use disorders and substance-induced disorders. A substance use disorder involves continued use even though consequences emerge and symptoms affect various areas of functioning (i.e., cognitive, behavioral, and physiological). A substance-induced disorder involves a reversible substance-specific syndrome (e.g., intoxication, withdrawal, or mental health conditions created through the substance use) that is caused by the recent consumption of a substance and is associated with significant problematic behavioral or psychological changes that result from intoxication (e.g., hostility, mood changes, and impaired judgment). To put it more simply, substance use disorders involve symptoms realized from continued use of a substance despite substantial consequences, whereas substance-induced disorders involve symptoms developed because of use (Hartney, 2013).

Sidebar 17.1 focuses on a philosophical and practical debate over the term *addiction* and its absence from the *DSM-5*. Consider the information in the sidebar as you review the remainder of this chapter.

SIDEBAR 17.1:   KEY POINT—WHAT IS ADDICTION?

The *DSM-5* no longer uses *addiction* as a diagnostic term in the substance use disorder category. The move away from the term addiction was completed to avoid stigma and because of poor definitions. However, the counseling world and professional literature have not responded in kind. A search of the professional literature under the term addiction resulted in over 91,000 entries with over 11,000 published since the *DSM-5* was released. Clearly, the behavioral health care world is not yet aligned with the *DSM-5* with regard to terminology. In addition to research, numerous professional credentials align with the term addiction. For example, the National Board for Certified Counselors issues the Master Addiction Counselor (MAC) credential, and the largest association for addiction professionals is named National Association for Alcoholism and Drug Abuse Counselors (NAADAC)—the Association for Addiction Professionals. These are only a small number of examples of the term addiction used in professional circles. As a counselor working with substance use disorders, how will you see your professional identity change because of the *DSM-5*? Will you consider yourself an addictions professional, or will you use a different term? How will you view the symptoms presented in your practice? Does the *DSM-5*'s elimination of the term change your perspective?

In general, substance-related disorders are tied to 10 classes of drugs (i.e., alcohol, caffeine, cannabis, hallucinogens, inhalants, opioids, sedatives/hypnotics/anxiolytics, stimulants, tobacco, and other or unknown substances not related to these 10 classes). We review each of these drug classes and discuss issues related to intoxication and withdrawal. Rather than differentiating between abuse and dependence (as promoted in the *DSM-IV-TR*), the *DSM-5* requires clinicians to focus on the broad range of severity (mild to severe) within problematic substance use behaviors that manifest in children or adolescents. Several course specifiers and descriptive specifiers are used in the *DSM-5* to help with targeted treatment planning.

DSM-5 Criteria

According to O'Brien (2012), the *DSM-5* criteria are a purposeful divergence from the *DSM-IV-TR* with the aim of creating an easier diagnostic process, improving diagnostic accuracy, reflecting experienced symptoms more accurately, allowing for a severity classification, and providing a more culturally sensitive representation. We first provide an

TABLE 17.1   **Key Points: Changes to Substance-Related Disorders since the *DSM-IV-TR***

DSM-IV-TR	*DSM-5*
1. 11 substance classes	1. 10 substance classes (amphetamine and cocaine merged into new stimulants class and phencyclidine merged into hallucinogens class)
2. Substance Use Disorders (included dichotomous Dependence and Abuse classifications)	2. Substance Use Disorders (no dichotomous classifications–conceptualized on a dimension of severity)
3. Substance-Induced Mood Disorder	3. Substance-Induced Bipolar Disorder
4. Substance-Induced Mood Disorder	4. Substance-Induced Depressive Disorder
5. N/A	5. Substance-Induced Obsessive-Compulsive Disorder
6. Substance-Induced Persisting Dementia and Substance-Induced Persisting Amnestic Disorder	6. Substance/Medication-Induced Major or Mild Neurocognitive Disorder
7. N/A	7. Caffeine Withdrawal
8. N/A	8. Cannabis Withdrawal
9. Nicotine-Related Disorders	9. Tobacco-Related Disorders
10. Polysubstance-Related Disorder	10. N/A
11. Recurrent substance-related legal problems (criterion)	11. Craving, or a strong desire or urge to use the substance (criterion)
12. With or Without Physiological Dependence (descriptive specifier)	12. N/A
13. On Agonist Therapy (course specifier)	13. On Maintenance Therapy (course specifier)
14. Early Full Remission and Early Partial Remission (course specifiers)	14. In Early Remission (course specifier)
15. Sustained Full Remission and Sustained Partial Remission (course specifiers)	15. In Sustained Remission (course specifier)
16. N/A	16. Mild, moderate, and severe (severity specifiers)
17. N/A	17. Separate criteria sets for withdrawal are provided for the drug classes (except for phencyclidine, other hallucinogens, and inhalants)
18. N/A	18. Exclusionary clause when symptoms of tolerance and withdrawal occur during appropriate medical treatment with prescribed medications

Source: King, 2014.

overview of criteria based on categories of disorders and then explore the criteria for each specific disorder. Our aim is to help conceptualize the criteria in the *DSM-5*. Clinicians should refer to the manual when considering a diagnosis in practice. Table 17.1 highlights the key changes to substance-related disorders since the *DSM-IV-TR*.

SUBSTANCE-INDUCED DISORDERS

The ingestion of substances can result in symptomology that ranges from the transient effects of intoxication to potentially importunate conditions of the central nervous system. In contrast with substance use disorders, substance-induced disorders are described throughout the *DSM-5* (American Psychiatric Association [APA], 2013) and are related specifically to the effects of substance ingestion rather than continued use despite consequences. For a substance-induced disorder to be diagnosed, a patient must present with a mental disorder that has manifested within one month of substance use, intoxication, or withdrawal. A substance-induced disorder must be tied to intoxication or withdrawal and must not be explained by delirium (a disturbance in attention and awareness). Like other mental health disorders, substance-induced disorder must produce a substantial degree of impairment or distress. Because substance-induced disorders are listed in the *DSM-5* along with the mental health disorder resulting from substance ingestion (see Table 1.1: Diagnoses Associated with Substance Class on page 482 in the *DSM-5*), our discussion is limited in this chapter.

SUBSTANCE USE DISORDERS

According to the *DSM-5*, there are 11 diagnostic criteria that must be considered for each of the substance use disorders, with criteria grouped according to "impaired control, social impairment, risky use, and pharmacological criteria" (APA, 2013, p. 483). Criteria 1 through 4 relate to impairment in the ability to control substance use (i.e., increasing amount of usage, inability to quit using, inordinate time dedicated to seeking the substance, and intense desire or urge to use). Criteria 5 through 7 relate to social impairment (i.e., dereliction of primary responsibilities, use in spite of social consequences and relationship problems, and reduction or discontinuation in activities because of use). Criteria 8 through 9 include risky use that can involve physically hazardous behaviors or use despite physical or psychological problems caused or exacerbated by the substance. The final two criteria (10 through 11) focus on pharmacological aspects of use (i.e., tolerance and withdrawal). When substance use is causing significant impairment across settings, but the minimum of two symptoms for a specific substance use disorder is not met, a clinician may classify the diagnosis as unspecified for the predominant drug category (e.g., unspecified phencyclidine-related disorder).

When a clinician diagnoses a substance use disorder, it also is necessary to indicate a level of severity: mild (two to three symptoms), moderate (four to five symptoms), or severe (six or more symptoms). The course (status of use) of the substance use disorder should also be specified. In cases where individuals have discontinued use, the clinician should indicate whether the child or adolescent is in early remission (i.e., three to 11 months of sustained abstinence and a regression below clinical significance in all criteria except for craving), sustained remission (i.e., when a child or adolescent discontinues use and regresses below clinical significance for criteria, except craving, for 12 months or longer), maintenance therapy (e.g., a prescribed psychopharmacological treatment to manage withdrawal symptoms and to reduce craving for use), or a controlled environment (i.e., access to the substance is restricted, such as in a correctional facility).

Substance Intoxication

Substance intoxication is a common phenomenon tied to the substances identified in the *DSM-5* and is caused by the recent use of a substance regardless of mode of delivery. To be diagnosed formally, intoxication must be clearly tied to changes in behavior or mental functioning and the symptoms must be independent of another mental disorder. The level of intoxication and the presenting symptoms can vary by the amount and type of substance ingested. When an individual uses routes of administration that have quick access to the blood stream (e.g., intravenous), intoxication is more intense and is more likely tied to physiological consequences such as withdrawal.

Substance Withdrawal

Withdrawal is a condition that is often tied to long-term, heavy use of a substance. The behavioral, physiological, and cognitive symptoms and severity of those symptoms vary by substance with the most pronounced tied to opioids, alcohol, and other similar classes of drug (Fisher, Grap, Younger, Ameringer, & Elswick, 2013; Muncie, Yasinian, & Oge, 2013). For example, some drugs, such as phencyclidine, can have long term but less severe withdrawal (Enomoto et al., 2005). The symptoms of withdrawal are directly associated with the effects of reduction or discontinuation of a drug on the central nervous system (APA, 2013). Although drugs that have a shorter period of action on the body tend to produce more significant withdrawal symptoms (e.g., cocaine), drugs that take longer for elimination (i.e., half-life) produce a longer withdrawal process (e.g., opioids).

Substance withdrawal and substance intoxication are strongly related to substance use disorders, and clinicians should be highly familiar with these phenomena. The remainder of this chapter focuses on the substances identified in the *DSM-5*, the related symptoms of specific substance disorders, intoxication, and withdrawal. The material following will provide specific information on each substance and the related consequences of use among children and adolescents. Because the primary criteria for withdrawal are similar across many substances, only those that differ will be reviewed in the following material.

ALCOHOL-RELATED DISORDERS

Alcohol consumption often begins in adolescence, and issues such as binge drinking occur in a large portion of the adolescent population. Johnston, O'Malley, Bachman, and Schulenberg (2010) reported 72 percent of high-school seniors in the United States have reportedly used alcohol, compared with 42 percent for marijuana and 24 percent for other illicit substances. Alcohol-related disorders during childhood and adolescence have a high correlation with a range of psychosocial issues within family, school, and peer groups. The highest prevalence of alcohol-related disorders occurs between the ages of 18 and 29 and thus crosses the barrier between adolescence and young adulthood (Lee et al., 2014). According to Lee et al., although many adolescents and young adults demonstrate problematic use, the patterns of use tend to peak in the early 20s and gradually dissipate in the ensuing years. Falck, Nahhas, Li, and Carlson (2012) conducted a study of almost 4,000 adolescents and discovered problem drinking occurring in over 30 percent of the sample. Furthermore, the researchers found that over 14 percent of the participants produced scores on a substance use screening inventory that indicated physiological dependence on alcohol and a range of other substances.

Alcohol Use Disorder

In the United States, children rarely present for treatment with a substance use disorder (Lee et al., 2014), they typically present differently than their adult counterparts, and they frequently report other substance use, comorbid mental disorders, and problematic family relationships (Thatcher & Clark, 2006). Although medical-based complications of alcohol use disorder typically develop slowly, adolescents can experience acute problems, such as alcohol poisoning (Thatcher & Clark, 2006). The potential for an alcohol use disorder diagnosis is much higher for those who begin alcohol use prior to age 14, and a clear genetic link is evident for those individuals who progress from early-onset drinking to a diagnosis–and the correlation is stronger for those children and adolescents who also use illicit substances (Chorlian et al., 2013).

Diagnosis of alcohol use disorder is somewhat problematic with regard to children and adolescents because the *DSM-5* criteria were primarily developed based on adult models and some of the criteria are not typical for adolescents. For example, one of the *DSM-5*'s criteria is tolerance for the effects of alcohol (e.g., requiring more alcohol over time to obtain the same effect). Although tolerance is a clear issue among adults, it may be difficult to measure in adolescents (Chorlian et al., 2013). Thus, the number of applicable criteria is restricted in the adolescent population. The *DSM-5* criteria are substantially improved over the *DSM-IV-TR* criteria because a diagnosis now requires two or more of the 11 listed criteria. Sidebar 17.2 is designed to raise awareness of the relationship between risky sexual behavior and alcohol use. Consider the information contained in the sidebar as you determine methods for assessment of alcohol use disorder.

SIDEBAR 17.2:   ALCOHOL USE DISORDER IN ADOLESCENTS

Alcohol use disorder among adolescents can affect several major life areas, including school, relationships, and health. One area that clinicians should be sure to explore is sexual sensation seeking. According to Oshri, Rogosch, Burnette, and Cicchetti (2011), adolescents who engage in treatment for substance use (including alcohol) will have high rates of sensation-seeking behaviors that are often tied to risky sexual acts (e.g., unprotected sex and multiple partners). The risky sexual acts reported by adolescents in substance use treatment are highly related to significant risk for HIV. As a result, it is critical to address sexuality in both prevention and treatment of alcohol use disorder as well as other substance use disorders.

If you were a clinician in a substance abuse treatment center, how and when would you incorporate the discussion of sexuality and protective factors into the treatment process? How would you determine the relationship between alcohol use and sexual acting out with your clients? Consider reviewing the professional literature for assessment instruments that identify risky sexual behavior as part of the evaluation for alcohol use disorder.

Alcohol Intoxication

Although cases of childhood alcohol intoxication may present for treatment, the primary cases are among the adolescent population. The typical onset of problem drinking occurs during adolescence, with up to 25 percent of high school seniors reporting binge-drinking behaviors (Spear, 2013). The prevalence of intoxication among this population is disconcerting because of the biological differences between adult and adolescent alcohol users. According to Spear (2013), adolescent brain development plays a significant role in the intoxication process. Alcohol intoxication can produce slurred speech, stupor or coma, an amnestic (blackout) effect, increased risky behaviors, impaired judgment, impaired functioning, higher potential for suicidal behavior, and other behavioral anomalies (APA, 2013).

Alcohol Withdrawal

Physical and psychological symptoms are typical during alcohol withdrawal, with manifestation typically among individuals who have a long history of alcohol use or intoxication, but it rarely occurs in individuals under 30 (APA, 2013). As such, child and adolescent clinicians will rarely treat alcohol withdrawal. In cases where it does present, clinicians should be aware that the withdrawal can produce significant medical-based complications (e.g., nausea or vomiting, psychomotor agitation, and anxiety) and may need medical supervision (APA, 2013). In cases where individuals have a moderate to severe alcohol use disorder, hospitalization may be necessary because of the potential for delirium tremens and seizures. Although hospitalization is reserved for severe cases, children and adolescents should have a lower threshold than adults when considering referral for inpatient detoxification (Stewart & Swain, 2012) to receive aggressive pharmacotherapy interventions (i.e., benzodiazepines, carbamazepine, clomethiazole, or lorazepam). In severe cases where patients are malnourished, there is a potential for the development of Wernicke's encephalopathy (i.e., biochemical lesions of the central nervous system caused by depletion of thiamine).

Caffeine-Related Disorders

Caffeine is not classified as a use disorder in the *DSM-5*, but there is potential for caffeine to be consumed with resulting intoxication and the potential for withdrawal. Although caffeine use is not a disorder, clinicians should attend to caffeine consumption by their child and adolescent patients because it can cause changes in behavior, cognition, mood, attention, sleep, and other areas (Jackson et al., 2013). From 1999 to 2010, caffeine consumption in the United States remained relatively stable, with the majority of caffeine intake resulting from soda, energy drinks, and tea (Branum, Rossen, & Schoendorf, 2014). However, a national focus on childhood obesity has produced a decline in soda use in recent years. In contrast, low-calorie energy drinks, with higher amounts of caffeine than soda, have increased dramatically within the child and adolescent population (Azagba, Langille, & Asbridge, 2014). According to Azagba, Langille, and Asbridge, the increased consumption of energy drinks should be viewed as an emerging health risk because it has been associated with reported depression symptoms, sensation seeking, and other substance use.

Because the increase in energy drink consumption is new, we know very little about the long-term effects. However, a number of recent studies indicate that energy drink consumption is highly related to risk-taking behavior (Arria, Bugbee, Caldeira, & Vincent, 2014). Researchers have also demonstrated an increase combination of energy drink use and alcohol consumption (Costa, Hayley, & Miller, 2014). According to Kaminer (2010), there are misconceptions about the use of energy drinks with alcohol (e.g., they reduce alcohol impairment) that may result in safety concerns and increased risk-taking behavior. In general, because energy drink consumption has risen dramatically, clinicians should pay careful attention to the relationship of consumption to any presenting behavioral issues among child and adolescent patients.

Caffeine Intoxication

This is a phenomenon that can occur with as little as 600 mg in daily dosage producing a range of symptoms that mimic psychiatric conditions (Aguiar, Gomes, Moreira, Henriques, & Silva, 2012). Although this occurrence has been relatively rare in the general population (APA, 2013), the rise in consumption of energy drinks may increase the potential among children and adolescents. In isolated cases, caffeine intoxication has resulted in death from seizures or cardiac arrhythmias and thus should be taken seriously by clinicians (Banerjee, Ali, Levine, & Fowler, 2014). When considering a diagnosis of caffeine intoxication, clinicians should screen for a range of symptoms related to anxiety and agitation (mental and physical) as well as other physiological responses, such as flushed face, diuresis, gastrointestinal disturbance, muscle twitching, tachycardia (APA, 2013).

Caffeine Withdrawal

Caffeine withdrawal syndrome is a fairly common phenomenon that occurs when caffeine users discontinue use abruptly (Küçer, 2010). According to Ozsungur, Brenner, and El-Sohemy (2009), the symptoms of caffeine withdrawal can be grouped under three headings (i.e., fatigue and headache, dysphoric mood, and flulike somatic). Symptoms of caffeine withdrawal are temporary and tend to occur among those users who habitually consumed more than 100 mg per day prior to discontinuation (Ozsungur et al., 2009). To avoid withdrawal, individuals can titrate the amount of caffeine consumption until gradually discontinuing use (Juliano, Huntley, Harrell, & Westerman, 2012).

CANNABIS-RELATED DISORDERS

Cannabis-related disorders are one of the few substance use disorders that are more common for children and adolescents than the remainder of the population. According to Haberstick et al. (2014), the greatest risk for cannabis use occurs during adolescence and young adulthood, with the onset of cannabis use disorder after age 27 being rare. This epidemiological factor is quite significant because of the relationship of cannabis use to behavioral health indicators, such as depression, arrest, and other substance use (Wu, Brady, Mannelli, & Killeen, 2014). A number of factors have been shown to predict cannabis use, such as childhood maltreatment, level of resiliency, ego strength, gender, race, and general personality functioning (Oshri et al., 2011).

Cannabis has been in use since before 2700 BC, but since the 1980s various synthetic forms have emerged throughout the globe that are more likely to produce an acute toxicity and can result in myocardial infarction, tachycardia, and hallucination (Evren & Bozkurt, 2013). These synthetic cannabinoids, which are created as herbal mixtures labeled as "not for human consumption," are known as *Spice*, *K2*, *Bonzai*, and *Jamaika* throughout the world. Synthetic cannabinoids are unregulated and may vary in structure from version to version (Evren & Bozkurt, 2013). Because of the variation across forms, the pharmacology and toxicology are unpredictable. In general, synthetic cannabinoids affect the same receptor sites in the brain and have the potential for many of the same symptoms of intoxication as natural cannabis. In addition to the major symptoms listed earlier, users may experience agitation, hypertension, low potassium, increase in blood sugar levels, and vomiting (Hermanns-Clausen, Kneisel, Szabo, & Auwärter, 2013). Synthetic cannabinoids also have a greater potential for creating acute toxicity, and medical staff should monitor patients experiencing acute intoxication (Hermanns-Clausen et al., 2013).

Cannabis Use Disorder

Adolescent users have viewed cannabis as having few harmful effects, yet research is growing that supports the notion that habitual cannabis use is related to risk for other compulsive substance use behaviors (Hurd, Michaelides, Miller, & Jutras-Aswad, 2014). De Bellis et al. (2013) examined differences in neural activation among adolescents with cannabis use disorder (CUD), adolescents abstinent from cannabis, and adolescents who did not experiment with cannabis. The researchers discovered that adolescents who use cannabis (even after abstinence) differ in neural processing from adolescents who never used the substance. These findings suggest a persistent neurological difference that exists in relation to cannabis use, which may create pathways for addiction. According to Hurd et al. (2014), the age of initial cannabis use can have even greater effects on neural pathways and is highly correlated with addiction during the adult years.

Cannabis Intoxication

Patients who present for treatment after recently using cannabis may be experiencing intoxication. Like intoxication with other substances, there must be significant behavioral or psychological changes that relate to some level of impairment for a diagnosis to be considered. At least two of the following symptoms must be present within two hours of cannabis use: (a) conjunctival injection (bloodshot eyes), (b) increased appetite, (c) dry mouth, and (d) tachycardia (APA, 2013). Hughes et al. (2014) found that individuals who were habitual users of cannabis reached intoxication levels often and used cannabis several times per day. This finding is important in light of the knowledge that heavy cannabis users develop tolerance for the effects of the drug and require greater amounts to reach intoxication (Theunissen et al., 2012). In several cases, emergency room patients have presented with seizures and depressed respiratory function (Jinwala & Gupta, 2012).

Cannabis Withdrawal

The *DSM-5* criteria for cannabis withdrawal require that a child or adolescent discontinue habitual use (i.e., heavy or prolonged use for at least a few months) and experience withdrawal symptoms within a week following termination (APA, 2013). Additionally, the child or adolescent must experience at least three symptoms of withdrawal and significant discomfort from physical reaction to the withdrawal (e.g., abdominal pain; APA, 2013). Clinicians addressing cannabis withdrawal issues should also consider the potential for vivid, unpleasant dreams as part of the process (Hesse & Thylstrup, 2013); cannabis withdrawal is also highly associated with substance use severity, additional consequences, and mood disorders (Greene & Kelly, 2014).

HALLUCINOGEN-RELATED DISORDERS

Hallucinogens are not typically the drug of choice for children and adolescents. Based on the results of a survey of almost 4,000 high-school students (Falck et al., 2012), hallucinogens ranked eighth among the list of substances eleventh and twelfth graders used. In that same survey, among the students whose scores indicated problematic use, hallucinogens were ranked twelfth. These results indicate that fewer cases of hallucinogen-related disorders should present in behavioral health care settings than almost all other classes of drugs.

Functional magnetic resonance imaging (fMRI) studies have shown that hallucinogens reduce blood flow in certain regions of the brain and that the highest degree of drug effect is correlated with the greatest reduction in blood flow and plays a key role in the effect of the drug on behavior and sensory experience (Lee & Roth, 2012). Because of the sensory experience associated with hallucinogens, they have long been drugs of use. In addition to the dissociative experience, hallucinogens can cause significant medical complications. Even at low doses, a hallucinogen can result in shock or coma (APA, 2013). The effects of phencyclidine can be long lasting. Enomoto et al. (2005) found that associative learning (i.e., Pavlovian paired learning) was still negatively affected eight days after the last use of the drug. In addition to medical issues, hallucinogens have been shown to produce violent reactions and are associated with incidents of intimate-partner violence (Crane, Easton, & Devine, 2013). To further your understanding of hallucinogens, we provide specific information about the various hallucinogen-related disorders in the *DSM-5*.

Phencyclidine Use Disorder

The primary phencyclidine-type of hallucinogens includes phencyclidine (PCP or Angel Dust) and Ketamine (Special K). Both of these hallucinogens were developed for medical use and continue to be used to treat chronic headaches, depression, pain, and other medical issues (Shen, Jiang, Winter, & Yu, 2010). Although these drugs have medical applications, they have become drugs of problematic use. Users of phencyclidines take the drugs orally, by snorting, by smoking, or by injection (APA, 2013). Individuals using phencyclidines may have lasting effects that resemble schizophrenia. The phencyclidine-specific symptoms of dissociation, violent behavior, and paranoia may aid clinicians in making an accurate diagnosis (Katayama, Okamoto, Suzuki, Hoshino, & Jodo, 2013). However, urinalysis is the best choice to determine the substance used (Lee & Roth, 2012).

Other Hallucinogen Use Disorder

Some hallucinogens differ in composition from phencyclidines and from each other. However, these hallucinogens produce the same excitatory and inhibitory responses on GABA-ergic neurons (Lee & Roth, 2012). The results of the decreased blood flow in the brain produce altered mind/body perception. As indicated earlier, hallucinogen use disorder is rare for adolescents and children. When the disorder does present among this population, patients will likely be using Methylenedioxymethamphetamine (MDMA) or ecstasy, dimethyltryptamine (DMT), or lysergic acid diethylamide (LSD).

Phencyclidine and Other Hallucinogen Intoxication

Intoxication from hallucinogens can produce serious symptoms and can even lead to coma or death. Although the *DSM-5* lists only coma and death under phencyclidine, researchers have documented brain death from MDMA use, along with self-mutilation, delirium, and renal failure from the use of novel hallucinogens (Aramendi & Manzanares, 2010; Gahr, Plener, Kölle, Freudenmann, & Schönfeldt-Lecuona, 2012; Jovel, Felthous, & Bhattacharyya, 2014; Tang, Ching, Tsui, Chu, & Mak, 2014; Vanden Eede, Montenij, Touw, & Norris, 2012). Symptoms of phencyclidine intoxication (e.g., rapid eye movements, tachycardia, and muscle rigidity) and other hallucinogen intoxication (e.g., tachycardia, sweating, blurred vision, and dilated pupils) are similar in nature. Although some cases of death have occurred because of using a hallucinogen, the most prevalent safety concern is related to the altered perception of reality. The *DSM-5* (APA, 2013) indicates that individuals who use hallucinogens are at a higher risk for accidents because of a sense of altered reality (e.g., believing they can fly).

Hallucinogen Persisting Perception Disorder

Although it is common for hallucinogen users to experience some effects of the drug long after use, in some cases, the lasting effects can cause significant distress. Perceptual disturbances for this disorder can last anywhere from weeks to years, and the symptoms can range from alterations in the visual field to geometric hallucinations (APA, 2013). The symptoms of hallucinogen persisting perception disorder (HPPD) may be treated pharmacologically with oral risperidone, olanzapine, benzodiazepines, or antiepileptic agents (Subramanian & Doran, 2014). In other cases where pharmacological intervention was claimed to be successful, the results are somewhat problematic because patients often experience spontaneous remission from HPPD symptoms (Hermle, Simon, Ruchsow, & Geppert, 2012). Thus, clinicians working with any children or adolescents who experience HPPD symptoms should consult with medical professionals and take an integrated health care approach to treatment.

INHALANT-RELATED DISORDERS

Generally referred to as inhalants, volatile substances are absorbed through a procedure known as huffing (APA, 2013). Inhalant-related disorders are established from the habitual inhalation of volatile substances (e.g., glues, fuels, paints, cleaning fluids, and other readily available products). Low-frequency inhalant users tend to experience less hedonic effects than their high-frequency counterparts but also experience fewer aversive reactions (Garland & Howard, 2010). As such, there is a potential reward system for increasing the frequency of use. Garland and Howard (2010) found that in those cases where aversive reactions occurred, users experienced symptoms such as chest pain, depression, and suicidal thoughts.

Inhalant Use Disorder

Inhalant use disorder is rare and almost nonexistent in U.S. children under age 12 (APA, 2013), and inhalant use typically remits before adulthood (Perron, Howard, Maitra, & Vaughn, 2009). According to Perron and Howard (2009), adolescents who are diagnosed with an inhalant use disorder are globally vulnerable to behavioral and mental health issues. Clinicians can likely predict that the severity of antisocial behavioral issues, other major depression, suicide attempts, conduct disorder, and other psychiatric symptoms increases stepwise with the increase in severity of inhalant use disorder (Perron & Howard, 2009). As such, clinicians should expect that treatment of this disorder is complex and likely involves intensive rehabilitation and mental health intervention, and clinicians should be aware that habitual inhalant users often present with rashes of the nose and mouth. These individuals will also have higher rates of involvement with the justice system, increased relational dysfunction, and polysubstance use histories (APA, 2013).

Inhalant Intoxication

As is the case with other substances, inhalant intoxication results from a recent, high-dose exposure to a volatile substance (APA, 2013). In general, the symptoms of intoxication are similar to those of alcohol intoxication (e.g., slurred speech, nausea, vomiting, and impaired motor functioning; Garland & Howard, 2011). However, individuals may also present with sore muscles, paralysis, lethargy, tachycardia, and fever (Cámara-Lemarroy, Gónzalez-Moreno, Rodriguez-Gutierrez, & González-González, 2012). Withdrawal from inhalants is considered mild and fleeting and therefore is not a diagnostic consideration (APA, 2013).

OPIOID-RELATED DISORDERS

Opioids are used by about 5 percent of the total adolescent population and are typically of the prescription variety (Substance Abuse and Mental Health Services Administration [SAMHSA], 2014). Prescription medications in the opioid category include hydrocodone, morphine, codeine, and oxycodone. According to the *DSM-5* (APA, 2013), opioid use typically begins in late adolescence, so treatment of child or adolescent clients for opioid use disorder is rare. For those cases that do present, the chances for physiological dependence are higher among white, adolescent, middle-class females (SAMHSA, 2014).

Opioid Use Disorder

When adolescents become involved in misuse of opioids, it predominantly stems from an attempt to alleviate pain-related symptoms (McCabe, West, & Boyd, 2013). In these cases, where misuse transitions to physiological dependence, many of the adolescents had experience with other substances, such as marijuana or alcohol (McCabe et al., 2013). Adolescents who develop problematic use of nonmedical opioids, such as heroin, have a higher involvement in drug-related crime, medical drug seeking, injection location scarring, and physical observations, such as track marks (APA, 2013). Regardless of whether the opioid is medical or nonmedical, patients often present with significant depression symptoms (SAMHSA, 2014). When considering a diagnosis of opioid use disorder, clinicians should differentiate endogenous dysthymia from substance-related symptomology (Nakawaki & Crano, 2012).

Opioid Intoxication

Substance-induced intoxication can present similarly regardless of the substance used. As such, clinicians suspecting an opioid intoxication should work with a behavioral health care team to verify the substance through blood analysis. Regardless of the type of opioid, intoxication can be life threatening. According to Fareed et al. (2011), the highest number of emergency room visits for opioid users is specifically related to overdose of oxycodone, hydrocodone, and methadone. The authors further indicated that drowsiness, stupor, and potential coma are high risks associated with opioid intoxication, along with extremely constricted pupils and depressed respiratory function.

Opioid Withdrawal

According to Hassanian-Moghaddam, Afzali, and Pooya (2014), opioid withdrawal is a syndrome that could be triggered by abstinence from habitual use or from treating opioid overdose with an opioid agonist, such as naloxone. In those cases, additional pharmacological intervention (e.g., clonidine) may be necessary to temper the effects of withdrawal (e.g., irritability, general dissatisfaction with life, insomnia, profuse sweating, nausea or vomiting, muscle aches, and diarrhea). Although typically not life threatening, withdrawal from opioids can result in significant distress and is associated with high incidents of relapse. In addition to the distressing withdrawal symptoms, most patients report fierce cravings (strong physiological or psychological urges) that drive them to use again within weeks after detoxification (Northrup et al., 2015).

SEDATIVE-, HYPNOTIC-, OR ANXIOLYTIC-RELATED DISORDERS

Some of the typical substances in this category include benzodiazepines, zopiclone, zaleplon, zolpidem, barbiturates, and others that do not have common prescription value (Ciraulo, 2014). Drugs from this class, especially benzodiazepines, are often used in conjunction with alcohol or other drugs to either enhance the experience of intoxication or help offset the side effects (Bond & Lader, 2012). The combination of drugs is important to note, because primary use of benzodiazepines is uncommon. Although not taken as the primary substance, problematic use of benzodiazepines can occur rapidly, and the withdrawal process can last for weeks (Bond & Lader, 2012). The *DSM-5* (APA, 2013) indicates that habitual use of substances from this category has an impact on general life functioning, including school performance, social activities, and family relationships.

Sedative, Hypnotic, or Anxiolytic Use Disorder

Occurring in 0.3 percent of adolescents ages 12 to 17, sedative, hypnotic, or anxiolytic use disorders are relatively uncommon (APA, 2013). According to a review of literature by Young, Glover, and Havens (2012), less than 4 percent of adolescents engage in non-medical use of this class of drugs. Although use disorders are rare for this category, it is important to understand that they are often comorbid with other substance use disorders (APA, 2013).

Sedative, Hypnotic, or Anxiolytic Intoxication

Because the use of sedatives, hypnotics, and anxiolytics is often in combination with other drugs of misuse, the potential side effects of intoxication can be compounded and potentially lethal. In a study Whiteside et al. (2013) conducted, 5.4 percent of the adolescents who received emergency room treatment in a single year indicated that they engaged in nonprescription use of a sedative, but only 12.3 percent of those individuals had a prescription for the drug. As a result, it is likely that many of the adolescents who present for treatment of sedative, hypnotic, or anxiolytic intoxication will have obtained the drugs through illicit means.

Sedative, Hypnotic, or Anxiolytic Withdrawal

A search of PsychINFO, Medline, the Psychology and Behavioral Sciences Collection, and Academic Search Complete did not produce any studies (other than those specific to alcohol) related to withdrawal from this class of substances. In addition, the *DSM-5* does not contain any prevalence data for withdrawal. Although withdrawal from any class of substances can be severe, it is unlikely that child or adolescent practitioners will face this syndrome.

STIMULANT-RELATED DISORDERS

According to the SAMHSA (2014), when children and adolescents age 12 or older initiate drug use, it is typically with marijuana or alcohol. In terms of initiation of illicit drug use, cocaine is the lowest reported substance at 0.1 percent (SAMHSA, 2014). It is important to report this information because stimulant-related disorders are relatively low incidence between the ages of 12 and 17, with prevalence being less than 0.3 percent for both cocaine and amphetamine-type stimulants (APA, 2013). For children and adolescents, it is more likely that stimulant-related disorders are based on misuse of prescription medications than cocaine. In a national survey of high-school students, 60 percent of the respondents who used stimulants indicated using them as prescribed whereas 22.9 percent reported abuse following prescribed use (McCabe & West, 2013). The highest rate of stimulant use occurs among 16- to 18-year-olds in rural settings (Cottler, Striley, & Lasopa, 2013). Stimulants are often used to treat obesity, attention-deficit/hyperactivity disorder (ADHD), and other medical issues.

Stimulant Use Disorder

According to Ersche et al. (2013), there is a higher potential for stimulant use disorder among individuals who have a familial history of substance use. In addition to neural differences, Ersche et al. (2013) found that individuals with stimulant use disorder have personality differences from nonusers, including a propensity for sensation seeking and higher obsessive-compulsive traits. Although stimulant use disorders occur in less than 0.3 percent of the adolescent population, it is important to be familiar with this disorder because it can have a rapid onset from initial use (APA, 2013). The *DSM-5* lists some of the typical signs associated with a stimulant use disorder as chaotic behavior, aggression, and paranoid ideation.

Stimulant Intoxication

In terms of stimulants, nonmedical use of prescription drugs, such as methylphenidate (i.e., Ritalin), is more likely among adolescents. In cases of prescription stimulant intoxication, individuals may present with a variety of symptoms similar to other intoxication (e.g., pupillary dilation) but also may demonstrate orofacial, stereotypic movements, such as tongue thrusting, which could resemble tardive dyskinesia (Gahr & Kölle, 2014). In addition, stimulant intoxication is associated with the failure to regulate temperature (i.e., hyperthermia) and can lead to stroke or death (Gahr & Kölle, 2014).

Stimulant Withdrawal

Individuals with moderate or severe stimulant use disorders are more likely to experience a withdrawal syndrome after reducing or discontinuing use of the substance (APA, 2013). To meet the *DSM-5* criteria for stimulant withdrawal, an individual must experience a state of dysphoria (e.g., an intense state of psychological discomfort) and at least two additional symptoms, such as fatigue, insomnia, or hypersomnia (APA, 2013). A resting heart rate under 60 beats per minute that results in physical distress (i.e., bradycardia) often accompanies withdrawal (APA, 2013).

TOBACCO-RELATED DISORDERS

According to the Center for Disease Control (CDC) National Center for Chronic Disease Prevention and Health Promotion (2014), almost nine out of 10 smokers begin the habit prior to age 18, and each day there are 3,200 new smokers under that age. Among today's youth, approximately 23 percent currently use some form of tobacco product (CDC National Center for Chronic Disease Prevention and Health Promotion, 2014).

Although the current use rate is high, it has declined greatly since the 1990s (Welte, Barnes, Tidwell, & Hoffman, 2011). Even though overall use has declined, the CDC National Center for Chronic Disease Prevention and Health Promotion (2014) found that the use of electronic cigarettes doubled from 2011 to 2012.

Tobacco Use Disorder

In the United States, tobacco involvement occurs more frequently in white adolescents from lower socioeconomic backgrounds than those from other races (Welte et al., 2011). According to Zhan, Dierker, Rose, Selya, and Mermelstein (2012), adolescents report experiencing individual symptoms of physiological dependence within the first 100 cigarettes. The adolescents in this study reported the need to relieve discomfort through smoking as well as having to increase the amount of smoking to attain the same level of satisfaction. Based on the criteria in the *DSM-5*, tobacco use disorder would be met for many of these participants within the first 100 cigarettes (Zhan et al., 2012).

Tobacco Withdrawal

Regardless of age, when individuals abruptly discontinue habitual tobacco use, they tend to experience the symptoms of withdrawal. Pergadia et al. (2010) conducted a twin study and found that withdrawal among adolescents was best conceptualized in two levels of severity. Based on their research, the severity of withdrawal could be predicted by difficulty with quitting, heavy use of tobacco, comorbid psychological and behavioral disorders, and alcohol-related problems. According to DiFranza, Ursprung, and Biller (2012), habitual smokers tend to experience a psychological sense of wanting to smoke as a first symptom of withdrawal. Soon after the experience of withdrawal, participants in their study reported experiencing a sense of craving, which had a physical component related to the experience (e.g., salivating and abdominal cramp). A majority of the participants also experienced a sense of needing tobacco that manifested in both psychological and physical forms (e.g., irritability and headache). According to the APA (2013), the symptoms of withdrawal are most significant in the first three days after cessation and tend to last up to three weeks.

OTHER (OR UNKNOWN) SUBSTANCE-RELATED DISORDERS

In this chapter, we reviewed the majority of substances and substance classes that result in use disorders. Although most children and adolescents presenting with substance use problems (e.g., use disorder, intoxication, or withdrawal) will fit within one of the specific categories, there may be occasions when the substance is not a clear categorical match. In those cases, the *DSM-5* provides for an Other (or Unknown) Substance classification. Abuse of drugs such as antihistamines or anabolic steroids would be examples that might fit into this category of substance-related disorders. In addition, various cultures throughout the world use plant substances that produce altered psychological states, and these drugs would fit into the Other category. Finally, when a clinician is not able to identify the substance used, the Unknown category is used as a diagnosis.

Differential Diagnosis

Differential diagnosis is a structured approach that clinicians should follow to increase the potential for arriving at an accurate diagnosis. According to First (2013), the following steps should be followed in the differential diagnosis process (i.e., rule out malingering, rule out substance as an explanation, rule out a medical explanation, consider an adjustment disorder, and determine whether the symptoms are significant enough to warrant a diagnosis). As we stated at the beginning of the chapter, clinicians must be able to differentiate between substance use disorders and substance-induced disorders (e.g., intoxication, withdrawal, or a substance-induced mental disorder). The etiology of each can be overlapping and complex.

Assessment Strategies

According to Fox (2014), clinicians begin the assessment process by gathering relevant information related to the presenting issues, examine the need for inpatient services or referrals, and determine whether any additional issues are relevant to the assessment. The clinician then summarizes all the assessment data to develop a treatment plan. A search of the professional literature resulted in thousands of resources for the assessment of substance use. However, not all assessment instruments are appropriate for adolescents. When selecting an assessment instrument it is important to determine the clinical utility, the assessment time frame, the target population, normative or psychometric data, methods of administration, and training requirements (Drummond, Sheperis, & Jones, 2015). We review some of the evidence-based assessment instruments appropriate for adolescents.

CAGE

The CAGE is a four-item questionnaire designed as a simple method to detect problem drinking (Ewing, 1984). The questions for the CAGE are: (a) Have you ever tried to *C*ut down on your drinking? (b) Do you get *A*nnoyed when people talk about your drinking? (c) Do you feel *G*uilty about your drinking? and (d) Have you ever had an *E*ye-opener (morning drink) to steady your nerves or get rid of a hangover? The psychometric properties of the CAGE have been studied extensively, and it has been shown to detect alcohol problems accurately. In a recent study, Skogen, Øverland, Knudsen, and Mykletun (2011) showed the CAGE had an overall internal reliability of 0.68, and factor analysis supported the use of a single factor of alcohol-related problems.

PERSONAL EXPERIENCE SCREENING QUESTIONNAIRE (PESQ)

The PESQ (Winters, 1992) is a 40-item screening instrument developed to reliably measure the severity of substance use, social or relational issues, and response distortion patterns. The instrument has demonstrated reliability with coefficient alpha ranging from 0.91 to 0.95. The instrument has been normed on a variety of adolescents, including juvenile offenders and drug users.

CRAFFT

The CRAFFT is a six-item instrument that is specifically designed to detect substance use among adolescent responders (Stewart & Connors, 2004). CRAFFT is an acronym standing for the following six items:

1. Have you ever ridden in a *C*ar driven by someone (including yourself) who was high or had been using alcohol or drugs?

2. Do you ever use alcohol or drugs to *R*elax, feel better about yourself, or fit in?

3. Do you ever use alcohol or drugs when you are by yourself, *A*lone?

4. Do you ever *F*orget things you did while using alcohol or drugs?

5. Do your family or *F*riends ever tell you that you should cut down on your drinking or drug use?

6. Have you ever gotten into *T*rouble while you were using alcohol or drugs?

According to Pilowsky and Wu (2013), the CRAFFT is the most researched brief screening instrument available, and the psychometric properties support its use for detecting substance use problems (e.g., Cronbach's Alpha = 0.68, sensitivity for risky use = 0.76, specificity for risky use = 0.94, sensitivity for dependence = 0.92, and specificity for dependence = 0.80)

SUBSTANCE ABUSE SUBTLE SCREENING INVENTORY–ADOLESCENT (SASSI-A2)

The SASSI-A2 (Miller, 2005) is a screening instrument designed to detect substance use issues among 12- to 18-year-old adolescents. The SASSI-A2 has been shown to be valid and reliable through numerous research studies. Scores on the SASSI-A2 have been reported to have adequate sensitivity for identifying individuals who meet diagnostic criteria for substance use disorders but may also include false positives for those who report nonuse of substances (Perera-Diltz & Perry, 2011).

Treatment Strategies and Interventions

Adolescent substance-related disorder treatment can occur in a variety of settings (e.g., inpatient, partial hospitalization, or outpatient) and take many forms (e.g., family therapy, group therapy, or individual therapy). Although innumerable psychological theories exist that drive substance use intervention processes for adolescents, the most common forms appearing in the professional literature include family therapy, motivational interviewing, psychoeducational approaches, and cognitive behavioral therapy (Tanner-Smith, Wilson, & Lipsey, 2013). In their meta-analysis of the research on adolescent substance use treatment, Tanner-Smith, Wilson, and Lipsey discovered that family therapy–based interventions proved the most successful treatment approaches—regardless of the method used. Although adolescents do tend to reduce use through treatment, abstinence is the common goal for most interventions. Unfortunately, adolescents have a high rate of relapse back into use after treatment (Winters, Botzet, & Fahnhorst, 2011).

SETTINGS

The determination of setting for substance-related disorder treatment, length of stay, intervention modality, and intensity of intervention are typically determined through the American Society of Addiction Medicine's (ASAM) Patient Placement Criteria, second edition-revised (Fishman, 2011). According to the ASAM's website (2015), over 30 states require use of the ASAM criteria to make placement determinations for substance use treatment. The ASAM criteria explore six dimensions (i.e., acute intoxication and/or withdrawal potential; biomedical conditions and complications; emotional, behavioral, or cognitive conditions or complications; readiness to change; relapse, continued use, or continued problem potential; and recovery/living environment) to guide the continuum of care. Clinicians should complete training prior to using the ASAM criteria.

Inpatient Services

Placement into substance-related disorder treatment is based on a six-dimensional assessment of problem severity. Clinicians use the ASAM criteria to navigate the decision-making process related to treatment setting. Those adolescents who are experiencing complications related to intoxication or withdrawal and a high number of problems in the other dimensions will likely meet the criteria for placement at inpatient services. It is important to note that the majority of substance use facilities are designed for adult services. In some areas of the United States, adolescent inpatient services may not be available. In those situations where facilities are not available but inpatient services are warranted, we recommend working with health care providers to consider general hospitalization in lieu of a specialized facility.

Outpatient Services

Services delivered on an outpatient basis can be delivered on a continuum of intensity from intermittent individual sessions to intensive outpatient throughout each week (Winters et al., 2011). According to Winters et al., a variety of service options is important to be able to address the individual needs of adolescents. With regard to the modality of outpatient services, Hogue, Henderson, Ozechowski, and Robbins (2014) found several well-established stand-alone treatments, including family-based ecological models; cognitive behavioral models; and combinations of motivational interviewing, family-based models, and cognitive behavioral therapy.

MODES OF DELIVERY

One of the key facets of effective substance-related disorder treatment for adolescents is development of a treatment plan that addresses the individual needs of the client (Rieckmann et al., 2011). Substance-related disorder treatment can involve individual counseling, family-based intervention, group therapy, psychoeducational training, self-help, and 12-step recovery groups. As we indicated in our discussion of outpatient services, research has supported the use of a variety of approaches, but the greatest evidence is available for family-based ecological interventions, cognitive behavioral individual therapy, cognitive behavioral group therapy, motivational interviewing, and combinations of evidence-based approaches (Hogue et al., 2014).

Evaluation Strategies

Because there are multiple risk factors for substance-related disorders, treatment of children and adolescents often includes intervention or prevention of other risk factors. Similarly, multiple factors place children and adolescents at risk for substance-related disorders. These factors include individual characteristics and cultural factors, such as low socioeconomic status, poor self-control, behavioral disorders, poor coping skills, peer group pressure, poor family relationships and inappropriate parenting style, childhood abuse, and other traumatic events (Okamoto, Ritt-Olson, Soto, Baezconde-Garbanati, & Unger, 2009; Prado et al., 2009; Thatcher & Clark, 2008). Furthermore, Cleveland, Feinberg, Bontempo, and Greenberg (2008) suggested that it is important to consider the individual, parents', teachers', peers', and community domains alike for reducing substance use among adolescents. Because of the myriad variables that could affect substance use, it can be difficult to determine effective treatments for these disorders. Further complicating the treatment of substance use disorders in adolescents is the comorbidity with other mental health disorders. In a study by Esposito-Smythers and Goldston (2008), 100 percent of the participants were diagnosed with a co-occurring mood disorder (major depressive disorder, dysthymia, or depressive disorder not otherwise specified), 54 percent an anxiety disorder (generalized anxiety disorder, social phobia, panic disorder, post-traumatic stress disorder, or acute stress disorder), and 54 percent a disruptive behavior disorder (ADHD, oppositional defiant disorder, or conduct disorder). However, over the past decade progress has been made in the treatment of adolescent substance use disorders, including the development of treatments specifically designed for adolescents (Deas & Clark, 2008). Donovan et al. (2011) indicated that evidence-based interventions have been developed. However, they also warned that there is little consensus about which outcomes are most important and how to define the efficacy of substance-related disorder treatment.

Adding to the difficulty of determining which treatments are effective is the volume of strategies and measurement tools. These variables add to the lack of consensus and make the comparison between studies difficult (Donovan et Al., 2011). Furthermore, a variety of outcomes are also of interest. Substance use is the primary measure, but other domains of functioning, such as educational and social functioning, are also important. Studies may measure reductions in symptom severity and improved quality of life. Another concern regarding the outcomes of intervention is that some studies focus on one substance whereas others focus on multiple. The aim of some studies may also differ. For example, the goal of some studies is complete abstinence whereas others focus on the reduction of use. All of these factors combined make comparison of treatments difficult. However, a variety of approaches have been found to be effective. This section will review these approaches.

TREATMENT EFFECTIVENESS

Adolescent treatment outcome studies fall into one of five categories: family-based interventions and multisystemic therapy, motivational enhancement therapy, behavioral therapy, cognitive behavioral therapy (CBT), and pharmacotherapy (Deas & Clark, 2009). More recently, Karki et al. (2012) suggested that treatment options fall into other categories: family-based intervention, school-based intervention, individual-based intervention, community-based intervention, and combined intervention. No matter what category studies are placed in, both reviews indicated that there are a number of interventions that have been found to be effective in the treatment of adolescent substance use disorders. For this section a combination of these categories will be used.

Family Based

Researchers showed positive outcomes for family-centered treatment approaches for adolescent substance users (Liddle et al. (2001); Rowe & Liddle, 2003). Under the category of family-based intervention is multisystemic therapy (MST). The search by Deas and Clark (2009) resulted in seven studies under this category. Of the seven studies reviewed, all had significant results. It is worth noting, however, that several of these reviewed studies included multiple treatments. Most notably, the addition of cognitive behavioral therapy (CBT) to MST demonstrated greater effects than MST alone. Similarly, the review by Karki et al. (2012) concluded that involving the family in the treatment of adolescent substance use disorders is effective. Sidebar 17.3 is designed to introduce you to a technique commonly used with multiple families in substance use treatment. Imagine that you are the counselor providing the services in this sidebar. Consider other techniques that might be effective.

SIDEBAR 17.3:　DENIAL AND THE FISHBOWL

Substance abuse treatment with adolescents can be a difficult process and may involve a high propensity to deny the presence of a substance use problem. How can you address this issue? Many substance abuse counselors involve family members in the treatment process. One method is to have multiple-family group sessions that also include the adolescents. To break the denial of problems, clinicians often have family members form an inner circle and have the adolescents form an outer circle. This fishbowl method allows the clinician to process the impact of substance use on the family while the adolescents sit on the outside and observe the process. By having the families take time to discuss the various ways the adolescents' use has affected them, it becomes more difficult for the adolescents to deny the problem. The clinician can then switch the inner and outer circles to process the experience with the adolescent clients, making connections among the experiences of the family members and adolescents. What other techniques can you discover that address denial in substance use treatment? What type of training might be required to use these techniques? How can you become certified to be a substance abuse counselor? Consider reviewing the professional literature as well as www.NBCC.org for more information.

Individual Based

Deas and Clark (2009) found two studies that used motivational enhancement therapy (MET), and the Karki et al. (2012) study found an additional two studies. All four of these studies found positive results for the use of MET. Deas and Clark (2009) also found cognitive behavioral therapy effective in treatment. The review by Karki et al. (2012) included an Internet-based program (ReelTeen; Schwinn et al., 2010). This program was found to reduce the incidence of drug use at three- and six-month follow-up.

School Based

Karki et al. (2012) reviewed five school-based programs. They were Life Skills Training Program, Female-Specific Motivational-Enhancement Group Intervention, The Climate Schools intervention program, Project Towards No Drug Use, and the Take Charge of Your Life program. In general, all but one program had positive outcomes. However, these positive outcomes were variable. For instance, Take Charge of Your Life had positive effects on those who used marijuana prior to baseline but showed a negative effect for nonusers (Sloboda et al., 2009). Similarly, the Female-Specific Motivational-Enhancement Group Intervention showed less consumption at a 10-week follow-up but not at a six-month follow-up. Furthermore, of the two studies of the Life Skills Training Program, one altered the views regarding the use of alcohol, tobacco, and other drugs (Anderson & Moore, 2009), but the other study (Spoth et al., 2008) found no effect at follow-up for nonprescribed medication.

Combined Interventions

Just as the heading implies, combined interventions comprise two or more interventions. One study found multidimensional family therapy superior to CBT, but both were effective in reducing use (Liddle et al., 2008). Another reviewed study (Slesnick & Prestopnik, 2009) combined ecologically based family therapy, MET, and the community reinforcement approach. The study revealed that negative family environment predicted motivation to change alcohol and drug use. Another study combined MET, CBT, abstinence-based contingency management (CM), and family management (Stanger, Budney, Kamon, & Thostensen, 2009). The study showed that combining MET, CBT, and CM enhanced abstinence, and it was maintained for longer periods compared with the control group.

Behavioral Treatment Approaches

There is not a distinct behavioral approach to treating substance-related disorders. Instead it consists of a variety of approaches, including coping skills training, relapse prevention, contingency management, couples and family approaches, facilitated self-change approaches, and aversion therapy. As noted in previous sections of this chapter, behavioral approaches have been adapted to a variety of settings (e.g., residential, outpatient, and computerized). Behavioral treatments are readily adapted to residential facilities, outpatient settings, schools, and community mental health settings (Witkiewitz and Marlatt, 2011). Similarly, these authors noted that behavioral interventions are also adaptable to differing delivery methods, such as by phone or Internet. Treatment modalities that are adaptable to multiple settings are particularly useful.

There are a number of reviews that have found behavioral approaches to be among the most efficacious. Similarly, meta-analyses have found small- to medium-effect sizes for both contingency management programs (Prendergast, Hall, Roll, & Warda, 2008) and cognitive behavioral treatments (Magill & Ray, 2009). The results vary depending on factors such as comparison group, definition of outcome, and follow-up time span. However, a number of studies have shown behavioral treatments to be no more effective than other more traditional psychotherapies (Imel, Wampold, Miller, & Fleming, 2008). Finally, there is scant evidence to support the efficacy of these behavioral treatments with minority groups and among patients with comorbid mental health disorders (Witkiewitz & Marlatt, 2011).

Despite the growing body of evidence that behavioral interventions are useful for adolescents with substance use disorders, getting adolescents to remain in treatment continues to be a challenge (Killeen, McRae-Clark, Waldrop, Upadhyaya, Brady, 2012). Similarly, these authors noted that there is a lack of consensus regarding which form of treatment is most effective. Contingency management programs coupled with cognitive behavioral therapy, motivational enhancement therapy, and family therapy have been shown to increase retention in treatment and reduce drug use in adolescents with marijuana use disorders (Kadden, Litt, Kabela-Cormier, & Petry, 2007; Stanger et al., 2009).

Similarly, Henggeler et al. (2006) found the combining of contingency management, multisystemic family therapy, and standard community treatment increased retention and abstinence rates in an adolescent drug court population.

In contrast, Killeen et al. (2012) did not find the addition of contingency management helpful without the use of a manual or checks on fidelity. Factors affecting the utility of contingency management included the magnitude of the reinforcer, schedule of reinforcement, and value of the reinforcer (Petry, 2000). Similarly, Stanger et al. (2009) noted that the value of the reinforcer must be sufficiently large to compete with the reinforcement of using the substance. Because Dougherty et al. (2007) found that adolescent substance users may have difficulty with impulsivity and deficits in delayed rewards, increasing the likelihood that adolescents receive the reinforcer may be beneficial (Killeen et al., 2012).

Diagnostic Challenges

Substance-related disorders occur in varying degrees based on the categories of substance, age, gender, cultural background, and other demographic variables. Our review of each substance-related disorder category in the *DSM-5* demonstrates a need for counselors and behavioral health care clinicians to be prepared to identify and treat these disorders. However, some considerable diagnostic challenges may affect the process. According to Cheng and Lo (2010), adolescents are more likely to present for treatment if they have a dual diagnosis (the comorbid presence of a psychiatric disorder along with a substance use disorder), have juvenile justice involvement, or if they are white male and from a more affluent background. Clearly a number of barriers exist to treatment for adolescents with substance use problems.

As Cheng and Lo (2010) indicated, dual diagnosis is a factor that increases the chances that an adolescent will report for treatment. Determining whether a substance causes a psychiatric symptom or whether two separate disorders are occurring simultaneously can be a difficult task. The accurate identification of presenting symptomology is important for any clinician. However, with dual diagnosis, clinicians must consider the dangerous nature of intoxication and withdrawal while recognizing the potential effects of psychiatric symptoms. One reason dual diagnosis is important to identify clearly is because comorbid depression and substance use has been shown to have a higher correlation with adolescent suicide (Effinger & Stewart, 2012).

Summary

Determining the effectiveness of treatments for substance-related disorders can be difficult because numerous factors influence treatment. Multiple considerations (e.g., individual, family, and cultural factors) must be accounted for. Similarly, outcomes to measure are also debated. Despite these factors, a number of promising interventions are available for the treatment of substance use disorders. Family-based treatments, motivational enhancement therapy, cognitive behavioral therapy, school-based therapy, and contingency management have all been demonstrated to be effective. Combining these treatments also has shown promise. Yet further study is needed to clarify the issues of measurement to compare studies and how to keep adolescents in treatment.

References

Aguiar, I., Gomes, S., Moreira, A., Henriques, V., & Silva, H. (2012). P-01—Cafeinism and psychosis—When the habit becomes a threat. *European Psychiatry, 27*, 1. doi:10.1016/S0924-9338(12)74168-8

American Psychiatric Association. (2013). *Diagnostic and statistical manual of mental disorders* (5th ed.). Arlington, VA: American Psychiatric Publishing.

Anderson, S. W., & Moore, P. A. (2009). The impact of education and school-based counseling on children's and adolescents' views of substance abuse. *Journal of Child & Adolescent Substance Abuse, 18*(1), 16–23.

Aramendi, I., & Manzanares, W. (2010). [Hyponatremic encephalopathy and brain death in Ecstasy (3,4-methylenedioxymethamphetamine) intoxication]. *Medicina Intensiva, 34*(9), 634–635. doi:10.1016/j.medin.2010.02.007

Arria, A. M., Bugbee, B. A., Caldeira, K. M., & Vincent, K. B. (2014). Evidence and knowledge gaps for the association between energy drink use and high-risk behaviors among adolescents and young adults. *Nutrition Reviews, 72*(S1), 87–97. doi:10.1111/nure.12129

American Society of Addiction Medicine. (2015). *What is the ASAM criteria?* Retrieved from http://www.asam.org/publications/the-asam-criteria/about/

Azagba, S., Langille, D., & Asbridge, M. (2014). An emerging adolescent health risk: Caffeinated energy drink consumption patterns among high school students. *Preventive Medicine, 62*, 54–59. doi:10.1016/j.ypmed.2014.01.019

Banerjee, P., Ali, Z., Levine, B., & Fowler, D. R. (2014). Fatal caffeine intoxication: A series of eight cases from 1999 to 2009. *Journal of Forensic Sciences, 59*(3), 865–868. doi:10.1111/1556-4029.12387

Becker, S. J. (2013). Adolescent substance abuse: National trends, consequences, and promising treatments. *Brown University Child and Adolescent Behavior Letter, 29*(5), 1–7.

Bond, A., & Lader, M. (2012). Anxiolytics and sedatives. In J. C. Verster, K. Brady, M. Galanter, & P. Conrod (Eds.), *Drug abuse and addiction in medical illness: Causes, consequences and treatment* (pp. 231–240). New York, NY: Springer Science + Business Media.

Branum, A. M., Rossen, L. M., & Schoendorf, K. C. (2014). Trends in caffeine intake among US children and adolescents. *Pediatrics, 133*(3), 386–393. doi:10.1542/peds.2013-2877

Cámara-Lemarroy, C. R., Gónzalez-Moreno, E. I., Rodriguez-Gutierrez, R., & González-González, J. G. (2012). Clinical presentation and management in acute toluene intoxication: A case series. *Inhalation Toxicology, 24*(7), 434–438. doi:10.3109/08958378.2012.684364

Centers for Disease Control and Prevention National Center for Chronic Disease Prevention and Health Promotion. (2014, February 14). *Youth and tobacco use.* Retrieved from http://www.cdc.gov/tobacco/data_statistics/fact_sheets/youth_data/tobacco_use/index.htm

Cheng, T. C., & Lo, C. C. (2010). Mental health service and drug treatment utilization: Adolescents with substance use/mental disorders and dual diagnosis. *Journal of Child & Adolescent Substance Abuse, 19*(5), 447–460.

Ciraulo, D. A. (2014). Sedatives, hypnotics, and anxiolytics. In H. R. Kranzler, D. A. Ciraulo, & L. R. Zindel (Eds.), *Clinical manual of addiction psychopharmacology* (2nd ed., pp. 199–260). Arlington, VA: American Psychiatric Publishing.

Chorlian, D., Madhavi, R., Manz, N., Wang, J. C., Dick, D., Almasy, L., … Porjesz, B. (2013). Genetic and neurophysiological correlates of the age of onset of alcohol use disorders in adolescents and young adults. *Behavior Genetics, 43*(5), 386–401. doi:10.1007/s10519-013-9604-z

Costa, B. M., Hayley, A., & Miller, P. (2014). Young adolescents' perceptions, patterns, and contexts of energy drink use. A focus group study. *Appetite, 80*, 183–189.

Cottler, L. B., Striley, C. W., & Lasopa, S. O. (2013). Assessing prescription stimulant use, misuse, and diversion among youth 10–18 years of age. *Current Opinion in Psychiatry, 26*(5), 511–519.

Cleveland, M. J., Feinberg, M. E., Bontempo, D. E., & Greenberg, M. T. (2008). The role of risk and protective factors in substance use across adolescence. *Journal of Adolescent Health, 43*(2), 157–164.

Crane, C. A., Easton, C. J., & Devine, S. (2013). The association between phencyclidine use and partner violence: An initial examination. *Journal of Addictive Diseases, 32*(2), 150–157. doi:10.1080/10550887.2013.797279

Deas, D., & Clark, A. (2009). Current state of treatment for alcohol and other drug use disorders in adolescents. *Alcohol Research & Health, 32*(1), 76–82.

De Bellis, M. D., Wang, L., Bergman, S. R., Yaxley, R. H., Hooper, S. R., & Huettel, S. A. (2013). Neural mechanisms of risky decision-making and reward response in adolescent onset cannabis use disorder. *Drug and Alcohol Dependence, 133*(1), 134–145.

DiFranza, J. R., Ursprung, W. W. S., & Biller, L. (2012). The developmental sequence of tobacco withdrawal symptoms of wanting, craving and needing. *Pharmacology Biochemistry and Behavior, 100*(3), 494–497.

Donovan, D. M., Bigelow, G. E., Brigham, G. S., Carroll, K. M., Cohen, A. J., Gardin, J. G., … Wells, W. A. (2011). Primary outcome indices in illicit drug dependence treatment research: Systematic approach to selection and measurement of drug use end-points in clinical trials. *Addiction, 107*(4), 694–708

Dougherty, D. M., Mathias, C.W., Liguori, A., Marsh, D. M., Dawes, M. A., & Moeller, F. G. (2007). Behavioral impulsivity in adolescent with conduct disorder who use marijuana. *Addictive Disorders & Their Treatment, 6*(1), 43–50.

Drummond, R. J., Sheperis, C. J., & Jones, K. D. (2015). *Assessment procedures for counselors and helping professionals* (8th ed.). Upper Saddle River, NJ: Pearson.

Enomoto, T., Noda, Y., Mouri, A., Shin, E. J., Wang, D., Murai, R., … Nabeshima, T. (2005). Long-lasting impairment of associative learning is correlated with a dysfunction of N-methyl-D-aspartate-extracellular signaling-regulated kinase signaling in mice after withdrawal from repeated administration of phencyclidine. *Molecular Pharmacology, 68*(6), 1765–1774.

Effinger, J. M., & Stewart, D. G. (2012). Classification of co-occurring depression and substance abuse symptoms predicts suicide attempts in adolescents. *Suicide and Life-Threatening Behavior, 42*(4), 353–358. doi:10.1111/j.1943-278X.2012.00092.x

Ersche, K. D., Jones, P. S., Williams, G. B., Smith, D. G., Bullmore, E. T., & Robbins, T. W. (2013). Distinctive personality traits and neural correlates associated with stimulant drug use versus familial risk of stimulant dependence. *Biological Psychiatry, 74*(2), 137–144.

Esposito-Smythers, C., & Goldston, D. B. (2008). Challenges and opportunities in the treatment of adolescents with substance use disorder and suicidal behavior. *Substance Abuse, 29*(2), 5–17.

Evren, C., & Bozkurt, M. (2013). Synthetic cannabinoids: Crisis of the decade. *Düşünen Adam: Journal of Psychiatry and Neurological Sciences, 26*, 1–11. Retrieved from http://www.dusunenadamdergisi.org/ing/fArticledetails.aspx?MkID=915

Ewing, J. A. (1984). Detecting alcoholism: The CAGE questionnaire. *Journal of the American Medical Association, 252*(14), 1905–1907.

Falck, R. S., Nahhas, R. W., Li, L., & Carlson, R. G. (2012). Surveying teens in school to assess the prevalence of problematic drug use. *Journal of School Health, 82*(5), 217–224. doi:10.1111/j.1746-1561 .2012.00690.x

Fareed, A., Stout, S., Casarella, J., Vayalapalli, S., Cox, J., & Drexler, K. (2011). Illicit opioid intoxication: Diagnosis and treatment. *Substance Abuse: Research and Treatment, 5*, 17–25. doi:10.4137/SART.S7090

First, M. B. (2013). *DSM-5 handbook of differential diagnosis*. Arlington, VA: American Psychiatric Publishing.

Fisher, D., Grap, M. J., Younger, J. B., Ameringer, S., & Elswick, R. K. (2013). Opioid withdrawal signs and symptoms in children: Frequency and determinants. *Heart & Lung: The Journal of Acute and Critical Care, 42*(6), 407–413. doi:10.1016/j.hrtlng .2013.07.008

Fishman, M. (2011). Placement criteria and treatment planning for adolescents with substance use disorders. In Y. Kaminer & K. C. Winters (Eds.), *Clinical manual of adolescent substance abuse treatment* (pp. 113–141). Arlington, VA: American Psychiatric Publishing.

Fox, C. M. (2014). *Assessing our youth: Clinician perceptions of assessment practices with adolescents in substance abuse treatment* (Doctoral dissertation). Retrieved from ProQuest Dissertations & Theses.

Gahr, M., & Kölle, M. A. (2014). Methylphenidate intoxication: Somnolence as an uncommon clinical symptom and proof of overdosing by increased serum levels of ritalinic acid. *Pharmacopsychiatry, 47*(6), 215–218. doi:10.1055/s-0034-1387700

Gahr, M., Plener, P. L., Kölle, M. A., Freudenmann, R. W., & Schönfeldt-Lecuona, C. (2012). Self-mutilation induced by psychotropic substances: A systematic review. *Psychiatry Research, 200*(2/3), 977–983. doi:10.1016/j.psychres.2012.06.028

Garland, E. L., & Howard, M. O. (2010). Phenomenology of adolescent inhalant intoxication. *Experimental and Clinical Psychopharmacology, 18*(6), 498–509.

Garland, E. L., & Howard, M. O. (2011). Adverse consequences of acute inhalant intoxication. *Experimental and Clinical Psychopharmacology, 19*(2), 134–144.

Greene, M. C., & Kelly, J. F. (2014). The prevalence of cannabis withdrawal and its influence on adolescents' treatment response and outcomes: A 12-month prospective investigation. *Journal of Addiction Medicine, 8*(5), 359–367.

Haberstick, B. C., Young, S. E., Zeiger, J. S., Lessem, J. M., Hewitt, J. K., & Hopfer, C. J. (2014). Prevalence and correlates of alcohol and cannabis use disorders in the United States: Results from the national longitudinal study of adolescent health. *Drug and Alcohol Dependence, 136*, 158–161.

Hartney, E. (2013). *DSM 5 criteria for substance use disorders: The symptoms used for the diagnosis of substance use disorders.* Retrieved from http://addictions.about.com/od/aboutaddiction/a/Dsm-5-Criteria-For-Substance-Use-Disorders.htm

Hassanian-Moghaddam, H., Afzali, S., & Pooya, A. (2014). Withdrawal syndrome caused by naltrexone in opioid abusers. *Human & Experimental Toxicology, 33*(6), 561–567. doi:10.1177/0960327112450901

Henggeler, S. W., Halliday-Boykins, C. A., Cunningham, P. B., Randall, J., Shapiro, S. B., & Chapman, J. E. (2006). Juvenile drug court: Enhancing outcomes by integrating evidence-based treatments. *Journal of Consulting and Clinical Psychology, 74*(1), 42–54.

Hermanns-Clausen, M., Kneisel, S., Szabo, B., & Auwärter, V. (2013). Acute toxicity due to the confirmed consumption of synthetic cannabinoids: clinical and laboratory findings. *Addiction, 108*(3), 534–544. doi:10.1111/j.1360-0443.2012.04078.x

Hermle, L., Simon, M., Ruchsow, M., & Geppert, M. (2012). Hallucinogen-persisting perception disorder. *Therapeutic Advances in Psychopharmacology, 2*(5), 199–205. doi:10.1177/2045125312451270

Hesse, M., & Thylstrup, B. (2013). Time-course of the DSM-5 cannabis withdrawal symptoms in polysubstance abusers. *BMC Psychiatry, 13*(1), 200–221. doi:10.1186/1471-244X-13-258

Hogue, A., Henderson, C. E., Ozechowski, T. J., & Robbins, M. S. (2014). Evidence base on outpatient behavioral treatments for adolescent substance use: Updates and recommendations 2007–2013. *Journal of Clinical Child & Adolescent Psychology, 43*(5), 695–720.

Hughes, J. R., Fingar, J. R., Budney, A. J., Naud, S., Helzer, J. E., & Callas, P. W. (2014). Marijuana use and intoxication among daily users: An intensive longitudinal study. *Addictive Behaviors, 39*(10), 1464–1470. doi:10.1016/j.addbeh.2014.05.024

Hurd, Y. L., Michaelides, M., Miller, M. L., & Jutras-Aswad, D. (2014). Trajectory of adolescent cannabis use on addiction vulnerability. *Neuropharmacology, 76*(Part B), 416–424.

Imel, Z. E., Wampold, B. E., Miller, S. D., & Fleming, R. R. (2008). Distinctions without a difference: Direct comparisons of psychotherapies for alcohol use disorders. *Psychology of Addictive Behaviors, 22*(4), 533–543.

Jackson, D. A. E., Cotter, B. V., Merchant, R. C., Babu, K. M., Baird, J. R., Nirenberg, T., & Linakis, J. G. (2013). Behavioral and physiologic adverse effects in adolescent and young adult emergency department patients reporting use of energy drinks and caffeine. *Clinical Toxicology, 51*(7), 557–565. doi:10.3109/15563650.2013.820311

Jinwala, F. N., & Gupta, M. (2012). Synthetic cannabis and respiratory depression. *Journal of Child and Adolescent Psychopharmacology, 22*(6), 459–462.

Johnston, L. D., O'Malley, P. M., Bachman, J. G., & Schulenberg, J. E. (2012). *Monitoring the future national results on adolescent drug use: Overview of key findings, 2011.* Ann Arbor: Institute for Social Research, The University of Michigan.

Jovel, A., Felthous, A., & Bhattacharyya, A. (2014). Delirium due to intoxication from the novel synthetic tryptamine 5-MeO-DALT. *Journal of Forensic Sciences, 59*(3), 844–846. doi:10.1111/1556-4029.12367

Juliano, L. M., Huntley, E. D., Harrell, P. T., & Westerman, A. T. (2012). Development of the Caffeine Withdrawal Symptom Questionnaire: Caffeine withdrawal symptoms cluster into 7 factors. *Drug and Alcohol Dependence, 124*(3), 229–234.

Kadden, R. M., Litt, M. D., Kabela-Cormier, E., & Petry, N. M. (2007). Abstinence rates following behavioral treatments for marijuana dependence. *Addictive Behaviors, 32*(6), 1220–1236.

Kaminer, Y. (2010). Problematic use of energy drinks by adolescents. *Child and Adolescent Psychiatric Clinics of North America, 19*(3), 643–650.

Karki, S., Pietila, A. M., Lansimies-Antikainen, H., Pirjovarjoranta, P., Pirskanen, M., & Laukkanen, E. (2012). The effects of interventions to prevent substance use among adolescents: A systematic review. *Journal of Child & Adolescent Substance Abuse, 21*(5), 383–413.

Katayama, T., Okamoto, M., Suzuki, Y., Hoshino, K. Y., & Jodo, E. (2013). Phencyclidine affects firing activity of ventral tegmental area neurons that are related to reward and social behaviors in rats. *Neuroscience, 240*, 336–348. doi:10.1016/j.neuroscience.2013.02.047

King, J. H. (2014). *Using the DSM-5: Try it, you'll like it.* Retrieved from http://www.continuingedcourses.net/active/courses/course081.php

Killeen, T. K., McRae-Clark, A. L., Waldrop, A. E., Upadhyaya, H., & Brady, K. T. (2012). Contingency management in community programs treating adolescent substance abuse: A feasibility study. *Journal of Child and Adolescent Psychiatric Nursing*, *25*(1), 33–41.

Killeen, T. K., McRae-Clark, A. L., Waldrop, A. E., Upadhyaya, H., Brady, K.T., Budney, A. J., … Higgins, S. T. (2006). Clinical trial of abstinence-based vouchers and cognitive behavioral therapy for cannabis dependence. *Journal of Consulting and Clinical Psychology*, *74*(2), 307–316.

Küçer, N. (2010). Günlük kafein tüketimi ile yoksunluk beiirtileri arasındaki ilişki: Anket çalışması [The relationship between daily caffeine consumption and withdrawal symptoms: A questionnaire-based study]. *TÜBİTAK*, *40*(1), 105–108. doi:10.3906/sag-0809-26

Lee, H. M., & Roth, B. L. (2012). Hallucinogen actions on human brain revealed. *Proceedings of the National Academy of Sciences of the United States of America*, *109*(6), 1820–1821. doi:10.1073/pnas.1121358109

Lee, J. O., Hill, K. G., Guttmannova, K., Hartigan, L. A., Catalano, R. F., & Hawkins, J. D. (2014). Childhood and adolescent predictors of heavy episodic drinking and alcohol use disorder at ages 21 and 33: A domain-specific cumulative risk model. *Journal of Studies on Alcohol and Drugs*, *75*(4), 684–694.

Liddle, H. A., Dakof, G. A., Parker, K., Diamond, G. S., Barrett & Tejeda, M. (2001). Multidimensional family therapy for adolescent drug abuse: Results of a randomized clinical trial. *American Journal of Drug and Alcohol Use*, *27*(4), 651–688.

Liddle, H. A., Dakof, G. A., Turner, R. M., Henderson, C. E., & Greenbaum, P. E. (2008). Treating adolescent drug abuse: A randomized trial comparing multidimensional family therapy and cognitive behavior therapy. *Addiction*, *103*(10), 1660–1670.

Magill, M., & Ray, L. A. (2009). Cognitive-behavioral treatment with adult alcohol and illicit drug users: A meta-analysis of randomized controlled trials. *Journal of Studies on Alcohol and Drugs*, *70*(4), 516–527.

McCabe, S. E., & West, B. T. (2013). Medical and non-medical use of prescription stimulants: Results from a national multicohort study. *Journal of the American Academy of Child & Adolescent Psychiatry*, *52*(12), 1272–1280. doi:10.1016/j.jaac.2013.09.005

McCabe, S. E., West, B. T., & Boyd, C. J. (2013). Motives for medical misuse of prescription opioids among adolescents. *The Journal of Pain*, *14*(10), 1208–1216.

Miller, G. A. (2005). *Substance Abuse Subtle Screening Inventory-3*. Springville, IN: SASSI Institute.

Muncie, H. L., Yasinian, Y., & Oge, L. (2013). Outpatient management of alcohol withdrawal syndrome. *American Family Physician*, *88*(9), 589–595.

Nakawaki, B., & Crano, W. D. (2012). Predicting adolescents' persistence, non-persistence, and recent onset of nonmedical use of opioids and stimulants. *Addictive Behaviors*, *37*(6), 716–721. 10.1016/j.addbeh.2012.02.011

Northrup, T. F., Stotts, A. L., Green, C., Potter, J. S., Marino, N., Walker, R., … Trivedi, M. (2015). Opioid withdrawal, craving, and use during and after outpatient buprenorphine stabilization and taper: A discrete survival and growth mixture model. *Addictive Behaviors*, *41*, 20–28. doi:10.1016/j.addbeh.2014.09.021

O'Brien, C. P. (2012). Rationale for changes in DSM-5. *Journal of Studies on Alcohol and Drugs*, *73*(4), 705.

Okamoto, J., Ritt-Olson, A., Soto, D., Baezconde-Garbanati, L., & Unger, J. B. (2009). Perceived discrimination and substance use among Latino adolescents. *American Journal of Health Behavior*, *33*(6), 718–727.

Oshri, A., Rogosch, F. A., Burnette, M. L., & Cicchetti, D. (2011). Developmental pathways to adolescent cannabis abuse and dependence: Child maltreatment, emerging personality, and internalizing versus externalizing psychopathology. *Psychology of Addictive Behaviors*, *25*(4), 634–644.

Ozsungur, S., Brenner, D., & El-Sohemy, A. (2009). Fourteen well-described caffeine withdrawal symptoms factor into three clusters. *Psychopharmacology*, *201*(4), 541–548. doi:10.1007/s00213-008-1329-y

Prendergast, M. L., Hall, E. A., Roll, J., & Warda, U. (2008). Use of vouchers to reinforce abstinence and positive behaviors among clients in a drug court treatment program. *Journal of Substance Abuse Treatment*, *35*(2), 125–136.

Perera-Diltz, D. M., & Perry, J. C. (2011). Screening for adolescent substance-related disorders using the SASSI–A2: Implications for nonreporting youth. *Journal of Addictions & Offender Counseling*, *31*(2), 66–79.

Pergadia, M. L., Agrawal, A., Heath, A. C., Martin, N. G., Bucholz, K. K., & Madden, P. A. F. (2010). Nicotine withdrawal symptoms in adolescent and adult twins. *Twin Research and Human Genetics*, *13*(4), 359–369.

Perron, B. E., & Howard, M. O. (2009). Adolescent inhalant use, abuse and dependence. *Addiction*, *104*(7), 1185–1192.

Perron, B. E., Howard, M. O., Maitra, S., & Vaughn, M. G. (2009). Prevalence, timing, and predictors of transitions from inhalant use to inhalant use disorders. *Drug and Alcohol Dependence, 100*(3), 277–284. 10.1016/j.drugalcdep.2008.10.017

Petry, N. M. (2000). A comprehensive guide to the application of contingency management in clinical settings. *Drug and Alcohol Dependence, 58*, 9–25.

Prado, G., Huang, S., Schwartz, S. J., Maldonado-Molina, M. M., Bandiera, F. C., de la Rosa, M., & Patin, H. (2009). What accounts for differences in substance use among U.S.-born and immigrant Hispanic adolescents: Results from a longitudinal prospective cohort study. *The Journal of Adolescent Health, 45*(2), 118–125.

Pilowsky, D. J., & Wu, L. T. (2013). Screening instruments for substance use and brief interventions targeting adolescents in primary care: A literature review. *Addictive Behaviors, 38*(5), 2146–2153. 10.1016/j.addbeh.2013.01.015

Rieckmann, T., Fussell, H., Doyle, K., Ford, J., Riley, K. J., & Henderson, S. (2011). Adolescent substance abuse treatment: Organizational change and quality of care. *Journal of Addictions & Offender Counseling, 31*(2), 80–93.

Rowe, C. L., & Liddle, H. A. (2003). Substance abuse. *Journal of Marital Family Therapy, 29*(1), 97–120.

Schwinn, T. M., Schinke, S. P., & Di Noia, J. (2010). Preventing drug abuse among adolescent girls: Outcome data from an Internet-based intervention. *Prevention Science, 11*(1), 24–32.

Shen, H. W., Jiang, X. L., Winter, J. C., & Yu, A. M. (2010). Psychedelic 5-methoxy-N, N-dimethyltryptamine: Metabolism, pharmacokinetics, drug interactions, and pharmacological actions. *Current Drug Metabolism, 11*(8), 659–666.

Skogen, J. C., Øverland, S., Knudsen, A. K., & Mykletun, A. (2011). Concurrent validity of the CAGE questionnaire. The Nord-Trøndelag Health Study. *Addictive Behaviors, 36*(4), 302–307. 10.1016/j.addbeh.2010.11.010

Slesnick, N., & Prestopnik, J. L. (2009). Comparison of family therapy outcome with alcohol-abusing, runaway adolescents. *Journal of Marital and Family Therapy, 35*(3), 255–277.

Sloboda, Z., Stephens, R. C., Stephens, P. C., Grey, S. F., Teasdale, B., Hawthorne, R. D., … Marquette, J. F. (2009). The Adolescent Substance Abuse Prevention Study: A randomized field trial of a universal substance abuse prevention program. *Drug and Alcohol Dependence, 102*(1–3), 1–10.

Spear, L. (2013). The teenage brain: Adolescents and alcohol. *Current Directions in Psychological Science, 22*(2), 152–157.

Spoth, R., Trudeau, L., Redmond, C., & Shin, C. (2008). Finding a path to more reasonable conclusions about prevention: A response to Midford. *Addiction, 103*(7), 1171–1173.

Stanger, C., Budney, A. J., Kamon, J. L., & Thostensen, J. (2009). A randomized trial of contingency management for adolescent marijuana abuse and dependence. *Drug & Alcohol Dependence, 105*(3), 240–247.

Stewart, S., & Swain, S. (2012). Assessment and management of alcohol dependence and withdrawal in the acute hospital: Concise guidance. *Clinical Medicine, 12*(3), 266–271.

Stewart, S. H., & Connors, G. J. (2004). Screening for alcohol problems: What makes a test effective? *Alcohol Research & Health, 28*(1), 5–16.

Subramanian, N., & Doran, M. (2014). Improvement of hallucinogen persisting perception disorder (HPPD) with oral risperidone: Case report. *Irish Journal of Psychological Medicine, 31*(1), 47–49.

Substance Abuse and Mental Health Services Administration. (2014). *Results from the 2013 National Survey on Drug Use and Health.* Rockville, MD: Author.

Tang, M. H. Y., Ching, C. K., Tsui, M. S. H., Chu, F. K. C., & Mak, T. W. L. (2014). Two cases of severe intoxication associated with analytically confirmed use of the novel psychoactive substances 25B-NBOMe and 25C-NBOMe. *Clinical Toxicology, 52*(5), 561–565. doi:10.3109/15563650.2014.909932

Tanner-Smith, E. E., Wilson, S. J., & Lipsey, M. W. (2013). The comparative effectiveness of outpatient treatment for adolescent substance abuse: A meta-analysis. *Journal of Substance Abuse Treatment, 44*(2), 145–158.

Thatcher, D. L., & Clark, D. B. (2006). Adolescent alcohol abuse and dependence: Development, diagnosis, treatment and outcomes. *Current Psychiatry Reviews, 2*(1), 159–177.

Theunissen, E. L., Kauert, G. F., Toennes, S. W., Moeller, M. R., Sambeth, A., Blanchard, M. M., & Ramaekers, J. G. (2012). Neurophysiological functioning of occasional and heavy cannabis users during THC intoxication. *Psychopharmacology, 220*(2), 341–350. doi:10.1007/s00213-011-2479-x

Vaiserman, A. M. (2013). Long-term health consequences of early-life exposure to substance abuse: An epigenetic perspective. *Journal of Developmental*

Origins of Health and Disease, 4(4), 269–279. doi:10.1017/S2040174413000123

Vanden Eede, H., Montenij, L. J., Touw, D. J., & Norris, E. M. (2012). Rhabdomyolysis in MDMA intoxication: A rapid and underestimated killer. "Clean" ecstasy, a safe party drug? *The Journal of Emergency Medicine, 42*(6), 655–658. doi:10.1016/j.jemermed.2009.04.057

Welte, J. W., Barnes, G. M., Tidwell, M. C. O., & Hoffman, J. H. (2011). Tobacco use, heavy use, and dependence among adolescents and young adults in the United States. *Substance Use & Misuse, 46*(9), 1090–1098.

Whiteside, L. K., Walton, M. A., Bohnert, A. S. B., Blow, F. C., Bonar, E. E., Ehrlich, P., & Cunningham, R. M. (2013). Nonmedical prescription opioid and sedative use among adolescents in the emergency department. *Pediatrics, 132*(5), 825–832. doi:10.1542/peds.2013-0721

Winters, K. C. (1992). Development of an adolescent alcohol and other drug abuse screening scale: Personal Experiences Screening Questionnaire. *Addictive Behaviors, 17*, 479–490.

Winters, K. C., Botzet, A. M., & Fahnhorst, T. (2011). Advances in adolescent substance abuse treatment. *Current Psychiatry Reports, 13*(5), 416–421. doi:10.1007/s11920-011-0214-2

Witkiewitz, K., & Marlatt, G.A. (2011). Behavioral therapy across the spectrum. *Alcohol Research & Health, 33*(4), 313–319.

Wu, L. T., Brady, K. T., Mannelli, P., & Killeen, T. K. (2014). Cannabis use disorders are comparatively prevalent among nonwhite racial/ethnic groups and adolescents: A national study. *Journal of Psychiatric Research, 50*, 26–35.

Young, A. M., Glover, N., & Havens, J. R. (2012). Nonmedical use of prescription medications among adolescents in the United States: A systematic review. *Journal of Adolescent Health, 51*(1), 6–17.

Zhan, W., Dierker, L. C., Rose, J. S., Selya, A., & Mermelstein, R. J. (2012). The natural course of nicotine dependence symptoms among adolescent smokers. *Nicotine & Tobacco Research, 14*(12), 1445–1452.

Chapter 18

Major and Mild Neurocognitive Disorders Due to Traumatic Brain Injury

Gregory S. Hupp, Richard J. Cicchetti, and Gary M. Szirony

Introduction

Traumatic brain injury (TBI) has gone by many different monikers over the years. Among some of TBI's aliases are head injury, concussion, brain damage, and more recently, post-concussive syndrome. For ease of discussion among both professionals and the public, any cognitive impairment caused by an external force or injury to the head is now most commonly identified as a traumatic brain injury (TBI).

TBI is a leading cause of death and disability worldwide (Goldsmith, 2014) and is the most common cause of death in children (Chen & Wu, 2011). TBI describes a range of injuries to the brain caused by a blow to the head or a penetrating injury to the skull. Results could include mild concussion, loss of consciousness, severe disability, and death, and TBI can affect virtually anyone at any age. According to the Centers for Disease Control and Prevention (CDC), about 2.5 million individuals suffering from TBI reach the emergency departments of hospitals or are hospitalized annually, and TBI is a leading cause of death in the United States. Approximately 30 percent, or just under one-third, of all deaths because of injury involve TBI. Approximately 138 people die daily from injuries that include TBI, and those who survive a TBI can face a lifetime of debilitating function that can include cognitive deficits, movement disorders, a loss of sensation, vision or hearing problems, personality changes, and depression (CDC National Center for Injury Prevention and Control, 2015).

From 2006 to 2010, leading causes of TBI included falls, being struck by or against an object (mainly unintentionally), motor vehicle accidents, and assaults. Falls accounted for 40 percent of all TBIs, with motor vehicle crashes accounting for about 14 percent. Assaults resulting in TBIs were responsible for about 10 percent of all cases, and nearly 15 percent related to unintentional blunt-force trauma in children and adults. Nearly 20 percent, or one in five, of all causes of TBI were listed as unknown. Among children and adolescents, approximately one in four TBI incidents in those under the age of 15 are because of unintentional blunt-force trauma. More than half of TBIs among children up to the age of 14 were caused by falls (CDC National Center for Injury Prevention and Control, 2015).

In recent years, much attention has been given to sports-related TBI (Halstead & Walter, 2010) and TBI among veterans returning from the wars in the Middle East. Sports concussions are frequent causes of TBI in older children, teenagers, and young adults. Head injuries are common in society, and although many do not lead to brain injury or cause only transient problems, the volume of head injuries alone suggests that neurocognitive disorders due to TBI are substantial (Simpson, 2014). Most disconcertingly, the rate of emergency visits for sports- or recreation-related injuries with a diagnosis of TBI rose by 57 percent among those 19 years of age or younger (CDC, 2011, as cited in CDC National Center for Injury Prevention and Control, 2015). However, it is interesting to note that many people who experience a concussion might not seek medical attention. Among the most common medical conditions for returning veterans from Iraq and Afghanistan are TBIs. Because of the frequent use of improvised explosive devices (IEDs), it is estimated one-third of returning veterans from Iraq and Afghanistan might suffer from a form of TBI (Okie, 2005, as cited in Veterans Health Initiative, 2010).

In general, TBI affects children and adolescents as well as older age groups disproportionately. The highest rates of emergency room visits were among children 4 years of age or younger. Among children and early adolescents ranging in age from 5 to 14, blunt-force trauma was the second leading cause of TBI-related emergency room visits. For adolescents and young adults, motor vehicle crashes ranked among the leading causes of hospitalization. According to the National Vital Statistics System mortality data (CDC National Center for Injury Prevention and Control, 2014), although TBI-related injuries have increased, deaths rates decreased slightly during the decade that began in 2001 and ended in 2010, from about 5.2 deaths per 100,000 to about 4.3 deaths per 100,000 among children less than 5 years of age. For the age group 5 through 14, death rates also decreased slightly from about 3.2 per 100,000 to just under two per 100,000. Sidebar 18.1 illustrates the extent of TBI as a major health problem in children and adolescents.

SIDEBAR 18.1: TBI—A MAJOR HEALTH PROBLEM IN CHILDREN AND ADOLESCENTS

- In 2010, among children and youth aged 0 to 14 years in the United States, more than half of all TBIs were because of falls.
- Assault accounted for 3 percent of TBIs in children under 15 years of age.
- In 2009, just under 250,000 children in the United States under the age of 21 were treated in emergency rooms (ERs) for sports- and recreation-related injuries resulting in a diagnosis of concussion or TBI.
- The greatest increase in ER visits during the years 2007–2008 through 2008–2009 increased the most for children 4 years of age or less.
- TBI resulted in more than 280,000 hospitalizations and 2.2 million ER visits in 2010 (CDC National Center for Injury Prevention and Control, 2015).

Description of the Disorder

Often, identifying the etiology of a TBI is fairly obvious—a baseball to the head, a car accident, or a fall out of a tree. Trying to identify the severity and functional impairment of TBI is an entirely more complicated process. Several classification systems for the diagnosis of TBI have been developed. Some are more simplistic than others, whereas some are more specific to the events that caused the TBI, such as for sports-related TBIs. In the case of pediatric TBI, the CDC identifies such an injury as "an occurrence of injury to the head resulting from blunt trauma or acceleration or deceleration forces," whereas the World Health Organization (WHO) identifies TBI as "an acute brain injury resulting from mechanical energy to the head from external forces" (McCrea, 2008, p. 23). The list that follows refers to the CDC's (CDC National Center for Injury Prevention and Control, 2010) case definition for TBI.

Traumatic brain injury (craniocerebral trauma) is defined either:

- As an occurrence of injury to the head that is documented in a medical record, with one or more of the following conditions attributed to head injury:
  - Observed or self-reported decreased level of consciousness
  - Amnesia
  - Skull fracture
  - Objective neurological or neuropsychological abnormality
  - Diagnosed intracranial lesion
- Or as an occurrence of death resulting from trauma, with head injury listed on the death certificate, autopsy report, or medical examiner's report in the sequence of conditions that resulted in death.

Previous editions of the *DSM* lumped the cognitive effects of a TBI into very narrowly defined conditions. It was either cognitive impairment because of dementia or because of (often drug-induced) delirium. Any other cognitive impairment was lumped primarily into a single diagnosis—that of a Cognitive Disorder Not Otherwise Specified. Fortunately, as our understanding and diagnostic capabilities of TBI have expanded, so have the diagnostic criteria in the *Diagnostic and Statistical Manual of Mental Disorders, Fifth Edition* (*DSM-5*).

DSM-5 Criteria

The *DSM-5* (American Psychiatric Association [APA], 2013) includes TBI under the Neurocognitive Disorders (NCDs) classification. NCDs include a range of cognitive difficulties, and their accompanied social-emotional effects, that range from congenital to adventitious disorders, organic to external etiologies, and static to progressive cognitive impairments. The *DSM-5* also makes a valid attempt to identify the emotional and psychological impact of such NCDs by a determination of severity of the neurocognitive impairment. New diagnostic classifications include both Mild Neurocognitive Disorder and Major Neurocognitive Disorder. It is important to note that any cognitive impairment is not otherwise attributable to another psychiatric condition, such as drug misuse or intoxication, schizophrenia, or neurodevelopmental disorders.

The diagnostic criteria for any of the NCDs are all based on key cognitive domains along with defined guidelines for clinical thresholds. Those key cognitive domains and their descriptions include the following:

Complex attention—Deficits in sustained attention, divided attention, selective attention, and speed of cognitive processing.

Executive function—Deficits in executive function, also frequently identified as *executive dysfunction*, may include difficulties with planning, problem solving, decision making, error correction, inhibition, and cognitive flexibility.

Learning and memory—Learning and memory deficits range from difficulty with implicit and immediate memory to very-long-term memory impairment for autobiographical information.

Language—Language deficits include both expressive and receptive communication difficulties. Deficits may include various aphasias, such as word-finding problems, lack of fluency, and improper use of grammar and syntax.

Perceptual-motor—Any difficulty in sensory perception or sensory processing may be included under the realm of a perceptual-motor deficit. Problems with visual perception, visuo-construction, and apraxias (inability to initiate or complete motor responses) and agnoses (inability to name or recognize objects).

Social cognition—Difficulties in social cognition are one of the newer areas of understanding. Social cognition includes the ability to recognize emotions properly and *theory of mind*, which is the ability to consider another person's mental state or point of view.

Major NCDs must include evidence of significant cognitive decline in one or more of the aforementioned cognitive domains that results in significant interference with activities of daily living and independence that are not the result of a delirium. Major NCDs should include specifiers that they occur either with or without behavioral disturbance, as well as the level of impairment that occurs because of the disorder, be it mild, moderate, or severe.

Mild NCDs, the most common of the two categories of TBI (Rao et al., 2010), must include evidence of a modest decline in functioning in one or more of the aforementioned cognitive domains, but those deficits do not necessarily interfere with independent functioning in daily activities and are not the result of a delirium or better accounted for by another mental health disorder.

Both major and mild NCDs can include specifiers that they occur either with or without behavioral disturbance, as well as the level of impairment that occurs because of the disorder, be it mild, moderate, or severe. Although no close correlation between severity of TBI and subsequent cognitive impairment can be seen, the probability certainly exists (Simpson, 2014). Behavioral features have been recognized in NCDs. Mood disorders, such as depression, anxiety, and elation, may occur, along with agitation, including confusion and frustration. Agitation is common, particularly in major NCDs. Sleep disturbances are common symptoms and can include insomnia, hypersomnia, and circadian rhythm disturbances. Apathy is common in both mild and major NCDs and can occur early in the course, when there is a loss of motivation to pursue activities of daily living (Jeste, Meeks, Kim, & Zubenko, 2006).

The *DSM-5* identifies under the Diagnostic Features section that "at the mild NCD level, the individual is likely to describe these tasks as being more difficult or as requiring extra time or effort or compensatory strategies" (APA, 2013a, p. 607) to accomplish daily tasks. For impairment at the major NCD level, "such tasks may only be completed with assistance or abandoned all together" (p. 607). Either of the categories, mild NCD or major NCD, may include mood disturbances, such as depression, anxiety, irritability, agitation, sleep disturbance, or elation.

With regard to culturally related concerns, especially the mild NCDs, those symptoms and subtle difficulties are more likely to be noticed in those individuals who engage in more complex occupational, educational, or recreational activities. NCDs with onset in childhood and adolescence may have broad repercussions for social and intellectual development, and in this setting intellectual disability (intellectual developmental disorder) or other neurodevelopmental disorders may also be diagnosed to capture the full diagnostic picture and ensure the provision of a broad range of services. In older individuals, NCDs often occur in the setting of medical illnesses, frailty, and sensory loss, which complicate the clinical picture for diagnosis and treatment. When cognitive loss occurs in youth, individuals and families are likely to seek care. NCDs are typically easiest to identify at younger ages, although in some settings malingering or other factitious disorders may be a concern. In younger individuals, NCD often co-occurs with neurodevelopmental disorders; for example, a head injury in a preschool child may also lead to significant developmental and learning issues. Persisting TBI-related impairment in an infant or child may be reflected in delays in reaching developmental milestones (e.g., language acquisition), in worse academic performance, and possibly in impaired social development. Among older teenagers and adults, persisting symptoms may include various neurocognitive deficits, irritability, hypersensitivity to light and sound, easy fatigability, and mood changes, including depression, anxiety, hostility, or apathy. Additionally, proficiency in one's native language versus his or her secondary language, as well as a cultural tendency to minimize somatic symptoms often associated with NCDs, are factors clinicians should fully examine.

Differential Diagnosis

The brain is the central feature of the central nervous system. It is common knowledge that the brain controls homeostasis of hormones and other neurochemicals within the body, that the brain receives sensory input and produces a response to such stimuli, and that the brain affects our ability to learn, laugh, cry, and remember. In essence, the brain controls every aspect of our lives. Damage to such an organ will, naturally, affect all aspects of our lives at some level. Damage to the brain will result in a complex array of symptoms that affect an ability to function on a daily basis. Those symptoms will fall into one of three categories: physical, cognitive, or emotional.

The *DSM-5* notes that differential diagnoses between normal cognition and mild NCD are challenging because "the boundaries are inherently arbitrary" (APA, 2013a, p. 610). In some cases, differential diagnoses should be considered when the reported neurocognitive symptoms appear to be inconsistent with the severity of the TBI. In such cases, biomedical and neuroimaging studies may help exclude organic conditions that may be affecting cognitive functioning. Once such biological markers are excluded, other considerations should turn to ruling out other psychophysiological conditions, such as somatic symptom disorder or a factitious disorder. Pathological emotional conditions, such as depression, anxiety, and posttraumatic stress disorder, often co-occur with NCDs, so identifying the presence and severity of overlapping symptoms, such as difficulty concentrating, behavioral disinhibition, attention deficits, and distractibility, is indicated. NCDs may also occur in individuals with substance use disorders, specific learning disorders, and other neurodevelopmental disorders, such as an intellectual disability, autism spectrum disorder, or an attention-deficit/hyperactivity disorder.

PHYSICAL DEFICITS

The physical aspects of a TBI are dependent on the location, extent, and nature of the injury. Often, for a major NCD, the TBI may be the result of a severe trauma combined with a significant physical injury. A child who is thrown from a moving vehicle is likely to suffer not only a head injury, but also some internal injuries, organ damage, and broken bones. For the more mild NCD, the TBI may be the result of shaken baby syndrome or falling out of a high chair or shopping cart. Children with a mild TBI are not likely to have external physical injuries but may suffer more internal physical problems related to the TBI, such as a persistent headache, sensitivity to touch at the site of the injury, or sensitivity to light. Mild TBIs also may include other structural injuries, such as a fractured cervical vertebra, pinched nerve, or herniated disc. Such biomechanical injuries may also result in persistent headaches, light sensitivity, and slowed cognitive processing more commonly identified as persistent migraine headaches.

Within the brain itself, a closed head injury, where there is no break in the skull or external penetrating injury, may result in widespread loss of blood or cerebrospinal fluid (CSF) and swelling of the brain. If such swelling becomes too severe, the child may need to have a hole surgically opened in the skull to give the brain some additional room to expand or have a drainage tube inserted into the subdural layer of the skull to drain off some fluid. These corrective surgical procedures may also result in some physical effects of brain damage, such as headaches and sleepiness.

Depending on the site of the injury, portions of the brain that regulate physical sensation and response (the sensorimotor cortex) or control motor movement (the occipital and parietal lobes) may be damaged. This may result in slowed response to sensory-motor stimuli—such as reacting to touching a hot stove, stepping on a tack, or repeatedly running into the left side of a door frame. Damage to the back of the head from falling backward may result in problems with balance, coordination, writing, or seeing. Damage to the occipital lobe may result in a condition known as *cortical blindness*—meaning that the child can visually perceive an object but cannot comprehend the meaning or usefulness of that object. Such sensory-motor deficits are part of the perceptual-motor domain of cognitive functioning.

COGNITIVE DEFICITS

By definition, both mild and major NCDs due to TBI also involve impairment to at least one of the six key cognitive domains. The more cognitive impairments are typically part of the key domains of attention, executive functioning, learning and memory, and language.

Children with cognitive impairments may have difficulty with multitasking (or shifting cognitive sets), planning and organizing their daily schedules and homework, or retaining and recalling information for their math test. Children with deficits in the language domain may complain of difficulty with reading, with comprehension, with solving math story problems, or with spelling. These conditions, often used by the educational community, are identified in the medical community as dyslexia, dyscalculia, dysgraphia, or as disorders of written expression. A student who is a slow learner may often be identified by her teachers as "lazy" or "not living up to her potential," when in fact, it is later discovered that the student might have suffered a mild concussion when she fell off the swing set in kindergarten. That child is likely to struggle academically until a proper diagnosis and appropriate treatment interventions are made.

EMOTIONAL-PSYCHOLOGICAL DEFICITS

The *DSM-5* (APA, 2013a) notes that "major or mild NCD due to TBI may be accompanied by disturbances in emotional function (e.g., irritability, easy frustration, tension and anxiety, affective lability); personality changes (e.g., disinhibition, apathy, suspiciousness, aggression)" (p. 625). For the child mentioned above who suffered a minor concussion back in kindergarten, her emerging academic difficulties and labeling by others (e.g., "She's lazy") are likely to create some defensiveness, irritability, and frustration. Often, children with mild TBI know that they *should* be able to perform a particular task but do not understand *why* they keep having these problems. This *not knowing why* factor is likely to manifest in a more pronounced *frustration factor*. It may actually be the frustration factor that gets the attention of the child's parents, who then seek some sort of mental health diagnosis for their child's behavior outbursts, irritability, sadness, tummy aches, headaches, and so on. A proper TBI diagnosis may help answer the why factor but must first rule out the emotional factors and determine the triggers for those emotional reactions. To diagnose a TBI properly, the *DSM-5* (APA, 2013a) states that, at a minimum, the following criteria must be met:

A. The criteria for a major or mild neurocognitive disorder must be met.
B. Evidence of a traumatic brain injury with at least one of the following:
   1. loss of consciousness
   2. evidence of posttraumatic amnesia
   3. disorientation and confusion
   4. neurological signs of injury that may include neuroimaging studies, onset or worsening of seizures, deficits in visual fields, hemiparesis, or evidence of aphasias (disturbances of the comprehension and expression of language) or apraxias (the inability to execute learned purposeful movements, despite having the desire and the physical capacity).
C. The NCD presents immediately after the occurrence of a TBI or immediately after recovery of consciousness and persists beyond six months.

Assessment Strategies

First, for a diagnosis of a major or mild NCD due to TBI, there must be evidence of, or strong likelihood of, a traumatic event involving the brain. To ascertain this, a strong family and developmental history is required. Ideally, a thorough assessment for an NCD due to TBI will include not only a strong history, but also review of medical records, academic achievement and performance, any neuroimaging studies, EEG studies, or other diagnostic information from allied health providers, such as speech, occupational, or physical therapists. Additional assessment should include a baseline cognitive assessment, neuropsychological assessment of the key domains to include motor development, behavioral, emotional, and psychosocial assessment of the child. Additional factors such as educational history, language history, and cultural history should be included as much as possible.

DETERMINING THE NATURE OF THE INJURY

Glasgow Coma Scale (GCS)

One of the most commonly applied scales for assessing general level of coma and impaired consciousness is the Glasgow Coma Scale (GCS). The scale was originally developed by Teasdale and Jennett (1974), professors of neurosurgery at the University of Glasgow's Institute of Neurological Sciences at Scotland's Southern General Hospital for the purpose of providing an objective method of assessing state of consciousness and level of coma following head injury. The GCS categorizes severity of TBI into one of three levels; mild, moderate or severe; and can be a useful indicator of severity in adults and some youth, but is not considered useful in children 0 through 4 years of age. A modification of the GCS is more appropriate in assessing younger individuals.

Children's Coma Scale

The Children's Coma Scale (CCS) is a modification of the Glasgow Coma Score designed for use with children less than 4 years of age although it is not as popular. Subscales assessing eye opening and motor response are identical to the GCS, although verbal response and behavioral aspects applied to younger individuals are adjusted in the CCS.

Rancho Los Amigos Scale

The Rancho Los Amigos Scale is a 7-level scale for assessing recovery in rehabilitation settings for those recovering from TBI related disorders. The Rancho Los Amigos scale is used to assess behavior, cognition, and response to the environment. Levels range from Level I, no response to the highest level, level 7, purposeful/appropriate response.

Abbreviated Injury Score/Injury Severity Score (AIS/ISS)

More commonly used in clinical settings, the Abbreviated Injury Score/Injury Severity Score (AIS/ISS) has been updated (AIS 98) to better assess children. The AIS score for the head is empirically correlated with GCS and has been shown to be a useful measure of TBI severity.

PHYSIOLOGICAL ASSESSMENT

Although there are some limitations to the various neuroimaging techniques, the information they do provide on positive findings can be invaluable. The easiest way to determine a head injury is to see a picture of it. If the damage is significant, has identifiable structural deficits, or shows evidence of brain tissue malformation (such as decreased ventricles, scarring, or hemispheric asymmetry), the evidence of those biomarkers can provide a valid interpretation of the functional deficits that are likely to occur.

Second only to the neuroimaging studies would be the results of an electro-encephalogram (EEG), a quantitative EEG (qEEG), or metabolic study such as Positron Emission Test (PET) or single-photon emission computerized tomography (SPECT) scan.

These types of tests are similar to the neuroimaging tests, but instead show abnormal electrical or chemical activity in the brain. The result is effectively the same—that if abnormalities are noted in these studies, then functional interpretations can be quite valid. However, similar to the neuroimaging studies, another limitation is that these physiological assessments often do not account for deficits in the social cognition domain or explain any emotional or behavioral reactions.

To help get closer to identifying the social cognition, emotional, and behavioral reactions, a review of notes from other allied health professionals and therapists is often quite beneficial. For children who experienced an early childhood TBI, those children often present with some form of developmental delay. All states have some form of federally-subsidized early childhood intervention services (ECI). ECI services typically intervene for child ages 0–3 and often involve speech, occupational, and/or physical therapy. For older, school-aged children, schools will often identify and provide speech therapy services, which can often provide some evidence regarding expressive and receptive communication deficits, how well a child responds to intervention, and how well the child retains newly acquired information. Sidebar 18.2 defines the acute physical effects of TBI.

SIDEBAR 18.2: ACUTE PHYSICAL EFFECTS OF TBI

Acute physical effects of TBI include:

- persistent headache
- repeated vomiting or nausea
- convulsions or seizures
- inability to awaken from sleep
- excessive tiredness
- slurred speech
- weakness or numbness
- loss of coordination
- increased confusion
- restlessness or agitation

Evaluation Strategies

INTERVIEWS

Parental interviews should be a cornerstone of any assessment procedure. However, parents can sometimes be less-than-desirable historians on their child's behavior. Many parents often confuse the developmental milestones of their children, might not have been present at certain critical stages due to work, health, or military obligations, or might not have been present when the brain trauma occurred. Therefore, interviews with multiple family members are preferred if possible. At the very least, the clinician should use one of the many structured developmental histories or interviews that are available, such as the Child Health Questionnaire (CHQ) or the Pediatric Evaluation of Disability Inventory (PEDI). Additional structured interviews, such as the Neuropsychological Processing Concerns Checklist for School-Aged Children and Youth (Miller 2007), would also be beneficial. Regardless of the interview instrument used, a comprehensive interview should include the following:

Birth history—length of pregnancy, complications, use of forceps, mother's health during pregnancy, mother's exposure to any chemicals or medications, and mother's use of drugs or alcohol.

Developmental history—age at which critical developmental milestones were reached and any type of developmental delays or interventions. Critical milestones include those for walking, speech development, and potty training.

Medical history—any medical or physical interventions, surgeries, or injuries the child has sustained. List of current and past medications. History of allergies, food sensitivities, and of course, head injuries of any type or intensity. Also include sleep history, sleep routine, history of insomnia, and sleep disturbances.

Family history—any history of mental retardation, developmental or intellectual delay, academic difficulties, substance abuse, and mental health history for parents, siblings, biological grandparents, and biological first cousins.

Academic achievement—current achievement levels, grades, study habits, test scores, and behavioral issues.

Social-emotional functioning—what the child's daily mood or disposition is; how well he or she handles changes in routine; number of peers; how well he or she interacts with peers, adults, and authority figures; level of child's prosocial behaviors; handling of disappointments; and leisure time activities.

For known head injuries—age of head trauma, method of injury, any loss of consciousness (LOC), length of LOC, any memory deficits, changes in child since injury, learning difficulties, and triggers to any emotional or behavioral outbursts.

Mental status examination—a mental status examination assesses a child's orientation to time, place, self, and purpose. Some structured, copyrighted measures attempt to provide normative information based on age and level of education. Other elements of a mental status examination assess a child's verbal fluency, memory, and cognitive flexibility at an age-appropriate level. Use of similar formats and noncopyrighted measures should also provide valuable insight to the child's cognitive functioning.

OBSERVATIONS

As Miller (2008) noted, children with a TBI will often display symptoms that vary greatly. Some of the more common commercially available standardized measures to assess current behavioral and developmental functioning include the Vineland Adaptive Behavior Scales, Second Edition and the Adaptive Behavior Assessment Scales, Second Edition. Sidebar 18.3 highlights deficits in various domains associated with TBI.

SIDEBAR 18.3:   TBIs' TYPICAL ASSOCIATED DEFICITS

TBI typically is associated with deficits in various domains that include:

- alertness
- attention and concentration
- intellectual functioning
- language skills
- academic achievement
- adaptive behavior

NEUROCOGNITIVE ASSESSMENT

Miller (2010) listed several possible consequences of TBI in children, identifying four primary areas of impairment: neurological (motor, sensory, and autonomic), cognitive, personality and behavior, and common lifestyle consequences. The first three areas are consistent with the key domains noted in the *DSM-5*. The fourth area, common lifestyle consequences, expanded on the functional abilities and impact as a result of a pediatric TBI. Common lifestyle consequences include inadequate academic achievement, lack of transportation alternatives, inadequate recreational activities, difficulties in maintaining interpersonal relationships, and a loss of independence and preinjury roles. These less objective consequences, coupled with differences in pediatric TBI compared with adult TBI, such as more extensive and diffuse brain swelling, exacerbated edema of brain tissue, and a more sensitive inflammatory response (Kochanek, 2006), suggested that the impact of pediatric TBI may possibly result in greater impairment and more neurocognitive domains that could be negatively affected.

With the increased likelihood of greater and more diffuse neurocognitive impairment, the need for a more comprehensive neurocognitive evaluation system arose. Because many pediatric patients with TBIs are already in school, or about to enter school, several different forms of legislation addressed this need. The No Child Left Behind Act of 2001 and the Individuals with Disabilities Education Act (IDEA) of 2004 resulted in sweeping changes in the determination and delivery of special education services (Miller, 2008). Teeter (2009) noted the importance of the need for school staff to assist in the coordination of ecologically based medication monitoring, home–school physician partnerships, and programs for children's services, suggesting "combined intervention programs for various childhood disorders" (p. 453). Coordination and regular communication among all professionals, including physicians and neuropsychologists, is required in cases of brain tumor or TBI. Teeter went on to note, "neuropsychological, cognitive, behavioral, and psychosocial factors are considered in the evaluation-intervention process," addressing the salience of accurate diagnosis and comprehensive evaluation of a full range "of the child's neurocognitive, academic, behavioral, and psychosocial needs" (p. 453).

This comprehensive need for neurocognitive assessment and monitoring of children with TBI forced a change in the practice of neuropsychological assessment. Historically, the assessment of cognitive functioning was in the purview of clinical neuropsychologists, who focused primarily on adults. The evolution of neuropsychology went from a single test approach to a battery approach to identify brain lesions and then to a more functional stage profile type of approach (Rourke, 1982), until Miller (2008) expanded this to label the current trends in neuropsychology as the "integrative and predictive stage." As the field transitioned from the fixed battery stage to the more flexible functional assessment stage in the 1990s, most neuropsychological tests were still geared toward, and normed on, adults. Although some prior attempts at neuropsychological assessment of children began to develop in the late 1960s, it was not until 2003 that the Dean-Woodcock Sensory-Motor Battery (Dean & Woodcock, 2003b, as cited in Miller, 2008) restandardized many adult neuropsychological tests on a broad-based national sample of pediatric patients. This occurred at about the same time other neuropsychological tests were being developed and normed specifically for school-aged children; tests such as the Test of Memory and Learning (TOMAL; Reynolds & Bigler, 1994 as cited in Miller, 2008) and the NEPSY (Korkman, Kirk, & Kemp, 1998) were among the earliest and most comprehensive neuropsychological tests for children.

More importantly to fully satisfy the comprehensive criteria for a diagnosis of mild or major NCD due to TBI, formal and objective assessment measures must include some sort of baseline measure and assessment of cognitive abilities across the various key domains of attention, executive function, learning and memory, language, perceptual-motor, and social cognition. The *DSM*-5 (APA, 2013a) provides details on cognitive domains on pages 593–595, noting, "The domains thus defined, along with the guidelines for clinical thresholds, form the basis on which the NCDs, their levels, and their subtypes may be diagnosed" (p. 592). Keeping consistent with other criteria, a comprehensive assessment should also include some measure of personality, behavioral functioning, and emotional lability (see Sidebar 18.4).

To establish a baseline measure, and more important establish some level of preinjury functioning, the commonly accepted approach is to use a comprehensive full-scale intelligence test. Because the function of the IQ test is to establish a baseline across a wide range of abilities, those tests that assess intelligence across several different domains are preferred. The more commonly accepted intelligence tests for children include the Wechsler Individual Scales for Children, Fourth Edition (WISC-IV) for ages 6 to 16; the Wechsler Preschool and Primary Scales of Intelligence, Fourth Edition (WPPSI-IV) for ages 3 to 6; and the Woodcock-Johnson Tests of Cognitive Abilities, Third Edition (WJ-III Cog) for ages 2 to 90 and older. Although other tests of intelligence exist, many are abbreviated forms, have too few subtests across the necessary domains, or do not contain enough items for valid and reliable factor analysis in the various domains. According to Miller (2008), the "*g* factor" of general intelligence is probably the least useful measure, whereas the qualitative and quantitative measures of performance are better used.

When considering appropriate neuropsychological tests for children, tests must be culturally relevant, situationally specific, and within socioemotional and environmental factors (Miller, 2008). Currently, similar to the IQ tests, although many single-function neuropsychological tests are on the market, only three major test batteries assess neuropsychological functioning in school-aged children. Those tests are the NEPSY-II, the WISC-IV Integrated, and the Delis-Kaplan Executive Functions System (D-KEFS).

As for the assessment of pediatric personality, behavior, adaptability, and emotional functioning, any test designed specifically to address those areas among children is generally acceptable. The primary goal is that those areas are considered an integral part of the diagnostic assessment. Sidebar 18.4 describes domains that must be included for comprehensive neuropsychological assessment to determine a major or mild NCD due to TBI.

SIDEBAR 18.4: COMPREHENSIVE NEUROPSYCHOLOGICAL ASSESSMENT DOMAINS FOR MAJOR OR MILD NCD DUE TO TBI

A comprehensive neuropsychological assessment to determine a major or mild NCD due to TBI must include the following domains:

- general intelligence or IQ
- measures of attention and concentration
- executive functioning
- learning and memory
- language
- perceptual motor
- social cognition
- behavioral adaptation
- emotional stability
- adaptive functioning

A Note on Neuropsychological Assessment

Neuropsychological assessment is a very complex, highly integrated process. The nature of major and mild NCDs due to TBI and other conditions is that every individual is different and that any two patients with the same condition may vary drastically in their presentation of deficits. The scores derived from any psychological test provide only a range of information and not a specific result. The interpretation of such comprehensive data should be done only by those licensed, qualified individuals with experience across a wide variety of NCDs and mental health conditions. The ultimate goal of a neuropsychological assessment is to provide ecologically valid interventions that can be implemented in the home and school environments, which should be priority the of all clinicians (Fletcher-Janzen, 2005).

Additional Concerns about Neuropsychological Assessment

Assessing children with different cultural backgrounds or those with special needs requires certain considerations. According to Nell (2000), although this is slowly changing, the majority of neuropsychological tests are "conceived and standardized within the matrix of Western culture" (p. 3). Assessing children from other cultures, or whose native language is something other than English, presents significant barriers. Considerations and accommodations must be made to account for the child's language differences and proficiency and his or her level of acculturation. The same concerns can also be expressed for children who have impaired hearing. The use of translators, either of verbal or sign language, presents several problems to the testing process: Some concepts do not directly translate from English to the native foreign language, there is no guarantee the translator will not embellish or alter the meanings of the questions or responses, and most neuropsychological tests lack appropriate normative data for different cultures and languages (Miller, 2008).

The nature of a neurocognitive impairment is that there are deficits. A TBI is typically not a focal, specific injury. The effects can be diffuse, spotty, and variable from one day to the next. Neuropsychology includes a procedure known as *testing the limits* of an individual's capabilities. Because of one's injuries or other complicating factors, sometimes adjustments to standardized testing procedures are necessary to obtain some information about that person's ability in a specific area. Although standardized procedures and normative data are used whenever possible, occasions exist whereby the *qualitative* assessment of an individual may provide more realistic data about the individual's true abilities. Such is the case when testing individuals with special needs. Children who have visual, hearing, or communication impairments require special accommodations and interpretations. Children with motor impairments are often tested without consideration for time constraints. Such accommodations and adjustments do not invalidate a neuropsychological examination, but those changes and alterations should be mentioned in the report; qualitative interpretations should be provided as to the patient's abilities in those areas.

Treatment Strategies and Interventions

Understanding issues secondary to moderate to severe TBI in children and adolescents can be a valuable asset. According to Rivera et al. (2011), children and adolescents with mild TBI who experienced intracranial hemorrhage experienced long-term reductions in quality of life (QOL) at all follow-up intervals measured in their study. Levels of activity assessed in individuals diagnosed with moderate or severe TBI during the first two years showed some improvement, although three months post injury, a significant decrease in the amount of activity was noted. Confounding the issue, an individual who has incurred a concussion might not realize the complications that can arise from an insult to the head and might underestimate the trauma that can result, particularly if the individual did not lose consciousness (DeMatteo et al., 2010; Halstead & Walter, 2010).

When determining a major or mild NCD due to TBI, it is important to consider that the most severe symptoms are evident within minutes of the injury and that delayed symptom onset is relatively rare. Most individuals will present with a combination of physical and cognitive symptoms. So-called classic symptoms of nausea and vomiting are relatively rare, but headache is the symptom that tends to linger the longest and tends to be the most problematic to manage. There is often a measurable improvement in symptoms within hours of the injury, and a gradual symptom recovery occurs over a period of seven to 10 days in 80 to 90 percent of cases. The recovery rate for both children and adults is fairly similar, and symptoms that persist beyond the expected recovery period are often attributable to noninjury-related factors (McCrea, 2008).

PSYCHOLOGICAL EFFECTS IN THE MANAGEMENT OF TBI

Gunstad and Suhr (2001) suggested in the *good old days* hypothesis that, following any negative event, people may attribute all symptoms to that negative event regardless of a preexisting history of that problem. In other words, even though an individual might have been good at remembering names, after a mild TBI he or she may attribute that problem to the TBI itself and use that as a primary example of "memory loss associated with a TBI." The importance of this for treatment is that the individual has now established a more global, external response bias to support his or her new role as a TBI survivor.

Wood (2004) offered another theory that generates and maintains new, possibly maladaptive behaviors. That theory is the diathesis-stress model, which suggests that external forces can reinforce misconceptions about deficits and impairments as a result of the person's brain damage (McCrea, 2008). Such reinforcement leads the individual to perceive that he or she will never get any better. One such real-life example of this is the aspect of learned helplessness that occurs immediately after a stroke. Strokes often result in partial hemiparesis. Without physical therapy or intervention of any kind, the patient may come to believe that the hemiparesis is a permanent condition and never attempt to reuse that limb, when in fact upwards of 75 percent regain full capability within a year.

COGNITIVE BEHAVIORAL INTERVENTION

Children with a major or mild NCD due to TBI typically display difficulties with an adaptation to weakness, secondary anxiety, and mood difficulties. These children also display problems with attention, processing speed, and executive processing. Strategies to address symptoms within the various domains seem to have the greatest impact.

For general acceptance of the impairment, Mittenberg et al. (1996) found that individuals who received cognitive behavioral therapy (CBT) and educational information about their mild TBI while in the hospital reported significantly reduced average symptom duration and significantly fewer symptoms than their untreated controls. Additional support for the efficacy of CBT in moderate to severe TBI is given by Hsieh et al. (2012). Earlier, Ponsford et al. (2001) concluded from their study that children with mild TBI who were provided a TBI information booklet showed reduced anxiety and a lower incidence of persistent symptoms associated with their TBI. WHO task force findings declared that early educational information "can reduce long-term complaints and that this early intervention need not be intensive" (McCrea, 2008, p. 179).

Cohen (1999) and Miller (2010) related that children with a history of brain injury are at a greater risk for developing depression and anxiety compared with their peers. These children often experience a loss of functioning and often have to participate in hours of physical rehabilitation that are often painful and frustrating. They need to continue frequent and numerous medical and therapy appointments and laboratory tests and to miss school, which disrupts their routine and could result in secondary mood dysregulation and anxiety. Recent literature supported these findings.

For example, Begyn and Castillo (2012) determined that it is extremely important to monitor children with TBI for depression, anxiety, social withdrawal, and decreased feelings of self-worth. Intervention should focus on helping the child identify personal strengths, learn appropriate coping skills, and develop sources of support. Although somewhat inconclusive, the researchers also felt that reentry into school and the reestablishment of a routine would serve to increase self-esteem and decrease depression. Sidebar 18.5 describes the relationship between depression and TBI.

SIDEBAR 18.5: DEPRESSION AND TBI

Depression has been linked empirically to TBI (Rao et al., 2010; Rapoport, 2012). Recognizing and treating depression secondary to TBI can help guide clinicians in determining optimal treatment options. A high level of variability exists in rates of depression associated with TBI, from 17 percent to 61 percent. Treatment of TBI also includes a collaborative effort to include all members of the family, medical, social, and school communities who interact with the child with TBI to reinforce the positive outcomes, decrease symptoms, and reestablish routines as soon as feasibly possible.

COGNITIVE REHABILITATION INTERVENTION

Cognitive rehabilitation is based on the idea that the brain is able to change and improve, given certain interventions. Early efforts at cognitive rehabilitation resulted in increased cerebral blood flow and improvements in cognitive, memory, and problem-solving skills (Miller, 2010). Research studies (Miller, 2010) revealed significant benefits to cognitive rehabilitation across several domains (Sloan & Ponsford, 2013). Research has been consistent in showing that cognitive rehabilitation should guide natural recovery, reinforce positive compensation, and suppress maladaptive behavior through restoration and compensation: restoration of diminished abilities to preinjury levels and compensation for lost abilities by supplementation and accommodation.

Various methods of cognitive rehabilitation include psychotherapy, medication, computer-assisted training, behavior management, and instruction in cognitive strategies. It is thought that cognitive rehabilitation strategies are best employed in multidisciplinary settings that include medical professionals; rehabilitation therapists, such as occupational, physical, and speech therapists; and mental health professionals, such as professional counselors and social workers. The collaborative efforts of this multidisciplinary team, in conjunction with the child's parents, teachers, and peers, are necessary to effect the greatest impact and improvement in the child's physical, cognitive, and emotional abilities.

People with brain injuries can experience multiple symptoms related to their injuries (Teeter, 2009). They may participate in a variety of programs, depending on their abilities and goals. People with a brain injury who are seeking to pursue a new recreational outlet may benefit from riding or driving programs. Participants develop skills needed to direct their equine partners through obstacles, through cones courses, or on trail rides.

Diagnostic Challenges

The *DSM-5* diagnostic criteria emphasize that there must be evidence of a TBI with at least the occurrence of a loss of consciousness, posttraumatic amnesia, disorientation and confusion, or a neurological sign of injury. This criterion, new to the *DSM-5*, clearly establishes the need for some form of objective evidence of a TBI. See Sidebar 18.6 for an overview of the addition of NCDs and TBI in the *DSM-5*. Diagnosing a TBI should be a fairly straightforward process. The nature of the disorder indicates that the cognitive impairments are the result of:

> an occurrence of injury to the head (arising from blunt or penetrating trauma or from acceleration/deceleration forces) that is associated with any of these symptoms attributable to the injury: decreased level of consciousness, amnesia, other neurologic or neuorpsychologic abnormalities, skull fracture, diagnosed intracranial lesions, or death. (Thurman, Coronado, & Selassie, 2007, p. 45)

Identifying blunt trauma is usually pretty easy—the bounce of a ball, striking a windshield, or hitting the ground. Many such incidents have witnesses to the injury, so gathering information about the location, impact, and immediate effects of the injury is easily accomplished. However, especially for the pediatric population, the initial trauma may not be known. In fact, the effects may not even manifest until several years later, such as when the child enters school. Knowing what these objective findings mean is essential, but perhaps more important is knowing that TBI does not necessarily have to involve many of these findings or that some of the neurocognitive signs may not appear until several years later. This creates some significant challenges to the proper diagnosis of a major or mild NCD due to TBI.

SIDEBAR 18.6: CHANGES FROM THE *DSM-IV-TR* TO THE *DSM-5*

Criteria for the diagnosis of delirium have been updated from the *DSM-IV-TR* to the *DSM-5*. Dementia and amnestic disorders are now subsumed under the new category of neurocognitive disorders (NCDs) in the *DSM-5*. The *DSM-5* now designates several criteria sets within the entity of major NCDs, one of them being traumatic brain injury (TBI). Diagnostic categories for major and mild NCDs are addressed separately. The *DSM-5* now recognizes less severe levels of impairment as mild NCDs. Major NCD syndrome remains consistent with current medicine and with previous *DSM* editions. Mild NCDs, new to the *DSM-5*, remain consistent with other medical fields, where care and research are focused in individuals diagnosed with TBI and other subtypes, such as Alzheimer's, cerebrovascular disorders, and HIV (APA, 2013b).

CHALLENGE 1: LOSS OF CONSCIOUSNESS (LOC) AND POSTTRAUMATIC AMNESIA

Loss of consciousness (LOC) can be defined as interruption of awareness of oneself and ones surroundings. LOC may last from mere seconds to months, possibly even years. Many mild TBIs result in periods of becoming dazed or seeing stars. In recent years, the blast effects of an improvised explosive device (IED) have resulted in very brief, or *mild*, ratings of lost consciousness, according to the most widely accepted standards for determining severity of concussion. Because of these wartime conditions, a greater understanding of the role of LOC in determining TBI is evolving (Veterans Health Initiative, 2010).

Posttraumatic amnesia (PTA) is a higher level of consciousness and awareness than coma but less than full consciousness. A mild concussion may also cause a brief period of PTA. According to Wilson, Herbert, and Agnes (2003), during a period of PTA, individuals may:

- Be disoriented—confused about where they are, who those are around them are, and the time, date, or year
- Be highly distractible
- Have difficulty with thinking, memory, and concentration
- Be afraid, disinhibited, agitated, and emotionally labile.

During PTA, individuals may be partially or fully awake but are confused about the day and time, where they are, what is happening, and sometimes who they are. They will not be able to store continuous or recent memory, such as what happened just a few hours or even minutes ago. If physically able they may wander, so it is important to make sure their surroundings are free of any hazards. The individual may exhibit some behavioral changes that include becoming quiet and passive or aggressive, abusive, and agitated. Often, patients have little or no awareness of these cognitive and behavioral alterations and will usually remember nothing of what happened.

Although PTA is useful in diagnosing and grading the severity of a TBI, it is difficult to document consistently and accurately within a hospital protocol, and the interrater reliability reporting PTA is low. Regardless, at this point, the presence and duration of a LOC "are noteworthy in diagnosing and grading the severity of TBI, but brief unconsciousness and amnesia are not predictive of recovery and outcome after TBI" (McCrea, 2008, p. 139).

CHALLENGE 2: NEUROIMAGING

TBI is a very complex interaction of idiopathic sequelae. McCrea (2008) identified that despite being objective measures to identify underlying structural or functional abnormalities in brain structure, many neuroimaging techniques lack the sensitivity to detect abnormalities related to milder forms of brain injury. For instance, a computed tomography (CT) scan can identify structural abnormalities or hemorrhagic lesions (think tumors and bleeds because of stroke) but cannot identify soft tissue bruising typical of a mild concussion from a soccer ball. In fact, for the child who suffers such a sports injury and is whisked from the playing field straight to the emergency room, the structure of the skull may remain intact, and there is no apparent bleeding or loss of cerebrospinal fluid (CSF) noticeable right after the injury. It may not be until 24 to 48 hours later when the child begins to complain of a persistent headache, sleepiness, or sensitivity to light. CT scans and magnetic resonance imaging (MRI) scans are very valuable for detecting structural injuries, but the absence of findings may often be incorrectly or inappropriately equated with a lack of evidence of a brain injury (McCrea, 2008). The other limitation is that neuroimaging studies often do not provide *functional* information about structural abnormalities. There are some advances as to the use of functional neuroimaging techniques, such as functional magnetic resonance imaging (fMRI) and positron emission topography (PET) scans, but the functional impact is often derived from general indicators that there is some sort of structural or metabolic abnormality in a part of the brain. In these cases, the functional interpretation is merely derived, not necessarily objectively and idiosyncratically measured for that individual.

CHALLENGE 3: MEASURING DECLINES IN FUNCTIONING

Primarily in the case of a mild NCD due to TBI, especially in the pediatric population, measurable signs and degrees of impairment may not be readily available. Very mild forms of a mild NCS due to TBI may also be revealed as a *postconcussion syndrome* (PCS). Iverson, Zasler, and Lange (2007) discussed the concept of PCS, positing that symptoms and functional limitations of a mild NCD due to TBI that seem to persist beyond expected recovery patterns "are due to neurologic, psychological, or other noninjury-related factors." According to the *International Classification of Diseases, Tenth Revision (ICD-10*; 2010), PCS occurs after a head trauma with a loss of consciousness and is characterized by symptoms that are present within four weeks after the injury. Those symptoms must fall into at least three of the following categories:

1. headache, dizziness, malaise, fatigue, and noise tolerance
2. irritability, depression, anxiety, and emotional lability
3. subjective concentration, memory, or intellectual difficulties without neuropsychological evidence of marked impairment
4. insomnia
5. reduced alcohol tolerance
6. preoccupation with above symptoms and fear of brain damage with hypochondriacal concern and adoption of sick role.

The *DSM-5* includes many of these conditions within the mild NCD and major NCD due to TBI criteria. For an infant or toddler who experienced a TBI due to shaken baby syndrome, a minor fall from the high chair, or a drop from the babysitter, the more significant cognitive impairments might not be revealed until much later. Because many children will not evidence these cognitive deficits until they are in school, they will be subjected to the Individuals with Disabilities Education Act of 2004. The IDEA defines TBI as the following:

> Traumatic brain injury means an acquired injury to the brain caused by an external physical force, resulting in total or partial functional disability or psychosocial impairment, or both, that adversely affects a child's educational performance. Traumatic brain injury applies to open or closed head injuries resulting in impairments in one or more areas, such as cognition; language; memory; attention; reasoning; abstract thinking; judgment; problem-solving; sensory, perceptual, and motor abilities; psychosocial behavior; physical functions; information processing; and speech. Traumatic brain injury does not apply to brain injuries that are congenital or degenerative, or to brain injuries induced by birth trauma. (Regulations: Part 300/A/300.8/c/12)

Although not technically a TBI because of blunt trauma or force, brain injury due to birth trauma can have significant impact on the pediatric patient. According to the IDEA,

TBI does not apply to brain injuries that are congenital or degenerative or to brain injuries induced by birth trauma. However, many birth traumas may, in fact, include an external traumatic element. In the case of an infant who experiences the umbilical cord wrapped around his or her neck at birth, it is likely that the cord has decreased or completely cut off oxygen to the infant's brain—a condition known as *anoxia*. Infants who experience this might have been called a *blue baby* because of the slightly bluish skin tone because of a loss of oxygen during birth. Other infants may experience episodes of being caught in the birth canal and lose oxygen, go into respiratory distress, or experience some form of biomechanical trauma (e.g., vertebral subluxation) during the crowning moment of birth that affected the spinal cord or brain. Some children develop brain damage because of the soft infantile skull bones placing pressure on the brain or a buildup of fluid on the brain—a condition known as *hydrocephalus*. Although most of the conditions resolve within a very short time after birth or through medical intervention, they may result in very mild neurocognitive deficits that are not revealed until the child enters school. Although the child may not technically meet the criteria for a NCS due to TBI, the cognitive and psychological effects and emotional and behavioral reactions are quite similar to a mild NCS due to TBI and should respond to similar interventions.

TBI at birth or as an infant can affect the developmental process. Abilities that have not yet developed at the time of the injury are the most vulnerable; those abilities may be delayed, be disrupted, or fail to develop. Some children may regain function lost because of a TBI but may have difficulty achieving higher developmental and cognitive function. Essentially, the earlier the onset of a TBI, the greater the impact on development.

The effects of an early childhood TBI can seriously disrupt higher-order thinking, executive functions, and social behavior. Often, previously developed skills will be preserved, but new learning may be difficult. For many of these higher-order factors, children who experienced an early childhood TBI may enter school at a level consistent with their peers but begin to fall behind despite early interventions. They tend to display more extreme discrepancies between their cognitive skills and academic achievement and are likely to experience uneven and unpredictable academic progress. See Sidebar 18.7 for a case study. The case of TJ describes an early adolescent sports-related head injury and possible ramifications of acute and chronic effects.

SIDEBAR 18.7:   CASE STUDY—SPORTS-RELATED HEAD INJURY

TJ is a middle-school student, attentive and with good grades. TJ plays soccer on her school team. At soccer practice after school one day, she runs head-on accidently into a teammate downfield and loses consciousness for a few minutes. The coach eventually notices and by the time the coach arrives, TJ regains consciousness but seems slightly disoriented and confused. TJ sits out the rest of practice and goes home. The next day, TJ has trouble remembering her locker combination, is somewhat less attentive in class, and is not able to recall simple lessons that she had previously mastered. The teacher notices a change in her behavior and asks TJ whether she is okay. TJ explains what happened at soccer practice to the best of her recollection but becomes frustrated trying to recall the details. Her teacher becomes concerned and escorts her to the school nurse. The nurse suspects a possible closed head injury and refers her for further medical and psychological evaluation, alerting her parents.

What might TJ have experienced? If she did incur a TBI, was it mild, moderate, or major, and what constitutes each? In other words, what are the diagnostic criteria, and what follow-up services would be recommended? What assessments would you administer quickly? Which assessments would be best to administer to determine short-term or long-term loss? Is her condition chronic or acute? Are there rehabilitative interventions that could help TJ? What can TJ expect over time?

Summary

TBI, also known as head injury, concussion, brain damage, and more recently, postconcussive syndrome, is a leading cause of death and disability worldwide and is a leading cause of death in children. Various names for cognitive impairment caused by an external force, such as blunt-force trauma or injury to the head, are now commonly identified as TBI. Complex and sometimes difficult to diagnose and treat, TBI can have wide-ranging and lasting effects or can resolve over time, depending on a wide variety of factors. Identifying the etiology of TBI can also be complicated and problematic.

Previous editions of the *DSM* combined the cognitive effects of a TBI into narrowly defined conditions of cognitive impairment because of either dementia or delirium. Any other cognitive impairment was given as a single diagnosis—that of a Cognitive Disorder Not Otherwise Specified. As the understanding and diagnostic capabilities of TBI have expanded in recent years, partly because of the increase in the number of cases seen, the *DSM-5* (APA, 2013a) now reflects TBI collectively under the categories of Mild and Major Neurocognitive Disorders (NCD). Diagnosis of NCDs is based on cognitive domains, including:

- Complex attention
- Executive function
- Learning and memory
- Language
- Perceptual motor
- Social cognitive.

Major NCDs include evidence of significant cognitive decline in one or more of the aforementioned cognitive domains that results in significant interference with activities of daily living (ADLs) and independence that are not the result of a delirium. Mild NCDs, the more common of the two, include evidence of a modest decline in functioning in one or more of the cognitive domains, but those deficits do not necessarily interfere with independent functioning in ADLs and are not the result of a delirium or better accounted for by another mental health disorder. The brain is a highly complex organism and is the key element of the central and peripheral nervous systems. Damage to the brain can affect aspects of daily living at some level. Physical, emotional, cognitive, and behavioral aspects can be affected, depending on the extent of the insult in combination with a complexity of factors that makes diagnosis and treatment complicated, particularly when the etiology is unknown or when long-term effects persist years later. Depression can be a major issue secondary to TBI and requires further research.

With the increase in cases presenting in hospital emergency rooms, additional research continues to bring deeper levels of understanding to the complex issue of traumatic brain injury. Advanced diagnostic tools, such as fMRI, EEG, SPECT and PET scans, and other such neuroimaging techniques, help identify damage to focal brain areas. With assessments, such as the Glasgow Coma Scale and its childhood adaptation, the Children's Coma Scale; the Rancho Los Amigos Scale; the Abbreviated Injury Score and Injury Severity Score; and a range of neurological, neuropsychological, and childhood and adolescent IQ instruments, a better understanding of possible effects of TBI can be pursued. The use of counseling and psychotherapeutic interventions, such as CBT combined with providing information to the client about the disorder, have shown promise in helping to reduce deleterious effects of TBI.

References

American Psychiatric Association (2013a). *Diagnostic and statistical manual of mental disorders* (5th ed.). Arlington, VA: American Psychiatric Publishing.

American Psychiatric Association (2013b). *Highlights of changes from DSM-IV-TR to DSM5.* Arlington, VA: American Psychiatric Publishing.

Begyn, E. L., & Castillo, C. L. (2010). Assessing and intervening with children with brain tumors. In D. C. Miller (Ed.) *Best practices in school neuropsychology: Guidelines for effective practice, assessment, and evidence-based intervention* (pp. 737–765). Hoboken, NJ: John Wiley & Sons.

Centers for Disease Control and Prevention, National Center for Injury Prevention and Control. (2010, April 1). *Traumatic brain injury in the United States: A report to Congress.* Retrieved from http://www.cdc.gov/traumaticbraininjury/tbi_report_to_congress.html#

Centers for Disease Control and Prevention, National Center for Injury Prevention and Control. (2014, February 24). *Rates of TBI-related deaths by age group—United States, 2001–2010.* Retrieved from http://www.cdc.gov/traumaticbraininjury/data/rates_deaths_byage.html

Centers for Disease Control and Prevention, National Center for Injury Prevention and Control. (2015, January 12). *Traumatic brain injury in the United States: Fact sheet.* Retrieved from http://www.cdc.gov/traumaticbraininjury/get_the_facts.html

Chen, C. Y., & Wu, H. P. (2011). Caring for traumatic brain injury in children can be a challenge! *Journal of Emergencies, Trauma and Shock, 4*(2), 161.

Cohen, M. S. (1999). Families coping with childhood chronic illness: A research review. *Families, Systems, & Health, 17*(2), 149.

DeMatteo, C. A., Hanna, S. E., Mahoney, W. J., Hollenberg, R. D., Scott, L. A., Law, M. C., … Xu, L. (2010). "My child doesn't have a brain injury, he only has a concussion." *Pediatrics, 125*(2), 327–334.

Fletcher-Janzen, E. (2005). The school neuropsychological examination. In C. R. Reynolds & E. Fletcher-Janzen (Eds.), *Handbook of school neuropsychology* (pp. 172–212). Hoboken, NJ: John Wiley & Sons.

Ford, E. G., & Andrassy, R. (1994). *Pediatric trauma: Initial assessment and management.* St. Louis, MO: Saunders.

Goldsmith, C. (2014). *Traumatic brain injury: From concussion to coma.* Minneapolis, MN: Twenty-First Century Books.

Gunstad, J., & Suhr, J. A. (2001). "Expectation as etiology" versus "the good old days": Postconcussion syndrome symptom reporting in athletes, headache sufferers, and depressed individuals. *Journal of the International Neuropsychological Society, 7*(3), 323–333.

Halstead, M. E., & Walter, K. D. (2010). Sport-related concussion in children and adolescents. *Pediatrics, 126*(3), 597–615.

Hsieh, M. Y., Ponsford, J., Wong, D., Schönberger, M., McKay, A., & Haines, K. (2012). A cognitive behaviour therapy (CBT) programme for anxiety following moderate-severe traumatic brain injury (TBI): Two case studies. *Brain Injury, 26*(2), 126–138.

Individuals with Disabilities Education Act, 20 U.S.C. §§ 1401(3); 1401(30) (2004). Retrieved from http://idea.ed.gov/explore/view/p/,root,regs,300,A,300%252E8,c,12,

Iverson, G. L., Zasler, N. D., & Lange, R. T. (2007). Post-concussive disorder. In H. D. Zasler, D. I. Katz, & R. D. Zafonte (Eds.), *Brain injury medicine: Principles and practice* (pp. 373–406). New York, NY: Demos.

Jeste, D. V., Meeks, T. W., Kim, D. S., & Zubenko, G. S. (2006). Research agenda for DSM-V: Diagnostic categories and criteria for neuropsychiatric syndromes in dementia. *Journal of Geriatric Psychiatry and Neurology, 19*(3), 160–171.

Janusz, J. A., Kirkwood, M. W., Yeates, K. O., & Taylor, H. G. (2002). Social problem-solving skills in children with traumatic brain injury: Long-term outcomes and prediction of social competence. *Child Neuropsychology, 8*(3), 179–194.

Kochanek, P. M. (2006). Pediatric traumatic brain injury: Quo vadis? *Developmental neuroscience, 28*(4–5), 244–255.

Korkman, M., Kirk, U., & Kemp, S. (1998). *NEPSY: A developmental neuropsychological assessment.* New York, NY: Psychological Corporation.

Max, J. E., Keatley, E., Wilde, E. A., Bigler, E. D., Schachar, R. J., Saunders, A. E., & Levin, H. S. (2012). Depression in children and adolescents in the first 6 months after traumatic brain injury. *International Journal of Developmental Neuroscience, 30*(3), 239–245.

McCrea, M. A. (2008). *Mild traumatic brain injury and postconcussion syndrome.* New York, NY: Oxford University Press.

Miller, D. C. (2008). *Essentials of school neuropsychological assessment.* Hoboken, NJ: John Wiley & Sons.

Miller, D. C. (2010). *Best practices in school neuropsychology.* Hoboken, NJ: John Wiley & Sons.

Miller, D. C. (2013). *Essentials of school neuropsychological assessment* (2nd ed.). Hoboken, NJ: John Wiley & Sons.

Mittenberg, W., Tremont, G., Zielinski, R. E., Fichera, S., & Rayls, K. R. (1996). Cognitive-behavioral prevention of postconcussion syndrome. *Archives of Clinical Neuropsychology, 11*(2), 139–145.

Nell, V. (2000). *Cross-cultural neuropsychological assessment: Theory and practice.* Mahwah, NJ: Lawrence Erlbaum Associates.

Ponsford, J., Willmott, C., Rothwell, A., Cameron, P., Ayton, G., Nelms, R., … Ng, K. (2001). Impact of early intervention on outcome after mild traumatic brain injury in children. *Pediatrics, 108*(6), 1297–1303.

Rao, V., Bertrand, M., Rosenberg, P., Makley, M., Schretlen, D., Brandt, J., & Mielke, M. (2010). Predictors of new-onset depression after mild traumatic brain injury. *The Journal of Neuropsychiatry and Clinical Neurosciences, 22*(1), 100–104.

Rapoport, M. J. (2012). Depression following traumatic brain injury. *CNS Drugs, 26,* 111–121.

Rivara, F. P., Koepsell, T. D., Wang, J., Temkin, N., Dorsch, A., Vavilala, M. S., … Jaffe, K. M. (2011). Disability 3, 12, and 24 months after traumatic brain injury among children and adolescents. *Pediatrics, 128*(5), 1129–1138.

Rourke, B. P. (1982). Child-clinical neuropsychology: Assessment and intervention with the disabled child. *Perspectives in child study: Integration of theory and practice.* Lisse, Netherlands: Swets & Zeitlinger.

Shulman, K. I. (2000). Clock-Drawing: Is it the ideal cognitive screening test? *International Journal of Geriatric Psychiatry, 15*(6), 548–561.

Silver, J. M., McAllister, T. W., & Yudofsky, S. C. (Eds.). (2011). *Textbook of traumatic brain injury.* Arlington, VA: American Psychiatric Publishing.

Simpson, J. R. (2014). DSM-5 and neurocognitive disorders. *Journal of the American Academy of Psychiatry and the Law Online, 42*(2), 159–164.

Sloan, S., & Ponsford, J. (2013). Managing cognitive problems following TBI. In J. Ponsford, S. Sloan, & P. Snow (Eds.), *Traumatic brain injury: Rehabilitation for everyday adaptive living* (pp. 99–132). New York, NY: Psychology Press.

Teasdale, G., & Jennett, B. (1974). Assessment of coma and impaired consciousness: A practical scale. *The Lancet, 2*(7872), 81–84. doi:10.1016/S0140-6736(74)91639-0

Teeter, P. A. (2009). Neurocognitive interventions for childhood and adolescent disorders: A transactional model. In C. R. Reynolds & E. Fletcher-Janzen (Eds.), *Handbook of clinical child neuropsychology* (pp. 427–458). New York, NY: Springer.

Thurman, D. J., Coronado, V., & Selassie, A. (2007). The epidemiology of TBI: Implications for public health. In H. D. Zasler, D. I. Katz, & R. D. Zafonte (Eds.), *Brain injury medicine: Principles and practice* (pp. 45–56). New York, NY: Demos.

Veterans Health Initiative. (2010, April). *Traumatic brain injury.* Retrieved from http://www.publichealth.va.gov/docs/vhi/traumatic-brain-injury-vhi.pdf

Wilson, B. A., Herbert, C. M., & Agnes, S. (2003). *Behavioural approaches in neuropsychological rehabilitation: Optimising rehabilitation procedures.* New York, NY: Psychology Press.

Wood, R. L. (2004). Understanding the 'miserable minority': A diasthesis-stress paradigm for postconcussional syndrome. *Brain Injury, 18*(11), 1135–1153.

Chapter 19

Other Conditions That May Be a Focus of Clinical Attention When Working with Children and Adolescents

K. Michelle Hunnicutt Hollenbaugh, Julia L. Whisenhunt, and Lee A. Teufel-Prida

Introduction

The *Diagnostic and Statistical Manual of Mental Disorders, Fifth Edition* (*DSM-5*; American Psychiatric Association [APA], 2013), includes a section specifically for issues that may be a consideration of treatment but are not actually diagnosable disorders. These conditions can be especially helpful in bringing attention to issues that may be important to address in treatment or are related to their diagnosed conditions. This chapter will discuss how and when to use these codes in diagnosis with children and adolescents, as well as discuss the focus and progress of treatment related to these conditions, and give examples of the related clinical issues that may be present in clients.

Using Z Codes with Children and Adolescents

The Other Conditions were formerly known as *V codes* and were coded on Axis IV in the *DSM-IV-TR* (APA, 2000). However, with the transition to the *DSM-5* and the alignment with *International Classification of Diseases, Tenth Revision* (*ICD-10*), codes, these conditions are most commonly referred to as *Z codes*, though there are also T, R, and E codes within this section. See Sidebar 19.1 for further explanation of the transition from V to Z codes. Z codes provide a more holistic clinical picture of the client and can help the clinician understand the factors that are possibly related to the client's diagnoses and assist the clinician in personalizing the treatment plan. There are nine categories of conditions and problems in this section, and there are several codes under each category. After completing a full biopsychosocial assessment with the client or family, the clinician should review the section in the *DSM-5* (pp. 715–727) for any other factors that may relate to the precipitating problem or symptoms of the diagnosable conditions. These factors may be problems the clinician would like to focus on in sessions with the client or notable aspects of the diagnosis, even if they are not going to be addressed imminently (APA, 2013). See Table 19.1 for a complete list of all the conditions that can be related to the diagnosis of a child or adolescent, including the previous *ICD-9-CM* codes and the corresponding *ICD-10-CM* codes.

SIDEBAR 19.1:   WHAT IS THE DIFFERENCE BETWEEN A V CODE AND A Z CODE?

V codes are associated with the *ICD-9, Clinical Modification* (CM). The *ICD-CM* is now in its tenth version, and the use of Z codes reflects a change that has occurred in the *ICD-10-CM*. The *ICD-10-CM* categorizes codes to represent reasons for encounters as Z codes instead of V codes. *ICD-10-CM* codes have three to seven characters, but Z-code categories Z00–Z99 consist of three to six characters. Additional *ICD-10-CM* information is available on the National Center for Health Statistics website at www.cdc.gov/nchs/icd/icd10cm.htm.

Differential Diagnosis

The first step in creating a differential diagnosis is data collection—taking a client's biopsychosocial history. Although the focus of this chapter is not to provide a summary of the steps involved in an intake interview, we want to direct the reader briefly to two helpful resources when working with children and adolescents. The APA has developed an informative Web page, which provides multiple *DSM-5* resources (www.psychiatry.org/practice/dsm/dsm5). Two of these include the Early Development and Home Background (EDHB) Form—Parent/Guardian and the Early Development and Home Background (EDHB) Form—Clinic. The APA identifies these as "emerging resources" and cautions that they should not be used as a singular means through which to identify diagnoses but rather as informative resources to use in the clinical decision-making process. These two inventories may assist in collecting history about children and adolescents that could inform the addition of relevant Z codes to their diagnostic profiles.

Identifying which Z codes to use, and when to use them, can be challenging. The challenge arises in two ways. First, it is important to remember that one would not use a Z code for an issue that is otherwise better accounted for by a standard diagnosis. For instance, one would not use Z63.4 Uncomplicated Bereavement for a client for whom major depressive disorder would be a more appropriate diagnosis. Second, a challenge emerges in regard to determining when it is appropriate to use Z codes. One should use Z codes only in situations in which the issue reflected by the Z code(s) either is a focus of the client's treatment or affects the client's treatment; Z codes should not be used in situations in which the client is not adversely affected by the issue reflected by the Z code(s). For instance, if a child is reared by his or her extended family members, but that child does not experience problems related to being reared by his or her nonbiological parents, the code Z62.29 Upbringing Away From Parents would not be appropriate. In considering whether to use Z codes, it is important to consider the implications for both the client's treatment and the client's medical history.

TABLE 19.1   Relevant Conditions That May Be a Focus of Clinical Attention for Children and Adolescents

Category	ICD-9-CM Code	Conditions	ICD-10-CM Code
Problems Related to Family Upbringing	V61.20	Parent-Child Relational Problem	Z62.820
	V61.8	Sibling Relational Problem	Z62.891
	V61.8	Upbringing Away From Parents	Z62.29
	V61.29	Child Affected by Parental Relationship Distress	Z62.898
Other Problems Related to Primary Support Group	V61.03	Disruption of Family by Separation or Divorce	Z63.5
	V61.10	Relationship Distress With Spouse or Intimate Partner	Z63.0
	V61.8	High Expressed Emotion Level Within Family	Z63.8
	V62.82	Uncomplicated Bereavement	Z63.4
Child Maltreatment and Neglect Problems	995.54	Child Physical Abuse Confirmed	T74.12XA
	995.54	Initial Encounter Subsequent Encounter	T74.12XD
	995.54	Child Physical Abuse Suspected	T76.12XA
	995.54	Initial Encounter Subsequent Encounter	T76.12XD
	995.53	Child Sexual Abuse Confirmed	T74.22XA
	995.53	Initial Encounter Subsequent Encounter	T74.22XD
	995.53	Child Sexual Abuse Suspected	T76.22XA
	995.53	Initial Encounter Subsequent Encounter	T76.22XD
	995.52	Child Neglect Confirmed	T74.02XA
	995.52	Initial Encounter Subsequent Encounter	T74.02XD
	995.52	Child Neglect Suspected	T76.02XA
	995.52	Initial Encounter Subsequent Encounter	T76.02XD
	995.51	Child Psychological Abuse Confirmed	T74.32XA
	995.51	Initial Encounter Subsequent Encounter	T74.32XD
	995.51	Child Psychological Abuse Suspected	T76.32XA
	995.51	Initial Encounter Subsequent Encounter	T76.32XD
	V61.21	Encounter for mental health services for victim of child abuse (specify physical, sexual, neglect, psychological) by parent	Z69.010
	V61.21	Encounter for mental health services for victim of nonparental child abuse (specify physical, sexual, neglect, psychological)	Z69.020
	V 15.41	Personal history (past history) of physical abuse (specify physical, sexual, neglect, psychological) in childhood	Z62.810

(continued)

TABLE 19.1 Continued

Category	ICD-9-CM Code	Conditions	ICD-10-CM Code
Housing and Economic Problems	V60.0	Homelessness	Z59.0
	V60.1	Inadequate Housing	Z59.1
	V60.6	Problem Related to Living in a Residential Institution	Z59.3
	V60.2	Lack of Adequate Food or Safe Drinking Water	Z59.4
	V60.2	Extreme Poverty	Z59.5
		Low Income	Z59.6
	V60.2	Insufficient Social Insurance or Welfare Support	Z59.7
	V60.9	Unspecified Housing or Economic Problem	Z59.9
Occupational Problems	V62.29	Other Problem Related to Employment	Z56.9
Other Problems Related to the Social Environment	V62.89	Phase of Life Problem	Z60.0
	V62.4	Acculturation Difficulty	Z60.3
	V62.4	Social Exclusion or Rejection	Z60.4
	V62.4	Target of (Perceived) Adverse Discrimination or Persecution	Z60.5
	V62.9	Unspecified Problem Related Social Environment	Z60.9
Problems Related to Crime or Interaction with the Legal System	V62.89	Victim of Crime	Z65.4
	V62.5	Conviction in Civil or Criminal Proceedings without Imprisonment	Z65.0
	V62.5	Imprisonment or Other Incarceration	Z65.1
	V62.5	Problems Related to Other Legal Circumstances	Z65.3
Other Health Service Encounters for Counseling and Medical Advice	V65.49	Sex Counseling	Z70.9
	V65.40	Other Counseling or Consultation	Z71.9
Problems Related to Other Psychological, Personal, and Environmental Circumstances	V62.89	Religious or Spiritual Problem	Z65.8
	V61.7	Problem Related to Unwanted Pregnancy	Z64.0
	V61.5	Problems with Multiparity	Z64.1
	V62.89	Discord with Social Service Provider, Including Probation Officer, Case Manager, or Social Services Worker	Z64.4
	V62.89	Victim of Terrorism or Torture	Z65.4
	V62.22	Exposure to Disaster, War, or Other Hostilities	Z65.5
	V62.89	Other Problem Related to Psychosocial Circumstances	Z65.8
	V62.9	Unspecified Problem Related to Unspecified Psychosocial Circumstances	Z65.9

TABLE 19.1   Continued

Category	ICD-9-CM Code	Conditions	ICD-10-CM Code
Other Circumstances of Personal History	V15.49	Other Personal History of Psychological Trauma	Z91.49
	V15.59	Personal History of Self-Harm	Z91.5
	V15.89	Other Personal Risk Factors	Z91.89
	V69.9	Problem Related to Lifestyle	Z72.9
	V71.02	Child or Adolescent Antisocial Behavior	Z72.810
Problems Related to Access to Medical and Other Health Care	V63.9	Unavailability or Inaccessibility of Health Care Facilities	Z75.3
	V63.8	Unavailability or Inaccessibility of Other Helping Agencies	Z75.4
Nonadherence to Medical Treatment	V15.81	Nonadherence to Medical Treatment	Z91.19
	278.00	Overweight or Obesity	Z66.9
	V65.2	Malingering	Z76.5
	V40.31	Wandering Associated with a Mental Disorder	Z91.83

Focus and Progress of Treatment Related to Other Conditions

Because the Z codes are listed in order of clinical importance in treatment, the focus of treatment will similarly focus on these codes in order of importance, in conjunction with consideration of symptoms of any other clinical diagnoses the client may have. Though as a clinician, you may use your clinical judgment in making decisions regarding the focus of treatment, it is often extremely helpful to engage collaboratively in the treatment planning process with the client to both increase commitment to treatment and empower the client to feel in control of his or her treatment (Sommers-Flanagan & Sommers-Flanagan, 2013).

Description of the Clinical Issues

RELATIONAL PROBLEMS

In consideration of the critical impact the family unit has on a client's mental health and well-being, nonpathological relational problems occupy a prominent place in the *DSM-5*. Within the chapter Other Conditions That May Be a Focus of Clinical Attention, the *DSM-5* identifies two broad categories of relational problems—Problems Related to Family Upbringing and Other Problems Related to Primary Support Group. Each of these categories includes multiple Z codes. These codes may apply to situations in which the respective relational problem is the primary treatment focus. However, some of these Z codes may also apply when problems within the respective relationship affect the course, prognosis, or treatment of a medical or psychological condition. As such, all of these diagnostic codes may function as stand-alone treatment issues, whereas others may be used either as a primary diagnosis or as additional specifiers (APA, 2013). See Sidebar 19.2 for a case study describing a situation involving relational problems.

Problems Related to Family Upbringing

Z62.820 Parent-Child Relational Problem. For the purposes of this diagnostic code, it is important to note that a *parent* is considered any person who serves as a child's primary caregiver (APA, 2013). Problems within the parental relationship may impair cognitive, behavioral, or affective functioning within both the child and parent (APA, 2013). Cognitive impairment may take the form of assuming others' intentions are malevolent, fearing abandonment, and expressing hostility (APA, 2013). A study by Mence et al. (2014) demonstrated the interaction between parental cognitive attribution of child affect and discipline among parents of toddlers. The researchers found that parents who interpreted their toddler's affect as overwhelming and unpredictable and who misattributed negative affect to their child's behavior tended to respond with hostile discipline measures (Mence et al., 2014). Behavioral impairment may take the form of arguments, violence, making threats, and avoidance of problems (APA, 2013). Specifically among parents, behavioral impairment may take the form of ineffective parenting practices, such as strict authoritarianism, overprotection, insufficient supervision, and lack of structure (APA, 2013). When using this diagnostic code, it is important to consider any relevant cultural issues and the child's developmental needs (APA, 2013).

Z62.891 Sibling Relational Problem. For the purposes of this diagnostic code, it is important to note that a *sibling* is considered any person who is related to the client through full genetic relation, half genetic relation, the blending of families, foster parenting, and adoption (APA, 2013). This code may apply to both minors and adults (APA, 2013). Furthermore, the level of distress within the sibling relationship must lead to one of the following three impacts on the individual client or family unit: (a) "significant impairment" within the client or family unit, (b) the emergence of symptoms within the client or a sibling, or (c) interference with the course, prognosis, or treatment of a medical or psychological disorder within the client or a sibling (APA, 2013, p. 716). Sibling conflict can take various forms and affect children and adolescents in multiple ways. A study by Campione-Barr, Greer, and Krusen (2013) examined types of sibling conflict and their impact on adolescents' emotional development. The researchers found, for instance, that adolescents who felt their sibling(s) invaded their personal domain were more likely to have increased anxiety and lowered self-esteem at a one-year follow-up (Campione-Barr et al., 2013). Moreover, adolescents who felt that they were given an unfair portion of the family resources tended to demonstrate elevated indicators of depressed mood (Campione-Barr et al., 2013). Therefore, incorporating sibling conflict in treatment planning may help address other mental health issues within the child client.

Z62.29 Upbringing Away From Parents. This code may apply to situations in which a child is, for a variety of reasons, not being reared by his or her parents (APA, 2013). These situations may include court-sanctioned placement (e.g., foster care or placement with a relative), non–court-sanctioned placement (e.g., living with family or friends), or state custody (e.g., group home or orphanage; APA, 2013). This does not include children who live in a boarding school, because a separate Z code exists for that purpose. It is important to remember that problems related to the child being reared away from the parents may be the primary treatment focus or may affect the course, prognosis, or treatment of a medical or psychological disorder. As such, unless one of the two above noted conditions is met, being reared away from one's parents probably does not warrant diagnosis under this code. McGoron et al. (2012) demonstrated that being reared away from one's parents does not necessarily produce marked psychopathology in children. In their study, the researchers found that small children who were reared in an institution and did not receive quality caregiving were significantly more likely to experience a variety of psychopathological symptoms (McGoron et al., 2012). Conversely, children who received quality caregiving and developed secure attachment were far less likely to experience psychopathological symptoms (McGoron et al., 2012). Accordingly, helping children to develop and maintain secure attachments with their caregivers may aid in preventing the onset of psychological distress in children who are being reared away from their parents.

Z 89.8 Child Affected by Parental Relationship Distress. This code may apply to situations in which children witness, or are otherwise impacted by, conflict between their parents (APA, 2013). These children may experience medical and psychological changes because of conflict between their parents (APA, 2013). As such, this code should be used in situations in which the primary treatment focus surrounds the negative impact the parents' conflict is having on the child (APA, 2013). Parental discord and its impact on children are highlighted by a study Hindman, Riggs, and Hook (2013) conducted. These researchers suggested that parental discord may interfere with secure attachment and, thereby, lead to increased symptoms of psychological distress in children. Additionally, although parental discord may not directly affect the course of treatment for adolescents, parental discord may interact with other client variables in ways that influence the most appropriate treatment modalities (see Amaya, Reinecke, Silva, & March, 2011). In consideration of these factors, it is important to address the impact of parent discord on the child client, namely in the area of attachment, and determine the degree to which the parents' conflict may or may not influence the course of treatment.

Other Problems Related to Primary Support Group

Z63.5 Disruption of Family by Separation or Divorce. This code may apply to situations in which adult intimate partners are either separated or in the process of obtaining a divorce (APA, 2013). According to the *DSM-5*, separation is specified by living apart (APA, 2013). Parental conflict during separation or divorce can have a significant impact on children. For instance, Sandler, Wheeler, and Braver (2013) found that children in high-conflict divorces tended to have high levels of mental health issues when they spent a large amount of time with a parent who practiced poor parenting skills but fewer mental health issues when they spent a large amount of time with a parent who practiced effective parenting skills. Furthermore, high levels of interparental conflict tended to lead to lower levels of effective parenting practices (Sandler et al., 2013). Similarly, Lucas, Nicholson, and Erbas (2013) found that children whose parents were experiencing conflict during marital separation were at marked risk of developing mental health problems; however, marital separation alone did not produce a risk of developing mental health problems. As such, it is important to remember that this code applies to situations in which the child is adversely affected by separation or divorce and the child's symptoms are not better accounted for by a different diagnostic code.

Z63.8 High Expressed Emotion Level within Family. This code may apply to situations in which a couple's or family unit's high level of expressed emotion either serves as the primary treatment focus or impacts the course, prognosis, or treatment of a medical or psychological disorder (APA, 2013). The *DSM-5* defines expressed emotion as a measure of the amount of negative emotion (e.g., criticism, aggression, and "emotional overinvolvement") exhibited within the family unit and directed toward a family member (APA, 2013, p. 716). Children who experience high levels of criticism from their mother may be particularly at risk for developing depression (Burkhouse, Uhrlass, Stone, Knopik, & Gibb, 2012), emotion dysregulation, and internalizing and externalizing problems

(Han & Shaffer, 2014). Working with parents to diminish expressed emotion or helping the child develop improved emotion regulation and adaptive problem-solving skills may be indicated.

Z63.4 Uncomplicated Bereavement. This code may apply to situations in which a client experiences a "normal reaction to the death of a loved one," which serves as the primary treatment focus (APA, 2013, p. 716). The client may present with symptoms that align clearly with a major depressive episode (APA, 2013). However, the client's symptoms are considered a normal reaction to a major life loss (APA, 2013). Two major considerations should be made when using this Z code. The first is in regard to differentiating a normal grief reaction from a major depressive episode (APA, 2013). The second is in regard to making appropriate cultural considerations surrounding the normality of grief reactions (APA, 2013). The addition of this Z code allows clinicians with a means through which to identify bereavement as a treatment issue without pathologizing the bereavement or invalidating the impact bereavement has on the individual (see Iglewicz, Seay, Zetumer, & Zisook, 2013).

SIDEBAR 19.2: CASE STUDY—RELATIONAL PROBLEMS AND OTHER PROBLEMS RELATED TO SOCIAL ENVIRONMENT

Maya is a 15-year-old female who identifies as Asian American. Maya's mother describes her as a "star student" but states that Maya is a "troublemaker" at home. Her mother further states that Maya has a hard time following family rules, such as demonstrating respect for her elders, arguing with family members, and doing her chores. Upon taking a client history, you learn that the family became U.S. citizens when Maya was 4 years old and her brother was 12 years old. Maya informs you that she got along with her parents until last year, when she entered high school. She can't identify any changes that occurred to initiate this conflict with her parents but tells you that her parents want her to be just like her older brother, who is enrolled in law school. Maya says that she wants to be a singer but fears that her parents will not let her pursue such a "childish" career.

At this point, four possible Z Codes may apply to Maya's treatment. Can you identify them?

To determine the most appropriate Z codes to use in determining Maya's treatment focus, you will need to gather more information. Where should you start, and how will you rule out the Z codes that do not best reflect the treatment focus?

Whenever you are working with clients who hold beliefs and values that may be different from your own, it is critical that you approach treatment in a way that does not impose your own values and assumptions about the client's culture. How will you address diversity in your treatment of Maya and your interactions with her mother?

Child Maltreatment and Neglect Problems

The APA (2013) identifies four categories of child abuse and maltreatment—child physical abuse, child sexual abuse, child neglect, and child psychological abuse. Each of these categories includes multiple Z codes. Similar to previous categories within this section of the *DSM-5*, these codes may apply to situations in which the respective abuse is the primary treatment focus. However, some of these Z codes may also apply when problems associated with abuse impact the course, prognosis, or treatment of a medical or psychological condition (APA, 2013). As such, all of these diagnostic codes may function as stand-alone treatment issues, whereas others may be used as the primary diagnosis or an additional specifier. As is often the case with the clinical issue of abuse and neglect, Z codes may be entered into the patient's clinical record as useful information on circumstances that may affect the patient's care. The Z code related to abuse or neglect could be the reason for the current visit or help explain the need for treatment.

The conditions of child physical abuse, child sexual abuse, child neglect abuse, or child psychological abuse tend to include a large portion of the challenges that child and adolescent clinicians address. Abuse and neglect are not regarded as a mental disorder (APA, 2013); rather, abuse and neglect can be a focus of clinical attention or part of an individual's mental health history. Teicher and Samson (2013) reviewed the literature on abuse with children and adults with the diagnoses of anxiety, depression, and substance abuse disorders. Those with abuse histories and psychiatric disorders had measurable changes in their brains, whereas those with psychiatric disorders but no abuse history had no brain changes. It is also worthwhile to note that those with a history of abuse and psychiatric diagnosis responded to different treatments from those without a history of abuse. As such, treatment of children and adolescents who experience abuse should receive targeted treatment intervention to help reduce the long-term negative effects of abuse.

With all the abuse and neglect codes, the seventh digit should be coded as either an *A* when the client is currently receiving active treatment for the condition or a *D* when the client is receiving routine follow-up care for the condition (APA, 2013). Under all three sections of abuse (physical, sexual, and psychological), there are codes for *Abuse, Confirmed; Abuse, Suspected; Encounter for mental health services for victim of abuse by parent; Encounter for mental health services for victim of nonparental child abuse;* and *Personal history (past history) of abuse in childhood*. Though the codes are different for each of these categories in each section, for brevity, they will not be repeated in the following sections.

In any situation in which the clinician believes (or has confirmed) that abuse has occurred, the proper child protective authorities should be contacted immediately, and the clinician should work closely with any child protective services caseworkers assigned to the client's case throughout treatment.

CHILD PHYSICAL ABUSE

About 49 out of 1,000 children nationwide experience physical abuse (U.S. Department of Health and Human Services, 2013). Risk factors for physical abuse include age of the child (older children are more likely to be identified as abused, possibly due to lack of identification in younger children), age of mother (younger mothers increase risk), mental health status of mother, marital status (single parents increase risk), and poverty level (children living in impoverished homes and neighborhoods are at higher risk; Zolotor & Shanahan, 2011).

CHILD SEXUAL ABUSE

Researchers have shown an average of 25 percent of children may experience some form of sexual abuse; however, this statistic may be larger due to the fact child sexual abuse is reported less frequently than other types of child abuse (U.S. Department of Health and Human Services, 2013). Fortunately, the frequency of child sexual abuse does appear to have declined dramatically over the past few decades, possibly due to prevention programs and awareness (Palusci, 2011). Risk factors for sexual abuse include gender (females are at higher risk), race, age (older children are at higher risk), and disability (Palusci, 2011).

CHILD NEGLECT

Child neglect accounts for up to two-thirds of cases reported to child protective services nationwide, making it the most reported type of child abuse (U.S. Department of Health and Human Services, 2013). There are many types of child neglect, which include medical neglect, inadequate supervision, and educational neglect (Dubowitz, 2011). Risk factors for neglect include parental substance abuse, child disability, and poverty (U.S. Department of Health and Human Services, 2013).

CHILD PSYCHOLOGICAL ABUSE

Though psychological abuse is often less reported and receives less attention than other types of abuse, it can be just as harmful as physical abuse and neglect (Hibbard et al., 2012). This type of abuse can include verbal aggression as well as isolation, exploitation, and emotional neglect. As with other types of abuse, risk factors include parental mental health problems, parental substance abuse, and multiple family stressors (Hibbard et al., 2012).

Housing and Economic Problems

HOUSING PROBLEMS

There are three codes under this section that may be of specific focus when working with children and adolescents. Z59.0 Homelessness may be the most imminent when working with minors. One in 45 children in the United States is homeless, and they often experience a multitude of mental and physical problems as result (National Center on Family Homelessness, 2011). Though addressing this issue in therapy may directly involve parents or guardians as well as community agencies and resources, homelessness is an aspect that must be addressed before the client will be able to focus on any other aspects of counseling (Maslow, 1943).

Z59.1 Inadequate Housing will be used when the client has housing, but there are serious dangers or deficits in the home. This may be subjective, and cultural factors related to this situation should always be considered (APA, 2013). However, it should also be noted if a child is living in a situation that can cause significant threats to his or her health. For example, living in a home with no running water or heat in the winter could be considered neglect and may need to be reported to the child protective authorities. Clinicians should be familiar with the rules and regulations regarding child protective services in the state in which they practice and the procedure for responding to issues of child welfare.

Z59.3 Problem Related to Living in a Residential Institution should be used when a focus of treatment will be directly related to any issues the child or adolescent may have living in an institutional setting. This can include children who are in a permanent residential situation via the foster care system or children who are receiving mental health or drug and alcohol treatment in a residential setting. This code should not be used if the issues seem to be related to an adjustment to a new living situation; instead, an adjustment disorder should be diagnosed (APA, 2013). Problems may include discord with authorities or other children living in the institution.

ECONOMIC PROBLEMS

Z59.4 Lack of Adequate Food or Safe Drinking Water is similar to Z59.1 Inadequate Housing in that both issues can affect children's well-being and jeopardize them medically. As previously mentioned, clinicians need to be aware of the rules and regulations in their state regarding child neglect and the circumstances under which they should make a report to child protective authorities.

Z59.5 Extreme Poverty and Z59.6 Low Income may be a focus of treatment for a child or adolescent in the event that the clinician wishes to link the client with community resources or case management services to assist the family in their current situation. Approximately 22 percent of children in the United States live in families with an income below the federal poverty level, and 45 percent live in families considered low income. Children living in low-income or impoverished homes are at higher risk for mental and physical health problems (Addy, Engelhardt, & Skinner, 2013).

Z59.7 Insufficient Social Insurance or Welfare Support would include a child or adolescent who might qualify for health insurance or social support but does not have this coverage due to lack of resources or documentation. As with other conditions in this section, the clinician may wish to focus on this aspect in treatment to link the client with the needed support agencies. Lack of preventative care can lead to an increase in physical and mental health problems or precipitate current mental health problems; therefore, this condition may be a foremost focus of treatment.

As with other unspecified disorders and conditions in the *DSM-5* (APA, 2013), Z59.9 Unspecified Housing or Economic Problem would be used when the clinician identifies a situation related to the child's or adolescent's housing and economic situation, but it does not fit in any of the other listed conditions.

OCCUPATIONAL PROBLEMS

Though Z56.9 Other Problem Related to Employment may not present often in diagnosis with children and adolescents, as many as 33 percent of adolescents enrolled in high school are also employed (Morisi, 2008). Though these positions are often part-time, adolescents experience problems similar to their adult employed counterparts, including harassment, stress related to work, and uncertainty about career choices. Furthermore, research shows that the ability of an adolescent to maintain employment is often a protective factor for at-risk adolescents. Individuals who maintain employment express higher self-efficacy, express positive views of the future, and are more likely to be employed in the future (Purtell & McLoyd, 2013).

OTHER PROBLEMS RELATED TO THE SOCIAL ENVIRONMENT

This section of Z codes focuses on issues within the client's social environment, excluding his or her family unit, that may affect the course of treatment.

Z60.0 Phase of Life Problem. This code may apply to both children and adults and can be used when a client experiences difficulty adjusting to a normal developmental life change, such as starting or graduating from school and individuating from one's parents (APA, 2013). This code should be used when the client's difficulty adjusting to life changes is either the treatment focus or when the difficulty adjusting impacts the course, prognosis, or treatment of a medical or psychological disorder (APA, 2013). As such, if the transition does not negatively impact the child, such as in the case of a child who is excited about beginning middle school, this Z code should not be used. When children experience problematic phase of life transitions, psychoeducation, normalizing, and a focus on coping skills may be helpful therapeutic interventions.

Z60.3 Acculturation Difficulty. This code may apply to situations in which a client experiences difficulty acclimating to a new culture and this is the primary treatment focus (APA, 2013). Acculturation can be particularly challenging for children when there exists a difference between the child and parental levels of acculturation. A study by Kim, Chen, Wang, Shen, and Orozco-Lapray (2013) demonstrated this when they found that adolescents whose parents experienced a discrepant level of acculturation were at increased risk for both depression and academic difficulty. These differences in acculturation may be the source of parent–child conflict, even though adolescents may not always identify cultural differences as the root of these conflicts (Bahrassa, Juan, & Lee, 2013). When possible, then, family counseling may be advantageous for children for whom this Z code is applicable.

Z60.4 Social Exclusion or Rejection. This code may apply in situations in which a client experiences persistent social exclusion or rejection (APA, 2013). The exclusion and refection may take multiple forms, all of which demonstrate an imbalance of power between the client and the perpetrator (APA, 2013). Examples include intentional exclusion from activities, bullying, mocking, intimidation, humiliation, and verbal battering (APA, 2013). The effects of social exclusion on children can be varied and marked. In a study by Hawes (2012), children who experienced ostracism also experienced threats to their primary needs (e.g., belongingness, control, self-esteem, and meaningful existence). Additionally, girls tended to report increased negative mood and displayed some aspects of lower cognitive functioning following perceived social ostracism (Hawes, 2012). The effects of bullying continue to garner increased attention in both the field of professional counseling and the lay community alike. Although prevention is the preferred treatment for bullying, early intervention is important to help reduce the negative impact of bullying on children. It is particularly important to create a safe and nonjudgmental therapeutic climate when working with children who have experienced social exclusion and rejection.

Z60.5 Target of (Perceived) Adverse Discrimination or Persecution. This code may apply in situations in which a client either experiences or perceives discrimination or persecution because of the client's membership to a specific group or people (APA, 2013). These groups may include, but are not limited to, gender, religion, race, culture of origin, political affiliation, socioeconomic status, ability or disability status, attractiveness, and sexual orientation (APA, 2013). Children experience, and are negatively impacted by, discrimination based on multiple diversity statuses. Unfortunately, the impact for children can be lifelong. A study by English and Lambert (2014), for instance, found a link between racial discrimination and onset of depression. Similarly, Benner and Graham (2013) conducted a study of minority adolescents to examine the impact of school personnel, peer, and societal discrimination on adolescents. The authors found that school personnel discrimination often resulted in diminished academic performance, whereas peer discrimination often resulted in symptoms of psychological maladjustment (Benner & Graham, 2013). Finally, societal discrimination was linked to increased racial awareness (Benner & Graham, 2013). Discrimination is not always rooted in race and ethnicity. One study examined the effects of parent and friend labeling on girls who were considered overweight (Mustillo, Budd, & Hendrix, 2013). The researchers found that, primarily for Caucasian girls, there were multiple short- and long-term indicators of psychological distress for girls who experienced weight-based stigma (Mustillo et al., 2013). So, although treatment may involve elements of advocacy when children experience discrimination or persecution, cognitive-based interventions may be useful in addressing elements of perceived discrimination.

Z60.9 Unspecified Problem Related to Social Environment. This code may apply to situations in which the client experiences a problem related to the social environment that is not otherwise better accounted for by the above-mentioned Z codes of Other Problems Related to the Social Environment. For some children, unspecified problems related to social environment may take the form of geographically relocating and changing schools. Experiences of this nature can produce feelings of anxiety, fear, and sadness in children and, as such, may warrant clinical attention.

PROBLEMS RELATED TO CRIME OR INTERACTION WITH THE LEGAL SYSTEM

The *DSM-5* states that all Z codes may be used if the issue is the primary treatment focus, the code helps support the need for treatment, or the issue may affect the client's treatment (APA, 2013). In this way, Z codes may be used even in cases in which they are not directly related to the primary treatment focus (APA, 2013). As such, although the following codes may not identify the primary treatment concerns, they may be useful to include in a diagnostic profile as a means of clarifying the client's complex treatment needs. See Sidebar 19.3 for more considerations regarding children and adolescents involved with the legal system.

SIDEBAR 19.3: SELF-AWARENESS—CLIENTS WHOSE TREATMENT INVOLVES THE LEGAL JUSTICE SYSTEM

By and large, mental health professionals probably describe themselves as nonjudgmental people who are able to compartmentalize their own feelings when working with challenging clinical issues. However, clinicians may sometimes not recognize the implicit ways in which their own values and beliefs influence the course of treatment. This is particularly the case when working with clients who have been involved with the legal justice system.

Throughout your clinical work, it is critically important that you become aware of and monitor your personal belief system. What do you believe about children and adolescents who have been perpetrated? Do you consider them *victims* or *survivors*, and what are the clinical implications of using these two labels? What do you believe about children's and adolescents' ability to change maladaptive and criminal behavior? Perhaps *especially* when we think our own belief system does not affect our work we are in danger of imposing our beliefs. As such, when working with children and adolescents who are involved with the legal justice system, seeking appropriate supervision and consultation is necessary.

Z65.4 Victim of Crime. This code may apply to situations in which a client is the victim of a crime. An alarming number of children are victims of nonsexual crime. These may include, for example, physical assault, intimidation, emotional victimization, property crime, and exposure to violence (see Finkelhor, Shattuck, Turner, & Hamby, 2014). Children who are victims of crime are often called upon to participate in a criminal trial against their perpetrator(s). Although participating, in moderation, in the legal justice process can have positive outcomes for some children, several factors may contribute to negative outcomes for children who testify in a court of law (Quas & Goodman, 2012). These may include, for instance, repeated testimony, multiple continuances, delays in proceedings, negligible rulings, and inadequate caregiver support throughout the legal process (Quas & Goodman, 2012). The focus of treatment may include helping the child manage the complex feelings that emerge following victimization but may also address the child's response to involvement in the criminal justice process.

Z65.0 Conviction in Civil or Criminal Proceedings without Imprisonment. This code may apply to situations in which a client has been convicted of a crime, regardless of whether the client was imprisoned for that crime. Children and adolescents who have been arrested for a criminal offense have decreased since 1980 but still represent an alarmingly large portion of the criminal offender population. Arrest rates for people ages 10 through 17 in 2011 totaled approximately four percent, or 4,367 for every 100,000 youths (Office of Juvenile Justice and Delinquency Prevention [OJJDP], 2014). Treatment with these children may focus on developing adaptive interpersonal, problem-solving, empathy, emotional regulation, and anger management skills. Treatment may also address managing the social stigma that often arises after a child has been charged with or convicted of a crime.

Z65.1 Imprisonment or Other Incarceration. This code may apply to situations in which a client has been convicted of a crime and, as a result, has been incarcerated. Children convicted of a crime may be incarcerated in a juvenile detention facility. Although the purpose of incarceration is rehabilitation, the outcome of juvenile detention may not always be positive; children may, during their stay in a detention facility, experience various forms of abuse that can have long-term negative effects (Dierkhising, Lane, & Natsuaki, 2014). A study by Dierkhising et al. (2014) found that over 96 percent of children and adolescents who were incarcerated experienced some form of abuse. Moreover, the more frequent the incidents of abuse were during incarceration, the more likely the children and adolescents were to develop posttraumatic symptoms, depression, and criminal recidivism (Dierkhising et al., 2014).

Z65.3 Problems Related to Other Legal Circumstances. This code may apply to situations in which a client has experienced other legal issues that are not better accounted for by the Z codes of Problems Related to Crime or Interaction with the Legal System.

Other Health Service Encounters for Counseling and Medical Advice

If severe relationship distress, partner violence, or significant stressors better explain the sexual difficulties, then an appropriate V or Z code for the relationship problem or stressor may be listed. Though it may seem inappropriate to include Z70.9 Sex Counseling in a diagnosis for a child or adolescent, this Z code also includes when an individual seeks counseling for sexual orientation, which may be a presenting concern for gay, lesbian, bisexual, transgender, questioning, and intersex (GLBTQI) adolescents. Sexual identity can be an important aspect to focus on in treatment—GLBTQI adolescents are three times more likely to attempt suicide than their straight counterparts, and 78 percent experience some form of teasing or bullying surrounding their sexual identity (Kosciw, Greytak, Bartkiewicz, Boesen, & Palmer, 2012). One major focus of counseling with GLBTQI adolescents may be the process of coming out, or disclosing their sexual identity to family members and friends. There are several developmental models that have been developed for the coming-out process; however, the most popular is the Cass Identity Model (1979). This model identifies the following six stages: identity confusion, identity comparison, identity tolerance, identity acceptance, identity pride, and identity synthesis. There are limitations to any developmental model, as every individual is different, and the process may not be linear. As a clinician working with a GLBTQI adolescent, it is important to be aware of one's own multicultural competencies, including attitudes and beliefs, knowledge, and skills, to work with this population (Arredondo et al., 1996). GLBTQI adolescents not only face the emotional struggles straight adolescents face but also often face additional bias, stereotypes, and verbal, emotional, and physical abuse from others (Kosciw et al., 2012).

Z71.9 Other Counseling or Consultation is a type of catchall for any situation that the clinician wishes to address in counseling but is not covered under any of the other Z codes.

PROBLEMS RELATED TO OTHER PSYCHOLOGICAL, PERSONAL, AND ENVIRONMENTAL CIRCUMSTANCES

Z65.8 Religious or Spiritual Problem relates to any issues the adolescent may have related to his or her spiritual beliefs and practices. Research shows that up to 95 percent of adolescents believe in God (Gollnick, 2005), and spiritual and religious beliefs can increase an individual's resiliency and overall wellness (Reutter & Bigatti, 2014). This aspect may be especially important if a child or adolescent is struggling with other diagnoses, such as depression and anxiety, as research has also found that religious and spiritual beliefs increase the ability to cope with mental illness (Brown, Carney, Parrish, & Klem, 2013). The APA (2013) notes that this condition should not be limited specifically to religious practices but can also include spiritual beliefs and values in general.

Z64.0 Problem Related to Unwanted Pregnancy will be used for an adolescent female when the pregnancy will be a focus of treatment. The rate of adolescent pregnancy has dropped drastically over the past years and reached a record low in 2011, with only about 3 percent of adolescent females experiencing pregnancies (Hamilton, Martin, & Ventura, 2012). Though these statistics are promising, adolescent clients experiencing an unwanted pregnancy are at higher risk for health problems, academic problems, and future employment problems (Hoffman & Maynard, 2008). When working with adolescent females who experience unwanted pregnancy, treatment may center on restructuring identity, developing coping skills, balancing motherhood with academics and employment, and managing any health concerns that may arise.

Z64.1 Problems with Multiparity, though likely less common, should be treated similarly to adolescents who experience a single-fetus pregnancy. Multiparity occurs when a woman is pregnant with more than one fetus at a single time. Multiparity, particularly when a woman is pregnant with five or more fetuses, can present hazards related to successful labor and delivery (Mgaya, Massawe, Kidanto, & Mgaya, 2013; Shechter, Levy, Wiznitzer, Zlotnik, & Sheiner, 2010). Additionally, reorganizing one's life to accommodate multiple new infants can be challenging for mothers and may impact their overall levels of happiness and satisfaction with their intimate-partner relationship (Gameiro,

Moura-Ramos, & Canavarro, 2009). As such, counseling may address both the mother's concerns regarding pregnancy and labor, as well as relational issues with the other parent. Psychoeducation regarding new parenthood may also help address some client concerns and better prepare the mother for her new role.

Though many clients with whom clinicians work may have other service professionals with whom they are working in the community, Z64.4 Discord with Social Service Provider, Including Probation Officer, Case Manager, or Social Services Worker should be used only if this discord is a specific focus of counseling or may impact the client's progress.

Z65.4 Victim of Terrorism or Torture and Z65.5 Exposure to Disaster, War, or Other Hostilities will likely accompany an acute stress disorder or posttraumatic stress disorder diagnosis, and therefore the treatment focus will be similar.

Z65.8 Other Problem Related to Psychosocial Circumstances and Z65.9 Unspecified Problem Related to Unspecified Psychosocial Circumstances will be used when there are other conditions related to the child or adolescent's psychosocial environment, but they do not fit any of the other coded conditions.

OTHER CIRCUMSTANCES OF PERSONAL HISTORY

Z91.49 Other Personal History of Psychological Trauma may be used if the client has experienced a psychological trauma other than those delineated in the psychological abuse category; however, treatment and diagnosis strategies will be similar.

Z91.5 Personal History of Self-Harm. Nonsuicidal self-injury can be defined as any action where the child or adolescent engages in bodily harm that is not intended as an attempt to take his or her life or is done for the purposes of body modification (Weierich & Nock, 2008). This can include, for example, cutting, burning, and hitting oneself. There are many reasons children and adolescents engage in this behavior, such as affect regulation, interpersonal influence, self-punishment, antidissociation, antisuicide, sensation seeking, and boundary setting (Klonsky & Muehlenkamp, 2007). Children and adolescents who self-injure may do so for multiple reasons, and the functions self-injury serves can change (Turner, Chapman, & Layden, 2012).

Studies have shown that up to half of adolescents in the United States might have engaged in nonsuicidal self-injury at some time (Lloyd-Richardson, Perrine, Dierker, and Kelley; 2008; Yates, Tracy, & Luthar, 2007). This behavior can be dangerous and can lead to accidental death. Additionally, there is a higher rate of suicide among people who self-injure (Brausch & Gutierrez, 2010; Toprak, Cetin, Guven, Can, & Demircan, 2011). If a client reports a history of these behaviors but denies engaging in these behaviors currently, clinicians should still discuss the events surrounding self-injury and functions it served as a means of identifying the client's triggers and coping style. This information may inform therapeutic work and provide valuable information to help the clinician identify signs of deteriorating functioning in the client. Moreover, it is important to remember that many clients who self-injure may not feel comfortable discussing self-injury with their clinician and, as such, may keep that information private until therapeutic rapport is well established.

Z91.89 Other Personal Risk Factors will include any risk factors under circumstances of personal history that have not been included in other categories and conditions in this section.

Z72.9 Problem Related to Lifestyle include aspects of the child's or adolescent's activities of daily living that may have an impact on any current mental health and physical diagnoses. These may include diet and exercise but also risky sexual behaviors and poor sleep hygiene (APA, 2013). Though wellness and preventative health care is on the rise, statistics show that only one in three children engages in physical activity daily, and most children and adolescents do not eat a properly balanced diet (Dietary Guidelines Advisory Committee, 2010).

Z72.810 Child or Adolescent Antisocial Behavior is to be included when the client is engaging in antisocial behavior that is not attributable to a diagnosable disorder, such as conduct disorder. Though these acts may be more sporadic, treatment may be similar to that of other disruptive, impulse-control, and conduct disorders (APA, 2013).

PROBLEMS RELATED TO ACCESS TO MEDICAL AND OTHER HEALTH CARE

Z75.3 Unavailability or Inaccessibility of Health Care Facilities, and Z75.4 Unavailability or Inaccessibility of Other Helping Agencies are both codes that would be used when the focus of treatment would be linking the client with other supportive agencies, similar to the previously mentioned codes Z59.9 Unspecified Housing or Economic Problem or Z59.7 Insufficient Social Insurance or Welfare Support.

NONADHERENCE TO MEDICAL TREATMENT

Z91.19 Nonadherence to Medical Treatment can include noncompliance with medication or any other treatment for medical or mental disorders that would be a focus of attention in counseling.

Z66.9 Overweight or Obesity, similar to Z72.9 Problem related to Lifestyle, should be used when the client's weight will be a focus of treatment, regardless of diagnosis with an eating disorder.

Z76.5 Malingering is defined as "the intentional production of false or grossly exaggerated physical or psychological symptoms, motivated by external incentives" (APA, 2013, p. 726). Differential diagnosis between malingering and factitious disorder is important, because one of the diagnostic criteria for factitious disorder is the absence of an obvious external motivation; instead the primary motivation is to assume a sick role. This should also be differentiated from somatoform disorders, where children are unconsciously producing symptoms via psychological concerns they are unable to verbalize (APA, 2013). Children and adolescents may engage in malingering for different reasons than adults. For example, adults may engage in malingering to receive financial compensation or to avoid work. However, children and adolescents may engage in malingering to avoid attending school or to receive attention from parents or guardians. It may be difficult to discern whether a client is malingering, and this Z-code should be included only when the clinician is certain, has a great deal of information regarding the client's biopsychosocial history, and has ruled out other diagnoses as a possible source for these behaviors (Morrison, 2014).

Z91.83 Wandering Associated with a Mental Disorder should be included only if the wandering is specific to a diagnosed disorder, as opposed to an intent to remove oneself from an unwanted situation. For example, a child or adolescent running away from home would not fit this code (APA, 2013). Wandering may be associated with a neurocognitive disorder, for example, autism spectrum disorder. Research shows that up to half of children and adolescents diagnosed with autism spectrum disorder engage in wandering behaviors, and the majority of those children entered into a dangerous situation as result (Anderson et al., 2012).

R41.83 Borderline Intellectual Functioning was formerly diagnosed for a child or adolescent who had received testing and whose IQ score was found to be above 70 but below 84 (APA, 2000). However, with the most recent publication of the *DSM*, IQ scores are no longer included in the use of this code. Instead, the clinician should include assessment of the conceptual, social, and practical domains in addition to standardized testing.

Treatment

The purpose of this section is to provide an overview of treatment modalities that tend to be efficacious when working with children and adolescents. A thorough review of these modalities is beyond the scope of this chapter. However, we have provided an introduction to five treatments that may be particularly useful for children and adolescents who experience complications surrounding the Z codes covered in this chapter. See Table 19.2 for a list of the Z codes and the corresponding treatment approaches that may be appropriate for these codes.

Cognitive Behavioral Therapy (CBT)

Cognitive behavioral therapy (CBT) has been around for decades and is by far the most researched therapeutic approach in the mental health field (Beck, 2012). An approach that focuses on identifying maladaptive thoughts, reframing those thoughts, and generalizing new skills to all situations in the clients' lives, CBT has been used for all varieties of diagnoses and problems in treatment (Sommers-Flanagan & Sommers-Flanagan, 2012). Though this may seem like a sophisticated approach for children and adolescents, there are numerous adaptations and approaches for children and adolescents. Rational emotive behavioral therapy (REBT), a form of CBT that includes specific automatic thoughts that are linked to core beliefs and schemas, has also been a popular approach, especially with regard to children and adolescents with self-esteem problems and disruptive behavior. In a meta-analysis of studies including REBT and children and adolescents, REBT showed significant improvement in mental health symptoms over other approaches (Gonzalez et al., 2004). CBT has also been used with mood and anxiety disorders, impulse-control disorders, and obsessive-compulsive disorder (Sommers-Flanagan & Sommers-Flanagan, 2012). CBT can also be adapted for culture as needed, and studies have found that CBT approaches are effective for Hispanic and African American youth with a variety of diagnoses and environmental backgrounds (Friedberg et al., 2014).

Dialectical Behavior Therapy (DBT)

Dialectical behavior therapy (DBT), considered a third-wave CBT approach, originated two decades ago and was developed for the treatment of borderline personality disorder

TABLE 19.2   Suggested Treatment Approach and Relevant Z Codes

Suggested Treatment	*Condition (Z Codes)*
Cognitive Behavioral Therapy (CBT)	Z62.820 Parent-Child Relational Problem
	Z62.891 Sibling Relational Problem
	Z62.29 Upbringing Away from Parents
	Z62.898 Child Affected by Parental Relationship Distress
	Z63.5 Disruption of Family by Separation or Divorce
	Z63.0 Relationship Distress with Spouse or Intimate Partner
	Z63.4 Uncomplicated Bereavement
	Z65.8 Religious or Spiritual Problem
	Z64.0 Problem Related to Unwanted Pregnancy
	Z64.1 Problems with Multiparity
	Z64.4 Discord with Social Service Provider, Including Probation Officer, Case Manager, or Social Services Worker
	Z65.4 Victim of Terrorism or Torture
	Z65.5 Exposure to Disaster, War, or Other Hostilities
	Z65.8 Other Problem Related to Psychosocial Circumstances
	Z65.9 Unspecified Problem Related to Unspecified Psychosocial Circumstances
	Z91.89 Other Personal Risk Factors
	Z72.9 Problem Related to Lifestyle
Dialectical Behavior Therapy	Z91.49 Other Personal History of Psychological Trauma
	Z91.5 Personal History of Self-Harm
	Z63.8 High Expressed Emotion Level within Family
	Z72.810 Child or Adolescent Antisocial Behavior
Play Therapy	Z63.5 Disruption of Family by Separation or Divorce
	Z63.0 Relationship Distress with Spouse or Intimate Partner
	Z63.8 High Expressed Emotion Level within Family
	Z63.4 Uncomplicated Bereavement
	Child Physical Abuse Confirmed/Suspected
	Child Sexual Abuse Confirmed/Suspected
	Child Neglect Abuse Confirmed/Suspected
	Child Psychological Abuse Confirmed/Suspected
	Z69.010 Encounter for mental health services for victim of child abuse (specify physical, sexual, neglect, or psychological) by parent
	Z69.020 Encounter for mental health services for victim of nonparental child abuse (specify physical, sexual, neglect, or psychological)
	Z62.810 Personal history (past history) of physical abuse (specify physical, sexual, neglect, or psychological) in childhood
Behaviorism	Z59.3 Problem Related to Living in a Residential Institution
	Z91.19 Nonadherence to Medical Treatment
	Z66.9 Overweight or Obesity
	Z72.9 Problem Related to Lifestyle
	Z76.5 Malingering
	Z91.83 Wandering Associated with a Mental Disorder
Expressive Therapy	Z60.0 Phase of Life Problem
	Z60.3 Acculturation Difficulty
	Z60.4 Social Exclusion or Rejection
	Z60.5 Target of (Perceived) Adverse Discrimination or Persecution
	Z60.9 Unspecified Problem Related Social Environment

(continued)

TABLE 19.2 Continued

Suggested Treatment	Condition (Z Codes)
Psychoeducation	Z65.4 Victim of Crime
	Z65.0 Conviction in Civil or Criminal Proceedings without Imprisonment
	Z65.1 Imprisonment or Other Incarceration
	Z65.3 Problems Related to Other Legal Circumstances
	Z70.9 Sex Counseling
	Z71.9 Other Counseling or Consultation
	Z75.3 Unavailability or Inaccessibility of Health Care Facilities
	Z75.4 Unavailability or Inaccessibility of Other Helping Agencies

(BPD) in adults (Linehan, 1993). Since that time, research has found it to be effective in reducing hospitalizations and nonsuicidal self-injury (NSSI) through several randomized controlled trials (Linehan, Armstrong, Suarez, Allmon, & Heard, 1991; Bedics, Atkins, Comtois, & Linehan, 2012; Linehan et. al., 1999). Many children and adolescents struggle with symptoms of BPD, including impulsivity, chronic emotion dysregulation, labile moods, and unstable interpersonal relationships, and these symptoms can lead to higher risk of suicide.

DBT is a complex, multifaceted treatment, based in dialectics, cognitive behavioral skills, behavioral techniques, and mindfulness meditation. DBT is founded on the biosocial model, which states that pervasive emotion dysregulation is a function of the interaction between a biological disposition for intense emotions, or inability to regulate emotions, and an invalidating social environment (Linehan, 1993). This can be especially clear when working with adolescents in the context of the familial situation. Modes of treatment in DBT include psychoeducational skills groups, individual treatment sessions, between session skills coaching, and between session homework and *diary cards*, a journal of the use of skills as well as emotions and engagement in problem behaviors (Linehan, 1993). Skills groups meet weekly and focus on four modules to help the client develop more adaptive methods of regulating emotions: mindfulness, interpersonal effectiveness, emotion regulation, and distress tolerance (Linehan, 1993). Though DBT with children and adolescents is similar to DBT with adults, some modifications are necessary to better suit their needs. The main focus areas in this adaptation are balancing change and acceptance, creating a structured environment, and generalizing treatment skills to all areas of the patient's life, as well as NSSI and emotion regulation (Miller, 1999; Miller et al., 2007).

Research on DBT in outpatient settings with adolescents has shown improvement in NSSI and emotion regulation skills (Hjalmarsson, Kaver, Perseius, Cederberg, & Ghaderi, 2008; Fleischaker et al., 2011). There is also research on using DBT specifically with adolescents struggling with eating disorders (Salbach-Andrae, Bohnekamp, Pfeiffer, Lehmkuhl, & Miller, 2008). There are studies that show effectiveness on inpatient units with adolescents, and in these studies, patients showed decreases in NSSI and higher levels of quality of life (Katz, Cox, Gunasekara, & Miller, 2004; McDonell et al., 2010).

PSYCHOEDUCATION

Psychoeducation is a blend of both psychological approaches and educational approaches to increase the functioning of a client struggling with mental illness (Lukens & McFarlane,

2004). Psychoeducation is an evidence-based treatment that emphasizes the empowerment of the client with knowledge of the disorder. For children and adolescents, this will often include the involvement of parents and family members. Psychoeducational approaches are often structured and are frequently delivered in a group setting. The focus of treatment is to educate the client regarding his or her diagnosis and symptoms, as well as to increase the client's coping skills, ability to manage symptoms, and knowledge and usage of support systems and resources (Lukens & McFarlane, 2004). Though research on psychoeducation has been primarily focused on schizophrenia, several studies show its effectiveness with children struggling with mood and anxiety disorders, as well as adolescents with conduct disorder and eating disorders (Fristad, Goldberg-Arnold, & Gavazzi, 2002; Gibbs, Potter, Goldstein, & Brendtro, 1996; Rocco, Ciano, & Balestrieri, 2001).

BEHAVIORISM

Though often criticized for its lack of insight-oriented techniques, behaviorism can be an important tool when working with children and adolescents specifically to decrease problem behaviors and increase positive behaviors. One of the most popular approaches, applied behavior analysis, was developed by Skinner in 1938 and includes reinforcement and punishment of a target behavior. It requires the clinician to be extremely knowledgeable of all the variables involved, including factors related to the target behavior (Spiegler, 2009). This approach can be especially useful when working to decrease disruptive behaviors or risk-taking behaviors with adolescents but has also been shown to be helpful in reducing symptoms of depression and anxiety in children and adolescents (Herson, 2002). However, development of a behavior plan must be carefully thought out and applied, and a functional assessment is often the first step. A clear idea of what will reinforce the client's behaviors can be extremely important, including consideration of all possible environmental factors and the involvement of parents, teachers, and other pertinent individuals as needed. When developing a behavior plan, it is important to assess background, identify antecedent events, determine relevant related environmental factors, develop hypotheses and action plans, and engage in constant reevaluation of treatment progress and outcomes (Spiegler, 2009).

PLAY THERAPY

Play therapy is way of "communicating therapeutically with clients" through play media and within the context of a safe relationship, through which clients can explore and learn more about themselves and the ways they engage in the world (Kottman, 2003, p. 1). Mental health professionals have used play therapy since the early 1900s, and although there has traditionally been relatively little empirical research on play therapy, several studies over the past 20 years supported its efficacy as a therapeutic medium (see Landreth, 2012). Literature provided support for the use of play therapy for children who experience obsessive-compulsive disorder (see Myrick & Green, 2012), problem behavior (see Ray, Stulmaker, Lee, & Silverman, 2013; Meany-Walen, Bratton, & Kottman, 2014; Schottelkorb, Swan, Garcia, Gale, & Bradley, 2014), low academic achievement (see Blanco, Ray, & Holliman, 2012), and social/emotional skill deficits (see Ahdieh, Mehrnoush, Masoumeh, Shirin, & Manijeh, 2014). These emerging results are consistent with notable play therapists' assertions regarding the inherent therapeutic qualities of play therapy. Landreth (2012), for instance, stated that "play is the child's symbolic language of self-expression and can reveal (a) *what the child has experienced;* (b) *reactions to what was experienced;* (c) *feelings about what was experienced;* (d) *what the child wishes, wants, or needs; and* (e) *the child's perception of self* " (p. 14). For many mental health practitioners, the healing and expressive powers of play therapy are undeniable.

Despite the seemingly simple nature of play, using this modality in clinical treatment requires significant knowledge and skill. One must be specifically trained in play therapy to refer to oneself as a play therapist. However, licensed mental health professionals may, with appropriate training and supervision, integrate play therapy interventions into their work with children and adolescents. For many children and adolescents who have not developed the emotional vocabulary to communicate their internal experience comprehensively, play therapy may prove particularly useful as a means of communication (Kottman, 2011). Indeed, Landreth (20121) stated that play is a natural form of communication for children. Moreover, play is nonthreatening and can help reduce the risk of retraumatizing survivors through the emotional distance play creates with the trauma memory (see Landreth, 2012). In this way, play may help trauma survivors express their thoughts and feelings, and perhaps even tell their trauma story, by expressing *through* play and play media. Although play therapy can be a powerful medium through which to facilitate growth and healing, it must be administered adequately. Failing to provide an adequate standard of care in the use of play therapy could lead to ineffective treatment and potential risk to the client.

EXPRESSIVE THERAPY

Expressive therapy is a category of creative approaches to mental health treatment. These approaches include art, music, drama, dance or movement, poetry, sandplay or sandtray, and integrated arts therapies (Malchiodi, 2005). Many authors categorized play therapy as a form of expressive therapy. In consideration of the focused training associated with play therapy, we have separated the two treatment modalities for the purposes of this overview.

Creative approaches to mental health treatment have been used to assist children and adolescents who experience a variety of mental health concerns. These include, for instance, grieving adolescents (Slyter, 2012), adolescents who experience anger management difficulty (Burt, Patel, & Lewis, 2012), children with chronic illness (Frels, Leggett, & Larocca, 2009), and clients who self-injure (Milia, 2000). As with play therapy, one must receive specialized training to refer to oneself as an expressive therapist. However, with appropriate training and supervision, mental health practitioners can integrate creative modalities into their clinical practice.

Also similar to play therapy, creativity is a powerful medium, and mental health practitioners must practice with caution to ensure the most appropriate and efficacious use of these treatment modalities. Inexperienced practitioners may inadvertently overlook the projective and communicative power of these media. Doing so can create risks to the client and interfere with the course of treatment. Additionally, a notable caution is that craft making is not equivalent to creative therapy. Craft making can be relaxing and perhaps even cathartic, but true expressive therapy allows the client to learn about himself or herself and the ways he or she engages with others. True expressive therapy helps clients find new ways of thinking about and reacting in the world.

Evaluation

There are numerous standardized, formal assessments that one might use in addition to a full biopsychosocial assessment, assessments that focus on specific symptoms and behaviors, if one has specific concerns about an assigned Z code. However, it should also be noted that the APA has provided numerous cross-cutting symptom measures via http://www.psychiatry.org/practice/dsm/dsm5/online-assessment-measures. These include assessments for parents and children for numerous symptoms, emotions, and behaviors (APA, 2013). See Sidebar 19.4.

SIDEBAR 19.4: ETHICS OF EVALUATION

If you are considering using a formal assessment, be sure to review the ethics of assessment and evaluation for your given profession:

- American Association of Marriage and Family Therapy (AAMFT) Code of Ethics
- American Psychological Association (APA) Code of Ethics
- American Counseling Association (ACA) Code of Ethics
- National Association of Social Workers (NASW) Code of Ethics

---

Summary

Though this chapter may seem overwhelming to the reader, Z codes are an important facet of the diagnosis process with children and adolescents. Z codes should be assigned after completing a full psychosocial assessment and any additional formal assessments as needed. Furthermore, Z codes should be included only when they will be focused on in treatment in addition to any other *DSM-5* diagnoses. Finally, these conditions should be included in the treatment plan based on level of importance, which can be decided using your clinical judgment and through collaboration with the client and his or her parents. See Sidebar 19.5.

SIDEBAR 19.5: DIAGNOSIS

"Diagnosis, is in the end, an expression of probability" (author of quotation is unknown).

The accuracy or certainty of your diagnosis rests on many factors, including but not limited to you (the clinician), the client, the current state of understanding for a given condition, the context within which the diagnosis is made, and the translation of coding changes into practice. Understanding the coding changes for Other Conditions that may be the focus of clinical attention in the *DSM-5* will influence the accuracy of your diagnosis.

References

Addy, S., Engelhardt, W., & Skinner, C. (2013). *Basic facts about low-income children: Children under 18 years, 2011.* New York, NY: National Center for Children in Poverty.

Ahdieh, C., Mehrnoush, K., Masoumeh, E., Shirin, C., & Manijeh, A. (2014). The effect of group play therapy on social-emotional skills in pre-school children. *Global Journal of Health Science, 6*(2), 163. doi:10.5539/gjhs.v6n2p163

Amaya, M. M., Reinecke, M. A., Silva, S. G., & March, J. S. (2011). Parental marital discord and treatment response in depressed adolescents. *Journal of Abnormal Child Psychology, 39*(3), 401–411. doi:10.1007/s10802–010–9466–2

American Psychiatric Association. (2000). *Diagnostic and statistical manual of mental disorders* (4th ed., text rev.). Washington, DC: Author.

American Psychiatric Association (2013). *Diagnostic and statistical manual of mental disorders* (5th ed.). Arlington, VA: American Psychiatric Publishing.

Anderson, C., Law, J. K., Daniels, A., Rice, C., Mandell, D. S., Hagopian, L, & Law, P. A. (2012). Spectrum disorders occurrence and family impact of elopement in children with autism. *Pediatrics, 130*(5), 870–877. doi:10.1542/peds.20120762

Arredondo, P., Toporek, M. S., Brown, S. P., Jones, J., Locke, D. C., Sanchez, J., & Stadler, H. (1996). Operationalization of the Multicultural Counseling Competencies. *Journal of Multicultural Counseling and Development, 24*(1), 42–78. doi:10.1002/j.2161-1912.1996.tb00288.x

Bahrassa, N. F., Juan, M. J. D., & Lee, R. M. (2013). Hmong American sons and daughters: Exploring mechanisms of parent–child acculturation conflicts. *Asian American Journal of Psychology, 4*(2), 100–108. doi:10.1037/a0028451

Beck, J. S. (2012). Why do I practice cognitive behavior therapy? In J. Sommers-Flanagan & R. Sommers-Flanagan (Eds.), *Counseling and psychotherapy theories in context and practice skills and techniques* (2nd ed., pp. 265). Hoboken, NJ: John Wiley & Sons.

Bedics, J. D., Atkins, D. C., Comtois, K. A., & Linehan, M. M. (2012). Treatment differences in the therapeutic relationship and introject during a 2-year randomized controlled trial of dialectical behavior therapy versus nonbehavioral psychotherapy experts for borderline personality disorder. *Journal of Consulting and Clinical Psychology, 80*(1), 66–77.

Benner, A. D., & Graham, S. (2013). The antecedents and consequences of racial/ethnic discrimination during adolescence: Does the source of discrimination matter? *Developmental Psychology, 49*(8), 1602–1613. doi:10.1037/a0030557

Blanco, P. J., Ray, D. C., & Holliman, R. (2012). Long-term child centered play therapy and academic achievement of children: A follow-up study. *International Journal of Play Therapy, 21*(1), 1–13. doi:10.1037/a0026932

Brausch, A. M., & Gutierrez, P. M. (2010). Differences in non-suicidal suicide and self-injury attempts in adolescents. *Youth Adolescence, 39*, 233–242. doi:10.1007/s10964-009-9482-0

Brown, D. R., Carney, J. S., Parrish, M. S., & Klem, J. L. (2013). Assessing spirituality: The relationship between spirituality and mental health. *Journal of Spirituality in Mental Health, 15*(2), 107–122. doi:10.1080/19349637.2013.776442

Burkhouse, K. L., Uhrlass, D. J., Stone, L. B., Knopik, V. S., & Gibb, B. E. (2012). Expressed emotion-criticism and risk of depression onset in children. *Journal of Clinical Child and Adolescent Psychology, 41*(6), 771–777. doi: 10.1080/15374416 .2012.703122

Burt, I., Patel, S. H., & Lewis, S. V. (2012). Anger management leadership groups: A creative intervention for increasing relational and social competencies with aggressive youth. *Journal of Creativity in Mental Health, 7*(3), 249–261. doi:10.1080/15401383 .2012.710168

Campione-Barr, N., Greer, K. B., & Kruse, A. (2013). Differential associations between domains of sibling conflict and adolescent emotional adjustment. *Child Development, 84*(3), 938–954. doi:10.1111/cdev.12022

Cass, V. C. (1979). Homosexuality identity formation: A theoretical model. *Journal of Homosexuality, 4*(3), 219–235.

Dierkhising, C. B., Lane, A., & Natsuaki, M. N. (2014). Victims behind bars: A preliminary study of abuse during juvenile incarceration and post-release social and emotional functioning. *Psychology, Public Policy, And Law, 20*(2), 181–190. doi:10.1037 /law0000002

Dietary Guidelines Advisory Committee. (2010). *Report of the Dietary Guidelines Advisory Committee on the Dietary Guidelines for Americans, 2010, to the Secretary of Agriculture and the Secretary of Health and Human Services.* Washington, DC: U.S. Department of Agriculture.

Dubowitz, H. (2011). Epidemiology of child neglect. In: Jenny, C. (Ed.), *Child Abuse and Neglect: Diagnosis, Treatment, and Evidence* (pp. 28–34). St. Louis, MO: Saunders.

English, D., Lambert, S. F., & Ialongo, N. S. (2014). Longitudinal associations between experienced racial discrimination and depressive symptoms in African American adolescents. *Developmental Psychology, 50*(4), 1190–1196. doi:10.1037/a0034703

Finkelhor, D., Shattuck, A., Turner, H. A., Hamby, S. L. (2014). Trends in children's exposure to violence, 2003 to 2011. *Journal of the American Medical Association Pediatrics, 168*(6), 540–546. doi:10.1001/jamapediatrics.2013.5296

Fleischaker, C., Böhme, R., Sixt, B., Brück, C., Schneider, C., & Schulz, E. (2011). Dialectical behavioral therapy for adolescents (DBT-A): A clinical trial for patients with suicidal and self-injurious behavior and borderline symptoms with a one-year follow-up. *Child and Adolescent Psychiatry and Mental Health, 5*(3), 1–10.

Frels, R. K., Leggett, E. S., & Larocca, P. S. (2009). Creativity and solution-focused counseling for a child with chronic illness. *Journal of Creativity in Mental Health, 4*(4), 308–319. doi:10.1080/15401380903372646

Friedberg, R. D., Hoyman, L. C., Behar, S., Tabbarah, S., Pacholec, N. M., Keller, M., & Thordarson, M. A. (2014). We've come a long way, baby!: Evolution and revolution in CBT with youth. *Journal of Rational-Emotive & Cognitive-Behavior Therapy, 32*(1), 4–14.

Fristad, M. A., Goldberg-Arnold, J. S., & Gavazzi, S. M. (2003). Multi-family psychoeducation groups in the treatment of children with mood disorders. *Journal of Marital and Family Therapy, 29*(4), 491–504.

Gameiro, S., Moura-Ramos, M., & Canavarro, M. C. (2009). Maternal adjustment to the birth of a child: Primiparity versus multiparity. *Journal of Reproductive & Infant Psychology, 27*(3), 269–286. doi:10.1080/02646830802350898

Gibbs, J. C., Potter, G. B., Goldstein, A. P., & Brendtro, L. K. (1996). Frontiers in psychoeducation: The EQUIP model with antisocial youth. *Reclaiming Children and Youth, 4*(4), 22–28.

Gollnick, J. (2005). *Religion and spirituality in the life cycle.* New York: Peter Lang.

Gonzalez, J. E., Nelson, J. R., Gutkin, T. B., Saunders, A., Galloway, A., & Shwery, C. S. (2004). Rational emotive therapy with children and adolescents: A meta-analysis. *Journal of Emotional and Behavioral Disorders, 12*(4), 222–235. doi:10.1177/10634266040120040301

Hamilton B. E., Martin J. A., & Ventura S. J. (2012). Births: Preliminary data for 2011. *National Vital Statistics Reports, 61*(5), 1–20. Retrieved from http://www.cdc.gov/nchs/data/nvsr61/nvsr61_05.pdf

Han, Z. R., & Shaffer, A. (2014). Maternal expressed emotion in relation to child behavior problems: Differential and mediating effects. *Journal of Child and Family Studies, 23*(8), 1491–1500. doi:10.1007/s10826–-14-9923-6

Hawes, D. J., Zadro, L., Fink, E., Richardson, R., O'Moore, K., Griffiths, B., … Williams, K. D. (2012). The effects of peer ostracism on children's cognitive processes. *European Journal of Developmental Psychology, 9*(5), 599–613. doi:10.1080/17405629.2011.638815

Herson, M. (2002). *Clinical behavior therapy: Adults and children.* Hoboken, NJ: John Wiley & Sons.

Hibbard, R., Barlow, J., MacMillan. H., Christian, C. W., Crawford-Jubiake, J. E., Flaherty, E. G., … Sege, R. D. (2012). Clinical report: Psychological maltreatment. *Pediatrics, 130*(2), 372–378.

Hindman, J. M., Riggs, S. A., & Hook, J. (2013). Contributions of executive, parent–child, and sibling subsystems to children's psychological functioning. *Couple and Family Psychology: Research and Practice, 2*(4), 294–308. doi:10.1037/a0034419

Hjalmarsson, E., Kaver, A., Perseius, K., Cederberg, K., & Ghaderi, A. (2008). Dialectical behaviour therapy for borderline personality disorder among adolescents and young adults: Pilot study, extending the research findings in new settings and cultures. *Clinical Psychologist, 12*(1), 18–29.

Hoffman, S. D., & Maynard, R. A. (2008). *Kids having kids: Economic costs and social consequences of teen pregnancy* (2nd ed.). Washington, DC: The Urban Institute Press.

Iglewicz, A., Seay, K., Zetumer, S. D., & Zisook, S. (2013). The removal of the bereavement exclusion in the DSM-5: Exploring the evidence. *Current Psychiatry Reports, 15*(11), 413. doi:10.1007/s11920-013-0413-0

Katz, L. Y., Cox, B. J., Gunasekata, S., & Miller, A. L. (2004). Feasibility of dialectical behavior therapy for suicidal adolescent inpatients. *Journal of the*

American Academy of Child & Adolescent Psychiatry, 43(3), 276–282.

Kim, S. Y., Chen, Q., Wang, Y., Shen, Y., & Orozco-Lapray, D. (2013). Longitudinal linkages among parent–child acculturation discrepancy, parenting, parent–child sense of alienation, and adolescent adjustment in Chinese immigrant families. Developmental Psychology, 49(5), 900–912. doi:10.1037/a0029169

Klonsky, E. D., & Muehlenkamp, J. J. (2007). Self-injury: A research review for the practitioner. Journal of Clinical Psychology, 63(11), 1045–1056. doi:10.1002/jclp.20412

Kosciw, J. G., Greytak, E. A., Bartkiewicz, M. J., Boesen, M. J., & Palmer, N. A. (2012). The 2011 National Climate Survey: The experiences of lesbian, gay, bisexual, and transgender youth in our nation's schools. New York, NY: Gay, Lesbian and Straight Education Network.

Kottman, T. (2003). Partners in play: An Adlerian approach to play therapy (2nd ed.). Alexandria, VA: American Counseling Association.

Kottman, T. (2011). Play therapy: Basics and beyond (2nd ed.). Alexandria, VA: American Counseling Association.

Lacro, J. P., Dunn L. B., Dolder, C. R., Leckband, S. G., & Jeste, D. V. (2002). Prevalence of risk factors for medication nonadherence in patients with schizophrenia: a comprehensive review of recent literature. Journal of Clinical Psychiatry, 63(10), 892–909.

Landreth, G. L. (2001). Facilitative dimensions of play in the play therapy process. In G. L. Landreth (Ed.), Innovations in play therapy: Issues, process, and special populations (pp. 3–22). New York, NY: Brunner-Routledge.

Landreth, G. L. (2012). Play therapy: The art of the relationship (3rd ed.). New York, NY: Routledge Taylor & Frances Group.

Linehan, M. M. (1993). Cognitive-behavioral treatment for borderline personality disorder. New York: The Guilford Press.

Linehan, M. M., Armstrong, H. E., Suarez, A., Allmon, D., & Heard, H. L. (1991). Cognitive behavioral treatment of chronically parasuicidal borderline patients. Archives of General Psychiatry, 48, 1060–1064.

Linehan, M. M., Schmidt, H., Dimeff, L. A., Kanter, J. W., Craft, J. C., Comtois, K. A., et al. (1999). Dialectical behavior therapy for patients with borderline personality disorder and drug-dependence. American Journal on Addictions, 8, 279–292.

Lloyd-Richardson, E. E., Perrine, N., Dierker, L., & Kelley, M. L. (2007). Characteristics and functions of non-suicidal self-injury in a community sample of adolescents. Psychological Medicine, 37(8), 1183–1192.

Lucas, N., Nicholson, J. M., & Erbas, B. (2013). Child mental health after parental separation: The impact of resident/non-resident parenting, parent mental health, conflict and socioeconomics. Journal of Family Studies, 19(1), 53–69. doi:10.5172/jfs.2013.19.1.53

Lukens, E. P. & McFarlane, W. R. (2004). Psychoeducation as evidence-based practice: Considerations for practice, research, and policy. Brief Treatment and Crisis Intervention, 4(3), 205–225.

Malchiodi, C. A. (2005). Expressive therapies: History, theory, and practice. In C. A. Malchiodi (Ed.), Expressive therapies (pp. 1–15). New York, NY: Guilford Press.

Maslow, A. H. (1943). Theory of human motivation. Psychological Review, 50(4), 370–396.

McDonell, M. G., Tarantino, J., Dubose, A. P., Matestic, P., Steinmetz, K., Galbreath, H., & McClellan, J. M. (2010). A pilot evaluation of dialectical behavioural therapy in adolescent long-term inpatient care. Child and Adolescent Mental Health, 15(4), 193–196.

McGoron, L., Gleason, M. M., Smyke, A. T., Drury, S. S., Nelson, I. A., Gregas, M. C., … Zeanah, C. H. (2012). Recovering from early deprivation: Attachment mediates effects of caregiving on psychopathology. Journal of the American Academy of Child & Adolescent Psychiatry, 51(7), 683–693. doi:10.1016/j.jaac.2012.05.004

Meany-Walen, K. K., Bratton, S. C., & Kottman, T. (2014). Effects of Adlerian Play Therapy on Reducing Students' Disruptive Behaviors. Journal of Counseling & Development, 92(1), 47–56. doi:10.1002/j.1556-6676.2014.00129.x

Mence, M., Hawes, D. J., Wedgwood, L., Morgan, S., Barnett, B., Kohlhoff, J., & Hunt, C. (2014). Emotional flooding and hostile discipline in the families of toddlers with disruptive behavior problems. Journal of Family Psychology, 28(1), 12–21. doi:10.1037/a0035352

Mgaya, A. H., Massawe, S. N., Kidanto, H. L., & Mgaya, H. N. (2013). Grand multiparity: Is it still a risk in pregnancy? BMC Pregnancy & Childbirth, 13(1), 241. doi:10.1186/1471-2393-13-241

Milia, D. (2000). Self-mutilation and art therapy: Violent creation. Philadelphia, PA: Jessica Kingsley.

Miller, A. L. (1999). DBT-A: A new treatment for parasuicidal adolescents. *American Journal of Psychotherapy, 53*, 413–417.

Miller, A. L., Rathus, J. H., & Linehan, M. M. (2007). *Dialectical behavior therapy with suicidal adolescents.* New York: Guilford Press.

Morisi, T. L. (2008). Youth enrollment and employment during the school year. *Bureau of Labor and Statistics Monthly Labor Review, 51*–63.

Mustillo, S. A., Budd, K., & Hendrix, K. (2013). Obesity, labeling, and psychological distress in late-childhood and adolescent black and white girls: The distal effects of stigma. *Social Psychology Quarterly, 76*(3), 268–289. doi:10.1177/0190272513495883

Myrick, A. C., & Green, E. J. (2012). Incorporating play therapy into evidence-based treatment with children affected by obsessive compulsive disorder. *International Journal of Play Therapy, 21*(2), 74–86. doi:10.1037/a0027603

National Center on Family Homelessness (2011). *America's youngest outcasts.* Needham, MA: Author.

Office of Juvenile Justice and Delinquency Prevention. (2014). *Law enforcement & juvenile crime: Juvenile arrest rate trends.* Retrieved from http://www.ojjdp .gov/ojstatbb/crime/JAR_Display.asp?ID=qa05200

Palusci, V. J. (2011). Epidemiology of sexual abuse. In C. Jenny (Ed.), *Child abuse and neglect: Diagnosis, treatment, and evidence* (pp. 16–22). St. Louis, MO: Saunders.

Purtell, K. M., & McLoyd, V. C. (2013). A longitudinal investigation of employment among low-income youth: Patterns, predictors, and correlates. *Youth & Society, 45*(2), 243–264.

Quas, J. A., & Goodman, G. S. (2012). Consequences of criminal court involvement for child victims. *Psychology, Public Policy, and Law, 18*(3), 392–414. doi:10.1037/a0026146

Ray, D. C., Stulmaker, H. L., Lee, K. R., & Silverman, W. K. (2013). Child-centered play therapy and impairment: Exploring relationships and constructs. *International Journal of Play Therapy, 22*(1), 13–27. doi:10.1037/a0030403

Reutter, K. K., & Bigatti, S. M. (2014). Religiosity and spirituality as resiliency resources: Moderation, mediation, or moderated mediation? *Journal for the Scientific Study of Religion, 53*(1), 56–72. doi:10.1111/jssr.12081

Rocco, P. L., Ciano, R. P., & Balestrieri, M. (2001). Psychoeducation in the prevention of eating disorders: An experimental approach in adolescent schoolgirls. *British Journal of Medical Psychology, 74*(3), 351–358.

Salbach-Andrae, H., Bohnekamp, I., Pfeiffer, E., Lehmkuhl, U., & Miller, A. L. (2008). Dialectical behavior therapy of anorexia and bulimia nervosa among adolescents: A case series. *Cognitive and Behavioral Practice, 15*(4), 415–425.

Sandler, I. N., Wheeler, L. A., & Braver, S. L. (2013). Relations of parenting quality, interparental conflict, and overnights with mental health problems of children in divorcing families with high legal conflict. *Journal of Family Psychology, 27*(6), 915–924. doi:10.1037/a0034449

Schottelkorb, A. A., Swan, K. L., Garcia, R., Gale, B., & Bradley, B. M. (2014). Therapist perceptions of relationship conditions in child-centered play therapy. *International Journal of Play Therapy, 23*(1), 1–17. doi:10.1037/a0035477

Shechter, Y., Levy, A., Wiznitzer, A., Zlotnik, A., & Sheiner, E. (2010). Obstetric complications in grand and great grand multiparous women. *Journal of Maternal-Fetal & Neonatal Medicine, 23*(10), 1211–1217. doi:10.3109/14767051003615459

Slyter, M. (2012). Creative counseling interventions for grieving adolescents. *Journal of Creativity in Mental Health, 7*(1), 17–34. doi:10.1080 /15401383.2012.657593

Sommers-Flanagan, J., & Sommers-Flanagan, R. (2012). *Counseling and psychotherapy theories in context and practice: Skills and techniques* (2nd Ed.). Hoboken, NJ: John Wiley & Sons.

Sommers-Flanagan, J., & Sommers-Flanagan, R. (2013). *Clinical interviewing* (5th ed.). Hoboken, NJ: John Wiley & Sons.

Spiegler, M. D. (2009). *Contemporary behavior therapy* (5th ed.). Belmont, CA: Cengage Learning.

Skinner, B. F. (1938). *The behavior of organisms: An experimental analysis.* New York, NY: Appleton-Century-Crofts.

Teicher, M. H., & Samson, J. A. (2013). Childhood maltreatment and psychopathology: A case for ecophenotypic variants as clinically and neurobiologically distinct subtypes. *American Journal of Psychiatry, 170*(10), 1114–1133.

Toprak, S., Cetin, I., Guven, T., Can, G., & Demircan, C. (2011). Self-harm, suicidal ideation and suicide attempts among college students. *Psychiatric Research, 187*(1–2), 140–144. doi: 10.1016 /j.psychres.2010.09.009

Turner, B. J., Chapman, A. L., & Layden, B. K. (2012). Intrapersonal and interpersonal functions of non suicidal self-injury: Associations with emotional and social functioning. *Suicide and Life-Threatening Behavior 42*(1), 36–55.

U.S. Department of Health and Human Services. (2013). *Child maltreatment 2012*. Retrieved from http://www.acf.hhs.gov/programs/cb/research-data-technology/statistics-research/child-maltreatment

Weierich, M. R., & Nock, M. K. (2008). Posttraumatic stress symptoms mediate the relation between childhood sexual abuse and nonsuicidal self-injury. *Journal of Consulting and Clinical Psychology, 76*(1), 39–44. doi:10.1037/0022-006X-76.1.39

Yates, T. M., Tracy, A. J., & Luthar, S. S. (2008). Nonsuicidal self-injury among "privileged" youths: longitudinal and cross-sectional approaches to developmental process. *Journal of Consulting and Clinical Psychology, 76*(1), 52–62.

Zolotor, A. J., & Shanahan, M. (2011). Epidemiology of physical abuse. In C. Jenny (Ed.), *Child abuse and neglect: Diagnosis, treatment, and evidence* (pp. 10–15). St. Louis, MO: Saunders.

Author Index

Subject Index

Page numbers followed by *f* and *t* refer to figures and tables, respectively.